HAMPSHIRE

The King's England

A New Domesday Book of 10,000 Towns and Villages

Edited by Arthur Mee

in 41 Volumes

NOTHING like these books has ever been presented to the English people. Every place has been visited. The Compilers have travelled half-a-million miles and have prepared a unique picture of our countryside as it has come down through the ages, a census of all that is enduring and worthy of record.

The Glory of Winchester

THE KING'S ENGLAND

HAMPSHIRE

WITH THE

ISLE OF WIGHT

EDITED BY
ARTHUR MEE

With 303 Places
and 180 Pictures

LONDON
HODDER AND STOUGHTON
LIMITED ST PAUL'S HOUSE, E.C.4

First published September 1939
Sixth impression 1956

It has not been thought desirable to note in this
volume the changes which the war brought about
in some churches and other buildings

*Printed and Bound in Great Britain for Hodder & Stoughton, Limited,
by Richard Clay and Company, Ltd., Bungay, Suffolk*

The Editor is greatly indebted to
JOAN BEGBIE
ANNIE JOHNSON and JOHN WILSON
for their valuable help with this book

For the pictures to
SIDNEY TRANTER, ART EDITOR
and to the following :
Messrs E. Bastard, B. T. Batsford, Ltd., S. J. Beckett,
W. A. Call, F. Crossley, J. Dixon-Scott, G. C. Druce,
H. Felton, A. F. Kersting, W. J. Nigh, T. Piper, J.
Reade, H. W. Salmon, J. Salmon, H. J. Smith, J.
Stone, E. W. Tattersall, W. Whiffin, F. R. Winstone,
and the City of Portsmouth Publicity Department.

PICTURES OF HAMPSHIRE

*Where the pictures are not on or facing the page given
they are inside the set of pictures beginning on that page*

vii

PICTURES OF HAMPSHIRE

HAMPSHIRE

This Realm. This Hampshire

IT is one of those pieces of England of which William Watson was thinking when he wrote in two of his stirring and immortal lines that

> Time, and the ocean, and some fostering star,
> In high cabal, have made us what we are.

We must count it a superb county, a favoured child of Nature and of History. Set in the middle of the coast by which the world's ships come and go, it stretches from our old sea-gate at Southampton to the borders of London's playground, Surrey. It has over a million acres and over a million people, and for beauty it is not surpassed by any county in the land.

It has not the kind of beauty that entrances us and draws the traveller like a magnet, the enchantment of the Sussex Downs, the grandeur of the Yorkshire Moors, the romantic appeal of the Cornish Coast, the unexpectedness of Shropshire, or the power to hold us spellbound as Lakeland does; but for a beauty that never fails, for country where we are never far from woodlands and never near a dull patch, Hampshire is unique. Its beauty is continuous; it never throws its character away.

Alfred began life as a neighbour of Hampshire, and in it is his capital and his grave. It was the heart of Wessex (this and not Dorset, as Thomas Hardy would have it), the stronghold of the Saxon kings, and there is a sense therefore in which we may say that it is very near the heart of England. Out of the overlordship of Wessex grew the overlordship of all England, and if we are to trace our monarchy back to a definite point in these islands it is in Hampshire that we find it beginning—Hampshire enveloped by the peaceful waters of the English Channel and the matchless counties of Old Dorset and pre-historic Wiltshire, Alfred's Berkshire, Surrey coming up to London, and Sussex like a garden by the sea.

3

Its delight is in its English beauty pure and simple, typical of the varied landscape of the south, with only two or three towering hills but with a succession of changing pictures which are a fascination to the traveller who knows what he is looking at. Everywhere the trees go marching up and down. With few great heights, it has a lot of little hills—highlands in the north and lowlands in the south. If we want the wind to blow us away we can go something like 900 feet up on the North Downs and the South Downs, both in Hampshire, and if we want a quiet day without the wind, sauntering in the haunts of Nature's children of the night, we can find it in a hundred places, but especially in the comfortable beauty of Alice's own wonderland, the New Forest in the midst of which she herself is sleeping.

It may be that the coast is not the most magnificent to look at, but what a marvellous piece of coast it is if we think of that long irregular line from Bournemouth to Southampton Water, and on to the greatest naval harbour in the world, guarded by the lovely Isle of Wight, which, by being where it is, gives these famous waters four tides every day. What pageants these waters have seen! Here came Henry the Fifth bound for Agincourt, here Nelson and his band of brothers, here that countless host of heroes who went to France in our own time, went out to the Seven Seas, and lie today in some far corner of a foreign field that is for ever England. For what the coast loses in beauty the spirit of History has given it abundant compensation.

History indeed has made its home in Hampshire. Portsmouth was the headquarters of Rome's rebel emperor Carausius, builder of the first British Fleet, and it has been a factor in the defence of England for sixteen centuries. Nearly every Hampshire town has had a long and stirring history. The Romans were at Southampton, the Saxons held it as a stronghold, and it was a walled medieval town, with the old walls still standing, looking down on the most impressive harbour works the 20th century has made anywhere in the world. It is under a field of wheat in Hampshire that the greatest Roman city in Britain lies, Sil-

4

PICTURES OF HAMPSHIRE

PICTURES OF THE ISLE OF WIGHT

HAMPSHIRE

chester; and over the border at Reading we may see the treasures found in its houses and its streets. If we would seek the biggest Roman monument above ground in this country, it is in Hampshire too, for neither the Roman wall of Hadrian across the North, nor the mighty walls of Richborough in Kent, can rival the walls of Porchester. Silchester and Porchester are Roman names to conjure with, and both are Hampshire's.

But in truth the map of Hampshire thrills with names like these. There is Bucklers Hard which built the ships for Nelson, about forty of them. There is Dogmersfield where Catherine of Aragon came, beginning her pathetic and dramatic career. There is Romsey, with the house King John built for his daughter, and Bishop's Waltham with the ruined palace of William of Wykeham, where he died, where Margaret of Anjou died after her unhappy reign with Henry the Sixth, and where Richard Lionheart was entertained after his crowning. There is Charford where the Saxon Cerdic fought his battles 1400 years ago, and Cheriton with the mounds in which lie 2000 Englishmen who fell when Charles the First and Cromwell were fighting the battles which saved our liberty. There is Ringwood where the Duke of Monmouth wrote his piteous appeal for life, and Warblington, home of Margaret Pole, from which she was dragged to her death, the last of the proud Plantagenets butchered like a dog. There is Milford, with Hurst castle from which Charles Stuart set out on his last journey, and Nursling where the monk Winfrith said goodbye to his brothers and set out to evangelise Germany and to become known in Europe for all time as St Boniface. There is Laverstoke, where a refugee family began making paper for Bank of England notes and makes it still. There is Basing, with the thrilling story of its great house and the story of Carlyle's magnificent man, William Paulet; he proclaimed Mary Tudor, received her here with Philip, and afterwards proclaimed Elizabeth, who declared that she could choose him before all the men in England. When Cromwell came himself to storm the house in the Civil War there were within these walls such men as Inigo Jones, Thomas Fuller, Wenceslaus Hollar, so famous a place it was. On the hill with the ruined chapel at Basingstoke lies the man who organised the Field of the Cloth of Gold, Lord Sandys.

If Hampshire had no other history but Winchester it would be enough. It is the unequalled town, with the longest cathedral in England, set in a bog in Norman days and set on a rock in ours, the crowning-place of the Conqueror, the resting-place of Saxon kings. Here we may sit in a matchless Norman transept on a bench used by the Norman monks. Here is the chair in which Mary Tudor sat when she was married to the King of Spain. Here is William of Wykeham's school, and the marvellous house of charity founded by the brother of King Stephen. Here the founder of our navy lies; here was sentenced to death the founder of our Empire. Here they laid the Conqueror's son William Rufus, slain in the New Forest by an arrow from Walter Tyrrell's bow; there is still in one of these Hampshire villages a family with the name of the man who took his body on a cart to the door of the cathedral.

For those who come this way in search of villages and churches regardless of their history Hampshire has a rich variety of appeal. We come upon Saxon work in a dozen of its churches, and it would seem that there is Norman everywhere. We remember about 30 fine Norman doorways, some of very great beauty, especially the north doorway at Crondall, the west at Vernham, the south at Winchfield, the north at Nately Scures, the west at Hurstbourne Priors, the south at Sydmonton, and the south at Wootton St Lawrence. The pilgrim through Norman England will find little better work than these. For architecture, indeed, it is a county no pilgrim can miss, with such noble monuments as Christchurch and Romsey and Winchester, such ruined splendour as we see at Beaulieu and Netley and Basingstoke. At Breamore, where there is still a curious little maze in the heart of a wood, the light still falls in the church through seven Saxon windows.

At Bramley, keeping company with glorious old glass, is a wall-picture of the martyrdom of Becket painted when men still remembered the event. At Chilworth are two bells old enough to have rung for Magna Carta, and probably the oldest bells in the South of England. At Chilton Candover the little crypt of a lost church has been found in our time. At Burley an enchanting painted ship is fading away after 600 years. At Hambledon the village boys are playing cricket still where the game of cricket was born. At Tichborne (linked with the sad tale of a young poet and one of the most romantic mysteries of all time) are the stately tombs of an ancient house, and at Titchfield are the tombs of the family whose patronage supported Shakespeare when he needed patronage. At Yateley is a delicate little bowl of rock crystal from Tudor days. At Brown Candover is the famous brass of two lovers arm in arm with a lily between them; at Crondall is a brass of 1381, the oldest in Hampshire; and at Nether Wallop is the only brass portrait in England of a prioress. At Abbots Ann are the wedding garlands which were carried at the funerals of maidens long ago—the "crants" the churlish priest objected to at Ophelia's burial. At Avington is a rare example of an untouched 18th century church. At Bishop's Waltham is the pulpit of Lancelot Andrewes, beloved by all and praised by Milton. At Crawley are rare timbered arcades. At West Meon are the graves of Richard Cobden's old folk, and of Thomas Lord whose name is given to our famous cricket pitch. In Brocken-hurst's beautiful churchyard sleep heroes of the war from three continents. At Clanfield, Colemore, Bramshaw, Hinton, Bighton, Headbourne Worthy, and Worldham are ancient bells. Boarhunt has a Saxon font, and there are too many Norman fonts to count, Porchester's being richly carved, and a remark-able group of four giving distinction to East Meon, St Mary Bourne, St Michael's at Southampton, and even to Winchester Cathedral. These four fonts are famous as belonging to a group of seven in all England made from the bronze-like marble of Tournai. At Odiham is one of England's most delightful streets and one of our most charming little homes of charity. At Bramshott is the crannied wall where Tennyson plucked a flower out of the crannies. At North Stoneham is the graveyard in which lie buried a company of hardy sailors of Dalmatia who perished here by violence or disease, strangers in a strange land.

If we would seek the villages and towns linked with great names we must traverse Hampshire from end to end. It may be doubted whether any county in the land surpasses Hampshire for the distinction brought to it by famous men and women who have passed this way. If we go back a thousand years and more it is Alfred's star that sets over this piece of England; across the border at Wantage he was born, and here at Winchester he lies. Here he set his scholars to work on the Anglo-Saxon Chronicle, and here he stamped his imperishable spirit for ever upon a city unique in the world. The Conqueror's son William Rufus, who lies not far away, perhaps lends the county infamy rather than fame, but his dust is in that great cathedral for ever associated with Hampshire's characteristic man, William of Wykeham. Here also was born that Prince Arthur whose death paved the way to the throne for Henry the Eighth and so changed the history of the world. This way came Edmund Spenser, living and writing at Alton for some time, and in this pleasant countryside there must have walked a greater than he, for Shakespeare must have been at Titchfield, where he would come to see his hero and patron; it is believed that he got the name of Gobbo from the registers here. At Odiham was born that William Lily who first taught Greek in London, and Otterbourne knew Sir Isaac Newton, who would stay there with his niece; here he said towards the end of his life that he felt he had been like a child picking up pebbles on the sea-shore, finding a shining one here and there, while the boundless ocean of knowledge lay unexplored before him. It is a noble roll of fame, but it is only beginning.

Here was Edward Gibbon as a boy, dreaming at Buriton of the pageant of Old Rome that he was to put into literature for all time. Here also was Gilbert White, watching his trees and his tortoises, and jotting down the small events of the Hampshire countryside, so that Selborne was for all time to be the haunt of Nature's pilgrims. Here at Hursley Richard Cromwell lived the life of a squire, and here in a little while he was again, son of our greatest English man of action, wandering about these fields, a broken man known as Tumbledown Dick, tumbled down from the seat next to the throne. Here at Burton the best man among the group of Lakeland poets spent some of his happiest days (the generous-hearted Southey), and at Lymington lies Caroline Bowles whose marriage with him in his declining years is one of the poignant chapters of our literature. From far away to this wonderful southern coast came the Wizard of the North, and it was within sight of one of Hampshire's noble headlands, Hengistbury, that Scott was moved, in writing Marmion, to one of the sublimest passages in his poetry, Now is the stately column broke.

Is there another small area of our countryside, we wonder, in which lie three such women as we find in three Hampshire graves—the brave Alice Lisle, butchered by Judge Jeffreys; the heroic Florence Nightingale, founder of our noble band of nurses; and the incomparable Jane Austen, whose novels will picture for many more generations yet the simple domestic life of the quiet homes of England in the days when France was seething in revolution. When these exciting days for France were ended by our Iron Duke, and the nation wished to give Wellington a great reward, it was a home in Hampshire that they gave him, Stratfieldsaye, where his famous charger lies. When in the course of time the Napoleons were done with, it was in Hampshire (at Farnborough) that they laid the last Napoleons to rest.

If we think of the smaller men whose fame is rather in our hearts than in our minds, we find in two Solent towns John Pounds, the poor cobbler of Portsmouth, and at Southampton Isaac Watts, whose hymn rings round the world whenever

Englishmen are gathered together in anxious days. And was it not a Hampshire boy who has worked his way into the human heart through books as no other man who ever lived has done? Almost within sight of the ships that come and go at Portsmouth stands the house in which Charles Dickens was born, and at Southampton was born Sir John Millais, whose pictures were hanging in our galleries while Dickens's books were issuing from the press. In the quiet little churchyard at Eversley lies a writer of another kind, Charles Kingsley, far from his Westward Ho!, and within sound of the crowded streets of Hampshire's finest seaside town lies the heart of Shelley. In the same town lies Lord Cromer, the maker of modern Egypt, so much esteemed by his country that he has a lovely medallion in Westminster Abbey.

But not yet are Hampshire's great names at an end. Lord Palmerston's home was at Romsey, and at Portsmouth the Victorian novelist George Meredith, the London novelist Sir Walter Besant, and the great Thames tunneller Isambard Brunel. From Portsmouth also came Vicat Cole, RA, who painted many sunny landscapes the last generation loved to see. This county of Jane Austen was also the county of Mary Mitford, who was born at Alresford, and Charlotte Yonge, who was born at Otterbourne, and it is not to be forgotten that in a grave at Lyndhurst, surrounded by the natural wonderland of the New Forest, lies the immortal Alice. This county claims also for its own the New Forest naturalist William Gilpin, and those two naturalists William Curtis and John Goodyer, Curtis remembered by a museum at Alton, Goodyer remembered as the greatest botanist of Cromwell's time. At Ropley was born the man who crowned Queen Victoria; at Oakley was born the man who crowned our bluebeard king, Archbishop Warham; and at Catherington lies one of our bravest and most reckless generals, Sir Charles Napier, conqueror of Scinde.

Of the makers of books Hampshire has seen a long procession passing by. We have looked at some of them, but here came Keats and loved it, here was George MacDonald, here

Darwin wrote, here Tennyson lived, here R. L. S. wrote his verses, here John Keble worked and wrote and built a church. Here Lamb and Coleridge came; here William Cobbett farmed. Here the fine poet Edward Thomas set out in our own time for the war from which he did not come back. At Southampton was born Charles Dibdin, who wrote over a thousand songs; at Upham Edward Young, the poet of Night Thoughts; at Bentworth George Wither, the poet who sold his lands to raise a troop of horse for Cromwell. At Hursley lies Thomas Sternhold, who set the Psalms to music; at Basingstoke lived Thomas Warton and here were born his sons, all three famous in poetry and education. And it is impossible to forget that the writer of some of the best hymns in our language was here, Thomas Ken, the bishop who refused to allow the king to bring Nell Gwynn into his house at Winchester.

We see that Hampshire has a noble place in our island story, a roll of honour thrilling to read, and we have seen that as a stretch of English landscape, reaching from the borders of London's neighbour down to the sea, it is as characteristic as any county in the land. In its natural endowment it is hardly less distinguished, indeed, than in its historic associations and its links with great folk. Its chief natural possession is the New Forest, an untamed stretch of country covering nearly the whole of the south-western area. It reaches from Southampton Water to the Dorset border, covering about 150 square miles.

It is the home of hare, fox, badger, and of rare butterflies and birds; 250 of our 350 species of birds have been seen within its precincts. In its long history it has known all kinds of men who have left with it tokens of themselves—implements of the Stone Age, graves of the Bronze Age, prehistoric camps, and pastoral earthworks; and within historic time Roman potteries have been found. It was the hunting-ground of the Conqueror, who hunted here so sternly that he ordained that whoever else killed a hart or a hind should be blinded. Two of his sons fell here while hunting, and near Canterton, in an oak glade at the foot of a steeply descending path, is a stone marking the spot where William Rufus fell there. Today there are few deer in the Forest, their place being taken by the shaggy little ponies that pick a scanty living among the heather, chewing the prickly furze-tops. They have owners who pay a grazing fee for them, and who know exactly where to find them when the time comes for the annual shows; but to most of us as we run through the Forest the ponies look like wild free things.

The villages of the Forest are few in number, but are mostly lovely or beautifully set. One of them is Beaulieu, with loveliness all round it, alive with nightingales, and with its exquisite ruined Abbey, its winding river, and its clustering woods of oak. Another is Boldre, with its old church, its old stone bridge, and the earthworks older than all. Bucklers Hard is in the Forest and launched 40 men-of-war made here from Forest oaks. Lyndhurst belongs to it, and is indeed the Forest capital, with its Verderer's hall, where hangs what is called William Rufus's stirrup through which all Forest dogs must pass if they would save their toes in old cruel days, and where the ancient court of Swainmote is still held to deal with Forest affairs. Brook, Burley, Bramshaw, Brockenhurst, Wood Green, and the rest, all have a claim on our hearts as children of the New Forest.

Then there are the little woods in the Forest: Sloden, where yews, crab-apples, and whitebeam mingle with oak and ash, holly and thorn; Eyeworth with a queen beech 17 feet round; beautiful Ocknell planted in the 18th century; Bushey Bratley brave with ancient beeches; Knightwood Inclosure, famous for its mighty oak 21 feet round; Mark Ash with two giant beeches six and seven yards round; Malwood Castle, site of an ancient camp; Ridley Wood, with beeches pollarded in Queen Elizabeth's day, still with the bank and ditch which enclosed it in the Middle Ages; and Whitley Wood, where oaks abound.

And then there are the plains of the Forest so glorious in the sun, so terrible under cloud: Beaulieu Hilltop Heath, Setley Plain, the wide heathery bottom of Latchmore with the treacherous bogs gay with white cotton grass, and the noble hills giving us such unforgettable views, as Pipers Wait, 422 feet high, and Bramshaw Telegraph, 419 feet.

The Forest has fine ponds—the so-called dewpond on the plain above Ocknell Wood, Hatchet Pond on Beaulieu Plain, and beautiful Sowley Pond graced with reeds and guarded by trees in which the herons live.

The Forest has singularly kept its laws, remnants of the forest laws that were once almost universal, and it has not only its own laws but almost a language of its own. Here we hear words and names familiar in these haunts since Saxon days, men speaking of the Swainmote, the name of the Forest Court held at Lyndhurst; of Estover, the right attached to certain houses of having fuel from the woods of the Forest; of Pannage, used for the beech and oak mast which makes food for pigs; of Torberie, the right of digging turf in a particular part of the Forest. Here and there we find a plain called a standing, such as Abbot's Standing near Beaulieu, and the word is traced to the custom of the Middle Ages when the game would be driven to a clearing in the woods where the sportsmen awaited it, concealed in branches on a stage or stand. Men still talk in the Forest of a Hat, which is a clump of trees on a little hill.

The woodlands of Hampshire are in all about 120,000 acres, and they are as typical of the county as the sheep and cattle on its downs, the horses on its uplands, the milch cows in the meadowed valleys, the fields aglow with corn, the poultry-runs that make patchwork on the hillsides. The hills come over the border from its county's eastern neighbours Surrey and Sussex, both the North Downs and the South Downs invading it and becoming linked together by the Alton Hills. Giving rise to the River Loddon and its tributaries, the North Downs run high across the north of Hampshire, mounting to within a mile or two of Inkpen Beacon just over the Berkshire border. Pilot Hill is their highest point in Hampshire, 874 feet. The South Downs are more broken than the North by rivers making for the Channel, and go west at a lower level by Winchester towards Salisbury Plain; but near Petersfield they rise in Butser Hill, the highest point in the county, 889 feet. From this great height we can look due north across to the Alton Hills and south to Broadhalfpenny Down, cradle of English cricket. The chalk downs cover a little more than half the county, and it may roughly be said that the county sinks slowly southward towards the sea. In every direction the downland area rises and falls, and in the hollows, where clays and loams take the place of chalk, are snug farms and a richer variety of trees than the yew, the beech, and the juniper of the downs.

Down the river valleys the deeper soil gives richness to the vegetation, giving us the northern woodlands, the eastern border called the Weald, and in the south-east the luxuriant growth of the early strawberry which loves the warm earth. A fine fruit garden is this. Nowhere in Hampshire is the country flat; a height of 200 feet gives the traveller a long range of view, and everywhere he goes he crosses river valleys with green meadows in which cows are browsing, field after field of strawberries in due season, and spreading acres of golden corn.

There are seven of these rivers running south, the most easterly of them being the Meon, which runs for 20 miles and descends 400 feet from springs at Oxenbourne, popping underground at West Meon and almost losing itself in the sands when it reaches the mouth of Southampton Water. Two miles up Southampton Water is the River Hamble, 12 miles long and one blaze of yachts. We must all love it for its good little ship Mercury, one of the best schools for the British Fleet. At the head of the great inlet we find the two rivers that have done so much to make Hampshire what it is, the Itchen on the east and the Test (known to anglers everywhere for its trout-fishing) on the west.

The Itchen is only 20 miles long, but is vitally important to the docks at its mouth. Rising near Hinton Ampner 240 feet above sea level, it is joined by the Candover and the Arle, and flows through the broad valley into Winchester, where Alfred must have walked along its bank. Twyford lies in the still wider valley the river has cut through the chalk, and at Eastleigh it leaves the downs behind for industry on its banks. The Test, flowing into the western horn of Southampton and becoming more and more valuable as the great seaport expands, is nearly 40 miles long. Rising below the North Downs near Ashe, it is joined by the Bullington, running through a valley delighting the naturalist, and the Anton, which gives its name to Andover, and carves its way through the South Downs to Romsey, where once it turned many mills before going slowly on to pour itself into Southampton Water.

Two rivers drain the New Forest into the Solent, the Beaulieu, 12 miles long, with Bucklers Hard on its banks and memories of our wooden men-of-war; and the Lymington, also running for 12 miles, a very lovely stream with Brockenhurst in the midst. These six are Hampshire's own rivers; the seventh is the Salisbury Avon which leaves the downs at the county boundary and flows through a valley in which lie such places as Ringwood and Fordingbridge and finally Christchurch, where, with the Stour coming over the Dorset boundary, it forms a remarkable estuary behind one of the most invigorating headlands on Hampshire's stirring coast, Hengistbury. It is Bournemouth which is guarding this noble headland for the nation; it is the eastern point of that great seaside town which has hardly a rival in the land, attracting a countless host that comes and goes, and a smaller host of intellectual folk who settle in this pleasant place for the evening of their days. Hampshire has indeed some remarkable estuaries, but the sea has had a share with the rivers in shaping its coast. Portsmouth Harbour has been from earliest times famous as a home of the British Fleet, and the eastern shore of this wide expanse of sea water is formed by Hayling Island, which on its farther side shares with Sussex the little harbour of Chichester.

The more we think of Hampshire and the more we look at its map or ride about its million acres, the more we feel that this central mass of southern England is something unique. Nature has richly equipped it with its share of common English beauty, and History, as we see, has adorned it beyond most other shires. It may seem to us that two things stand for its uniqueness—the New Forest for its natural beauty, and the Victory at Portsmouth for its place in history. In all our goings round England, seeing its famous and dramatic things, we have seen nothing more moving than the sight of Old England's Wooden Walls in Portsmouth Harbour—Nelson's flagship set out in all its glory as he saw it.

Hampshire goes back a long long way, with 400 prehistoric burial mounds, a dozen Saxon monuments and scores of Norman ones, and more old bells and ancient dials than we can remember; but among all these things (even if we count such splendours as Romsey Abbey, Christchurch Minster, the Hospital of St Cross, and Winchester itself), these ships stand out as perhaps the most romantic of all its possessions.

And yet this county is very much alive, with all its roots in the past. Come to Bournemouth in the summer and see. Come to Aldershot and see the British Army. Come to Portsmouth and see the British Navy. Come to Basingstoke and see a British workshop. Come to Southampton and see the Queen Mary, the wonder of the 20th century world, keeping touch week by week with the two great families of the English-speaking peoples. We shall feel in any of these places (and in 300 more) that Hampshire is alive with energy as well as beauty, with the work of the day as well as with her trees and flowers and the music of her nightingales. And then we can go to the Isle of Wight, and find that she has one more wonder yet, a little kingdom of serenity in this most troubled world.

Ophelia's Garland

ABBOTS ANN. One of Nature's exquisite little places, exquisitely named, it has been an inhabited corner of these islands since Caesar's legions came. One of the beautiful things found in a Roman villa here is a tessellated pavement now in our national treasure-house. And long after that this village on the little river Pill was one of the many estates of Thomas Pitt, Diamond Pitt, grandfather of the great Earl of Chatham. An extraordinary man, he enriched himself in India, where one of his transactions was to buy for £20,000 a diamond he sold for £135,000, now one of the national jewels of France. Settling down after a life of adventurous money-making, he became a Commissioner for building new churches, and set an example by rebuilding in classic style the church of his own village, Abbots Ann. A medallion under the tower tells of his munificence.

We reach the church by paths in the shade of yews and chestnuts, and find it an odd little place with panelled box-pews, a handsome gallery, a font lid decorated with acorns, and an altar table and a chair in the vestry which are thought to belong to Shakespeare's day, when the bells in the tower were first rung. The chair is carved with the heads of two grotesque lions.

High up in the nave two rows of white paper garlands hang on the wall, with white paper gloves dangling from each. To those who do not know their significance they are nothings, but to those who know they are touchingly human things, for each of these white garlands has followed to the grave some maid who led an unspotted life and died before she could be a bride, or some young man who died too soon. The earliest garland dates from 1740, and the two latest we saw were those of a boy of 15 who died in the last year of the war and of a woman who died in 1921. It seemed to us remarkable not only to find these garlands here but to find the custom still existing.

The honouring of a blameless life with these garlands is a very ancient custom and was once common in our countryside. Gilbert White witnessed it when he was a boy in Selborne, but he records its decline, and though we have found the garlands in perhaps half a dozen churches, as far as we know Abbots Ann is the only place where the practice continues. The most thrilling memory it brings to mind is in Shakespeare's picture of the graveside of Ophelia. Ophelia is depicted in Hamlet as being awarded these tributes to her virtue (called crants then) in spite of the vehement protest of the churlish priest who buried her, who was ruthlessly chastened by her brother with a scorn that stirs us still as we read his words:

> Priest. *She should in ground unsanctified have lodged*
> *Till the last trumpet ;* . . .
> *Yet here she is allowed her virgin crants,*
> *Her maiden strewments, and the bringing home*
> *Of bell and burial.*
> Laertes. *Must there no more be done?*
> Priest. *No more be done!*
> *We should profane the service of the dead,*
> *To sing a requiem, and such rest to her,*
> *As to peace-parted souls.*
> Laertes. *Lay her i' the earth;*
> *And from her fair and unpolluted flesh*
> *May violets spring! I tell thee, churlish priest,*
> *A minist'ring angel shall my sister be,*
> *When thou liest howling.*

What Happened to a Village

ALDERSHOT. It has grown from a small village of Crimean War days to be the chief military centre of England, with a camp of 4000 acres. Its famous barracks are relieved by trees, and the big garrison church of All Saints is set among fine evergreens. Its walls are crowded with memorials to fallen soldiers, and hanging in it are the tattered colours of the regiments.

One of its striking possessions is a gigantic statue of Wellington on horseback by Matthew Wyatt; it is by the Royal Pavilion. The Iron Duke (who is here in bronze) has come from Hyde Park Corner. There he was looking out on the moving throng long before it became the busiest corner in the world. The statue stood at the top of Constitution Hill before the great arch now crowned by the Quadriga, and it was taken to pieces and drawn to Aldershot by horses.

The first Lord Baden Powell used to tell an odd story of this statue. While it was being put together, only the horse's head remaining to be fixed, the men knocked off work for their midday meal. The call "Feed" came from the stables near by, and a cavalry man who was there with his meal snatched up his dinner and rammed it down the throat of the bronze horse. Whether he himself was not hungry that day, or whether an excess of good humour led him thus to give the duke's horse a meal, we do not know, but down the throat of the bronze horse his dinner went, and there, we believe, it still remains.

The old village church of St Michael stands by a fine park and has been made new except for its 15th century tower (with a bell of Shakespeare's day), an old chapel, and some medieval windows. On the walls are kneeling figures of two ladies of the days of Queen Elizabeth, one Lady Mary Tichborne (who kneels with seven sons and six daughters), the other Lady Ellen Tichborne, wearing a flowing black dress and a ruff, and with this fine rhyme about her:

> *Who lived (and now is dead)*
> *A life prepared for dying,*
> *Who died (and now she lives)*
> *A death prepared for living,*
> *So well she both professed*
> *That she in both is blest.*

The church has some good modern woodwork, a beautiful window of Christ among the Children, and a tiny sculpture of the Madonna and Child brought from the battlefields of France in the first year of the Great War.

Aldershot has six churches in all, public gardens with an obelisk of Cornish granite and some captured guns in memory of the men who fell in the war, and one of the biggest open-air swimming pools, covering an acre and holding a million gallons. A mile away is Caesar's Camp, and an entrenchment which it is thought might have been occupied by King Alfred when he defeated the Northmen at Farnham.

We can hardly expect to find the characteristic beauty of England here, but perhaps it may be said that this scathing picture of the way Aldershot village was made into a camp seems a little too scathing; it is by Mrs Ewing, who was writing her stories for children then:

Take a Highwayman's Heath. Destroy every vestige of life with fire and axe, from the pine that has longest been a landmark to the smallest beetle smothered in smoking moss. Burn acres of purple and pink heather, and pare away the young bracken that springs verdant from its ashes. Let flame consume the perfumed gorse in all its glory and not spare the broom, whose more exquisite yellow atones for its lack of fragrance. In this common ruin be every lesser flower involved: blue beds of speedwell by the wayfarer's path, the daintier milkwort and rougher red rattle, down to the very dodder that clasps the heather; let them perish and the face of Dame Nature be utterly blackened! Then: shave the heath as bare as the back of your hand, and if you have felled every tree, and left not so much as a tussock of grass or a scarlet toadstool to break the force of the winds, then shall the winds come, from the east and from the west from the north and from the south, and shall raise on your shaven heath clouds of sand that would not discredit a desert in the heart of Africa. By some such recipe the ground was prepared for that Camp of Instruction.

Nelson's Admiral and Cromwell's Little Dick

ALRESFORD. This trim and prosperous-looking little country town has 800 years experience of English ups and downs. It was a Bishop of Winchester, Godfrey de Lucy, who founded the town at the head of what he hoped would become a great trade waterway through Winchester to Southampton. He built a dam across the river and dug a reservoir of 200 acres to make the Itchen, into which the Arle flows, navigable at all seasons. In going direct from New Alresford to Old the traffic still crosses over Bishop Lucy's dam, lined with tall trees through whose tapering trunks the waters of his reservoir twinkle in the sun. The reservoir has shrunk to a mere 60 acres, but is beautiful and big enough to make us wonder at the skill of the men who made it so long ago.

Besides the Causeway and the Reservoir, Alresford has a bridge of the 14th century, tucked away below the houses at the bottom of Broad Street, which in itself is altogether enchanting. The street is very wide, as its name informs us, and runs between two grass banks shaded with limes. Little shops and charming little houses smile across at each other from behind the limes, and the church looks down from the top of the town.

In one of these houses, grey blue with green windows and doors when we called, a girl was born about 200 years ago, who grew up to give us some of the most intimate glimpses we have into the quiet side of 18th century life. She was Mary Russell Mitford, and she wrote Our Village. Dr Mitford was a spendthrift, a worthless sort of fellow, who not only went through his own fortune and that of the heiress he married, but managed to squander £20,000 won by his little daughter in a lottery when she was ten. Most of her life Mary had to work hard to support him. Their house has been enlarged, but its owners have always taken pains to preserve it as it was. We may be sure that Mary knew the lovely mantelpiece in the drawing-room and that the room behind, with its delightful William and Mary window, was her father's study, the room where she would read the leading article in The Times to him. A rare window it is, for it is hard to find one like it now. It can be pushed up till it disappears into the wall above, allowing us to walk through into the garden.

The church of St John the Baptist has suffered with the rest of the town in a plague of fires, and has been extensively restored, yet the oldest part of the tower comes from Norman times and it is more than probable that there was a Saxon church on this very site. Above the west door is another piece of ancient craftsmanship, a tiny clear-cut stone crucifix whose age must be about 700 years. Within all is neat and looking new, but there is a 13th century tower arch; a pretty Jacobean table given by the son of James Sait, who was sexton and clerk here 50 years: and a glazed case full of pieces of old carved masonry, including two very good faces. The big east window is brightly coloured with many figures.

An orderly line of five gravestones rises up in the churchyard, each at the head of a grave like a flower-bed, wired off from the rest of the ground. Here sleep five of Napoleon's men, four soldiers and one sailor. The town is full of stories about French prisoners billeted here. One says they gave the church its clock in 1811; another that they were most unpopular until one night a fearful fire broke out, and they rose to the occasion in such fashion that they were looked upon as heroes. The handsome churchyard gates to the highroad are in memory of a lady who worshipped here for half a century.

Old Alresford was long ago outdistanced in the race for prosperity by its namesake beyond Bishop Lucy's Causeway, and is content to drowse by a sedgy green divided by a trickling stream. Its 18th century brick church has an imposing wall-monument in the nave. Two lifesize figures at the sides seem slightly to embarrass, by their flamboyancy, the lovable young woman whose bust looks at us a little shyly from the top. She is Jane Rodney, the wife of one of Nelson's band of brothers, who lies in St Paul's; she died at only 27, leaving two little ones behind.

Admiral Rodney built the great house by the church, raised on the foundations of the old manor house, and it is hard to believe, as we look at this house and the impressive monument he raised to his wife, that at one time he was so pressed for money that he had to fly from his creditors.

We may think it a pity that Nelson's admiral pulled down the old manor house, for in it lived a man Oliver Cromwell loved, whom he affectionately called Little Dick. Richard Norton, a Puritan to begin with, was one of those men who could not stay the course, and he dwindled ultimately into Royalism. But before he left the Puritans he helped to deal the Royalist cause one of its severest blows while serving under Sir William Waller. When the two armies were at grips at Cheriton he was able, by his knowledge of these lanes and byways, to bring up his troop of horse unseen behind the king's men and to charge down on them from the rear, flinging them into confusion.

There was a rector here who shepherded his flock for 52 years last century, Henry Hubbard; and we noticed in the churchyard a most attractive little classical building put up not long before we called. It covers a family vault, and inside it is a marble altar below a sculpture of the Madonna and Child. When we called Mr Walter Spiers was about to celebrate his 75th anniversary as a bellringer here; he started as a ringer when he was nine, and had rung the bells of nearly every church in the county.

It was the wife of a rector of Old Alresford who founded the Mothers Union, which has 600,000 members all over the world pledged to uphold the sanctity of marriage. There is a Mary Sumner House in Westminster built as a memorial to this lady of the rectory. The first card of membership of this widespread union was drawn up here, and the work went on quietly in this village for its first nine years. Then Mary Sumner moved to Winchester, her husband being made archdeacon, and afterwards appointed Bishop of Guildford.

Here Lived Edmund Spenser

ALTON. It is a delightful country town of good repute in the world of healing, for it has one of the best homes for cripples in England. It should be of good repute to those who love courage, for it has a dramatic tale to tell of the fall of a gallant little host in the Civil War. As a place of pilgrimage, it was the birthplace of a man considered to be the best botanist in England in his day (John Goodyer), and it is believed to be one of the few places in England where we know that Edmund Spenser lived.

Hidden in a crowded narrow street in the marketplace is a brick house now made into two cottages, their doors sharing the same pediment. It is said that when these houses were one, back in the days of our Golden Age, it was the home of one of the most choice spirits of our literature, the man who wrote the Faerie Queene and died for want of bread. John Aubrey says that "Mr Spenser lived some time in these parts, in this delicate sweet air, where he enjoyed his muse and writ good part of his verse." The house is in Amery Street and has a tablet saying that Spenser lived there in 1590. We know that he was in England at this time and it has been calculated that this would be the date when he would be down at Alton. He was also for some time at Penshurst with Philip Sidney, starting the Faerie Queene and finishing the Shepherd's Calendar in that famous house. John Aubrey's information is all we have bearing on that point, but it was written only half a century after Spenser's death and may therefore be accepted. If the tablet is true this house is the one in which he may have written not only the Ruines of Time but possibly Mother Hubbard's Tale, which, attributed to his youth, is so melancholy and intimate a picture of the disappointments of Court that it must have sprung from the disappointment attending his visit to Elizabeth with the Faerie Queene, which brought him, not great State office as he had hoped, but only a £50 pension.

The church is very old and full of beauty; the central tower of the early Normans remains, rising on four arches with capitals carved a few years after the Conqueror came. The carvings are crude but deeply interesting, and it is stirring to think that this dragon, this dove, these asses, this hyena, and this cockerel upside down, with all the figures carved round about, were done by men who would hear the news of the Battle of Hastings. There are two Norman windows over the arches of the tower. Inside is a little Norman doorway into the vestry, and the font, which was found lying abandoned on a farm, is also Norman.

Alton's is one of the rare churches with two naves and two chancels, one nave and chancel 15th century, the others having grown up round the church the Normans built. They are separated by a noble medieval arcade running the whole length of the church, with stone heads looking down from the corbels. In the south chancel are several things about 750 years old, a big canopied piscina, an aumbry, and a carving of a hand grasping a pastoral staff. The chancel has become the peace memorial chapel and is resplendent with coloured sculptures of St Michael and St George.

From the 15th century come paintings of figures fading away on one of the pillars of the nave; they represent a bishop, a king, and a saint. From the same century comes part of the screen, and there are fragments of old glass in the vestry. There is a small brass on a pillar to the memory of Christopher Walaston who was Groom of the Chamber and Master of the Goshawks to four sovereigns, and near it is a 16th century brass of a lady and her three daughters. A stout almsbox fitted to a pier has received the charity of many generations, for it was here in early Stuart days, and an almsdish has kept it company all the time. A splendid 18th century candelabra hangs under the tower, and in the porch (which has a Tudor doorway with a fine old door) are two elaborately wrought parts of a Jacobean torch-holder.

But not all these things, ancient and lovely as they are, thrill us like the bullet marks on the pillars and the doorways and the door itself, some of the holes having still the actual bullets in them. A brass with the name of Colonel Boles reminds us that the bullets come from the Civil War. It was standing in this magnificent Jacobean pulpit that Colonel Boles died for Charles Stuart. It is a thrilling story.

Alton was held for the king by Lord Crawford with a troop of horse and a small company of infantry under Colonel Boles. General Waller lay at Farnham with 5000 men of the Parliamentary Army. The two commanders amused themselves by sending jesting messages to one another, and Lord Crawford sent to General Waller an invitation to exchange a butt of wine for an ox. On receiving the wine Crawford answered that he would bring the ox in person, to which the answer was that he need not trouble, as General Waller would fetch it himself. That night the General marched round and came upon the Royalists suddenly from behind. Lord Crawford galloped away for reinforcements, leaving Colonel Boles to hold out as long as he could with his infantry. The Parliament men fired the thatch of several houses, and under cover of the smoke fell on the Royalists in the marketplace. A loyal Alton man set fire to his own house so that the smoke might confuse the Puritans, and it served its purpose by enabling Boles to withdraw his men to the hillside under the church. They fought bravely from dawn till noon, but the odds were against them, and under the heavy fire of two regiments they were forced back first to the churchyard wall, then to the churchyard, then into the church itself. Barricading the door, the colonel told his men the fight was to the death. The cannon of the Parliament men battered down the door, and of the eighty Royalists who went in sixty were soon dead. The twenty living men gave up the fight, but not Colonel Boles. Step by step he was forced back thrusting and parrying, to the foot of the pulpit and up its steps; and then, crying aloud the name of the king, he fell.

The inscription tells that this memorial was set up to this renowned martialist Richard Boles, who for King Charles did wonders at the Battle of Edgehill and whose last command was at Alton, where he was surprised by five or six thousand of the rebels, which caused him to fly to the church with near fourscore of his men, who there fought them six or seven hours:

The rebel breaking in upon him, he slew with his sword six or seven, and then was slain himself with sixty of his men about him. His gracious Sovereign, hearing of his death, gave him his high commendation in this passionate expression, Bring me a mourning scarf; I have lost one of the best commanders in this kingdom.

> *Alton will tell you of that famous fight*
> *Which this man made and bade the world Good-Night.*
> *His virtuous life feared not mortality,*
> *His body must, his virtues cannot, die.*
> *Because his blood was there so nobly spent*
> *This is his tomb, the church his monument.*

Alton has a modern church of All Saints, and its lady chapel has been dedicated by its townsfolk to one of the old vicars, a butcher's errand boy who grew up to be the shepherd of the flock. The church has a pulpit and a font carved by members of the congregation, and an 18th century lamp from Italy hanging in the sanctuary. There is a second modern church on the road to Medstead, the church of Alton Abbey built by eight monks who 40 years ago walked from South Wales with their priest to found an abbey in Hampshire. They had no money to pay for lodging, and the first night they slept under trees in the pouring rain. The next day they started to make themselves huts of wattle and daub and a tiny wattle church to worship in. Then they began work on the abbey church, picking up flints from the estate for its walls, with only a ship's carpenter to help with the woodwork. It is a humble place compared with the abbey built by the monks of Buckfast, but the same idea is behind both. Alton's monks added a gatehouse and quarters for themselves which had to be enlarged as their number increased; and, because the chief work of their Order of St Paul is to care for destitute seamen, there is a house attached to the abbey where live 20 old sailors home from sea.

Alton (which has an avenue of beautiful chestnut trees by the green) has known two famous botanists, John Goodyer born in Queen Elizabeth's time, whom we meet again at Buriton, and William Curtis, who lived through the last half of the 18th century. Curtis was first interested in plants by an ostler at the Crown Hotel, and lived to be a veritable Hampshire Linnaeus. He was a doctor, but most of all he loved botany. He published his own researches and translated those of Linnaeus, and was claimed as one of the foremost naturalists of his day. His work on grasses was of the utmost value to farmers, and he tested and popularised new vegetables, and wrote plainly and practically on every species of the vegetable kingdom, linking botany with medicine in a masterly way. In his day the countryside was seized with panic over a plague of browntailed moths. The farmers, slow to believe in new ideas, believed the caterpillars would eat the crops bare, but William Curtis quietly investigated the habits of the parasite and found that England was experiencing one of those tidal waves of insect life which recur from time to time and ebb as surely as they rise. He was right.

The manuscript lectures and notes of William Curtis, with fine

drawings by Sydenham Edwards and Moses Harris, may be seen in
Alton Museum, and here, too, is a brown ware jug beautifully
moulded with hops and ears of barley, specially made for Curtis
in 1781. In this museum we are reminded of another famous
Englishman, for here is a page from the diary of Gilbert White of
Selborne, four miles away. It gives us a glimpse of the famous
naturalist in his vicarage garden, and above it hangs a framed bill
from the Swan Inn for the hire of a post-chaise White took from
Selborne to Alresford on December 8, 1787. The museum has a
collection of Roman and medieval antiquities, agricultural implements, and documents relating to the town's history.

A row of fine old almshouses still stands in Church Street, and the
gabled grammar school founded in 1638 by John Eggar is still used
as a school for girls. William Pinnock, who wrote several school
books last century, was an usher here.

We do not know how many Alton folk could quote a few lines
from Edmund Spenser's Faerie Queene, but time was when all good
Alton folk could quote a line or two from Kipling's Absentminded
Beggar, for it was thanks to the fund raised by this poem during the
South African War that Sir William Treloar, the generous-hearted
Cornishman who became Lord Mayor of London, was able to
snatch a hospital here from ruin and turn it to magnificent use again.
The hospital was built for the wounded, and after the war the War
Office abandoned it, so that the grass grew up to the trees and there
was one more wilderness of peace in our fair island. It was the end of
a movement of great enthusiasm which had presented the hospital
to the nation; and yet it was not the end, for Sir William Treloar,
remembering the little cripples for whom he gave his life, and
hearing that the hospital was falling into ruin, begged the War
Office to give it to him. The War Office referred him to the Charity
Commissioners. The Charity Commissioners were astonished at
such an appeal for charity, and it appeared that a thing given to the
nation for one purpose could not be diverted to a new purpose. In
the end, however, Democracy found a way, and an Act of Parliament
was passed, transferring this gift to the nation to Sir William Treloar's cripples. In the midst of the buildings today is a bust of Sir
William, once a beloved figure here as he is still an honoured
memory. It will be long before his familiar figure is forgotten on

Ludgate Hill, for he was part of it; he had been in London as a business man and a civic ruler for over 40 years. In his college days he travelled to town from Blackheath in a railway carriage with no roof, no windows, and no seats.

The five great blocks of his hospital now span a distance of a thousand feet, and there has been no nobler work in England than the work done here for some of the saddest children ever born. There was no hospital anywhere for these little ones with a disease in their bones which strong men shudder to think of; but for years now they have been arriving here and going home again, 92 out of every hundred of them made whole.

One cripple passing through this place is the heroine of one of the most remarkable little stories of the Great War. This is it.

A Wonderful Story of the Great War

IT happened that in 1912 a South African lady living in Windhoek sent her little daughter, three years old, to a famous hospital in Berlin to be treated for tuberculosis of the spine. She was cured, and arrangements were made for her return home when suddenly the Great Shadow fell upon the world.

As the mother was preparing to leave Windhoek the German army invaded Belgium, and Germany found herself at war with the British Empire. Windhoek is in South-West Africa, which was then German territory, and the child's father, a British subject, was imprisoned in a concentration camp. Mrs Phillips was left with two children to provide for.

It is not difficult to imagine her distress, for her daughter was now alone in an enemy land and the mother was not allowed to write or even to send the fees to the hospital. It seemed suspicious to the German authorities in Africa, and as her home had been burned down the mother could not produce the papers showing that her child was in a Berlin hospital. It was not very long before South-West Africa became British and the father was released from camp; but his freedom made little difference as far as the child was concerned, for still they could not communicate with an enemy country. They heard nothing and could find out nothing. They waited in an agony of suffering all through the war; theirs was one of the millions of small tragedies arising from the calamity that overwhelmed mankind.

They were bitter days for this poor mother, and more bitter still they would have been had she known the truth about her child, frail subject of the British flag. The truth is that this little one was *wandering in the streets of Berlin in the middle of the Great War.*

What had happened was as remarkable in its way as what was about to happen. When the child's father took her to the Berlin hospital he was naturally unhappy at leaving her there alone, and begged one of the nurses to watch over her. The nurse was faithful to her trust. She took a personal interest in her charge as long as she remained in hospital; but the time came when the pressure of war conditions drove the patients from the hospital, which was needed for wounded soldiers, and our little South African, now cured, was handed over to a charitable institution.

The nurse was drafted to duty elsewhere, but continued to watch over her little friend. At last came the time when the strain of the war was almost too much for Germany to bear, and the child, now eight, was handed over to somebody unknown, a woman who appeared to be respectable but treated the child so harshly that hard work and low diet brought a return of the spinal trouble. The nurse lost sight of her. Then happened a very remarkable thing. Walking in the streets of Berlin one day, the nurse noticed a crippled child, and, her heart full of pity, she went across the street and received the surprise of her life, for the cripple was no other than her little hospital friend. The child was very ill from starvation and harsh treatment and the effects of scrubbing floors. It was not easy to hold the child of an enemy country in Berlin in those late years of the war, when every mouthful of food was twice precious, but the nurse took the cripple under her care, and at length was able, some time in 1917, to exchange her for a German officer who had been taken prisoner and was in Belgium.

Now this little one, unknown child in a strange land, found her way to England and to Alton, where she was cured again of her spinal trouble in the Treloar Hospital. Here she lay, and one day a South African soldier, on leave in London, saw her picture in an advertisement of the hospital, came down to Alton, and identified her, so that she was soon with her mother again. An appeal in the Children's Newspaper was the means of discovering the German nurse, who was put in touch with the friend she had snatched so miraculously from the peril of the war.

By Portsmouth Harbour

ALVERSTOKE. Tucked away between the Solent and Haslar Creek, running up from Portsmouth Harbour, is this old haven of rest, with gorse-sprinkled common and a crescent of white-fronted old houses that were young when Queen Victoria was in her nursery. How many admirals, home from sea, have come here to end their days?

The white-fronted crescent, built when the place had ambitions to become a spa and have a pump room, is almost its greatest antiquity. The church by the Georgian rectory, standing on a slight rise with the shallowing creek coming almost to its foot, is a building of the 19th century on the site where a much older church had stood. But all seamen know the place, for between the shore and the church stands the lofty three-sided column of brick, faced with white stone and called the Gilkicker, which marks for ships the sunken spit that begins from there to stretch towards Spithead. Westwards is Stoke's Bay with the naval station at the end of an Admiralty pier, and on the shore the line of bathing-boxes each year stretching farther toward Lee-on-the-Solent. Towards Gosport, the common merges into the grounds of Haslar Naval Hospital and its old tree-shaded cemetery.

There are older hospitals than this great naval establishment, as well as newer ones, but few join more effectively a spacious old dignity with the modern demands of light and air. It has many great wards fitted with every modern device of the art of healing for the reception of 2000 patients. It has rows of old houses of Georgian brick for its principal officers, and a front and wings and chapel raised in the fine tradition of Georgian architecture.

Lord Sandwich, First Lord of the Admiralty, irreverently called Jemmy Twitcher by the Navy, was its foster-father, and he was happy in persuading the Government to spare no expense. Its architect had the idea of designing it after the model of Greenwich Palace, and if his hopes were not quite fulfilled he at any rate built well. Its foundations, of immense strength, were laid in 1746 and the building was completed in 1762. Its walls are of great thickness, four feet in the lower stories, with vast cellars below. The buildings occupy more than seven acres, the airing-grounds (where convalescents were allowed to walk and take the air) comprise 33 acres; and this is only a third of Haslar Hospital's holding. It has a magnificent sea-front, which is in itself more attractive than any esplanade.

Over the main entrance is a remarkable piece of sculpture in Portland stone. In the middle are the royal arms of George the Second, on the left a woman's figure leans on a rudder and pours oil on the wounds of a sailor, the north star above her head and the compass at her feet. On the right-hand side Commerce sits among bales and chests, distributing money, fruit, and flowers, and at the corner is a sailor in distress.

The museum has received for a hundred years or so contributions from naval captains and surgeons, specimens from all parts of the world, a miscellaneous collection of weapons and many curious objects from distant seas and islands. Among them may be mentioned a grisly assembly of tattooed heads from New Zealand. The most historic relic of all is Captain Cook's speaking-trumpet.

The beautiful cemetery has many sad memories but few notable memorials. The sick and wounded of Sir John Moore's army were brought to Haslar and large numbers died. They were buried here. Many of the brave who perished in the wreck of the Royal George were laid in the paddock, and it is possible that the remains of Admiral Kempenfelt himself are among them:

> Brave Kempenfelt is gone
> His last sea fight is fought,
> His work of glory done.

These members of the eight hundred for whom the bell would toll (Toll for the brave, the brave that are no more) are in the old cemetery. In the new one is a monument to the memory of the 311 officers and men who perished in the Eurydice when she foundered off the Isle of Wight in 1878.

At one end of the sea wall is Fort Monckton, and at the other is a narrow spit where stands Fort Block House guarding the western entrance to Portsmouth harbour. From it in old times the great chains were stretched to the opposite side of the harbour, and tightened in time of danger by capstans.

The story of Haslar hospital would be incomplete without reference to the curious old bridge linking it with Gosport. It has a long and curious story of vested interest, and when we crossed it last we had still to pay the toll.

The church has an interesting link with naval history, for here lies Captain George Bligh, who as a lieutenant on the Victory was wounded by a musket ball at Trafalgar. Unlike Nelson, he made a good recovery and lived to serve his country for eleven more years. He was buried here in 1835; six of the oldest watermen in Gosport carried his coffin to the tomb, and each received (by his desire) a sovereign and a new suit.

There is at Alverstoke a branch of the National Children's Home, which has a little chapel in front of which stand a bird sanctuary and a lily pond, presided over by the Saint of Little Brethren, St Francis. It stands amid tall trees and within call of the sea. The architect said that when he was asked to design a church for children there came to mind the little hill churches of Italy mellowed by southern suns.

A Great Lady

AMPFIELD. A tiny place in lovely pastoral country, we remember it because a great lady sleeps here. A red granite stone under one of the loftiest Wellingtonias we have seen marks the resting-place, in a churchyard filled with noble trees and banks of rhododendrons, of Elizabeth Webber Harris, and tells us nothing more about her than that she died at 83 and was the wife of General Webber Desborough Harris of the Royal Fusiliers. That is all. We are not told she was a hero. But we should never forget her, for a hero she was, and she lived into our own time.

She was born in Victorian England and went out to India with her husband. The regiment was attacked by cholera, and in one night 27 men went down with it. Although she knew how frightful and deadly the disease is, and though she could easily have been sent away to wait until it was all over, this delicately nurtured young woman chose to stay by the regiment and to nurse its sick, which she did with the skill, courage, and devotion of Florence Nightingale herself. All the other nurses died, but she kept on, and when the fighting was over she was still at her post. The officers decided that her courage merited the highest reward and recommended her for the VC, and on learning that only men could receive it they sub-

Alton   Abbey Gatehouse

Bucklers Hard   Beaulieu River

Bucklers Hard   The Tiny Village

Andover   The Lofty Church Tower

Bishop's Waltham   The Ruined Palace

scribed to have one made for her in gold, and Sir Samuel Brown, VC, presented it to her.

The 19th century church has one thing of beauty which it owes to this great woman, the window she put here in memory of her husband. Its colour is quiet and harmonious, and it shows an armoured knight with roses at his feet.

The Little Altar

AMPORT. It has many charming thatched cottages, but it is dominated by the great house whose entrance we see on the way to the church, long the home of the Marquess of Winchester. On the walls of the church we come upon many names from this family, kinsfolk who were admirals and generals, and among them Lord William Paulet, one of the commanders in the Crimean War who became a Field-Marshal. Here, too, are tattered flags, old swords, and a portrait medallion of the 15th marquess who fell in South Africa after 20 years with his regiment. Though this 14th century church was greatly altered in the 19th century, much that is old and beautiful remains. There is a canopied piscina with what seems to be a rose in the basin, three canopied stone seats for priests, some 17th century chairs, richly traceried 14th century windows, a line of flowers round the parapet of the 14th century tower, and a notable stone head 600 years old. But the most rare and interesting possession hangs in a case under the central tower, an alabaster carving about 18 inches high, found in a cottage in the neighbouring hamlet of Cholderton. It is one of the portable altars made by the Chellaston alabaster workers of Derbyshire, and is about 400 years old. In the centre is John the Baptist's head on a charger, on either side stand saints, below is Christ rising from the grave, and above are angels carrying the Baptist's soul to heaven. Very beautiful is the workmanship of the delicate and exquisite canopy, the whole altar being the biggest of these small altars known.

But there is here a touch of our vanished past far older than all this, for in Cholderton Park are graves dug before history began.

Tales of the Old Folk

ANDOVER. It has its place in our Saxon history, for a Witenage-mot was held here, a Viking king was feasted here in 994, entertained by Ethelred and converted by Alphege, promising never

D 33

again to visit England as a foe. But life was going on in Andover long before this, for it has monuments of the people who made their home on the banks of the River Anton in the Stone Age; it has long barrows where they lie, ancient and mysterious ditches made by men before history, buried villas in the tracks of ancient roads made by the Romans, a beautiful gateway tucked in between two shops and a few feet of ivied wall left in the churchyard from an ancient priory. Standing with the old priory was a Norman church, and one of the arches built by the Normans stands as a gateway to the churchyard, all that is left of the church pulled down last century.

The church we see has lofty arches, vaulted roofs, and little stone angels with musical instruments guarding the seats of the choir. Among its many coloured windows is an attractive one of St George, a vigorous figure with a face of a young man apparently a portrait from life. Two wooden crosses from Flanders hang on the wall and there is a memorial to Reginald Norton Knatchbull, who died commanding his regiment in Mesopotamia and sleeps in Bagdad. As a young man he helped to defend Ladysmith, winning the DSO and the Queen's Medal with five clasps, and in the Great War he fought in two countries.

Several monuments there are from the old church. Richard Venables, a London merchant, kneels by his wife, with cherubs about them, both in black Elizabethan clothes, and Dorothea with a captivating bonnet. We learn that Richard was a generous man:

> *A hundred pounds he gave the poor*
> *Which as a stock should still remain*
> *To buy them bread for evermore,*
> *Their hungry bodies to sustain.*

A very quaint 17th century board is written with all the benefactors of the town, set up, we are told, "that all persons may be satisfied how that matter stands, that the towne and public officers may be freed from the scandal thrown on them by ill men."

Hidden away by the organ is the monument of Richard Kemis, crowded with little figures. His wife had three husbands and Richard was the last; he is sitting holding her skull, a prayer desk separating him from his children and their mother, a handsome woman.

One of the sons of this place in the 19th century was the botanist, Charles Baron Clarke, who brought back from India a collection of

25,000 plants which he presented to Kew. He helped Sir Joseph Hooker to compile the Flora of British India and was president of the Linnean Society.

Above the town runs a long path shaded by trees, it is called Lady's Walk and has splendid peeps of the great hills fortified by some of the very first men who thought this country worth defending with their lives. In the museum is an interesting geological and archaeological collection, and among its many curiosities is the cloak that was wrapped round Nelson as he lay dying on his flagship at Trafalgar.

An odd story is told in the registers of a marriage which took place here in 1762 when Jean Drouett, a war prisoner, was married to Elizabeth Adkins. Their son grew up to be a postmaster in France, and it was he who recognised the king and the royal family as they were escaping in the Revolution, and betrayed them to their doom. Another tragic tale of Andover is that of John Body, a Somerset man who was tried at Winchester in the days of Queen Elizabeth and hanged, drawn, and quartered here for denying that the queen was the head of the Church of God. He had not committed any other treason, he told the people in his dying speech, unless hearing mass and saying Hail Mary were treason.

An odd little industry has been carried on by an Andover family since the beginning of last century, and we found them fulfilling an order for 1000 bundles of birch twigs. The twigs are used in the brewing of malt vinegar, and the fulfilment of the order involves cutting them, tying them neatly into faggots, and sending them by rail. We understand that in olden days Surrey was able to supply all the twigs needed by the manufacturers, but the spread of building in the Home Counties has involved the cutting down of so many birches that the vinegar brewers must go farther afield for them. The twigs must be cut when dry, but green, and here in Andover the family which cuts them [in Doles Wood] cuts four truckloads every winter, weighing about 12 tons. They must be cut with much skill, neither too heavy nor too spindly, and there is a natural pride among the men who carry on this small craft in our countryside.

Robin Redbreast's Church

ASHE. A green haven off the noisy road where motors fly past all day, we remember it as the home loved by a robin, a robin much beloved. It is in the church, and we cannot help feeling how delighted Mary Russell Mitford would have been to know his story when she was writing Our Village in this countryside, for this was her mother's village; here her mother grew up at the rectory.

We open a tiny iron door in the wall close by the screen and find Robin behind it, a wooden bird on a wooden nest, the memorial of a welcome little chirper when they were rebuilding the church last century. The bird would hop in, as robins will, and came to feed from the hands of the men, and to be so unafraid that it made a nest of shavings indoors. The workmen fed and protected it while the little ones were hatched and flew away, and before they left a carpenter made this little cupboard in the wall and set Robin inside it. It is the second robin we have come upon like this; there is one in Dorset, in the sanctuary at Wimborne St Giles.

Robin's church has kept something of its ancient past, for it has a 14th century piscina and another in the vestry, set on a pillar by a Norman craftsman 700 years before the carpenter carved the robin. The new screen has parts of the old one worked into it, and hanging close by is the rectors roll with the names of two men who gave lifelong service to the village. One is Simon Holdip, who came four years after the Armada and stayed until the Civil War, 53 years; the other is Richard Russell, who was rector for 63 years in the 18th century, and was succeeded by three Lefroys, a father and two sons, one the husband of a Jane Austen, niece to the immortal Jane. There are tablets to all three of them.

It was one of the Lefroys, born here two years after Waterloo, who dug up the body of Napoleon on his lonely island. He was John Henry Lefroy, a descendant of Huguenot refugees who found safety here from the persecution after the revoking of the Edict of Nantes. He sleeps at Crondall a few miles away.

Near Ashe rises the Test, a river flowing its entire length of nearly 40 miles through Hampshire. Rising in the peaceful chalk hills, it flows into Southampton Water. The first tributary on the right bank is the Wiltshire Bourne, at Fullerton the little River Anton arrives from Andover, and at Bossington the Wallop Brook comes down from three villages which have been named after it. Then the Test enters a broad valley, dividing itself in wide irrigation through several channels. Romsey stands on its banks some five miles from its entry into Southampton Water, and in the course of that five miles the Test receives the united waters of the Blackwater and Cadnam Rivers and the Bartley Water from the New Forest.

From Norman Days

ASHLEY. It has a company of splendid ash trees, as it should have, and its cottages are charming, but its chief delight is in the little church, where it has memories of its people for eight centuries. Those who peep inside the door will be greeted by a quaint and solitary head on the opposite wall, 500 years old. Outside are two mass dials. The oldest possessions are two tiny windows in the chancel and a simple chancel arch four feet wide. They belong to Norman England and are probably 800 years old. On either side of the little arch is an unusually big peephole. There is also a Norman window made still more precious by a 600-year-old painting on one of the splays, showing a saint holding what looks like a book. Norman, too, is the font, square and simple, rising on a single pillar from its base. A stoup inside the door is probably 13th century, and near by is an almsbox with a heavy-topped canopy carved from a single piece of oak, still taking care of alms as it has done for 350 years. In this simple and ancient chancel, quaintly sloping uphill to the altar, it is odd to find the airs and graces of the 18th century, yet here they are. On one ornamental tablet we read of Abraham Weekes, whose love of mankind was part of his constitution, and on another of two Thomases of the Hobbs family, the father a doctor in three reigns and the son, a student of 17, drowned in the Rhine in Queen Anne's day. Near the church are earthworks of a Norman castle and not far off are remains of a Roman encampment.

The Faded Pictures

ASHMANSWORTH. It has lost some of the oldest pictures in Hampshire, painted on the Norman walls of its church and round the Norman chancel arch, and faded almost away when we called. Traces of three schemes of painting could still be seen, some at least 600 years old, some painted over in the 15th century, and some of the black-letter texts which covered our church walls after the Reformation. On one wall we can still see St Christopher, with a very odd black and white face near by, and close to the chancel arch are ancient reddish paintings and a blue medallion of the arms of Charles the Second. Full of age it all is, with two Norman windows in the chancel, two square peepholes looking at the altar, four consecration crosses where the Norman bishop anointed the walls inside, two 17th century windows with wooden frames, a Georgian altar and a pulpit, a bell that was ringing ten years after the Armada, and a 12th century font now recut. But oldest of all are some fragments kept here of pottery and glass from Roman England.

Shelley's Brother

AVINGTON. It stands on the River Itchen beside Itchen Abbas, rich with trees and meadows, charming cottages and gardens, and the wide park of Avington House with its lake. It was in the old house in this park, now happily pulled down so that the memory of her deed may fade away, that the terrible Lady Shrewsbury dressed herself up as the Duke of Buckingham's page while he fought a duel with her husband, and looked on calmly at his death.

The church is an almost untouched example of the 18th century place of worship. It is pretty much as it was when people went about in powder and patches, when sedan chairs were used for taxis, when rapiers were worn as a matter of course, and when Dr Johnson and Tobias Smollett were still pointed out in the street.

Then it was that Margaret, Marchioness of Carnarvon, rebuilt the church of Avington, a neat red brick building giving little outward hint of the stateliness within. Great box-pews, a beautiful pulpit with a dove resting on its shapely canopy, and a splendid reredos, all made from mahogany, greet us as we enter. The squire's pew is so big that the Sunday school used to be held in it. There is a slender 18th century marble font, a delightful 18th century candelabra, and, peering over the gallery, a little organ so old that it is worked on the hurdy-gurdy system. The best touch of colour is the beautiful Crucifixion in the east window, all the more attractive for having clear glass all round it. One of three books in a glass case in the chancel, all bound in velvet and embroidered in silver, is a copy of the rare Vinegar Bible, considered valuable by collectors because in the parable of the vineyard the printer changed vineyard into vinegar.

A white marble memorial to the Lady Carnarvon who built the church (but did not see it finished) has one of the queer old inscriptions. It tells us that she was blessed with beauty, rank, and fortune, all of which she made the best use of; it adds that the complacency of her features showed the innocence of her mind; and it tells us that she was religious without enthusiasm—a phrase which shows how time changes the meaning of words, for enthusiasm here means fanaticism. In something of the same spirit is the tablet to a 19th century Duchess of Buckingham, which says that her virtues would have adorned a cottage.

Near the gaily painted pulpit (matching the chancel panels and the reredos) is a monument of a charming young man who seems to have walked out of Dickens, with the high collar and flowing hair of a hundred years ago. He shared a nursery with four sisters and an exciting elder brother who used to terrify them all by scientific experiments and make up for it by telling them wonderful fairy-tales. The elder brother died far away in Spezia Bay, but his heart is in a grave in Hampshire; he was Percy Bysshe Shelley. Another memorial shows a niece of his being received into heaven by an angel; it was put here by working men in Lancashire, where her husband was MP.

The Work of the Centuries

BARTON STACEY. In this countryside by Bransbury Common, where wild life has sanctuary and may build or burrow in peace, cave dwellers lived in the long ago, leaving their flint axes behind them, and there is an ancient British Dyke. The noble tower of the church was built just before the Reformation and has big carved pinnacles at the corners and a row of grinning heads running round the top. It is built partly within and partly without the church, so as to leave room for the pathway outside where the processions used to walk. The church was begun by the Normans and the font they made is its oldest possession. The aisles and chapels were thrown out by the English builders following them who finished the chancel as we see it. There are three consecration crosses and two mass dials, and a fragment of the medieval roodloft stairs remains. Century after century has given something to this church. From the 12th comes the font, from the 13th and 14th the tiles by the altar; from the 15th the chapels and the aisles; from the 16th the altar plate, some tombs, and a statue of the Madonna; from the 17th the altar rails and two plain stools on which the coffins would rest; from the 18th two candlesticks (which have been remade), and from the 20th a peace memorial with 16 names that live for evermore—a fine and original piece of work like a canopied recess carved with flowers and linenfold. The font has a painted cover made by a vicar from remnants of the ancient chancel screen. On the boldly carved altar are three sculptured figures of Faith, Hope, and Charity, done by 17th or 18th century men; it is the centrepiece of the fine sanctuary panelling in memory of Michael and Maurice Hodgson, two brothers killed within the same week of the war in 1915.

The Proud House of the Paulets

BASING. It has lost one of the greatest houses in the land, but it has found a thrilling place in history. The great house and the spacious church were both in the very heart of the Civil War. The church remains, but the house is a ruin, with a story of courage and sacrifice, of loyalty to a king and treachery to a brother, and finally of a great act of mercy.

The church was taken by both sides in the Civil War, and restored at the Restoration. The top of the tower was made new, but the lower part remains Norman, with the original arches. The charming font and the aisles are 15th century, the two chapels and the richly carved pulpit are 16th. The 17th century bier is now used as a seat. The lovely piece of needlework hanging on the wall is old Italian. There are some 14th and 15th century tiles, and a 16th century statue of the Madonna.

Under the arches between the chapels and the chancel are the sculptured tombs of the Paulets, one 15th century with Sir John and his wife Eleanor, two with 16th century Sir Johns, and one of the remarkable 16th century Sir William who built the great house; a magnificent kind of man Carlyle called him, "whose best bed excited the wonder of the world." The great Sir John of the siege is buried at Englefield; the greatest Paulet here is Carlyle's magnificent William, the builder of the house.

On the wall of one of the chapels hang helmets and gauntlets, and there is a fine portrait bust by Flaxman of the sixth Duke of Bolton. Rich in noble blood is this small chapel, for a brass on the wall tells us that under our feet six dukes of Bolton lie. They were Paulets too, the first duke being the Marquess of Winchester who simulated madness to cover a disagreement with James the Second, and had a leading part in bringing over William and Mary. The last five dukes were undistinguished men, the sixth being an admiral with a reputation for lacking courage and audacity.

The ruins of Basing House stand on the site of a Norman castle which made way for the wonderful home of old Sir William. Here still stands the proud gateway through which there must have passed a remarkable procession of historic figures, from Philip of Spain dreaming of his Armada to Oliver Cromwell who brought the great house down. To this place came Inigo Jones, Thomas Fuller, and Wenceslaus Hollar, all sheltering in the siege. Here still is the old dovecote which must have been a good friend to the garrison, with its 500 nests and the old turning-ladder from which a man could reach a bird in any one of them. Here are mighty earthworks and fragments of walling, and wild strawberries were growing among the brick and stone of the cellars when we called. On one cellar wall are fading away old charcoal drawings, among which we could just make out a ship and a cavalier's head. Across the way the great brick barn in which the Paulets learned to ride still stands, with the marks of Cromwell's guns still on its walls. In a small museum are fragments of carvings, tiles, and firebacks from the fallen house, with swords, bullets, cannon balls, and other relics of the siege.

Here long before Basing House was built, before the Normans raised their castle, King Alfred was fighting in his youth against the Danes; and round about are the earthworks of Pyotts Hill and Winklebury Circle, scars of wars older than history.

Carlyle's Magnificent William

WILLIAM PAULET, born in 1485, the year of Bosworth Field, was one of the most extraordinary men of his age, Carlyle's magnificent man. He lived through the reigns of four Tudor sovereigns and died in a fifth, advising Queen Elizabeth to the last. He married twice and lived to see 103 descendants.

He was the eldest son of Sir John Paulet, who commanded a force against the Cornish rebels in 1497. In 1512 he was Sheriff of Hampshire and in the Reformation Parliament of 1529 sat as its representative. Henry created him controller of the household in 1532, the critical year before Catherine's divorce, and it was left to

William Paulet to convey the commands of the king to his unhappy wife. After Henry's death he shared power with Northumberland on the fall of Protector Somerset, whose white staff as Lord Treasurer he took, retaining it until the end of his life, 22 years after.

When the boy king died the Marquess of Winchester, as he now was, wished for the observance of the Act of Succession, but the Duke of Northumberland proclaimed Lady Jane Grey queen and it was Winchester who placed the crown jewels in her hands on July 12. But he was carefully watching his ducal rival, and persuaded him to lead the forces about to set out to subdue Mary Tudor, who had raised her standard at Framlingham. Telling Suffolk, Jane's father, to keep Winchester and the rest of the Council under his eye in the Tower, the mighty duke set out the next day. Winchester and other nobles made an excuse to visit Baynard's Castle on July 19, on the pretext of levying more troops, and there they declared for Mary, Winchester riding through London to proclaim her accession. Mary made him Lord Privy Seal, and when she married Philip of Spain (in Winchester Cathedral) she took her husband to Basing House five days after the wedding and they feasted there.

When Mary died the old man rode through London again proclaiming Elizabeth, who confirmed him in his high office and visited him at Basing, being so delighted with him and his wonderful house that she said: "By my troth, if my Lord Treasurer were but a young man I could find it in my heart to have him for a husband before any man in England."

This proud old Marquess of Winchester was vigorous to the last, dying at Basing House in 1572. Of himself he wrote in his old age:

> Late supping I forbear.
> Wine and women I forswear;
> My neck and feet I keep from cold,
> No marvel, then, though I be old;
> I am a willow, not an oak,
> I chide but never hurt with stroke.

Willow indeed he was, weathering the storms of five reigns.

The Great Siege of Basing House

THE long-drawn-out siege of Basing House was one of the most notable events of the Civil War. This stately home of the Marquess of Winchester quickly attracted the attention of the king's advisers as a strategic post for controlling the trade route to the West. Winchester was a Roman Catholic and to his home came many an old adherent of the queen. The marquess set about fortifying the house, and on the last day of July a hundred musketeers marched in as its trained garrison under Lieutenant Peake, who had serving under him two men who were famous as craftsmen then and are now, the engravers Hollar and Faithorne. Within the ramparts of Basing they were gathered with some other famous men of the time. Old Thomas Fuller was here as chaplain, and Inigo Jones was in the house for the last dread fight.

Inigo Jones, distraught with the confusion of the times, had buried his money in Lambeth Marsh and taken refuge with the marquess because he was a patron of art. Inigo was the foremost architect of his day, having established the new classical style. He had designed Lincoln's Inn Chapel, St Paul's Covent Garden, the "handsomest barn in England," York Water Gate, Chilham Castle in Kent, many country mansions, the Palace at Greenwich, and, best of all, the Banqueting House in Whitehall.

The time he spent here must have been sad days for Thomas Fuller, who by his wise tolerance and ready wit had been doing his utmost to allay the rising passions on both sides. So temperate was he in all he said and wrote that he was accused of being lukewarm in his adherence to Charles Stuart. As chaplain to the Royalists he wrote prayers and meditations for the men, and when suspended from preaching during the Commonwealth he wrote Histories and his well-known Worthies of England, which he left uncompleted.

The governor of the troops was also a famous man, Robert Peake, son of the serjeant-painter to King James. He and his brother William had a printseller's shop on Snow Hill where they employed young Faithorne. So able a soldier was Peake, and so often were the besiegers repulsed, that during a lull in the siege in March, 1645, King Charles made him a knight on a visit to Oxford. After the king's death he was exiled for refusing to take the oath to Cromwell.

William Faithorne, a younger man of 27, had marched with Peake, under whose guidance he was studying the art of engraving of which he was to become so supreme a master. Banished for refusing to take the oath to Cromwell, he worked at his craft in Paris and obtained permission in 1650 to return to London, where he set up a print shop. He drew crayon portraits of many of the most famous men of his time and engraved a wonderful map of London six feet long, which is of great interest today.

Faithorne's fellow musketeer, Wenceslaus Hollar, was born at Prague in 1607. His drawings attracted the attention of Thomas Howard, Earl of Arundel, ambassador to the German Emperor, and he brought him to England in his suite. Hollar taught drawing to the Prince of Wales, and two years later made engravings of Vandyck's royal portraits. He published two splendid books of costume, and when his patron fled abroad he stayed to fight for the king. Luckier than his two friends, he escaped from his captors at Basing House. His works number nearly 3000. Evelyn described him as a friendly and good-natured man, but shiftless as to the world, dying not rich.

Another member of this besieged band was Thomas Johnson, the first man to write a book about all our British plants. So unusual was his occupation that on one occasion he was arrested as a wanderer at large. He enlarged Gerard's Herbal and fitted 2766 illustrations into it. His record at Basing House was one of great bravery; he was shot while defending it.

A few days after the arrival of Robert Peake the siege began, and for three months colonel after colonel of the Parliament attacked the house, but failed. The marchioness and her womenfolk made bullets from lead stripped from the roofs and hurled stones and tiles on the attackers. At the end of 1643 the losses of the army of Parliament were so severe that they had to retire, even though General Waller, who was called the Conqueror, had endeavoured to force his way in with 7000 men.

In the following spring Parliament again sent forces to deal with the stubborn Basing stronghold, and from then up to October 1645 the attacks and skirmishes were nearly ceaseless. A crushing blow to the marquess was the discovery that his brother Edward Paulet was in treacherous communication with Waller with a view to surrendering. The traitor's punishment was terrible, for he was made to act as hangman to his confederates, but was spared himself. Smallpox appeared to add to the misery of starvation; yet the defenders held on. Then came a bitter blow by the desertion of five hundred men on May Day, 1645; but still the heroic remainder stuck to their guns. It is curious to reflect that the deserters were Protestants who changed sides on account of religious differences.

Now the battle of Naseby came, and the victorious Cromwell himself marched into Hampshire. He captured the castle of Winchester and led his army to Basing. The fate of the gallant band of defenders was sealed. Cromwell, it is said, first climbed to the top of Winklebury Circle, a prehistoric encampment overlooking the house, and from there took note of its plan and defences. At 5 o'clock on October 14, after offering a prayer, he suddenly attacked, breaching the walls with cannon and pouring in his overwhelming forces. Hopelessly outnumbered and weak with hunger and disease, the garrison had little chance, but they put up a gallant fight, losing 100 men killed and 300 prisoners; Inigo Jones was among them, and was carried out wrapped in a blanket because the victors had stripped him of his clothes.

Dr Hugh Peters, the Puritan preacher, came along to survey the scene and torment the vanquished marquess, who was goaded to reply that if the king had no more ground in England than Basing House he would still adventure as he had done and maintain it to the uttermost. Suddenly fire broke out and Loyalty House became a ruin. Cromwell gave orders that anyone might carry away its stones, and allowed looting as a warning to his enemies; but he spared the brave old marquess, committing him first to the Tower and finally allowing him to leave the country in peace.

The Ruin on the Hill

BASINGSTOKE. The motorist may think of it as a workaday town to get through quickly (if he can), yet indeed it is not without its temptation to a traveller, and it is admirably placed as a central point for reaching historic towns. Within an easy run are Gilbert White's Selborne, the Hog's Back and Guildford, Winchester and Salisbury, the fine old town of Newbury, Silchester and Reading, the ruins of Basing House, Charles Kingsley's village, Jane Austen's country, and much more.

The great Thornycroft engineering works fill the streets with a throng of working people twice a day, and indeed it is a busy town, yet there are quiet oases, restful places indoors and out. The River Loddon rises a little above the town and flows to the Thames through the fields, and one of the most interesting quiet places in Hampshire is the ancient burial ground about the ruins of the Chapel of the Holy Ghost, which was built about 700 years ago in a graveyard made for those who died in that bitter time when the Pope laid England under an Interdict for the evil doings of King John. There were no christenings in our churches, no burials in our churchyards in those six years from 1208 to 1214, and there was set apart then a graveyard known as the Liten, where the people who died in Basingstoke could be laid to rest in consecrated ground. When the Interdict was raised, and life became normal again, the ground was consecrated and the Chapel of the Holy Ghost was built. It has fallen into ruin, but to this day the headmaster of the grammar school bears the title of the Chaplain of the Holy Ghost.

The ruin stands attractively set on the hill near the station, with something of the apse, a piece of wall with beautiful niches in it, fragments of tracery, and two stone figures which have faded out of recognition in the winds and rains of centuries. One is a 13th century knight with his legs crossed and angels supporting his head, and of him no guess can be made at identity; but of the other, a man in a long Elizabethan gown, we may believe that it represents Lord Sandys, who was buried in this chapel under a tomb which he ordered to be made, part of which can still be seen. He built the great house now called The Vyne at Sherborne St John close by, and was the chief man of Basingstoke in his day, one of the founders of this chapel. Henry the Eighth believed in him, and he helped to organise the marvellous pageantry of the Field of the Cloth of Gold. He was at the coronation of Anne Boleyn, who stayed with the king at The Vyne, but he was accommodating enough to conduct the queen to the Tower when her time came to lose her head.

One witness we still have of the beauty of this chapel in its great days, for the east window of the peace memorial chapel of the great white church of Basingstoke has in it today the medieval glass through which the light would be pouring when they brought Lord Sandys to his rest. The window has delicate tones of blues and greens, ruby and gold, with faded figures showing Our Lord's Agony in the Garden, and Elizabeth bringing the good news to the Madonna. It was during the Civil War and after that the chapel on the hill became a ruin, the lead was stripped from its roof by the Parliament men, and was shaped into bullets, and long after that the grammar school boys (when Gilbert White was one of them) delighted to throw stones and bring down great pieces of the chapel wall. They held their lessons often in a room made in the tower.

The 16th century church of St Michael has a great array of strange gargoyles looking down from its tower, and inside is much fascinating work in wood and stone, ancient roofs, a fine old screen, an altar with a dozen figures set in niches, a very long peephole, a recess over the doorway full of stone angels, a font with a tremendous cover, and an almsbox as old as the church. There are stately clerestory windows with fine figures of saints; a window of St Stephen with three stones on a Bible, and St Clare with lilies and a basket of loaves; and another window to two Hampshire captains who fell in the war, with portraits of Aldhelm and Geoffrey of Bouillon in which are set small scenes from Jerusalem and the Euphrates. In the chancel (which has preserved one of the earliest English arches leading into a chapel) is a brass portrait of Robert Stocker, a yeoman who led a virtuous life all through Elizabeth's reign and made a godly end in 1606; and there is another brass portrait of John Hilliard, a dear little lad with a long frock and girdle who died a few years after Shakespeare.

St Michael's (which has a room over its porch) has had its excitements in ancient and modern days. In ancient days it had a miracle-working statue of the Madonna which nobody dare destroy when the decree went forth against these superstitions, so that Thomas Cromwell himself came down and shattered the figure to fragments. In our own time the south aisle was burned down while it was being renewed, and a better miracle than the old statue ever performed was witnessed then. The vicar was to sit in the church on St Michael's Day to receive contributions for the rebuilding; it had been so arranged before the fire, and he resolved to sit in the ruined aisle. It was in the autumn of 1938, when Europe seemed rapidly to be verging on war, and suddenly the Prime Minister announced in Parliament that he was going to see Herr Hitler. The relief throughout the country was indescribable, and the next day, when the vicar of St Michael's sat in the burned-down aisle, he received not the two or three hundred pounds he had expected, but more than enough to pay for the work that had been done and for the work that was to be done. It was a noble thanksgiving.

There is in the church an 18th century monument to a vicar here, Thomas Warton, himself a man of no mean repute but with two sons who both won fame, one as Poet Laureate and one as Headmaster of Winchester. The father himself was Professor of Poetry at Oxford before he came to Basingstoke as vicar and master of the grammar school. He put his sons into the school, and Joseph, the elder boy, was Gilbert White's great friend. All three Wartons were deeply interested in poetry and all wrote it more or less; it was what they said about it that had wide influence, marking a turning-point in literature. Pope was then the poet's idol, and Joseph Warton boldly declared that Pope was stilted, and that all his moralising was not poetical. The poet, he said, should have imagination and be inventive and romantic, and have freedom in style, and none of these things had Pope. Joseph went to Winchester as headmaster for 27 years and lies in the cathedral. His younger brother Thomas mixed architecture with literature, became Poet Laureate and Professor of History, and was the first man to set himself the task of seriously gathering the whole story of English poetry into one book.

In the red brick vicarage in which young Thomas Warton was born there also lived a vicar who lies buried in Durham Cathedral; he was Sir George Wheler, the famous traveller born in Cromwell's time while his Royalist parents were in exile in Holland. He became vicar of Basingstoke after the Restoration, and it was while he was vicar here that there was born his son Granville, who made some of the first-known electrical experiments at Otterden in Kent. An ancient brick and timber house by the church stores a library collected by this interesting vicar.

Much of the history of Basingstoke can be seen in its museum. Starting from the chalk fossils which prove the foundation of the town to have been an old sea floor, we see the story of the earliest inhabitants of 100,000 years ago who left their crude flint tools on the local hilltops; of the later inhabitants whose better implements are freely found in the surrounding fields; of the Roman occupation of the district which dotted it with country villas and farms round the great city of Silchester; and of the medieval courts of justice where the tything men brought their fellow-citizens before the

Basing   The Castle

Basing   The Church

Basingstoke   **The Ruined Chapel**

Pamber   **Priory Church**

magistrates for throwing rubbish into the street or the town brook, for selling short-weight bread, and in the case of women offenders for scolding and railing at their neighbours. There is also to be seen in the museum the actual post office of 70 years ago, when all the postal business of the town was effected through one small window.

Basingstoke has remembered its heroes in a Memorial Park with a fine gateway crowned by a bronze statue of Victory, by Mr L. F. Roslyn; it stands as a tribute to 234 men who did not come back, and it is delightful to see their memory honoured in a park so well timbered and so picturesquely ordered, with a children's playground, a pond for toy boats, tennis courts, bowling greens, football ground, bandstand, and the old mansion of the Goldings transformed into municipal offices. The town hall itself is an imposing building with a fine clock tower raised on eight elegant arches.

The town has a noble roll of honour. It gave birth to the 13th century Greek scholar John of Basingstoke and to the 13th century Chancellor of England who founded Merton College.

John was one of the first Englishmen to master Greek thoroughly. He travelled in Greece, and a curious story is told of an archbishop's daughter there who instructed him; it was said that she had power to foretell eclipses, storms, and earthquakes "with unerring certainty." John brought home with him the first knowledge in England of the famous apocryphal book The Testament of the Twelve Patriarchs, originally part of the Bible but hidden away for centuries. Matthew Paris records that it was a great grief to Simon de Montfort when John of Basingstoke died in 1252. Of Walter de Merton's birthplace we cannot be certain, but his parents are buried in St Michael's, and he held lands here. His college at Oxford became the model for university colleges everywhere.

More famous than either of these men is an old boy of the grammar school, the great seaman Sir James Lancaster, who commanded a ship against the Armada and whose voyages of trade and discovery contributed largely to the foundation of our Empire in India. Basingstoke was his school.

A Sailor to Rank with Drake

SIR JAMES LANCASTER was one of the greatest of all the Elizabethan adventurers, a sea captain inspired by Drake and a pioneer of the trade which brought to our shores luxuries till then beyond the reach of our people. The name of this great seaman is on the map, not in the sun-drenched Indies of his toil and gain, but at the Sound that opens from Baffin Bay and is the gateway into the North-West Passage, in search of which he sent forth William Baffin himself when his own adventurous voyages had ended.

Sir James left no descendants and of his parents we know nothing. He arrives in England out of Portugal shortly before the Armada. He was a man of considerable ability, for we find him commanding a vessel of Drake's squadron, the Edward Bonaventure, in the great conflict with the galleons of Spain. He had old scores of his own to pay off against a race he declared to be lacking in faith and truth, so he was a willing leader of the first expedition that left our shores for those distant islands of mystery, commanding the 300-ton merchant ship in which he had trounced the Armada. All told, they were not more than 300 men who set out in 1591 for the Far East. A month in the doldrums played havoc with their health, and disaster followed disaster. In the end they were driven to seek refuge on an island, and while most of the crew were ashore one day the ship broke adrift and was driven before the wind with only five men and a boy on board. They could not take the ship back to the island, but miraculously succeeded in navigating her, with the rich looting intact, safely across the Atlantic to England! As for Captain Lancaster, a French ship brought him home and he landed at Rye in 1594, after three years of daring fit to rank in fame with Drake's voyage in the Golden Hind twelve years before.

Lancaster had shown the way and the East India Company was formed in London. The brave pioneer was sent out with three more ships, and he captured Pernambuco, with so much spoil that he had to charter seven French and Dutch vessels to bring it home. Again he was sent out, this time with letters from Queen Elizabeth to see the kings of the East. By dosing his men with lemon juice (a preventive of scurvy which was not used again for over a century) he warded off sickness on his own ship, but 105 out of 280 men on the three other ships died before the Cape was reached. In Sumatra he was welcomed as a deliverer by the native king, who gave him a letter to Queen Elizabeth whose fame had reached his ears, and helped him to surprise a Portuguese ship in the Malacca Strait. Pushing on, Lancaster established a trading factory in Java, and returned with his ships "entreasured with bags of spices full" to anchor in the Downs. He arrived home in autumn, to learn that Elizabeth had died in the spring.

He was knighted for his exploits and settled down to direct the new trading company and help William Baffin to fit out his expedition to the North-West. He himself lived on 15 more years, dying two years after Shakespeare, and he left his wealth to charity.

As Long as the World Lasts

BAUGHURST. It is on Hampshire's beautiful north border, and has one or two things saved from the past. Its babies receive their names at a pretty font, decorated with quatrefoils, which has seen the children come and go for 500 years; and the rebuilt church has a chancel screen, rich in carving, said to have been the gift of a Lord Chancellor of England who rose rapidly to power under Henry the Seventh but lost his influence to Cardinal Wolsey. He was Archbishop Warham. A window in the nave has attractive glass of Our Lord in memory of David Williams, rector for 20 years last century. The church has a chalice used here when Shakespeare was a boy, and a brass telling that a 17th century man left money for the poor as long as the world shall endure.

A Bad King's Good Deed

BEAULIEU. Beaulieu Abbey has come down to us in history as King John's Good Deed. We may never know the truth of his quarrel with the White Monks, or of the dream which induced him to make peace with them, but we do know that he took a personal interest in the founding of the Abbey of the Beautiful Spot in 1204, that he visited it while it was building, and gave it rich endowment.

Where the New Forest came down to meet Beaulieu River as it enters on its tidal journey towards the Solent a little company of French monks chose the site of their dwelling-place. It is about 700 years since it rose complete, and King John's son, Henry the Third, came to the dedication of the abbey his father had founded, bringing with him his queen, his children, and many of his nobles. Amazed must the few peasants in this solitary place have been as the magnificent procession swept through the great door, monarchs and courtiers, four bishops with their trains of chaplains, priests, and monks, and crowds of retainers and servants, all flooding the church with the vivid colour of their robes and vestments, while amid the clanging of armour the voices of the choir pealed forth in the triumphant Psalm : *Let us go into the House of the Lord; our feet shall stand within Thy gates, O Jerusalem.*

Three hundred years later it was another King Henry who destroyed the abbey, and from that day to this it has stood as it is, one of our loveliest ruins. Not a stone of its beautiful church was left in place; the materials were carried away to build houses and castles and smaller places. What was left of the abbey passed as a house to Thomas Wriothesley, Earl of Southampton, Lord Chancellor to Henry the Eighth.

We come to the village across the wide open spaces of Beaulieu Plain with its 54 barrows, its stretches of ever-flowering gorse, and its lovely views of forest and sea, the haunt of the rangers of Beaulieu. Passing the neat cottages with timbered walls and overhanging gables, and the old watermill used by the monks for grinding corn and sawing timber, we cross the bridge between the old Mill Pool and the quay of Beaulieu River, and find ourselves before the Outer Gatehouse.

In the days when this wall was intact, enclosing 58 acres of grounds, this was the only entrance, and there is no finer 13th century gatehouse, perhaps none so perfectly preserved, in the country. The Great Gatehouse within, thought by some to have been the Abbot's Lodging, has been carefully restored and modernised and is now known as Palace House. Other buildings still standing are the Dormitory of the Lay Brothers and the apartments below, the Domus, restored by Lord Montagu in memory of his parents, who are buried near the lovely ruins they did so much to guard and save. Well into our century this dormitory was but a lumber room, and there are few other rooms of its period in England on so magnificent a scale and so perfect in detail.

We walk up some of the original steps of the wide stone staircase. The roof has massive tie-beams, and the oak floor, dense and black as iron, gives an impression of lasting strength which will outlive as many generations as have trod it down already.

In the Lay Brothers Refectory are gathered many relics mutely telling the past story of the abbey and its people. A unique and pathetic treasure is the small coffin which held the hearts of a husband and wife, a touching souvenir of wedded love found last century near the Great Gatehouse. The gravestone of the Lady Isabella, the wife of one of King John's sons, is here still. The daughter of William Mareschall, Earl of Pembroke, she died at Berkhampstead in 1230, and was buried here before the altar. We can read a few broken words in Latin with her pretty name Ysabella. The grave of another English princess was marked by a stone to Eleana, little daughter of Edward the First, who did not grow up. The stone is nearly ten feet long, and has a dainty border of white squares, each with a letter cut into it. Many of these are illegible, but the words Jesu Christ Omnipotent can still be traced. Among the papers of Edward the Second scholars have found the bill for the burial at Beaulieu of this little royal maiden.

Here are the troughs, used as water pipes, hollowed out from trunks of trees by the monks, and there is a collection of tiles from the floors in many charming designs and colours. There is a large-scale model of the abbey and all its buildings. The place is lit by electricity, and the last act of Lord Montagu's crowded and public-spirited life was to inspect this completed model before he left Palace House to enter the nursing home in which he passed away.

Is there anything lovelier in all the ruins of our English abbey than the great cloister of Beaulieu, nearly 140 feet square? Was ever a more perfect setting for the elegant pointed arches of the 13th century craftsmen, bordering this smooth carpet of emerald green? The inner wall of the cloister has gone, but its foundations are visible here and there. From every crevice of the crannied walls spring tiny flowers, ferns of many kinds fall in graceful cascades over old brown stones, while myrtle, magnolia, laburnum, and flowering trees of every season add charm to the scene.

One of the rarest gems is the north-east doorway, with many orders of mouldings, by which the monks entered the church. We can imagine the long line of white-robed figures moving slowly round the cloister and disappearing beneath this lovely archway as the bell called for morning or evening prayers.

At the demolition of the abbey the dining-room was left practically untouched so that it might serve as the village church, for which it is still used. As it was not built for a church it stands north-to-south instead of east-to-west. The old oak door has part of its early ironwork. There were three lancet windows on the north and south walls, but of the three behind the altar on the north the middle one has been blocked by a buttress to strengthen the gable. A string-course runs all round the building and there are six more lancet windows with double-mullioned arches on the east wall. On the western side of the church is its rarest treasure, the beautiful stone pulpit which clings to the wall like a swallow's nest beneath the eaves. Its only entrance is by an archway leading to a tiny lobby from which a narrow flight of steps cut inside the wall mounts to the pulpit. The lobby and the stairway are lighted by an exquisite miniature arcade of six pointed arches, and behind the pulpit an early traceried window has two trefoil-headed lights below a quatre-foil. The pulpit itself is an artistic masterpiece; it is shaped like the corbel of an arch, the stone panels decorated with leaves and flowers. Though now used as a pulpit it was built for a rostrum from which during the meal the monks in turn read to their brothers below.

There is a triptych of the Crucifixion on the south wall. A medallion in white marble, with a woman's face in profile, is in memory of the wife of Mr Justice Darling. Lady Cross, their home, was near to Beaulieu and she sleeps in the churchyard.

Here in this matchless garden of peace the trail of war must come and a tragic trail it is. It is told in an inscription set up in the lifetime of the second Lord Montagu, recalling that during the war, when he he was engaged on transport service, his ship was torpedoed. He was saved after being in the water for 18 hours, while his secretary lost her life. This is what we read:

Erected by John, 2nd Lord Montagu of Beaulieu, in thank-fulness for his miraculous escape from drowning after the sinking of the P. and O. S.S. Persia, torpedoed by a German submarine near Crete; and of Eleanor Velasco Thornton, who served him devotedly for 15 years; drowned December 1915.

Above is his portrait in bronze, placed there at his death, with the words "In happy remembrance of the 2nd Baron Montagu, who passed to a fuller life March 1929."

A noble record of service had the vicar here when we called, for the Revd R. F. Powles, then in his 87th year, came as a curate 54 years before we found him still preaching. Thankful was the good old man for the help of his Toc H friends, for our friend Tubby Clayton is frequently here visiting his home at Little Hatchett.

A monument to Mary Do, who died in 1651, seems almost modern in this 13th century world. A Calvary in the churchyard has oak figures of St John and the Madonna on either side of the Cross. It is to the memory of Philip Armstrong and his brother officers and shipmates, who lost their lives on a submarine during the war, and to the men of Beaulieu who did not come back.

Surrounded by all this wealth of beauty in cloister, window, and arcade, the heart of Beaulieu lies in the mysterious charm of its invisible church. The whole plan of nave, aisles, transepts, and chapels is outlined on the soft turf which covers the space where once this abbey rose in stately splendour. We are filled with a deep emotion as we pace the lost nave and chancel, or halt with reverent step before the simple cross where the high altar stood. Where pillars sprang in massive pride to a vaulted roof, cypresses now taper to the sky; and where all heads were bowed at the silver note of the sanctus bell, nothing now breaks the silence but the song of birds.

Old Yews

BEDHAMPTON. It gives Portsmouth fresh water from its springs. Bordering a busy highway, it has a quiet corner where the church stands away from the village, with beautiful old houses and noble trees. There are two old yews in the churchyard, one leaning on a staff when we called, though his sturdy mate needs no support, being over 20 feet round and still growing. The church has a beautiful chancel arch resting on graceful pillars and decorated with diamonds and chevrons by some of the earliest Norman craftsmen. On the walls is a mass dial from the days before clocks, and in the chancel is a medieval piscina. There is a massive 13th century bench carved with flowers, and among the other old work are traces of the medieval screen, and timbers in the roof of the nave.

The Chief Scout's Village

BENTLEY. It lines the highway west of Farnham with pretty cottages, old houses, hop gardens, and trees. Every boy knows it because it is the Chief Scout's village, where for years he lived at Pax Hill; a finger-post points up a drive lined with fruit trees as if to say, what we know quite well, that all the world is welcome there.

It was the Chief Scout who gave Bentley its quaint history sign, one of the forerunners of the history posts which have sprung up in many villages since. This one is oldfashioned and not one of the best, but it has all the interest of the pioneer. It is in the form of an open book, set under a thatched roof with a little green archer in red hose and hood perched on the ridge shooting an arrow into the air. The open pages of the book have a plan of the village on one side and notes about Bentley's history on the other. We learn from these notes that General Waller paraded his troops on Bentley Green before marching to the attack on Basing House, that Bentley means the green by the forest, that the yew trees here probably originated in the days when Bentley supplied the king with an archer every year, that Domesday Book says that William the Archer was lord of the manor then, and that Gilbert White of Selborne used to stay at Marlands on the outskirts of the village.

We think it must have been one of Baden-Powell's bright boys who went out blackberrying here a little while before we called. He went for blackberries and brought home broken pots. He had come upon a Roman grave of the first century, and in it were 12 keel-shaped urns containing bones and charcoal. It had long been known that there were burial grounds about, but nobody could find them until the blackberrying boy went out and brought home history. The land where the grave was found is called Bury Court Farm, the name for which is clear at last, for in a document of 976 which describes the boundary of Crondall Manor are these words: "Then to the Bentley boundary, on to the heathen burial place; then to where Elstan lieth in heathen burial."

Bentley has a small church with a low tower about 500 years old at the base and younger at the top. It stands on a hill among the hop gardens with a noble avenue of beech trees behind it (said to be about 900 years old) and seven ancient yews leading to its doorways. They are not huge in girth, but some of them have such a mighty spread of branches that props and timber arches have been built to hold them up. The font comes from the days when some of these trees were saplings; it is Norman, shallow and square with an

arcaded bowl resting on four little pillars. Two piscinas are from
the 13th century. The chancel is interesting for having clerestory
windows, some of them with fragments of gold and white glass of the
15th century. In the tracery of the east window are little gold and
white angels of the same time, one announcing the glad news to
Mary. There are three Marys in modern glass under medieval
canopies, the old and the new beautifully blending. The north arcade
of the chancel has fluted capitals and is Norman. The simple south
arcade is 13th century. The sturdy oak balustrade before the altar
was made in Milton's time, having then belonged to a gallery which
has now disappeared. On a grey slate set in the south aisle wall are
engraved 17th century portraits of Margaret Windsor and her
husband, he in a short cloak and both wearing ruffs.

The Poet of a Hundred Books

BENTWORTH. The 13th century font of this beautiful little
church, with an oak cover which has been over it since Shakespeare's day, must draw many pilgrims to it, for at it was christened
a boy destined for a remarkable career, George Wither. He wrote
poems of delicate fancy, rose to be a fiery Puritan, was stripped of
his estates at the Restoration, and died after writing about 100 books,
his long life stretching from the year of the Armada to the year after
the Great Fire. His poems were forgotten, and were brought back
to fame by Charles Lamb; but one of the things he is remembered
for at Bentworth is that he sold his lands in this place to raise a troop
of horse for Cromwell. Often he must have been in this small
church, so delightful with all its ancient arches, and he may well
have looked up curiously at the small monument with the little figure
of Nicholas Holdip on the sanctuary wall. The oak seats in the
aisle were made in the poet's century, and so was the little chest
under the tower. He would hear the four bells ring when they were
new, but the nave arcades and the chancel arch were four centuries
old when George Wither was baptised, being built about 1175.
The 13th century chancel has a pointed doorway and a richly
decorated piscina, and in a built-up doorway is a group of stones
moulded by the Normans. The modern glass includes figures of the
Archangels Gabriel and Michael, and two scenes of the Madonna.

We read on these walls of a father who served in the Crimean War, and of one of his sons who fell in the first weeks of the Great War; but it is outside, on Bentworth's simple peace memorial in the shadow of the tower, that we come upon the name of the chief hero this place has known in our own time. He was Colonel Neville Elliott-Cooper, and he had three distinctions; the Military Cross won in 1916, the DSO won early in 1917, and the Victoria Cross awarded for a gallant act of leadership at Cambrai. News was brought to him in his dugout that the enemy had broken through. He jumped on to the parapet, calling on the Reserve Company to follow him. Quite unarmed himself, he led them toward the advancing enemy, who were actually forced back 600 yards; but he fell severely wounded, and realising the hopelessness of the position, signalled to his men to retire, knowing well that he would fall into the enemy's hands. His gallant act gained time for other reserves to occupy the line. For three months he lingered as a wounded prisoner of war in Hanover, where he died.

The forgotten poet rescued from oblivion by Charles Lamb was George Wither. He was born a poet, and as such the Bentworth neighbours of his father did not understand him. They seriously advised that he should be "put to some mechanic trade" to clear such unpracticalness out of his head, but the father sent him to Oxford. Then he went to London to conquer the world by his poetry. His bosom friend was William Browne, author of Britannia's Pastorals, and he knew Michael Drayton. All three were ardent lovers of their country. The time was just before the death of Shakespeare, and poets were at a premium.

When King James's son Henry died both Browne and Wither wrote elegies, and when the Princess Elizabeth married Frederick the Fifth George Wither pleased her so by his Nuptial Poems that she remained his friend in need, and soon had the opportunity of serving him. He also won the admiration of King James, so much so that years later, when Wither had written some very useful and devout Hymns and Songs of the Church, the king actually issued a patent for them to be bound up with the Prayer Book, and was only finally restrained by the firm resistance of the Church authorities.

So George Wither and William Browne had made their way by poetry and had won the notice of the Court, and they went on writing about each other admiringly in the pastoral form made popular by Spenser. But there was another side to Wither. He was a religious man, a Puritan and a patriot, and he saw things in the life of the Age that he thought he might remove by the use of satirical denunciation, so he published his Abuses Stript and Whipt. They were general warnings and not personal, but somebody with power fitted the cap on himself and promptly the poet was clapped into prison. Who did this against him, and why, has never been found out. Yet it did not daunt him, for he went on writing in prison, and the Princess Elizabeth used her influence to secure his release. The poems he wrote in prison are among the brightest and most graceful from his pen, and include his best known song:

Shall I, wasting in despair,
Die because a woman's fair?

These early experiences were repeated in later years. Wither was full of the joy of life and a master of lyrical expression, writing with an intimate love of nature; but then his public spirit drove him into satire against what he regarded as wrong, and over and over again he was silenced. When the Civil War broke out he sold his property to equip a troop of horse for the Parliamentary side, and served with distinction. His later years were years of protest and of doleful prophecy, and the grace of his early work had quite disappeared when he died, an old man nearly eighty years old, at a house in the Strand, and was buried in Savoy chapel.

The Perfect Hamlet

BICKTON. A turn on the road to Ringwood brings us to a lane which joins hands with the Avon at this perfect hamlet. A watermill greets us with the pleasant sounds of tumbling water and rumbling grindstones. Up past the mill are lovely thatched cottages with hive-like porches and gardens bright with lilac and fruit trees. Nearly hidden by soaring elms, and standing on a small green whose trees accompany it down to the water, is a fine old farm with comfortable barns and byres. Here the river spreads out lazily as if tired of its battle with the mill, and among the small islands streaking its shallows wild swan, duck, and sea-gulls idle away the hours.

The Ancient Bell

BIGHTON. It has an old church with a wonderful bell which has been heard in Hampshire since the time of Joan of Arc. It raised its voice in thanksgiving for the destruction of the Armada. The church has also a Norman font, a Norman window in the chancel, a canopied piscina made in the 13th century, arcades with staunch round pillars and decorated capitals about 750 years old, and an ancient pillar piscina near the door. The screen and the roof are painted and brightly gilded.

A Kitchener of Long Ago

BINSTED. Here sleeps a warrior of 600 years ago, and here sleep the far-off ancestors of a famous warrior of our own time, Lord Kitchener, for we have come upon a gravestone in Suffolk to a Kitchener ancestor who came from this place in 1693. The sleeping knight is believed to be Sir Richard de Westcote, who founded a chantry here in 1332, and lies within the 14th century walls of the church, his face worn away by the centuries. His crossed feet rest on a lion and over his suit of mail he wears a coat with a belt.

Binsted, high up in the hop-growing country round Alton, has given to the British Museum terracotta works of art made by the Romans, and there has also been found here a stone coffin with a skeleton in it.

In a delightful village corner the church stands with an overhanging timbered house across the way. Entered through a 14th century doorway, it will strike the traveller as very long and spacious for a village church. The arches in the chancel are Norman. The tower is a generation or two younger, and so are the arches of the nave, above each of which is a 15th century lancet in the clerestory. Under a 14th century arch in the lady chapel is a tomb lightly carved with a cross. In a lancet window by the door is a little medallion of heraldic glass made in 1578, showing the arms of Sir Henry Wallop, who impoverished himself as a patriot in the days of Queen Elizabeth and lies in St Patrick's cathedral in Dublin. There is a Jacobean altar with baluster legs and a chest of the same period; but what we thought more thrilling is a door into the vestry, still on the hinges on which it first swung open 500 years ago.

Hanging on the wall is the simple wooden cross of an officer who died for us in the Great War, one of those pathetic memorials more moving than anything else our own generation has put in our churches. It belongs to William Wickham Ogilvy, of whom his padre wrote these noble words :

He realised perfectly that he would not live, and was wonderfully calm and brave about it.

We see his name again on the peace memorial in the churchyard, where also, among the heroes of Binsted, is Ernest George Cox, who died of gas poisoning three years *after the war was over.*

The Last Seat on the Last Boat

BISHOP'S SUTTON. In a field by the church are the foundations of the kennels where the hunting bishops of Winchester kept their hounds. On the church walls are the crosses where the bishops touched the stones on Consecration Day and the mass dials by which the villagers told the time before clocks came. The church is charming with two Norman doorways, one decorated with the heads of weird half-human birds. The nave has little Norman lights, the belfry rests on splendid medieval timbers, and the 650-year-old chancel has by the altar the brass portraits of two delightful people who seem to be smiling at one another, as if sharing some lovely secret. They lived 400 years ago but that is all we know of them. He is in plain armour; she has on elegant costume, a fine headdress, a long robe, and a beautiful girdle clasped with three Tudor roses. The sanctuary rails are old. The altar has a rare plate said to have been given by William of Wykeham, founder of Winchester School. For 500 years every priest of St Nicholas has handled it and must have loved this precious piece of silver. Under the 12th century chancel arch is a quaintly written tablet to William Cowper, a London surgeon of Queen Anne's time, who worked himself to death at his studies; but it is a tablet with an unfamiliar name which is the thrilling possession of this small place. In the churchyard sleep a father and his son having the name of McNeile; the tablet is to the memory of Ethel Rhoda McNeile, one of the world's unknown heroes. She gave up the last seat in the last boat of a sinking ship.

A gold sovereign brought up from the sunken Egypt lies on our desk as we write; it went down in the bullion room of the ship, with courageous women aboard, after the collision 25 miles south-west of Ushant in 1922. In the panic which followed the collision of the Egypt there was a mutiny among the stewards. It was quelled, but the time left for getting out the boats before the ship went down was short. A number of passengers had failed to get their lifebelts. The water had reached their cabins and they could not get to them. A Marconi operator took off his own life-jacket and gave it to a lady who had none, and that brave man did not come home. The women and children were lined up. They could not stand on the deck; the ship had heeled too sharply. They lay along the rail, edging their way as best they could toward the waiting boat.

The Chief Purser, who was superintending the loading of the boat and counting heads as the passengers were helped into it, called "Three more." Miss McNeile was Number Three in the line. Hers was the last place. On her right was a married woman who murmured something. It was "Oh, my children! What will they do without a mother?" Miss McNeile put her arm under the woman and hoisted her across, saying, "If you don't mind we will change places." There was no time for anything else to be said. The woman who had been given her place was seized by the sailors and pushed into the boat, which was cut adrift. A minute afterwards the Egypt turned turtle and went down. The one was taken and the other left.

"My sister naturally gave her place," her brother said, "because it would have hurt her more that the children should be motherless than that her own life should be at an end. Had she not done what she did all her life would have been haunted by that thought. She was always capable of rapid thinking and quick decision, and used both in that hour of peril in order not to miss her opportunity. If she had been slow about it she would have been grabbed and put into the boat. Her chance would have gone." Miss McNeile was a graduate of Girton College, and the Church Missionary Society and India knew her as Sister Rhoda.

Lancelot Andrewes and William of Wykeham

BISHOP'S WALTHAM. On these chalk downs, ten miles from their cathedral, the bishops of Winchester had a noble palace and a park of 1000 acres. It was begun as a castle by Henry de Blois in 1136 and finished as a palace by William of Wykeham. Bishop Thomas Langton built the brick wall round it, and the garden house, in the 15th century.

There are imposing ruins of the palace, where Henry the Second called on his nobles for supplies for his Crusade, where Richard Lionheart was entertained after his coronation, where Margaret of

Anjou slept in a blue and gold bed, where William of Waynfleete and William of Wykeham died. Here is the massive tower, with the walls of the great 14th century building where the retainers were housed, and a wall pierced by five great windows with embattled transoms, part of William of Wykeham's hall.

The road winds down between the ruins and the lake, fringed with willows and rushes and decked with water crowfoot; it is called Abbot's Pond. The lake was made by damming one of the Hamble's tributaries and is now the headwater of the river. There are pike in the lake and trout in the Hamble.

A narrow street of delightful oldfashioned houses brings us to the flint church high above the town, some of the houses with wistaria and magnolia on their walls. The tower of the church, built after the old one fell down in 1582, has a stair turret ending in a little round tower with big stone crosses on the walls. We found wallflowers blooming in its crannies. The square porch has a simple door with a huge wooden lock, and it is still possible to make out the year 1613 cut near the top of the door.

The pride of the church is the pulpit, given in 1600 by the famous Lancelot Andrewes, Queen Elizabeth's Dean of Westminster and one of the remarkable group of men who translated the Authorised Version of the Bible. Its panels are carved with gabled arches and foliage, and it has a canopy with cresting. From this pulpit William Brook preached for 59 years last century. Preserved near the pulpit is an old hourglass which has come back to the church after long absence, and near it we found, among fragments of stone carving, the plain old font, also rescued and returned after straying away. In front of the altar under a plain stone lies the old tutor of Andrewes, Dr Ward, once rector here. He also was one of the translators of the Authorised Version.

It is thought that William of Wykeham built the chancel, for his rose is carved at the top of the east window. The altar rails and a handsomely carved chair, with angels carrying the crown, are 17th century. A second chair is a wonderfully good copy of the first. In an aisle is a Tudor altar richly carved; a sculptured coat-of-arms and four cannon balls from the walls of the castle; a quaint carved and painted wall-monument to Elizabeth and Robert Kerby of the 18th century; and a bust of Thomas Ashton dressed in black, with a black beard, and long hair, as his friends saw him in Elizabethan days.

In this village were kept many French prisoners during the Napoleon wars and one of them was Garneray the painter, the story being told that while on a prison ship he tried to escape with a friend but sank into the mud and was recaptured, his friend being drowned.

The Youngest Son

BLACKMOOR. It has a church designed by Alfred Waterhouse in the 19th century and given to the village by Lord Chancellor Selborne, who was laid to rest beside it in 1895. A tablet on the wall tells of Blackmoor's gratitude to this great lawyer and great churchman, who with his wife did so much for the village in which they worshipped. There are many memorials to soldiers and sailors, one of them a window shining with figures of the Madonna and St George.

Yet this dignified church is not the only thing Blackmoor owes the Selbornes, for close by it is a peace memorial as charming as any village could have, a delightful cloister surrounding a little garden and a cross. Within it are a fountain and a seat for the children, and among its inscriptions is one which says:

Remember, Children, the glory and the sadness of War, the courage of the men, and the sorrow and suffering of all the people.

It was all given by the second Earl of Selborne and his wife, whose youngest son is among the names that live for evermore.

Lord Selborne was a friend of Tennyson and of the famous Dr Jowett, master of Balliol, who told Tennyson, in a conversation the three were having together, that the philosophy in his poems was more to be considered than any regular philosophy in England, adding that he believed In Memoriam and Crossing the Bar would live for ever in men's hearts. Lord Selborne, who lived through 83 years of last century, was a great lawyer and a great churchman, who went into Parliament and refused a post in Mr Gladstone's Government rather than agree to the disestablishment of the Irish Church. He represented England at the enquiry into the Alabama incident, making the most of our bad case. He bought 1800 acres in Hampshire and built his house on the site of an old farm, discovering a hoard of Roman coins and pottery in the excavations. He gave the village not only its church, but the parsonage and schools.

Beaulieu   **View Across the River**

Beaulieu   **The Abbey Cloisters**

Cloister Doorway

Refectory Doorway

The Wonderful Pulpit

BEAULIEU ABBEY AND ITS ANCIENT ARCHES

The son he lost in the war was a poet of great promise, Robert Stafford Palmer. He went out from the house in the park as a captain in the Hampshires, and in the first year of the fighting he wrote this Battle Prayer:

> *How long, O Lord, how long before the flood*
> *Of crimson-welling carnage shall abate?*
> *From sodden plains in West and East the blood*
> *Of kindly men streams up in mists of hate*
> *Polluting thy clean air; and nations great*
> *In reputation of the arts that bind*
> *The world with hopes of Heaven, sink to the state*
> *Of brute barbarians. . . . Lord, how long*
> *Shall Satan in high places lead the blind*
> *To battle for the passions of the strong?*
> *Oh touch Thy children's hearts, that they may know*
> *Hate their most hateful, pride their deadliest foe.*

Alas, the hate and pride of war were very soon to consume him.

Saxon England

BOARHUNT. It lies apart from its wonderful little treasure-house, which stands near the top of a hill, hidden by trees. A prosperous-looking farm and two cottages share the narrow path which brings us to a piece of Saxon England.

Perhaps the first thing we notice about this quiet grey building is its bell-turret, shaped like an archway with lovely pillars and roofed with stone tiles. It has held its own against the storms and furies of 700 winters. But older than the belfry is the church itself, for it was raised by men who had never heard of Norman William. The Normans made their mark on it, but left for our delight the tall chancel arch, only seven feet wide, the round and massive font at which Saxon babies were dipped, and a charming small window decorated by a Saxon mason with a delicate fragment of cable moulding. On the eastern gable is a narrow pilaster strip, the hall-mark of the Saxon builder. From the 13th century come the odd half-arch to the left of the chancel arch, the image brackets on either side of the altar, the piscina and aumbry, and the blocked-up priest's doorway. The same century gave the chancel a fresco, now only a dim suggestion of figures behind a wall-monument to the Henslowe family. The monument, raised in 1577, is handsome with heraldry and has jovial little angels clasping shields. On the cornice stand three headless figures.

F

In the churchyard is a huge hollow yew, 27 feet round. We heard that it was once the home of a family for a whole winter.

Mr Jenvey's Wheels

BOLDRE. For the loveliness of its situation, for the beauty man and nature give it, but especially for its human story, it is one of the much-loved places. It stands astride the small valley whose stream gives the village its name. It is the central river of our greatest woodland, the New Forest, and is first the romantic Highland Water above Brockenhurst, then Boldre River, and finally Lymington River, navigable for steamers below that town.

The village is here, there, and everywhere. It follows three or four winding wooded lanes, climbing any hill it takes a fancy to, and extends along the stream thinly from the church for a mile or more to Vicar's Hill, where lived William Gilpin, the remarkable vicar who, with Caroline Bowles (who was to marry Southey) gave Boldre its touch with literature. For his intimate and detailed knowledge of natural things he was called the Gilbert White of the New Forest.

The quaint simplicity of Boldre is altogether charming. At the bottom of the hill is a bewitching timbered cottage whose owner loves it so much that he would not have a straw of its thatched head hurt. Myrtle and wistaria clamber over its face; its garden is alight with flowers, and on its tiny lawn is a tread pump 200 years old, decorated with hares and a stag. Its doors hang by hand-forged hinges, and the key turns in ancient wooden locks. A Roman road runs past its orchard and a trout stream meanders by.

On the way to the church, close to the old five-arched bridge across the swiftly-flowing Boldre, is a self-respecting sunburnt house next to a wheelwright's shop. Both belonged, when we called, to Mr Jenvey, and had been in his family 200 years. For 200 years the wagons of Boldre have gone about their business on Jenvey wheels. But the Jenveys were not only wheelwrights; there were musicians among them, and in Boldre church we found, fixed to the wall in a glass case, a weird and wonderful instrument. It is the 14-holed bassoon played by Jesse Jenvey in the choir in the far-off days before the organ came.

These are the kind of things that are typical of Boldre, a place full of interest, and yet with an interest deeper still for the things not seen, for here it was that Caroline Bowles, a poet herself, married Robert Southey, in 1839. It was here that the tragedy of those few years began, a tragedy for which no one was to blame.

The church, the 13th century successor to a church in the Conqueror's Domesday Book, stands on a hill half-hidden by ash and elm. In it is a bust of a 17th century MP, John Kemp, shown with a book and a skull, his long hair over his shoulders. The font is 15th and the altar table 17th century. The windows have lost their old glass, but one of the small ancient possessions of the church has a fascinating interest for the antiquary. It is a huge iron key with which it is believed the monks of Beaulieu Abbey used to unlock their great door. There is a beautiful old panelled chest, and a Breeches Bible of 1579 in a glass case.

By the withered trunk of an old maple in the churchyard is a grave with an epitaph by which all must pause who would feel the true spirit of this place, for here lies the old vicar William Gilpin, one of England's gentlemen, one of Boldre's truest friends. It is Gilpin and Southey who give this place its fame. This is the epitaph we read, and it is his own, as we shall see:

In a quiet mansion beneath this stone, secured from the afflictions and still more dangerous enjoyments of life, lie the remains of William Gilpin, sometime vicar of this parish, together with the remains of Margaret his wife.

He goes on to say that they await patiently the joy of waking in a happier land, and adds quaintly, in words grown over with moss:

Here it will be a new joy to meet several of their good neighbours who now lie scattered in these sacred precincts around them.

He was 80 when he died, in the year before Trafalgar. About a mile away at Vicar's Hill, in the garden he planted and loved, his great plane tree still stands. The view from his lawn, across sloping green fields and over beautiful woods to the hills of the Isle of Wight, is a noble one. On a chest we found an old engraving of the vicar.

The Poignant Tragedy of a Poet

THIS is the pathetic story of Robert Southey and Caroline Bowles, whose marriage took place in Boldre Church. She was born at Lymington, and lived always at Buckland, except for the three sad years at Keswick as Southey's second wife. He lived only a few weeks at her Buckland cottage after his marriage. He was a family man, a devoted husband and father, a most industrious literary worker, depending domestically on wifely care. But by the time he was 60 his mental energy had waned. Then, for three years, he had the loss of his first wife's help and the anxiety of her illness and complete mental failure. Her death left him the wreck of his earlier self.

For 20 years he had had a literary correspondence and friendship with Caroline Bowles, whose tastes and aims were like his own, and 19 months after his wife's death he went from Keswick to Boldre and they were married. He was in his 65th year and she in her 53rd. It seemed singularly suitable, and would have been if he had retained his mental fitness, but his noble life was broken, and his brain failure was swift and tragic. He did no more effectual work, and his wife was ill at ease among his family, who resented her presence at Keswick. Three years later Southey died, a melancholy ruin.

It is Southey's wife who honours Boldre, where she spent a useful life. Eleven years after her husband's death she was laid to rest at Lymington. She had been the poorer for her marriage. When she was left an orphan her adopted brother settled on her £150 a year till she should marry. This lapsed when she married Southey. By his will Southey left her £2000, but she was less well provided for than before her marriage, till she received a crown pension of £200 a year two years before her death. Caroline deserved her pension, for her writings in prose and verse were sympathetic in spirit, pure in tone, and always had the aim of social helpfulness. No one was to blame for this matrimonial tragedy, for neither Southey nor Caroline Bowles realised the seriousness of his breakdown when they married. He had been the noblest human character of all the Lake poets, and deserved a better reward.

Wonderful William Gilpin

ONE of our forerunners in the Grand Tour of England, William Gilpin was much more than a country parson with a picturesque and powerful personality. He was 53 when he came to Boldre, and had had before that nearly thirty years of schoolmastering, during which he used his holidays for rambling through England. He had also written the life of his famous ancestor Bernard Gilpin, the Apostle of the North, as well as Lives of Latimer, Wycliffe, and

Huss. Seven Gilpins are in the Dictionary of National Biography and all were descended from the same Westmorland family. Bernard was great and heroic, and ranks first in the family, in influence as in time, but William Gilpin of the New Forest has quite an original claim to distinction.

He was the first Englishman to set himself the task of picturing by prose and pencil the abounding beauties of his native land, as Michael Drayton had attempted in rhyme in Elizabethan days. He was ordained at 22, and after a few years of curacy took over a school at Cheam in Surrey, which he conducted on lines strangely different from the school methods of his day. Discipline was maintained by a jury of boys who, under supervision, imposed fines which were spent in buying books, improving games, and in feeding the poor, so giving the boys practice in managing things. The school was popular and successful. One of its scholars (Henry Addington) became Prime Minister. It was another of Gilpin's old boys, William Mitford, the historian of Greece, who presented his old master with the vicarage of Boldre.

Boldre gave him plenty to do, for it had been neglected and was remote and backward. His energy soon stirred up the parish. He was prolific in plans and in deeds. He promoted a new poorhouse, and built a school out of the profits made from the books he now began to write with enthusiasm. To the children he supplied clothes as well as learning, but his idea of fitting education to the real wants of life led him to limit the education of village girls to reading and sewing.

His love of nature was only equalled by his hatred of sin. Notorious ill-doing had no quarter from him, and he went so far as to compel two of his parishioners, one a rich man, to do public penance in white sheets. But what interests us today is his delight in scenery and the charm of its variations, what he called picturesque beauty. Not only did he revel in the New Forest, but he knew, described, and drew the Eastern Counties with as much zest as Hampshire, Sussex, and Kent; he wrote of the Wye and South Wales as eagerly as of the Lakes and the Scottish Highlands. There have been better descriptive writers than William Gilpin, but none so early and so copious.

The Radical and the Parson

BOTLEY. It lies on the upper reaches of the Hamble, a delightful old town with quaint shops, handsome houses, and pretty inns. Two possessions we found here of the remote and recent past, both in the market hall. One is a carved block of timber about three feet high, part of a Danish war galley found embedded in the river mud last century, 110 feet long; the other is a huge china jug covered with ships and pictures, said to have been the punch jug used at the Farmers Club dinners when Botley was a thriving market town.

There are two churches, the old one far off with its chancel only, the other just a centenarian; the newer one has dormer windows with carved bargeboards, a stone frieze, and in its tower a diamond-shaped clock with a gilded crown. The clock came from the stables of William Cobbett, the Radical farmer, who used to live at Botley in a house called Fairthorn Farm. Often this famous man, as he left his stables on horseback for one of his rides about England, must have looked to this clock for the time. His old gardens and outbuildings are in the grounds of Botley Hill.

Cobbett declared that Botley had everything in it that he loved and nothing that he hated—it had neither workhouse nor barber, nor attorney, nor a justice of the peace; but he could walk along a field with the primroses and bluebells spangling on the banks on both sides of him, a thousand linnets singing in a spreading oak above his head, and he could hear the jingling of the traces and the whistling of the ploughboys saluting his ears from over the hedge. It was at Botley, where he lived for some time, that this bluff country-man quarrelled with the parson. He would go to hear his sermons, but he would ride outside the rectory trying to attract his attention in unpleasant ways; and he frequently declared that he longed to horsewhip him in the pulpit for talking such nonsense. Again and again we come upon the Botley parson (Richard Baker) in Cobbett's Rural Rides. He was one of two men who were the only rectors here from 1803 to 1903, he for 54 years, John Morley Lee succeeding him. Baker was such an enemy of Cobbett that he would not let the villagers have the key of the church when they wanted to ring the bells on Cobbett's release from Newgate, he having been imprisoned because he expressed in public his indignation at Englishmen being flogged under a guard of Hanoverian soldiers. Cobbett tells us how a legacy hoax once got the parson up to London to a hotel. "Up went the parson on horseback [he says], being in too great a hurry to run the risk of coach. The hoaxers, it appears, got him to some hotel and there set upon him a whole tribe of applicants—wet nurses, dry nurses, lawyers with deeds of conveyance for borrowed money, curates in want of churches, coffin-makers, travelling companions, ladies maids, dealers in Yorkshire hams, Newcastle coals, and dealers in dried night-soil at Islington. They kept the parson in town for several days, bothered him three parts out of his senses, compelled him to escape, as it were, from a fire, and then, when he got home, he found the village posted all over with handbills, giving an account of his adventure under the pretence of offering £500 reward for the discovery of the hoaxers."

The font in the new church came from the old one and was carved by a Norman mason. It is thought the sculptor was a local man, for his work is not very skilful. Cable moulding runs round the top and bottom, joined by herringbone strips, the panels left being filled with crude arcading. It has been through unknown adventures, for it was found in the river. Here is one of the rare arcades we have come upon with timber in them. Crawley and Gosport have others. Both nave and aisle have timber roofs, and the aisle has timber piers. In a handsomely canopied recess lies the full-length figure of John de Botley. He wears a long plain gown, his hair is long, and his mouth is smiling. He walked about here in the 14th century. The little 13th century church stands a long way off among farm buildings and cottages, at the end of an enchanting lane. It has trees all round it and a pond by its gate, and is entered through a doorway made up of simply moulded Norman stones. There are two narrow deep-set 13th century lancets, and a 600-year-old canopied piscina.

The Beautiful Garden of Shelley's Heart

BOURNEMOUTH. It is one of our wonderful towns by the sea, with a name a thousand years old and a history little more than a hundred. Millions of people know that there is no more delightful seaside town for those who love to be in touch with nature and to see her unspoiled. Here if we come in the busy months is an endless throng of people winding through the Central Square, but those who know feel that it is not unfitting that there should rest within sound of them all the heart of the poet of the Skylark, the Winds, and the Clouds. It is not unfitting that the heart of Shelley should lie here, for if Bournemouth is crowded it is beautiful, fit garden to have so precious a thing in its keeping. Its romantic chines, the little ravines planted with trees and shrubs running inland from the coast, carrying sea breezes into the streets, are unmatched anywhere, captivating places. The far-spread spaces of Bournemouth's parks (Meyrick Park 194 acres and Queen's 175) offer an endless delight of heather, gorse, and open common. The Overcliff Drive follows the cliffs for five miles without a shop. The bathing beach is six miles long; it must have been this fine stretch of golden beach that suggested Thomas Hardy's name for Bournemouth—Sandbourne; he calls it so in Tess. Where shall we find such rhododendrons in a town, where such glorious walks for mile upon mile in a perfect natural paradise?

The little Bourne runs through a chain of lovely gardens (miles of them) cut through the middle of the town, growing more lively as we approach the sea, the quiet upper gardens shaded with trees, the tennis courts below. Then comes the noble column in memory of Bournemouth's heroes, guarded by four lions. Trickling through a pretty water garden, the stream plunges under the crowded Square, the busy hub of Bournemouth, and beyond, as if it were glad to be free from its gloomy tunnel, it tumbles swiftly on to the pleasure garden below, through a glorious rockery. We have not seen a better laid-out pleasure space than this, ending in the grand Pavilion with its windows looking on to the Channel. Here is the Bourne Mouth; it pours itself into the sea under a pier a thousand feet long. Surely this town of 140,000 people is a happy place, with miles of sand dunes without a fisherman, a town without an industry except that of making people happy. It caters for a vast multitude all the year round, and it is known to travellers everywhere as a seaside town without a rival.

From the day when Mr and Mrs Tregonwell drove across the rough moorland track from Mudeford and came upon the lovely spot then known as Bourne its growth has been extraordinary. Mr Tregonwell has left us the story of his impression as he suddenly came upon it. He was delighted, bought land, built a house, and made a decoy pond up the Bourne. He planted all the valley and much of the coast with the pines that have made Bournemouth famous. In 20 years a village was scattered among them and many of these pines are still left by the road and in the woods at the back of the town. One of them, in Stourwood Avenue, is a centenarian. Time has proved that Mr Tregonwell was right. His houses have been followed by so many thousands more that their rateable value is now £2,000,000. We do not wonder, for Bournemouth attracts more and more people. It has had living in it Robert Louis Stevenson, who lived here "like a weevil in a biscuit," coming for his health but ill all the time in spite of all that this healthy town could do. It has had John Keble, who died here, and Lord Cromer, who is buried here, and for years George Macdonald the poet and James Payn the novelist and W. H. Hudson the naturalist were familiar figures in these streets. Bournemouth is the sort of town that will always attract men and women with imagination and a love of romantic beauty.

It grows and grows, and new pleasure buildings rise to meet the growing needs of the multitude coming here to spend its leisure or to seek its pleasure.

It has made the whole nation its debtor by taking in Hengistbury, the noble headland which is now the eastern point of Bournemouth. It has taken in Holdenhurst, where the Stour winds in and out among low-lying fields before it enters Christchurch. Here the thatched village of Holdenhurst has kept its rural character and still stands apart from the far-reaching lines of villas and bungalows which have swept around and swallowed up so many villages and hamlets. Among its farms and thatched cottages the western end of the little 19th century church rises in a wide gable to an open bell chamber, and many dark cypresses stand like sentinels in the church-yard, flowered like a garden. Here for more than fifty years one man lived and laboured as curate and vicar, and died at 90. The organ installed to his memory was subscribed for "by friends, visitors, and a grant from the Carnegie Corporation of New York in 1913." A memorial window given by his wife represents the Presentation in the Temple, and a similarly beautiful one on the opposite wall, showing the Annunciation, was the gift of a family in memory of their father and mother.

Two other places Bournemouth has drawn unto itself: Boscombe, which continues its charming cliffs and has the old home of the Shelleys, now public, with a little theatre Tennyson and Robert Louis Stevenson used to go to; and Southbourne, where the sea is rapidly encroaching and eating away houses and land—we may see the huge stones it has overthrown lying on the beach, and just beyond it is the impressive headland of Hengistbury, which thus comes into the range of Bournemouth's attractions. The civic spirit of the town is worthy of it all, as anyone can see who stands on this six miles of bathing beach or in these pleasure grounds, with a magnificent entertainments pavilion, baths and swimming pool, two piers, and a new hall used in the summer for exhibitions and in the winter as an indoor bowling green said to be the finest in England. Though Bournemouth had the first electric trams in England it has given them up for modern trolley buses, and another mark of its public spirit is the municipality's use of waste. It hates all waste and litter, and turns it into profit and beauty. After being sifted all that cannot be used is burned in destructors, and the heat provides power for crushing the unburnable matter and mixing it with cement to form 30,000 paving stones a year. The heat from the destructors also warms the water in the public baths. Old cans and kitchen utensils are treated and used to the extent of hundreds of tons to form foundations for new roads. As for the old tramlines, they have come in most opportunely to reinforce the concrete of huge sea walls. Useless hollows are filled and levelled to form children's playgrounds. Marshy swamps by the River Stour are being reclaimed. Bournemouth must have been reading Dickens, and is apparently believing in the Golden Dustman.

Loving old things as well as new, the town has saved the medieval bridge across the Stour at Iford, over which we may still walk on our way to Christchurch, the noble minster which Bournemouth has within easy reach by one of the best seaside walks in England.

Many familiar names come to mind as we stroll about the pleasant streets and gardens of the town. Skerryvore, in Alum Chine, where Robert Louis Stevenson lived for three years (it was named after a lighthouse built by Robert's grandfather and his sons) is alas! now but a memory, for it was damaged during the war and afterwards demolished. Its old summer house may perhaps have seen the birth of Kidnapped, Dr Jekyll and Mr Hyde, and a Child's Garden of Verse, all of which were written here. We think here, too, of Miss Adelaide Ann Boodle, whose death in 1934 broke one of our last links with Robert Louis Stevenson. Her friendship with him and Mrs Stevenson began when they came to Bournemouth and continued when they went to Samoa. Some of Stevenson's letters to her are included in the Vailima Letters, and she herself wrote about the friendship in Flashlights from Skerryvore. Stevenson called her the Gamekeeper because she looked after his pets when he was away from home, and in return she named him the Squire. In the Wimborne Road Cemetery sleeps Rob Roy MacGregor, who wrote A Thousand Miles in a Canoe, the story of his wanderings, and here, too, lies Canon Twells, whose undying memorial is his touching hymn, "At even, ere the sun was set," sung on Sunday evenings all round the world.

Standing with wide windows and balconies overlooking the bay is the Russell-Cotes Art Gallery on the East Cliff, once the home of Sir Merton Russell-Cotes. In this gorgeous home he stored the treasures he gathered on many journeys in many lands, bequeathing it all to the town with an endowment for its upkeep. Porcelains of many periods and countries, crystals and precious stones, miniatures and enamels, English, French, and Dutch furniture, prehistoric stone weapons and native implements, Japanese and Burmese treasures, cases of miniatures and butterflies, are in rich profusion in this fine museum, and in one case are autographed letters of Sir Walter Scott, Garibaldi, John Ruskin, and Florence Nightingale. An Irving Room holds many relics of Sir Henry, including costumes and jewels he used on the stage, letters he wrote and received, portraits, playbills, and so on.

Other fascinating relics of famous men include a letter written by Nelson on the Victory seven days before he died, a lock of his hair cut off by Hardy and set in a small brooch, and a necklet of hair given by him to Lady Hamilton. A crimson leather dispatch case with gilt tooling belonged to Napoleon, and was found on the field after the Battle of Waterloo, and an inlaid octagonal table here was used by him in his exile on St Helena. A suite of stately galleries opened by Princess Beatrice in 1919 was added to the ground floor by Sir Merton and Lady Russell-Cotes on the 59th anniversary of their wedding day, and another gallery was given by their son and daughter in 1926. They contain a fine collection of pictures, including many by the best-known artists of the 19th and 20th centuries. There are works by Landseer, Poynter, David Cox, David Murray, Herkomer, Frith, Woodall, Lucy Kemp-Welch, Edwin Long, Luke

Fildes, Etty, Leader, Aumonier, Fragonard, Orchardson, and many other painters. A charming group of water-colour drawings by Walter Crane illustrates the Round Table of King Arthur. There is a landscape by Corot, a moonlight effect by old Crome, a replica by Turner of his St Michael's Mount, and a bust of Cromwell by Roubiliac. Yet, lovely as are these crowded galleries, we must remember the view from the wonderful windows across the bay, where the sun sets in a glory of green, rose, and gold.

The history of Bournemouth's mother church of St Peter's is bound up with the history of the town, and especially with the life of its first vicar, Alexander Morden Bennett, who came here when the Victorian Era was but eight years old and Bournemouth yet an infant. He found a poor little church, no school, no parsonage, and a living so scanty that it was going begging. To the single-minded devotion and the thirty years incessant work of this brave man is due the dignified and beautiful church which was completed with a great service of thanksgiving in 1879. One month more, and, having seen his work accomplished, the vicar laid down his task and passed peacefully away. The lovely church of St Stephen was raised to his memory, and many other churches in the town owe their existence to his boundless energy and his quenchless enthusiasm. He sleeps in the shadow of the church he loved and served.

The stately church, designed by George Edmund Street RA, architect of the Law Courts in London, is one of his most effective works. Its fine spire is seen all over the town. The simplicity of the lofty nave is in marked contrast with the elaboration of the chancel, where polished marble columns support the roof and gleaming mosaics and glowing frescoes give an indescribable richness of colour. The pulpit (which has been at an international exhibition) is in itself a masterpiece, the book-rest supported by an angel in alabaster, and carved heads of the Apostles adorning it.

It was a happy inspiration that the first vicar of this beautiful church after its completion, Alexander Sykes Bennett, should be the son of the man by whose labours it had been built and dedicated; he carried on the devoted work of his father for the churches of Bournemouth and was vicar for thirty years. There is a window of four saints to his memory.

It was in St Peter's, in the Keble Chapel, that there was often seen in the closing years of last century one of the century's noblest figures. Here Mr Gladstone sat as an old man when staying at Bournemouth for his health. Noticing his difficulty from deafness in following the service, the sacristan found him a seat in the choir, and on one of the oak stalls a brass plate tells us that "from this stall Mr Gladstone made his last Communion in church on Thursday, March 3, 1898." It was known while he was here that his end was not far off, and one of his biographers has told us that his desire was to die at home, where he had spent his best years:

So he made his last journey from Bournemouth to Hawarden. The news that he was leaving spread about the town and some inkling of the truth as to his condition had leaked out. When he reached the station there was a crowd awaiting his arrival, and as he walked with almost vigorous steps across the platform someone called out, "God bless you, Sir." Instantly he turned and, facing the uncovered crowd, lifted his hat, and in the deep tones which men knew so well, said, "God bless you all, and this place, and the land we love."

It is not easy for young people of this generation to understand the emotion which came to those who heard these words, for Mr Gladstone was a hero almost unparalleled among his countrymen. His was the voice of Europe in the days when a statesman's voice rang round the world as none does now; and this Goodbye to Bournemouth was the farewell to public life, the farewell to life itself, of one of the most beloved, most esteemed, and most magnetic figures who have ever crossed the stage of history. Of this dramatic passing St Peter's church and the town of Bournemouth have a pathetic memory.

The founder's window in the tower of St Peter's pictures other great builders: Aaron and the Tabernacle, Solomon and the Temple, Lanfranc the builder of Canterbury, Walkelin who rebuilt Winchester, and Flambard with the model of Christchurch Priory. Also to his memory is the Bennett Memorial Window, with scenes from Revelation. This church built with so much devotion has also a window to a sacristan, set up in honour of 40 years of service. We found the sacristan still in active service, respected and loved by all who knew him. His window shows the Annunciation in softest blues and greens, and is worthy to rank with the other fine glass of

77

this proud place. A three-light window in the Keble Chapel, where the author of The Christian Year would often sit in the last years of his life, is from the William Morris workshops, showing Our Lord's appearance at the Sea of Tiberias after the Resurrection. The five-light Minstrel Window, exquisite in colouring and unusual in subject, pictures the place of music in worship, and has the Angels of the Nativity, the Song of Miriam, the Children Singing in the Temple, the Sweet Psalmist of Israel, the songs of Paul and Silas in prison, and the Worship of the Lamb. We cannot forget the homely group of carol singers in the snow, where a little dog waits patiently at his master's side. In the Te Deum Window of the Keble Chapel the portrait of Keble is in a group of saints of all ages. Most of these are by Clayton and Bell, and there is a charming window of scenes in Our Lord's life by Percy Bacon, thought by many to be the finest glass here.

St Peter's stands nobly above the Central Square of Bournemouth, and by it is one of the loveliest of our churchyards, terraced and climbing a steep hillside planted with shrubs and firs. On the lower slope a churchyard cross rises 22 feet; it was carved by the same master-hand as the pulpit, and the six panels show the martyrdom of St Peter and scenes from Our Lord's life. Here lies Lewis Tregonwell, the founder of Bournemouth and builder of its first house; he died in 1832. Not only one of the most beautiful, this is one of the most interesting churchyards, too. By the side of the steps leading up to its almost precipitous slope is a vault in which rests the heart of our great but hapless poet Shelley. The vault, under a grassy mound topped by low monumental erections which tell who rest beneath, is the burial-place of Shelley's second wife Mary Godwin, mother of the poet's son and heir, Sir Percy. When Sir Percy died and was buried here beside his mother, his father's heart was buried with them. Here, too, were reburied Mrs Shelley's father and mother, William Godwin and his wife. Mary Godwin died when her daughter was born and William Godwin 38 years afterwards, both being buried in old St. Pancras churchyard in London and removed here after Mrs Shelley's death.

All the Godwins had literary prominence in their day—Mrs Godwin (Mary Wollstonecraft) for her Vindication of the Rights of Women, a pioneer book; Mr Godwin, the philsophical Radical, for his Inquiry Concerning Political Justice and his Adventures of Caleb Williams; and Mary Shelley for her grim story Frankenstein. Mrs Shelley, by her anxious care for the unpractical poet, made some amends for her impecunious father's sponging on him. Here the strange assortment rest together, three queer people with the heart of Shelley as a bond which links them to each other, as to us all.

Bournemouth has a fine group of modern churches, with towers and spires and attractive interiors. St Clements was designed by Mr J. D. Sedding, the architect to whom Ruskin said that he must keep a pencil or a chisel in his hand if he were to be more than a mere employer of men; the church has a tower and six bays, an aisle, and a chapel, and among its possessions is a pair of Italian candlesticks. Richmond Hill Congregational Church has a fine tower with a spire rising 130 feet; this was the spiritual home of the famous and beloved Free Church leader Dr J. D. Jones, who in 39 years made it a Mecca of the English-speaking Nonconformist world.

The Oratory of the Sacred Heart has an altar of grey sculptured Italian marbles inlaid with lapis-lazuli, and steps and floor of white marble. The lofty reredos of white marble has Our Lord with angels, and the unusual decoration of the Communion rail is of beaten brass with marble medallions of saints. Holy Trinity is built of brick in the Byzantine style, and its tall bell-tower stands apart. It was Bournemouth's second church, and has a rose window in memory of Bishop Sumner of Winchester and a fine chancel window by A. K. Nicholson representing the orders set forth in the chorus of praise of the Te Deum. A triptych of the Ascension on the high altar glorious in gold and colour is a tribute to the devoted service of Canon Eliot, 15 years vicar here.

St Stephen's church on Richmond Hill, the memorial to Bournemouth's first vicar, is of singular beauty, one of the finest works of Mr J. L. Pearson, architect of Truro Cathedral. Looking across the twelve arches of the double aisles on either side of the nave, we see a graceful and ever-changing perspective of clustered columns and moulded capitals. One block of marble forms the font, and the dazzlingly white pulpit is carved with figures of saintly women. The richly decorated chancel is of cathedral-like proportions. There is a silver crucifix of the 16th century and an illuminated manuscript.

Proudly on the hill towards Poole stands the church of St Michael,

79

with its dignified tower 150 feet high, a landmark for the western side of the town. The wide chancel is covered with wall-paintings of the Te Deum and there are two beautiful screens, one of iron with panels of foliage, the other of oak in the style of the 15th century. The centrepiece of the marble pulpit is a white alabaster figure of St George and the Dragon. A bronze figure of Fortitude by Sir George Frampton and a charming series of windows picturing King Arthur and the Knights of the Round Table give a rich dignity to the memorial chapel for those who did not come back (designed by Sir Thomas Jackson); and majestic angels glorify the great west window by Christopher Whall, the artist in glass who raised the whole standard of his craft in the early years of our century.

We can almost think ourselves in one of the hill cities of Northern Italy as we approach the Church of St Francis of Assisi, a replica of an Italian Church, standing out clearly against a blue sky on the northern edge of Bournemouth, overlooking the slopes towards Wimborne and Ringwood. The roof of bright red tiles, the square tower and white walls, strike an exotic note which harmonises well with the clear skies and bright sunshines of this sunny town. The interior is white and wide and simple. No stained glass cuts off the bright light streaming in, intensified and reflected by the white walls. Under a canopy 24 feet high the high altar stands on marble pillars. A daring use of colour on the roof, almost crude in blue and green, accentuates the primitive effect. We find ourselves almost waiting for the heavy door to swing open for some contadina from the vineyards coming to count her beads before the blue-robed Madonna or the kindly St Francis. Birds, beasts, and flowers in the carvings of the porch remind us of the love of the Little Poor Man for his Little Brother.

It is good that this fine monument of faithful devotion in memory of a saint beloved by all mankind for his simplicity should strike the note of sacrifice and pure unselfishness. The entire cost of the church was borne by one giver who remains unknown, and all about us little gifts speak of loving sacrifice in its service. We have found in our journeyings precious stones set in chalices in memory, and wedding-rings on which is hung the Lenten Veil; here in this church of St Francis we found another lovely thing—three once-treasured silver teapots transformed into lamps before the altar. The Christ on the

The Zigzag Walk

Peace Memorial

St Stephen's Church

BEAUTIFUL BOURNEMOUTH

Durley Chine

West Cliff

'BOURNEMOUTH'S LOVELY COAST

Crucifix was brought from the battlefield of the Marne. The heavy Norman bowl of the font was rescued from a Welsh farmyard.

Southbourne has two notable modern churches, the church of St Catherine, with an 18th century carpet in the sanctuary and Joan of Arc in one of the windows, and Immanuel Church, one of the finest small Congregational buildings of this century, mentioned by the President of the Royal Institute of British Architects as one of the outstanding buildings of its year. Its massive lines are carried out in mellowed red brick against which a lily pond in a grassy setting forms a graceful contrast, and a gentle figure of St Francis, designed by Mrs G. F. Watts, looks down in benediction on his little feathered brothers bathing and fluttering about his feet. The lofty and spacious interior is chaste and beautiful, its pale stone pillars and the purple hangings of the apse flooded with golden light from the windows. A pleasant tablet on the wall records the thanks of the congregation to Frederic Lawrence the architect, F. A. Grigg the builder, G. Eaton the foreman, and all the men who built the church. Can it be wondered at that Bournemouth, with its equable climate, its clear air and abundant sunshine, its many flowers and thousands of fragrant pines, its golden sands and delightful surroundings, attracts crowds of visitors who come back year after year, and that many who retire from active work in harsher and bleaker parts of our island decide to spend their later years in this sheltered garden city by the sea?

The Mystery of Shelley's Heart

SHELLEY'S heart has been the subject of one of the most baffling literary mysteries, and there are few matters of fact on which more errors have been printed. Men have discussed for years in the newspapers whether the heart is buried in Italy. It has been said to be in Boscombe church. Travellers have declared that it is in the museum at Keats's house in Rome. Even Mr T. J. Wise, the great bibliographer who was supposed to know next to everything declared just before he died that Lady Shelley had told him she had sent the heart to Rome. It would be possible to make up a list of quite fifty misstatements about it, and the confusion is increased largely by the extraordinary fact that Captain Trelawny, who rescued the heart from the fire when the body was burned, never mentioned it until many years after, and that Leigh Hunt, who quarrelled about the

G   81

heart with Mrs Shelley and had it in his possession, never mentioned it in his autobiography. It has all been very mysterious, but the truth is that it lies in Bournemouth having come to this corner of Shelley's Motherland in the curious way we will now describe.

Shelley was drowned on July 8, 1822, while sailing in a boat, the Ariel, from Leghorn to Lerici on the Gulf of Spezzia. He had been living for some time on the Italian coast near Lerici with his wife and his friends, Mr and Mrs Williams. Byron was living at Pisa, and his sailing-boat, the Bolivar, was at Leghorn under the command of Captain Trelawny, another friend.

Leigh Hunt and his family arrived at Leghorn, and Shelley crossed the bay in the Ariel to greet them. His companions in the boat were Williams and an English sailor boy, Charles Vivian. Shelley had no knowledge of the management of a boat, Williams a little knowledge, and the boy more. They joined the Hunts at Leghorn, and went on to Pisa to visit Byron. With him the Hunts stayed, but Shelley returned to Leghorn, and, with Williams and the boy, set sail for his seaside home. Trelawny, in the Bolivar at Leghorn, saw the start. The day was threatening, and quickly a heavy summer storm burst on the bay. When it cleared the Ariel could not be seen, and Trelawny hoped it had reached Viareggio on the other side. But either it had been sunk by the storm or, as came to be suspected, had been run down by a local fishing boat in the hope of booty.

Ten days passed and then the bodies of Shelley, Williams, and the boy were all cast ashore by the sea. They were discovered by Trelawny, who had been searching the coast, and he at once sent the news to Byron and Leigh Hunt at Pisa. They came by land to Viareggio, near where the bodies lay, three miles apart. The remains of Shelley and Williams were undistinguishable by their features, owing to the battering of the waves; but in one pocket of Shelley's coat was a book by Sophocles in Greek, now in the Bodleian Library at Oxford, and in the other pocket a volume of poems by Keats, who had died more than a year earlier. Trelawny buried the bodies temporarily in the sand by the shore, broke the news to Mrs Shelley and Mrs Williams, and awaited the arrival of Byron and Leigh Hunt.

More than six weeks after the drowning the bodies of Williams and Shelley were cremated, Williams on August 15 and Shelley on August 16. They were burned on the wild and lonely shore by arrangement with the Italian authorities, Byron, Hunt, and Tre-lawny being present. The bodies, drenched in spirits, were burned in an iron furnace, and the ashes of Williams were sent to England, while those of Shelley were taken to Rome by Trelawny, enclosed in a box lined with velvet. They were buried there, on December 7, in the Protestant cemetery beside the graves of Keats and of Shelley's child William, who had died not long before. On a flat gravestone an inscription was engraved, the Latin provided by Leigh Hunt, with this quotation from The Tempest suggested by Trelawny.

Percy Bysshe Shelley
Cor Cordium

Nothing of him that doth fade
But doth suffer a sea-change
Into something rich and strange.

Cor cordium, heart of hearts, has probably suggested to genera-tions of casual observers that Shelley's heart was buried here, but it was neither burned at Viareggio nor buried here. During the cremation the poet's heart was observed to be resisting the fire, and Trelawny snatched it from the flames, burning his hand in doing so. Leigh Hunt, as Trelawny afterwards revealed, received the heart and gave it to Mrs Shelley after Mrs Williams had expostulated with him for appropriating it. Later Mrs Shelley returned to England, Trelawny providing her with the money for the journey.

Mrs Shelley, who was Mary Wollstonecraft Godwin before her marriage, was meanly treated by Shelley's father, Sir Timothy, until her son Percy, four years after the poet's death, became heir to the baronetcy. Then the grandfather provided more generously for the boy; but his mother, who brought him up, maintained herself largely by her writings. When Sir Timothy died, in 1844, and Sir Percy inherited the estate, his devoted mother was rewarded by affectionate devotion from her son, and she lived largely at Boscombe Manor in Bournemouth, where Sir Percy had a country house. There she kept, with sacred care, the heart of her husband; she preserved it wrapped in a page of Adonais, Shelley's immortal poem on the death of Keats, and it was found so wrapped up at her death in 1851. When Mrs Shelley died her son Percy proved faithful to the memory of his mother in a conspicuous degree. He provided a family vault in the hilly churchyard of the first church built in Bournemouth, St

Peter's, and not only buried his mother there, but brought from St Pancras Church the bodies of William and Mary Godwin, her father and mother; and there, when in 1889 he was himself buried,

In his coffin his father's tired heart found its last resting-place.

Hengistbury Head

HENGISTBURY is the extreme eastern part of Bournemouth, and has with great public spirit been placed by the town under the National Trust. Looking from the sea like a monstrous whale stranded on the edge of the English Channel, this mile-long headland, lofty and sheer, is the most romantic viewpoint on the Hampshire coast. Behind it lies Christchurch harbour, the estuary of the Avon and the Stour.

Approached across agricultural land and some heath between the Avon and the sea, the headland is cut off at the neck by an ancient earthwork fortification between the harbour and the Channel. This earthwork, known as Double Dykes, makes a camp of the whole headland and the flat land at its foot, a camp enclosed between sea and harbour and dyke. The Double Dykes, which must have been a lofty rampart when first raised, belong to the Iron Age, and certainly were thrown up more than 2000 years ago. The headland, 300 yards behind it, reaches a height of 180 feet, with a sheer drop down to the sea, and has on its summit a coastguard's lookout. The steep grassy ascent to it is in spring thickly carpeted with bluebells.

The view from the coastguard's cabin is magnificent in its extent and beauty. It embraces, besides a stretch of the Channel where ships from Southampton can be seen on their way to all parts of the world, the Isle of Wight from the Needles to Yarmouth; the Hampshire mainland with Hurst Castle and the entrance to the Solent, the bright cliffs of Milford and Barton and Highcliffe, backed by the New Forest; near at hand, the waters of Christchurch harbour, generally like a sheet of glass in which Christchurch Priory is often reflected a mile away; St Catherine's Hill, the watershed between the Avon and the Stour; the whole coastal line of Bournemouth to the Haven of Poole; and the Purbeck Hills of Dorset to Durlstone Point.

So much for the view from this always breezy height; but there are fascinating features on the hill itself. It is closed with heather and bracken, and down its landward side we may scramble through all kinds of bushiness into a wood. Every part of it is soaked in history. On the summit, just where the coastguard's neat wooden shelter stands, stood a battery in the days of Nelson. It was put there when it was anticipated that Napoleon would attempt his threatened landing somewhere on this sandy beach from Hengistbury to Poole. So there was a battery here, another at Southbourne, and martello towers at Branksome. He did not come, for Nelson destroyed his fleet at Trafalgar. Hengistbury has a close association with that great victory.

Anyone walking halfway along the top of the headland comes to a deep excavation on the Christchurch harbour side. From it much ironstone has been removed. It was conveyed by barges up the Solent to close by Bucklers Hard, and there smelted and used wherever iron was needed in the construction of ships. More than sixty vessels were built at the Hard on the Beaulieu River, and four were battleships at Trafalgar. The first battleship Nelson commanded as its captain had been built there. This headland is therefore linked with Nelson's meteoric career through the iron it contributed to his ships.

There is also a literary association between the headland and the time of Trafalgar. When Napoleon found he could not invade England, and so strike at the heart of the European alliance Pitt had formed against him, he moved his army from Boulogne, crossed Europe, and crushed our ally Austria at the decisive battle of Austerlitz. It was a fatal blow to Pitt, who saw his plans shattered. Sir Walter Scott was shortly afterwards visiting a friend at Mudeford, a fishing village on Christchurch harbour opposite Hengistbury, and was there writing his poem Marmion, which he dedicated to his host, who was a strong supporter of Pitt. In his introduction to the poem, written on the scene of the anxieties that had preceded Pitt's death, the poet included the lament of great dignity and beauty beginning, *Now is the stately column broke*, and wrote of Pitt and his great rival Fox as patriots in death:

> *Speak not for these a separate doom*
> *Whom Fate made brothers in the tomb,*
> *But search the land of living men,*
> *Where wilt thou find their like agen?*

The poet was looking at Hengistbury as he wrote; the headland was his inspiration. That is the part Hengistbury was playing in the days of Sir Walter Scott. Did he know its history? Probably not. But if he had known what we now know how charmed he would have been! It has been studied afresh and discoveries have been made that take us back far beyond the days of written history. On its northern edge, near the summit, two round graves have been worked over, and round the base of the hill it has been found that before the arrival of the Roman legions in Britain there was a British mint here. The hearth used for the minting of coins, the dies, and some of the coins have been unearthed, showing that there was then a degree of civilisation quite unexpected. Later invaders of the Viking type used the rivers as passages inland, and the ancient camp behind the earthworks as a defensive base for their raiding operations.

The camp was then much bigger than now, the Double Dykes and the headland itself extended far into the encroaching sea, for the coast and the hill are being steadily disintegrated and washed away, and the engineering staff of the Bournemouth Corporation are to defend the time-enchanted land which the town has given to the nation. In recent years children in hundreds, from Poplar and elsewhere, have camped in open-air holidays in the ancient camp under the hill, but not one in a thousand who ramble over the headland and wonder at its excavations, now weathering down into miniature hills and valleys, know of its history or feel the thrill of its past. It is one of England's noblest natural spectacles, slowly vanishing before the onslaught of the sea without being understood.

The River Itchen Starts on its Journey

BRAMDEAN. It has some delightful old houses, and has given Winchester a pavement from a Roman house found in Brookwood Park. Another beautiful estate has a peep of the Elizabethan Woodcote Manor through the tall trees. At the end of a quiet lane, with a farm for its neighbour, is the 700-year-old church with a wooden bellcot. Thomas Durnford, who was rector for 51 years of the 18th century, found it little altered from the days when Giles the Englishman began his ministrations here in 1289, and the church remains to this day a very simple place.

The chief distinction of Bramdean is that here rises the River

Itchen, a delightful river for people who love to watch Nature in quiet meadow scenery edged by little hills and occasional woods. About 27 miles long to its remotest source, the Itchen teems with history, as might be expected, for its waters run through Winchester. The River Alre, a tributary from the east, has supplied a pool at New Alresford since the year 1200, when it was formed to assist the navigation of the Itchen by ensuring a sufficiency of water; it is still there, covering 60 acres of its original 200.

The Itchen's own topmost spring is at Bramdean, and two miles on its way the stream passes Cheriton, one of the battlefields where Charles Stuart's hold of his misgoverned people was loosened. It was on the river's banks at New Alresford that Mary Russell Mitford was born; there she lived while her father squandered her mother's fortune. Mary's sketches of village life will never be forgotten; her village was Three Mile Cross in Berkshire. At Twyford poor little deformed Alexander Pope went to school, and as quite a small boy was withdrawn after he had written satires on his schoolmaster and been soundly whipped for his impertinence. Hursley, though three miles away from the river, lies in its valley westward. There John Keble was vicar for more than 30 years, and there lies, with his wife and children, Richard Cromwell, Oliver's pathetic son and for a brief space Lord Protector of England, a good man who has been spitefully scorned because he was not a great man.

The Glorious Colours From the Civil War

BRAMLEY. It has some wonderful pictures in its windows and on its walls, frescoes painted perhaps 700 years ago and stained glass by Continental artists of the 16th century. They are all, of course, in this charming church, watched over by a mellow red tower about 300 years old. We enter it by a 15th century doorway with a door on two hinges older still.

The most interesting wall-picture is of Becket's martyrdom, fading away after its 700 years, but showing him on his knees with a suggestion of the faithful Grim behind him, trying with outstretched arms to protect his master. Painted about 50 years after the martyrdom took place, this picture is remarkable and valuable for the accuracy of its detail, the four murderers having shields which are very early examples of heraldry, one showing the muzzled bear of the treacherous Reginald FitzUrse. It is a vivid and awful scene, simply drawn, with one sword cleaving Becket's skull and another viciously driving its point in.

Facing it is a faded 15th century picture of St Christopher, with a little photograph beside it taken before it had faded. We can still make out curious fishes in the stream, and two mermaids, one of whom is obviously distressed because a young angler on the bank has hooked her by the tail. A bearded hermit on the bank is holding a lantern to light the way.

On a wall profusely decorated with masonry patterns, flowers, and graceful spirals, are two more 13th century pictures, a tall bearded man with a staff, and the Madonna with her Child on her knee. Fixed over these when we called were very clear copies of the originals in the same colours, and there was an excellent copy of the Becket picture elsewhere in the church.

The old glass is beautiful still. At the top of a window in the nave are 15th century crowns, radiant heraldic suns, and the feathers of the Prince of Wales—devices suggesting that the window was perhaps set up in celebration of the Yorkist victory at Tewkesbury. Below are 14th century coats-of-arms and exquisitely drawn little figures—three musicians with violin, pipe, tabor, and tambourine; three men with halos; and a woman with a Crown of Thorns in her hand, standing on a fallen king. The same window has a few rich fragments among which we see a fish on a dish.

But the great pageant of colour in Bramley is in the big south window of its Brocas chapel, filled with lovely 16th century glass. It is the work of Flemish craftsmen, and was saved from the destruction of the Civil War by being buried in the moat at Beaurepaire House, the ancient home of the Brocas family not far away. The harmony of the colours is beautiful, a warm gold running through it all, binding together the quiet blues, gentle greens, and deep reds of the whole. The glass, arranged in our time in memory of Henry Welch Thornton, has a row of three Bible pictures at the top, showing the finding of the coin in the fish's mouth, the visit of the Shepherds, and St John writing Revelation with his eagle at his side. Then comes a row of five charming medallions, one with St Martin on horseback dividing his cloak with the beggar, another with Death and Time on either side of a tree, and a third with the Holy Family. Ten panels show Gideon and the Fleece, David and Goliath, David's Coronation, the healing of Naaman in the Jordan, Tobit and the Angel, the Birth of the Madonna, the Visitation, the Crucifixion, St Benedict with a monk, and a knight kneeling before John the Baptist. The knight is golden-haired, and handsome in grey-blue armour and a short coat with crescent moons on it. Among these big panels are many small ones, one of them all gold, showing the Almighty creating the World. At the bottom of all are three other panels with the Holy Family, the Madonna and Child and St Anne, and Noah sleeping. Two panels are filled with ancient fragments, and altogether it is an astonishing window gallery.

On the floor of the chapel are the 16th century brass portraits of Richard and Alys Carter, and of Gwen Shelford, who died in 1504 and has a long gown and a girdle fastened with three flowers. In a glazed case on the wall are the oldest things we see in Bramley—Roman tiles found when a chancel window was restored. With them are medieval tiles, pieces of alabaster, and a fragment of oak from the Norman foundations of Winchester Cathedral.

But the great centrepiece of the chapel is the 18th century marble monument of Sir Bernard Brocas by Thomas Banks. He was, said Sir Joshua Reynolds, the first English sculptor to do figures with classic grace, and this figure appealed greatly to Mary Russell Mitford when she visited Bramley and described its country games. Sir Bernard, a stout man in drapery, expires in the arms of a graceful lady who seems scarcely equal to the task of holding him. At both ends of the monument there are figures carved in relief.

In the chancel is a marble tablet to Thomas Shaw, who died as vicar here in 1751 after a life of many adventures, having been out to Algiers as chaplain of an English factory there. He made excursions to Carthage, Egypt, and Palestine, collecting plants, coins, and antiquities, and four companies of Turkish soldiers were needed to protect his caravan from wild Arabs.

The core of the church is Norman, and on the wall below one of the three Norman windows is a 12th century consecration cross, the oldest of all Bramley's paintings. The 13th century chancel has a shaft piscina, a traceried 16th century screen, and lovely 17th century altar rails. There are some 16th century benches, a Norman font with an old wooden cover, and an 18th century pulpit. Also 18th century are the nave panelling and the panelled gallery on fluted pillars. High up in the roof is a window cut before the Reformation to light the rood. There are five mass dials on the walls.

Bramley has one proud distinction; it is in the pages of Gibbon with Thomas Shaw, its famous traveller vicar.

The Truthful Traveller

THOMAS SHAW, the splendid man who gave the last years of his life to the service of Bramley as its vicar, was deemed by many merely another creator of Traveller's Tales.

Never did a more faithful recorder wander from the ways of civilisation into the dangerous wilds. He explored Egypt, Sinai, Cyprus, Jerusalem, the Jordan Valley, and Tunis; he wandered spellbound along ways that Hannibal had trodden in his conquering marches, and among the ruins of Carthage; he investigated the interior of Algeria, Tripoli, and Morocco.

Yet he was back in England before he was 40, took his degree, became a clergyman, and turned author. Naturally his travels and collections formed the subject of his pen and brush. The story he had to tell, related by a scrupulous and gifted scholar, was a revelation to his generation. He cared nothing for politics but was a born observer of natural phenomena, and so strange were the things he had to describe and picture that stay-at-home critics in armchairs fell upon him and rent him.

It is delightful, therefore, to find in Gibbon's Decline and Fall of the Roman Empire, in a chapter scarifying the average traveller-author, this footnote: "Our blind travellers seldom possess any previous knowledge of the countries which they visit. Shaw deserves an honourable exception." Even more romantic than that is the fact that his unvarying accuracy is splendidly vindicated by Bruce, who in turn came to be impeached and vilified and himself in need of vindication as the author of marvellous tales of adventure.

Shaw's reputation for truth and accuracy was completely established in his own day. Distinctions attended him, his works were translated and widely read abroad; he did magnificent work at his university, and settled down as vicar of Bramley to enjoy the fame of one of the most illustrious travellers of the day.

William Lawrence's Beautiful Writing

BRAMSHAW. Its delightful common is now the nation's, in the hands of the National Trust. Ringing out over it is one of Hampshire's oldest bells, hung in the 13th century or perhaps before; it may have rung for the victory of the Barons at Runnymede. Ever since those days this bell has been heard in its quiet corner of the New Forest. Only 20 inches high, it is so excellently made that its voice is still clear.

The church sits on a hill, its graveyard shadowed by beautiful trees, among them an old yew. The plain old font bowl has probably kept the bell company all the time. The noble roof of the nave is made of chestnut trees hewn down in the 15th century. The registers, written on vellum, were begun in 1597 by William Lawrence, who kept them carefully in writing so beautiful that it is a joy to look at them, and we are saddened when we find this penmanship coming to an end, broken off by the entry "William Lawrence, vicar of this parish, died Julie 1616." He gave his people something to read for all time, and well may Bramshaw boys be shown this scholar's pages in an age when handwriting is little thought of.

Twice here we are reminded of the sea, once by a white marble tablet with a steamship and a lighthouse on it, in memory of a young cadet, and again by a tablet which tells us of as pitiful a bereavement as any village ever had, for seven young men from here went down in the Titanic.

Two great hills tower up not far from Bramshaw. Pipers Wait, reached by rough tracks through lovely woods, is 422 feet high and renowned as the highest point of the New Forest. From its heathy top we have splendid views, with what is known as Bramshaw Telegraph, the other big hill, 419 feet high in the near distance. Bramshaw Telegraph was in the 19th century a small station for sending and receiving semaphore messages, one of a long line of hilltop stations running from Plymouth to London, each manned by three men. In those days, almost inconceivable in this age of instant communication, news was flashed from point to point as far as men could see, and we may look on Bramshaw Telegraph as a landmark in the march of man towards the Wireless Age.

The Flower in the Crannied Wall

BRAMSHOTT. There are villages that can proudly boast of their great ones, as if they said: "Here in my beauty and peace he first saw the light." Bramshott is the birthplace of a poem of 47 words, a gem to be proud of. It was born here one summer's day in the sixties of last century, when Tennyson, who loved this country-side and was to build in it a house to die in, came to a chain of lovely wooded pools called Waggoners Wells, not far from the village, and its chief charm. Near one pool is a little wishing well with ivy-leafed toadflax growing out from the crevices of its grey stones. To this secluded haven Tennyson came walking, and pulled a flower from a cranny. Then he wrote those famous six lines which everybody knows:

> *Flower in the crannied wall,*
> *I pluck you out of the crannies,*
> *I hold you here, root and all, in my hand,*
> *Little flower—but if I could understand*
> *What you are, root and all, and all in all,*
> *I should know what God and man is.*

So these small pools half hidden from the eye have sent a message round the world. Waggoners Wells are man-made pools, and one of them, called Hammer Pond, was once harnessed to the great hammer used for beating out the slag of an old ironworks. Odd that they should begin by turning the wheels of industry as falling water and should end by coming into literature.

The church stands attractively among yews and trimmed bushes in a very well-kept churchyard, and the view of its 13th century chancel and 15th century transepts is charming. It has a medieval font, two peepholes looking at the altar, an 18th century candelabra, and a case containing two ancient pottery bowls found embedded in the mortar of the tower. One of the lancets in the chancel has delightful little figures in ancient glass, and there are some ancient tiles. Among much modern glass we liked best the dignified figures of Paul and Barnabas in memory of the 32 years service of a 19th century rector, and the figures of Mercy and Love in memory of one of his successors in the 20th century.

A touching monument in the chancel is carved with graceful figures of a boy and a father who was "most loved when best known." Set up here by the sorrowing mother, we read on it how

Sir James Macdonald died a few months after his little son. In the low tower are six bells made in Chelsea, one boasting:

When from the earth our notes resound
The hills and valleys echo round.

One of the rare possessions of the church is its altar plate. There are three pieces of 17th century silver and a pewter flagon made about the time when Cromwell lay dying, shaped like a soldier's water-bottle, with a long neck and a knobbed screw top. Portrait medallions grace its sides and two dragons cling to its shoulders, gripping the chain by which it is carried. It is said by an expert to be unique and to resemble the pilgrim flasks of early days.

When the charming house by the church was new in the 15th century they brought here to sleep John Weston and his Elizabeth. We see their portraits in brass. Their clothes are lovely, and Elizabeth is fortunate in her headdress, draped with gauze.

The Little Son of the House

BRANSGORE. From Avon Tyrrell, the country home of Lord Manners, we come to Thorney Hill and its little chapel by a road so lovely that it might lead to Fairyland. In a deep belt of trees on either side the sombre mystery of fir trees blends with the slender grace of silver birches, draped in due season in a shimmering veil of early green, cherry trees laden with their snow-white tassels, and wood violets and bluebells peeping out from the banks of gorse.

The chapel is 20th century, built for the tenants on the estate and the dwellers of Thorney Hill by Lord Manners and his wife "in memory of their daughter, who was called from them in the 18th year of her life to worship Him in a temple not made with hands." She died in India and was laid to rest at Clovelly. The chapel lies off the road beyond a small plantation of pines, the interior of stately classical design. The walls and ceiling of the apse are covered by an exquisite painting in memory of Lady Manners by a Scottish artist, Mrs Traquair. In the apse itself is a group of figures, modern yet mystic in treatment, symbolising the Te Deum, and among the saints, apostles, soldiers, and worshippers are introduced the faces of friends and members of the Manners family. The little lad with tunic and staff is the son of Lord Manners, the dignified woman is his wife, and among others we recognised the Prime Minister Lord Salisbury and his son the Bishop of Exeter. Against a glorious gold background in the ceiling of the apse is seated the Madonna with angels adoring, and a low frieze of many heads all lovely in colour and design. The whole church is paved with black and white marble, and the altar is unique in our experience, an immense block of polished grey marble resting on two lions.

Two pathetic reminders of the Great War we found here. On a table tomb is the bronze figure of the son of the great house, the boy in the painting; he grew up to be a lieutenant in the Grenadier Guards, and when he was only 22 he gave up his life for England among the woodlands of France with a hundred British soldiers, his comrades of a devoted rearguard, "at peace in the silence of the Forest." The figure is the work of Sir Bertram Mackennal and the modelling of the figure and of the brave young face is very beautiful. On a stone panel behind the tomb are two angels bowed in grief. The New Zealand coat-of-arms in colour above a touching and grateful inscription was set up here by 400 officers of the New Zealand Force who were patients in the house of Lord Manners at Avon Tyrrell. "We fought for England," it says, "and, wounded and sick, found at Avon Tyrrell healing and a home."

The village church was made new last century. We found the sanctuary hung with blue and gold, fragrant with great boughs of cherry blossom before the altar steps. The graceful 16th century font came from Christchurch Priory, a mile or two away, its basin deeply carved with shields and quatrefoils and its pedestal in canopied niches. The rusted slots of the old hinged cover are here and on the modern cover is the carved figure of Our Lord with a child. The oak stalls are rich with poppyheads and vine leaves, and the plain oak Litany desk is in memory of Henry Nicholson, "a chief musician in this House of God." In a tiny chapel is an oak shrine beautifully carved with linenfold pattern below; it bears the names of the Bransgore men who died for us.

The 17th century Beech House looks across the countryside from its fine position on a hill, surrounded by woods and with lakes in the park, and its tower has wide views of the New Forest.

Written by the Saxons

BREAMORE. It had a history before the Conqueror came, for it is one of our Saxon villages. Its church was more than half-way through its first century when the Normans began building castles and cathedrals in these islands. It has three mass dials on the walls. The church is on the lines of the famous church at Dover Castle, and is 32 yards long and 20 wide, all its walls Saxon except the porch. The light falls through seven Saxon windows and we plainly see the pilaster strips which are the Saxon builder's certain sign.

For many generations old men of Breamore have sat on the benches in the porch looking at the remarkable sculpture of the Crucifixion over the doorway. It has been cut away to the level of the wall and the figures are sadly damaged, but they were still fairly clear when we called, with the painted landscape of some later artist behind the tragic group. The most remarkable piece of Saxon antiquity, however, is the Saxon writing on one of the arches, the only original arch left in the tower; it is 54 inches wide and the pillars are decorated with cable moulding. The writing is on the arch, a few of the oldest words still found on any English wall, meaning, *Here the Covenant becomes manifest to thee.*

Below the Saxon rood over the door the Normans carved a round medallion of the holy lamb, but except for three scratch dials on the walls most of the later work belongs to the 14th and 15th centuries; the arches of the tower and the chancel are 15th, their capitals carved with faces and foliage, grapes and acorns, oak leaves and thistle.

The mother of one of our heroes has put a tablet to him by the pulpit and hung his sword below it; he was Sir Edward Hulse, who fell at Neuve Chapelle. He lived at the great house here, built by the first baronet whose name he bore, physician to George the Second. When a famous man was ill Sir Edward Hulse declared that he would die if a certain rival doctor had his way, but the patient declared for the rival doctor and lived. On his retirement Dr Hulse bought the estate at Breamore, which his successors have held since, and it was here that he grew melancholy with the thought that he would die of want and his servants would pop guineas into his pockets to save him from this delusion.

There is a giant yew in the churchyard and a huge cedar over-hanging from the beautiful garden of the manor house, which has a

Tudor wing. We found the stocks (with two pairs of holes) in a garden in front of the school.

Approached by a long lonely path at the back of Breamore House is the mysterious maze in the heart of a dense little wood, its age unknown and its use unrecorded. We must walk half round the copse to find its single narrow opening, and in the middle of the trees we shall find a grassy path three feet wide winding to a low mound in the centre. The whole maze is nearly 30 yards across, and at each curve the path slopes slightly towards the middle to afford a firmer footing to runners. It is said that a man could run to Gallons Hill and back, a distance of more than a mile, while another was reaching the middle of the maze.

Those Who Gave Themselves

BROCKENHURST. With a glorious piece of the New Forest to itself, it is as lovely a corner of Hampshire as we can find, charming with thatched cottages, a fine old manor garden famous for its clipped yews and beautiful avenues, and a small church on a green hill. We come to it along delightful lanes from the Lymington or Beaulieu roads, an enchanting spot which the poet would call the veriest school of peace. Here two grand old giants are coming to the end of their days, a magnificent oak in crutches and a yew with a hollow trunk 17 feet round, nearly a thousand years old and still vigorous. The yew was here when the oak was an acorn; it may have seen the Norman builders lay the foundation-stone for the church, and the carvers marking out the mass dial on the wall. It may have seen the Normans bring the doorways through which we enter still, beautifully carved in the Conqueror's day. The plain chancel arch is by the same builders; and they made the font where the children of Brockenhurst have been baptised for eight centuries. Amid all this that is so old stands the quaint pew where squires have sat in lonely dignity for many generations.

Slight traces remain of 12th century painting on the walls, but more attractive are two windows in lovely colours, one in memory of Cecil Gill with a ship sailing over rough seas towards a sparkling sun, the sails filled with the breath of a cherub and on the deck a mitred bishop; the other, to George Knipe Gandy, filled with heraldry, a banner, and a globe.

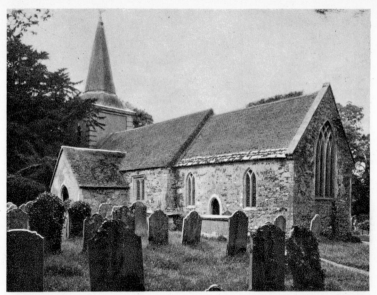

Brockenhurst   A New Forest Church

Breamore   The Saxon Church

North Warnborough   Roman House

Brading   Roman Mosaic Pavements

The churchyard, in which the ends of the earth have met, is famous for its gravestones. Among them is one with a quaint carving of a hut in the trees, in memory of Brusher Mills, a familiar figure in the New Forest. He was given his name because of the careful way he brushed the New Forest cricket ground between innings, but earned his living in a very queer way, suggested by the snakes carved on his stone. His work was to catch snakes alive for the cannibal hamadryads at the London zoo. He had no fear of adders, and picked them up with his bare hand.

Behind the hut carved on his stone is a pathetic story. There is an old forest law which gives a man the right to claim a piece of land if he lives on it for 30 years. Brusher Mills lived in a hut in the forest for one day under 30 years; and it is pathetic to think that only a few hours before his 30 years were over he came home to find his hut burned to the ground. It broke the old man's heart, and he died soon afterwards.

It is not the only story in this beautiful churchyard, nor the most moving. In this quiet spot sleep heroes of three continents. There are three unknown Belgians, three Indians who gave their lives for us, and about 100 New Zealanders who died in a hospital here and sleep as far from their own land as the world's wide bounds will allow. Can any place in Hampshire stir us more than this small plot of ground, with its tale of heroism and sacrifice? It was magnificent of the New Zealanders to pay so great a price; and wonderful of the Indians to leave the East to serve the West. Two of them have simple crosses above their graves; but one has a stone that must thrill all who read it. He was Sukha, who worked in the hospital and was known and loved by everyone in Brockenhurst. He died in the first year of the war, in the darkest hours of 1915, and we read that, although he was not a Christian, his life was sacrificed for others. Then comes this fine word which seems to be for all who sleep here, Belgians, English, New Zealanders, and Indians: "There is one God and Father of us all." It might well have been written in letters of gold over the gateway of this Garden of Remembrance.

It seems to be fitting that in this churchyard there lies Miss Diana Genevieve Harvey, of whom a beautiful tale is told. This kind old lady went from her woodland home at Brockenhurst to the breezy slopes of Tunbridge Wells for a little change, and there her kind

H 97

heart led her to call and see Dr Barnado's crippled children. They were at play, as eager as could be, and the most eager of them was a sharp little fellow with one leg that had been weak as long as he remembered. He was not as nimble as some, but no one played more keenly, and his face was bright and winsome. The lady spoke to him, and his manners were charming. She fell in love with him at first sight.

Might she take some of the children for a motor-ride? she asked. Of course she might; and of course red-headed Percy Perrin was one of them. The more the lady saw of the little fellow the more she liked him. She called to see him again. At holiday times, Christmas, and Easter she wrote to him, and he wrote back as well as he could. The spelling wasn't much, but she liked it.

Two years passed by, and they were not years of forgetfulness on the old lady's part. The life of the little lad had been brightened by the friend he had found and by his memory of the talks he had had with her during her visits to the Home.

Then the news that the dear lady was no more seen in her accustomed haunts at Brockenhurst, and the kind people at the Home were made sad by the thought that Percy Perrin had lost his friend. But he had not lost her. Her care for him was going on. When her will was made known it was found that she had left £1200 to provide for his education and then to go to the Homes.

Between Two Cathedrals

BROUGHTON. It lies by the Roman road between two of our most wonderful cities, halfway between two cathedrals, and while Nature gave it this high dignity Time has left it three legacies.

From the Saxons it has, on Broughton Hill, a warrior's grave in which was found a shield, a sword, and the bones of the warrior who wielded them. The Romans left it a road, the foundations of a house, and fragments of glass and pottery. The Normans, in whose day it was already famous for the honey it still sells, gave it a fine church.

A great part of the Norman fabric remains, including three worn but sturdy pillars in the nave, with sculptured capitals and strong arches above them, but the 13th century men gave the church a doorway in the tower, with a canopied niche on either side, battered but still beautiful. In the chancel are several lovely things. A 15th century pillar piscina rests on a graceful shaft, decorated under its shallow bowl with queer monkey-faced people, one a little man squatting with his hands on his knees. Facing it is something of 17th century England, a magnificently carved table from the early part of the century, and on it three pewter vessels, a bowl, an alms-dish, and a handsome flagon made at the end of the century. The painted panel of the reredos is 13th century. The pews, cut down from their original stature, were all put up in 1638 after a fire had burned the old ones. They are dark and panelled, fine against a delightful brick floor, and fit company for the rugged old beams in the roof. An old door remains, with its lock and key, and there is a dovecot in the churchyard.

Broughton has a roll of rectors far back into village history, from which we gather that Giles Dowse was here 57 years in the troubled 17th century and Stanlake Lee 54 years in the 19th. The village has a Baptist chapel proudly announcing that it was founded in 1655, almost within the first generation of the Baptists in this country.

The Lovers

BROWN CANDOVER. We found two people of Brown Candover, two unknown 15th century folk, whose love for one another was so pure that the artist who engraved their portraits in brass set a lily between them as the symbol of their affection, and engraved their portraits on brass like lovers, arm-in-arm. He drew the man in a full-sleeved coat, a purse hanging at his waist, and strap shoes on his feet. The lady he gave a kennel headdress and a long and graceful gown. A happy couple they must have been in their Tudor home. They died the year after Queen Elizabeth's crowning. The old church in which they laid them was pulled down last century, but the new one has some of its treasures. It has, besides this lovely brass of these dear people, two treasures from other lost churches in Hampshire. One is a fine set of altar rails carved with vines and cherubs by an Italian craftsman; the other is a big chair in the chancel, its back curiously carved with figures of Adam and Eve, who stand on each side of the tree of knowledge, down which the serpent glides on its way to that fell deed which, we must believe, has brought the world to this.

The Street Forgotten by History

BUCKLERS HARD. A famous street forgotten by history, it lies not far from the beauty and wonder of Beaulieu, and at first the pleasant country lane leading to it, bordered by oak coppices and flowery banks, seems no more exciting than any other of Hampshire's pretty roads.

The first hint it gives us of something more to come is when the tree tops begin to assume the stiff angles which only fierce sea-gales can give. Then the woods stop, and across the fields comes the memory-haunting sight of jumbled russet roofs showing above the curve of the ploughland; beyond them the grey-green waters of Beaulieu Creek, winding and twisting among its cream-coloured reed beds; and beyond that, again, the low-growing oak woods which gave W. H. Hudson "a green thought in his soul" and Nelson three good ships to fight at Trafalgar. The timbers for the Agamemnon, the Euryalus, and the Swiftsure grew up on the banks of Beaulieu Creek and into ships on the slipways of Bucklers Hard.

This tiny village, now two rows of cottages in a short wide street, was in the 18th century important and busy with shipbuilding. The beginning of its industry was due to the fact that John Duke of Montagu owned the island of St Vincent, and his argosies from Bristol and the Thames were often delayed by contrary winds while ships from the Solent were free to sail. Beaulieu River had inherited from the Abbots of Beaulieu the privileges of the Cinque Ports as a free harbour, while there was ample timber in the oak woods of John Montagu's manor of Beaulieu. Accordingly the duke offered land beside the river as sites for shipyards at a very cheap rental, with three loads of timber for every new house erected. In September 1743 the Wyatts came here from Southampton to build, and two years later the Surprise, a 14-gun ship, was launched, to be followed by 50 more ships before Trafalgar had been fought and won. The first ship Nelson commanded came from here.

When a big man-of-war was to be launched the street so silent now would be thronged with a gay and fashionable crowd, and Henry Adams, the master builder, built on to his house a splendid banqueting hall for the sole purpose of entertaining these "genteel gatherings." Here he entertained two kings. This house is now a small hotel and its owner has tried to preserve it as it was in the heyday of the village, when the wide street was lined with stacks of green timber lying there to weather, piled so high that it overtopped the houses. It took a thousand oaks to build a ship for Nelson; and it was this dramatic thought that led his friend Admiral Collingwood to keep his pocket full of acorns as he walked about the countryside planting them where he could.

It is sad to think that the brothers Adams, who succeeded their father in business, were ruined because they failed to deliver to date four ships commissioned by the Admiralty, for with them failed Bucklers Hard, grown up round the ships it had built for the Bristol Fleet; and when the work went the workers went with it. Left to themselves, the cottages had not the heart to stand empty after they had once been happy homes, and one by one they crumbled and fell, and now all that remains of the thriving village of other days is a double row of cottages, a wide grass-grown street, and down in the reeds the remains of two of the slipways.

Yet in the creek we found charming yachts cruising, showing that our own sailors still find these waters, with their 17-foot draught, good and pleasant sailing; and so perhaps prosperity may come to Bucklers Hard by way of sails again.

Nelson's Agamemnon

THIS is the story of the most famous ship built at Bucklers Hard, Nelson's Agamemnon. Launched in April, 1781, the Agamemnon was a powerful man-of-war, with a gun deck 160 feet long; she was nearly 1400 tons and carried 64 guns. Early in 1793 Horatio Nelson, who had been chafing for four years as an unemployed officer at Burnham Thorpe, was summoned to the Admiralty, who offered him active service in command of the Agamemnon in the impending war with France. Nelson stepped on board the ship exactly a week after the head of the French King had fallen at the guillotine, and he declared that she was without exception the finest 64 in the service.

By the middle of July he was off Toulon, and when this naval station was occupied by the Allies he was dispatched to Naples to convoy troops. Here he met for the first time Lady Hamilton; but the meeting was brief, for word came that a French warship was in the neighbourhood and Nelson put to sea at two hours notice and soon had the Frenchman blockaded in Leghorn.

The Agamemnon first tasted battle in October, when she was engaged in a running fight with four French frigates. Her rigging was so badly cut about that the French escaped; but the Melpomene could only just crawl into Calvi harbour in Corsica, where Nelson was to have the satisfaction of capturing her.

It happened thus. The Corsicans had risen against the French and asked aid of England. Lord Hood evacuated Toulon and blockaded the three strongholds of the French in the island, San Fiorenzo, Calvi, and Bastia. The first of these soon fell, but the English general Lord Dundas wished to delay for fresh troops. Not so Nelson, who declared that his seamen of the Agamemnon cared no more for bullets than peas. Nelson was forthwith made a brigadier, and with soldiers and 250 seamen he dragged the guns up a precipice and captured Bastia with the loss of only 14 men. Calvi alone remained. Nelson and his men dragged the guns up the cliffs once again, and poured shells and shot into the town, losing the sight of an eye during the bombardment. With the surrender of the town came the prize of the Melpomene sheltering in its harbour. Before the end of the year Lord Hood was succeeded by Admiral Hotham, and the Agamemnon took a distinguished part in sea-fights in the Mediterranean, though Nelson did not think much of them, as they were fought at longer range than he liked. In July the Agamemnon led a group of frigates to co-operate with the Austrians in the Gulf of Genoa; and so strenuous was her service, capturing privateers and destroying the French coastal trade, that in the following June she was sent home to refit, and Nelson hoisted his new Commodore's pennant on the Captain.

On the eve of Trafalgar the Agamemnon was one of the ships set to watch for the enemy; she then formed up in the line led by the Victory, being seventh in station. The next year she was with Sir John Duckworth off San Domingo, but she did not long survive the hero who had made her famous, for in May 1809 she was totally wrecked off Uruguay.

Such was the end of a ship which in 28 years saw more fierce fighting than any of its predecessors or any of its successors bearing the name of that Homeric hero who gathered round him

> *a thousand ships*
> *And burnt the topless towers of Ilium.*

BULLINGTON. It is a charming little place in the pastoral country near Whitchurch, not far from Tidbury Ring, a prehistoric camp where many coins have been found. The small church, reached from the road by an avenue of limes, is near a poplar-lined stream in a cluster of byres and barns, close to a pretty farmhouse. In the modern brick tower are charming traceried windows, and there is a blocked-up Norman doorway with a simple arch. The chancel is 13th century and the font is 14th.

Two Shrines

BURGHCLERE. It has two doors that take us into notable places, a Norman doorway into the 12th century church and a doorway opening from a lawn into a shrine of the 20th century. Eight hundred years between and so strangely different, both these shrines have in them the spirit of an infinite trust.

The small church has altogether three lovely doorways, two Norman and one made by our first English builders, with mass dials on the walls. The Norman doorways are on either side of the nave; the one we come in by has a big decorated arch, the other is tiny and has a tympanum scaled like a sea monster. The third doorway has charming foliaged pillars and a graceful arch with rows of moulding. The high and lofty nave is 800 years old. The altar has an enchanting silver plate with scallop handles and a rose-patterned centre; it was made to hold sweetmeats, but was presented to the church by a lady of 200 years ago.

The preacher here has a rostrum neat and rare, for he stands in a neat hand-wrought steel pulpit. The chancel screen is a thankoffering for the safe return of a son from the war. The peace memorial has a row of nine enamelled badges. The roof has traceried beams with spandrels. The sanctuary has a 17th century chest.

Four windows have good glass, showing Charity with three loaves; a singing choir and musical angels in memory of Marion Arkwright who trained the choir, gave the organ, and played it 30 years; St George and St Helena in a pair of chancel lights; and a window to a member of the India Civil Service who

> Died and left so sweet a memory
> That still he seems to live.

This quiet village was greatly loved by Dean Field, who toward the end of his life became its rector, seeking rest among these hills with their ancient earthworks and their group of Seven Barrows.

He was one of the finest preachers of his time. Queen Elizabeth made him her chaplain and King James cried "Is his name Field? It is a field for God to dwell in." The king sent for him to come to Oxford to take part in a discussion, and when he died, in the same year as Shakespeare, James added his name to the Fellows of Chelsea College, saying "I should have done more for that man." His vast learning is stored in five great books and his body rests in St George's, Windsor, where his brass portrait is on his tomb.

The 20th century shrine at Burghclere is the Oratory of All Souls, rising like a tower between two wings, two houses of charity. The Oratory is a memorial, and it is now in the keeping of the National Trust. It is notable for the pictures which cover its walls, painted on canvas by Mr Stanley Spencer, who gave six years of his life to them.

We should come to them willing to receive a great shock from what is called stark realism. In the medley of innumerable objects that make up these huge canvases are soldiers rising from graves to deliver up their wooden crosses, white mules, men tidying their uniforms, bakers coming with loaves, men making beds and filling water bottles, others reading maps or bathing, pictures of teatime with piles of bread and butter; extraordinary heaps of unrelated oddments. We cannot think it beautiful, but it must be regarded as the work of a distinguished artist of our time who offered his life for his country and set all this down as symbolic of that time, when he was on the Macedonian front. Many will see it as a representation of the nightmare of war.

The Historian and the Botanist

BURITON. Butser Hill, climbing up to nearly 900 feet above the sea and crowned with an ancient camp, towers over this small place near Petersfield, with its tree-shadowed church, its old rectory, the manor house, the farm, and the pond. At the rectory was born the great 18th century Hebrew scholar Bishop Lowth, and the manor house was the home of the father of Edward Gibbon, who gave the world the famous history of the Decline and Fall of the Roman Empire.

The great historian loved the quiet of this place when he was a boy; here, he used to say, he spent many light and some heavy hours. Here he began to form a library of his own, developing his love of books in his father's library—"stuffed with old trash, High Church divinity, and politics." He grew to love books so much that he always remembered with delight the day when he exchanged a £20 banknote for 20 volumes. He would recall the elegance of the dinners at his father's house, and rejoiced in being occasionally transported from the avarice of his tutor's foreign wife to the daily neatness and luxury of an English table.

The church has Norman arches on pillars carved with water lilies, foliage, and scallops, and the quaint low font is also Norman. The chancel and the tower are 13th century. In the sanctuary are two richly carved old chairs and on the walls are traces of painting 600 years old. There is a beautiful marble on the wall curiously like a brass, engraved with the figures of Thomas Hanbury and his wife Elizabeth, with their children kneeling above them in Elizabethan costume.

In one of the windows are the arms of the Goodyers, a crest of a partridge holding a good ear of wheat in its beak; it is a tribute to the famous man who lies here with his wife in a nameless grave, John Goodyer, the botanist. He was a man who did honour to Hampshire in his day and for all time, for there has been found in our own time, discovered lying on an old beam in 1907, an order signed by a Royalist General, giving protection to Goodyer when the town was garrisoned with troops in the Civil War. The order was given by Sir Ralph Hopton, and it commanded all officers and subjects "not to fail on all occasions to defend and protect John Goodyer, his house, servants, family, goods, chattels, and estates of all sorts from all damages, disturbances, and oppressions whatsoever."

John Goodyer was considered the best botanist in England during the Commonwealth. He lived from 1592 till 1664, born at Alton, and living for some time in a house on the little green now called The Spain, at Petersfield. He found a wealth of natural interest in this countryside, for it is rich in plants and flowers as well as in bird life (we have counted 110 birds in a list noted by people here). Goodyer knew every lane and field for miles round, and made countless notes on scraps of paper, afterwards compiling his knowledge in a mass of papers which were lost till our own time when they were discovered in the archives of Magdalen College, Oxford. He was building up botanical knowledge years before John Ray, 40 years before Linnaeus, and a century before Gilbert White. He worked on till he died, when he left his village £75 a year for charity. He had spent here many years of profitable toil, a pioneer and friend of learned gardeners, always peeping and botanising, noting down for the first time as novelties flowers which are now in every child's nature book; discussing the cultivation of Drake's new weed, tobacco, watching the first English potatoes grow, naming and describing plants to which he first gave a place and a name. His diaries, kept year after year, record his friendships and his visits, telling us who had gardens and what the gardens grew at a time when flowers and ornamental shrubs were first establishing themselves amid the simples for medicine and herbs.

Remembering his father's association with Magdalen, he bequeathed all his papers and an incomparable botanical library to the College, but his bequest was lost and forgotten until 1920, when Mr R. T. Gunther edited the manuscripts in a volume which at once took its place as a classic of botany.

Sir Walter Scott in the Wild Country

BURLEY. The village is nearly all new, like its church, but Castle Hill, at the end of Burley Beacon Ridge, was a defence camp before Julius Caesar came to Britain. From its summit we can look over the Avon valley and to the Dorset and Wiltshire hills. Above the village is the wild and lovely Holmsley valley which Sir Walter Scott loved for its wildness; he said it reminded him of his native moors. Although the railway runs across it now, and most of the trees have gone, it is still a free and beautiful stretch of country.

Quite near is the fine colony of beeches called Ridley Wood. In the deep hollow way approaching it on the west smugglers used to meet their customers, coming up from the Avon valley and over the heath by Smuggler's Road. These beautiful beeches were unlawfully pollarded in 1571 by the tenant who had the enclosure, and the recording of this misdeed has enabled us to learn that the trees are over 350 years old. Some of the younger beeches are self-sown. At Burley Lodge are the few survivors, battered and forlorn, of what were once known as the Twelve Apostle Oaks.

The Ship Which Carried Nelson

BURSLEDON. Here the pleasant River Hamble widens into a harbour encircled by low hills and trees; here the yachts winter.

The church, Norman before it was restored last century, stands halfway up a hill overlooking the red roofs and the boats in the bay. It has a charming timber shelter for its west door. In an outer wall are two beautifully carved 17th and 18th century tombstones, the 17th century one decorated with spades, flaming torches, cherubs, and hourglasses. The big and handsome font is Norman, decorated with interlaced arches 800 years old; the chancel is 13th century and has two delightful corbel heads, smiling. Here is one of our rare 20th century brasses, a fine portrait of Loraine Estridge, Canon of Truro. There is a small sculptured tablet with reliefs of Eastern scenes in memory of Gilbert Spencer Smith, who fell for his country far from home, and two other monuments tell of the days of sails and timber ships. One is flanked by columns surmounted with a coat-of-arms, a painted ship's hull carved at its base. It is to the memory of Philemon Ewer who died in 1750, a shipbuilder who "during the late war with France and Spain built seven large ships of war," and "in the execution of that important trust gained and deserved the reputation of an ingenious artist, an excellent workman and an honest man." The other monument is a plain tablet saying that in the churchyard sleeps George Parsons, from whose Bursledon yard came not only the 74-gun ship Elephant but the ship which carried Nelson in the battle of Copenhagen.

Southey's Village

BURTON. A green valley, a shining river, and a dark hill clothed with pines—this was what Robert Southey saw when he looked from his window in Burton, his palace as he called it, though it was but a cottage with a big garden, a fish pond, and a pigeon house. He loved this place and turned it into song:

> The beauty of the place, yon healthy hill
> That rises sudden from the vales so green.

He bought two cottages and made them into one, and here he wrote his English Eclogues and entertained his poet friends. They were Southey's happy days, when he was in his twenties, and he and his young wife first saw the New Forest in the full glory of Spring. They came down in the stage coach, and there is a letter in which we can almost hear the poet (the most human of all the Lakeland poets) chuckling as he tells how all but he were sleeping when something fell off the roof, and he had the unutterable pleasure of waking everybody by bellowing for the coachman to stop. "This New Forest is simply lovely (he wrote). I should like to have a house in it and dispeople the rest like the Conqueror."

He found rooms at Burton, where his brother came to tell him stories of his life as one of Napoleon's prisoners. Here Charles Lamb came to see him, but the love for London was too strong for the green spell of the Avon valley, and the East India clerk went home again.

Southey's cottage is all that Burton has to show. The big garden is a small one now, the pigeon house is gone, the fishpond is a drinking-place for cattle, but the cottage is in loving hands and is a charming place. The church is modern, but at the cross roads on the way to Christchurch is a ruin of a stone cross where the monks of Christchurch used to come to preach; and in the churchyard we found the medieval font.

The Red King

CANTERTON. This is not a village but a hamlet of the New Forest, with alternations of thick copses and open grazing glades, small farms and an old manor hall, in the neighbourhood of the spot where 800 years ago an unpopular King of England met a tragic death. In this out-of-the-way place stood for centuries the cottage where, it was said, lived Purkis the charcoal burner, who found in one of these forest glades a red-haired, brutal-faced man lying dead with an arrow piercing his breast. It was William Rufus, second king of the Norman line, the most cruel of the kings who looked on England as a hunting-ground and valued a deer more highly than an Englishman.

The Red King lay there alone. His hunting companions had galloped away to find his brother Henry, who also was hunting that day in the New Forest, and they and Henry rode swiftly to Winchester, where Henry was proclaimed. Purkis the charcoal burner put the dead King's body on his cart and took it to Winchester, where it was buried without a mourner, or the tolling of a bell, or a prayer, or any sort of funeral service, or any inscription on his tomb, for, as the old chronicler wrote, "He was loathsome to his people."

How he was shot will never be surely known. The tradition is that the Norman knight Sir Walter Tyrrell shot an arrow which glanced from a tree and accidentally hit the King. Tyrrell denied that he shot the arrow, but he did not ride with the Red King's retinue to find and proclaim the heir. Instead, he rode out of the great forest westward, and is said to have reached safety by crossing the River Avon at Tyrrell's Ford, so named to this day.

The tree which was thought to have deflected the arrow was long kept in mind, but in course of time it perished and then, in 1745, Lord De la Warr marked the spot by an upright stone, which is still there but encased in iron because it was suffering from the hands of those people who go about the world chipping off bits of wood and stone, carving their names in sacred places, and throwing litter everywhere.

The probability is that Walter Tyrrell purposely shot the unwanted King, hoping Robert, Duke of Normandy, the King's elder brother, would be his successor, for he crossed to Normandy at once with the news that the throne was vacant. The scene of the tragedy lies with forest scenery of great beauty all about it, but it loses its seclusion more and more as every year goes.

When the arrow struck him everyone who knew what had happened vanished from the place, some to find his younger brother Henry and make him King rather than have his elder brother Robert, others to be away from his dangerous presence. That had become a habit with his people. When he appeared they disappeared to avoid him. It was best not to be seen. So, when the fatal arrow laid him low he was left alone, to be found later by people living in the forest, to be taken on a cart to Winchester, and buried without a word of Christian hope, in a tomb on which the cathedral tower crashed down seven years afterwards.

Yet this king had begun his reign with the hearty support of his English subjects. They welcomed him with hope. They were quivering under the tyranny of the Norman barons to whom the Conqueror had given a large part of the land of England. The Conqueror himself had found these alien helpers, whom he had enriched, a danger to his throne, and he had been obliged to check their tyranny. He knew that his weak and sluggish eldest son Robert would be utterly unable to hold the land against the horde of rapacious Frenchmen who had followed him to England, and who were now building defensive castles everywhere. So on his deathbed he had nominated his grim son William the Red as his successor, and the native English knew that such a successor was needed if the country was not to be harassed by a horde of petty tyrants. So they had rallied unitedly to put Rufus on the throne and he had promised them everything they desired.

Never was a betrayal more complete. As soon as he was firmly seated on the throne he broke all his promises to his English supporters, ruled them and the Norman barons with a rod of iron, fleecing them all alike for money to carry on his wars and buy support from others who were beyond his power. The Norman nobles looked with longing eyes at the lazy, ineffectual Robert as his possible successor, and the English saw fresh hope in his younger brother Henry, who was capable, scholarly, and by comparison a gentleman.

No wonder a mysterious arrow removed this tyrant, who regarded neither God nor man, and for whom no good thing can be said.

Two Admirals

CATHERINGTON. It has great possessions. One of them, made in the 14th century, once stood outside the church, tall and splendid for all to see, with an old mass clock on the wall near it; now it is inside near the chancel, a wonderful stone cross with a small Crucifixion carved at the head of it. By it stands its broken base, a rusty cannon ball resting on it. On the wall of the nave, above the arcade built by the Normans, is a painting of the Archangel Michael weighing the souls of men. It is 700 years old, and the red colour is vivid and clear. The soul is represented by a round and smiling face peering out of one scale against a potful of demons and vices in the other. Another demon has crawled on to the arm of the scale to pull it down, but is baffled by the Madonna, a tiny figure holding down the soul's end of the scale. There is a monument with a showy figure of Nicholas Hyde, who defended the Duke of Buckingham when he was impeached. He lies by his wife, both wearing ruffs and gowns, and with them are their ten children.

In the churchyard lie the wife and the son of Edmund Kean, whose name was magic to the ears of Londoners in the days of Thackeray and Dickens; and there is a pathetic memorial to six children of one family who died before they were eight years old. Here also lies a famous Admiral, Sir Charles Napier. He was laid to rest here in 1860 after a life of great adventure. When he was still a young man he was nearly ruined by his faith in the invention of steamboats, and he had another tragic experience about the time he was made an admiral, for cholera broke out in his squadron and on his flagship, and in five days he buried fifty men. He rendered immense service to Portugal during a revolution there, being put in command of the Portuguese fleet, and hailed as a liberator of the country, "cheered, kissed, and embraced by everybody," as he said.

Not far from his grave is a monument to Admiral Cradock, who lies in the bed of the Pacific. He shared in the pride and tragedy of the Great War. In the first week of it he drove two German cruisers off the Atlantic trade route, so that the Admiralty was able to declare that the Atlantic was safe and British trade was going on as usual. His tragic experience was the Battle of Coronel, when his squadron met disaster at the hands of Admiral Von Spee's ships, and the heroic Admiral Cradock went down with his men.

Brother to Chaucer's Good Parson

CHALTON. It is on the Sussex border and has a view of a windmill on the top of a great hill, looking as if Rembrandt had etched it there. It grinds no corn but proves once more the truth of Milton that they also serve who only stand and wait. From the top of the hill is a fine view of Spithead and the Isle of Wight. The small 700-year-old church is so beautifully proportioned that it gives us a feeling of loftiness and space. Its east window is of unusual design, having four tall lancets of equal height. There is a little old glass. The font is 15th century, decorated with shields, flowers, and a furious lion with a bristling mane. In the south transept is an old panelled chest carved with foliage. One of the three bells is medieval, and is said to have been brought from Nuneaton Abbey; and there is a mass dial which would be on the wall here before the bell came. There are two 18th century candlesticks.

On the chancel wall Richard Ball is kneeling in prayer. He died in 1632 and this is the gem of unknown literature they graved for the shepherd of this flock:

> *Reader, blest is that Priest which doth not preach*
> *God's sacred lore alone, but's flocke doth teach*
> *By's pious life: this Reverend Divine*
> *That's here interred did both . . .*

In alms to poore, to God in prayer and prayse
With syncere heart he wholly spent his dayes,
He lived beloved a compleat age and then
He payed Death's due, bewailed of all good men.

Dear Richard Ball was surely brother to Chaucer's good parson:

All that Christ and His Apostles taught
He preached, and first himself their lessons wrought.

Bricks and Cherries

CHANDLER'S FORD. It is very long since they buried their people in the old barrows hereabouts; long since people came to it from miles round for the Merrie Feast held in Ramalley; not so long since the schoolmaster complained that the boys were no good in the morning because they had been up all night making bricks for the Law Courts. The contractor was Mr Bull and he ran one of the biggest brickfields in England here, making 35 million bricks for the great courts which now stand in the Strand, with his statue in the quadrangle looking on. Now it has grown into a big place and has a small new church, but still we find here the name of Purkess, descended from "one Purkis" who found the body of William Rufus and carted it to Winchester. The place has that historic memory, and one more memory of the Merrie Feast. Merries were small black cherries of the sort now rarely met with, and the hills of Chandler's Ford were once white with their blossom. In those days young Richard Cromwell brought his youthful bride to feast on merries here.

It is good to think of one happy day in that unhappy life of unwanted power and ungrateful daughters. Richard's wife was from Hursley, where she lies with him and their eight children, only three of whom grew up. We read that when they were married Dorothy Major's father, in considering settlements, had a strong preference for such moneys as had come to Oliver by inheritance rather than by grants or confiscated estates!

A Tale of Saxon Days

CHARFORD. The south-east corner of Wiltshire plunges like a dagger into Hants, the point of the dagger reaching No Man's Land in the New Forest. On the very edge of the intruding land, but in Hampshire, is a place with a name in history more than 1400 years

The River Test near Stockbridge

The River Wey near Bentley

The Nave

The Lady Chapel

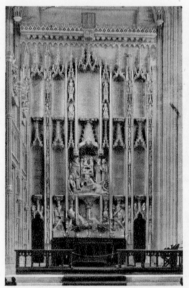

14th Century Reredos

The Salisbury Chantry

CHRISTCHURCH PRIORY

ago. It is Charford, the ford being over the Avon just where it leaves Wiltshire.

It is the scene of a battle fought by Cerdic, a Saxon pirate chief, and his son Cynric, against the Britons of Hampshire. It has been claimed that Cerdic's victory at Charford in 519 "set the crown of the West Saxons on his head." What happened then at Charford is certainly of importance, but does not make it a main turning-point in England's story.

Charford itself is now little more than a name. It is not a village. It has no church. Here the Avon spreads over water meadows in fast-running streams, which push their way through stocky little locks and over tiny weirs. It is a place of laughing waters, gathered in from the whole width of Salisbury Plain. Possibly it was the highest place to which the flat-bottomed boats of the English invaders could ascend the Avon. And here Cerdic and Cynric won such a victory that they decided they would be sea-rovers no longer, but would settle in the land they had conquered, calling themselves kings. Though it is extravagant to say that the England of Englishmen was born at any particular time or place, such as in the year 519 at Charford, this time and place are rather central for looking round and seeing what happened.

Our forefathers, the northern pagans, who were the terror of the seas, had harassed the coasts of Britain for centuries while the Roman legions were its defenders, and they had wintered on the shores of Kent and Sussex for half a century before Cerdic took part in these popular adventures. He came in 508 and won a great victory somewhere on Southampton Water, or the course of the River Itchen, and he spent a good part of the next dozen years in conquering the Isle of Wight and extending his domination over the Hampshire coast. Then, in 519, he and his son Cynric moved westward to Christchurch Bay and up the Avon to complete their hold of the coast and overthrow the opposition offered them at Charford. Further advance inland was not attempted for the moment. Cerdic was content to consolidate his seaside Hampshire kingdom between Southampton Water and Christchurch Bay, so he gave the Isle of Wight to his nephews and set up as a permanent kinglet, with a strip of Hampshire coast as his possession. He did not "set the crown of the West Saxons on his head." Between him and any such ambition lay the whole line of hill forts from Old Sarum to Badbury Rings and the Dorset Heights. The idea of a West Saxon Kingdom was two centuries ahead.

Cerdic quickly found how narrow were the limits of his power. He lived 14 years as king of his little coastal domain, gave up the practice of a summer return to his northern haunts, and introduced tribal laws and government. His son and his grandson succeeded him and a kingly line of relationship was sustained in what became Wessex, but it was not for 32 years after Charford that the English under Cynric succeeded in capturing the fortress of Old Sarum.

When three centuries had passed, and civilisation and Christianity were flourishing under Alfred, and attempts were made to write up the records of the early years of English conquest in England, a good deal was made of the story of kings descended from Cerdic. They had been ruthless in their conquests, and particularly in destroying towns, like Bath and St Albans, founded in the Roman Era. This period of strife following Cerdic, viewed from the standpoint of British defence against fiercely aggressive paganism, comes to us in the dim form of legendary verse with the shadowy figure of Arthur as the champion of Christianity against the assaults of implacable foes.

Jane Austen's Last Home

CHAWTON. It is made delightful by meadows and trees, mellow village roofs, and a splendid old mansion, but it is made historic by a red brick house at the fork of the highways to Winchester and Southampton. A little way from the village stands the great house, built in the 16th and 17th centuries, an impressive sight with noble trees and a church to complete the picture. Chawton lost its old church by fire last century, and this one, designed by Sir Arthur Blomfield, has many beautiful things: a screen crowned by rood figures, a reredos finely painted, attractive altar rails, and nine delightful candelabra bought with the earnings of the village carving class. In the lovely Book of Remembrance we noticed the names of three officers who won the DSO. Rescued from the old church are a 15th century bell, a tablet to John Hinton who had been rector 58 years when he died in 1802, and a rather pompous monument to Sir Richard Knight who lived at the manor house in the 17th century; it shows him in armour, with lace at his throat and a curly wig on his head as in Jacobean days.

Bramshott : John and Elizabeth
Weston, 1430

Nether Wallop
Mary Gore, 1436

West Tytherley
Anne Whitehead, 1480

Dogmersfield : Anne Sutton and her children, 1590

Odiham
William Goode, 1498

South Warnborough
Robert White, 1512

Bramley
Gwen Shelford, 1504

BRASSES OF HAMPSHIRE PEOPLE

The little red house at the meeting of the roads was Jane Austen's last home. Here she lived out the last seven years of her life. Here were born of her rare fancy those characters whose fame outlasts all human lives. Here she finished Emma and Persuasion. Here began her last illness, yet here she spent some of her happiest years with her mother and her sister Cassandra. She loved this garden with its peonies and pinks, sweet williams and columbines. She would note the first coming of the strawberries and the blossoms. Here she would sit for hours at the piano, and from this house she would walk a thousand times to the manor, where her brother Edward lived. She overtaxed her strength in nursing her brother Henry, and died in Winchester, where she went with her sister to seek advice. There is a tablet on her cottage here with a bronze inscription given by her admirers, and on the walls of this church are memorials to the two Cassandras, her mother and sister, who sleep in the churchyard.

Here lies, as a tablet reminds us, Sir Edward Bradford, who gave the London police their good name. He was born in 1836, son of a parson, and sailed as a youth for India, where he gave over 30 years of brilliant service as soldier and administrator. He gained the hearts of princes, rulers, and native soldiers, and it was said that good men loved him and bad men feared him.

He fought in Persia and throughout the Mutiny, and was repeatedly commended for spirit, gallantry, tact, and discretion. His career was arrested by a grim tragedy. Attacked by a wounded tiger, he found his gun impeded by the branches of a tree, and so dropped it and leapt into the bed of a stream, intending to dive. The water proved only knee-deep, and the tiger seized him by the shoulder. Bradford kept his presence of mind and, with the tiger biting him, walked round a boulder, so enabling his companion to approach and shoot the animal dead. The adventure cost him an arm.

Returning to his Indian duties Bradford filled many important posts, suppressing crime, introducing good government, and popularising railways. At 53 he was recalled to London for duties in the India Office, but had been there only a year when the grave demoralisation of the London police led to his appointment as Commissioner.

He did wonders. He checked a strike, restored discipline, introduced many reforms, built new stations and signal offices, reduced superfluous labour, and raised the efficiency of the force while carefully safeguarding the moral and physical well-being of its members. He made London's police a model to the world. He retired in 1903 but continued his efforts for social reform; he rode, drove, and enjoyed himself as if he had never known physical disablement. A very brave man of sterling character, he died in 1911, and was laid to rest here with his first wife, who was born at Chawton House.

Here Lie 2000 Englishmen

CHERITON. It is entrancing in a shallow valley where the Hampshire Itchen is young. Its little church keeps watch from the top of a green hill where men first raised a church 700 years ago. The lovely cottages have been homes so long that when Cobbett rode through the village he said it all seemed as old as the hills around it.

The church has been made new, but not too harshly, and it keeps the massive 12th century tower with its arch, and some beautiful 14th century tiles by the altar. The porch has fine heads looking down, and let into the walls on either side of the entrance are two pieces of exquisite 14th century carving. Under the tower is a very fine chest, perhaps a little older than the 17th century silver chalice, and there is a 13th century piscina and an ancient mass clock.

But the chief sight of the village is the group of mounds which for 200 years have been part of the landscape here. They are all that is left of that spring day of 1644 when there was fought here a battle which "broke all measures and upset the whole scheme of the king's counsels". Waller, the Parliamentary General whom Clarendon called "a right good chooser of vantages," was marching from London and Lord Hopton, who held Winchester as his base, moved out with the Royalist Army to meet him, occupying Alresford. Not far from Cheriton is Cheriton Wood, sloping to the top of a hill, and in manoeuvring for position Waller occupied this wood, and from it his old campaigning friend Hopton tried to dislodge him. The armies were about equal in numbers, 10,000 men in each, and there was stubborn fighting for hours before a Cavalier officer led his horsemen down a sunken lane in a charge towards Cheriton. It was a movement Waller had anticipated, and his artillery swept the lane, while his cavalry met the shattered charge in the open ground below.

Hopton's men advanced to the rescue and were involved in the same overthrow. In the meantime Hopton fought desperately to cover the retreat of the foot and the artillery. The slaughter was terrible, and Lamborough Lane, where the battle culminated, ran with blood. The fallen were buried in heaps together and the mounds we see are the mounds raised over them. There lie 2000 Englishmen, a tragic memory in Hampshire's green and pleasant land.

CHILBOLTON. A delightful village on the Test, its beautifully kept church has a built-up Norman window high in the wall, 13th century nave arcades, a 13th century chancel, a charming chancel screen with part of the original 15th century screen in it, two desks with linenfold panelling, and three piscinas. The handsome pulpit is Elizabethan, splendid with patterns, flowers, and linenfold, and above it is the upper doorway of the ancient roodloft. For a communion flagon the village has a 17th century cup of silver beautifully chased, with delicate handles and a cover to match.

CHILCOMB. Set below the downs near Winchester, Chilcomb has much to make its people love it. There are timbered cottages, tall trees, and, best of all, a little Norman church. Its first known priest, Henry Rowadone, lived here as long ago as 1289. In the high Norman chancel arch, decorated with a modest carving, is the simple old screen scored by the mark of its maker's adze. The chancel is paved with tiles all brave with lions, griffins, eagles, and fleur-de-lys, the work of 15th century men, and has fragments of coloured glass 500 years old. There is a mass dial by which the villags would tell the time in the days before clocks.

We were sorry to see on the green of this quiet village a big German gun, pointing to Winchester. From Deacon Hill, 471 feet high, is a fine view of the cathedral city and of the village spread before us.

The Little Crypt of the Lost Church

CHILTON CANDOVER. It has one of the noblest yew avenue in Hampshire, 40 feet wide and running for half a mile. Nearly every tree touches its neighbour, and many of them are 12 feet round. A fine sight are these sombre yews, certainly as old as Cromwell.

But across the way is something far older, the buried crypt of a vanished church. It is one of the discoveries of our time, unsuspected until ten years after the Great War, when the rector received information from a venerable parishioner which set him dreaming. The old man declared that there was a church underground and that he remembered being taken into it by his father when he was a boy. Mr Gough set to work with pick and shovel and soon found himself spellbound in a vaulted Norman crypt, with an apse and narrow windows. It was empty but for a big stone coffin and piles of earth. About 40 feet long by 11, it is divided by a wall with an archway, a sort of nave and chancel, and it seems to belong to the middle of the 12th century. It was the crypt of a church which stood by the ancient manor house, and the church and the house have both disappeared. Now the crypt has come to light again, a very rare example of a crypt belonging to a village church.

It has become a tiny church itself, with an altar and an 800-year-old font found in a heap of rubbish. A few 13th century gravestones were on the floor when we called, and it was thought that one of them was that of Jehan de Andeley, who held the manor almost seven centuries ago.

It has been suggested that the crypt may possibly be the remains of a Mithraic Temple, Mithras being the sun-god of Persia worshipped by many of the Roman soldiers who came to Britain. In spite of his being a god of the sun his temples were partly or completely underground, to resemble the cave into which he was dragged when fighting with the sacred bull. For some time there was a contest between Christianity and Mithraism in Roman Britain, but Mithras (if indeed he was worshipped here) has lost his temple at Chilton Candover, for soon after we called a Christian service had been held first on the roof and then in the crypt below, every member of the congregation carrying a candle.

Hampshire's Oldest Bells

CHILWORTH. It is one of Southampton's little neighbours, with a grey church by the busy highway. Made new in 1812, the church has kept three treasures belonging to its ancient origin. One is the square Norman font supported on five pillars, and the others are two bells which are at least 700 years old and may have been made in Norman times. Each weighs almost a hundred pounds, and they are the oldest bells in Hampshire, probably in the south of

England. A photograph of them hangs on the wall by the font, near a case containing their old clappers, which have been replaced.

A Pearl of Great Price

CHRISTCHURCH. From Lyndhurst over the perfect roads of the New Forest, by purple heather and yellow gorse and dark mysterious tracts of woodland, we come to this place of many waters, over three bridges across the Avon and its branches. The old town lies in the narrow strip of land between the channels of the Avon and the Stour, both rivers meeting in Christchurch harbour before they reach the sea.

In summer the main street is crowded with folk on their way to the Priory or to the sandhills beyond the river at Mudeford. Along the shore of the little quay are moored gaily painted houseboats, and small yachts, motor boats, canoes, and rowing boats dart to and fro filled with laughing youth. But when the last rose of summer has faded the spirit of the past awakes again in Christchurch, above the flaunting shop fronts the little dormer windows and the roofs green with moss and lichen come once more into the picture; and neighbour greets neighbour as they pass in the quiet life of the little country town. A solitary boy trails a fishing line on the low sea wall; the boats lie high and dry; and the waters are undisturbed but for the sudden swoop of wild birds wheeling and calling.

British and Roman races have lived here, but the earliest known record of Twynham, the old name of the town between the streams, is in the Saxon Chronicle. When the Conqueror made his Domesday Book the old mill was here with 21 houses. The castle, of which the keep still stands, has come down to us from the 12th century, and is the work of the Normans.

Its east and west walls rise from the top of an artificial mound about 20 feet high, with 9000 cubic yards of earth in it. The walls are 10 feet thick and 30 high, and give us some idea of how a Norman noble set to work to build himself a fortress. Close by, and at one time connected with the castle, the so-called Constable's House is a rare example of Norman domestic architecture in England, one of the most perfect. It stands picturesquely on the bank of that branch of the Avon which was at the same time the castle moat and the mill stream. We can hardly realise that this treasure of Norman handiwork was preserved almost unimpaired until the later years of the 18th century. Its destruction was then begun, and but for the heroic vicar William Jackson the building would have disappeared. He so roused public opinion that the vandalism was stopped and the beautiful ruin saved.

This Norman house has an area of 80 feet by 35. Though the roof has gone the walls are almost intact except where the north-east turret has fallen. There were two storeys, and the great gable is almost perfect. The lower room is lit by narrow loopholes but the lovely windows of the upper room are of exquisite work. Part of the stairs remain, and the circular chimney which was connected with the great fireplace. The walls are five feet thick.

Has any English town, we wonder, a fairer scene than this from the narrow Convent Walk below the priory and the castle ruins? On one side flows the rivulet, so shallow and crystal clear that every polished pebble of its bed gleams in the sun. From the castle enclosure a mighty cedar throws its dark branches almost to the farther bank, and an evergreen oak towers above it in stately pride. Against the sky stand out the pinnacled tower and the long lines of the priory roof, the massive masonry of the keep, and the green-clad walls of the Norman house, and in the distance are the five low arches of the grey bridge that has weathered the storms of centuries. Just before the mill stream joins the Stour to enter the harbour it flows below a two-arched bridge built by the Normans, and the Priory Mill that was here in the Conqueror's day is still on the banks as a boathouse.

Leaving the castle, we pass the old court house, which is now a fine bookshop with a deeply thatched roof, carved bargeboards and a plaster-work front; and the wide street narrows like a cathedral close, with round windows and low-eaved houses, to the entrance of the priory. It was Roger Flambard, evil genius of William Rufus, one of the greatest of the Norman bishop-architects, who designed the church, which with Durham Cathedral is a lasting witness to his architectural skill.

The unforgettable gem of the original Norman exterior is the north-east turret of the north transept. On the lowest stage an arcade of linked arches surrounds the whole transept; the next stage of the turret is an arcade rising from decorated shafts; and a third arcading above (with a steep stone roof) completes this exquisite masterpiece. In its delicacy and miniature proportions it is a remarkable exception to the usual massive character of Norman work.

An avenue of elms brings us to the north porch, 700 years old, and almost as big as some village churches. It is a noble entrance to this noble building, and has no parallel in any English minster. It is 40 feet long and its walls rise almost to the clerestory. There is a stone seat along each side and an arcading of pointed arches. Slender shafts of marble rise between them and form the capitals of the beautiful double doorway with six orders of mouldings.

The entire building, nave, choir, and lady chapel, is of great length, 333 feet, and within the church the seven Norman arches of the nave are impressive almost beyond words. They are Flambard's work, and as an example of decorated Norman style there is nothing in the kingdom to surpass them. The arches rise from bold and massive clustered columns, the capitals ornamented with foliage; and between the arches other clustered columns rise to the roof, giving an impression of soaring loftiness rarely seen in a Norman interior. The majestic character of the nave is continued in four lofty arches which once supported a central tower. The clerestory has plain pointed arches built by Prior Peter about 1200, with a passage running through the arches known as the Nun's Walk. The spandrels above and below the triforium are elaborately covered with ornament, giving a further richness to the effect of the beautiful nave.

The 14th century stone screen between the nave and the choir is a rare and beautiful possession. Quatrefoiled panels with shields below the canopied niches are separated by buttresses with a wonderfully rich effect. Lovely detail abounds in every part; each empty niche has its daintily vaulted roof, and tiny creatures creeping and flying along the buttresses add to the charm of it all.

It is the 15th century choir which is considered by many judges to be the finest part of the church. Everywhere about us is beauty expressed in a thousand ways. From the elegant roof hang bosses and pendants supported by angels in gold and colours, bearing monograms, figures, shields, and flowers. The carving of the 36 stalls is superb. As if the artists could not bear to leave their task, the wealth of imagery in the miserere seats flows over the ends of the benches and the arm-rests, while even from under the pinnacled parapet which crowns these lovely groups the faces of animals and birds, portraits of kings, queens, and cardinals, look down.

In this marvellous work, perhaps the work of a lifetime for them, the medieval craftsmen dared to hold up to satire the world in which they lived. They were no respecters of persons, and the follies and failings of the Middle Ages are reflected as in a mirror. The crafty fox in a monk's cowl is preaching to a flock of geese, while his clerk, a cock, crows the responses below. While a clown is performing a dog steals his porridge; devils consort with angels; monsters, mermaids, dragons, and griffins, strange beasts from land and sea, are some of the hundreds of devices in this picture-book of olden times. Most of this work dates from the time when Henry the Seventh was king, but two or three of the stalls are probably from the second half of the 13th century, one of these being specially fine with curled foliage.

Yet all this profusion of loveliness is but the setting for the rich pearl of the choir, the matchless 14th century stone reredos. It has been considered by one authority as the finest in England without any exception. It was here before the choir was built about it, and it rises in three tiers of canopied niches, five niches in each tier, and all magnificent.

The original plan of the unknown artist of this English masterpiece was to combine the genealogy of Christ and the scenes of the Nativity. As in a Jesse window, the lowest group shows the reclining figure of Jesse on a majestic scale; David with his harp is on the left hand and Solomon on the right. The branches of the vine, symbol of the stem of Jesse, intertwine with the lower figures and end at the feet of Mary at Bethlehem. In this upper group the Heavenly Child is seated on Mary's knee, a quaint little figure, while the Wise Men offer their gifts. The ox and the donkey are looking on, and in the background shepherds with their sheep are looking upward listening to the message of the heavenly host.

The buttresses dividing the niches are covered with tiny figures of delicately carved saints, but the niches are empty. The elegance of the whole conception and the vigour of the carvings are astonishing, but imagination is powerless to visualise its transcendental beauty in its first freshness, when in every canopied niche stood a silver figure. It is a wonder of artistic devotion to a beautiful idea.

A small and ancient door on either side of the reredos once led to a gallery behind and was opened for processions; a glorious scene the choir must have presented with the light from the windows (long since vanished) falling like ruby, sapphire, and topaz on all this brilliance, and the long train of priests in gorgeous vestments rising from aisle to choir to mount the steps of the altar and become lost to view until it reappeared in splendour on the farther side.

The vaulted roof of the lady chapel is beautiful like that of the choir; it is 14th century and the angels supporting the pendants are holding instruments of music. There are five consecration crosses on the old altar stone here, one of the biggest altar stones in England, 11 feet long and nearly 4 feet wide. There is here also another richly tabernacled reredos of Henry the Seventh's time. A room over the lady chapel known as St Michael's Loft has a staircase of 82 steps running up inside the wall; who cannot sympathise with the Christchurch grammar school boys who up these stairs went creeping like snails unwillingly to school?

The finest of all the monuments at Christchurch is the Salisbury Chapel, a chantry set up in her lifetime by the tragic Countess of Salisbury, Margaret, lady of the manor here. Of all the tragic stories of the ever-changing fortunes of the White and Red Roses, hers is one of the saddest, touching the depths of poignancy. At the Battle of Wakefield her grandfather fell, and her father, Duke of Clarence, was killed by the treachery of his brother, Richard Crookback. Her brother and her first-born son perished at the block, and when the last and most brilliant of her race, her young son Reginald Pole, Dean of Wimborne at 17 and later Archbishop of Canterbury, roused the anger of Henry the Eighth, the king avenged himself on the remaining members of his family. The aged countess was condemned to death after two years of imprisonment, and in the Tower, when she, the last of the proud Plantagenets, refused to bow her head before the axe of the executioner, the head was severed from her body as she stood, and her poor corpse was laid to rest in the burying ground for traitors. So it is that this lovely chapel in Christchurch, which she had meant to be her grave, is tenantless. Well might Macaulay write that the Salisbury chantry "still pleads in its empty grandeur for the stately lady whose bones lie in unhonoured burial."

Built of Caen stone, one of the hardest of building materials, much of the exquisite decoration of this chapel is as white as if carved yesterday. It rises in three stages from floor to roof of the north choir aisle. Above the panelled base are four-light windows on the second and third stages with battlemented transoms. Bands of lacelike moulding adorn the tomb and the slender buttresses in endless variety. The steps leading into this miniature chapel have been worn by the feet of pilgrims, and much wanton destruction (as with the rich canopied niches and the painted bosses hanging from the roof) is due to the superstitious ignorance which attributed miraculous powers to stone chippings from the chantry.

The alabaster figures of Sir John and Dame Chidioke lie on an altar tomb; he died fighting in the Wars of the Roses, and is in armour, the lady having an elaborately mitred headdress. The angel once supporting her head has vanished save for a tiny hand. A panel of sculpture by Chantrey, in memory of John Barnes, who died in Waterloo year, has two women kneeling in grief, and to one of them a little dimpled child is clinging. In the choir is one of Flaxman's loveliest pieces, a portrait group in memory of Viscountess Fitzharris of Heron Court. The young mother, who died in 1815, is sitting with a baby in her arms, and two boys in long trousers and ruffled collars are looking into her face as she reads to them. The graceful composition of the group and the features of the mother and her children are not easily forgotten. Under a chantry in the south aisle sleeps Robert Harys, a rector of Strowston who died in 1525; on the carved screen is one of those playful designs our forefathers loved, a rebus on his name Harys, with the carving of a hare and a twisted monogram YS.

The last Prior of Christchurch was John Draper who died in 1552 and sleeps in the little Draper Chapel behind a graceful screen. We owe him an eternal debt, for at the Dissolution his reputation as an honest man and his friendship with Thomas Cromwell induced Henry to leave the church intact, though the monastic buildings were destroyed except for the porter's lodge, which is still here. A little model of the early priory is above the door of this chapel, showing the early central tower. Here is hidden away one of the most perfect and graceful piscinas in the country; the miniature grace of its fan vaulting is a delight to see.

The Shelley monument under the tower is of deep interest. Designed by Henry Weekes, it was set up by the poet's son, having been intended for St Peter's Church in Bournemouth, where the poet's heart lies. As there was no room there for so imposing a monument it was set up here. The white marble panel shows the poet lying on his wife's knee, and below it are the immortal lines from Shelley's Adonais, written for Keats but a fitting elegy for Shelley's own memorial :

> *He has outsoared the shadow of our night,*
> *Envy and calumny, and hate and pain,*
> *And that unrest which men miscall delight,*
> *Can touch him not and torture not again.*

Of the precious glass which was one of the glories of the choir a few fragments only are now left. They are in the clerestory windows and in the lady chapel; we noticed an angel's face among them. In one Norman window are some bits of old French glass. There is no glass of outstanding merit in the 19th century windows. The blue east window of the lady chapel has scenes from the life of the Madonna; four warrior saints shine in the south choir aisle, and on the north side are charming panels of St George and St Elizabeth of Hungary. Above the great west window is a canopied niche with a figure of Christ wearing the Crown of Thorns, a hand raised in blessing.

There are several unusual and interesting inscriptions in the churchyard; this one on a brick tomb of 1641, near the great porch has never been explained :

> *We were not slayne but raysed,*
> *Raysed not to life,*
> *But to be buried twice*
> *By men of strife;*
> *What rest could the living have*
> *When dead had none?*
> *Agree amongst you,*
> *Here we ten are one.*

It is thought that ten men were drowned in a shipwreck off Christchurch harbour and first buried without the consent of the owner on other ground, being reburied in this grave owing to his resentment.

Of the eight bells in the tower two rang over Christchurch meadows before this 15th century tower was built. Two others were here when our men marched to Agincourt, and rang for joy when Henry the Fifth came home again. The views from the tower are far-reaching and of great beauty. Inland the courses of the Avon and the Stour, the harbour, and the narrow run between the sandhills and the shore of Mudeford can be followed as in a map; from Hurn and St Catherine's Hill in the west the land extends to the borders of the New Forest on the east, and the lovely sweep of the coastline from Hurst Castle to Swanage is broken only by Hengistbury Head and Poole harbour, while the Isle of Wight lies fair and mysterious in the open sea.

A mile out of the town is St Catherine's Hill, where, according to the legend, the priory was to have been built; from its height Southey wrote his verses on the distant view of the Avon. The remains of a British camp have been found there, and we see still the foundations of an ancient chapel of St Catherine. To the west is Heron Court, home of the Earl of Malmesbury, famous for its rhododendrons; they are a sight to hold us spellbound.

But perhaps the scene which will live longest with us is of the quiet east end of the churchyard known by the lovely name of Paradise, where the green bank slopes down to meet the river, and the priory stands as if "looking at its own beauty in a crystal mirror."

CLANFIELD. It lies under the downs near a mound called Rowland's Castle, and still it sends out, ringing over the hills, the music of two bells from its medieval church, first rung in 1448. The 19th century church also keeps the 15th century font from the old church, a beautiful old window, and a 17th century chalice.

On the hill above the village is the grave of a prehistoric warrior, the unknown sleeper of the downs.

The Ancient Bell

COLEMORE. One of the bells in its little turret has called the people of Colemore to prayer for nearly 600 years. It was made in the time of Chaucer. Approached by a grass path near a yew weary with age, the small church was partly built in the 12th and 13th centuries and looks across the road at a great stone barn. It has a chancel screen with a Tudor craftsman's work in the heart of it, and a Norman font lightly carved with arches and designs.

The roodloft stairs are still in the wall and by the doorway leading into them are the hooks for the iron hinges, older than the Reformation, and a long square tunnel for peeping through at the altar. In the transept, by a tiny Norman window, is a curious oblong brass with a decorated top, pillars engraved at its sides, and a winged cherub at its base. On it is the epitaph of John Greaves, rector in the days of Shakespeare. Two of his successors in Colemore were laid to rest beside this altar where each of them had ministered for 59 years. One was James Cookson who died in 1835, and the other Richard Pocock of 1718, a man of "singular probity, eminent piety, and great charity." A rare place for long service Colemore seems to be, for just outside in the churchyard sleeps Thomas Hervey, who saw the dawn of the 20th century after he had been rector 49 years, and we were shown all these graves by a sexton whose father and grandfather had served the church before him, the three of them already covering a span of over 120 years.

Little Goldfinch

COMPTON. It lies in the hollow of the downs near Winchester, and it has two doorways as old as the cathedral; they lead into the church, both tall and narrow, one of them beautifully carved and with an old oak door swinging on massive hinges. Here too is the chancel of those days, now a chapel, and in it by the altar is a window rich in gay fragments of old glass with its light falling on a 13th century painting of a bishop. He is carrying a staff and is probably St Theobald. In the chapel is a stout pillar piscina which seems to be a miniature column with the interior of its capital hollowed out. In a glass case is an odd white christening bowl with blue flowers, a little basin presented to the church 300 years ago. The font itself is 13th century. There are two fine old chairs with tall backs. In the chapel is a 15th century bench-end, and high on the wall is a good portrait bust of an engaging man called John Harris, who died about the time when Charles the Second came back. The 17th century balusters in the pulpit appear to be part of the old altar rails.

There is a floor-stone to a wise old man who began his career here and became famous in two bishoprics, and, though he might have lain in either of his cathedrals, wished to come back to lie where he once once a curate. He was George Huntingford, a Greek scholar,

Christchurch   **The Tower Across the Waters**

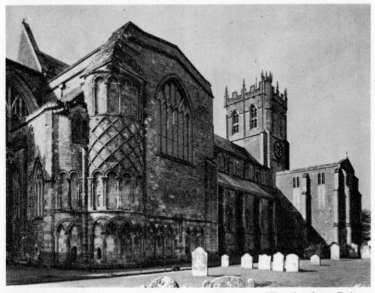

Christchurch   **The Ancient Priory**

Carved Stalls and Bench Ends in Christchurch Priory

once so poor that he became a schoolmaster to support a brother's family. At Winchester he had as a pupil Henry Addington, one of the few undistinguished men who have become Prime Minister, and it was owing to his friendship that Huntingford became first Bishop of Gloucester and then Bishop of Hereford.

By the church is a beautiful house called Manor Farm, once the home of a Goldfinch family. The family invariably christened their sons either Richard or John, but one little Goldfinch there was who broke the rule. He was born during the Civil War, and one day a troop of soldiers came demanding shelter and food and plenty of ale. As it happened, the only ale in the house was that set aside for the christening festivities of the new little Goldfinch, and poor Mrs Goldfinch, much put about, explained the dilemma to Captain Barnard. The kindly captain forbade his men to touch the ale, and asked his hostess to give the little one his name. So it is that one of the gravestones bears the name of Barnard Goldfinch, a relic of the days when the Roundheads had their guns in a Roman burial-ground here, still known as Oliver Cromwell's Battery.

Compton has no stone for its great hero John Philpot, who was burned at Smithfield. He was born here in 1516, and went to school at Winchester, where it is said he once wrote 200 verses in a night without more than three faults. After graduating at Oxford his religious views led him to leave the country and travel on the Continent. As the result of an argument with a Franciscan friar between Venice and Padua he nearly fell a victim to the Inquisition, but he managed to get home and at last became Dean of Winchester. It is recorded that the bishop was set against him, and Philpot was nearly murdered by an official of the cathedral. After Mary came to the throne he was thrown into prison, convicted of heresy, and burned, suffering with great heroism.

From the Conqueror's Century

CORHAMPTON. It is one of Hampshire's wondrous Saxon places. The remains of a stockaded village have been found in it in our own time, and its church has been called the oldest in Hampshire. There are those who think it was founded by Wilfrid when he came to convert the Jutish settlers in the valley. It is pure Saxon of the Conqueror's century except for the chancel wall, which has been made new. One thing it has which must set any mind thinking, a sundial which has been here 900 years. Before the Conqueror came people passing through Corhampton would look up at this stone clock on sunny days, and here it is today. Beautifully sculptured leaves radiate from its centre. It has lost its hand, but the hole is here in which it was fixed.

Two other sacred stones from far-off days this small place has. One is the stone seat of the priest by the altar, very old and very wide, thought by some to be Saxon; the other is the original stone altar with five consecration crosses on which a Saxon bishop placed his hand in blessing. We cannot be sure about the font; it has a single band of cable moulding round it and may be the work of Saxons or some early Norman craftsman.

How thrilling are these walls of Isle of Wight stone! Outside them are the narrow Saxon pilaster strips, and the great stones at the corners are laid long and short as the Saxons always laid them. Inside is the original plastering with the mason's marks all rudely drawn, crosses in circles. In the north wall is a beautifully arcaded Saxon doorway with capitals of projecting moulding of a rare design, a pilaster strip rising above the arch. The tall chancel arch is Saxon, of fine simplicity. On the walls of the chancel are many traces of wall-paintings in red, green, and yellow, probably 13th or 14th century. In this place so old the pulpit and altar rails seem new indeed, but are Jacobean. There are Jacobean panels carved with foliage in the back of the pew by the door, and one is in the lectern.

The great yew throwing its shade on the porch is 26 feet round its trunk, and has seen the people come into this church for perhaps 20 generations. Grouped about it when we called were fierce-looking gargoyles rescued from a well near by, and not far off lay a huge stone coffin which must have been here for centuries when the Saxons put their sundial on the wall. It is Roman, and still keeps its lead lining. It was found in a field in Meonstoke in May 1917, and in it was the skeleton of a man.

The Old Tree Trunks

CRAWLEY. We may say that it has noble trees indoors and out, for here, in one of the neatest and most prosperous-looking villages in the county, are charming timbered houses and rare timber arcades in the church. These stalwart wooden columns, eight great uprights and cross-pieces, were cut from trees felled, it is believed, by men who swung their bright axes and made the forests ring 500 years ago. They are a sight seldom seen, those at Warburton and Lower Peover in Cheshire being notable examples of the same kind. We have found other sets at Gosport and Botley in Hampshire.

Shaded by a splendid yew, the church has several friendly old faces at the windows outside, a fine and massive old chest, and a chancel arch of the 12th century. On the wall is a brass inscription in memory of Crawley's famous rector Dr Michael Renniger, a man who must have seen Drake and Raleigh, for he was chaplain to our romantic Queen Elizabeth. He was rector of Crawley for all but 50 years, from 1560 till he died in 1609, and they laid him here in the church he had served so long. He was one of the stout defenders of Protestantism, who suffered exile in the reign of Mary Tudor, and came back when he had an opportunity of doing good and being free.

You Earthly Imps

CRONDALL. It is a delightful village in itself, and its avenue of limes is surely the grandest that ever led to a church door, slender giants like poplars forming a narrow aisle as high as the tower. There are 12 pairs, and the line is started from the churchyard gate by eight pairs of youngsters with pollarded heads.

And what a church they lead us to, a big and splendid Norman place. The porch at the end of the avenue has a sweeping horseshoe arch framing a doorway carved deeply by the Normans, its sides cut with crosses by pilgrims or crusaders. The church has three Norman doorways, the west one simply carved, the north one not at all, and blocked. Enormous buttresses flank the west door, and there is another pair of them south and north, so big that aisles have been built between them with windows in the buttresses themselves. The pinnacled tower in no way matches the great grey Norman mass. Its 17th century builders took for a model the tower of Battersea church, and Crondall's church accounts detail the fourpences paid for ferrying masons across the Thames for a look at the model. Their names, the paysheets, and the hours the men worked are all set down faithfully, making a very interesting document, and we read that £76 was given towards the new tower by Nicholas Love, a judge at the trial of Charles who refused to sign his death-warrant. Built of red brick, the tower is curiously placed to the east beside the chancel, its bells and bell-ropes being reached by outside balconies from the stone newel staircase which once led to the roodloft and central tower, and now continues up till it brings us into a long low room lit by a single Norman window. It is like a lumber room in an old house. Inside a clerestory lights up a noble array of stalwart Norman arches with scalloped capitals. The chancel has a vaulted roof made lovely with mouldings, and two richly decorated arches rebuilt as they were 700 years ago, though wider at the top than the bottom. In the roof is a big boss with a holy lamb which is of a type rare in country churches, and was probably carved by the 12th century craftsmen of Canterbury cathedral, where there is another boss like it.

In the keeping of this splendid church is the oldest brass portrait in Hampshire, showing Nicholas Caerwent, a sad-faced vicar who died in 1381. He wears his robes and holds in his hands the chalice which in Elizabethan times was melted down to make the silver cup in the church today. On his robes is a swastika.

Old Parson Caerwent must have preached to the Giffords from Itchet Manor House, whose descendants are in brass above a canopied tomb. Sir John kneels in 16th century armour with above him his charming crest of a hand grasping a bunch of flowers. His wife's portrait has gone and that of his sons, but his eight little daughters are still with him. The tomb opposite is carved and coloured with the arms of the Paulets. In one of the aisles is a grisly little brass of John Eager, showing a shrouded skeleton lying on a rush mattress and begging   *You earthly imps that here behold*
This picture with your eyes

to remember where man's glory lies. In a recess in the wall hangs a wooden cross from Flanders.

There is an old oak altar table of about 1550, a large tub-shaped Norman font, a 17th century almsdish, and in the vestry a little marble font of 1648. But there is a far greater treasure locked in the vestry, a fine chest so old that it was in need of repairs a generation before the Spanish Armada. It was made about 1400 with six layers, leather, plaster of Paris, sheet iron, oak, sheet iron again, and then iron bands all round. No safer guard could be found for the interesting church accounts, which are perfect back to 1543.

CURDRIDGE. It is in the strawberry district, and has a 19th century church designed by Sir Thomas Jackson, though its tall tower, beautifully panelled with flint, is later than his time. Here under a granite tombstone in the churchyard lies Nowell Salmon, who won the VC at the second Relief of Lucknow and lived on to the eve of our own time. It was of great importance that a certain tree should be climbed for the purpose of directing fire on the enemy, and several had given their lives in climbing it when Lieutenant Salmon volunteered. He succeeded where they had failed, became a VC, and lived to become an admiral. Under a rose tree in the churchyard lies another admiral, Cyril Everard Tower, DSO.

Three Treasures

DAMERHAM. It has a Norman church on a hill above the River Allen, with three rare treasures. The first treasure we see as we come in, for it is a queer Norman relief over the door, showing a knight spearing a fallen enemy. It was found in the vicarage walls and brought here long ago. The second treasure is on the altar, a beautiful metal cross fashioned in Italy while Michael Angelo was alive. At the back of it is a glazed hollow made for a holy fragment in the days when it was believed there were pieces of the true cross in the world. Round the hollow are engraved the words "This is a piece of the true cross." The third treasure we must ask the vicar to show us, for it is a beautiful chalice fashioned in the year when Drake set out to encircle the world in the Golden Hind.

The north arcade was built by the Normans. Two newcomers came into the belfry in the year after the Great Plague, and they bear the date 1666 and this rhyme: When few did thrive we three became five. There is a scratch dial beside the porch, and the stump and base of an old cross in the churchyard.

Mr Austen's Church

DEANE. Here lived Mr Austen, father of the immortal Jane; he was preaching here and at Steventon when she was born.

He would come with her through this porch in which she would look at the glowing figure in rich robes, the work of a 15th century artist. Another window over the altar came from Belgium. It is dramatic and moving, showing Christ on Calvary against an angry sky threatening that darkness which came over the whole land until the ninth hour, and heavy with the storm that rent the veil in the temple. One of the great possessions of Deane is its altar plate. There is a 16th century flagon, a chalice of 1570, and a rare silver bowl with a helmeted head in the centre and the words Give God Thanks For All engraved round the rim. The short stem is decorated with faces and roses and joined by a thick corded moulding to the foot, which is lovely with lilies. The bowl was made in 1551 when Edward the Sixth was on the throne, but it did not come to Deane until the reign of Dutch William, when it was presented to the church.

Made From Old Yew

DIBDEN. It stands on the edge of the New Forest and over-looks Southampton Water. The small and charming church is about 700 years old and a great part of it has sunk. The capitals of the 13th century arcade are only shoulder high on the south, and still lower on the north, while the piscina is level with the chancel floor. The font is as old as the church. There are fragments of 14th and 15th century glass in the windows, a 17th century chair in the chancel, and a splendid old chest with carved panels reminding us of cathedral windows. In the vicarage is a table made from the old yew which has vanished from the graveyard; it was bequeathed by the vicar who had it made to his successors at the vicarage. It has been said that the fine altar rails were also made from the yew, but we do not know. By the tower wall near the font is a tapering medieval tombstone with a foliated cross.

Catherine of Aragon Comes

DOGMERSFIELD. In this quiet countryside those who know what happened here must be strangely moved by the thought of the thread of history that winds its way so curiously about the world. It was down these quiet Hampshire lanes that Catherine of Aragon came, "a most poor woman and a stranger"; here began that train of great events that were to fill the world.

The church in so historic a place is young indeed, for it owes its inspiration to the interest of John Keble, whose friend Charles Dyson was parson here. Keble, who was making a little money out of his Christian Year chose the land for the church and gave the altar and two small windows in the vestry which have his initials on them. A more recent window in the north wall is from the workshops of Christopher Whall, who did so much to raise the standard of glass in our churches, and in the west window is a medallion of Jacob and the Angel which was painted by Lady Canning. The altarpiece is precious not only because it is charming in itself but because it is the work of an artist of the Flemish School in the 17th century, long believed to be the work of Vandyck but now thought to have been inspired by Rubens. It is a Lamentation, showing the taking down from the Cross, and the portrait of Nathaniel and the rough vivid face of Peter both appear to be by a master hand. We found another delightful work of art hanging on the wall, a small water-colour copy of Raphael's Transfiguration.

There is a Tudor brass of a handsome woman kneeling at a prayer desk on which lies a baby in swaddling clothes and a book of devotions. The young mother is Anne Sutton, and behind her kneel three children at prayer in Elizabethan dress. The prayer of the mother (who died two years after the Spanish Armada) is, Not by merit but by mercy, judge me, O Lord, and at the foot of the brass is this:

> *Earth hath her corps, heaven hath her soule,*
> *Her fame remaynes behynde,*
> *The dew desert, by trew reporte*
> *Of lyfe well ledd, to finde:*
> *Of love her husband settes*
> *This monument to showe*
> *Her birth and death, and leves the reste*
> *For others to bestowe.*

Here are the pathetic white figures of a sorrowful father and his little boy wrought in marble by an Italian craftsman; they are the mourners of the bride of a year who lies below, Lady Charlotte Mildmay. Here is one of the saddest tales in all the world. Charlotte Bouverie had married Henry Mildmay with high hopes, and a son was born to them at the end of a year. She gave up her life to bring him into the world, and died when he was five days old. The boy was to grow up to be the fifth baronet and owner of 10,000 acres. His mother was born in the 18th century and he was to live into the 20th, and in all these years they were together but five days. His father married again and his marriage led to a sensational divorce case with damages heavier than had ever been known in an English court. The marriage was unhappy, and in the end the husband shot himself in the year of revolutions, 1848; the son lived to be 91 and died in 1902.

Here lies another Sir Henry Mildmay and his wife Jane, he dying at 44 just after the Battle of Trafalgar, and she at 92 just after the Indian Mutiny. She was a remarkable lady, and it is remembered that to the end of her life she would sit upright in a chair doing fine needlework without glasses.

There was a day at the beginning of this century when the rectory of this small place was in every paper in the land, for Richard Mildmay Foot, the rector's son, went out from here to the South African War and became the chief figure in an incident which greatly thrilled the public. He was wounded in the head on Tugela Heights, with the Boers near enough to call on him to surrender, but he shouted back to them, "No, I'll die first," and in the end he was rescued by his regiment.

Dogmersfield House is today a Queen Anne structure and has been much modernised, but here was the great house 400 years ago, a bishop's palace to which Henry the Sixth and Henry the Seventh came. It happened that the bishop living here was the king's secretary, and one of the duties that fell to him was to fix up for Henry the Seventh the marriage between his son Arthur and the Spanish princess from Aragon. Catherine sailed from Spain and landed at Plymouth after a stormy voyage, and the king with a gay company set out to meet her. It was here that they met, the princess worn out and travel-stained, the king all impatient and brooking no delay, and neither king nor prince able to speak with the princess in either of their mother tongues. But we read that all ended pleasantly, the party dancing together to the music of the minstrels, and in a few weeks they were married with great splendour in St Paul's; and in a few months the prince was in his grave. The history of the world was to be changed, for Henry the Eighth was to come to the throne, was to marry Catherine and grow tired of her, to marry half a dozen and grow tired of them, and to turn the court and the world upside down by a tyranny nothing could gainsay.

The quiet life of Dogmersfield went on. The house which had seen this fateful meeting was transformed, and a formal garden laid out in the 18th century, when the dovecot was built. The park and the woodlands have grown to over 1000 acres. But the quiet lanes are quiet no more, though an old bell rings out over them from the new church tower as it has rung for 500 years.

The Stone Lady From the Moat

DROXFORD. Men remember here that an old man used to come fishing on the banks of the lovely Meon, for he was Izaak Walton, staying at the rectory with his daughter. The little river becomes doubly dear to Droxford for this memory of the great lover of Hampshire's streams, sleeping in Winchester Cathedral in the heart of the county which he said "exceeds all England for swift, shallow, clear, pleasant brooks and store of trouts." He married the rector's daughter, Anne Hawkins.

We found on the walls of the church four mass dials from the days before clocks, so old it is. The fine 15th century tower rises in three stages above a church which is still much as the Normans left it—a richly carved doorway in the porch, a simpler doorway in the north wall, powerful piers holding up the arcades, and the chancel arch itself. All this the Normans gave to Droxford. From the 13th century come three piscinas and the arches of the chapels, the 14th century gave them their windows, and the 15th century gave one of the chapels an exquisite canopied niche. The dignified and massive altar rails are Jacobean, as is the little oak altar table. There are some old books, and trace of wall-paintings.

In the chapel with the beautiful niche is the stone figure of the mother of John Droxford, a 14th century bishop. The stone lady has had an adventurous time since she came here. When the statues of saints were being broken into dust in the Civil War she was secretly removed from her altar tomb and buried in a moat close by, and there, having been forgotten for about 200 years, she was found last century and brought back to the church. We may think her a little worldly at a first glance, for she clasps what appears to be a purse or a pendant hanging by a ribbon round her neck; but we do her wrong if we think so, for to her breast she is pressing no purse, no pendant, but the jewel of her husband's heart.

Here John Goodyer of Alton, the 17th century botanist, spent many of his early years, giving the village the odd distinction of being the first place in England to popularise the Jerusalem artichoke. Early in our own century a Jutish burial ground was discovered here, and most of the interesting finds are in the British Museum or at Winchester.

George Whitefield, Curate

DUMMER. In this small place, in the ancient pulpit with traceried panels which has been in the church over 500 years, was heard a voice that rang through England, for Dummer was the first curacy of George Whitefield, who rode through our towns and cities and villages with John Wesley preaching to the English people.

His church is 700 years old, but Dummer is much older. Far back in the days before history this was the home of a people who cremated their dead and buried the ashes in urns, for their urns have been found and we may see them in the fine museums of Reading and Southampton.

A very rare thing we came upon here, set above the chancel arch and curving round under the nave roof. It was made in the 15th century, a great wooden canopy decorated with gilded bosses to be a background to the crucifix on the old roodloft. Here by the altar is the brass portrait of William Dummer, who must have seen this canopy in its place; he is with his son, who died almost as soon as he was born. Except for a few years at the beginning and a few years at the end, William lived through the whole of the 16th century, serving the City of London for over half of it, and then they laid him here, the last of the long line of Dummers of Dummer who had been in this place since the Normans came. A brass by the lectern tells of another William Dummer in the 15th century, and their old home is not far from the church, a lovely place with massive walls centuries old.

One of the windows has a tiny fragment of ancient glass, but more interesting for the antiquarian is a brass used twice over, a palimpsest fixed to a hinge so that we may see both sides; it has an inscription to Allys Magewik of 1591 on one side, and one to Robert Clerk, a priest a hundred years before, on the other side. The church has spiral altar rails of the 17th century, a 17th century gallery filling half the nave, good modern pews made by a local carpenter, a charming little canopied niche in the 15th century doorway, traces of wall-paintings 500 and 700 years old, a 17th century chest, and a big niche by George Whitefield's pulpit.

George Whitefield was here six weeks, coming to this small place from Oxford as a penniless parson, yet proud in his heart, as he wrote to John Wesley, for these were poor and illiterate people, and his pride was hurt. It is true that a squire had just given him ten guineas and made it possible for him to pay his debt at a bookshop, but he mourned for his scholarly friends in this lonely village as a dove that has lost her mate. And yet, he said, he followed the plan of a very old parson and went among the folk from house to house, and in a little while he was learning as much in an afternoon's visiting at Dummer as in a week's study at Oxford.

He gave up the chance of a profitable curacy while he was here, and evidently found himself at home in the end, for about Christmas time in 1736 he wrote to Wesley that he had just returned from a weeping flock at Dummer.

The Painted Ship

DURLEY. What most of its people believe to be its oldest possession is still alive and flourishing in its churchyard—Old Yew, a giant said (but wrongly, we believe) to be mentioned in Domesday Book, yet in any case a giant indeed. Hidden away down winding lanes is one of the loveliest watermills in Hampshire, and everywhere is something beautiful, meadows, trees, bridges, streams, and barns. But perhaps its chief possession is an enchanting painted ship with a sailor swarming up the rigging. He has been here about 600 years and unhappily is fading away on the splay of a transept window in the church. A fine little picture he must have made when the church was new (when its two crusaders were laid in their tombs), and we could wish that Time would be more kind to him. Fading away also is the portrait of an Evangelist on the chancel wall.

There is a 12th century font, a 13th century holy water stoup, a 14th century piscina, an old panelled chest, a handsome Jacobean pulpit with a hanging canopy; the magnificent roof is of Spanish chestnut and there are ancient beams in the belfry. We noticed that Thomas Scard was curate and rector for half of last century.

The Wooden Walls of Old England

EAST DEAN. A homely little place under a fine ridge with bushy trees, it has a church to match, built 700 years ago in an England trying to get itself in the habit of building its own kind of church, free from the Normans. Much has gone but something remains, and there have been found traces of the older Norman church, the round head of a Norman window built into one of the buttresses, and something of a Norman piscina and of a stone niche from the same time. The oldest part of the existing church is the 13th century stonework of the east window, but the walls stand as they have stood for centuries, some of the stones perhaps a thousand years old. As the church is mentioned in the Conqueror's Domesday Book, a Saxon church probably stood on this site and part of these walls may possibly have belonged to this original church. Many of the roof timbers are said to have been used in ships. New timber was taken from the neighbouring woods to the shipbuilding yard, and the wagons would return here with loads from the shipbreakers, where the wooden walls of England were broken up when no longer seaworthy, so that it is probable enough that these timbers of the sea may have come to rest in the old roof.

There are old oak benches in the nave, and we come in by an old door made in Cromwell's day, still with its massive ring and its ponderous wooden lock, and set in a heavy oak frame of rough-hewn timbers. The little gallery, which has been here since the 17th century, is now fitted up as a Children's Corner, and has panelling from the old manor farm, and the font, with eight carved panels round its bowl, is 500 years old.

The church is an interesting monument of the centuries in this small place with only 50 houses, and it was sad to find so small a village struggling to save the ancient timbers of its church from the little beetle which lives on our antiquities.

EASTLEIGH. It has little history except that the railway made it, but its carriage and engine works are famous. They cover 70 acres and employ 3600 people. They work in fine shops and play in the finest sports ground for a hundred miles round, to which we came by one of the avenues of young trees which lead to the town. The ground is Fleming Park, and is backed by a low but beautiful tree-covered hill. It has delightful flower beds, and a lilypool with goldfish. The church is 19th century, one of the many churches built by George Edmund Street, architect of the Law Courts.

At the Rise of the River Meon

E AST MEON. A delightful corner of Hampshire, it lies with its interesting old cottages in the rich meadows of a winding valley, the chalky hills about it crowned with lovely trees. On these downs, 400 feet above the sea, the little River Meon rises, passing to a belt of woodland, the western end of the Forest of Bere, on to Wickham, and then through six miles of orchards and farms to the Solent. It was on the banks of this trout stream that Izaak Walton spent much of his time. All about us on the downs are ancient burial mounds, and there is an old camp on Winchester Hill.

Here still remains the old Court House, the lovely medieval manor in which the Bishops of Winchester held their courts for many generations. It has stonework four feet thick in its walls, old timbers, corbels of bishops and kings, beautiful windows, and charming red-brown roofs.

Along the road by the churchyard is a fine row of limes backed by a steep hill covered with bushes and trees. The lychgate, with a stone roof covered with moss, is in memory of a much-loved doctor. It brings us to as fine a village church as we shall find in Hampshire, its walls four feet thick and going back 800 years, for it is said that they were built by the cousin of the Conqueror, Bishop Walkelin. On its sunny wall is a mass dial by which the people would tell the time in the days before clocks. There is a grand 12th century central tower with zigzag round the windows, supported on four fine Norman arches with scalloped capitals, open all round inside and outside and now crowned with a lead spire. The 12th century arches were painted in the 13th century, and there are still faint traces of the painting on them. We noticed a crowned head and a Crucifixion under a canopy. We may come in by two fine Norman doorways with zigzag arches resting on round pillars; the west doorway has four orders of moulding. Two heavy arches 700 years old lead from the chancel into the lady chapel, and the east window, by Mr J. N. Comper, has a fine group of patron saints in memory of the men who did not come back from the war. They are the saints of the fighting countries, and with them is St Michael for the Air Force, and for the Navy St Nicholas with the three children in the tub. There is a small triangular window 600 years old in the nave, flanked by stone faces of a man and a woman. The dignified oak pulpit was decorated with inlaid patterns in 1706, and is interesting because it was brought here from Holy Trinity Church near the Tower of London, where Sir Isaac Newton must often have listened to sermons from it when he was Master of the Mint.

But the glory of East Meon is the font, one of a group of four to which the famous font in Winchester Cathedral belongs. It is over a yard square, borne on pillars carved with leaves. The upper surface is rich with foliage, bunches of grapes, and doves drinking from vases, and two sides have an ornamental frieze of doves and dragons, while the other sides have reliefs of Adam and Eve in the garden. They show us the familiar story in the quaint figures of the Norman mason, and we see the Creator forbidding Adam to eat of the fruit of Knowledge, and then creating Eve. We see Eve taking the apple from the serpent in the tree and Adam eating it. In another scene an angel with a huge sword is expelling them from a great church which seems to have been the sculptor's idea of paradise, and in the final scene Eve is holding her distaff and the angel is teaching Adam to dig. This remarkable font, fashioned of black marble from Tournai in Belgium, is thought to have been given to the church by Henry of Blois, the Conqueror's grandson, who built St Cross at Winchester.

On one of the walls is a tablet of 1633 which tells us that

> *Here lieth the body of Richard Smytter*
> *Who departed this life in hope of a better,*

and in a small cavity in the walls was found a bone which had evidently been carefully put there when the walls were built. From the days of the Civil War comes a stone in the floor of the transept on which is the curious inscription "Amens Plenty," said to mark the hurried burial of Cromwell's soldiers who fell in a skirmish here a few days before the Battle of Cheriton in 1644.

Mother of Five Bishops

EASTON. Its cottage gardens were like a rainbow when we called at this delightful Itchen valley village, and doubly interesting it becomes when we learn that its manor belonged to Sir Philip Sidney.

Dymoke House opposite the church was built with the stones of the old manor house.

The church is Easton's jewel. It is as different as can be from other churches hereabouts, and looks, with its quaint tent-roofed tower, as if it had been picked up in France and dropped on English soil. The nave has two Norman doorways, the north one simple, the south one heavy with moulding. Norman windows pierce the north wall, and above a 13th century arch is a small Norman doorway leading on to the floor of the belfry, which is reached from below by a Norman stairway worn down by many generations of ringers. There is a handsome 17th century pulpit, and near it a narrow doorway leading to a turret up which for hundreds of years a priest would climb, catching glimpses of the lovely valley through the slender windows on his way, to proclaim the good news from the roodloft. The chancel, which has a 13th century piscina, is vaulted and rounded into an apse. It has two great arches, shaped like slightly pointed horseshoes, one lovely with decoration, and both resting on capitals beautifully carved when the Norman style was passing away.

On the chancel wall is a dignified monument telling of Agatha Barlow who lies below the chancel floor by the side of her son William's grave. She was once a nun, but she married William Barlow, who, before he was made a bishop by Henry the Eighth, was prior of a monastery in Berkshire. When Queen Mary came to the throne he was treated harshly and went into exile for safety's sake; when Elizabeth succeeded he returned and was appointed Bishop of Chichester. Below the monument is a brass plate taken from Agatha Barlow's grave, saying in Latin:

> *Barlow's wife Agatha doth here remain;*
> *Bishop, then exile, then Bishop again.*
> *So long she lived; so well his children sped,*
> *She saw five bishops her five daughters wed.*

The inscription on the monument tells us who these bishops were. One of them, Toby Matthew, was famous for his wit and became Archbishop of York; of another, Herbert Westfayling, it was said he was never betrayed into laughter! Agatha was 90 when she died in 1595 at the house of her son William Barlow, who was rector here for 48 years. He was for a time tutor to Charles Stuart's brother Henry, and was "noted for his skill in navigation, being the first to write a treatise on the properties of the magnetical needle." Close to the Barlow memorial is a very charming brass portrait of Algernon Wodehouse, the rector who beautified the church last century, and equally charming in the nave is the memorial to a lady of Dymoke House, two panels carved with scenes in the life of the Madonna. On the roll of rectors are two men who became headmasters of two great schools, Rugby and Winchester.

One of Cromwell's Men

EAST TISTED. Its houses and gardens, on the Alton road, have great dignity and charm, and its handsome 19th century church has risen in place of its old one. Hanging on the wall is a remarkable painting by a village boy of 14 showing the village and the old church as they were in his time just before Waterloo.

The new church has a fine tower screen and font cover, and an attractive east window showing the Wise Men at Bethlehem above a choir of angel children. All that is left in it of the past is its collection of beautiful monuments, the 17th century bells, the altar plate, and a 17th century chest. There is a pewter flagon a foot high, made in 1702, and two old pewter almsdishes.

Most imposing of the memorials is the great tomb of Sir John Norton, with his marble figure in armour, his plumed helmet at his feet. He was one of Cromwell's men, though his epitaph says he was of unshaken loyalty to his king. He lies gazing down one of the aisles, looking at all who worship in it and also at a beautiful tomb with the kneeling figures of another Norton generation, Anne and John of the 16th century. Facing down the other aisle are Elizabeth and Richard Norton, a hundred years before Sir John, kneeling on either side of Christ rising from the sepulchre. They have a lovely canopied tomb with coloured shields, and their 17 children kneel in rows behind them, dressed in the costume of 400 years ago. At the foot of their monument is a 14th century gravestone with the head and shoulders of a woman; we see that she is a widow, for she carries her husband's heart in her hands. At the west end of the church are 19th century busts of two men of the Scott family, from Rotherfield Park across the way.

A few minutes along the Alton road we catch a glimpse of Pelham, a great house with one of the best tulip trees in England in its grounds.

East Meon   Looking Down on the Church

West Meon   Looking Up at the Church

East Wellow   **Where Florence Nightingale Sleeps**

Monk Sherborne   **The Medieval Church**

Weyhill   **The Little Church**

EAST TYTHERLEY. Here, among the secluded byways between Salisbury and Winchester is a 700-year-old church with a 19th century tower. Three panels of its original glass have figures of St Peter, an archbishop, and a bishop. Robert Owen, the great social reformer, knew the place well for hereabouts was established one of the many high-minded but ill-fated communities with which he was associated. Queenwood, which he called Harmony Hall, afterwards served as an agricultural college and then as a school, and here Professor Tyndall was a teacher with Henry Fawcett in his class.

Here Lies Florence Nightingale

EAST WELLOW. It has Florence Nightingale in its keeping. Here she sleeps. She knew this village as a child, and she was here when all England rang with her praises. She knew Hampshire chiefly in winter, for most of her summers were spent at her Derbyshire home, Lea Hurst; but she came to know these lanes in every season and loved to visit the people in the cottages.

Her home in Embley Park, one of the two houses she loved best, is little changed since she knew it. It has fluted pillars in the hall, a spacious staircase up and down which she ran in that swift silent way of hers, and a beautiful drawing-room where still hangs a mirror in which she would often see her earnest face. Still as lovely as when she walked in them are the avenues in the park, and the gardens that gladdened her heart would gladden any heart still. There is a letter from her sister to a friend which says:

If you would ask learned men they will tell you June at Embley is poetry ready made, and the first thing I shall do when I go to Heaven is to celebrate the pomps and beauties of the garden. It is so beautiful that you cannot fancy anything so near Eden or Fairyland. I never conceived anything so exquisite as today lying among the flowers, Flo reading and talking.

In the 45 years she lived in London her friend Sir Harry Verney would often lure her from her room in South Street and take her for a drive, and it was always easiest to persuade her to go in rhododendron time, for she was eager to be thinking of her Hampshire garden. Her last visit to the house she had known for 70 years was on a summer's day in 1891, and the glory of the gardens must have given her a lasting memory. She lived another 20 years and was 90 when she died, and, though the nation would have laid her in the

L   145

Abbey, this remarkable woman, who had given the world a new ministry of healing, wished for no other place to sleep in than this.

It must have pleased Florence Nightingale to know that Wellow once belonged to another great lady of England, King Alfred's daughter Ethelfleda, the lady of the Mercians; it was bequeathed to her in the king's will.

The church of St Margaret, which has kept seven of its consecration crosses and bells of 1450, is a small and simple 13th century building with a belfry of what Gilbert White would call the dovecot type. The doorway is 700 years old and the door has been swinging in it for many generations. The attractive interior owes much to the five great wooden pillars and the heavily timbered roof. The chancel is panelled with Jacobean oak and has a rector's desk made from fragments of an ancient screen. There is a lid of a 14th century priest's coffin below the lovely Jacobean pulpit, which has a panelled stairway and a newel post richly carved with leaves. The walls have traces of old painting. On the canopy of the pulpit are words which must often have stirred Florence Nightingale, so fitting that they might have been chosen for her.

For Sion's sake I will not hold my peace,
and for Jerusalem's sake I will not rest.

Resting in one of the windows we found here a little cross made of bullets picked up in the Crimea, and beside it a simple framed text with the words, *It is I, be not afraid*, which was hanging in the bedroom of Florence Nightingale in Park Lane when she died; it would be the last promise her eyes fell on.

If the old legend is true we are safe from harm for the day as soon as we open the ancient door into St Margaret's, for our eyes fall at once on St Christopher carrying the Child across the stream. On the wall near him is something like a golden-haired princess with a distaff in her hands looking appealingly to St George who is approaching with a sword and carrying keys. Often must Florence Nightingale have looked up to these red and yellow pictures and wondered at their quaintness. We might wish perhaps that Florence Nightingale's grave had something to mark it as noble and as beautiful as the bronze statue of her in the Crimea group in London, but perhaps she would have wished it free from grandeur. Her grave-stone has nothing but her initials and the year of her birth and death.

We look in vain in this churchyard for any memory of the little Russian prisoner Florence Nightingale brought home with her. He came into one of her hospitals, an orphan named Peter Grillage, and Miss Nightingale took charge of him and had him taught. One of the nurses asked him where he would go when he died if he were a good boy, and the little lad answered, To Miss Nightingale. He grew up at Embley, the Nightingale home here, acting as a man-servant in the house; and he married one of the maids, Temperance Hatcher. They had two children, to whom Miss Nightingale sent presents from time to time, and she remembered them in her will. Peter lies in Plymouth cemetery.

The Lady of the Lamp

ALL the world knows her as the Lady of the Lamp, the angel of mercy who glided at night through the hospital at Scutari where the wounded of the Crimea were lying, and where rough suffering soldiers would kiss her shadow as she passed.

All that is history and the truth, but it is only part of the truth about her. She was the Woman with the Torch, casting its blazing rays on the dark places of the ignorance, the blundering, the official slothfulness which had made the hospital a pest-house and had subjected the sick and wounded of the army to a cruelty of neglect that was one of the worst blots on War Office administration.

She fought the War Office then and thereafter with all the resources of her formidable will, and was not content till she had pierced the armour of official obstinacy and established an organisation of Army Nursing. It is hardly too much to say that the Army Medical Service in its modern form owed its foundation to her relentless zeal.

She was a gentlewoman, the clever, handsome daughter of a well-to-do family which hoped for her a brilliant marriage; but almost from her youth she had other ideas, and the dominating one was that her life should be devoted to some high purpose. She sought and found it in nursing and when she was a young woman no profession could have seemed less desirable for one of her up-bringing, for the general run of nurses were Sairey Gamps of the kind depicted by Charles Dickens. But she stuck to her point.

When she was over 30 she at last got her way and spent her days as the superintendent of a charitable nursing home in London. When the Crimean War had broken out, and some idea of the terrible condition of the wounded had been made known in England, she was the one woman equipped to meet an extreme need. The letter she wrote to her friend Sidney Herbert at the War Office suggesting that she should go, crossed one from him inviting her to go. Within a week she had set out for Scutari and she arrived between the battles of Balaclava and Inkerman. She found the overcrowded pestiferous hospital worse even than The Times correspondent had described it.

She set herself to redeem its horrors with all the energy at her command. She had taken money and medical stores with her. She fought the officials who hindered her. To the soldiers she was an angel, to those who resisted her she was a fury. The nursing was only part of her task. She was the responsible administrator. Her correspondence alone occupied her far into the night. She got things done. Once a doctor ventured to remark, when she had given some direction, that the thing could not be done, and she said quietly, "But it must be done," and it was done. She put the Scutari Hospital in order and cleanliness, she became inspector of the other Crimean hospitals, she made herself the common soldier's banker. She was the wounded soldier's General.

Yet all this was no more than the prelude to what she hoped and strove for during a number of years of her long life, so many of them spent as an invalid on her couch in South Street, Mayfair. When she came back to London, recipient of every honour that could then be given to a woman, she crept back quietly and alone to her home in Derbyshire while all London was seeking her, and when she had settled down she set herself to fight the War Office phalanx once again. She succeeded, with the help of her friend Sidney Herbert, in having the Army Medical Department reorganised, and if Sidney Herbert had not died she would probably have reorganised the War Office itself.

That dream faded. But, though her flaming energy had burnt down her vitality to its socket, she continued through the rest of her life to exert herself in nursing, and all the English institutions of Nursing Sisters own her as their foster-mother.

Bishop Ken's Church

EAST WOODHAY. It has a lovely yew planted by Bishop Ken when he was rector here, before he became famous as one

of the Seven Bishops who refused to read the Declaration of Indul-
gence and was driven into retirement for refusing to take the oath to
William of Orange. His yew still throws its shadow on the doorway
through which he would pass, and as we follow in his steps we look
across the nave to a window in which he stands in his black gown
with a brown fur border, above a small panel showing him confirm-
ing two girls. With him is another famous rector here, William of
Wykeham, holding in his hand a toy model of Winchester Cathedral;
he wears his red and gold robe and carries his crozier, and in the
panel below he is christening a child. The figure of Bishop Ken was
given by many admirers of his morning and evening hymns, now
sung everywhere; and that of Bishop Wykeham by a rector's children
in memory of their parents. Besides these, two other rectors of this
little place lived to become bishops.

The window is East Woodhay's chief possession and it has another
splendid window worthy to keep it company—the east window by
Louis Davies with stately figures in gorgeous colours in memory of
a Harrow master, Walter Guillemard, and his daughter Phyllis. The
window shows St Christopher carrying a Child looking somewhat
alarmed, the Madonna, and the archangel Michael, and has five
charming small panels associated with the father's college and the
daughter's school. Two other rich windows show Christ receiving the
sword of a soldier who fell on the Somme, and St Martin dividing
his cloak, in memory of 24 men who did not come back. On the
nave wall is a pathetic memory of three people drowned at Studland
in our time, two dying in trying to save the third; the tablet shows an
angel and a child writing the words of Laurence Binyon, They shall
grow not old as we that are left grow old.

There stands by the altar a man who may have known Bishop Ken,
for he was living in his day; he is Edward Goddard, and he stands
lifesize in a coat of many buttons with big cuffs, his hand on two books
and his wife standing by him. Thomas Douglas Hodgson served at
this altar for 59 years with these pompous figures at his side.

EAST WORLDHAM. It stands on the top of a great hill not
far from Alton, with wide views where its road goes over the
edge. The walls of its church have been built up again with the stones
the 12th century builders used, and here still are their two fine door-

ways, north and south, one blocked and the other used, but both deeply moulded and ornamented. Every window in the church is a lancet. The communion cup was made in the 17th century, and in a canopied recess in the nave lies a sleeping woman who has been here in stone six hundred years.

The Smallest Parish

ELDON. Was ever so small a place, so odd a corner of a great country? It is said to be the tiniest parish in Hampshire, and we do not doubt it. Reached by winding lanes climbing and dipping between the hedges, its quaint church stands on the top of a hill with an old farmhouse to keep it company. For about 700 years the church has been looking out across the woods and fields near Romsey; it has been a fowl-house and many other things; but we found it a church once more, kept spotless and bright. It is about eight yards long and has half a dozen pews. There are stone medallions in the walls which once held consecration crosses, four mouldings inside and two out, reminding us of that proud day when the bishop came to Eldon and put his hand on these six places. There was another great day in 1729, but we do not know what happened then; all we know is that the date and the initials W. H. are set in black bricks. The font must be one of the smallest in the country; it is hardly bigger than a goblet, but it is a copy of the beautiful 15th century font in St Mary Magdalen at Oxford.

Little Isaac Watts

ELING. Standing on the fringe of the New Forest and at the head of Southampton Water, it has an inn whose hospitality has been unbroken for 500 years, an ancient mill with a wooden wheel which has been turning for centuries, and a charming hilltop church. In the church is an arch made before the Conqueror landed in England, near which hangs a splendid helmet with a crest—a castle with crimson flames pouring from its battlements. On either side of the altar is an old chair richly carved, and above the altar hangs a fine picture of the Last Supper painted by the Venetian Marziale, an artist who may have known Michael Angelo. The chancel arch is a noble tribute to the 13th century masons who raised it. The organ-blower sits on a 17th century stool; there is a delightful candelabra of the 17th century with a dove carrying an olive branch, a dove of which we heard an odd story from the vicar, who, seeing that it was 300 years old, saved it from a passing tinker's melting pot. The tower is 15th century, and lovely is the blessing of one of its bells *Peace and good neighbourhood*, once a familiar salutation of neighbours passing in Worcestershire. We have come upon it inscribed on a public seat at one of the great heights of Kent, looking down the Darent Valley.

But the greatest pride of Eling is in its ancient registers, among the earliest in England, going back to 1538. In them we find this interesting note:

Thomas Burgess the Sonne of William Burgess and Elizabeth Russell the daughter of the now wife of Stephen Newland were asked three Sabbath days in the parish church of Eling, Aprell 16, Ap. 23, Ap. 30 and were married by Richard Lord Crumwell.

A great day for the village it must have been when Cromwell's unhappy son gave happiness to two young lovers, hoping, we may be sure, that their lot would prove a happier one than his.

One of Eling's rare treasures is the superb set of 17th century silver plate, some of the very finest to be found in Hampshire. It is in perfect condition and decorated with beautiful acanthus leaves. In the set is a chalice, a paten-cover, a paten, and a flagon holding seven pints.

Many fine headstones, some carved with heads and ships and some with cherubs, have been brought indoors to be saved from rough weather. One still in the graveyard is the stone of William Mansbridge of Cadnam with an epitaph telling of the tragic fate which befell him in 1703:

Stop, reader, pray, and read my fate,
What caused my life to terminate.
For theivs by night when in my bed
Broak up my house and shot me dead.

More appealing to most of us is the grave where lies one of Eling's vicars, John Pinhorne, for to him the whole world owes something, little though it knows it. As headmaster of Edward the Sixth's School in Southampton he had a share in the education of Isaac Watts, and so great was Isaac's affection for his old teacher that he addressed a Latin ode to him. It is an ardent salutation, in which Watts felicitates his old master on the kindly skill with which he has smoothed the rough ways of his pupil through Greek and Latin and Hebrew, permitting him to enjoy not only the glories of Homer and Virgil but the sublime truths of the Scriptures. Vicar here for a far longer time was William Phillips, from 1803 to 1855, his 52 years of service only equalled here by James Olding, who was sexton from 1744 to 1796. He would dig the grave of Susanna Serle, whose bust is here by Rysbrack, keeping company with one of Peter Serle who died 12 years before her in 1741.

Not far from Eling is Testwood, which has a strikingly modern church built of brick with a great cross on the face of its sturdy tower, huge arches outside, and inside two brick arches with a span of fifty feet. It is built from the designs of Mr N. F. Cachemaille-Day.

The Pitiful Story of Alice Lisle

ELLINGHAM. Even if it was not on the fringe of the New Forest, with all the natural beauty about it, it must for ever be a place of pilgrimage to Englishmen who love their freedom. Nature has given it a great oak which has grown to be over 20 feet round its trunk, shading a stream with a footbridge and a ford, and there is a hill covered with heather and topped with vigorous firs. Standing where their roots make a bony pattern on the ground, we have a magnificent view. But it is not for this that we come. We come because Dame Alice Lisle sleeps here. She lived across the stream at Moyles Court, to which a beautiful avenue runs from the church by a way Dame Alice must often have come. It was her Elizabethan home, where she lived as the wife of one of the judges of Charles Stuart and from which she came to the court which led her to be butchered by Judge Jeffreys. She sleeps here in the churchyard with her daughter Anne Harfell, both in a low stone tomb. Facing the pulpit (which was new in those days) is the old pew in which she would sit. It has a canopy rising on slender pillars decorated in 1626 with pierced carving.

The chancel screen is the graceful work of medieval craftsmen, and on it is an hourglass, one of the small number of old ones still left in our churches; it is from 1650. It is believed that the wall above the screen may hide the old roodloft, built over after the Reformation. The chancel floor has 13th century gravestones with raised crosses on which gilded and painted bosses look down from the roof. In the sanctuary are two finely carved chairs. The font is 15th century and there are traces of wall-painting of the same age. At the west end of the nave is a fine piece of panelling which was once at the altar, skilfully carved with cherubs, drapery, and foliage; and above it all a dove hovers over a lamb. In the centre is a picture by a Flemish artist showing the Last Judgment, in a frame believed to be by Grinling Gibbons. It was brought from the church of St Mary in Cadiz after a siege in 1702: a speck of war loot falling into the hands of Admiral Lord Windsor, who brought it back to his home at Moyles Court and gave it to the church. It is 16th century.

The old door of the church is made of two layers of planks studded with iron nails, and keeps its ancient ring. By it is an old scratch dial, and there is a blue and gold sundial which has been marking time since 1720.

We noticed on the peace memorial a notable inscription following the names of men who fell and expressing thankfulness for the safe return of those who came back, none of them blinded or maimed.

Alice Lisle, to whose grave pilgrims must always come in this peaceful churchyard, was the victim of one of the foulest crimes that stain the infamous record of Judge Jeffreys. She was 71, widow of John Lisle, the judge who is believed to have drawn up the form of sentence read out to Charles Stuart, though she declared that she had shed more tears over the execution of the king than any other woman in England.

She was charged at Winchester with having, after the Battle of Sedgemoor, harboured a dissenting minister named John Hickes and another man named Nelthorp, both of whom had taken part in the engagement on the side of Monmouth. Thirty years before (and nine years before he himself was murdered) Judge Lisle had sentenced to death as a rebel John Penruddock; and it was this man's son, Colonel Penruddock, who was now to bring Alice Lisle to death.

She did shelter the two men, and Colonel Penruddock, notified by a village spy, went to Moyles Court and arrested the two fugitives and Alice Lisle herself. But she swore that she had known Hickes only as a dissenting minister, that she did not know Nelthorp's name until he was arrested, and that she had no knowledge of their having been in the battle. Jeffreys was in his element as judge and prosecutor; to a reluctant witness for the prosecution he shouted: "It is infinite mercy that for these falsehoods of thine God does not immediately strike thee into hell! Jesu God! Thou art a strange prevaricating, shuffling, snivelling, lying rascal. Hold the candle to his face so that we may see his brazen features." As the candle was thrust nearer and nearer his face the witness protested: "I am quite cluttered out of my senses; I do not know what I say."

The summing up by Jeffreys was a model of judicial unfairness, and the jury had grave doubts. The evidence was insufficient, they said. Jeffreys stormed at them as if they had been in the dock, and in the end they had no alternative to returning a verdict of Guilty. Thereupon he sentenced Dame Lisle to be drawn on a hurdle to the place of execution and burnt alive, adding: "Mr Sheriff, take notice, you are to prepare for this execution of this gentlewoman this afternoon." The horrified clergy of the cathedral went to him in protest, and the sentence was postponed for five days. In that time James the Second was moved to change the penalty into death by beheading, and this sentence was carried out on September 5, 1685.

Four years later the two daughters of Alice Lisle petitioned the Government, which by special Act of Parliament annulled the conviction on the ground that the verdict was "procured by the menaces and violences and other illegal practices of Lord Jeffreys."

Queen Elizabeth Awakes

ELVETHAM. The church is with the great modern house in the 300 beautiful acres of Elvetham Park, where herons fly about. It was made new in 1841, but has still a 13th century canopied piscina and marble portraits of Reynolds Calthrope and his Priscilla. They are high up in the gallery, Priscilla, with her hair curled about her forehead in the fashion of Queen Anne's day, and Reynolds handsome in a curled wig. Each monument has a canopy of festooned drapery. There is a striking reredos with painted and gilt tracery forming a background to three delicately wrought figures, Our Lord in the centre and the Madonna and the Archangel Gabriel beside him. The ancient Elvetham House has vanished, with its memory of Queen Elizabeth, who was lavishly entertained here by the Earl of Hertford. The lake near the church was the scene of a display in which three maidens appeared in a boat playing Scottish jigs; and among the buildings raised in the park for the queen and her retinue was a green bower of ivy and hazel used as a presence chamber. Each morning the queen was greeted on waking with pastoral songs.

The Pews of Chaucer's Day

EMPSHOTT. It is surrounded by hills and is perched on one itself, near Liss. By a charming old house its church stands in great peace, a simple shrine mostly built when the Norman style was changing into English. The chancel with its lancet windows is 13th century. The nave arches and the chancel arch are outlined with carving and have a variety of beautiful capitals, one arch ending with a quaint priest's head. The interior is remarkable for its very narrow aisles and its collection of old woodwork, much of which gives the impression of being done by village craftsmen. There are rows of beautiful pews probably made in Chaucer's time, a Tudor pulpit with linenfold panels, an old sanctuary seat and carved altar rails, an oak box 500 years old and a few poppyheads. The 700-year-old font has an elegant wooden cover of the 17th century, and at the west doorway is an ornamental screen painted with the arms of the man who gave it 300 years ago.

There was born in this village the famous Hampshire cricketer John Small, who had a little shop in the great square at Petersfield with a sign outside offering to play any man in England for five pounds a side. He was a member of the original Hambledon Club, Hambledon being the cradle of cricket.

Charles Kingsley's Grave

EVERSLEY. In the quiet lanes a little way off the great road where the cars rush by, it is still part of the quiet countryside Charles Kingsley knew, where he loved to walk about and be one with his neighbours. He went to school every day, and taught as long as he could stand the heat and smell of a low room ten feet square crammed with children. He came here as curate when there was a cracked kitchen basin in the font for the holy water and a broken chair by the altar. He stayed as rector all his life, and here he lies in as simple a grave as a man could have, sleeping among his flock. Over him is a white marble cross with passion flowers and three Latin words which stand for this expression of his faith, *We love: We loved: We will love;* and it may be that at some time of the day the shadow will fall on it from the great rough wooden cross in memory of those who went out from his village and did not come back.

He sleeps between the house he lived in and the shrine he loved, the rectory looking on the road across the small lawn and the simple church in which he preached for 33 years. The chancel has a painted screen with lilies he designed, and there is a brass which has brought many antiquarians to this place for something curious and unusual about the intricate lacework engraved on its cross. It is here in memory of Richard Pendilton, a faithful servant of that 15th century soldier-statesman who figured at the Court of Henry the Seventh, and arranged for the marriage of Prince Arthur with Catherine of Aragon.

But the loveliest thing in the church is a charming old Victorian lady lying in the chancel, with her feet against a prick-eared dog. She is Dame Marian Cope who was probably buried by Charles Kingsley, for she died a year or two before him. It may very well have been that Dame Marian was in the church that day when Charles Kingsley was on his way to the pulpit and saw a butterfly on the floor in danger of being trodden on. He stooped and picked it up, putting it out of the window, and went back to his pulpit, preaching, we may be sure, in the spirit of that poet who went before him:

He prayeth best who loveth best
All things both great and small.

As Charles Kingsley lay dying his daughter heard him exclaim, "How beautiful God is," and as he looked out from his window for almost the last time, the snow having cleared away so that he could see the grass, he said, thinking of his youngest son, "Tell Grenville I am looking at the most beautiful scene I ever saw." The last morning at five o'clock, when he thought himself alone, he was heard repeating the words of the Burial Service:

Thou knowest, O Lord, the secrets of our hearts . . . Thou most worthy Judge Eternal, suffer us not, at our last hour, to fall from Thee.

He never spoke again. He was carried to the grave by villagers he had known. There were three VCs there, and the great Max Muller wrote this picture of the scene in this place on January 28, 1875:

There was the representative of the Prince of Wales and the gipsies of Eversley Common. There was the squire of his village and the labourers young and old. There were governors of colonies, officers and sailors, the Bishop of his diocese and the Dean of his abbey. There were leading Nonconformists and his devoted curates, peers and members of the House of Commons, authors and publishers, and huntsmen in pink.

All that he had loved and all that loved him were there, and few eyes were dry when he was laid in his own gravel bed, the old trees he had planted and cared for waving their branches to him for the last time, and the gray sunny sky looking down with calm pity on the deserted rectory.

The great house in the park is Bramshill, designed by the builder of Hatfield and Holland House; he built it for Lord Zouche, a powerful man at Court who meant to give it to James the First's son Henry when he was Prince of Wales. Nobody can say how different the course of England's history might have been if Henry had lived in it, but he died and left the throne to Charles Stuart, who was to think of him as he walked to the scaffold that winter's morning, for he turned at Spring Gardens and said to his servant, "I remember my brother Henry planting a tree there." The house was seven years in building, spectacular with terraces outside and rich in treasure inside. Some of the great firs go back to the days of Queen Elizabeth, and Charles Kingsley used to say that Bramshill was the only place in England where a painter could learn what Scots firs are.

A hero of long ago came to the park as lodgekeeper after leaving the army, and here he died. We may think that the proudest thing in the park was his VC. He was Francis Wheatley, who was in the trenches before Sebastopol when a shell fell among his comrades. He tried to put out its burning fuse with the butt of his rifle, and, failing in this, picked up the shell and threw it over the parapet.

One of the stories of the great house is of an archbishop ancestor of Kingsley, whose portrait he always looked at with interest. In the days of Shakespeare, when Archbishop Abbot was trying his hand at the crossbow, he aimed an arrow at a stag and killed a keeper. There was such an outcry in the country that the archbishop was suspended from his office, though James the First declared that nobody but a fool or a knave would think worse of a man for an accident. One of Kingsley's letters refers to it:

I went the other day to Bramshill Park, the home of the lord of the manor here, Sir John Cope. And there I saw the very tree where an ancestor of mine, Archbishop Abbot, in James the First's time, shot the keeper by accident!

I sat under the tree, and it all seemed to me like a present reality. I could fancy the noble old man, very different then from his picture as it hangs in our dining-room at Chelsea. I could fancy the deer sweeping by, and the rattle of the crossbow, and the white splinters sparkling off the fated tree as the bolt glanced and turned—and then the death shriek. He never smiled again ! And that solemn form always spoke to me, though I did not then know what it meant.

It is strange that that is almost the only portrait saved in the wreck of our family. As I sat under the tree there seemed to be a solemn and remorseful moan in the long branches, mixed with the airy whisper of the lighter leaves that told of present as well as past!

Bramshill is reached by an avenue a mile long, and has a lake of five acres through which the woodlands spread for 1000 acres. The great gallery is over 40 yards long, hung with tapestries and crowned with a magnificent ceiling, and all the rooms are of vast size. But it is the wonderful setting of the house that is its chief glory; it stands in 4000 acres and has been described as "a noble and mellowed medieval pile set in rolling parkland, bracken-clad heath, and woods, falling to the river where it widens into a sheet of ornamental water."

The Historian's Friend

EXBURY. It lies in the trees on the edge of a heath where Beaulieu River pierces with many channels the narrow strip of marshland separating it from the Solent. The old church has been made new, but is true to the severe simplicity of the 13th century builder. It has an Elizabethan chalice, a font made in the last year of the 12th century, and a delightful timber roof painted blue and green. In a fine setting under the tower is the bronze figure by Cecil Thomas of a young soldier lying on a tomb, with tall bronze candlesticks at the corners. It is the memorial of John and Alfred Forster, both slain in the war. A bronze plaque of John Forster is on the wall near by; he is in officer's uniform. Near it is the roll of honour, also in bronze, ending with the noble lines of Sir John Arkwright:

> *O valiant hearts who to your glory came*
> *Through dust of conflict and through battle flame,*
> *Tranquil you lie, your knightly virtue proved,*
> *Your memory hallowed in the land you loved.*

Lord Forster outlived his sons and set up their memorial; he himself, dying in 1936 after having been Governor-General of Australia, has a memorial in the form of a stone cross carved and painted with arms unique in heraldry in that the supporters are lieutenants of the regiments in which his two sons gave their lives. In the centre of the cross is a casket chamber containing his ashes; it is behind an elegant bronze grille with a floral design.

There is a plain tablet to William Mitford, the historian of Greece, who lies here. His friendship with Edward Gibbon did much to help him to make a success of his History. The Mitfords lived in the big white house hidden by trees, the woods glorious with bluebells in their season, and the garden famous for its rhododendrons.

The Bookman's Last Visitor

EXTON. The river Meon, the meadows, trees, and pretty cottages make Exton a charming place. The church, with a 13th century chancel and a 14th century nave, has an old bell which rang before the Reformation, a silver cup made in 1648, a 13th century canopied piscina and aumbry in one, and a charmingly simple Jacobean altar. Saved from the weather's rough handling is a battered headstone by the font. Its inscription is illegible, but its sculptured top is in good preservation. It shows Death coming to a booklover, who sits up in bed to greet his last visitor, surrounded by the Chippendale cases which hold all that he has cared for in the world.

The Champion's Daughter

FACCOMBE. It is hidden away where the North Downs begin to run up towards their highest point, near Inkpen Beacon above the Bourne valley. Its old church has been superseded but there are remains for which we may be grateful. A handsome old font richly decorated with chevrons continues the baptism of babies which has been going on here for 800 years; it has still the two staples used for fastening down its cover in the days when men were afraid of witchcraft. By the door is a delicate scene cut in grey stone showing a lady kneeling at a table. Before her is her son, with one knee on a cushion and a book in his hand, wearing a turned-down ruff, a short coat, and breeches with a knot of ribbons, and behind her are three daughters. We read that she is Anne Reade, daughter of the "Knight Champion to the late Queen Elizabeth and to King James that now is." Another memorial is to a baronet whose constant study, we are told, was Truth, and whose name, if Virtue can preserve a name, will be Immortal, though his title died with him.

In modern glass the east window shows Our Lord on high with St Michael and St Barnabas, and another window has St John in a beautiful blue robe in memory of a 20th century rector.

A Terrible Day

FAREHAM. Its long wide street of old houses and new shops make a pleasant broken line, and other houses descend to the head of the creek. The place scarcely looks its age, for it is as old as the Conqueror. The creek runs up from Portsmouth Harbour, and on the tide barges and small ships come to the wharf and make a pretty sight. A mill once stood beside the winding water with a pond which for time immemorial has been drained on St Peter's Eve for everybody to pick up fish.

Today many roads radiate from Fareham, one to Titchfield where Margaret of Anjou was married, one to Porchester Castle, and one to Southwick where Henry the First's Black Canons migrated from Porchester Priory. But the antiquity proper to these noble names has fled from Fareham, where the ancient church was rebuilt just before Waterloo, and the town's oldest memories are that on the Portsdown Hills above it. Lord Palmerston built the red brick land defences of Portsmouth, and survivors of Trafalgar raised an obelisk to Nelson. There is one other memory, for where the bus depot is so busy now stood a leisurely Georgian house in which Thackeray lived as a boy. At Fontley near by Henry Cort, the iron puddler of Gosport, built in the 18th century the first iron mill. There are no ironworks now, nor much trace of them, but the brickworks that have made "Fareham Reds" since William the Third came to England are still prosperous.

A Georgian tower which might have been built of the bricks, now mellowed by time, is the chief ornament of the church of St Peter and St Paul. Its north chapel is the chancel of the far older church which stood here from the 13th century till a gale destroyed it in the 18th, and has in it traces of the Saxon. There are two armchairs with richly carved backs, two benches of 1400 and a piscina of 1500, a fragment of a medieval reredos, an old stone coffin, and in a new chapel the panelling and the altar are made from beams 600 years

Hursley
John Keble's Church

Eversley
Charles Kingsley's Rectory

Sopley   **The Little Church on the Hill**

Corhampton   Saxon Church

Boldre   13th Century Church

Idsworth **Medieval Hilltop Church**

Farnborough **Tomb of the Last Napoleons**

old. On the walls are two busts and a sculpture in memory of one of the most terrible days in the history of the British Fleet. One of the busts is of Richard Collins who died in 1831, the other of Admiral Sir Edward Bruce, with two sailors mourning over it; the marble relief shows a ship with a broken mast tossing on an angry sea. It is HMS Hero, which went down in 1811 with all her 600, not one man surviving.

The church of Holy Trinity has three pictures on its walls painted by Spanish and Russian artists; the Spanish picture is 16th century.

The Amateur Builder

FARINGDON. It is in a pleasant country of thatched roofs near Selborne, and by two ancient yews in the churchyard is a cross from which Gilbert White would preach when he was curate here. The church has a new chancel but keeps its 13th century tower, three Norman arches, two mass dials, and five 17th century bells. The plain pulpit, also from the 17th century, has a remarkable distinction, for in 122 years only two rectors preached from it, one being here 60 years and the other 62. It was the second rector (T. H. Massey) who, with the help of only one man, built the extraordinary red brick school facing the church. Seemingly as big as the church, it is a fantastic building with little towers and battlements, but it stands as a mighty monument of two men's labour. Massey's Folly the people used to call it, but it has now been reshaped a little and serves as a school and a village hall.

An Old Man's Prayer

FARLEIGH WALLOP. The grey Georgian house of Sir John Wallop, who was created Earl of Portsmouth by his friend George the First, stands in this charming village by Basingstoke. It rests on the foundations of an ancient building which had been the home of the Wallops since 1414, and where Sir Henry Wallop entertained Elizabeth. The Wallops have been a great family for many centuries. One Sir John was a doughty admiral and a much-travelled ambassador in Henry the Eighth's reign. Sir Oliver was knighted on the field of battle in 1547, and Sir Robert was one of the men who signed Charles Stuart's death-warrant. At the Restoration he was imprisoned in the Tower, where he died an old man. His prayers for mercy, and for permission to breathe pure air once more before he died, were ignored by the son of the man he had sent to the block.

The little 14th century church, with light streaming through all its windows, stands solitary among the trees, reached by a winding way made lovely in spring with banks of primroses and violets. The chancel, newly panelled with linenfold, is paved with the heraldic stones of generations of Wallops, and the walls bear their monuments. By the altar is a handsome 15th century tomb with quatrefoils on its sides and a top scarred by vanished brasses. Near the wall-monument of the first Earl of Portsmouth is his grandson's, with the forlorn figure of a woman mourning by a weeping willow.

The Gallant Steed

FARLEY CHAMBERLAYNE. It is a steep hill which brings us to the hazel avenue leading to its green hilltop, with a church full of the memorials of the St Johns. The road to it is planted with peace memorial trees. The walls of the church have been standing since the 12th century, and there are consecration crosses and a mass dial on them. The doorway has two strange heads cut in the capitals. Three of the bells rang out in thanksgiving for the scattering of the Great Armada. The tower is supported by massive timbers, and the roof has a regiment of old beams. Here they laid to rest John and Susannah St John, who died young within a year of each other three centuries ago. We see them kneeling in black on either side of a small hooded basketwork cot tilted at a perilous angle so that we may see their baby son, of whom we read a sorrowful note that he was "borne after his father's death and died before his mother." Near this pathetic tablet is a canopied monument on which lies a gracious old man, Sir William St John, who died at the beginning of the 17th century, and here wears armour such as Sir Walter Raleigh might have worn. There is a pewter almsdish of Sir Walter's day.

On Farley Down is a pointed stone monument 30 feet high which Paulet St John raised to his horse (Beware Chalk Pit). It tells us that one day in 1733, when out hunting, Paulet came suddenly upon a chalk-pit and, too late to avoid it, let his gallant horse take the leap over a terrible drop of 25 feet. The daring steed leaped safely over and in a year the same pair won the Hunters Plate on Worthy Down.

The Horns Are Sounding

FARLINGTON. Four churches have been built in eight centuries at this point on the road from Chichester to Portsmouth, and there is still a fragment of one of them, the ornamental drain of the Norman piscina. There is also something that must make a pathetic appeal to any pilgrim, a stone like a small coffin lid carved with a cross. It comes from 700 years ago, when it is thought that the heart of a crusader was buried here. In the sanctuary is a charming marble tablet with the kneeling figure of a woman, her head bowed, her left hand shading her eyes, her right arm holding a child. Clinging to her, and looking up at her, is a little boy. It was a tragedy. She was the wife and they were the little ones of the rector, Edward Richards, who lived through most of last century. He came here as rector in 1825 and had been here eight years when his wife died. She died in August, leaving him with these two little boys, and one of them followed her in September and the other in December. The bereaved rector lived on into the Victorian Era and was still preaching here when our fathers were keeping Queen Victoria's Jubilee. He was rector 62 years. They lie in the churchyard shaded by fine yews, with a view across the marshes to the sea.

Here also lies Luke Kent, the first mail-coach guard. He left a small charity to his successors on the Chichester Coach so that they should sound their horns on passing his grave. The Chichester Coach has passed away but still the horns are sounding morning, noon, and night by Luke Kent's quiet grave.

The Last of the Napoleons

FARNBOROUGH. Here ends the long story of Napoleon. From the throne of France to this quiet corner of Hampshire came the last of this famous house. Here has been laid in our own time the Empress Eugenie, full of years and sorrows; she lies in the chapel she had built for the third Napoleon and their son Prince Imperial.

It was to Chislehurst in Kent that they fled from the throne of France in the terrible days after Sedan, and in the course of time the widow Eugenie came to Farnborough and took the great house called Farnborough Hill. She was a remarkable woman. "I tell you I died in 1870," she would say, but long after that she bought this place, enlarging it and adding an abbey, with St Michael's Church attached, and to the vault below the church she transferred the tombs of the last Napoleon and his son. Now she is with them.

The house in which she lived for 40 years is a remarkable spectacle with its gables and turrets; the abbey is the home of a group of monks; and the church crowning the hill above the rest of the buildings is a place of dazzling splendour with a marble pavement and a lantern dome. In the sanctuary is a Crucifix made from a single piece of ivory and presented by the Pope at the christening of the Prince Imperial, who was to grow up and die on a British battlefield in Zululand, and so earn his right to an English grave.

He was scouting with a party of soldiers when they were ambushed, and his restive horse prevented him from mounting. When at last he got into the saddle the girths broke and he fell to the ground. His right hand being injured by a kick from his horse, he defended himself against the Zulus with his left till he fell, wounded 17 times. He lies with his father and mother in the crypt, the most striking part of this striking church, impressive with its massive piers with carved capitals rising from a floor of coloured marble. The three granite tombs weigh five tons each; those of the Emperor and his son were given by Queen Victoria; the third was added when the Empress Eugenie died in 1920, aged 94. She was buried here in the presence of King George the Fifth and Queen Mary, with whom stood the Kings of Spain and Portugal. Three vacant chairs gilded and painted are kept in the crypt. Above the Emperor's tomb hangs a bronze wreath in memory of the Battle of Solferino, where Napoleon joined with Italy and 20,000 Austrians were slain.

By the doorway of the vault is a grave that is here by the wish of the Empress Eugenie. It was her desire that her much-loved and faithful Corsican secretary should lie as near to them as possible. He was the faithful hero and servant of the royal exiles to the end. If guests should arrive Franchescini Pietri would surrender his apartments and in a single room would live, sleep, and conduct the business of the fallen sovereigns. He stood between them and begging impostors or annoying conspirators. He knelt with the Empress at the bedside of the dying Emperor and heard Napoleon's last words, "Were you at Sedan?" The young Prince Imperial left him £5000 in his will.

It is strange that when the Empress Eugenie arrived at Farnborough she found in the village church, painted on the wall, the only old portrait known in England of St Eugenia. The discovery was a great delight to her in the new home she made for herself, and often she would bring her friends to the church to show them her saint, with her halo of stars and the crescent moon. With St Eugenia are Mary Magdalene and St Agnes, all three painted about 800 years ago. They are on a Norman wall, and still plain on this wall is a painted consecration cross.

The church stands in a charming setting of trees, and we come into it by a door probably as old as the church itself and strong enough for centuries to come. The timbers of the porch (oak or chestnut) are 700 years old, and in the porch are solid benches almost untouched by time or weather. Two of the doorways are Norman, and the timbers of the quaint wooden tower are believed to come from ships that were on the seas when the Golden Hind was sailing round the world. The tower rests on four massive oak posts. The high chancel screen and the high balustrade of the gallery are Jacobean. The font is a beautiful copy of one of the 14th century. The pulpit is 17th century and the reredos, like the chancel, is 19th; it has three panels with onyx from Mexico, marble from Siena, and spar from Derbyshire. The chancel has the sin of darkness, but has much dignity and colour in its windows, one of which shows the Holy Family and the Wise Men. On a tablet on the chancel arch we read of the five Earls of Anglesey buried here, the first of them Arthur Annesley, who sat in Richard Cromwell's Parliament and became Treasurer of the Navy to Charles the Second. The tablet tells also of the Earl of Tyrone, who married the first Earl of Anglesey's daughter and died a prisoner in the Tower, having helped to defend Cork against Marlborough soon after the Revolution of 1688. We noticed outside, the gravestone of John Richards, who was rector for nearly half a century in the time of the greatest Napoleon of all.

The Little Slave Boy

FAWLEY. Its fields run down to Southampton Water, its wide heath is lovely with gorse, and away behind it stretches Beaulieu in all its glory. It is said that the big wall round the rectory was built with stones from the ruins of Beaulieu. We were told that the rectory has 37 rooms, and that a summerhouse in the grounds has been built with shells picked up on the shore by village children. Here we saw a beautiful thing and heard a beautiful story.

The beautiful thing is a little piece of beaten silver scarcely bigger than a man's hand, the choicest of Fawley's treasures. In the centre of it, surrounded by a scalloped edge, is an engraved head of Our Lord. It is believed to be part of the church plate given to Fawley in the 14th century by William of Wykeham, and it keeps company with a handsome Elizabethan chalice.

The story is of a little slave boy, Irby Amelia Frederick, Irby Frederick for the captain and Amelia for the ship which saved him. He was ten years old when he was carried off from his African home and put on the French frigate Arethusa, to be sold in South America. On its way the Arethusa was challenged by HMS Amelia, commanded by Captain Frederick Paul Irby of Fawley. The slave traders were overpowered and the gallant captain brought this boy home with him, sending him to school and baptising him here.

We come into this church (with a mass dial on its wall) through a splendid Norman doorway, with a richly decorated arch, to find the work of Norman craftsmen everywhere about us. The chancel arch is Norman and on its eastern face are traces of a gable of the Saxon walls the Normans rebuilt. There are two Norman arches with nobly carved capitals on the north of the chancel, and the tower is little changed since the Normans left it. The arcades are 13th century, and there are two 13th century chapels. The deeply carved pulpit is 17th century, and shows arches over tiled floors. One of two chests is carved with the date 1636. There are some precious fragments of 15th century glass in the vestry, one with a sad face of Our Lord, and another with St Nicholas.

Here by Fawley stands what is left of Calshot Castle, hid by the shining hangars of the RAF at the end of a shingled beach at the mouth of Southampton Water. From the water it can be clearly seen, sturdy as the monarch who built it with the stones he stole from the beautiful abbeys of Beaulieu and Netley. The tongue of land it stands on is thought to have been the landing-place of Cerdic the Saxon, who, like Julius Cæsar, came and saw and conquered.

The big house called Eaglehurst has in its grounds a tower known as Luttrel's Folly, after the name of its builder. From it there used to be an underground passage to the beach.

FLEET. It has the biggest pond in Hampshire, about three-quarters of a mile long and covering 130 acres. The monks of St

Swithun's at Winchester used to get their fish from it, long before the railway cut it in two. In the dignified modern church are the marble figures of the founder and his wife. They lie under a canopy decorated with angels swinging censers. At their feet are two dogs, one a little terrier with his paw on a ball.

John Chubb's Epitaph

FORDINGBRIDGE. The best thing in this charming little town is the sturdy church, mostly 700 years old, and the best thing in the church is the roof of the lady chapel, a wonder of medieval craftsmanship of remarkable beauty. It has prophets and kings, and beams adorned with clusters of flowers, the middle one showing the artist's conception of the head of God enveloped in clouds. He is bearded and has a benevolent and dignified expression.

Besides the handsome roof the church has a lofty 13th century chancel and a lovely arcade on clustered shafts. The nave and aisles are 14th century, and the clerestory and the tower 15th. The font is 700 years old, and was found in the vicarage garden. We are told that at it on September 4, 1664 the eight children of Samuel Harris were baptised together! The royal arms over the door is a fine piece of 18th century woodcarving. Near the chancel, set in a queer and cumbersome frame, is a brass to William Bulkley who died in 1568, he in armour and his wife in a tight-waisted dress, three boys kneeling behind their father and five girls behind their mother. An altar tomb in the outside wall of the lady chapel contains a stone scored with grooves said to be made by the sharpening of swords in the Civil War.

The 15th century porch has an old mass clock near it, and a room over it is approached by an avenue of limes. The tower has a fine view of the Avon valley. The Avon flows by Fordingbridge, and as it is famous for its chub it is interesting to see the many gravestones bearing the name in the churchyard. John Chubb, who died young in 1784, has a sad epitaph:

> Death like an overflowing stream
> Sweeps us away: Our life's a dream:
> An empty tale: a morning flower
> Cut down and withered in an hour.

There are ancient earthworks on Castle Hill not far away from Fordingbridge, from whose summit are splendid views of the county.

FREEFOLK. It shares a new church with Laverstoke, but it has its own little 13th century church in a field behind the rectory. In this old church is an imposing and sumptuous monument, coloured and gilt, on which the figure of a bearded man lies stiffly in silver painted armour, with his two daughters kneeling in black in front of the tomb. He is Sir Richard Powlett of Shakespeare's time, a sculptured helmet by his side and a real one hanging with a spur above. At the west end of the church is a handsome screen apparently by 15th century craftsmen, and on the wall is a trace of ancient painting. Much younger is the huge painting of two bearded figures with tablets bearing the Commandments, and the painted cherubs holding up the Creed and Lord's Prayer beside the altar. There are traces of wall-painting and hanging on the wall are two iron candlesticks, elegant and 18th century.

Witnesses of Ancient Days

FROXFIELD. It bears the mark of ancient times in two sets of earthworks of prehistoric origin, traversing the valley sides. The plough turns up in these fields the flint tools of these early people, and of fossils and sea-urchins belonging to the days when sea covered the hills and no man walked here. The Romans also left behind them a peaceful memory, the remains of a villa with a bath having been discovered here.

There are two new churches which have memories of the old church gone. St Peter's, High Cross, has three Norman arches in the arcade, with scalloped capitals; and St Peter's-on-the-Green has some tablets to the memory of old Froxfield folk. Among them is the memorial of kind Richard Love and his Barbara, who died in 1690 but whose charity still lives and helps in the schooling of poor children. Garlands of carved flowers hang on either side of the tablet, with delightful cherubs below. Mistress Honor Neale, daughter of Sir William Uvedale of Wickham, whose ancestors helped William of Wykeham in his poor and struggling youth, has a tablet. Two old yews stand as sentinels by the path to the porch.

In St Peter's, High Cross, is a tablet by the altar rails in memory of John Silvester, the last of a family living in Froxfield 350 years until 1928.

For a little walk from Froxfield we go to Petersfield, the road winding through the beautiful hanging woods on the side of the hill.

Froxfield is high up in the hills, with a towering neighbour in Stoner Hill, 758 feet high, from whose summit we have a magnificent view.

The Glowing Window

FROYLE. It has one of the best windows in Hampshire, the east window of its church. In the quatrefoils of its tracery blazes the original 14th century glass, a glorious company of glowing shields of the Plantagenets and of the Confessor. It is almost unbelievably beautiful when the sun pours through its deep blues and rubies and gold, as it has been pouring for 600 years. In splendid modern glass below the tree of Jesse branches into kings and prophets, till Our Lord lies in his Mother's arms above them all. There are two other windows which also have 14th century glass in fragments. The modern windows are rich in colour. In one St John writes his Revelation, the angel standing behind him, and in the distance is a vision of the Madonna with a seven-headed serpent under her feet, each head crowned, a vivid picture against the deepest of blue skies. Other windows are charming with Bible scenes, one just above a choirboy's head showing the journey from Bethlehem, with Joseph going ahead with a lantern, his bundle of belongings slung on a stick over his shoulder, while Mary and the Child follow on a donkey led by an angel, and other angels hover over them with lanterns to light the way.

The royal arms of King Charles add yet another touch of colour to these shining white walls, where gilded angels stand on brackets, and old Italian and Spanish statues stand round the organ.

We step down from a 19th century nave into the fine 14th century chancel, which has altar rails 300 years old and the brass portrait of an English gentleman, John Lighe, who was a boy of 13 when Drake drove back the Armada. There is a fine chalice engraved in those days, and another richly and wonderfully wrought which came from Spain in the days when Drake was no more troubling her. It is a very unusual cup; the British Museum has another like it.

Gilbert White's Brother

FYFIELD. Here sleeps Henry White, brother of Gilbert White of Selborne and rector here for 26 years before he died in 1788. He was devoted to music, but spared no time in noting certain facts about nature after the manner of his famous brother. In a letter to a friend Gilbert White says that Henry tried all the owls in his neighbourhood with a pitch-pipe set at concert pitch, and found that they all hooted in B flat! The rectory that Henry turned into a private school is here still, and the churchyard where he lies is secluded and delightful, with a magnificent beech shading our approach to the little church whose walls were first raised 700 years ago. It has massive oak pews, and a font well carved with quatrefoils like some we have seen 500 years old. There is a memorial to an officer who served the Motherland in India for 40 of his 56 years, dying in 1847 on his way from Cawnpore to Dum Dum; and a handsome peace memorial tablet with the names of 37 who came through the Great War, as well as of 11 who died. Among the survivors we noticed two who won the DSO.

A Roman villa has been dug up not far away, and among the finds were a tessellated pavement, gateposts of green sandstone, and coins belonging to the time of Carausius, the rebel who made himself a sort of Emperor of Britain.

God's Field Wakes From Its Long Sleep

GODSFIELD. It may have been the Black Death which sent it to sleep, but certainly its medieval glory lay unguessed at or in ruin. Most of it has passed away, but a little of its treasure all may see in one of our national treasure-houses at South Kensington, and something of its beauty still remains on its own green hill. We find it by a neat farm, a small grey building with a handsome chimney battered by time, an arched doorway, a bricked-up window, and four pretty windows still letting in the light. Here, under one roof, are the two rooms of a dwelling-house (one above the other) and a larger room that was once a chapel. The altar was by the bricked-up window, and on the wall are two brackets for images. The roof has its original beams and a few of the original rafters. We were delighted to find the whole of this little place set up as a hostel for those who love to walk about our incomparable English countryside. One room was a kitchen, another a bedroom, and the chapel itself was a most attractive lounge.

Nearly 800 years ago Bishop Henry of Blois gave land here to the Knights Hospitallers, but it was not until about 1360 that they set up this building for the management of their estate. It has changed little since that pathetic day when the knights deserted Godsfield and moved to North Baddesley, bidding it farewell and leaving it forlorn on its green hill, never again to be the home of prayer and praise. The lower room of the house has two pointed doorways, and both rooms have wide fireplaces and windows looking out on woods and fields. In the upper room is a peephole from which we look through to the chapel. Perhaps this was the priest's room, or perhaps the hospital: in either case the peephole was to give a glimpse of the altar down below.

It is dramatic to think that something from this altar may still be seen, for here a great discovery was made and a treasure found which is now in the Victoria and Albert at South Kensington. A labourer working at a hedge felt his billhook strike hard metal, and found a round bronze box and its domed and decorated cover. It was a holy pyx, the casket in which the Host was kept after consecration; Godsfield had yielded up its sacred memory after many centuries.

So we have a glimpse of this long lost gem, a jewel sparkling on this altar 500 years ago. It is one of the best examples of the beautiful work of 14th century craftsmen South Kensington has. Not far from the farm which has these memories is the ancient earthwork called Oliver's Battery.

In Three Chapters

GOODWORTH CLATFORD. Three great chapters of our Island Story it brings to mind. One is of the days when the Conqueror's men and the English builders after them were raising our noble heritage of church architecture. Here are two arcades, one as the 14th century builders left it with two weird faces on a pillar, the other with Norman piers and 13th century arches resting on them. Beautifully decorated are these Norman capitals, and one of the arches is outlined in familiar ornament. The Normans made the font, the chancel is 13th century, the tower with its comic gargoyles is 13th or 14th, and the sedilia are 15th. The nave has a kingpost roof of old dark beams, and on the wall are two fine pictures: Our Lord and the Sinful Woman, and a scene of Bethlehem.

The second chapter is brought to mind by the great beech avenue of Red Rice House, which was planted to mark the Battle of Malplaquet. It was one of those battles of which Southey was thinking when he wrote the lines that are so familiar to us all:

Pray tell us all about the war,
And what they fought each other for,

and the result of it was the capture of Mons from the French at the cost of 30,000 lives.

The third chapter comes to mind at the sight of a plain wooden cross which still had the soil of Flanders clinging to it when we called. It hangs near the roll of honour, and was brought from the grave of Sergeant Charles Tilley of Clatford, one of the eight men of this village whose names live for evermore, with the screen under the tower as the memorial.

The Storehouse of the Navy

GOSPORT. As the crowded ferry boat leaves Portsmouth the broken line of Gosport roofs is uplifted above the dancing waters of the harbour. In front are moored luxurious white steam yachts and sailing yachts with tall spars, and on either side of Gosport pier is the yard where the yachts were built and where the sails are made for all the big racing cutters of the world. Two of the Shamrocks were born here.

Gosport, we may almost say, floats on its yachts, for it has a sailing lake where the model yachts of the world meet in international encounter. But it is also the Stores of the Navy. Everything the navy needs is stored in the Victualling Yard. From Nicholson's Yard the shore goes round to Blockhouse Point, now a submarine base, and then, with as pretty a background as Gosport has to show, passes over a bridge, still levying a toll, to old Haslar Hospital, the Sick Bay of the navy, built in the 18th century. It is entered through a pair of handsome gates.

This is Gosport in its most attractive guise, for most of it is far from glorious. Among some of the poor old houses, yet surrounded by fine trees and with a lime avenue to its gate, is Holy Trinity church, built of red brick in 1696 when Dutch William had come to replace the Stuarts. Its bell tower of the last century stands four feet from the wall. About that time its interior was so remodelled as to leave little of the 17th century atmosphere. But the church has two distinctions that it retains; it has timber arcades which the eye can hardly believe, and it has an organ on which Handel played. His master hand rested on these pipes and flute stops when he was organist to the Duke of Chandos. The organ was in the private chapel of the Duke at Little Stanmore, in Middlesex, and there Handel composed or first performed his oratorio of Esther. When the duke died, Gosport, with rare intuition, bought the organ for £117, and so acquired the memory of the birth of these immortal chords. As for the timber arcades, they are these 14 round white columns that give such a striking aspect to the nave. Actually they are painted oak, being 14 trunks made from trees grown at Farnham Castle and given by Peter Mews, the great Bishop of Winchester at the time of the building of the church. The chancel screen, iron on an alabaster base, was designed by Sir Arthur Blomfield. Whatever else the 17th century church has lost it has kept from the beginning its altar silver, a chalice, a paten, two flagons, and an almsdish.

These are traditions of the town's middle age, and it has others. Where Nicholson's Yard stands on the beach was once the old fort where the Parliamentary guns were planted to bombard Portsmouth in the siege of 1642. At that time iron chains stretched from Block-house Point to a round tower on the Portsmouth side of the harbour. The last time the chains were tightened was in 1778, during the American War when a French fleet was sighted off Plymouth.

Somewhere among these Gosport byways Henry Cort of Lancaster set up his forge and mill for iron puddling. His experiments gave a tremendous impetus to the iron industry. In 1740, the year he was born, we produced 48,000 tons of pig iron; he died in 1800, a poor brokenhearted old man, but in 1884 we were producing eight million tons, all owing to his invention. There is a tribute to his work in a sculptured panel over the entrance to the public library and secondary school, a fine block of buildings. The panel is one of three and represents the work of Henry Cort, the other two showing the landing of Henry of Blois, and Lady Alwara, who gave all her possessions to the church at Alverstoke.

Old Glass

GRATELEY. The chief pride of this enchanting village is the beautiful 13th century glass in its small church, with a nave of the 12th century and a chancel of the 15th. There are only fragments, but they are in wonderful deep blues and glowing reds and golds, the best piece being a medallion in the nave showing the martyrdom of Stephen. In the centre lancet over the altar is part of the figure of the Archangel Gabriel. The glass was rescued by some forgotten lover of beauty when the destroyer Wyatt was restoring Salisbury Cathedral. Some of the old glass has been found in our time and fragments are now brightening Grateley's little church. The font is ancient, and stands on a stone said to have been the base of a cross, while the font itself may be of Roman origin and possibly recut. The group of three coloured figures forming the rood is a lovely tribute given to the father of a family in 1934.

The bells in the old tower have been ringing since Shakespeare's day. The ancient silver chalice is thought to have been made by a local craftsman. A bracket for an hourglass is fixed by the ancient window that lights the pulpit.

Near the church is a dovecot, and an old manor house now a farm, with its Tudor barn still left; but not far from the village was discovered a ruined house compared with which a Tudor barn is a mushroom. It had a tessellated pavement and a well, and belonged to a family living here when the village was an important station on the Roman highway, running straight as a die from Silchester to Sarum. From Quarley Hill, topped by a prehistoric camp hidden by beeches, both these places can be seen on a clear day.

Long after the Romans left it Grateley was important, for in Saxon times a Parliament was held here by King Athelstan.

Dame Caryll in Her Solitude

GREATHAM. Its old shrine is all but forsaken, the scene of its joys and sorrows for more than 600 years. The broken walls of the nave were richly clothed in nature's green when we called, as if to heal their wounds. Across the road the village has a handsome modern church, but the 13th century chancel of the ruined church, though seldom used, still has its 17th century altar and its old altar rails; and, lying in magnificent solitude in this deserted sanctuary, is Dame Caryll in alabaster on a splendid panelled tomb. The great hollow yew outside would be a sturdy youngster when they laid her here in Charles Stuart's days.

A little way off is Longmoor Camp, where officers and men of the regular army are trained in railway transport. An old forage barn has been adapted as the garrison church, and five windows have been presented to it by the four railway companies and London Transport, in memory of the men of the Railway Troops who fell in the Great War. The windows are the work of Mr Martin Travers and are exceedingly attractive. The L.M.S. is suggested by St Mungo, patron saint of Glasgow, and St Alban; the G.W.R. by St David and St George; the L.N.E.R. by St. Andrew and St Peter; and the Southern Railway by St Augustine and the cathedrals of Salisbury, Chichester, and Canterbury. The Transport Board is represented by St Paul and St Edward, with the coats-of-arms of the 12 counties which the board's vehicles cover.

The Old Roodloft

GREYWELL. Many of its houses might have come straight from a fairy story. They bulge out, they lean over, and still the old timbers somehow manage to hold them up. The church (which has kept five of its consecration crosses) is small, but, like the rich young ruler, it has great possessions: a silver chalice from Elizabethan England, a bell which has been ringing from its wooden turret since the Wars of the Roses, a font 500 years old, a doorway much patched since the Normans made it, a dwarf 13th century chancel arch, and something which only one other village in Hampshire has, a roodloft that survived the Reformation. The screen and the loft and the turret stairs leading to it, all 15th or 16th century, were quite new when the Reformation came and carved figures of Calvary were taken from such lofts and thrown out of the churches. Many of the lofts disappeared at the same time, but on the top of this screen is a perfect panelled alcove, the panelling of the six-feet wide roodloft continuing up the walls and arching over the roof. The choir would sing from here on special occasions, and later it became the men's gallery. Up to 1870 the men used to sit up here, but then the screen, with its lower panels cut out, was raised on a stone base, and no longer could the loft be reached by the turret stairs.

King Cerdic

HALE. It looks down from a hill above the Avon a little way from the ford named Charford after Cerdic who set up here as a Saxon king on winning a famous victory over the Britons. Its church is tucked away below the manor house in Hale Park, which has two lovely avenues of limes and chestnuts. The church was built when few were being built in England (in 1715), and on the floor is a beautiful heraldic brass to Sir John Penruddocke, who died in 1600. In one of the transepts are three 18th century monuments. A huge marble statue of Thomas Archer shows him in classical costume reclining on some books, with a woman holding a skull and another a book. A white urn and pedestal by Richard Westmacott, with rams at the corners, is to Joseph May and his mother, who died within a few weeks of him in 1796; and beside it is a wall-monument of a woman with a sorrowful and beautiful face, letting fall a flaming torch against an urn, on the base of which is a fine medallion portrait of Henry Archer in wig and cravat. The font may be Norman.

The Home of the Good Ship Mercury

HAMBLE. Here where the River Hamble (ten miles long and dotted with pleasure craft) slips down into Southampton Water with the tide, was the landing-place of many an enemy of England, from Saxons who gained their first foothold on the southern shore to Frenchmen who raided and burnt, and, last scene of all, to Frenchmen of a later day who were brought here as prisoners of war.

Turn back the pages of the history book where each leaf is a century, and see first the yellow-haired Saxons who came with Cerdic and Cymric in 495, landing on the beach of the country they were to make the new England. Another page, and the warring Jutes follow hem in 514, and after them the longships of the Danes thrust their beaks in the sandy estuary and land the ruthless pirates who carry death and terror to the defences of Winchester. Other pages still, and the French come in 1377 to raid this village which hides so peacefully behind its sheltering trees.

Peace came to it long ago, when the Benedictines built their priory on the rising ground above the common, where now the church is the only fragment remaining of their piety. William of Wykeham rebuilt in the 15th century the priory founded in 1109, and traces of both builders are plainly seen. The long narrow nave of the church has a fine Norman doorway with round columns and zigzag, and there is a Norman arch in the south wall which led to the priory with the remains of another facing it. The east window and the double piscina, enriched with a carved canopy, are the work of master masons of the 14th century.

Highclere   19th Century Castle

Titchfield   The Abbey Gatehouse

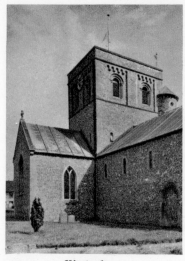

Kingsclere

Crondall

Avington

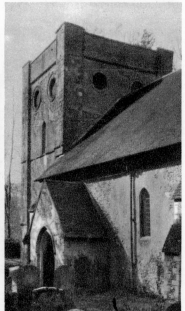

Warnford

FOUR HAMPSHIRE CHURCHES

The high tower begins as Norman and ends with William of Wykeham's work. It has a bell which can count five centuries of service. A younger bell has the name of James Bradley, lord of the manor, and another Bradley carved his name on one of the great beams of the barn close by. But there are other names carved there which tell a more significant tale. They are those of exiles cut deep in one of the cross-beams high in the roof. An old Hamble man who lived nearly to this century had the tale from his father of how they came to be there. He could remember seeing 2000 French prisoners landed at Hamble and marched to the barn. Some of them swarmed up the posts and sat astride the cross-beams. There Jacques and Pierre and Jean and the rest cut their names in the hungry intervals of waiting before they were marched off to prisons.

Two of Hamble's old houses have much interest. One is 16th century, known as the Gun House, perhaps because it has cannon buried by the door; the Olde House is much older and has a 12th century doorknocker.

On the common is an earthwork which is said to have been a promontory fortress. Another fortress which can be seen when the tide is out was built by Henry the Eighth as one of his coast defences.

Raider, pirate, scholar, saint, and prisoner have all known Hamble, some too well. Today the aeroplanes which circle over it all day are the only reminder of war's alarms. It is said that in the mud of the tidal river lies embedded a Danish ship which came sailing up against the England of King Alfred, and in the estuary is Commander C. B. Fry's ship Mercury, on which boys are trained to be good sailors and worthy Englishmen.

The great grey ship swings at anchor in midstream in the Hamble river, a waterway on whose green banks are trees and a village or two devoting most of their energies to the care of and building of pleasure craft. She is the successor to a graceful three-masted ship which began life as a tea-clipper in the African trade, became a training ship, and sank at sea after being bought for service in the war.

The business of the Mercury is to fit boys for the sea life they wish to follow. Its name is known and honoured in the navy and the merchant service, for her record is a fine one and many of the lads who began life on the lower decks with their Mercury training fresh in their spirits have attained not only to Masterships in the merchant service and to responsible non-commissioned ranks in the navy, but to the quarter deck itself.

The reason for this honourable record is not far to seek. Those responsible for the actual training of the boys are convinced, as was the founder, that to be of true service to his country a man must be master of himself and must develop all that is best in his nature to the utmost of his power. Thus the basis of the training is religious, and every gift for beauty that a boy may possess, such as love of poetry or an aptitude for drawing, is encouraged directly it is perceived. Music is particularly fostered, and is taught by a master who has been making Mercury musicians for nearly fifty years. To boys who at the end of their training have found themselves debarred by some physical misfortune, such as colour blindness, from following the career on which they had set their hearts, this musical education has proved a great blessing. They have been able to enter bands in the navy, army, and air force and many have become bandmasters.

The Mercury owed its beginning to Charles Arthur Hoare, whose generosity provided a ship, shore establishment, and plant, and who paid for their upkeep for 23 years. After his death in 1908 the fate of the Mercury hung in the balance but, thanks to the courage of Commander C. B. Fry, the famous cricketer, it was saved. He was given permission to run the ship for two years and was promised that if he carried on successfully it should not come to an end but be made an Educational Foundation. The Commander and his wife succeeded in making those two years worthy of Mercury tradition, and it is due to their devotion and courage that the Mercury is still providing British shipping with some of the best of its personnel.

Today this great ship where the boys sleep at night, and where they practise gunnery, lies in the Hamble, and on the banks above are their church, their beautiful little theatre, their fine playing-fields, and the building wherein are airy schoolrooms, a messroom where every table has its flowers, and a recreation room made beautiful with panels painted by a gifted artist.

Commander Fry long served his country by his example on the playing-field; here he has served her longer still by his exertions.

The Lusty Fellows of Broadhalfpenny Down

HAMBLEDON. It is charm itself; very old and very beautiful is this village sheltering under great hills protected by deep woods. It has a big yew, a ruined windmill, fragments of Saxon England, and a noble piece of Norman England; and it has a warm place in the heart of every Englishman. For Hambledon is the home of the game of games, Cricket.

While our army was fighting the American colonists Hambledon was fighting nobler battles in its fields. The Hambledon Eleven won fame on the top of Broadhalfpenny Down, having been born in the little brick inn, whose landlord, Richard Nyren, made the club, and whose son John became its historian. The Bat and Ball Inn still bears its old name, and its sign still speaks of Hambledon delight, for on one side is painted a batsman and bowler of the 18th century, and on the other Richard Nyren is still smiling. There were some queer names in his Eleven—Aburrow, Leer, Lumpy, and Hogsflesh. They were lusty fellows and gallantly they played on Broadhalfpenny Down and on Windmill Hill.

Opposite the inn is a granite obelisk on which are two bats, a ball, and stumps marking the site of the pitch of the cricket club from 1750 to 1787. It was unveiled in 1908 when 5000 people came to see a match here after an interval of a hundred years.

The nave of the church was once a Saxon place of worship. The Normans came and enlarged the tiny building, cutting arches in the walls and adding aisles. The Saxon strips are still seen at the west end of the north aisle and there are some mason's marks; but far more beautiful is the exquisite and delicate sculpture of the four Norman arches, the loveliest things in this most lovely village. Two consecration crosses have survived on the church walls, and there is a mass dial from the days before clocks.

We are surprised to see, high up on the wall, a piscina out of reach; then we notice a timber ledge, a window, and a narrow archway. We are looking up into what was once a hermit's room; there is still to be seen the stone spout for carrying away the water when the hermit scrubbed his cell. The tower of the church was built in Tudor days, and from the same days comes the magnificently carved pulpit, with its plain steps going up in a low and beautiful curve. There is a richly carved old chair in the sanctuary, and the names of 33 Hambledon heroes are on a piece of wood from HMS Britannia, the Dartmouth training ship.

Under the tower is a tall stone with the name of Symonds. The family still holds a bowl given by Charles the Second to a tipsy host who gave him lodging for the night. In the days when Charles was being hunted he hid about these wooded uplands, and was brought by Colonel Gunter to the Hambledon house of the colonel's drunken brother-in-law Symonds, who came home finding the colonel in his house with "some Roundheaded rogue's son," he would be bound.

Here Cricket was Born

IT would take a great deal of writing to prove the statement that cricket was born at Hambledon. Nowhere can the eternal principle of evolution be seen more clearly than in that noblest of games, and cricket of a sort has been played in England for 600 years. The first formal rules for playing the game, in essence amazingly like the present rules, were made by the London Club, playing on the Artillery Ground at Finsbury, before the Hambledon Club was formed. How then can Hambledon be said to have given it birth?

The answer is that the game of the older centuries had been a crude beginning, a vulgar game of a scratch character; but it kept on evolving, notwithstanding legal persecution for playing it, with a penalty of two years of imprisonment and a £10 fine, and it emerged, shortly before the Hambledon Club was formed, as "a legal and very manly game, not bad in itself, but only in the ill use made of it by *betting more than ten pounds on it*."

People who play on village greens have not ten pounds to bet with, and the legal decision just quoted shows that when that decision was given (1748) cricket had become a game that was attracting the attention of the well-to-do, and was being betted on in an age eager to bet on anything. Now of all popular sports cricket is the least betted on. It has passed through that stage. The moneyed sportsmen of the mid-eighteenth century picked their players, some of them playing themselves, and played their matches for heavy stakes. But as the rules of the game were fixed, and local play was organised, the game itself proved so inherently interesting that victory by skill became a sufficient reward. Cricket itself triumphed. It cast off the lure of betting. Honourable competition sufficed. The game was the thing that mattered. Club met club. Teams were formed from all England. Play became nationalised.

And this is where Hambledon comes in. It was the pivot point on which this purifying change turned. Rural Hambledon, in a remote part of Hampshire, had a local team which could and did challenge and beat, again and again, teams picked from the whole of England. From Hambledon came the impulse that made cricket the purest and most honourable and most English of all games, and in that sense modern cricket was born there.

The Saxon Builders

HANNINGTON. One of the far-away places high on the downs, it takes us back a thousand years, for here we see the fine workmanship of the Saxons still strong and true. It is at one of the corners of the church (on the left of the porch), where the stones are laid in the long-and-short manner of the Saxons. The chancel arch, with a peephole beside it, was built by 12th century men, and so were two of the arches in the nave. The lovely little pulpit was carved 300 years ago; the graceful chalice is older still; the reredos is a piece of old panelling; and there still ring out from the tiled and shingled spire three 17th century bells. We noticed that some of the pillars here are of solid chalk, with little crosses on them.

The village has a pond, a roofed well, and several old houses.

The Village Thankful

HARBRIDGE. A score of tiny streams meander between the low-lying meadows of the Avon, a tapestry of green shot in due season with the gold of cuckoo flowers and kingcups. Beyond stands the battlemented church tower with its graceful little corner turret. The church was made new a century ago by the Earl of Normanton, and the older part of the tower in grey stone contrasts delightfully with its new brown and grey. There is an imposing wall-monument to the memory of an Earl of Normanton who died in 1868, his wife, and their youngest son "who fell at Sebastopol and was buried on the hill fronting his division, where his comrades erected a tomb." Four windows in memory of the countess in 1855 have a series of medallions picturing scenes from the life of Our Lord. A touching inscription on the peace memorial records the names of four men who fell and "thankfulness to God for the return of 52 men, none of them blind or maimed." There is a lovely bit of colour on the wall in a 17th century coat-of-arms.

An avenue near the church leads to Somerley, the home of the Earls of Normanton, beside the Avon in a splendid park of eight hundred acres. The great house had, when we called, fine paintings by Sir Joshua Reynolds and an organ worked by water-power.

HARTLEY MAUDITT. Its wide pond keeps lonely company with its church, of which the nave walls and the chancel arch were built by the Normans. The beautifully decorated doorway, with its deep mouldings, was fashioned when the Norman style was passing away. There are two rows of ancient tiles in the floor of the 13th century chancel, and a handsome 15th century font carved with flowers, window tracery, and a horseshoe. In the chancel are several 17th century heraldic memorials to the Stuart family, and in the nave is a simple tablet to Thomas Lightharness, who was for 25 years servant to Sir Nicholas Stuart. One of the windows is a tribute to an old lady who died in 1908, Emily Plummer. It has two figures, one an attractive Madonna in blue.

John Keate of Eton

HARTLEY WESPALL. Reached by lovely lanes, Hartley Wespall has an old church like no other in Hampshire; its west wall has a bold pattern made of mighty timbers black with age. The high-pitched roof rests on moulded timber pillars felled in the 14th century. The handsome pulpit is Jacobean, and there is an attractive screen crowned by a crucifix. Two of the bells were ringing when the first English books were printing. The curious will be drawn to a touch of grimness and beauty on one of the walls, a lady and a skeleton. She is Abigail, Lady Somerton, who died in 1692 and has a fine monument with her portrait, two charming little boys weeping at the sides, and a leering skeleton with folded arms at the base. On the wall we read of two brother captains killed in the war, one of them, Robert Durnford, laid to rest in Persia after he had won the DSO. In the chancel lies a remarkable man who was rector and schoolmaster here about 25 years, John Keate.

Son of a parson-schoolmaster, he was born at Wells in 1773, and, entering Eton at 11, passed to Cambridge at 18. A distinguished classical scholar, he gained a fellowship, took orders, and at 24 returned to Eton as assistant-master.

The school was a hotbed of turbulence and disorder. Boys gambled, drank in public-houses, went to dog-fights and cock-fights, poached, and smuggled drink into school. There were eight or nine masters for 500 boys, and Keate was responsible, during his early years, for the control of 170 boisterous scholars. In 1809 he was elected headmaster, and in that capacity he trained some of the most famous men of the age; yet he scorned mathematics, and under him history, English literature, science, and geography (except so far as it bore on the classics) were unknown. Yet in spite of his curriculum Keate was one of the greatest masters Eton ever had.

It was said of him that he flogged "half the ministers, bishops, generals, and dukes" of the century. He was faced by organised defiance and hooliganism, which found expression in rowdy choruses during lessons, in the smashing of his desk, in a fusillade of bad eggs, stone-throwing, and persistent insubordination.

Keate was a midget of five feet, but, as one of his pupils said, in him was concentrated the pluck of ten battalions, and twice he suppressed formidable rebellions. One day he birched 72 boys, on another 100. Once, mistaking the list of candidates for confirmation for the usual roll of offenders, he flogged the lot, and became all the more furious in face of explanations. In spite of his severity he was as a rule just, and was beloved even by those he birched. Retiring from Eton after fruitful service, he came here as rector in 1824, and proved an ideal parson. Towards the close of his life one of his old pupils found him on the rectory lawn, an old man with his coat off, playing cricket with little boys and girls, and exclaiming to his wife, "Mrs Keate, that's not fair—petticoat before wicket!"

One of Our Worst Generals

HARTLEY WINTNEY. The trees that were being planted when William Cobbett rode by in 1821 are flourishing on the green. He put down in his diary that it was impossible to overpraise the act of Lady Mildmay in planting them. The village has a new church with attractive coloured windows in the chancel, and with a dignified peace memorial chapel whose panelled walls bear the names of those who died for us. Each name has a panel of its own, and tragic it is to read of all those corners of a foreign field that are for ever England. Three men, we noticed, died at Jutland, two of them in the tragedy of the sinking of the Black Prince, and two others died with Lord Kitchener in the Hampshire. To France and Mesopotamia and the Dardanelles they went from this little place, and honoured among them is the name of Emily Judd, a munition worker.

A tablet on the wall, put here in 1932, has a moving story to tell; it is a tribute to the beautiful and courageous life of Catherine Alice Griffith, who, though herself an invalid with failing sight, devoted her life to the blind.

The new church has put the old one out of action except for funerals, but the old church is a place to see. It stands away from the village in a beautifully planted churchyard with fine views of woodlands and distant hills. Both nave and chancel have 14th and 15th century work in them, and the doorway is about 700 years old. There is a Norman piscina on a slender pillar, with a head carved on its basin; there are carved and twisted altar rails from the 18th century; and there is an ancient ironbound chest.

The old priory on Wintney Moor has vanished and left no trace, but standing where it stood is a huge 16th century barn, and a smaller brick and timber building built about the same time.

A brick house with lions on the gateposts is the house Hangman Hawley built. He was one of the men who are best forgotten, of whom Wolfe of Quebec wrote that the troops dreaded his severity, hated the man, and held his military knowledge in contempt. He left a will revealing to the world the meanness of his spirit, and ordered that his carcase should be put anywhere with no more fuss than if a poor soldier were being buried. A poor soldier indeed, a poor man, one of the worst generals our Army has known.

Parchment for the World

HAVANT. It has lost one of the most interesting little trades in England, which was carried on here for about a thousand years. We found sheepskins hanging here in one of the little streets outside the place where it was turned into some of the best parchment in the world. What precious documents have gone about the earth on parchment made in Havant no man knows; they must be found in safes and strong-rooms, in Parliaments and palaces, and in archives everywhere. Now, we understand, this little industry is at an end in Havant.

This busy little town overlooking Langston Harbour sets us thinking of invasions, of two that happened and one that did not, for we find here, in its church, memories of the Roman invaders who came to stay 400 years, the Norman invaders who welded us into a nation, and the Napoleon invaders with whom something went wrong. It is the church which reminds us of Rome, for it has been found that these mighty Norman piers supporting the tower are resting on Roman concrete. Here must have stood a Saxon church, and before it must have stood a Roman building. We are in the presence of the Romans, the Saxons, and the Normans on this spot.

It would seem that all our great centuries have left their mark on this place, for the tower piers are 12th century, the chancel 13th, the vestry 14th, and the stair turret of the tower 15th; the registers begin with the 17th, a bell has been ringing since the 18th, and the nave was made new in the 19th. There is a Norman window still left in one of the transepts, and both transepts are unusual in having aisles; the north is the original transept of the 15th century, the south is a copy. The chancel also is curious for having a vaulted roof of chalk, which has not crumbled in 700 years.

In his old chancel lies Thomas Aileward, who was preaching here in William of Wykeham's day. He would talk over William's plans for Winchester with him for rebuilding the nave and founding the school, for he was the great bishop's secretary. His brass portrait is in the chancel floor, and from it we imagine him an honest, pleasant-faced man in a cope decorated with roses, lilies, wheat sheaves, and lions.

The tower, resting in its Roman bed, has a bell which has had a great adventure. It was cast in 1714 and came to Havant by road in the days when a horse with a post-chaise was the fastest means of transport, when people travelled by daylight for fear of lurking highwaymen. In 1930 the bell needed attention and was sent away to be recast. It left the dimness of the tower to find an England utterly changed; it travelled in a noisy horseless carriage at a breakneck speed, passing hardly a horse on the road. It was recast and sent down to Havant again, and here it swings, dreaming of the different Englands it has known. Under it is a flag of the volunteers who banded themselves together in Havant to resist Napoleon when the mothers of England were fearing for their little ones because men said the French monster ate little children.

By the 19th century font is an old piece of carved stone set in the wall, seeming to be a fragment from a Norman font. It has a curious decoration of something like a leopard between two rosettes. The lady chapel, in the south transept, separated from the chancel by a carved oak screen matching the altar and the reredos, has a stone figure of the Madonna with the Child, and a pillar piscina in memory of Elizabeth Richardson and her son, a naval captain.

The Alabaster Panel

HAWKLEY. It lies in a valley near Gilbert White's Selborne, its church and many of its houses looking on to a pleasant green. Beyond them are green slopes and a tree-clad cliff called Hawkley Hanger, the scene of a landslip in 1764 described by Gilbert White. William Cobbett climbed it in 1822. The new church was built on the site of the old one, with all its windows and arches in Norman style and richly decorated. Its most striking feature is the tall tower with a round staircase turret and a steep four-gabled cap, reminding us of the Saxon tower at Sompting in Sussex. Its greatest treasures are a font 700 years old, four 15th century bells, and a 15th century alabaster panel of the Betrayal of Jesus, with eight figures (including Peter with his sword and a fallen Roman soldier) all beautifully sculptured. It is a splendid piece of medieval art.

The Island Older than History

HAYLING ISLAND. It is a little island older than History, four miles long with but ten square miles in all, yet with much that stirs the mind of an Englishman, for it is full of wonder. It has an earthwork which may have been thrown up in the days before Christianity and moated in some later day—Tournebury. It has a living yew tree which may have been here when the Conqueror came. It has a font at which children may have been christened in Saxon days. It has bells which have been ringing for about 600 years. It has dials which have been telling the time since the days before clocks. Rich indeed is this small place, a veritable treasure island in itself, with two churches which have seen the centuries go by and kept something from many of them.

St Peter's of North Hayling welcomes us with a solid timber porch made by 15th century men, and lets us in by a medieval door with long hinges. The doorway itself has small crosses probably cut in the stone by pilgrims. Inside is a simple 12th century arcade; altar rails 300 years old; four poppyhead benches probably made in the 14th century; a font carved 700 years ago; two 17th century chests,

15th century roof beams, and, up a short stair through an ancient timber doorway, three wonderful old bells still hanging in their original frames, where they have been ringing since about 1350, a marvellous musical trio. There are very few of our English churches with three bells so old still ringing. Among the many wall-memorials is one of Sarah Rogers who died in 1812; it has an endearing little seraph and this pathetic epitaph:

> *Ye virgins fair, your fading charms survey,*
> *She was what'er your tender hearts can say.*
> *Let opening roses, drooping lilies, tell,*
> *Like these she bloomed, and ah! like these she fell.*

In the graveyard is a row of stones marking the graves of others of her family. Thomas Rogers, who died in 1791, has a beautifully carved wheatsheaf on his; John who died in 1808 has the oddest imaginable pair of weeping figures, a classically clad woman and a man in a tall hat and mourning streamers. Over these graves falls the shadow of a yew 19 ft round and perhaps 500 years old; and on the walls of the church those who search diligently will find two little sundials older still pricked in the stone.

But Old Yew has a neighbour which must make it feel young, the wonder of St Mary's of South Hayling. It is a living giant guarding the spacious timber porch, a mighty yew which must surely be the oldest in Hampshire, for it is no less than 34 feet round, and we imagine that it is well on its way to its millennium, much older than the 15th century porch or the 13th century church. Nobody knows how old it is, but it must surely have been here when the Conqueror came. An iron railing protects its great trunk, and some of its huge branches are borne on timber props.

St Mary's, built by 13th century men who may have sat eating their frugal meal by this old tree, has a clerestoried nave. The central tower arches and the nave arcades rest on pillars with capitals and bases rich in masterly carving, with all kinds of leaves, battling dragons, and heads of kings and bishops. The 12th century font has two faces carved on it. The lancets of the east window are filled with beautiful figures of saints. Near the pulpit is a marvellous stone bowl which is claimed as either a washing bowl or the Saxon font of the island's first church. It was dug up in a field and rescued by a vicar of Hayling. Its rim has been greatly damaged in the course of its adventures, but the remarkable design running round it is plain. The church has three small sundials like those of St Peter's, and the old stocks are by the lychgate.

Here Before the Conqueror

HEADBOURNE WORTHY. Almost within sound of Winchester, separated from the road by a brook, is one of the oldest churches in Hampshire, here before the Conqueror landed at Hastings. It has its Saxon witnesses inside and out. On the outer walls are the narrow pilaster strips of these old masons, keeping company with much younger buttresses and windows, one buttress being hollowed so that we may see the Saxon long-and-short work in the wall.

Inside, in a room built on to the end of the church in the 15th century, are the remains of what must have been a noble work of art when the sculptor stepped back to look at it a thousand years ago. It is on the wall above a perfect little Saxon doorway, a sculpture of the Crucifixion whose figures were destroyed by order of a Bishop of Winchester soon after the Reformation. So battered are they now that hardly more than their shadowy outline can still be seen, yet it is thought that in medieval times this two-storeyed room was built to preserve their sanctity, and to save them from the wind and rain that had already beaten against them for 500 years. On the floor of this room are some medieval tiles and in one of the windows is a 15th century portrait of St Matthew brought from a Devon village.

The 13th century gave the church its plain font, the sedilia, and a tall piscina with a lovely canopy. In the chancel are three stone seats at least 500 years old, and a window of which the lower part was once unglazed and closed with a wooden shutter. On the wall is the brass portrait of a 15th century scholar, a Winchester boy wearing the long and simple gown of the school of his time, and standing with joined hands, a flame-like scroll issuing from his lips with the words "I will sing of the mercies of the Lord forever." Below is an inscription telling us that he is John Kent, who went to Winchester School in 1431 and died there in 1434. An attractive modern brass portrait shows a naval officer's wife of the 19th century. The church (which has a mass dial for telling the time in the days before clocks) has two bells which have come down from about 1380 and one made about 1420, so that it possesses some of the oldest of Hampshire's iron singers. The very original modern pulpit, with its two carved heads and delicate tracery, is the beautiful work of John Henry Slessor, who was rector 44 years.

In the graveyard, among lawns like velvet in front of the chancel, is the plain table tomb of Joseph Bingham, a fine old scholar of Stuart days who made a name for himself by his book on Christian Antiquities. He was sometime rector here and was ruined by the South Sea Bubble, the forerunner of the huge financial swindles of later times, in which financiers took over part of the national debt, forced £100 shares up to £1000, and ruined vast numbers of people.

HEADLEY. It is in a little realm of pine trees, and its church, though much rebuilt, still has a stalwart medieval tower looking across the fields near the Surrey and Sussex borders. It has a great array of smart oak pews, but as token of its antiquity it has preserved a panel of 13th century glass showing a saint kneeling for execution, some Elizabethan altar plate, and brasses of an unknown couple in the costume they wore in 1510.

Anthony Trollope's Mother

HECKFIELD. It has a place all its own for its quiet charm, and it comes into books as the birthplace of Frances Milton, who married a Mr Trollope and became the mother of the famous Anthony, whose peaceful tales of Barchester delighted a great number of people in his day. There was nothing peaceful about Mrs Trollope's life. Her rather eccentric husband sent her off with three children to start a store in Cincinnati. It failed, and Mrs Trollope took up her pen to retrieve their fallen fortunes, writing many books that have been forgotten.

The church, with a 16th century tower, has something from most of our building centuries. It has one of the old crusading chests, a small plain chest with a slot in the lid through which people would drop coins for the next Crusade; it may be 700 years old. It has a beautifully sculptured font of the 14th century, some walls of the 15th, and an Elizabethan chalice and paten. It has some benches and a brass portrait of the 16th century, the brass showing Elizabeth Hall in a long dress: her husband built the chapel, in which was an ancient helmet when we called. There are several sculptures of people who died when Shakespeare was spending his last days by the Avon. One is Henry Tomworthe, who kneels at a desk dressed in a black gown and a ruff. Another is the monument set up in 1609 by Prudence Humfry to her most dear husband and parents and children, showing them all at prayer in their black clothes. A third shows Thomas Creswell on his knees with his two wives and ten children, one a baby. An 18th century heraldic monument is to Anthony Sturt, and there is a 19th century brass inscription to Lord Eversley, who was Speaker of the House of Commons and died here; he built in the village the almshouses his wife had planned before she passed away.

Heckfield came into history in 1940 as the scene of the passing from this world of Mr Neville Chamberlain. He had been Prime Minister at the outbreak of the Hitler War, and in broadcasting to the nation that we were at war with Germany he declared that on that sad day everything he had worked for, hoped for, and believed in, had crashed into ruins, adding: "I cannot tell what part I may be allowed to play myself". He played his part for twelve months like an English gentleman and a brave statesman; then, having already surrendered the Premiership to Mr Churchill, he resigned on the breakdown of his health, and a few weeks later died at Heckfield.

The Stately Avenues

HERRIARD. It is simplicity itself, but with the noblest of approaches. Scarcely a road is without its avenue of stately trees, and grandest of all are the beeches across Weston Common, a green nave nearly two miles long. A Queen Anne manor house stretches its parkland round the church, which, though refashioned, has kept through the centuries some of its consecration crosses and its ancient mass clocks. It has a narrow doorway with carved arch and leafy capitals and a splendid wide chancel arch with row upon row of moulding, both 700 years old. In a window in the chancel a patchwork of ancient glass shows a golden-haired saint with a crown on her head and the King of Beasts crouched at her feet with a kindly countenance. The organ fits into a pew screen made when Charles Stuart was king.

Defender of the Seven Bishops

HIGHCLERE. Proud of the park, which it declares to be the loveliest in southern England, with trees and lakes and the timbered beauty of Sidown Hill 872 feet high, it was for generations one of the country seats of the Bishops of Winchester, and its 19th century castle is now the seat of the Earl of Carnarvon. The great William of Wykeham loved Highclere, and not until Edward the Sixth was king did the bishops lose it. One of its owners was Sir Robert Sawyer, who has a handsome monument on the chancel wall of the church built towards the end of his life when the old one was pulled down. Pepys tells us that he went to the House of Commons to see Sir Robert Sawyer taking part in an impeachment and was "glad to see him in so good a play." He was one of the most eloquent lawyers of his day. He appeared in a prosecution under Jeffreys before that name began to stink in men's nostrils. He prosecuted the Earl of Shaftesbury in 1681. He appeared against Algernon Sidney and the young John Hampden. He got Titus Oates convicted for perjury. He was bold enough to resist James the Second in seeking dictator powers, and he made England ring with his brilliant defence of the Seven Bishops, for which he took no fee. He moved a resolution in Parliament that it was inconsistent that a Protestant kingdom should have a Popish prince.

Sir Robert Sawyer's monument has a skull crowned with bays below a draped curtain. Another of these fashionable monuments, with a figure leaning on an urn, is by Roubiliac, in memory of an 18th century Bishop of Waterford; and a charming 18th century medallion is a tribute to William Coleman, who was, "as far as consistent with human imperfection, an Honest Man."

But for many the most exciting thing here will be the great tomb of Sir Richard Kingsmill, for this man's only child Constance married Sir Thomas Lucy of Charlecote, grandson of the man who drove Shakespeare to London. Sir Richard's epitaph tells of 25 years of faithful and honest service to his queen and informs us that he was a most worthy professor in common law. He lies full-length, clad in the black robes and cap of a Tudor magistrate. His son-in-law kneels at his head in armour, with Constance by his side, the monument being given, we read, "for the witnessing of their grateful minds towards him"; and kneeling below are six boys and four girls.

It was the fourth Earl of Carnarvon who built this church in 1870, and his memorial in it is a pair of windows showing a choir of angels, put here "by those most loving and most beloved by him."

A tablet on the wall tells us that he recovered the remains of a 17th century kinsman whose body had been torn from its grave in the French Revolution. He is buried in a chapel in the grounds. He lived a crowded public life which seems to have begun when he was seven, for at that early age he made a speech on kindness to animals. He was a great friend of imperial federation, and introduced the Confederation of Canada Act in 1867, introduced a Bill for the union of South Africa in 1877, and is said by Parnell to have proposed an Irish Parliament in 1866. This he denied, but what he certainly did propose was the setting-up of the Parnell Commission with its sensational consequences.

The Kaiser and His People

HIGHCLIFFE. It has a lovely golden coast, topped by fine trees and gorse-capped cliffs, with the Isle of Wight smiling across a changing sea, Hengistbury lying westward like a black sleeping whale, and the dimly distant Dorset headlands.

Here are the fine grounds of the magnificent Highcliffe Castle, a 19th century structure in which is some stone from a 15th century abbey on the winding River Seine above Rouen. The stones may well have been handled by men who saw Joan of Arc burned in Rouen marketplace. The castle is on the site of a house belonging to the third Earl of Bute, the unpopular Tory minister of George the Third. Bute retired to it after he had resigned the Premiership (the mob having repeatedly tried to burn down his London house), and he declared that a life on bread and water would be luxury compared with the life of a Prime Minister. The lodge gateway remains of the old house of those days.

We do not know how much History will say about the part this castle played in the events which led up to the Great War, but it comes into the story. In 1907 the Emperor William (the Kaiser of the war) rented the castle to recuperate, and spoke with great frankness to General Stuart-Wortley, his host. The General was so impressed with the fervour of the Kaiser's friendship for England that he asked the visitor's permission to publish their talk as an interview. The Kaiser was willing, a representative of the Daily Telegraph put the interview into proper form, and that paper published it to the world.

It created a great sensation; a very friendly feeling in this country but a feeling of sensational resentment in Germany, and in the end the Kaiser shrank before the storm, and the interview was officially denied, although it was perfectly true. It is significant that it was suppressed *but it was friendly to England*, and it remains for all time as a remarkable example of a sovereign made to lie to calm the passions of his people.

The church was built in 1843 by Lord Stuart of Rothesay, who built the castle. It has a bell from Russia which is said to contain a great quantity of silver. In the pulpit is old wood richly carved with fruit, foliage, cherubs, and a figure of Christ holding an orb. The massive old altar rails are richly carved with lions and foliage; as is also a table in the sanctuary, where there is an extraordinary old chair boldly carved with eagles and the figure of a man.

The Baby in Scarlet and Gold

HINTON AMPNER. From its hilltop it looks out to Gander Down, the Meon Valley, and Cheriton Field, where Waller defeated the Royalists in 1644 and 2000 Englishmen lie sleeping. The traces of Saxon walls have been made almost unrecognisable, but there is still a Saxon or Norman arch in which the vestry door has been opening and shutting since Nicholas Lacy gave it in 1643. The richly carved pulpit is a generation older. The chancel is full of the memorials of the Stewkleys, among them a splendid heraldic brass to Sir Hugh who died in 1642, and the marble monuments of two children. One is a baby wrapped in scarlet and gold who lived for a few of the first days of the 17th century; the other is a boy in long petticoats, lying on his back and looking towards some angels who appear through the clouds. One of the windows is to Bishop Wilberforce, and has in it the Good Shepherd. The bishop would come often to stay at Hinton House among the lofty beeches, the home of his friends the Duttons.

HOLYBOURNE. Were it not for the traffic which races through on its way to Portsmouth, we could wish that every other house here were ours, so charming are they. In one of them lived Mrs Gaskell, friend of the Brontës and author of Cranford ; her house is called The Lawn. The church by the pond has a Norman tower capped with a tiny spire, and on the sunny wall a mass dial for telling the time in the days before clocks. The five finely carved stone heads supporting the nave roof have been looking down for 700 years. In the tower is an ancient bell with a lion's head stamped on it. Justice, Charity, and Mercy are fine bold figures in the windows.

Forgotten Place

HORDLE. All that is old is far away, the little graveyard in which its old folk sleep. It lies by a Roman camp and near a modest farm on the road from Christchurch to Milford, ringed by trees and overgrown with brambles. It is a forgotten little place, its stones heeling sideways on their forsaken graves. Shouldering their way through the rough undergrowth are a few massive greywethers, mighty stones like those at Stonehenge, all that is left of the church the Saxons built, pulled down last century. Most of the stones were carted away but the great foundations remain for us to trace the outline of the shrine where bells once rang and voices sang in praise, and the voice of an old parson would say:

All flesh is as grass. The grass withereth, the flower falleth away, but the Word of the Lord endureth for ever.

The sea is eating away the cliff, and the life of Hordle with its modern church has sprung up farther inland; here now we come upon some old geologist, or those stirred by old memories. In the cliff below Hordle House is the famous Crocodile Bed in which we find remains of crocodiles and fish. The village is summoned to the new church by the bells from the old one.

The Epitaph From the Ring

HOUGHTON. It has piers and capitals in its church from the 12th century, and other old things to see. There are consecration crosses and mass clocks, two peepholes into the 13th century chancel, three simple piscinas, and two plain wooden stools on which coffins have been rested for many generations. A fine painting of Our Lord is believed to be by Francesco Albani, who was born at Bologna in 1578. Here in the 17th century John Stubbs was rector, and he lies in the graveyard with a curious epitaph. With him in the grave lies his wife, who followed him after 30 years of widowhood, and their stone tells us that their son restored her to him to fulfil the tender vow recorded in the elegant inscription on her wedding ring, in some of the tenderest words ever written:

Intreat me not to leave thee, or to return from following after thee, for where thou goest I will go, where thou diest I will die, and there will I be buried.

For 15 years John Stubbs watched over this flock, and with him in the churchyard is a charming brick and timber canopy set up over a village pump, the tribute raised in 1931 to Lionel Wells.

A Moving Fragment

HOUND. It seemed to us a rather moving fragment in the great mosaic of our Motherland. Old Yew stands by the church, silent sentinel of its comings and goings for perhaps 20 generations, and in the church, built 700 years ago (with a wooden belfry added later), there rise from floor to roof four mighty timbers roughly hewn by axes, making the west end something like a picture of one of the primitive stables beloved of the old Nativity painters. It is all very simple, with a nave and chancel only, and a big square font 700 years old; the chancel has a piscina and an aumbry.

A stone on the wall tells a heartbreaking tale; it is sacred to the memory of four 18th century babies, two brothers who died in their infancy and a brother and sister who died in six months.

John Keble's Church

HURSLEY. It was odd to be here and see an old man trundling a wood on the bowling green, and to be told as it rolled slowly towards the jack that Richard Cromwell used to play with it. Odd, surely, that the drama and tragedy of so long ago should come to mind on a bowling green.

Hursley is a delightful place among the trees and meadows lying off the road to London, with every form of domestic architecture, thatch and tile, Tudor brick and plaster, timbered fronts and roofs golden with lichen, quaint gables, deep eaves, and lovely dormer windows, all giving a touch of old England to this place. The woodland bordering Hursley Park has glorious beech arcades which John Keble used to call Hursley Cathedral, and the fine house in the park has a lovely garden, and magnificent panelling in its hall which is believed to have been carved by Grinling Gibbons. A mile away are the scant remains of a 12th century castle built by a king's brother, Henry de Blois. All that is left of it is a deep well, a towering wreck of a gatehouse, and fragments of windows and doorways. It is well kept, and little deer come tripping up to it. Several yews grow round it, and one of them has seen the centuries go by, for it is 25 feet round. It may be as old as the church tower, a handsome structure built in the 14th century, the only thing old about the church, which was built when men were not particularly in love with beautiful buildings.

It is interesting because it was built by John Keble out of the profits he made from The Christian Year. He was vicar here and in love with the place and with his work. Here he preached for about a generation. He climbed up to the summit of the tower and put the weathercock on the steeple with his own hand. The red granite stone with a cross and a chalice and a book near the tower marks the grave where they laid him in 1866. He being dead yet speaketh, for at the end of the village is a school built in his memory out of money sent from all over the world to mark the centenary of his Christian Year, the collection of sacred poems which became a best-seller, largely perhaps because of its association with the Oxford Movement.

There lies here also one of those two Gloucestershire men who wrote out the Psalms so that they could be set to music, and dedicated them, much to the young king's delight, to Edward the Sixth. John Keble's Christian Year may have sold well in its hundred years, but the metrical version of the Psalms by John Hopkins and Thomas Sternhold have had a sale unparalleled by any book except the Prayer Book and the Bible. Sternhold saw only 19 of his translations in print, but he had the satisfaction of seeing them launched successfully; he was fired by the growing desire of the English people to have their church service in their own tongue, and the book became the first sacred song book of Protestant England. Here they laid him to rest in 1549, he having lived for some years in the hamlet of Slackstead close by.

A little white cross in the tower has come from the battlefield round Ypres; it has on it the name of Lieutenant Hewitt, VC, who gave his life for England there. He was wounded by a piece of shell which set his clothes ablaze, but he put out the flames and led on his men through machine-gun fire, achieved his object, and then fell to a sniper. His magnificent example of coolness and his contempt of danger stirred the whole battalion.

In the chancel lies the old man who used to play with the bowl that has been preserved and is brought out once a year for the tournament on Cromwell Day. It is said that he planted the limes round the churchyard. Certainly he was long a strangely pathetic figure here, one of the immortal nobodies of our English history, Tumbledown Dick, Richard Cromwell. Here he found his wife, the daughter of Richard Major who lies in the chancel. For years Richard Cromwell lived here a pleasant country life, apparently not greatly in love with his father's view of things; and there is a letter in which Oliver speaks of his idle ways and begs Richard Major to look after him. "I would have him mind and understand business," Oliver said, "read a little history, study the mathematics and cosmography. These are good, with subordination to the things of God, rather than idleness or mere outward worldly contentment. These fit for the services for which a man is born." We know that Richard ceased to be idle, but he was unequal to his task. He came back to live here after the collapse of the Commonwealth, while his father's head was stuck on a pike for 25 years outside Westminster Hall. To this church he came on Sunday mornings, and in the afternoon he would ride alone to a Baptist meeting-house a few miles away. He spent part of his time with the Pengellys at Cheshunt and the rest with his daughter Elizabeth here. He died at Cheshunt, and they brought him to rest in Hursley chancel. He had been alone and sorrowful, and it must have been pitiful for him to be walking about this place, for here he had seen nearly all his children die. He lies with his wife and eight of their children of whom only three grew up. This is the list: Ann, an infant, 1651; an infant son, 1652; Mary aged 2, 1654; an unnamed infant, 1655; Dorothy, an infant, 1658; Dorothy Mortimer, 20, 1681; Oliver, aged 48, 1705; Elizabeth, aged 82, 1731. It is part of Richard Cromwell's tragedy that he has no memorial.

Poor Richard Cromwell

WITHIN two generations after Oliver there were Cromwells begging for bread. It was bound to be. It may be doubted if any man in the Commonwealth could have followed Cromwell without losing what reputation he had, and yet that is no excuse for the gross discourtesy which Richard Cromwell suffered from those who owed everything to his father. "I thought those whom my father raised from nothing would not so soon have forgotten him," Richard complained, and on the same day he was writing to Fleetwood, who had married Oliver's daughter: "Let me beg you to remember how his late Highness loved you; how be honoured you with the highest trust by leaving the sword in your hand which must defend or destroy us. Let us remember his last legacy, and, for his sake, render his successor considerable, and not make him vile, a thing of naught, and a byword."

It was in vain; the appeal of Cromwell's son to those whom Cromwell loved fell on deaf ears. Richard opened Parliament for the first time in January, 1659; three months later, on April 21, he resigned the office of Protector of his own free will, and disappeared from history.

He was the most unenviable man in England. Involved in debt, surrounded by enemies, he took refuge in flight. The ingratitude of Parliament was amazing. England owed the Protector £29,000. Money advanced for the purchase of coats for soldiers and for the use of the Army had not been repaid, and Parliament recognised its liability by appointing a committee to set matters right. As a result of their deliberations Richard was granted six months exemption from arrest, and when the inquiry was over he was compelled to flee by the failure of Parliament to carry out its promise. It was decided to sell the plate, hangings, and furniture of two palaces to pay Richard, but the arrangement was never carried out, and for twenty years he was an exile in Europe. He wandered homeless in a strange land, a fugitive from the law. In his trunks were the congratulations he had received only a few months before from many of the crowned heads of Europe. A dozen years before his father's name had made the world tremble; now it was a name to which his son dare not answer. His wife waited fifteen years for his return and died without seeing him again; his favourite daughter Dorothy was married and buried in a few months. She was the only Cromwell, somebody has said, "born in the purple." Richard came home at last to live in lodgings at ten shillings a week. Nobody guessed at first that the Mr Clarke who lived simply and quietly at Cheshunt was the man who had been Protector of the Commonwealth. Mrs Pengelly, his landlady, kept his accounts in great detail. He smoked a good deal, paying 2s 8d per gross for his pipes; and he was generous even in his poverty. On one occasion he borrowed £2 from his landlady, who entered it down for the day "when you had your feast."

When his daughters came to see him from Hursley, his home in better days, Richard would treat them to a comfortable dinner in Westminster, borrowing the money from the good Mrs Pengelly, who seems to have done something to soften his hard fate.

But generally he seems to have been a tolerably happy man, blessing everybody in spite of circumstance, and blaming none. When Queen Mary died he spent half-a-crown, we are told, on a pair of mourning gloves. His last days were made unhappy by a painful quarrel with his daughters concerning property at Hursley, and in his old age Richard was driven from his own home. A law-suit established his rights at last, and before his death the family was at peace again. "Live in love: I am going to the God of Love," he said to his daughters, as he lay dying on a summer's day in 1712.

There is a story of a great ceremonial in which Queen Anne was the central figure. The queen was surrounded by a host of gaily-dressed courtiers, and in the throng was an old man of 83, wearing the plain dress of a country farmer. "Have you ever seen such a sight before?" asked a looker-on, and the throng was startled to hear him reply, *Never since I sat in her chair*. It was Cromwell's son.

The Track Older Than the Romans

HURSTBOURNE PRIORS. Old Yew nods by its church, dreaming of the vanished fane and all they saw together. They saw the bringing to this place of many of the treasures of the wisest man of his day, Sir Isaac Newton. They were brought to a house in this deer park, which Charles Kingsley thought the most beautiful park in the south of England; the big house standing there now was raised on the site of the home of a girl whose mother was Catherine Barton, the niece of Sir Isaac Newton. Catherine married John Conduitt of Otterbourne and the daughter married Lord Lymington, and brought here with her many relics of Newton: Kneller's two fine portraits, with the spirited sketch he did for one of them, a copy of the bust of Newton by Roubiliac, and many manuscripts. Towards the end of last century a fire broke out, consuming pictures by Reynolds, Hoppner, Holbein, and Vandyck, but happily all the Newton relics were saved.

The church, with a mass clock on its sunny wall, has two richly carved Norman arches, one at the west doorway and one leading into a chapel. Near the second arch is the ornately canopied tomb of Sir Robert Oxenbridge, who lies, a black-bearded man in black and gold armour, by his sombrely clad wife, with their 14 sons and daughters round the tomb. Beside the tomb are two helmets. The tall Norman font is covered with zigzag, and the lectern is a graceful angel carved in oak as a tribute to the 6th Earl of Portsmouth, who would read the lessons here.

The wide grass-grown track passing the village is so old that it was probably well-worn when the Romans came, and may have been familiar to those misty prehistoric folk whose villages have been found hereabouts. They dug themselves round pits in the ground, about 4 feet deep and 13 wide, and paved them with flints. Near these pit dwellings have been found pot-boiling stones and millstones for grinding, along with pottery and bones.

The Old Door

HURSTBOURNE TARRANT. It is a big village nestling in a valley so steep that those who climb up the churchyard can look over the top of the shingled tower and spire. William Cobbett thought it a sight worth going miles to see. At every turn of his head he found fresh beauty. He would have found it also in the church, for it has wonderful possessions. The walls are chiefly 12th and 13th century, pierced with windows of many shapes and sizes, and a little chapel with a piscina is most unusually placed at the west end of one of the aisles.

The 700-year-old font rises on a group of pillars from a dais of ancient tiles. The reredos is made of Jacobean panelling rescued from a doomed cottage, and by it is a graceful weeping woman carved in memory of a 19th century lady. A fine doorway has a bird's head over one pillar and a dragon over the other, both approaching 800 years old; and a door in the west wall of the tower, studded with nails, is still swinging on fleur-de-lys hinges that have borne it to and fro 600 years. The belfry stairs are enclosed in 15th century woodwork, and near them is one of the huge poles with a steel hook used for raking thatch off burning roofs.

But perhaps the most important possession of the church is what is left of its 13th century wall-paintings, shadowy remains but not yet lost, for we see something of the Wheel of the Seven Deadly Sins, and near it the parable of the Three Living and Three Dead, three kings facing three skeletons. The kings are in a reddish tint, the skeletons in a ghostly yellow.

The peace memorial is a brightly coloured window of Our Lord crowning a soldier, with St George on one side and St Martin on the other, and another memorial is to Samuel and Mary Heskins of the 18th century, who lived together "a happy pair" 45 years, he being vicar 47 years. Mary died one winter's day in 1731, and Samuel followed her in a few weeks.

In our own time the church has received a bequest of an organ built by Mr Henry Prosser of this village, who bequeathed it himself and, following the traditions of benefactors of long ago, provided for certain inhabitants to receive five pounds of English beef, tea or tobacco, and five shillings in money each Christmas.

IBSLEY. It has the Avon and a sparkling weir, with wild duck wheeling by, and a lovely new bridge. The 19th century church has an amusing painted monument. A father and mother kneel facing each other, in their hands a vine whose spreading branches bear not only green leaves and purple fruit but the faces of five children, all looking as if they were there under protest. The monument is to Sir John Constable and comes from the happy days of Charles Stuart. It was sad to see here a glorious elm avenue, said to have been planted by prisoners from the Napoleon wars, being laid waste on the altar of this great Motor Age.

The Paintings on the Walls

IDSWORTH. It has one of the grandest and loftiest avenues of limes in the county at the bottom of a hill, and standing lonely on the top of the hill, in a meadow on the Sussex border, is the creeper-covered church, with some of the most wonderful pictures in Hampshire painted on the walls and in the window splays 600 years ago. On the splays of the east window are paintings of Peter and Paul, Peter being in papal robes. On the north wall are two pictures, a hunt and a feast. In the vigorous hunting scene men and dogs sweep through a forest to meet a fearful object half-human and half-beast, standing at bay on all fours. One of the hunters winds a horn and carries a bow. St Hubert raises a front paw of the beast, and restores it to human form, and we see the restored man being clothed and counselled as to his future life. Below the hunting scene is the feast of Herodias. In the background is part of a castle—the prison of John the Baptist, and the figures of the martyr and his hideous executioner. The table has a cloth laden with viands and goblets of wine. Among the guests at the table are two crowned ladies. Two servants attend Herod and Herodias, and one offers the head of the Baptist on a charger.

The nave of this tiny church was extended in the 16th century but was first built about 950. The Jacobean pulpit is charming and the font has flowers carved by a 15th century mason. In the east window is an old medallion of yellow glass showing a man kneeling under a tree, his horse and dogs standing by; it appears to be Flemish. There are two mass clocks on the wall.

The Weekend Cottage

ITCHEN ABBAS. The pathway to its Georgian church was lined with roses when we called, and it brings us to a giant that may be the oldest thing we see here, an ancient yew of great beauty, about 25 feet round the trunk. Hale and hearty still, this marvel of Itchen Abbas has for companion another lovely tree, one rarely found in graveyards, a graceful walnut. We do not wonder that Charles Kingsley loved to come to this village of clear streams, green meadows, and noble trees.

In one of these fields is all that is left of the home of a Roman family. After the Romans came the Normans, and they gave the church its west doorway and its chancel arch, and a style the modern builders have copied. In the sanctuary is a tablet to Robert Wright, who was rector for the first 50 years of the 19th century; and hiding in the porch are memorials to the two sons and the grand-daughter of an 18th century rector who was Dean of Chichester. All died young, one boy from a lingering illness, the other snatched away by a fever in the same year, and the girl with all the beauty of youth still about her. The charming lychgate was set up in 1933 in memory of a father and a mother. There are four consecration crosses.

In the churchyard is the grave of John Hughes, who was hanged at Westminster for horse stealing, and is said to be the last man in England hanged for that offence.

It was this corner of Hampshire, his biographer tells us, which became as dear to Lord Grey of Fallodon as Fallodon itself, and here for a full generation he enjoyed the wild life of the countryside on half an acre of land, on which he built a small cottage. It was his weekend place, and he used to say that he paid his rent in the form of bread thrown on to the grass for the birds in front of his sitting-room window. Here he would come when the worries of Parliament drove him to seek relief, and it was here that he wrote in 1895 "I shall never be in office again, and the days of my stay in the House of Commons are probably numbered." All the world knows that 20 years after this he stood by Mr Asquith's side when these two old friends stood for the spirit of England in its darkest hours.

Once he wrote to his wife from here that he felt as if his heart was too full and might burst:

I feel as if I must come in every half-hour to write to you. I have been on the bridge and eaten my figs on it and thrown the stalks into the river. I can hardly breathe for the sacredness of the place.

Another time he was disappointed that the birds did not come to him freely; he had seen only seven out of the twelve sorts that should have come, and he felt "as offended as a Sovereign whose levee has been badly attended, and as anxious as a parent whose children have stayed out too late."

In those bitter years when the storm of adversity seemed as if it would not cease about him, one of the blows came from this place so beloved. In 1917 Fallodon was burnt to the ground; in 1923 his post brought him a pathetic letter from the woman who looked after his cottage at Itchen Abbas:

My lord, what can I say to you? I am sore vexed, but your pretty cottage is burnt to the ground. What will you say, my lord?

It was the end of the Hampshire weekends which had brought relief to the man who for so long bore the burden of our Foreign Office on his shoulders.

ITCHEN STOKE. We remember a charming little lady in brass greeting us as we came to the church in this simple countryside. She is almost all the beauty that is left, with good taste in dress, and altogether pleasing in a dignified gown and a sort of Tudor hat, her only adornment a rich girdle and deep fur cuffs. She was Joan Batmanson, and they laid her to sleep in this place 400 years and more ago. Though sadly ornate within, the 19th century church is striking outside for its tall lancets and a great rose window. There is a gracious little sculpture of Our Lord over the porch, and a big font in memory of the architect's little girl of ten, with a father's pathetic wish written round the base:

> *Oh! for the touch of a vanished hand*
> *And the sound of a voice that is still.*

A Queen's Dowry

KIMPTON. Here was found a little Roman hut with a floor of rammed earth and roof-stones lying about it, and near by, at Shoddeston, the manor which was part of the dower of Edith, last of the Saxon queens. There are brass portraits of a lord of the manor and his family on a decorated tomb in the church; he is Robert Thornburgh and has with him two wives and their nine children, all in the charming dress of the early 16th century. The church is chiefly 13th century with 14th century transepts; but its tower was cased in brick in the first half of last century. Very attractive the interior is, with all its old stonework, the piers of the arcade merging without capitals into the arches themselves. There are lancets in the chancel, fine beams spanning the roof, and a peephole from each transept to the altar; and tucked away behind the organ there is a piscina and a charming little low window, still with its old iron grating. A 17th century wall-monument has one of the grimmest skulls we have seen.

The Norman Church in Downland

KINGSCLERE. We must call it one of Hampshire's fortunate places, a sleepy little town set in splendid downland, with delightful houses bordering its streets, and a staunch Norman church to safeguard its treasures.

The church was once paved with medieval tiles, and the walls of its chapel are now hung with them in cases. They were made in the 13th and 14th centuries and show various devices and quaint animals. On the sunny wall is a mass dial from those far-off days. The chapel is divided from the chancel by a 13th century arcade and contains one of the best monuments in Hampshire, that of Sir Henry and Lady Bridgett Kingsmill, who lie side by side in alabaster. Sir Henry is a handsome man of noble and sensitive countenance, who died long before his wife. He lies on a plaited rush mattress in armour and Cavalier boots, and Lady Bridgett, who set up the monument two years before she died, lies in flowing garments with a shawl over her hair, holding a book and a tasselled handkerchief. In striking contrast to this rich memorial is a very massive and ancient stone coffin, shaped for the head and shoulders. There are tablets on the chapel wall to Sir Robert Kingsmill, an admiral who died in Trafalgar year, and to Edward Webbe, a vicar who was deprived of office in the Civil War and later became chaplain to Charles the Second. His successor, Ambrose Webbe, was vicar 50 years, a record equalled (if the old archives can be trusted) by Thomas Hunte in the 15th century.

Seen from outside, the walls of the church have been renewed in modern times, but their age is seen within. The chief architectural splendour is the group of Norman arches supporting the central tower, those east and west having lovely patterns not all of which are old. The 17th century pulpit is handsomely arcaded and carved with much detail; the Norman font bowl has two sides decorated afresh in the 15th century and an oak cover of Shakespeare's time; and there is a brass candelabra of 1713 with a bird on the top. The north wall has a beautiful Norman doorway built into it.

Two of the treasures of the altar are silver chalices of the days of Drake and Raleigh, and there is a silver flagon given by Lady Bridgett Kingsmill in 1670.

The Two Unknowns

KING'S SOMBORNE. Its peace memorial stands proudly on a charming green, and behind its church is a field covered with queer ridges, with the grey stones of low walls showing here and there. The ridges are the foundations of some ancient building which has been called King John's Palace for hundreds of years; probably the John concerned was John of Gaunt. One of the things the church has to show is believed to be the oldest of its kind in Hampshire. It is the mutilated stone figure of William Briwere, who lived in the days of Thomas Becket. His head has gone, with most of the little winged figures supporting it, but his priest's robes are almost as they were 750 years ago. He lies under a 14th century canopied niche. He would see the consecration crosses and the mass dials on the sunny wall; there are four of them. Not far from this ancient sculpture is a huge stone with brass portraits of two unknown civilians of the 14th century, men with short swords, wrinkled brows, and cloaks flung over their shoulders. The font, made of stone quarried in the Purbeck hills 700 years ago, has nine pillars to support it. Two of the arches in the nave are 13th century and there is a fragment of very old glass. The delightful rails under the chancel arch were shaped in the 17th century; and the great ornamental beams in the nave roof look like Tudor work. An unusual sight we noticed on the stones of the doorway, which have ornamental crosses and sacred monograms of the letters IHS, all old and very lightly cut.

A Famous Liberal

KING'S WORTHY. It lies on a busy highway near Winchester, a village fit for a king indeed. Although much of its church has been built anew it is all in harmony with the 15th century flint tower. The fine 500-year-old font remains, and in a window is a little round panel of medieval glass showing two mitred bishops with croziers drawn in gold. On a wall is a pathetic tablet with the names of four brothers lost in the Great War, Ernest, Charles, Reginald, and Cecil Baring.

In the churchyard, and within sight of the winding River Itchen, sleeps Lord Eversley, a great Liberal of the days of Mr Gladstone. He was one of the best reforming spirits of the great age of Liberalism, known in those days as Mr Shaw Lefevre. He was unrivalled in his knowledge of affairs and used to say he had known 37 Prime Ministers, Lord Chancellors, and Primates. In his youth he had carried the coronet at the funeral of the Iron Duke, and ridden a horse from Vienna to Constantinople. He championed the cause of public commons, defended footpaths, started sixpenny telegrams, supported Free Trade as the source of England's prosperity, warmly advocated Peace and the reduction of armaments, and was long regarded as a possible Prime Minister. He died at 97, having lived from the reign of King William the Fourth into the reign of King George the Fifth.

On the Old Highway

KNIGHTS ENHAM. It has a grassy track which was once a busy highway of the Romans, leading them from Winchester into Wiltshire. There was a Roman village here. Now there is another kind of village, built up since the Great War by men broken on the battlefields, who here seek to keep their heads above water. They learn carpentry, basket-weaving, and cabinet-making, and have a shop in London where those they fought for may buy their wares.

A little way off still stands the 13th century church, now but a chancel and a nave with its old aisle arches built up in the wall. It has a shingled tower, and a porch entrance of great timbers. In the place of honour stands a new font, while the old one of which it is a copy waits humbly at one side, carved by Norman craftsmen.

The Refugees

LAVERSTOKE. Here has been made for two centuries and more the paper for Bank of England notes. The family owning the mills is descended from the first man to run a paper mill here. He was young Henri Portal, son of a Huguenot family whose chateau was attacked by the soldiery of Louis the Fourteenth after the Edict was revoked in 1685. The children were hidden in an oven by their old nurse, and there they cowered, terror-stricken by the sounds of fear and death on every hand around them. When all was quiet they came out.

It must have been a fearful sight which met their eyes, and they sought freedom by escape. After many adventures Henri reached Southampton. He learned the art of paper-making from fellow refugees at South Stoneham mills, and there he met Sir William Heathcote, squire of Hursley, who obtained for him the lease of a tiny mill on the Test near Freefolk. From this small beginning this earnest and brilliant young man became the owner of bigger and better mills, and at last, in 1727, Sir Gilbert Heathcote, Governor of the Bank of England and uncle of Henri's good friend, placed with him the order for the Bank's paper. The little mill near Freefolk is now Portal property, and though it is unemployed it stands well cared for and enchanting on the clear, smooth-running Test. On its front is a sculptured coat-of-arms. Laverstoke mills have been rebuilt and brought up to date, but preserved on an inside wall is a stone telling of their first building in 1719 by the gallant Henri Portal.

The road runs by the Test for a while, and across the river a beautiful park slopes up to Laverstoke House, rebuilt in 1798 under the direction of the great architect Bonomi. The park is famous for its beeches and has one of the oldest walnut trees in England.

The church shared by Freefolk and Laverstoke stands between

the villages. It is big and new, with lovely ironwork on the door and with two things of great beauty inside. One is the delicately carved screen with its fan tracery, rich vine band, and rood figures up above; the other is the noble reredos copied from a medieval one, with eight painted panels of the life of Jesus, four on each side of a central group of carved figures gathering about Our Lord on the Cross. Above the figures is a rich array of golden canopies, the highest pinnacle reaching almost to the roof.

But Laverstoke, like Freefolk, still keeps its old church. It is in the park and has been greatly restored, but it still has its old bell dated 1624 and one or two old monuments besides those of the Portals, whose mausoleum it has become. Chief among the older monuments is the beautiful marble bust of Katherine Stewkley who died in 1679. Her face is full of charm and character, and her epitaph suggests that she was more intelligent than the average woman of her day, with a love of learning that made many envious and unkind. It ends bitterly:

The dull oblige mankind
And all their love engage,
While tis a crime to be refined
Above the present age.

We may like better the epitaph on the dignified wall-monument of her parents, John Trott and his wife, who died about the same time as Cromwell. It is graced with these lines, a gem of gems from the literature of our churches:

He wrongs the dead who thinks this marble frame
Was built to be the guardian of his name,
Whereas twas for his ashes only meant:
His name was set to guard the monument.

The Old Stone

LECKFORD. A village of plaster and thatch, gardens and trees, it stands below the meeting-place of the Anton and the Test. A very ancient building with remarkable possessions is its church. It has some of the original 13th century flint walls (on which is a mass dial), an unusual timber tower rising from wooden pillars within the church, and a rare possession in its sanctuary. By the altar is a simple table which used to be the altar, but has now given place to a stone of great antiquity, returned home after long banishment. The original stone at which the bishop would stand to give his blessing on Conse-

Lyndhurst   Forest Cottages

Canterton   The Rufus Stone

THE STATELY TREES OF THE NEW FOREST

Milford-on-Sea

Lymington

TWO MEDIEVAL HAMPSHIRE CHURCHES

cration Day, it rests on four pillars cut from the same kind of stone, and the only covering we found on this rare altar was a piece of delicate and lovely lace. The altarpiece is richly decorated with fruit, and there is a marvellous display of old choir-stalls, with wide arm-rests and tip-up seats. They were brought from Venice in our time but were made when Venice was gay with ships and merchants and precious cargoes from all over the world. The font is Norman. The splendid canopied pulpit and the charming altar rails are 17th century, and the handsome screen is modern.

Over the choir-stalls is a small wall-monument to a husband and wife who lived and loved in the troubled times of the Civil War, Sir John and Lady Jane Thornburgh. Their epitaph tells us of their anxious lives, speaking of wealth-wasting lawsuits and life-wearing care, and ends:

> *Lament their loss, ye poor, ye sick and lame,*
> *God hath their souls, the world will speak their fame.*

The Oldest Inhabitants

LINKENHOLT. They have taken their oldest inhabitants and set them in two half circles round the top of two windows, fossilised sea urchins found in fields and gardens here, relics of the days when Linkenholt's population went its way on fins. One of the windows is by the church porch; the other is a Norman window on the north side. Here from a great historic period was found an egg-cup lying unbroken, made and glazed and used by the Romans; and after the Romans came the Normans, walking through this very doorway into the church, and baptising their little ones at this very font with its band of carving done 800 years ago. After the Normans the Tudors; they built the noble gabled manor house which still keeps company with these pretty cottages.

Nelson Breakfasts and Blucher Dines

LIPHOOK. It lies just within the Hampshire boundary from Sussex, with only an inn for the traveller to see, but an inn with a history. For centuries men have been coming and going, gladly and sadly, to this charming inn, the Royal Anchor. The cobbled space in front of it is shadowed by a great chestnut tree 300 years old. It was a hostelry in the time of Edward the Second, who came here with his acrobatic cook riding before him, entertaining him with equestrian antics. Queen Anne came 400 years afterwards and reclined on a bank in the forest while the keepers drove past her 500 deer. Samuel Pepys, travelling this way to inspect shipping at Portsmouth, found to his relief "good honest people" at the inn when he arrived after losing his way in the forest.

The Anchor has the distinction of being one of the last places to attend to the wants of the heroic Nelson, who breakfasted here on his way to Portsmouth and Trafalgar. When Napoleon had been finally disposed of, and Blucher came to London to share the honours of Waterloo with Wellington, (it was then he made his comment on London: What a city to sack!) he dined on the way at the Anchor with the Allied Sovereigns; and on a dresser in the lounge is now displayed the flowered Spode dinner service they used. Upstairs, in a room with a magnificent Jacobean door, Queen Victoria slept when she stayed here as a girl with her mother. She sent the door, years after, as a memento of her visit.

A secret stairway behind the fireplace in the lounge once led down to wretched little cells, five feet by three. In these dark cellars, in the bad old days when people were transported for small offences, many wretched convicts spent the last night on their way to the coast and the agony of Botany Bay.

In the Hollow Trunk

LISS. Its tower is as old as the Conqueror and may be Saxon, but life was going on in Liss thousands of years before the Saxons came. We found a lofty old yew still vigorous in the churchyard.

Wonderful things have been found hereabouts belonging to those ancestors of ours who left no other records than their graves and the treasures buried with them. Those who have searched for ancient history here have found flint arrowheads, spearheads, and axes, some of them now in the British Museum; but the most remarkable discovery at Liss was the hollowed-out trunk of a tree in which men found a hard black lump looking like a piece of coal. The discoverers say that after it had been in the house some time this black fragment unfurled itself and proved to be hair, the hair of some dark lady who lived in the world and was buried at Liss before Jesus Christ was born.

The church (St Peter's) that has grown up about the Norman tower is the work of 13th and 15th century builders. The beautiful little south doorway and parts of the tower are 13th century. The tall pointed arches of the nave arcade, the lovely traceried window in the north wall, some of the timber in the porch, and the font, are all 500 years old. In the 19th century church of St Mary there is an old chest, and two 17th century coffin stools.

The fine old farmhouse called Place House, a little way from the village, is an ancient nunnery made new in the 19th century. What is believed to be the refectory still stands, a lofty building now used as a lumber room, and the hall has some beautiful panelling thought to have been the reredos of the altar from the old chapel.

The Seven Barrows

LITCHFIELD. Nature has given it its most inspiring monument, for it has Beacon Hill rising sheer and bare to the height of 858 feet above the sea, crowned with the defences of a British camp that may be older than Caesar. At the foot of the hill are the grassy hillocks called Seven Barrows, though a ruthless railway has depleted their number. They are the graves of a people who may have seemed as far off to the builders of the camp as the builders of the camp seem from us, for in these barrows sleep the ancient folk of this countryside who used flint tools and burned their dead.

The church is set in what is like a lovely garden rather than a graveyard, as all our churches should be set, and Litchfield's herbaceous border is a sight we shall not soon forget. There are Norman pillars in the nave, filled-up arches from a vanished aisle, a massive font of the 12th century, three old faces looking out in the chancel, and a chalice from Elizabethan England. Delightful and striking is the 17th century chancel screen, which rises to the roof and is supported halfway by beautiful stone brackets.

The Saxon Walls

LITTLE SOMBORNE. Its small church has braved about a thousand years of rough weather and has still the hall-mark of the men who built before the Conquest. Some of the outer Saxon walls still stand, having outlasted the vanished 13th century chancel. The chancel arch has been built up and has become a beautiful frame for the altar, with two lancet windows above it saved from the lost chancel, and a tiny built-up window near by through which the light must have fallen on Saxon worshippers. On the outside of the north wall is a slender pilaster strip, and some of the unmistakable long-and-short work seen everywhere in Alfred's England.

LITTLETON. Its little ones are christened in a noble font that has seen such ceremonies for over 700 years. It is square and shallow, with five supporting columns, and is richly carved. The chancel arch is Littleton's peace memorial, but it is on its old base of the 13th century. Two graves we noticed in Littleton, one inside the church belonging to John Smythe who died just after the Tudors came to the throne; the other outside the chancel, that of William Butler, a faithful servant in the village in one house for 55 years.

The Daffodil Crosses

LOCKERLEY. It was old when Domesday Book was written, for there it is mentioned as belonging to the Archbishop of York, its ancient church being a chapel of ease to Mottisfont, as is the church of the neighbouring East Dean. These small churches were probably built by the Saxons with wattle and daub, and nothing remains of them save the ancient font of a rough-hewn circular stone preserved in the porch at Lockerley. The Saxon churches were probably pulled down about 1200 and rebuilt by William Briwere, who founded Mottisfont Abbey about that time. Unfortunately Lockerley's old church was pulled down last century and very little remains of it save a Norman window, which it is hoped to work into the south transept, now the Children's Corner. The fine new church was built by Mr F. G. Dalgety of Lockerley Hall, who bought from his forests in New Zealand giant logs of Kauri timber to be made into pews. A beautiful model of the ancient church is preserved in the porch and there are a few other relics of it, notably the bells (dated 1676), the crude old weathercock, and the tub font.

The churchyard is remarkably interesting and kept with loving care. In it is an ancient yew tree, nearly 25 feet round. The site of the old church has been levelled, and the ground plan marked out by an edging of box, and in due season it is gay with daffodils, which have been planted in the form of crosses on the old graves. The parish registers of Lockerley go back to the days of Queen Elizabeth, and the church has ancient communion plate presented to it in the year before Charles the Second was crowned. The vicarage stands next to the church, and part of it was once the tithe barn.

Dead Man's Plack

LONGPARISH. It has a tall grey cross set up last century, with a grim tale to tell of Dead Man's Plack, for here it was, in a wood on the road to Andover now reached by an avenue of beeches, that Ethelwulf was slain. He was a Saxon earl and all unworthy of his trust, for Edgar the Peaceful, friend of Dunstan, sent him to see a beautiful girl to report on her charm before his royal master came to offer her the crown, and Ethelwulf hid his mission from her and took her for himself. The king was moved to such anger that it is said he struck Ethelwulf dead with his own hand; though the bride is not held guiltless, for she was ambitious and eager to be queen. She was, moreover, the guilty Elfrida who, when Edgar died in 975, murdered her stepson in Corfe Castle to set her own child on the throne. The funeral casket of the unhappy Edward has been found at Shaftesbury in our time and we have seen his remains in a leaden casket there.

It is the cross that tells the story, but it is the tower of the church that has seen the centuries go by. It is 500 years old, and the nave arcades with their scalloped capitals are 13th century. The south doorway is 14th century, the pulpit has an old hourglass which has been brought here in our time, and the font has a remarkable pinnacled cover about nine feet high. The interior is dark and ornate, and the traveller will find it hard to believe that some of these red and blue windows, shining so vividly, were beloved by our Victorian ancestors, though we may like the Bethlehem east window standing out brightly in the dark chancel, and an aisle window showing the Miraculous Draught of Fishes, in memory of Admiral Durnford, who died in 1919. By the lychgate we found the old stocks, crumbling.

The village lives up to its name, having one of our longest streets straggling along with some charming cottages for over a mile.

Here Came the Danes

LONGSTOCK. It is as delightful as can be, with its smiling water-meadows before it and its thatch and plaster cottages, one of them overhung by a graceful walnut tree. It has rebuilt its old church, and in our search for beauty we find little here beyond the charming fluted altar rails, a Jacobean desk, a few rows of medieval tiles behind the altar, eight wooden angels watching over the chancel, two fragments of old sculpture in the vestry, and a 600-year-old font.

Yet behind a prosperous farm by the river is something exciting enough to stir the dullest imagination, for the river runs past earthworks 1100 years old, whose marshy bottoms are now filled with tall reeds but were once noisy with seafaring voices and talk of ships. We should not understand what was being said if we could step back across the centuries among the tall, fair-haired men we should find here, for their tongue was harsh and foreign. Here in Longstock was a Danish dock, and here came the long, dark, evil ships, bringers of fire and sword and death, back from their raiding. Here, too, more keels would be laid to replace those lost at sea and the peaceful valley would echo with the sound of hammer and saw shaping them. Terrible they must have looked gliding down the clear waterway, their savage figure-heads staring fiercely forwards, straining to catch their first glimpse of the sea, the oarsmen idle behind their shields, letting the breeze and current carry them down. Now, in the grassy, reed-grown basins, the only builders are the sedge-warblers and the reed-buntings; the only navies known to the whispering river are silent finny things going their way under water.

Whatever may be thought of the Danes who left their name on several prominences to the west of Longstock and doubtless came there up the river, there are on the hills on either side of the Test at Longstock clear evidence of stern activity before the Danes were heard of hereabouts. On Danebury Hill are the ruins of massive earthworks of a kind familiar to those who know these far-flung downs, and a track runs from them across the Test valley to the 500-feet-high Woolbury Ring on Stockbridge Down. There must have been many people about on these downs, people commonly called Britons, when the lofty places of defence were planned, but how long ago who can say?

Come Where the Fields Are Gay

LONG SUTTON. Away from the bustle of the world, fortunate is the traveller who comes this way when the fields of sainfoin are in flower, covering acre after acre in a drift of pink, reminding us, with the yellow patches where the crop is mustard, of the Norfolk tulip fields.

Whether the church or its old yew sentinels are older is something of a puzzle, but the two yews are veterans, both hollow and beginning to feel weary of the centuries, and one measuring 20 feet round. The charming lines of the little church remain much as they were when it was new at the beginning of the 13th century, with round pillars and a simple Norman font. Four posts inside the nave help to support the little grey wooden turret which sits astride the roof with three old bells averaging 400 years. A chapel has a charming 14th century canopied niche, and a plain timber chest nine feet long which has endured 600 years and seems strong enough for 600 more. Beside it we found a wooden bier which bore its first sad burden before the Reformation.

Everywhere in this bit of Hampshire are delightful old brick and timber cottages, farms, and oast-houses, and as charming a collection of odd-shaped gables as we remember. The village has its full share of them. Looking out on the church through latticed windows is the old parsonage, now two cottages, each ending in a group of two gables and three chimneys. Farther down the road a little cottage almost roofed over with creeper shares one of its walls with an ancient chapel. Best of all is the farm just beyond the church, one side of which is a piece of Tudor England left unspoiled. On the wall of the church is still the old mass dial by which the village folk would tell the time in the days before clocks.

The Pathetic Story of Southey's Wife

LYMINGTON. A smiling little town on the estuary of the Boldre river, its ancient streets, still delightful with their Georgian houses, have seen exciting days. Its dockyards provided the navy with more ships than Portsmouth. There are few slipways now, but graceful yachts are still built by the river, and they ride her on their moorings, dipping and bowing when the steamer from the Isle of Wight comes up the narrow Channel. Here still is the handsome Georgian house in St Thomas Street known as Quadrille Court because dashing officers from Germany, brought over in fear of Napoleon's invasion, would here make merry by dancing with Lymington's young ladies.

Rising through the trees across the river is a gleaming white shaft to a courageous admiral of the Burrard family, who took his wife's name and was known as Sir Harry Burrard Neale. He was in command of the San Fiorenzo which was at Weymouth in attendance on the king, and soon afterwards was with the ship at the Nore when the mutiny broke out. His men refused to join the mutineers and the revolted ships opened fire on her. The San Fiorenzo managed to escape and the mutiny collapsed, the admiral being publicly thanked at the Royal Exchange in London. The Burrard baronetcy has lapsed for half a century, but the name is honoured still in Lymington, for they long served the town. One of them, General Burrard, suffered in reputation through the man-oeuvring of politicians, he being sent out to supersede Wellington, a task for which he was not fitted. He was the victim of a bad system, and made an unhappy appearance in the limelight of history through no fault of his own.

There is a fine view down the street of the church with its great west window and the tower rising behind it with a little wooden cupola over the clock. The cupola was built in 1670. Inside are traces of the 700-year-old arcade. The Courtenay Chapel is 14th century, and has a timber roof with 15th century carved bosses. The chancel has a canopied piscina, there is a fine heraldic carving in memory of Richard Hopkins Miles, who died in 1682, and two busts by artists more famous than the men they represent—a Rysbrack bust of Charles Colborne and one of Captain Rogers by John Bacon RA. In a glass case on the wall are preserved some bosses from the old roof, some ancient pewter almsdishes, and a small christening bowl. There is some 18th century Spanish glass.

In the churchyard lies Caroline Bowles, the second wife of Robert Southey. She lived nearly all her life in a cottage here near Buckland Rings, a round British camp, leaving it only to marry Southey and returning to it after a few tragic years.

Her mother, who was a sister of General Burrard, died when Caroline was 30, leaving her alone in the world, but she was enabled to keep her cottage by an annuity allowed to her by her father's adopted son. With this and with the occasional help of her pen she managed to live. It happened that she had sent one of her poems to Southey, who encouraged her so much that they met and formed a sort of literary partnership, which came to nothing much but led to a correspondence of 20 years. Then Southey's wife's mind gave way and she was released from her anguish by death, and in eighteen months after that Southey wrote to Caroline Bowles an offer of marriage. She accepted it, but within three months came the collapse of Southey's intellectual powers. Caroline's position was one of utmost misery, for she was not welcomed by Southey's children, and the poet's condition rapidly became worse. His death put an end to three years of great unhappiness. While doing justice to his children Southey left Caroline £2000. It was less than she had sacrificed by surrendering her annuity to marry him, and she returned to her cottage worse off than she had left it. For the last two years of her life the Government allowed her a pension.

Francis Joseph Mary Epiphanius Patmore

THERE is still remembered at Lymington, though he died far away, a man who bore a remarkable name and was a familiar figure here. He was Francis Patmore.

We must count it as one of the countless crimes of the Great War that this fine man was taken from us before he was fifty. He was the son of Coventry Patmore, a poet better known to the Victorians than to our own time.

"Piphie" the poet called this little son, whose full name was extraordinary: Francis Joseph Mary Epiphanius Patmore. "Piphie is a continual delight, beyond all I ever dreamed of," his father once wrote.

We do not wonder that such a boy grew up to love his country. He was in the war against the Turks, and was taken prisoner by them. Glorious is the tale his comrades tell of how he behaved when the prisoners were marched 1700 miles from Bagdad to Kastamuni in Asia Minor. On that terrible journey he was constantly carrying another man's pack or helping a lame comrade along. But for the cheerful burden-bearing of this heroic soul many another man would have fallen out to die.

Afterwards Francis Patmore managed to escape from prison, but he was caught, and was flung into the horrible gaol where he got typhus. Then he was carried out, half-conscious, tied back downward across a mule, and thus made the journey to another prison.

Byron has described in his own thrilling way the terrible ride of Mazeppa, tied on the back of a horse; but it can hardly have been more terrible than this ride of Francis Patmore. The dragging ropes injured him so badly that it soon became obvious that he could never take part in the war again, and so the Turks were willing to exchange him. He spent a year in hospital, and for long afterwards was an invalid who constantly had to submit to operations. But he kept up his heart and was brave enough to live through all these fearful adventures. In his captivity he would think of the little English villages he knew, and it was then that he wrote these lines, with their memories of our countryside:

In England the leaves are falling from chestnut and beech and oak,
Where once mid mossgrown tree-trunks the ringing echoes woke.
Oh, for the smell of the mudflats when the autumn tide runs low,
As over the darkening waters the plovers come and go.
When the haunting smell of the wood-smoke hangs low o'er the village
  street,
And the dust drifts gold in the sunset stirred by the children's feet.

After his release he went to Kenya, where he started a coffee plantation and became a magistrate respected by all who knew him; but in the end he died a victim of the war no less than if he had died on the battlefield. War does not always kill outright; sometimes it lets its victims go and plays with them like a cat with a mouse.

Alice's Wonderland

LYNDHURST. Here is the heart of the New Forest. From this place, where seven roads meet, the life of the Forest has pulsed and flowed through its thousand arteries for centuries. Here grew up a settlement of a few houses, a church, and a court where five times a year since the 14th century 40 chosen Verderers have met in the ancient Verderers Hall to discuss the government and upkeep of the Forest, to assign the tasks of verderers, marksmen, woodwards, colt-hunters, and keepers of this vast area, and until the 17th century to deal out awards and punishments.

And now through all the summer months across wide tracts of unspoiled heath and moorland, or through woodland districts where every kind of English forest tree has its wild unfettered home, along the seven roads and the many bypaths, motorists, sightseers, and ramblers pour into the picturesque street of this small town.

At one end of the long street the Verderers Hall stands next to the King's House, which was built in the time of Charles the Second for the Forest Warden. The Verderers Hall has panelled walls and a floor of unpolished red and white tiles mellowed by age. Before the

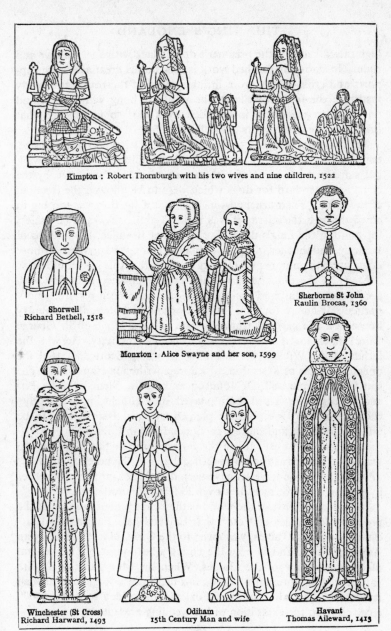

Kimpton : Robert Thornburgh with his two wives and nine children, 1522

Shorwell
Richard Bethell, 1518

Monxton : Alice Swayne and her son, 1599

Sherborne St John
Raulin Brocas, 1360

Winchester (St Cross)
Richard Harward, 1493

Odiham
15th Century Man and wife

Havant
Thomas Aileward, 1413

OLD HAMPSHIRE BRASSES

219

high raised bench is the prisoner's dock, black with age, massive and rude. No smoothly finished work is this, but its great axe-hewn supports and cross-beams are a fitting symbol of the rough and ready justice of the forest dwellers. The walls are hung with antlers and one fight to the death is recorded by a pair so interlocked that neither of the combatants could free itself.

Tradition has assigned to William Rufus a stirrup of unusual size, ten and a half inches by seven and a half, still hanging on the wall, but actually it is a piece of 17th century work, and was used by the court as a standard for dogs which were to be allowed the freedom of the forest. Their cruel custom was that if the dog was too big to crawl through the stirrup it was maimed so that it would be useless for hunting the king's deer. The Abbot of Beaulieu, the Abbess of Romsey, and the men of Lymington were among the privileged whose dogs, up to the number of 32, were exempt from this ferocious law.

Many of the old houses of the town which keep company with the Verderers Hall and the King's House have been restored and a particularly fine restoration is that of one of the hotels, like a country house in a fine garden. Cuffnells Park was the home of Sir George Rose, much loved for his kindly heart and honesty. He was the father of the William Stewart Rose to whom Scott dedicated the opening stanzas of Marmion, which were written in Hampshire. The son knew Hume and Dr Johnson and was a friend of Pitt; Pitt and George the Third both stayed at Cuffnells, and loved its rhododendrons. One of these planted by Lord Bute is said to be one of the oldest and biggest rhododendrons in England.

A mile or two westward in the Forest is the mighty Knightwood Oak, its trunk measuring over 21 feet; and in the beech plantations of Mark Ash Wood, which have been described as the finest beeches in Europe, one tree measures over 20 feet and another 18.

In this lovely part of the world is the country house of one of the proudest companies of Youth that England has. Foxlease, with its estate of nearly 70 acres, was given to the Girl Guides in 1922 by an American lady, and is now the country headquarters and general place of assembly of the Guides. When the Marys of the Empire gave a wedding present of £6000 to our Princess Royal she handed it over for the maintenance of Foxlease and added to it the £4000 received from the exhibition of her wedding presents.

The church stands high above the roadway near the King's House; it is 19th century, a little 13th century chapel and a later church having been replaced by this modern Gothic building in red brick. From its high position and its towering spire of 160 feet it is a well-known landmark. One of Charles Kingsley's New Forest Ballads tells of an ancient tragedy here:

> *They dug three graves in Lyndhurst yard,*
> *They dug them side by side;*
> *Two yeomen lie there, and a maiden fair,*
> *A widow, and never a bride.*

The interior is richly decorated, the pillars of the nave being exquisitely carved, and supporting the timbered roof are angels and the heads of great reformers; Luther, Cranmer, Latimer, and Melanchthon. The chief treasure of the church is a magnificent wall-painting of the Ten Virgins over the altar, by Lord Leighton, painted when he was staying here with his poet friend Hamilton Aidé. The picture is badly lighted, and it is difficult to appreciate its beauty and rich colouring; the stern dignity of the restraining angel and the distress of the Foolish Virgins are a lasting memory. The artist painted his Biblical characters from local models.

In the windows is some fine glass by William Morris. Small panels of women's figures show Hannah and Rachel, Elizabeth and Monica, the Madonna and her mother. In another lovely group are the Angels of the Nativity and the Angels at the Tomb.

There are two lovely memorials. A panel by Flaxman, removed from the older church, is a sister's tribute to Sir Charles Philip Jennings; on it a woman's form is bowed in grief over a broken column. An exquisite monument to Anne Frances Cockerill has a girlish form in white marble lying on a couch, her hands clasped, the dazzling whiteness of the slender figure in high relief against a background of gold mosaic on which a butterfly is poised.

To thousands who come to this church it will be chiefly interesting because in the churchyard lies Mrs Reginald Hargreaves, born as Alice Liddell but known to all the world as Lewis Carroll's Alice in Wonderland. She was the second of the three daughters of Henry Liddell, Dean of Christ Church, Oxford. On July 4, 1862, a professor of mathematics at Christ Church took the three little girls on the river. Alice was ten. It was so hot that they left the boat and rested in the shade of a hayrick, and the grown-up friend, Charles Lutwidge Dodgson, had to amuse them. A story was demanded:

> *Imperious Prima flashes forth*
> *Her edict "to begin it"—*
> *In gentler tones Secunda hopes*
> *"There will be nonsense in it!"*
> *While Tertia interrupts the tale*
> *Not more than once a minute.*

So the mathematical professor turned storyteller and began:

> *And ever, as the story drained*
> *The wells of fancy dry,*
> *And faintly strove that weary one*
> *To put the subject by,*
> *"The rest next time"—"It is next time!"*
> *The happy voices cry.*

Here under that hayrick the story of Alice in Wonderland, with nonsense in it far beyond all that Secunda (who was Alice) could have expected. On following excursions Mr Dodgson had to continue the adventures with the White Rabbit who had a waistcoat pocket, and the Mouse with the long tale, the savage Queen of Hearts, the Duchess with the sharp chin, the Cheshire Cat, the Mock Turtle, and the rest. Often he would tease his listeners by pretending to fall asleep at an exciting point.

Alice particularly was thrilled with the story, and Mr Dodgson decided to give her a surprise at Christmas. He put the whole of Alice's Adventures Under Ground (as he first called it) on to paper, giving it an illuminated title-page and 37 drawings, while at the end was a photograph of Alice herself. Seldom can a girl have received a more precious gift and never a more delightful dedication:

> *Child of the pure unclouded brow*
> *And dreaming eyes of wonder,*
> *Though time be fleet and I and thou*
> *Are half a life asunder,*
> *Thy loving smile will surely hail*
> *The love gift of a fairy tale.*

Alice Liddell grew up to marry Reginald Hargreaves of Lyndhurst, and to have children of her own to whom she must have told the story many, many times, reading over and over to herself the

little bit at the end where her friend made Alice's sister dream of the
time when Alice would be a grown woman,

*How she would keep through all her riper years the simple and
loving heart of her childhood: and how she would gather about her
other little children, and make their eyes bright and eager with
many a strange tale, perhaps even with the dream of Wonderland
of long ago: and how she would feel with all their simple sorrows
and find a pleasure in all their simple joys, remembering her own
child life and the happy summer days.*

Twenty years passed from the time the tale was told, and then
George MacDonald, fine poet and himself a writer for children,
suggested to Mr Dodgson that the story should be published. So
Alice was asked to lend the manuscript, Mr Dodgson promising
that no one should handle it but himself. The famous illustrations by
Sir John Tenniel were based on the author's own drawings. The
book was immediately successful, and brought the mathematical professor with the queer name worldwide fame under his pen name of
Lewis Carroll. The original manuscript was sold in 1928 for the
astonishing price of £15,400, a record for any English book.

Alice Hargreaves had three sons and two of them were killed in
the Great War. Her husband died in 1926, but Alice lived on here.
She lived to visit America for the centenary celebrations of the man
who made her immortal, and her last home was at Westerham in
Kent, where she died in November 1934 at 82; but what is mortal
of her rests in Lyndhurst, Alice in Nature's Wonderland.

We do well to leave this lovely town with the peaceful thought of
Wonderland. Sir John Millais and his friend Lord Leighton both
loved to make their pictures here, and the place is haunted with
lingering and kindly memories. One of the loveliest of all that we
carry away is in the words with which Lyndhurst salutes her brave,
those who gave their lives for us: *To the Unconquered—Peace.*

Motor Age to Cart Age

MAPLEDURWELL. We leave the Motor Age at Polecat
Corner and turn up rough lanes into the Cart Age, to be
welcomed at the end of one of them by a shapely little church and a
charming cottage or two. The church has been much refashioned,
but fragments of the 15th century chancel screen are in the little new
one, and it still has (hidden under the organ) the brass portraits of

John and Agnes Canner and their family, who saw the old screen when it was new. Massive oak beams make the roof the most impressive thing here. The door has an old lock and key and there is a Bible box 400 years old.

MARTYR WORTHY. One of its bells has been ringing for over 500 years, but we can come into its little church by one tall Norman doorway and leave by another; and the walls of its nave are Norman too. The chancel apse is panelled, and the modern pulpit and reading-desk are both carved; but the chief interest of the church is in the memorials to a woman of our own century and a man of the century before. We may read on these walls how Miss M. E. Bishop, who knew Martyr Worthy in her youth, went on to become headmistress of two schools and the first Principal of Royal Holloway College; and how Admiral Sir Thomas Pasley, who died here in his retirement, lost a leg on his flagship the Bellerophon when Lord Howe's fleet beat the French in 1794. Here the old admiral sleeps his last sleep, the memorial being the tribute of his grandson, who bore his name and was an admiral too.

He Went Down With Kitchener

MATTINGLEY. It lies just off the Reading road, a delightful company of old cottages with a green. The builder of the most unusual 15th century church is thought to have been Bishop Waynflete. It is made of brick and timber, and its chancel is practically untouched since its original builders left it. The walls are of narrow bricks wedged aslant between silvery timbers standing only seven inches apart, herringbone fashion. The nave arcades are of beautifully moulded timbers too, and we may think of the whole church as a timber structure, except for the tiles on the roof and the bricks filling the walls.

In one of the windows are fragments of ancient glass including a little tree and parts of a flowery background; and in a case is part of the old crimson altar cloth, resplendent velvet with beautiful silver embroidery and fringe. It is a delightful piece of work, done by a lady who may have been discussing the news of Charles the Second as she sat doing it. It was used in this church for over 200 years. Two of the bells are very old, one among the oldest in Hampshire. This ancient bell was possibly made in the 12th century, and the

The Ruined Grandeur of Netley Abbey

Freefolk

The Village and its Church

Meonstoke

13th Century Church

other about 1450. There is an altar frontal of the 17th century, and the font is the same age.

Among the names of Mattingley's heroes we noticed a stoker who would be tending the boilers of his ship when she was mined, one of the 600 who perished with Lord Kitchener on the Hampshire.

The Nine Builders

MEDSTEAD. It has two sturdy Norman arches with round piers and moulded capitals to dignify the nave of the little church it has rebuilt, and in the chancel is the memory of a touching friendship of long ago. It is a plain marble wall-memorial to John Downes, a native of Carmarthen, who was curate of this parish and of Wield. He died in 1770 still young, and his epitaph gives us a touching picture of the life of two curates who loved each other in the villages about, for we read that this small but sincere memorial of a long and affectionate friendship was erected by his afflicted countryman and friend, Robert Thomas, curate of New Alresford.

The church has an unusual poor-box, made about 500 years ago, probably in France. A charming window in the nave shows Joan of Arc and St Elizabeth, and is in memory of a mother who died one winter and of her baby daughter who followed her in the spring.

On the road to Alton some monks have built themselves a small abbey church and gatehouse. They started 40 years ago, when eight brothers and a priest walked from South Wales and settled on this uncultivated bit of land. With the help of a ship's carpenter they built everything we see here. More monks have joined since, and there is a home attached to the abbey, where 20 old sailors are comfortably quartered.

It happened that we were here just after the funeral of an old lady of 82, who had (in accordance with an ancient custom we were told) been carried for a mile between the house and the churchyard, the bearers wearing white smocks and black skull-caps.

The Price of War

MEONSTOKE. It has a church on the bank of the river, which was white with water crowfoot when we called. It would seem that all the cottages and old houses here have been made gracious by hands which knew only how to make things beautiful. The 13th century church has lost its clerestory, the signs of which we see in a row of round windows above the arcades and in the corbels remaining on the walls. The nave and chancel, the graceful arcades, the tower, and the splendid chancel arch, are all 13th century. The sculptured font is Norman. In the chancel are two stone coffins found in the churchyard. The handsome pulpit with its wide armrests and delightful twisted columns is 17th century, though it has modern panels. It may be that the old panels are now hanging in the aisle, for here is a vigorous piece of carving by a German craftsman of the same time as the pulpit, showing Jacob wrestling with the angel. There is a consecration cross on one of the walls.

We were told here that it was thought the village suffered in proportion to its size more than any other in England from the war, losing 22 men out of its hundred families.

Two Fine Old Men

MICHELDEVER. When the train from Waterloo has reached this place it has climbed higher than the cross on St Paul's. It is worth the climb, for if there were nothing else there are two fine beech avenues, one of them the first thing they see who come by rail. But the best thing they see is the tower which has been standing here 400 years, the finest possession of the village and one of the most notable towers in the county. From its embattled top fierce gargoyles look down, and charming windows pierce its belfry.

Two fine names we come upon in this small place. The chancel has a monument by the famous Flaxman showing a woman with eyes uplifted in memory of Sir Francis and Lady Baring. Facing it is another big monument to the Barings, guarded by two charming angel figures; and hanging on the wall is the faded flag of HMS Captain, lost in a gale in the Bay of Biscay in 1870. Among the 470 men who perished with their ship were Cowper Phipps Coles, her designer; Hugh Talbot Burgoyne, her captain (one of the first men to win a VC); and Arthur Baring, a midshipman of 16 and the great-great-grandson of old Sir Francis Baring, who rebuilt much of this church.

The Barings came from Bremen, where Franz Baring was a Lutheran pastor. His son John set up as a clothmaker in Devon and represented Exeter in Parliament. John's son Francis, who sleeps here, born in 1740, was all his life deaf, but being sent to London for training he showed a genius for finance. A man of insight and indomitable courage, he laid the foundations of a firm that was to become world-famous as Baring Brothers, he became chairman of the East India Company, and his advice was frequently sought by the Government. He raised great loans for national purposes and made a fortune for himself. Experience made him a Free Trader, and he advocated the remission of taxes on a variety of imports. When he died in 1810 he was acclaimed the first merchant in Europe, and he left a fortune of more than two millions. His second son was created Lord Ashburton, his grandson was the first Lord Northbrook, and from Sir Francis himself descended Lord Cromer, the maker of Modern Egypt, who lies in a Hampshire grave (at Bournemouth).

The other famous name is that of a brave Huguenot marquis who sleeps in this churchyard, the Marquis de Ruvigny, who died while staying with his cousin at Stratton House close by.

It has been said that never grave closed over a braver or more modest soldier than this old man, whom they laid in this place in 1721. He had sacrificed his French estates to join the English Army for the defence of his faith. He had done all he could to stop the revocation of the Edict of Nantes. At 43 he came to England, and for 25 years he served our army in Ireland and Flanders and Spain. Though the French once caught him, they let him go in admiration of his character. Once a Spanish enemy on the field sent his own physician to attend him. He lost an eye and an arm in the service of his adopted country, and, after his stirring life, he was living quietly at his Hampshire home, Rookley Manor House, when he came to visit his cousin here, and died.

Micheldever had a church a thousand years ago, and under its tower there are still two arches 600 years old as well as fragments of Norman fonts found in cottage gardens hereabouts. The village archives go back to 1538, the oldest book of them being bound in a piece of parchment manuscript of the 13th century.

Here were the Romans, and here was a Saxon burial ground, but before either Romans or Saxons came the great earthworks were raised on Norsbury Ring, within a walk of this place.

We found here when we called two farm workers who had been on the farms for over half a century, Richard and David Hall; yet even their long service was exceeded by Thomas Clarke of whom we read in the church, for he was vicar 54 years last century and saw his three wives and three children go to the grave before him.

The Handsome Knight

MICHELMERSH. It crowns a high hill near Romsey, hiding itself in trees over whose tops peers the rare 15th century tower, weather-timbered down to the ground. In this church Michelmersh keeps its chief treasure, the 13th century font, shallow and cup-shaped, with flowers and faces. It is an original and delightful piece of work. A stone knight lies in the chancel, looking, in spite of the loss of his nose, a handsome and honest young man not likely to pick quarrels, but ready with his sword and lance when called upon. Geoffrey de Canterton (so they believe he was) lived at a time when it was well to be master of both, in the 14th century days of the barons against the kings. Now his hands are folded, his crossed feet rest on a buck with an eel-like neck and long antlers, and his head is supported by what were once small angels. Near this peaceful warrior is a quaint and unusual stone wall-tablet to Trustram Fantleroy and his wife, with two enchanting kneeling figures in relief in the simple dress of a Tudor squire and lady. They have been here 400 years. Opposite them, in a beautiful window, are lovely fragments of ancient glass, with the heads of two bishops and two bearded men. On both sides of the arch, over the organ, is fine stone carving, one piece seeming to be the cross of a 13th century coffin lid, probably from one of the stone coffins here. There are traces of medieval painting on the walls.

The Solitary Grandeur of Hurst Castle

MILFORD-ON-SEA. It has a noble view across the Solent and sees the sun set on the Isle of Wight, with Hurst Castle in solitary grandeur on the marshes, guarding the seaway up the Solent and lighting it by night. A delightful corner of England is this breezy cliff, with its seascape, the wooded valley, and the village trying to look like a little old town. Charles Stuart must have looked out on it all with strange emotion, for it was from his captivity here that he set out on the journey that ended on the scaffold.

The church (with the unpardonable sin of darkness) is one of the most distinctive of the small churches of Hampshire, with an exquisite 14th century doorway and a unique tower. It started as a wide Norman building and still has two arches in the nave and a small doorway in a transept made by its Norman builders; but the greater part of it is 13th century. We noticed a little stone man playing bagpipes by a window near the porch.

The extraordinary tower is 13th century, with a 14th century leaded spire. The tower spreads out near its base into extensions of the aisles, looking rather like a broody hen squatting over her chickens, with her long neck stretched up high looking out for danger. Round the top are carved heads.

There are three coffin lids 700 years old, two sad little ones. On a wall is a much-worn but graceful carving of the Annunciation, found under the floor and thought to be part of an ancient reredos; it is nearly 600 years old. In the sanctuary is a fine pair of old chairs with carved backs. There is a 13th century piscina and an 18th century chest. In a rich gilded frame on the wall of the nave hangs a brilliantly clear picture painted for an Italian church by Pietro Perugino. It shows the Madonna and Child sitting on a throne, with John the Baptist and John the Evangelist on either side. On a transept wall is a beautiful white tablet by J. H. Foley showing kneeling figures of a woman and a girl, the woman with her left hand to her face and her right arm round the girl. It is to Admiral Sir William Cornwallis, who died in 1819 and desired that no monument should be raised to his memory. On the chancel wall is a sculptured marble by P. MacDowell, RA to Sir Rivett Carnac who entered the East India Company in 1801, and was called the Friend of the Natives; the artist shows his relations weeping over his deathbed.

In the churchyard lies William Saville Kent, the biologist and author, who died in 1908. His grave is covered with a wonderful assortment of fossilised sponges, grown over with moss when we called. In front of the church, in the churchyard, stands a lofty modern cross on mossy old steps.

It is the peep of Hurst Castle we remember here. It was built by Henry the Eighth to defend the Solent, and in it is stone from Beaulieu Abbey. It is heavily armed and has a light 76 feet above high water. Liners bound for Southampton are signalled from it. The approach is from Keyhaven to the ford near Sturt Pond, and then on foot along the bank of shingle which has been thrown up by the breaking down of the cliffs. It is a dull track for about two miles, bringing a sense of grim isolation.

The Last Journey of Charles Stuart

IT was his wanderings after the vital defeat at Naseby, in June 1645, that brought Charles eventually to Hurst Castle. What he had lost in the war he tried to regain by intrigue.

Meantime the real power in England was the Army, which was impatient with all this intriguing. It was the first thoroughly trained standing Army England had ever formed, and it was master of the situation. Its respect for a Parliament which was unrepresentative and out of date was very small, and its disgust with Charles, and its contempt for him, were deep.

The war went on round various towns and castles garrisoned for the King, but the Army was closing in on Oxford, his temporary capital. To avert capture Charles rode north and surrendered himself in 1646 to the Scots, who met Parliamentary Commissioners to discuss terms of settlement. But nothing came of it, and Charles, left in the hands of the Commissioners, was conveyed to Holmby House in Northamptonshire. There negotiations were carried on, but no agreement could be reached, for the King held that he had absolute right of government and that the people had no such right. In fact, he said on the scaffold that "a share in the government did not appertain unto them." While he negotiated he plotted continually, feeling that time was on his side.

At last the Army felt that its victories were being frittered away. Cromwell was in an awkward fix. He believed in Parliamentary government, and favoured the reinstating of the King with a Parliamentary system; but he knew the Army put the blame on the King, and that Charles was deceiving his opponents at every turn. Accordingly on June 3, 1647, he sent Cornet Joyce with a troop of horse to remove Charles from Holmby House to Hampton Court, and London was occupied by the Army. Then the Army, which was now definitely taking the lead, drew up its proposals for a settlement, the soundest and most moderate proposals yet made. But Charles would not agree. He was arranging for an invasion of England by the Scots and a renewal of the war, and he sought greater freedom for himself by escaping from Hampton Court to Carisbrooke Castle, where the Governor, Colonel Hammond, was known to the King. Charles felt he might count on his allowing him, if need be, to escape to the continent; but Hammond did not read his duty in that way. He reported the King's arrival to the Government.

Charles was a prisoner at Carisbrooke for more than a year, and all the time the Army ruled. It interfered with Parliament itself and excluded members it regarded as obnoxious. It demanded that "the capital and grand author of our troubles be speedily brought to justice for the treason, blood, and mischief he is guilty of." It called the Colonel from his post to come to headquarters, and on November 29, 1648, Carisbrooke Castle was seized by Colonel Cobbit and Charles was lodged the next day in Hurst Castle, where no escape was possible.

His captivity in this lonely stronghold on the margin of Keyhaven mud-flats marked the fixed determination to send him to his doom, and he was beheaded in Whitehall on January 20, 1649, the pathetic victim of his Stuart incapacity to be a straightforward king.

The Wonderful Sword

MILTON. It looks across the restless Solent to the Isle of Wight, and sees the coast from Swanage to Hurst Castle. In crumbling Barton Cliff are found fossilised alligators, lizards, tortoises, and turtles; there is a big collection from here at South Kensington.

It has a strange possession in its church porch, a wonderful sword with a long wavy-edged blade bearing the famous mark of Andrea Ferrara who made swords for the gallants and soldiers of the 17th century. It is chained to the monument of the man who collected them, a silly-faced fellow bewigged and in armour, clutching his helmet in one hand and a stone likeness of the sword in the other. He was Thomas White, who died in 1720, and the inscription tells us that he served under three kings and Queen Anne in the wars. The tower is 300 years old, but the chancel is modern, and of fine simplicity. It is divided from the nave by an oak screen and three impressively simple round arches.

The Old Politicians

MINSTEAD. The cottages follow one another in a free and easy way down the slope they are built on, itself all ups and downs, till they reach the extraordinary little church standing on a hill of its own, with a big yew at its gate. It is like a cottage, with gabled windows peeping out of its roof, except that it has an odd little cupola, a small timber spire, and a golden vane. One of its bells has been ringing for 600 years and another for 400.

A heavy ancient door with what seems to be its original iron handle, hangs in the 12th century doorway, and it opens on an interior Sir Roger de Coverley would have been at home in. Here is that rare survival a three-decker pulpit, plain, 17th century, and sturdy, and just such a one as the old knight must have sat under. Here are two extraordinary pews, entered by a small door in the 17th century porch, like small rooms, one with a fireplace and both furnished with comfortable chairs. The humble oak pews in the nave show adze marks 300 years old; the rare double-tiered galleries are so low that a man must bow his head to pass. The base of the medieval screen has been preserved. The font is Norman and has a story, having been dug up in a garden. It is curiously carved with the Baptism, the holy lamb, a lion with two bodies, and two eagles and a tree.

We noticed that one of the rectors, John Compton, was here for 56 years last century; and on the walls we noticed the hatchment of the Earl of Erroll who lies in the chancel, and of whose death an odd tale is told. It is said that the squire sat by the bedside to prevent creditors from removing his body and then brought it first to his manor house and later to the family vault for burial.

Near the church is an inn with the old signboard bearing the figure of the Trusty Servant, a copy of the picture in Winchester College showing a man with a pig's snout, the ears of an ass, and the feet of a stag. Above the village rises the oak-covered mound of Malwood Castle, once a British camp.

Here is Malwood Lodge, still a home of the Harcourts when we called, and once the paradise of that Sir William Harcourt who was one of the bluff, burly figures of the political days of Gladstone and Disraeli. He was Chancellor of the Exchequer, and one of his Budgets introduced the Death Duties, which have had so striking an effect on our countryside by leading to the transformation of great estates.

Here Sir William loved to come from the rush and strain of Westminster; he would scream with joy, his biographer tells us, as he entered the gates of this paradise. He used to say that he had had a good year with his farms when he lost £3 an acre, entering an item in his accounts such as health and pleasure to set off the loss. He built the house "Queen Anne in style and cottagey in feeling," and its visitors book has a host of interesting names. One is the name of Joseph Chamberlain, written in a margin, and thereby hangs a tale. They had come from a Round Table Conference in the exciting days when Mr. Chamberlain was a thorn in the side of his Liberal chief and, the page in the visitors book being full when Chamberlain's turn came to sign, Harcourt said to him, "Now you can turn over a new leaf." But it was not his habit, and Chamberlain signed in the margin of the crowded page.

The Ancient Door

MONK SHERBORNE. Its church is a little way from the village, and we enter it through a solid timber porch which has been on duty 500 years, its heavy beams partly obscuring the chevron moulding of the Norman doorway and the painted trellis of the tympanum. The ancient door has fine elaborate hinges.

The church is charming itself and is full of lovely things: a Norman chancel arch resting on slender pillars whose capitals have two half-human faces with pointed ears, a curious patched-up Norman font with three heads under the bowl, a Norman pillar piscina in the vestry, a charming chancel screen still with some of its 15th century carving, and a carved pulpit set up by the man whose heraldic brass is on the wall near it, the old rector William Dobson, described as a painful servant of God who exchanged Earth for Heaven in 1653. The iron hinges and the spring latch to his little door are still here.

All the woodwork in this well-kept church is delightful. There are massive old pews, 17th century altar rails now under the belfry, and beams that have been supporting the belfry for 500 years. Some of the bells were ringing in the days of Queen Elizabeth and some of the windows were made about 1300.

The Great Old Lady and the Queer Old Rector

MONXTON. One of the villages along the Pillhill Brook near Andover, it has in its refashioned church two pillars 700 years old. They have sculptured capitals and support the chancel arch. On the wall is the brass portrait of an old lady who saw the

233

most astounding reigns in English history, born under Henry the Seventh, living through the reigns of Henry the Eighth, his pathetic son and his fearful daughter, and seeing most of the reign of the dazzling Elizabeth. Her name was Alice Swayn, and she was 98 when she died. Here she is kneeling with her son, both portrait and inscription superbly kept and polished when we called.

Near by is a brass inscription to Richard Pore, the kinsman of an Elizabethan rector, and a glazed case with two metal flagons, one of them made in 1682.

In the early part of the 18th century the village had an extraordinary rector with such a mania for mathematics that he took no interest in anything else, never leaving the house to carry out his duties in the church, nor giving himself time to be shaved, but "letting his beard grow till he was a spectacle." So, we gather, he brought on himself the illness from which he died.

MORESTEAD. The bell rings out from the open turret of its church as it has been ringing for more than 300 years, but this downland village has something much older; it lies on a Roman road and has a font which was made in Norman England. On Hazeley Down is a small wayside cross in remembrance of the men of the London Regiment who came here in the Great War, and we found the trees they planted flourishing in their memory.

Goodwill From Germany

MOTTISFONT. The best thing we found here is the big east window of the church, entirely filled with 16th century glass said to have come from the ruined chapel at Basingstoke. In it is a Crucifixion with St Andrew and St Peter on either side, the Coronation of the Madonna, and Christ in Majesty. This rare window does not exhaust the old glass of Mottisfont, for there are bright and lovely strips older still, made by craftsmen of Chaucer's England. The chancel arch is Norman, finely moulded with zigzag, and in the nave is a Norman font. In the sanctuary is a nameless tomb with a row of little battered figures. There are consecration crosses on the walls, and carved in stone near the door are two coats-of-arms and two helmets which may be regarded as an odd example of goodwill between two countries. They come from Bremen, from a church built in 1693. When that church was rebuilt in 1898 the carving was sent over to the English descendants of one of its German founders.

Near the church is a varied group of some of the tallest trees we have seen. At Brook near by is a stream called the Farburn, used by the Abbess of St Mary at Winchester to drive a mill and to supply fish when river-trout were unseasonable. There was probably no earlier artificial reservoir in England than that made in the valley of this river, and in dry winters we can trace the bank on the hillsides. We can still see the great artificial dam about 25 feet high stretching halfway across the valley, and within the last few years the lake has been partly restored, being now a beautiful sheet of 15 acres swarming with trout.

Sir Walter Scott Writes Marmion

MUDEFORD. It is a fishing village with a history, at the mouth of Christchurch harbour, and it has kept singularly unchanged its old-world character. Side by side with dignified Victorian and Georgian houses, half hidden in their charming grounds, are the cottages of the fishermen who in the early spring of the year go down to the Run (a narrow channel formed by the Stour and the Avon on their way to the sea) there to net the Christchurch salmon. In 1803 King George called at Mudeford in his yacht and sampled the place on his way to Weymouth, with the Scots Greys, the Yeomanry, and the Christchurch Volunteers firing salutes on the beach. After that Mudeford brightened and increased the number of its bathing machines. Among those who bathed there was a Dorset Squire named Tregonwell, driving from Cranborne Lodge. Going home he passed Bourne Chine, a pretty valley with a decoy pond and a spacious sandy shore. Why should there not be a bathing resort here? he thought; and he built himself a house there, now the nucleus of the Exeter Hotel. So Bournemouth began. Now there are houses all the seven miles from Bournemouth to Mudeford, and Bournemouth has long passed its 100,000 residents, while Mudeford has still the air of a fishing village with a scattering of houses of impressive respectability. It is the part of Christchurch where people build huts on the sandhills and bathe.

A mighty and ancient cedar almost hides with its great sweeping branches the little church founded in the second half of last century by one of the neighbouring Ricardo family, to whose sons and daughters there are numerous tablets and memorials. Here in recent years it has been the custom to hold a Spring service for the fishermen and their families followed by a simple ceremony of Blessing the Waters, when the vicar and the choir go out in boats to offer prayers of thanksgiving and dedication for the harvest of the sea. In Autumn, when the church is decorated with fruits and flowers, an appropriate background is provided by the fishermen's nets.

Rowing boats ply to and fro across the Run carrying passengers to the great bank of fine sand beyond, which forms a delightful little Lido for Christchurch holiday makers. Though the village has remained much the same the Run itself has seen many changes during the centuries in its course and outlet. The constantly shifting sands under the influence of wind and tide have altered the direction of the channel again and again. As recently as 1935 a great storm broke through the eastern end of the sandbank forcing the waters through an almost entirely new opening.

When Mudeford still had hopes of being a wateringplace it won for itself a rather curious place in an immortal page of literature. Here Coleridge used to come for rest and change, and here came Sir Walter Scott, both as friends of the member of Parliament for Christchurch, William Stewart Rose, who had a house called Gundimore. Scott was here in 1807 and was writing Marmion at the time. Gundimore, surrounded by trees, is the last house in the village where the road turns down to the beach by the Run beyond the little quay. The room in which Scott wrote is recessed in a passage-way and has a lovely view across the lawn to the Isle of Wight. It was the view of Hengistbury from here which inspired him. Having written the beginning of Marmion, he would be moved by what Mr Rose had to tell him of Pitt, for Rose had been Pitt's friend and his follower in the House. Scott was a Tory and a patriot, and the impressive sight of Hengistbury, and the knowledge of the part it had played in frustrating Napoleon's plans, would move him we do not doubt to these noble lines on Pitt:

> Now is the stately column broke,
> The beacon light is quenched in smoke,
> The trumpet's silver sound is still,
> The warder silent on the hill.

John and Mary

NATELY SCURES. A stone's throw from all the rush of the Basingstoke road to the west, one of the busiest in England, a little Norman church has been standing, a shrine of peace, for 800 years, with roses climbing up its walls, and a mermaid coyly flicking her tail on one of the capitals of the handsome Norman doorway. It is nearly our smallest church, so tiny that 18 paces take us from end to end. Rounded into an apse at the east end, it has two bells hanging exposed in a tiny turret at the west, and is lit by only deep Norman windows. Inside is an arcaded Norman font. The walls are covered with tablets to all the Carletons buried here. We read of Dudley Carleton, the 4th Lord Dorchester, who served in the Crimea; Richard Carleton, rector here for half a century; General Thomas Carleton, first Governor of New Brunswick when it became a separate province in 1784; and the General's only son William, who fought as a boy at Trafalgar and lived on another 69 years, one of the last survivors of the battle.

But it is a brass tablet under the west window that captures our fancy. It is to a happy couple who died within seven months after living through the Civil War. The wife went first, and in 1661 the husband followed her, and the village engraver painfully and conscientiously wrote out their last words to each other; we imagine that he was much moved, for apparently he left out letters and went back to put them in and somehow he got all the Ns the wrong way. As naive as his printing are the verses themselves. They begin:

> Here lies John Palmer and Mary his wife,
> Prisoners of hope to eternal life.

Then John says to Mary:

> Mary make room!
> To thee I come
> And my last home
> Till the Day of Doom.
> Then shall we wake, rise, live for aye
> With Christ a never-dying day.

And Mary lovingly replies:

> I went before
> To ope the door;

I could not stay
But now give way.
Come then, my dear, we'll sleep in bliss
And in the dust each other kiss.

And then together these two dear people tell their simple tale:

Twice sixteen years we lived together
In sunshine and in stormy weather,
In wedlock bands husband and wife,
In joy, love, peace, void of all strife,
And ten times changed our habitation
And here at last we fixed our station,
Where after ten years spent we have
Obtained at last a quiet grave.

Painted Walls

NETHER WALLOP. Enchanting with willow and brook, thatched roofs, and plaster walls, it is good at taking care of lovely things, and has a medieval church worth taking care of, with rugged old pews, an old screen in the tower, sculptured capitals in the nave, 14th century niches in the wall, and Tudor timbers in the roof. We come in by an ancient door and find ourselves in the presence of many rare things. One of them is the only brass portrait of a prioress in this country, hidden under a mat in the nave. There are two brass portraits known of abbesses, but Mary Gore, who died just after Joan of Arc had led the French king to be crowned at Rheims, is the only prioress whose portrait we have in brass. She is tall and elegant, and has a small prim face.

But it is up and not down that we must look for some of the greatest treasures of this place, the medieval paintings uncovered on these ancient walls by Professor Tristram and his men from the Royal College of Art, who had been here not long before we called, removing layer after layer of plaster. There is a great bell painted over the tower arch, a little saintly figure very clear on the splay of a window, a suggestion of angels over the chancel arch, and a jumbled patch of colour in which we can make out a pair of scales. Most impressive of all is the St George in the nave, with part of a castle close by, and two faces looking over its wall. St George is in armour, piercing the dragon with his lance. He is vividly drawn in ochre and black, and it is interesting to find him here because at the time we called this was the only case known to Professor Tristram in which a St George has been found in a village associated with miracle plays. It may be that the figure was taken from life, representing one of the players. They are probably 500 years old.

An oddity seldom seen in a churchyard is the great pyramid, about twice the height of a man, set up in memory of an 18th century "Doctor of Physick." It bears his coloured arms, and has red stone flames rising from the point.

It is said that Cromwell passed through Nether Wallop on his way to the dramatic siege of Basing House, but great folk must have passed this way before Cromwells or Caesars were dreamed of, for in the neighbourhood is Danebury Hill, with the wonderful prehistoric long barrows in which lie our far-off ancestors.

The Abbey of the White Monks

NETLEY. We are greeted here with these beautiful words: "Approach with reverence, for there are those within whose dwelling place is Heaven." For 700 years it has sheltered in a dip of the land near the shore of Southampton Water, protected by elms from the rough sea winds, and for 400 of these years it has stood a memory-haunted ruin, mute witness of its ancient glory.

It was as long ago as 1239 that a little company of White Monks led by Peter des Roches set out from Beaulieu in search of a place to found a new colony. They settled here. The Abbey was endowed by Henry the Third as a tribute to Peter des Roches, who had been his tutor. With his Queen Eleanor of Provence, the King was at the dedication of a magnificent group of buildings. The early grounds of the abbey went down to the shore, and after the Dissolution the Gatehouse, now on the other side of the road, was converted by Henry the Eighth into a fort commanding the entrance into Southampton Water. The house known now as Netley Castle was built in the 19th century on the foundations of the Tudor fort.

The abbey here was never so completely dismantled as most other religious houses. Much of the domestic part was adapted as a dwelling-house and was used until the end of the 17th century. Patches of red brick show the additions made by 16th or 17th century owners. The desertion of the place began in the 18th century, when the owner sold the church to a Southampton builder. Tradition tells that, though warned in a dream against the sacrilege, the builder persisted and was killed by a falling stone before he could complete the outrage. However that may be, we can never be thankful enough to whatever or whoever saved this jewel of rare beauty.

A glorious group of grey stone, it rises from a charming setting of lawns. We come first to the domestic quarters, where at every turn lovely vistas beckon us till we reach the Cloister Court, 114 feet square. Here we see the moss-grown base of the central fountain, the slender lancets of the dormitory, the exquisite pointed arches of the eastern wall next to the chapter house, and the eye, leaping from charm to charm, is arrested by that superb miracle of Netley, the frail arch poised high in the air, so delicate and fairylike against the sky that we almost hold our breath lest the wind should shatter this ethereal vision. We do not wonder that the abbots chose for their last resting-place the gracious chapter house, inmost heart of all this beauty. We feel, after seeing its exquisite proportions, that the sight of the windows through the cloister arches is a memory that can never fade. There is a hooded chimney reaching nearly to the roof in what is called the Guest Room, with a wide open drain on one side communicating with the fishponds. As we look into its depth of 15 feet we are amazed at the tremendous strength of the foundation walls.

But all else is dwarfed before the awe-inspiring majesty of the abbey church. No imagination is needed, as at Beaulieu, to build up this House of God. The walls are here in their magnificent proportions, 211 feet long, 58 wide, and 115 feet from transept to transept. The bases of four great piers mark the position of the central tower; on two of them rough inscriptions and designs are partly legible—two hearts below a cross and banner. A fragment of a spiral stair shows where the monks would climb to light the lamp high in the tower, a landmark and beacon to ships as they entered the narrow passage from the Solent. The two great windows, east and west, are silhouetted on a background of trees; the mullion of the west window has gone, and the ravages of time and storm have worn away the mouldings of the east, but the sheer beauty of their outline is a wonder still.

We can trace the altars in the chancel aisles, and of the south transept enough is left to give a slight idea of the perfection of the whole interior. Clustered slender columns rise to a great height, and from the delicately-moulded capitals spring the narrow pointed ribs upholding the vaulted roof. The triforium is still in place, and on every side piers, mouldings, quatrefoils, and recesses charm us by their ornament and grace.

The Office of Works has happily stripped the ivy from the ruined walls, and the stark splendour of the grey stone, the revealed detail of archway and doorway, window and pillar, is more than recompense. As dusk falls on this quiet scene, disturbed only by the mournful cry of wheeling seagulls, we turn away wondering if some of those whose dwelling-place is Heaven are here again, stealing silently into their great church, seeing the lamp aglow before the altar and hearing the deep-voiced chant of *Ora pro Nobis* ringing down the solitary aisles.

Between the abbey grounds and a small modern church are the remains of the moat and the fishponds, and at a little distance from the ruins the abbot's lodging and the infirmary stand apart. From here we have one of the finest views of the whole group.

The biggest English military hospital was built at Netley to receive a thousand wounded soldiers from Florence Nightingale's beds in the Crimea. Its front is a quarter of a mile long and more; it is perhaps the longest building in the land. But it is something far older than this that we remember here. We remember a peace that can almost be felt, something that will not pass away.

NEWNHAM. The church has one 12th century doorway and the pillars of what we imagine to be another, one carved at the top with a queer beast; but a finer possession is the Norman chancel arch with its lines of moulding and traces of medieval painting. On the wall of the panelled sanctuary is the portrait of a bearded man engraved on a 14th century gravestone. He appears to have a halo, and wears the robes of a priest. One of the bells has been ringing since the century of Agincourt and Joan of Arc.

Heroes

NEWTON VALENCE. Its church stands by an impressive manor house built in various styles, some of it centuries old. A great yew about seven yards round rivals the tower in height, and a 700-year-old font stands outside the church door. The chancel is 13th century and has in the sanctuary a pillar piscina which must have come from an earlier church, for it is Norman. There is a very neat 13th century piscina in the side chapel. A brass inscription tells of a vicar's little boy who died in the same year as Shakespeare, and on the roll of victory is the name of Edmund White, who served the village for 53 years. All the lancet windows are bright with coloured glass, two showing the warrior saints Martin and George in memory of three warrior brothers, Neil, Ronald, and Alexander Maclachlan. Neil fell in India in 1908, and both his brothers won the DSO in the Great War. We see their names again on the peace memorial by the roadside, together with Colonel H. A. Lemprière, the third DSO hero from this quiet corner of Hampshire.

A Wrong Put Right

NORTH BADDESLEY. To find its chief beauty we must go through the village and follow a green lane. In about a mile we shall come to a manor house and a tiny church which is believed to stand on the site of a pagan temple. Its quaint brick tower was built in 1674. The 15th century timber porch, resting on low walls made of big stones, has a door with a curious sliding iron bolt for a handle. Inside is beauty simple and unspoiled. The font was here in Chaucer's time, and may be Norman. There is a little glass 600 years old. The lovely screen was the gift of Lord Chief Justice Fleming, who lived in the neighbourhood and is buried at North Stoneham; his initials and the date of its erection (1602) are on the chancel side of the screen. The beautiful pulpit, believed also to have been his gift, is panelled, and has a canopy carved with foliage. By the font, safe under a glass case, is a great Bible with chains hanging from it; it was given by Thomas Tompkins, a blind rector from 1693 to 1702, and in it is the "genealogy of the line of our Saviour Jesus Christ observed from Adam to the blessed Virgin Mary" compiled by John Speed, a historian of Charles Stuart's reign who was entitled to two shillings for every Bible which used it. Below the pulpit is a 15th century chest with a rounded lid cut solid from an oak.

In the chancel is a richly carved 14th century tomb, and in the window above it is a 15th century pane of glass with a gold T in it. Both the tomb and the initial belong to Galfridus de Tothalle,

Knight Hospitaller and rector here for 50 years, for the Hospitallers' Hampshire headquarters were at North Baddesley after the Black Death drove them from Godsfield. A bulky wall-monument in a corner of the chancel is attributed to Inigo Jones. Below an inscription to John More, who died in 1620, stands a cherub on a skull, holding a winged book.

Just inside the churchyard here are two gravestones raising an interesting point concerning gravestone history. We have seen in one of our Kent villages a false claim on a tombstone blotted out; here we see a wrong on one stone righted on another. The first stone has this inscription:

In memory of Charles Smith who suffered at Winchester on the 23rd March 1822, for resisting by firearms his apprehension by the gamekeeper of Lord Palmerston when found in Hough Coppice looking after what is called game, aged 30 years.
If thou seest the oppression of the poor, and violent perverting of judgment and justice in a province, marvel not at the matter for he that is higher than the highest regardeth, and there be higher than they.

By this stone stands a stone set up in 1906 in justice to the memory of Lord Palmerston, who, it seems, wrote to the judge to ask for mercy and also appealed to the Home Secretary on Charles Smith's behalf. The new stone has this inscription:

Charles Smith was convicted at Winchester Assizes of attempting to murder. A watcher named Robert Snellgrove approached Smith to identify him, Snellgrove, quite a youth, was alone and unarmed; Smith, with a companion and armed, fired at close quarters the whole contents of his gun into Snellgrove's body. In 1822 attempt to murder was a capital crime. Copies of the original papers connected with the case are deposited in the church chest. E.A.

As a record of village life this is unique in our experience, and surely a remarkable example of insistence on English fairplay.

By the church is the manor house with some of the old bricks of the Knights Hospitallers' building in its walls, and in its garden is a very old fig tree said to be descended from a tree in the garden of the Knights.

Though hundreds of years have passed since the last of the Knights Hospitallers bade farewell to this beautiful part of Hampshire, their memory is kept literally green by the woods and meadows they knew so long. From a mound near the fig tree we look out to Knight's Wood, Zion Hill, and Little Prophet's Wood, heavenly places with heavenly names. Long may they flourish in this land so fair.

Famous Folk

NORTHINGTON. It has one of the best 19th century churches we have seen in a village, with pinnacles and amusing grotesques on the tower and chancel, and with much beautiful woodwork inside. Fine, too, is the stone pulpit, round whose stem an extraordinary beast is clinging perilously. This splendid church was the gift of the fourth Lord Ashburton, who did not live to see it finished; he now lies in a corner of the churchyard. In the nave, with the mud of a foreign field still clinging to it, is the wooden cross of his son Guy Victor Baring, brought back from the Great War to "the beloved home of his childhood." A big monument with two delightful angels under the tower tells of the first, second, and third lords, and of others of their family. Alexander Baring, first Lord Ashburton, was born in 1774. He was the son of the great financier Sir Francis Baring, and was himself a financier and a leading statesman of his day. He went to America as British Commissioner when trouble arose over boundaries, concluded the Ashburton Treaty at Washington in 1842, and is said to have "spread a social charm over Washington and filled everybody with friendly feelings toward England." Facing the monument is a big tablet to Robert Henley of the 18th century, who became Lord Chancellor and first Earl of Northington, and to his son Robert, the second and last earl, Lord Lieutenant of Ireland "in times very difficult."

The site of the old church close by has a veteran yew among the gravestones, and a memory of the great Gilbert White, who was curate here before he went to Selborne. The mansion of Northington is the Grange, a splendid house of many columns and fine pediments, low, irregular, and 380 feet long. It is said to be the work of Inigo Jones and Sir John Soane, the great architects of the 17th and 19th centuries, and is set in a beautiful park with lakes kept filled by an Itchen tributary flowing through to Alresford. The grounds were laid out by the first Earl of Northington, and in the great house George the Fourth lived when he was Prince of Wales. It became a meeting-place for famous men during the life of Lady Harriet (the first wife of the second Lord Ashburton), Carlyle, Thackeray, Kingsley, and Wilberforce being among her guests.

The Strangers in a Strange Land

NORTH STONEHAM. It is touched with the spirit of progress which is making Southampton one of the most remarkable ports of the world, but it struggles to keep itself a village, and we found a thatcher here lamenting the new red roofs, and the smith still at the forge which his family had run 200 years, though his brother had taken his Oxford degree and was engaged in research into the question of Anglo-Saxon dialects. We found also a descendant (making pegs) of the great Nicholas Wadham who founded a college at Oxford; and one other remarkable fact we found—that from the end of the 18th century this place had had, when we called, only five rectors. Two were father and son: Edwardes Beadon who was rector for 49 years and was chaplain to George the Third, and his son, who followed him for 68 years and died in 1879, after holding a hundredth birthday party at the rectory.

Away from the village, on the edge of a park, we come to the church by a lychgate made from the timbers of HMS Thunderer. The church has much to give us pleasure and stir our imagination. Outside it is almost entirely the work of men who lived in the days of the Wars of the Roses, and the fine buttressed tower, which has a curious wooden clock face that has only one hand, is 15th century. Its oldest possession is the 13th century font. It has some monuments of great historic interest, and windows notable for their heraldic glass.

It is for a remarkable stone, unlike anything else we have seen, that the lover of antiquity comes; it is in the middle of the chancel floor, a gravestone of grey marble cut to imitate a brass. It has on it a shield with a doubleheaded eagle, and at the corners are the emblems of the Four Evangelists. Round the edge is a strange inscription. It is probable that there is hardly another tombstone like this in England, for the medieval Italian words on it tell us that here is the burial place of the Guild of Slavonians, the hardy sailors of Dalmatia who manned so many Venetian ships in the Middle Ages. This is a witness of the great trading days when Venice "held the gorgeous East in fee." Its men came much to Southampton and carried on a busy trade with Winchester, passing along the Roman road through North Stoneham. The people of Southampton were bitterly hostile to them, and so it came about that not there, but in this little village church, under the symbol of their protecting eagle, were laid to rest those who perished by violence or disease so far from their native land.

The year on the tomb is 1491, and the trade with Venice came to an end 40 years later. Then it may have been that the iron rings by which the stone was raised at each burial were removed, and the holes filled with lead, as we see it.

In striking contrast with this modest stone is a huge tomb calling to life the dark days of James the First, for this man who lies in it in scarlet and ermine was Sir Thomas Fleming, Chief Justice under Elizabeth and James. He made his home here and died suddenly after entertaining his tenants. He it was who decided that as the king owned all the seaports he might impose what duties he liked on goods. He was also a member of the council which tried the Gunpowder Plotters. With him, rather grim in her black hood, lies his wife, a prayer book in her hand, and below kneel their eight children. The elder sons are in armour and the heir who married Oliver Cromwell's aunt is a size larger than his brothers and sisters, to show his importance. A pompous inscription tells us everything about him except that his father was once a small mercer in the Isle of Wight. A 19th century John Fleming has a bust on the wall.

On the wall of an aisle is a memorial to a worthy man and his delightful wife. Lord Hawke was Admiral in the days when England's prowess at sea was so great that Horace Walpole found it necessary to ask each morning what new victory there was. He gained one himself, the mastery of the Channel, and his memorial has a panel with a stirring relief of a battle, with flying clouds and smoke and an angry sea. His wife, we are told, was "the best wife, the best mother, and the best of friends; for truth, engaging tenderness, and good nature: the delight of all who knew her"; and his inscription says: "The annals of his life compose a period of naval glory unparalleled in later times, for wherever he sailed victory attended him."

It is said that this quiet village may have been in 686 the scene of the cruel deed of which we hear in the story of the Abbot of Redbridge, for here, it is thought, fled Arwald and Atwald, sons of the king of the Isle of Wight, who were betrayed to Cadwalla, king of Wessex; he allowed the abbot to teach them the truths of Christianity and baptise them, and then had them executed.

NORTH WALTHAM. It has kept alive a play 800 years old, a village troupe of mummers still acting it in neighbouring villages at Christmas time; and it has a 500-year-old font, decorated with flowers and quatrefoils, and brought from its neighbour Popham. It is the prettiest thing in the refashioned church, a building with arches in the style of the 12th century. The oldest possessions of the church apart from the structure are the 600-year-old piscina and the mass dial of the same age, which marked time for the village in the days before clocks. There are 16th century bells and altar plate of Tudor and Stuart days.

The Lonely Fortress

NORTH WARNBOROUGH. A walk by the old Basingstoke canal, where yellow waterlilies float and wild roses trail the towpath hedge, leads us to a group of slender firs marking the ruined keep of King John's Castle.

Nature has made it her own. Ivy and little trees grow from its flint and rubble, but there is still left to it something of the great strength for which it was famous. It is a grey ring of wall rising about 40 feet with a diameter of over 30, the walls 8 feet thick. Some of the eight buttresses have crumbled away, and here the great wall has fallen. Great gaping holes mark round windows and arches through which King John looked out. He built this place, and it was here he set out one morning on the way to Windsor fuming at the thought of what was coming, for his journey ended in Magna Carta.

There is no roof, and nettles grow on the floor; but curiously intact is a chimney in the wall, with slanting tiles still marking the fireplace. Deep ditches curve round this grim sentinel from a grim past. A group of houses collected round it to accommodate nobles and their retinue, but the tower has outlived them all. When Louis the Dauphin came over to help the English barons the castle held out against the invader for about a fortnight and surrendered only on condition that its garrison should march out unharmed with the honours of war. The Dauphin agreed, the gates were opened, and out marched the heroic garrison—three knights, three squires, and seven men-at-arms. They were loudly cheered by their astonished foes, who nobly kept their word and let them go their way.

For a short time these walls sheltered the Frenchman who founded our Parliament, Simon de Montfort. His wife, the Countess of Leicester, was granted the use of the castle by her brother Henry the Third, and in the British Museum is the diary she kept during the six months she was here till her husband was killed fighting against the king in the summer of 1265. The diary, written on a parchment roll 20 feet long by one foot wide, is chiefly concerned with prices paid for food, clothes, and services, an interesting peep into the life of the Middle Ages.

In remarkable contrast with this lonely fortress, where no one has lived since the 16th century, is the friendly little hamlet, with its charming row of ten brick and timber cottages with overhanging storeys, and an old mill house with the Whitewater stream running past. It once turned eight mills. The one here and Castle Mill are now private houses; Poland Mill stands unused by its Tudor farmhouse, while another Tudor farm called Potbridge is half a mile away, with a big beam in one of its upper rooms stretching from wall to wall only three feet from the floor. Lodge Farm is Elizabethan with a most unusual gable and a timbered granary raised on stone mushrooms to protect it from rats. It is as charming as most old farms, but it has history as well as charm, for in one of its barns is a Roman museum, and the trees in its orchard grow from the foundations of a homestead of 1600 years ago.

The farmer came upon these foundations by accident in 1929, and enthusiastically had them all laid bare, as we found them. Two Roman homes were here, and we can see where they had their central heating apparatus, and how the hot air was carried through the house. Here are tesserae from the floors, patterned plaster from the walls, and tiles from the roof. Hundreds of shells still testify to the Roman's love of oysters, though 65 pounds of them have already been gathered up. We saw two tiles on which a dog and a goat stepped while the tiles were still soft, leaving their imprint for 16 centuries. We found smaller things in cases: coins of the Caesars, a complicated padlock, Roman keys and nails, pots and dishes, a comb, and many relics also of ancient Britons.

Such was the harvest of the past yielded in this Hampshire orchard; and these are not the only museum exhibits of North Warnborough, for something else beside the countess's diary has found its way from here into a London museum. It is a copy in the Victoria and Albert of a bit of Tudor painting inside a Tudor cottage, on the road to Greywell. Roughly sketched in red on a wall are two men on horseback with a simple design round them.

The Wonderful Monk

NURSLING. It is scattered about the banks of the River Test not far from Southampton, with a creeper-covered water-mill, a small 14th century church, and a towered and gabled Tudor house. The great house is Grove Place, a wonderful sight when the terraces of daffodils are ablaze with gold and in the meadow the lovely chalices of nature are blowing in the wind. It is approached by an avenue of lofty limes. The house took ten years to build in the time of Elizabeth, who is said to have stayed here. There are splendid plasterwork ceilings and oak panelling, a noble staircase, and the arms of Elizabeth and Charles Stuart are on the walls.

But fame reached this small place long before the days of the great Elizabeth, for here came a boy who was to be known throughout Europe as St Boniface. He was born as Winfrith at Crediton in Devon, but he came to the monks of the monastery at Nursling, among whom he reached his intellectual prime. He was one of the rarest gifts of Saxon England in the dark and barbarous age of the seventh century.

He must have been one of the few men of his time who mastered all the learning then available. When he was 30 the fire of the missionary blazed in his heart, and as Abbot of Nursling he travelled about Europe with the zeal of a crusader, entering into a fruitful alliance with Pope Gregory the Second, who sent him into Germany. Here his passionate fervour found full vent, and like a patriarch of the Old Testament he strode into Paganism's holy places and smashed the idols. Thousands flocked to baptism under his persuasion. His holy life gained him wide fame, and when the father of Charlemagne sought a saintly man to crown him it was Boniface he chose. But the day came when he met a hostile multitude with murder in their hearts. He would not allow his friends to attack them or to defend themselves. "Let us not fear those who may kill the body but cannot touch the soul," he said, and he met his death unflinchingly, kneeling with the Gospel in his hands and awaiting the onslaught. Fifty disciples were with him and their dead bodies were left to bear him company. Though his life took him so far away he never forgot this village of his youth, and when his sight was growing dim he wrote to one of his friends, the blind Bishop of Winchester, asking that a fine manuscript of the Prophets, so fairly and cleanly written by an Abbot of Nursling, might be sent out to him.

There is a tablet in memory of Boniface on the wall of the church porch. The church itself has window tracery from the 14th century, a pulpit decorated by an Elizabethan craftsman, and 14th century tiles in the vestry wall. Nearer these times is a big gravestone with three brass plates of the 17th century, engraved with a sun, a globe, a book, a skull, and some stars above the clouds.

On a splendid canopied tomb in the vestry lie Richard Mille and his wife. They died about the same time as Shakespeare, and they lie here propping up their serious faces on their hands. He is in black and gold armour, and she is finely dressed, with a big ruff and red shoes. A tablet on the wall of the nave has white marble curtains drawn back to reveal for us the busts of Colonel Warren Hastings Frith and his wife Ellen, both with earnest faces, she wearing a lace cap.

The Man Who Crowned Bluebeard

OAKLEY. It is William Warham's village. This village boy saw his star rise and lead him on to dazzling heights. He was trusted and much loved by Henry the Seventh, who made him Lord Chancellor and Archbishop of Canterbury; and then the star of Cardinal Wolsey rose with Henry the Eighth, and Warham's star set.

The high tower in the grounds of Malshanger, the new house, is all that is left of his home; but the church he rebuilt for his native village has kept through another rebuilding his arms carved on stone over a handsome Tudor doorway, and has given him a memorial window. It shows him in brown and golden robes, one of his hands raised in blessing, the other holding a cross. Above the archbishop's arms on the tower is a piece of sculpture whose origin nobody knows, a simple relief of a man with a dog's head and one hand raised. It is a very old and curious fragment. There is some 16th century glass, altar plate of Tudor and 18th century days, and a font set on the base of an old churchyard cross.

Here sleeps Warham's father Robert, under a canopied tomb with the brass portraits of himself and his wife. They are both in simple clothes, and William kneels at the head of their four sons. Close by is another tomb with two sleeping alabaster figures on it, probably other Warhams, richly dressed in Tudor clothes with many rings on their fingers, the lady's fingers half covered with them. Both wear charming little chains and have curious square-toed shoes. The Warham arms are on this tomb, with the three shells and the odd-looking goat. Two old arches seem to have been used again in the south arcade; one, supported on round pillars, we imagine to be about 750 years old; the other, finely panelled, may well have been in the church William Warham built. High on the wall between them is a charmingly sculptured boy keeping watch over a family tablet of last century.

What a contrast between the peace of this village and the turbulence and terror in which Warham ended his days! Few men have filled more offices in the State than he, his 82 years embracing one of the most exciting and dangerous periods in English history.

One of the most trusted advisers of Henry the Seventh, he had a share in arranging the marriage of Prince Arthur with that lady of sorrows Catherine of Aragon. He figured in all the State functions of the closing years of the reign, and then, in June 1509, Prince Arthur being dead and his brother Henry having succeeded him as husband of Catherine, Warham crowned the young couple in Westminster Abbey.

With Bluebeard's development Warham had a thousand occupations, but a new star soared in his firmament and, with the ascent of Wolsey, Warham gladly receded into a position of less prominence. He was a scholar. He had an abiding affection for Erasmus, who dedicated to him some of his work. Many were the gifts of money with which the good archbishop mitigated the poverty of his friend.

Warham never was a reformer, but it went against his grain to persecute those who wanted reform. He became involved in the strife which grew out of Wolsey's towering ambitions and the disputes arising from Henry's repeated demands for loans and subsidies.

We trace the old primate defending the rights of his see against the haughty cardinal; see him hurrying along the coast of Kent to prepare defences against a threatened invasion; hear him half-heartedly urging the men of Kent to give of their wealth for the king's wars. We picture him at Otford and Knole successively receiving with lamentable countenance the petitions of the hard-hit landowners for the return of loans which the king refused to pay.

Wolsey easily imposed on the simplicity of Warham to make him believe that there really was ground for Henry's divorce from Catherine, yet such was his inherent kindness that he was made counsel for her assistance. Towards the end he drifted into opposition to Henry over ecclesiastical prerogative, and finally found himself in exactly the position which had brought Becket to his doom. But he was aged and failing, and to the boundless delight of Anne Boleyn he died before his scruples regarding the divorce could stiffen into irrevocable opposition.

A munificent friend of education and of church building, Warham poured out his vast wealth on objects dear to his heart, and died so poor that he left only just enough to pay for his decent burial in the cathedral over which he had presided thirty years.

Street of Delight

ODIHAM. One of the most delightful of Hampshire's small towns, it has houses older than the Reformation, set in a countryside made fair by Nature and made notable by history. In this wide street of charming houses are two St Georges, fitting for a place that has seen so much history go by. One is the painted sign on the 16th century inn and one on the peace memorial (which has two women's names on it and was fragrant with rosemary for remembrance when we called). Next to the George Hotel is a house with a lofty front room as big as a chapel, where Charles Kingsley used to lecture, coming over from Eversley.

The Tudor vicarage, a charming gabled place with tall chimneys, has an interesting neighbour on each side. One is the farm called Palace Gate, which has in its barns and cellars and the fine avenue of limes behind it all that is left of an old palace visited by Queen Elizabeth; the other is a beautiful house of which parts go back to Chaucer's day, with a yew hedge which was growing in Milton's time.

A mile out along the Winchfield road is an old tree called Frenchman's Oak because it showed prisoners in the Napoleon wars that they had reached the limit of the walk permitted them. Then there is the great chalk pit with its towering white cliffs and hosts of jackdaws, and the cottages where the humbler ranks of prisoners were quartered to be near their work of quarrying. But we can take a walk from Odiham which brings us to a scene more thrilling, for it leads to the banks of the old Basingstoke canal by the neighbouring hamlet of North Warnborough, where stands all that is left of the castle from which King John set out on a summer's day in 1215 for the meadows of Runnymede, where he threw himself on the ground in his rage and gnashed his teeth and gnawed chips and straw before he sealed Magna Carta.

Those who love the quiet corners which keep alive so many of the charities of our countryside will linger by the friendly bit of 17th century England behind Odiham church, a group of almshouses forming three sides of a garden. Close by them is a tiny cottage with a chimney almost as big as itself. It is still called the Pest House, as it was in the days when the sick were tended here.

On these small homes of the old folk falls the shadow of the red church tower, built of brick in the Civil War and looking with its red and white pinnacles rather like the tower of a Tudor house. There is a grim head over the clock, and stone corbels are everywhere. On a south buttress are scratched two mass clocks, unusual in having the hours numbered on them.

The church rises in the square known as the Bury, and we come to it through a short avenue of limes. It is the biggest church in North Hampshire, refashioned in the 14th century. One of its stately arcades has three piers of slender clustered 15th century columns, the other is 14th century, with arches springing so airily as to need only two columns to carry them from end to end of the nave. The galleries, lavishly carved and reached by their original steps, were built in Charles Stuart's day; the 17th century pulpit, carved with scrolls and vases of flowers, is one of the handsomest in the county. The chancel has delicate 15th century screens, Jacobean altar rails, and low arcades of the 13th century. The pillar piscina is 700 years old. The font, made about 1500, is remarkable for being hewn from chalk; it has a lily carved on it and an odd bracket at the edge of the bowl, such as we have seen in a few other fonts, probably for a little shelf.

A chest in the tower has the date 1662 set in nails, and one in the vestry has four keys marked with the initials of the vicar and three churchwardens. There is a beautiful silver chalice of 1618 and a sanctus bell of 1558.

The church is rich in brasses of men and women of the 15th and 16th centuries, confused in some cases by wrong inscriptions. There is a civilian with his wife dressed in the quiet clothes fashionable about 1480, a gaily-clad lady of the 16th century kneeling with her nine daughters, and another lady with six daughters; a handsome young man in armour, and a civilian in square-toed shoes; a 15th century priest named William Goode, and a fine heraldic brass of the 17th century to Edward Seagar. But most charming of all the brasses is the little one of Margaret Pye on the vestry floor. It is the portrait of a baby in swaddling clothes as worn 300 years ago, with a long pleated bib and pretty headcloth. Outside the church door is the old altar tomb of Robert May:

> Stop, gentle reader, hither turn thine eye
> To learn whose mortal part beneath doth lie.

We are told that Robert founded the grammar school for Odiham's poor boys, and are urged to copy his virtues:

> Thus taught, good reader, to thy home retreat,
> With rival ardour let thy bosom beat.

In the shadow of the north wall lie the graves of two French prisoners. It is a noble tradition in Odiham that their stones are scrupulously kept, and we found them, like the thatched cottage in the poem, wondrous neat and clean. One of them has these touching words: He was a prisoner of war; Death hath set him free.

Protected by a timber roof against the churchyard wall are the old stocks and whipping-post. The post has still its iron grips for the wrists, made in three sizes so that they would fit whoever came. An odd thing we heard here was the tale of a calendar found in the smoke loft of a chimney in Hillside Farm, another old house about a mile from Odiham. It was being repaired a few years ago when a calendar for 1666 fell out from a niche in the chimney, black with smoke but unburned. It marked off the days of the Great Fire of London, but had itself escaped the little fire burning below it for 250 years.

Lighting a Lamp in the Dark Ages

THERE was born at Odiham in 1468 a man who is still unforgotten for his great learning in the Dark Ages. He was William Lily, who while still at Oxford obeyed some mysterious call to the East. Like a true Crusader he went to Jerusalem; then returned to Italy and settled down for five years in Rhodes. Here he was in the midst of hapless companies of scholars who had fled in terror when the conquering Turk captured Constantinople in 1453.

For centuries Constantinople had been the last sanctuary of classical learning. Here scholar recluses had hoarded manuscripts which had come down from ancient days. Here in a quiet backwater when all was storm, fire, and barbarism in the outer world, the world of the scholars had quietly brooded over its treasures, rich only in possessions of the intellect.

Like a thunderbolt the Turks broke into this great academy of culture, and the scholars fled in all directions. But they carried with them seeds to fertilise all Europe. Under their cloaks and in hastily gathered packages they brought away their precious manuscripts, so that wherever two or three refugees from Constantinople were gathered together there was learning in the midst of them; and each gathering was as a river sending off streams of inspiration and teaching in every direction.

It was one such company of exiled scholars with whom this son of Odiham took up his residence at Rhodes; he became a Rhodes Scholar 400 years before Cecil Rhodes thought of his great idea! For five years Lily laboured with delighted ardour at Greek language and literature; then he came home with volumes of learning in his head and stacks of manuscripts under his arm. The profoundest scholar in his native land, he established a small school and was the first man to teach Greek in London. It is difficult for us now to realise the importance of this man with his Greek; it meant that England now shared to the full the Renaissance of Learning, and that whosoever would might familiarise himself with the fruits of the most splendid age in the history of mankind.

The value of his work was quickly perceived. When Dean Colet in 1512 founded St Paul's School he made Lily its first master, and there for 11 years this great scholar moulded and enriched the minds of

Young England. The illustrious Leland was one of his pupils; Sir Thomas More and Erasmus were among his friends and contributed to his work on Greek grammar, the preface to which, it is believed, was written by Cardinal Wolsey.

The plague of 1523 swept him into the grave; but his Grammar was in use at his old school for the next four centuries, and the seed he sowed has not yet yielded its last harvest.

Sir Isaac Newton and His Niece

OTTERBOURNE. Lying on the western side of the green valley of the Itchen this lovely village draws us to it for its own sake, and for its links with famous folk. Here sleeps a gracious lady among the scenes into which she was born, and here towards the end of his life came one of our immortals, the great Sir Isaac Newton. The lady was Charlotte Yonge, who wrote many novels and charming books about this part of England, and lies near the granite cross in memory of John Keble, who was rector of three villages roundabouts.

The quiet life of Charlotte Yonge in this remote countryside is one of the most remarkable proofs of the influence that may be exerted over a wide part of the world by people making little fuss. She lived at Otterbourne House and for 71 years she taught in the village Sunday school; most of the time she also taught the Bible in the day school. She was the daughter of the local squire, and when she began writing books it was felt that she should only make profit out of them if she gave the money away. One of them, the Heir of Redclyffe, was a great success, running through 22 editions in 23 years. She used its income to build a schooner for Bishop Selwyn's mission work in the South Seas, and the profits of another book helped to build a missionary college in New Zealand. Altogether she wrote 160 books, many stories with an historical basis, and she covered English history to the end of the Stuart period in eight volumes which she called Cameos. Her views were largely shaped by John Keble, who was vicar of Otterbourne, and her life centred on the new church here to which she gave much of her income.

She built the lychgate, her last gift before she died in 1901. There is a cross over the chancel rails in memory of her; the rails themselves are an odd mixture of praying saints and fat little cherubs brought over from an abbey in Flanders. The screen is 17th century. This warm-hearted lady did much to break down the prejudice against

A Roman Wall

Norman Church

Porch in the Castle

PORCHESTER'S FORTRESS AND CHURCH

The Massive Walls and Bastions

The Norman Keep

PORCHESTER CASTLE

fiction in many strict circles of those days. She lacked breadth of outlook, but the very essence of purity was in her books.

She was greatly interested in the planting of the holly hedge round the churchyard, which sprang from the berries decorating the altar at the first Christmas of the church. Perhaps she would feel it a little pathetic to come down the lane to where a farm keeps company with all that is left of the ancient church. Standing in a small graveyard is the old chancel, with three blocked-up arches which were in the nave. A service is held here once a year. Some of the graves about it have been here 300 years, and a little yew tree near the gate keeps them company shading a stream that trickles past.

Near the grounds of Otterbourne House is an old clay pit called Dell Copse from which clay was dug to make bricks for the bishop's palace at Winchester built by Christopher Wren. One of the last things Miss Yonge wrote was a description of the beauty of the daffodils in this little dell.

Hid in the trees of Cranbury Park (to which we come past a keeper's lodge built with materials from Netley Abbey) is the long low red and white Cranbury Hall, where the wisest Englishman of his day and one of the wisest of mankind loved to be.

It was towards the end of his life that Sir Isaac Newton came to Cranbury Park as the friend and guest of the man who lies on his right hand in Westminster Abbey, John Conduitt. The story which brought them together has given the gossipers something to write about for generations, and we must suppose that the mystery will remain a mystery to the end. It concerns Sir Isaac Newton's niece Catherine Barton, a brilliant woman for whom Charles Montagu, Earl of Halifax, had a great affection. After the earl's wife died in 1698 the relations of Lord Halifax and Catherine Barton were for years the subject of much speculation, and not even yet is it known whether Catherine was his wife or his friend. Professor de Morgan, who investigated the matter at the end of last century and wrote a book on the subject, came to the conclusion that the earl and Catherine were privately married, the marriage being kept secret for some reason unknown, and certainly at his death Halifax left her an income sufficient to keep her in dignity. Two years afterwards she married John Conduitt, and so it was that her home at Cranbury Park would often shelter her famous uncle.

It is easy to imagine this immortal man strolling under these glorious trees, looking across the green slopes of the park to the lake beyond. He loved it all, and himself superintended the fixing of the great sundial which is still in the garden. He himself devised the unusual dial, which has on it the names of places where the hour coincides with our noonday all round the world. Conduitt was a most suitable companion, and Newton delighted in the company he found at Otterbourne. His host was an old Westminster School boy and an old pupil of his own, he had travelled on the Continent, and was a Member of Parliament, yet he is chiefly interesting to us for his assistance in gathering materials for the biography of Newton which he meant to write but did not. We must always be grateful to him, however, for he put into English literature one of its smallest but most precious gems, for it was he who preserved among many fragments of Newton's conversation the most famous of all the things he said about himself, expressing his own humility in the presence of the infinity of knowledge. He saw himself, he said, as "a boy playing on the seashore, diverting myself in now and then finding a smoother pebble or a prettier shell than ordinary, while the great ocean of truth lay all undiscovered before me."

Cranbury Hall was sold to a curious man called Lee Dummer, who sought to add to its interest by setting up in it the medieval Cross of Winchester. It was all successfully arranged, until the Dummerite labourers arrived at Winchester with their wagons and horses and weapons for dismantling the cross, when they were so pelted by indignant apprentices and citizens that they returned home with their wagons empty. Finding that he could not get the Winchester Cross Mr Dummer had a copy of it made in plaster, which stood in Cranbury Park until wind and rain demolished it.

A Talk With the Village Cobbler

OVERTON. It has a stable with a memory and a church with a story. The stables are at the manor house, a fine place for horses yet with better days behind them, for they were once a Norman chapel, parts of which remain. We must have seen about a hundred of these lost churches. The church with a story has 13th century walls, 14th century arches resting on Norman piers, and a remarkable possession of a grand old door still on its original hinges, folding back oddly on its centre as it has been doing 600 years. It was probably this very door that let poor frightened John Bentley into the church when he came for sanctuary in the time of William of Wykeham, having by accident killed a man. He was a stranger and did not know of whom he should beware, and after evensong the village cobbler kept him in conversation while others stole upon him unawares, dragged him through this doorway, and sent him captive to Winchester, very pleased with themselves. But they had reckoned without William of Wykeham who, angered at the violation of the ancient right of sanctuary, sent to Overton to seek out the offenders.

There is an old inn in the village with a fireplace in which fires have been burning since the days of Queen Elizabeth.

OVER WALLOP. A pretty village near the Wiltshire border, its church has been made new and has some of its original stones still in the walls and arches. We noticed two or three old capitals used again, and four attractive heads gazing eastward up the church; but the chief treasure this place has is its fine font, the elegant workmanship of 15th century men. Adorned with flowers and a shield in quatrefoils, it has also a dove among other carvings under the bowl, and small panels like windows round the stem. There is one 17th century bench, a piscina and an Easter sepulchre of the 13th century, and bells of early Tudor and Stuart days. On the walls is a tablet to a chorister who sang in the choir for 64 years, Charles Shadwell.

OVINGTON. It is a lovely little neighbour of Alresford, with three streams meeting, their waters crossed by small bridges. In the 19th century church is a grey font on five pillars, made of Purbeck marble and lightly carved by a Norman mason.

The Wooden Knight

PAMBER. An avenue of oaks leads across a field to the church, all that is left (save for a length of broken wall and a fishpond) of one of Hampshire's biggest priories. What we see of it is 12th and 13th century. It is the chancel of the old monks; the massive tower at its west end once stood at the junction of nave and transepts. A splendid building it must have been, for this chancel is long and lofty, with rows of lovely, deeply splayed windows and a nobly proportioned triple window over the altar. Painted on the wall are the remains of a line of angels with outspread wings, and near the pulpit is a consecration cross almost as clear as the day it was painted 500 years ago. The solid and dignified screen, most of the plain old benches, and the font panelled with gay flowers, are all the work of men living in the 15th century. By the altar is a beautiful canopied piscina about 700 years old, and all about the church are many medieval gravestones, some with unusually fine floral crosses. There is an ancient bowl, possibly the original Norman font. Under an arch in the wall is a rare wooden figure of a knight, the treasure of the church. He wears chain mail and a coat, and his crossed feet with their spurred heels rest against a lion. It is a fine piece of work, fashioned by an artist in the 13th or 14th century from some enormous oak which must have been growing in Saxon England. There are only about a hundred of these old wooden figures in the country.

Under a gravestone near the gate sleeps Thomas Chandler, woodman, who died in 1880 and was for nearly 50 years a most faithful and well-loved servant of Queen's College, Oxford, for centuries the owners of these lands and buildings.

PENTON MEWSEY. The neighbouring aerodrome of Andover has taken away some of its quiet, but not its charm, and it remains a beautiful farming village with creeper-clad cottages. Its simple 14th century church has been well cared for and keeps from its earliest days a mass dial, two aumbries, an octagonal font, and fragments of glass with gold patterns and foliage. The two bells in the turret are 16th century, and the little oak chest is Jacobean.

Round the Old Square

PETERSFIELD. It is dominated by the natural bulwark of Butser Hill, 900 feet up and the highest point of the South Downs. It is on the London-to-Portsmouth road, and it had nine inns in the coaching days; Pepys tells us that he slept at one of them in a room Charles the Second had slept in. It has a fine old Square presided over by a king on horseback, and a common of 80 acres bordering a lake of over 20, a delightful scene with the hills rising behind it and graceful trees shading its banks. It has traces of the 700-year-old Durford Abbey—something of the moat and the fishpond remains, with stone fragments, old tiles, and a stone coffin. It has fine old houses with overhanging fronts and timbered facades, and as we walk about its streets we come upon names that set us wondering. Frenchman's Lane reminds us of a camp of prisoners taken in Napoleon's wars. Music Hill (so rare but so suitable for a town with a musical festival of high repute) speaks of a military camp in the 18th century when bands played on the heath. Sheep Street reminds us that in the 16th century Petersfield was said to maintain 1000 poor people in the clothing trade "without begging." The peaceful spot known by the curious name of The Spain is a mystery, but may have something to do with a Spanish market for wool.

The Dutchman who sat on our throne sits on horseback on a high stone pedestal, a Dutch king of England looking like a Roman! He was given by a benefactor of the town, and was moved into the Square a few years before Waterloo. The statue is of lead and shows him with a laurel wreath on his head, a scroll in his hand, and a bow on his horse's tail. The inscription pays tribute to William of Orange for steadfastly upholding the State when its fall was imminent.

The pilgrim through Norman England is bound to come this way, for off the Square stands the old church, with a grandeur that has lost much since the Normans fashioned it but is still impressive. What the church has lost was a central tower which long kept company with the western tower, both Norman, so that 800 years ago this church must have been a noble spectacle. The towers were early 12th century; the aisles were added as the Norman style was passing into English, but the north aisle has an impressive series of pure Norman arches. In the course of time the western tower received its Tudor battlements and the walls of the central tower were taken down, leaving its western arch to divide the nave and chancel. It stands today as a Norman wall unique in our experience. Looking down the stately nave from under the round arch of the western tower we see beyond the Norman chancel arch three narrow east windows, and in the wall over the arch are three narrow arches set in a mass of slender round columns. The chancel arch has three depths of decoration, one with two rows of zigzag; the three arches over it are intricately and beautifully carved. The middle one has a cross set in it; the others are glazed as windows, and above them is another small window. Seen from the tower it is not only unusual but beautiful. Much of the pure Norman work has been taken down and rebuilt in the same style in modern times; the south arcade has been rebuilt, and only the western arches on the south are old, while much of the western tower, including the fine doorway with zigzag, has been completely restored. The Norman font vanished long ago and its medieval successor is in the churchyard, a modern one being now used.

There is a monument with a spirited relief of a sea fight in memory of George Joliffe, who was at the Battle of Aboukir, and on the wall is a tribute to Commander Loftus Jones, who went down with his torpedo destroyer Shark at Jutland. The Shark was heavily damaged by shell fire, and Commander Jones was wounded in the leg, but nothing could daunt him. He stood by the only gun the ship had left, and helped to keep it in action. A shell then took off his leg above the knee, but he continued to give orders while a stoker attended to him. As something had happened to the ensign he ordered another to be hoisted, and then gave orders to the crew to put on lifebelts. The Shark was now struck by a torpedo, and though a few survivors were picked up in the night the Commander went down. He was awarded the VC for his great courage.

All round Petersfield's graveyard are beautiful headstones which have been removed and set up as a wall, an example all our churches might well copy. Here lies the famous criketer John Small, an original member of the first cricket club at Hambledon, the cradle of cricket. We read on his stone that

> Praises on tombs are trifles vainly spent,
> A man's good name is his best monument.

He used to have a linen draper's shop in the Square, and it is remembered that he put these lines on the front of it:

> The said John Small,
> Wishes it to be known to all,
> That he doth make both bat and ball
> And will play any man in England
> For five pounds a side.

Petersfield is rich in old and new buildings. Its town hall is very modern, but some of its religious denominations have good churches. The Methodist Church has a turreted tower and a spacious west window, and the Roman Catholic Church of St Laurence is attractive in Italian style, with a conspicuous dome. By the little green called The Spain is one of the oldest houses in the town, in which lived John Goodyer; there is a plaque on it paying tribute to this botanist who built up so great a fame in his day. He came to live in The

Spain when he married Patience Crump, and botanists from all parts came to visit him here. He was born at Alton and lies at Buriton, where we come upon him again.

A familiar figure in Petersfield was Edward Thomas, one of the poets killed by the war. It was from here that he went out to the front. He lived in the neighbouring village of Steep, where there is a hillside monument to him. Mr Walter de la Mare wrote of him that "when he was killed in Flanders a mirror of England was shattered."

PLAITFORD. In its small church, for the most part 700 years old, is a plain font, an ancient chest, and, let into the wall, some lovely old tiles decorated with lions and dragons.

The Greatest Roman Monument in England

PORCHESTER. Companionable old houses comfortably settled in their gardens have come closer and closer to the flinty walls and bastions of Porchester Castle since the last tokens of war and men-at-arms disappeared from it. Peace has settled on it after the whole pageant of British history has marched through its gates.

Today we pass through either of its gates to find a greensward like a village green. Children race one another over the grass; old people sit under the shade of the trees. In one corner is a grey church which had a delightful flash of red roses about it when we called. In the opposite corner are the drawbridge, the ruinous walls, and the square keep of a Norman castle that frowns no more but seems to smile on a scene that is so English and so enchanting.

We may seek it by the Landward Gate, rejoicing at the sight of so much beauty; but even before our steps turn to church or castle they take us, whether we will or no, to the Water Gate on the opposite side. This is the gate through which we see the marching centuries come, and seem to hear the tread of all the peoples who have helped to make this England. If we had chosen to come to the castle by boat from Portsmouth we should have followed in their wake. The castle stands by the northern extremity of Portsmouth Harbour, the waterway's natural guardian. We look across the tide to the distant cranes, three miles away, of Portsmouth Dockyard and the bristling row of steel monsters, the bulwarks that have replaced Old England's wooden walls and walls of stone.

Here at the head of the long water a British chieftain raised his camp on a site flanked on one side by the water and on the other by its ramparts, raised earthworks, and ditches encircling 19 acres, well fitted to bear the brunt of any land attack from tribal enemies. But there was a fiercer, more subtle foe to come. From these earthworks, whose lines we still see about the green setting of the castle, the Britons watched with doubting eyes the Roman galleys sweeping up the lagoon. Here they learned the lesson that he who commands the sea may have as much or as little of war as he likes.

It was of small avail to them, for the Romans drove them forth, and where the camp had been they set up this great castle with twenty round bastions about a huge fortress. Their work stands and has stood since the Roman Carausius, the usurping Emperor of Britain, made it the home and cradle of the Britannic Fleet, our first organised navy.

No wonder the walls have stood. They are six to ten feet thick and 25 feet high. They are studded all about their outer side with huge bastions commanding the approaches. Once there were 20, now there are 14 with the towers at the angles, and the places where others stood can easily be seen. This Roman castle, though now but a shell enclosing nine acres, is the most extensive and complete remnant of Roman architecture in these islands.

We do not know why it was built, but Carausius was the first Count of the Saxon Shore, which meant that he was the guardian of Roman Britain from the raiders sailing from Jutland and thereabouts. The shore under his supervision extended from here round the coast to Caister in Norfolk. As part of the supports to the Roman fleet nine forts were established. Eight of them can be identified, and this at Porchester was the westernmost, Portus Adurni.

Its walls have an interest of their own because of a peculiarity of the material. Here and there we see those flat red tiles so common in our Roman walls, but their main substance is flint with bonding courses of yellowish limestone and the pink mortar like concrete. From the walls the Romans built the Roman Britons saw with dismay a new invader come when the legions and the fleet had gone away. The Saxons were at last sailing up the Sound to ravage and plunder.

This was the second lesson for Britain. It is some tribute to the Roman tradition that the invaders left small mark on the fortress. There is no Saxon architecture here, though one part is called the

Saxon Tower. The Saxons came and settled down; the centuries rolled on. Then came another invader, though not by this entrance, and what had been British, Roman, and Saxon in turn was now Norman. It is a strange thought that to both Saxon and Norman invaders, though long centuries intervened, the Roman fortress must have looked almost as old as it looks to us. A Saxon thane or a Norman knight would probably recognise it now.

Yet the Normans, as military as the Romans, saw the castle's possibilities. They had no mind, like the Saxons, for open fields; they were engineers, and in their castles their plan was to multiply the lines of defence. So within the half-mile of flinty walls they built a square keep with a much lower fore-building to contain a chapel and guard-room, and walled off a small space to form an inner court surrounded by a ditch. They strengthened the Water Gate and rebuilt the Land Gate. Ruinous as much of their work is now, we can, thanks to our twentieth-century Office of Works, make out their plan. Henry the First began it, the Plantagenets completed it; but it is to Norman Henry that we owe the church at the opposite corner. It was for the use of a priory founded in 1133.

Let us stand at the Water Gate where a causeway runs into the creek and the waters come lapping close up to the walls twice a day, partly filling the outer moat. The gate is ruinous, but we easily see where the Normans added triple defences, with guardrooms, a place for the sentry, and a stair mounting up. Up that causeway strode the Saxon Portha from his ship in 501, and 600 years later Robert of Normandy trod the same rough stones. King John went out from it when he would sail to France. Margaret of Anjou came this way to marry Henry the Sixth. But it has had less happy visitors—ship-wrecked galley slaves, a fierce miserable rout, shepherded through this gate, and Dutch sailors and French prisoners by the thousand.

The castle is like a story within a story. The Normans looked on these walls not with any veneration for their age, but with a keen eye to their possibilities as a fortress, and strengthened them by a moat filled with water from the Roman moat outside. This, with many additions by later kings, is what we see. The Roman moat has been trimly scooped out by the Office of Works, the inner moat restored, the crumbling walls secured and propped, and a lawn, trimmed and mown, made to cover the inner court. Access to the castle was by the gateway still fronting us, with a drawbridge over the moat, and there was and is a small sally-port overlooking the Roman moat.

When we now cross the wooden bridge to enter the inner castle the additions are at first perplexing. King John was the first to modify the original plan. He raised the keep from fifty to a hundred feet, and remodelled the domestic buildings. Richard the Second had palatial ideas. He pulled down most of John's work, though we may find traces of it in a passage leading from the Great Hall to the King's Chamber. Richard made the Knighten Hall, used as a banqueting room. At one end was the royal dais, at the other the minstrel gallery; we find our way to both by a handsome porch with a pointed arch which is still beautifully groined and pillared.

A flight of steps through the porch used to lead to the banqueting hall and we may see the spiral stairway giving entry to the guardroom and the minstrel gallery. We may find the kitchen and the buttery, where so many fine feasts were prepared, and can discover the queen's parlour and the king's solar and the counting-house.

The plain Norman keep is split by a crack from base to summit on its northern side, but seems now to be at rest. There are four storeys connected by a spiral stairway. On entering through the gateway, with the arms of Henry the Seventh over the portal, we find it divided into two chambers, with some of the old timbering of their roofs remaining. King John used them as a wine cellar. In the wars with Napoleon prisoners slept here till the place became a plague spot. Continuing up the stairway we can still reach the state apartments, guardrooms, and garrets.

When the castle was in its heyday a broad rampart ran along the summit of all the outer wall. The only remnant is that between the keep and the tower on the same north side of the castle. It is plainly built, 50 feet high, and in four floors. In the 18th century its basement was used as a cell for prisoners. There is a breach still to be seen in the wall, said to have been the work of Spanish prisoners who tried to escape during the Seven Years War. It also has a sunken dungeon. No stairways seem to connect the ground floor with the chambers above; ladders may have served. There is a window on the south front with the Tudor rose; it gives light to an apartment of unusual importance, which figures in the story of The Three Mus-

keteers. The next builder was the Elizabethan Sir Thomas Cornwallis, who built the apartments for Court officials and the kitchen,
pantry, and servants lodgings. These, leading to the Barbican Gateway, complete the castle in all its stages and throughout its history.

The Barbican Gateway sprang from the curtain wall built by
Henry the First. The Norman gate is in a square tower 28 feet
broad, projecting outward from the Norman curtain and pierced by
a round-headed arch. On the front of the tower is a turreted barbican
with a beautiful porch, begun in the reign of Edward the Second and
completed by Edward the Third. The vaulted and carved roof is
perforated with holes to permit an outflow of boiling lead on the head
of an enemy. The next section consists of stout buttresses defended
like two others with a gate or portcullis; and the fourth and last was
formed by two parallel walls projecting forward. The whole length
of this composite gateway is a hundred feet, and the way in was
barred by a moat, a drawbridge, two portcullis gates, and three
open ones.

It is even more elaborate than the Landward Gate in the Roman
walls, though that was greatly strengthened in the reign of Richard
the Second and was given a drawbridge and a portcullis. It has a
handsome decorated portal with a drop arch ending in carved
corbels, said to represent Richard the Second and his queen. Within
the archway the inner and outer arches are curved into a vault with
four heavy corbels on which are carvings of a cat, a cock, a bat, and
an owl. Over the entrance is a tower with a chamber reached by a
vaulted stairway. It became an 18th century prison and its walls and
passages are covered with names of prisoners.

These walls, these stones, these rooms have the interest of architecture and a vast antiquity, but their greater interest arises from the
men and women with whom we may people them. Here kings and
queens held their Court. The trim lawns stand between the crumbling
walls; knights and ladies, men-at-arms, pages and scullions, maids
and kitchen wenches, passed over the cobbles for centuries. In the
keep Edward the First loaded the bishops of St Andrews and of
Glasgow with chains. In the Knighten Hall the Earl of Cambridge,
Lord Scroop, and Sir Thomas Grey were arrested for conspiracy
against Henry the Fifth on leaving for Agincourt.

Long after all but the names of these had been forgotten the castle renewed its sordid tradition as a hold for prisoners. In the 17th century Dutch prisoners of war were housed here and set fire to the church. In the 18th century 7000 Frenchmen were lodged within the walls; and we are glad to think they were not altogether unhappy, for they spent a good deal of their time making models of ships from the bones of their rations. Hundreds of their names are cut on the walls of the gateway, the tower, and the keep.

Such is the fortress. The church has cut its name far less deeply in history. When the monks had left their priory the Norman church seems to have sunk almost out of mind. It had to wait till Queen Anne before a gracious hand was extended to it; then it became an object of reverent care, while its proud companion the castle relapsed into something worse than a barracks. This reversal of fortune has preserved for us the saintly dignity and charm of the church we see standing in its little acre of trees and modest graves. One of the last of these was added in our own day, when Mr W. L. Wyllie, the painter-historian of the Navy, was borne through the Water Gate and laid to rest.

It is best to enter by the noble west doorway, a round Norman arch of three orders resting on twisted shafts with carved capitals. Above the capitals on either side are the fish and the bowmen of the Zodiac. Above the doorway are three round-headed arched recesses, the middle one a window. The long nave seen from here is plain but spacious; the Norman windows have no ornament. There are walled-up doorways that led into the cloisters when the church was part of the priory. Within and without are scars and signs of its earliest structure and employment, but the effect is one of whitewashed plainness.

The arms of Queen Anne hang on the north wall; the arms of Elizabeth face them on the south. To the right of a window in the chancel is a curious bust of Sir Thomas Cornwallis, groom porter to Queen Elizabeth, her governor of the castle. The chancel is surrounded with Norman arches resting on shafts with carved capitals, these also, like the rest of the church, too trim and neat to show their age. But when we remember that prisoners of war were once housed in the church and its greater part was destroyed by fire in 1665 we may be grateful for the care that has still left to us so much beauty undestroyed.

One magnificent relic has survived through every century of the church's history; it is the Norman font. It is round, resting on a solid base of interlaced arches faithfully restored. The upper part is as it was when it left the hand of some Norman stonemason who carved the Caen stone in its intricate spirals with serpents, flowers, and figures, after a pattern older than any Norman king. Its symbolism may be variously interpreted, but its splendour needs no explanation. Like Porchester itself, it is the link between the Romans and the peoples of Europe and Britain whom they first taught and who in turn became their heirs.

Alone on a bleak windy ridge near Porchester is a monument to Nelson, an obelisk with the words: "Consecrated to the memory of Lord Viscount Nelson by the zealous attachment of all those who fought at Trafalgar, to perpetuate his triumph, and their regret."

The Greatest Naval Port in the World

PORTSMOUTH. It is one of our old sea-gates, from which England's fleets have sailed to victory and to which they have never returned from defeat. It is the greatest naval port in the world, called in ancient times "the glory and the bulwark of these kingdoms."

Portsmouth and Gosport face each other across the harbour. On the Portsmouth side are the Round Tower of Edward the Third and the Square Tower of Henry the Seventh. From King Edward's Tower a mighty chain of iron was drawn across the mouth of the harbour in the olden days to a tower on the Gosport side, and within this chain lay Portsmouth, its approaches, its harbour, its creek, its docks near and far, spread in a prospect stretching for miles up to the Portsdown Hills (with their tree beacon to guide our ships and airmen). Old Portsmouth lies about King Edward's Tower, and in these few acres is packed all the historic interest of the little world centred here in Nelson's day. Away to the east of it is the spacious splendour of the Southsea front, and behind it all the new Portsmouth spreads; but it is down on the front, round about the High Street, that the heart of old Portsmouth still seems to beat. Here are the narrow streets and the old houses, the little dock called the Camber where tramps and small barges tie up to the quay; the Hard where they brought ashore the body of General Wolfe from Quebec; the houses in which a remarkable group of Portsmouth men were born; the inns so well known to Nelson and his band of brothers; the churches with so much history in their walls.

Behind all this a red brick gate leads us into the dockyard, the buildings of which stand high and clear. We may wander about its 300 acres with their pleasant old Georgian houses, the church built in Queen Anne's day and named after St Anne, and the tall masts of Nelson's Victory safe from storms or war's alarms in the oldest dry dock in the world. Here she is resting after 47 years of active service, having flown the flags of 14 admirals.

On the left of all this is the long line of grey-blue monsters—battleships, destroyers, and cruisers of Old England. They seem to stretch endlessly down the vast harbour, but beyond the end of the line, dim unless it is a very clear day, the low line of a wall broken by high towers stands up ghostlike above the water and below the encircling Portsdown Hills. On these hills are shadowy grey walls which it is hard sometimes to believe are real, yet they are Roman, for they are Porchester Castle, perhaps the most spectacular structure the Romans left behind in Britain 15 centuries ago. They have stood through all these centuries and seem likely to stand another thousand years, yet one shell from these grey monsters would shatter them to dust. That old Roman castle stands at the beginning of the history of Portsmouth and of England. It was the first port here when the Roman galleys came and the Roman engineers built their westward castle to protect the British shore against the Saxon.

Farther west the creek runs up to Fareham out of our sight, but within our view the waters of the harbour lap Whale Island (the Naval Gunnery School), and on the other side the Clarence Victualling Yard, the broken front of Gosport, and the creek of Haslar, the Navy's hospital.

Let us come back to these old streets where the seamen lived in Nelson's day and before it. Where Broad Street ends the captain's barge would await the admiral, and if it should be Nelson or some other great commander the people would be leaning from the casements of these old bow windows to see him pass. The houses are not what they were, yet some keep still their handsome fronts, and all are interesting because they were known to those great seamen who kept the seas for England; they passed this way and heard the cheers and saw the waving handkerchiefs. We saunter about Broad Street and High Street thinking of what has happened in these old houses. Within a few minutes walk of us were born men of such extraordinary genius in varying fields as would make Portsmouth famous if nothing else had happened here. One was George Meredith, who would not be understood. One was Jonas Hanway, the reforming spirit chiefly remembered now because he was the first man to carry an umbrella. One was John Pounds, the crippled cobbler so beloved. One was Sir Frederick Madden, who did much precious work for early English literature. One was Brunel the tunnel man, one was Sir Walter Besant the novelist, one was the incomparable Charles Dickens. In one of these houses lived Admiral Anson, who knelt on Southsea beach to give thanks for a safe return from his journey round the world. In the old inn which is now the Soldiers' Institute Captain Marryat's heroes, Midshipman Easy and Peter Simple, took their ease. At the Old George Nelson slept before he sailed for Trafalgar. The room is as he left it, with the old four-poster bed he slept in, the oak chair he sat in, the mirror he looked in. After Nelson came Wellington, entertained at a banquet given here to the Allied Sovereigns after Waterloo, so that this old inn has links with both these battles. In this same High Street is Buckingham House, so called since that tragic day when George Villiers, Duke of Buckingham, here ended his strange life. A half-demented soldier bought a tenpenny knife on Tower Hill, rode down to Portsmouth, tethered his horse outside the walls, loitered about outside this house, and as the duke came out from breakfast and stooped to take leave of a friend the soldier's arm stole over his shoulder and stabbed him to the heart. He had negotiated the marriage of Charles Stuart to Henrietta Maria.

Across the road is what is now a Unitarian Chapel, in which John Wesley preached, and that Simon Brown who made dictionaries and said we should be thankful to God for all things, even for dictionary makers. Here also preached John Hicks who fled from Sedgemoor and was sheltered by Dame Alice Lisle, who was butchered to death for her charity by the foul Judge Jeffreys. But what will interest many travellers most about this little chapel is a grave at the back of it, in which lies John Pounds, who mended Portsmouth's shoes and took care of its Ragged Robins. He was crippled for life as a boy by falling into a dry dock. Beginning with a crippled nephew, he started a school, tempting the young desperadoes of Portsmouth's streets by giving them hot potatoes. They came to the little shop that Portsmouth has preserved, a queer little place with a wooden fronted chamber over it; we may ask for the key next door. In time he had 40 ragged pupils, and he would sit cobbling in their midst, cobbling shoes and building minds, teaching them reading, writing, and arithmetic. He would feed his waifs and clothe them, and he kept a wardrobe from which he would dress them up on Sundays. From his work sprang the Ragged School Union which is now the Shaftesbury Society, and Lord Shaftesbury himself was proud to say "I am a disciple of John Pounds." Not far from the site of John Pound's little shop is a most oddly shaped house which Portsmouth keeps well painted and in good order because it is the oldest house now standing in the town; it is a queer little place in Highbury Street.

Here in the High Street is one of Portsmouth's small group of museums, known as the City Museum and Bashford Portrait Gallery and housed in the old Guildhall. Its career as a portrait gallery began with the gift of six family portraits by Miss Bashford, and there are now also works by W. L. Wyllie, Vicat Cole, Rex Vicat Cole, and George Cole, the Coles having been born in the town. The museum rooms have exhibits of model boats ranging from the Santa Maria to a river gunboat, prints illustrating naval history and the growth of Portsmouth, and a growing collection of obsolete domestic and agricultural implements. The museum has memories of two great tragedies, the flag of the Birkenhead and two candles from the Royal George.

The house in which Charles Dickens was born is away from the rest, up beyond the dockyard in Commercial Road, a modest house of two storeys and an attic. Here he was born on February 7, 1812, being christened at the same font as Isambard Brunel; it was then in Kingston church but is now in St Alban's at Copnor near by (Copnor being one of the places Portsmouth has swallowed up). One of the things many people will learn for the first time about Dickens from the papers we see at his birthplace is that he was christened as Charles John Huffham Dickens; it is probably true that never before have two such unknown names come between two so widely known. The birthplace is now a museum with relics of Dickens, engravings and photographs, and valuable editions of his works; but the most interesting of all its possessions is the couch on which he died on June 9, 1870. It was brought from the house at Gadshill, near Rochester, and is fittingly kept in the town which had his cradle.

Petersfield
William the Third

Aldershot
Duke of Wellington

Southampton
Pilgrim's Memorial

Southampton
Memorial of Mary Rogers

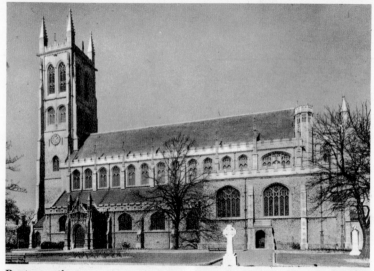

Portsmouth

St Mary's Church, Portsea

Yateley Church

Titchfield Church

At the seaward end of High Street stands the Square Tower, and on its landward side is a lead bust of Charles the First by Hubert Le Sueur. An oak and laurel wreath surrounds it, and it was set up on his homecoming from making arrangements for his Spanish marriage, the inscription telling us of his travels through France and Spain, with many dangers by sea and land. The Governor of Portsmouth in those days used his authority to make everybody take off their hats when passing the bust. The Square Tower is part of the fortifications which continue towards the King's Bastion on one side and the Round Tower on the other. Not far from the Round Tower is the Sally Port opening on to the harbour, the old place for taking boats to the ships at Spithead. We are sure that Nelson would see it, and it is an historic spot.

Portsmouth has two old churches, one now the cathedral in the High Street, the other now the Garrison church on the Grand Parade, close by. The cathedral is one of the smallest in the land, and one of the few seen from the sea; the Garrison Church is the ancient Domus Dei, a House of God for Christ's Poor, founded by the Bishop of Winchester in the year before Magna Carta. It was known as the Hospital of St Nicholas, the nave being then the hospital in which the brethren lived, and the chancel their chapel. The chancel has beautiful 13th century vaulting, and the lofty nave has five bays. It has stone seats and piscinas of the 12th, 13th, and 14th centuries. There are 42 oak stalls, some given by our public schools, Eton and Harrow among them. Sir Charles Napier lies outside the west door with his figure on a tomb, having died at Portsmouth at the end of a long life of adventure in which he conquered Scinde (telegraphing home the word Peccavi, *I have sinned*).

The old church had a tragic day in 1449 when Margaret of Anjou passed this way to her tragic marriage with poor Henry the Sixth at Titchfield. The country was on the brink of the Wars of the Roses, and rebellion was lifting its ugly head. The Earl of Suffolk who proposed the marriage, the Bishop of Salisbury who performed it, and the Bishop of Chichester (Moleyns) who arranged it, were all murdered. Moleyns had come down to Portsmouth to pay the soldiers, and they dragged him out of Domus Dei and made an end of him on the beach. That was the end of Portsmouth for two generations, and after about 60 years a vicar of Domus Dei and his flock marched to and fro all day between the hospital and the church of St Thomas, being whipped on the way, and at last set free to build a chapel of penitence on the site of the murder. Henry the Seventh made peace, and built the Square Tower and the first dry dock ever known. Henry the Eighth completed his father's work. The master and the brethren of the hospital surrendered it at the Dissolution of the Monasteries, the master being made Dean of St Paul's and the chapel becoming a war store. Elizabeth turned it into the Governor's house, and here the governor lived in the days when Catherine of Braganza arrived to marry Charles the Second; she stayed here several days before Charles found it convenient to come, and here they were married, the bride cutting off the ribbons from her wedding dress and handing them out as souvenirs.

On the south wall of the chancel is a brass in memory of John Mason, who lies in Westminster Abbey. It was at his house that the Duke of Buckingham was slain. Mason had been Governor of Newfoundland, and drew the first English map of our oldest dominion, writing a pamphlet describing its climate, and even the sort of vegetables grown there. He went out again and founded New Hampshire, taking with him 100 Danish oxen and a set of church furniture, for he was a devoted churchman, and when he died he left 1000 acres for a school and another 1000 for a church out there.

There lies in the Garrison Church one of Nelson's great captains, Sir Thomas Foley, who went round the world with Anson. He led at the Battle of the Nile, and compelled the first surrender of a French ship there. At the Battle of the Baltic Nelson went aboard Foley's ship, and with the fighting at its height Admiral Parker's signal to "Cease action" was reported, Nelson turning his blind eye to it and refusing to obey. "You know, Foley (he said), I have only one eye and have a right to be blind sometimes; I really do not see the signal." Foley never forgot that experience on his ship (the Elephant), and when it was broken up he managed to get some planks from the deck and kept them for his coffin, in which he lies here.

Portsmouth Cathedral is being fashioned out of the church of St Thomas, built in memory of Becket soon after his death. It is a strange old place being shaped into a modern cathedral with much skill and ingenuity and is destined to be the most captivating building in the town. Its tower was built as a watch tower in 1691, the date being on it with the star and crescent, and the initials of the mayor, John White. The original church itself is the oldest building in Portsmouth, finished in 1196. It was the Civil War that destroyed the old tower, and when the war was done and the Protectorate had also run its course, the new tower was raised at the west end, its cupola being added in the first year of Queen Anne. The golden barque which crowns it as a weather-vane has an odd story, for it was put up by the churchwardens to celebrate their victory over a quarrelsome vicar who spent a fortnight in Winchester gaol. What is now called the Martyr's Chapel, the south transept, is part of the original church. The vaulted chancel with round arches on octagonal piers, divided into smaller pointed arches on a central shaft, is beautiful 13th century work.

Just within the chancel aisle is the monument set up by the Countess of Denbigh to her brother the Duke of Buckingham. It has figures of Fame and Glory and a marble urn in which the heart of George Villiers was supposed to have been placed. On the wall kneels the figure of Sir Charles Blount, a kinsman of Queen Elizabeth's Essex, and there is a tablet to Sir John Kempthorne, who fought under General Monk and Prince Rupert and was knighted for his brave sea fight with seven pirates. In a table tomb lies Benjamin Burgess, a vicar of Richard Cromwell's time. When the Committee of Safety opposed Richard and turned out the Commons, some of the members came down to Portsmouth to consult the governor about restoring Parliament, and they took up their quarters at the Red Lion next door to the church. Benjamin Burgess was present. A small army was got together and marched on London and at the critical moment they turned the scale, Parliament assembling once more and Burgess preaching the sermon.

In the chancel is the gravestone of Jonas Hanway's parents; he was christened here in 1712. Though we remember him as the umbrella man, he lies in Westminster Abbey because he had other titles to fame, having been a noble and persevering philanthropist and founder of the Marine Society. He was commissioner for victualling the navy, and used the Square Tower as a storehouse.

Since the church of St Thomas became the cathedral Portsmouth has continually striven to add to its dignity and beauty. The mayor's pew, remnant of four spacious boxes once used by the corporation and their wives, is enriched with a great shield. The processional cross has been carved from a design by Mr Harold Wyllie out of oak from the Victory; on it are small copies of the figureheads of four ships, and immediately below the cross itself are the figures of four Bishops of Winchester: St Swithun, William of Wykeham, Lancelot Andrewes, and Edward Talbot. The bishop's throne is an oak copy of the stone chair at Canterbury. The organ was built by Abraham Jordan in 1718. The pulpit cloth is 17th century, the pulpit itself of the same age, with a gilded canopy crowned with a golden trumpeter. The poor-box is made from old battleship timber. The registers record the christening of George Meredith, whose grandfather Melchizedeck was churchwarden. Here is kept a copy of the wedding certificate of Charles the Second, whose marriage to Catherine brought him the possession of Tangier, though he had to abandon it and sent out Lord Dartmouth to withdraw from the fortress. They brought home the church plate, and it is now here. Hanging on the wall is a long lost portrait by the famous Italian Carlo Dolci; it is 17th century and represents Philip Benizi.

The windows of the nave tell us the story of Portsmouth. Beginning with Wilfrid of Selsey, who brought the Gospel to the south Saxons, they continue with Alfred, Father of the British Navy, and Richard Lionheart, who gave the town its first charter; Thomas Becket, John de Gisors, and Bishop Toclive of Winchester carrying on the tale into the 12th century. Other windows show us the last prior of Southwick (William Norton), Thomas Carpenter who built the first town hall, Thomas Heather, a 17th century vicar, and Lord Dartmouth and Bishop Ken, who went to Tangier to bring back the plate, taking Samuel Pepys with them.

The cathedral has galleries in which Charles Dickens and Captain Marryat placed some of the more shadowy characters of their novels, and an epitaph tells us of Ambrose Stanyford, who died in 1694, having been "the happy instrument of contriving, framing, and finishing the inside beauty of this house." The beautifying goes on, for there hang in this cathedral ensigns flown in the Great War from some of our great warships, the Princess Royal, the Invincible, the Ceres, and the Mary Rose. The flag of the Invincible was flown in the Battle of the Falkland Islands, and was hoisted into position by the widow of Commander Townsend, who went down with the ship at Jutland with 1025 officers and men. With these flags hangs a model of the historic ship in which Sir Kempthorne defeated seven Algerian pirates. It was the Mary Rose, the fourth man-of-war of that name.

Long before his day a Mary Rose was the pride of the fleet of Henry the Eighth, only surpassed by the Great Harry, but while war was threatening with France in 1545 she sank in the Solent before the eyes of her royal master. The second Mary Rose fought against the Armada and carried Raleigh to the Azores, the third was wrecked off Flanders in 1650, and the fourth was Kempthorne's ship. Two and a half centuries went by, and then came the fifth Mary Rose which sank with her colours flying on October 17, 1917.

It is a model of Kempthorne's ship which hangs here as a memorial "of all those officers and men of his majesty's navy who through many centuries have worshipped in this holy place, and who have upon the high seas served with faithfulness and at the cost of their lives." The brave Sir John lies in this cathedral, having lived long to tell the tale of the fight with the seven pirates:

Two we burnt and two we sunk, and two did run away,
And one we carried to Leghorn roads to show we'd won the day.

This model ship was a gift to the cathedral from Mr Clement Langford, a Portsmouth-born Australian. It is made of Australian wood and hangs with a white ensign above it. Admiral Jellicoe hung the ensign and Sir Roger Keyes placed the ship in position, and to him was given in memory of the occasion a book bound in boards taken from the first Mary Rose when it went down here before the stricken gaze of King Henry the Eighth.

Portsmouth has a group of modern churches of which the most magnificent is St Mary's which replaced the ancient church of Portsea, the district outside the dockyard. It was entirely rebuilt in the middle of last century, a spacious and impressive place to hold 2000 people, the seven bays of the nave each having two clerestory windows. The chancel screen is of hammered iron. The font is made from one piece of alabaster, with niched figures of Our Lord and the Children, and the scene of the Baptism. There is a hammerbeam roof with winged angels looking down. The exterior of this great place is a remarkable spectacle and it is good to see that the churchyard has become a garden and a playground. In it is a memorial of the Royal George which sank in sight of Portsmouth one day in 1782. Some of its 800 men lie in the churchyard here, and the ship's bell is in the dockyard church. As we hear it the words of Cowper come to mind: Toll for the brave, the brave that are no more. It has been suggested that the brave Kempenfelt himself lies in a Portsmouth grave, but we do not know. It was perhaps the most tragic day in Portsmouth's history when this ship heeled over and its rotten timbers fell to pieces. The truth was not known, and Cowper's poem gives us the popular belief that the ship capsized in the wind:

> Her timbers yet are sound,
>   And she may float again,
> Full charged with England's thunder,
>   And plough the distant main.

> But Kempenfelt is gone,
>   His victories are o'er,
> And he and his eight hundred
>   Shall plough the wave no more.

The truth is that brave Kempenfelt and his 800 men were murdered, victims of the Admiralty's neglect in allowing the navy to rot. St Alban's church, in the part of Portsmouth called Copnor, has fragments of 14th century glass, the Dickens font with a lovely painted cover, an 18th century flagon, an Italian chalice, 16th century altar plate, two 17th century chests, and a medieval censer; and St Agatha's is unusually planned on the lines of San Miniato in Florence, with decorations by Mr Heywood Sumner. In Holy Trinity, the Royal Naval Church, are two chalices from the Victory.

The most spectacular building in Portsmouth is its magnificent Guildhall, opened in 1890 by the Prince of Wales for Queen Victoria, who is said to have been frightened by the steps. Its great tower rises 210 feet, the front has six columns with a lion at each side of the portico, and in the tympanum Britannia sits with Peace and Plenty about her. In the square in front is Queen Victoria by Alfred Drury, his first big sculpture, and behind the Guildhall is the Municipal College, a fine block of buildings, crowned with a ship as a weathervane. The Guildhall has a superb collection of plate, one of the richest collections of its kind in England. Its maces are historic, a

Tudor one with James the First's arms added to it, another with the arms of the Commonwealth, and those of Charles the Second. There are many fine bowls, and a loving cup of the time of Henry the Eighth, two magnificent flagons of Charles the Second silver, and a fine salt bowl given by a Gosport blacksmith who in 1664 made a great chain for the defence of the harbour.

Hereabouts is Victoria Park with many memorials. A great column with a lion at the top is in memory of Sir Charles Napier, conqueror of Scinde; a granite column is to the men of HMS Centurion, who fell in trying to relieve the Pekin Legations; a piece of an anchor is from HMS Sultan, having broken off at the Siege of Alexandria. The memorial to the 6000 men of Portsmouth who fell in the Great War is a cenotaph crowned with an urn surrounded with stately masonry and two groups of sculpture, another memorial is to Sir George Tryon and the men of HMS Victoria who went down with the ship as the result of one of the most incredible mistakes ever made in naval history. One day in June 1893 the Mediterranean Fleet was formed in two columns 1200 yards apart, the Victoria and the Camperdown leading, with Sir George Tryon commanding the Victoria. The Admiral gave the signal for the Victoria and the Camperdown to turn inwards, and it was clear to all that the distance was too small. They collided. The Camperdown struck the Victoria, which turned over and plunged headfirst to the depths. Tryon went down saying "it is entirely my fault," and 320 officers and men went down with him.

The main gateway into the dockyard was fashioned in Queen Anne's day. Keeping company with the clock tower near it is the signalling tower which sent semaphore messages twinkling from Spithead on their way to Whitehall. Ahead of us are eight acres of Henry the Eighth's dockyard, in which is Number One dock, the oldest of all, opening directly into the harbour. The dockyard has many relics and memorials. In front of the Georgian houses where the Port Admiral has his headquarters in Sunny Walk, William the Third stands on the road from the main gate to the Victory. Captain Scott stands in bronze (done by his wife) on the dockyard parade facing Harmony Row, which the houses of the officers are called. He stands, cap in hand, wearing his naval overcoat and sea-boots, with one of the dogs of his expedition at his feet. Near by is the church built by Telford, St Anne's, with the bell from the Royal George. By the admiral's house is the Navigation School.

The great dockyard is the workshop of the Royal Navy, its repairing and fitting rooms, its experimental laboratory, and in many ways its executive headquarters. It has a furnace that can heat a bar 100 feet long, and a Nasmyth hammer that can give a blow of 200 tons. It has 60 acres of enclosed basins, 15 dry docks, three miles of wharfage, and ten miles of railway. About 90 acres of its area have been reclaimed by using the mud excavated from the basins.

One of the most interesting attractions in the dockyard is the panorama of the Battle of Trafalgar painted by Mr W. L. Wyllie, a labour of love for years; it shows the battle in the afternoon when the Victory and the Temeraire and the French Redoubtable were all jammed together, rolling and crashing as they fought. Here is also a museum second only to the United Service Museum in Whitehall.

It contains the most valuable ship's model anywhere in the world, the actual scale model from which the Victory was built. The museum has a sea chest belonging to Nelson, and the death mask of the admiral taken on the Victory by the ship's surgeon. There are pictures, plans, engravings, old letters, Fleet orders, figureheads of the fighting ships, and a chronometer belonging to the Victory.

The museum is, indeed, a sort of annexe of Nelson's Victory, and we may think there is no more captivating place for any sailor than here, for we have the panorama of Trafalgar, the museum with all its relics of the great sailor, and the Victory itself for us to visit.

Truly, for the student of Trafalgar there is no place anywhere to equal this famous city.

Portsmouth has many striking gateways (its Landport Gate, the King James Gate the Naval Barrack Gate, and the Memorial Arch at the hospital), and many striking buildings, such as the Seaman's Orphanage, the Roman Catholic Cathedral, the Navigation

Portsmouth

Nelson's Victory

Portsmouth   The Guildhall

Portsmouth   The Cathedral

Portsmouth   **Entrance to Harbour**

Portsmouth   **The Spacious Southsea Front**

The Implacable

The Camber Dock

Home of John Pounds

Birthplace of Dickens

FAMOUS SIGHTS OF PORTSMOUTH

School; and away from the old streets and the dockyard is her attractive pleasure ground, Southsea, a little apart from Portsmouth, but necessarily of it. Southsea has one of the finest sea fronts of any of our holiday towns, bright and flourishing and gay with tennis courts and looking across the dancing waters of the Solent where they open up to sea beyond the green breakwater of the Isle of Wight.

Long ago when these inviting pleasure grounds were marsh and sandy wastes Henry the Third assembled his armies here to reconquer France, and from Southsea Castle above the common Henry the Eighth witnessed a two-day fight at Spithead between the French and English fleets and the sinking of the Mary Rose. Near the Clarence Pier the old anchor of the Victory is set on a granite base, for all to see, and close by is an obelisk marking the place where the murderer of Buckingham hung in chains. Dominating the front is the magnificent Naval Memorial on the edge of the common. It is a landmark for ships at sea, being a soaring stone column with a copper sphere resting on the top in the style of those at Plymouth and Chatham. At the corners round the base are four lions, and at the four corners on the top are bronze figures representing the four winds of Heaven, holding up the copper globe. There are other memorials to ship's officers and men, one to the Crimean dead having a gun from Sebastopol in front of it. Of Southsea Castle, originally a Tudor fort, nothing remains but the enclosing ramparts.

There are three Southsea churches with something notable among their possessions: St Matthew's with an altar painting of 1666; St Stephen's with a Danish silver beaker of 1646; and St Michael's with a Spanish censer made of copper.

Southsea has on its eastern parade the beginning of what may come to be developed as a great museum and art gallery for Portsmouth, Cumberland House. It suffers from lack of space as many museums do, and is today chiefly a natural history museum and a circulating art gallery. On the ground floor is a fine collection of Hampshire birds and animals, with rocks and fossils of the neighbourhood, and there are aquarium tanks showing the smaller forms of sea-life around the shore, and an observation hive of honey bees. The circulating art gallery, of course, comes and goes, but here is the nucleus of a permanent gallery of pictures, including works by W. L. Wyllie, Frank W. Wood, Martin Snape, and Preston Cribb.

In front of Southsea lies Spithead, the roadstead between Portsmouth and the Isle of Wight. At times we may see here our great steel monsters, and at all times we may watch the white-sailed yachts skimming its surface between the black and white chequered forts spacing it at intervals. These round forts are obsolete, though they are still manned, and each has its own deep well. In the channel between the coast and the island the huge Atlantic liners pass.

In our own century Portsmouth has gathered to itself a few of its outlying villages and hamlets: Cosham, Fratton, Milton, Eastney, Great Salterns, and Hilsea. Hilsea has a barracks and garrison church which has preserved a Norman doorway and a 12th century font, and Cosham has still a little Norman work, which came to it with the old church of Wymering, now much restored. It has, however, kept a 13th century arcade, and sedilia and piscinas from the same time.

Two Ships from Trafalgar

WE may wonder if there was ever a more dramatic spectacle anywhere by the sea than the two ships that fought each other at the Battle of Trafalgar and long lay as neighbours in peace, the Victory in dry dock, the Implacable afloat.

The Victory is a national monument, restored so that we see her as Nelson knew her; the Implacable was alive with Boy Scouts, floating at the head of the harbour in Fareham Creek within gunshot of the Victory. In 1805 the shot would have been fired, for the Implacable was then the Duguy Trouin, and when her first commander, Admiral Dumanoir, sighted Nelson's flagship her first shot tore the Victory's topsail. When the battle had been lost for France the Duguy Trouin withdrew with a parting shot from the fighting Temeraire; but she was afterwards captured and entered the British navy as the Implacable. She was the last ship afloat which fought at Trafalgar. After many years in Falmouth Harbour where the generosity, of Mr Wheatley Cobb equipped her as a holiday training ship, the ship was brought to Portsmouth to rest by her great adversary. They met again after 127 years had passed since they met in action, and as the Implacable was towed past the dockyard the marine guard of the Victory stood to attention and returned her salute, for this was no enemy ship that was coming, but a friend who had put in a hundred years of service as a king's ship. As she sailed into Portsmouth Harbour all the warships dipped their flags. Now, alas, she has vanished beneath the waves—for ever.

Nelson's Victory lies in the oldest dry dock in the world, and if Nelson the seaman would miss the salt water Nelson the admiral would look with pride on his flagship's graceful bulk, the swelling lines of the hull, the three great lanterns aft, the soaring masts, the yards, the hempen rigging, the lines of fluttering flags. All is there as Nelson saw it at Trafalgar, except the shot-torn sails.

It is as he saw it, not indeed altogether as it was, for masts and rigging and even guns had to be replaced. But the replacement which began when, at the instance of Admiral Sturdee, the ship was rescued from the peril of foundering at her moorings and was moved into dry dock, has been carried out by the Society for Nautical Research with the most painstaking accuracy. So far as is humanly possible this proudest memorial of the British Navy is the ship Nelson loved, the ship that carried his flag to victory, the ship in which he died.

Impatience to reach the spot where he yielded up his life perhaps hastens the necessary tour of the four decks of the ship, their guns and their fittings, yet these are of immense interest, both because they bring back to us every feature of a fighting ship of those fighting days and because we are sure the admiral knew them all. Nevertheless, we descend from the poop (where in fine weather Nelson walked up and down the weather side) to the upper gun deck, with the cabins occupied by him for two years without setting foot on shore; then to the middle gun deck with the 24-pounders, the lower gun deck with the 32-pounders, till we come to the cockpit.

Here we meet history face to face. Here Nelson died. Here he consummated Victory with Sacrifice. The cockpit is well lighted now, but in that hour of fate the fitful gleam of a ship's lantern was all that lighted up the heavy beams and the pallet on which the hero was laid. We cannot hear the thunder of Trafalgar's guns, the surge of the waves is silent, but we can picture all else. The surgeon's fingers are on the failing pulse. The chaplain lays his hand on the admiral's chest. The purser supports his head. The steward scans the surgeon's face to see if he may read a sign of hope. Captain Hardy towers over the group. Even the carpenter has crept down to watch the group in breathless anxiety. The minutes flow swiftly by, the admiral's life is ebbing, though he opens his eyes and smiles when they tell him that 20 prizes have been taken and the victory won. Captain Hardy kneels down and kisses him. The dying man murmurs, "Now I am satisfied. Thank God, I have done my duty." Another moment and Hardy stoops again. The admiral says, "Who is that?" The captain answers, "It is Hardy," and Nelson says, "God bless you, Hardy," and enters on his immortality.

There are a hundred other memories that this great ship awakens, a hundred pictures of the navy of Nelson's day that it presents to us. The surgeon's quarters where Nelson died are themselves a reminder of the desperate hardships under which men risked their lives. They are dark, they must have been foul, the surgeon's instruments were of the crudest kind.

Compared with this dark cubby-hole the gun decks are almost cheerful. The whole of the ship lies open to us now, neat from poop to forecastle. We see the wheel ropes, the pumps, the hempen cable, the capstans, the store rooms, the quarters of officers and men. We must employ our imagination to fit into this background the scene on the day of the Battle of Trafalgar. All is here to be awakened by the touchstone of imagination. During the Great War a proposal was made to move the Victory to the Thames and the First Lord of the Admiralty was willing, but it was found impracticable for the ship to make the journey, and she remains in the harbour where she is most at home, the most dramatic possession of the greatest naval port in the world.

Three Generations

PRESTON CANDOVER. Its new church stands for all to see; its old church hides behind the trees, gazing sadly across the meadows. It is the ancient chancel, all that is left of one of the first churches built in Hampshire when Norman influence was ceasing to be dominant. By the old priest's doorway, now built up, is a very old mass dial, probably Saxon, and over the west doorway is a Saxon coffin lid carved with a wheel cross. The nave was burned down in the 17th century, and the new 19th century church has been built on another site. On the floor of the old chancel are ancient tiles and memorials of people who knew the church when it was loved and cared for. There is a fine brass portrait of Katherine Dabridge-court who worshipped in the old nave in the time of Shakespeare. She is charming, in the beautiful clothes she wore in the reign of Queen Elizabeth. Her family at one time owned the estate the nation bought for Wellington, Stratfieldsaye.

Not so charming but of great interest is a brass inscription near this lady on the floor; it is to one of the three generations of vicars here who preached in this old chancel for 99 years, Peter, William, and John Waterman. Peter preached his first sermon here in 1626 and all but 100 years later John Waterman preached his last. John was the shepherd of his flock for 54 years and seven months, and his record has never been equalled in the history of this old place. It has been nearly reached, however, for there was laid here during the war Sumner Wilson, the beloved vicar of 54 years and four months.

The People of the Manor House

PRIORS DEAN. It lies among wild hills, its brick manor house looking as if it had been here nearly as long as the mighty yew shading the church door. The floors of the house have yielded many thrilling finds, among them two toy lead cups and saucers, a Stuart stirrup-iron, and a clip thought to be the top of a chatelaine. In the garden and the field near by have been found Roman tiles, a lovely tear bottle (in which it is said wives used to catch their tears when their husbands were away) and a burial urn much older than the Romans. The tiny church is 13th and 14th century, but is entered by a Norman doorway. It has an old and heavy door and an ancient timber roof, and its belfry rests on great baulks of timber.

In the chancel floor are brass portraits of people from the manor house of Shakespeare's day. John Compton is full-bearded and wears a long gown over his doublet and hose, his wife having a lovely ruff and plain sleeves with neat cuffs. Grouped round the chancel walls is a sculptured gallery of the Comptons in the 17th century. There is the bust of a stout young man, Compton Tichborne, and next to him is the monument he raised to his grandparents, Sir John and Dame Bridget, with portrait busts of them. Sir John has a little beard and a cloak over his armour, his lady wears a scarf over her hair. Opposite them kneels Elizabeth Tichborne, Compton's mother, wearing a long veil and a wreath; she died at his birth in

1623. Near her is her sister Bridget Stoughton, richly dressed and very delicately sculptured, her sleeves bound with rosettes. She also died young, being 21, and left four children who are here with her.

PRIVETT. Under the trees by the cross-roads is a notable group of round barrows called the Jumps, in which, we think, lie men of the Celtic race the Romans found in Britain. The beautiful modern church was designed by Sir Arthur Blomfield; its lofty tower has a spire rising nearly 170 feet. Its mosaic pavements of Italian marble were laid by workmen who came from Italy to lay them. The lychgate is from the timbers of one of the ships used for Arctic exploration by Admiral Parry.

QUARLEY. We may walk round its church outside to see some of its oldest possessions, the doorway and the little window high up, both built by the Saxons and now blocked up; the curious 18th century east window flanked by square pillars with elaborate capitals; and three bells kept in a frame in the churchyard, one of them 300 years old and another older than the Reformation. The church has an Easter sepulchre in the sanctuary, and its font is about 700 years old. The pulpit has spiral balusters in the same style as the finely carved 17th century rails across the chancel arch. One of the 19th century rectors, we noticed, was Charles Mackie who ministered here for 51 years.

Quarley has given its name to the great tree-capped hill near by, a well-known landmark in Hampshire 561 feet high. It is ringed with entrenchments made before history, and from its summit wide stretches of country may be seen. The Port Way passes near.

The High Hearts of the King's Sons

REDBRIDGE. It stands where the River Test enters the highest reach of Southampton Water, after it has wound its way there through quiet reeded channels. It once had considerable trade by small ships, but it is now swallowed up by Southampton. The passage of the Test has been greatly improved in our time by new bridges, and today there is a beautiful 17th century stone bridge by the fine modern one of concrete. Certainly there has been a bridge here since the tenth century. For its most distant history we have to go back to Bede and his jottings about the uneasy times when the Saxon hordes were fighting for a permanent hold on southern

286

Britain. In the seventh century Redbridge already had an abbey, whose abbot was named Cynebert, and of him Bede tells a story curiously illustrating the convulsive changes in kingship and in religion.

Cadwalla, the grandson of one of the most resolute Saxon invaders, took up his grandfather's warfare against the Jutes, who had seized the Isle of Wight and the eastern part of Hampshire, as well as Kent. He captured the Isle of Wight, but two of the sons of the King of the Island escaped to the mainland and took refuge at Redbridge monastery. Cadwalla seized them and demanded their death. The abbot Cynebert pleaded that at least he should delay their execution until they had been converted to Christianity and Cadwalla agreed. So the abbot, "after teaching them the word of truth, and washing them in the font of salvation, gave them assurance of being received into the heavenly kingdom"; and though they did not escape death the lads were able to meet it with high hearts.

A Duke's Appeal for His Life

RINGWOOD. It stands on the banks of the River Avon, where the fine salmon river curves through flowered meadows to Christchurch and the sea. It has in its High Street a little white building of sad memories, Monmouth House. Here the unhappy Duke of Monmouth, dragged out of a ditch after the Battle of Sedgemoor, was brought as a fugitive, a king's son looking like a labourer. Under this roof he sat down and wrote a piteous letter to James the Second. He was filled with remorse, he said, for the wrong he had done the king, but his misfortune was such as to meet with some horrid people "that made me believe such things of your majesty and gave me so many false arguments that I was fully led away to believe that it was a shame and a sin before God not to do it." He declared that he would rather die a thousand deaths than excuse anything he had done, and confessed himself in the wrong as much as any man had ever been. He prayed that God would strike the king's heart with mercy and compassion and that he might see him to speak one word. The duke was taken from this house for one of the most pitiful interviews ever known with a king, at which Monmouth fell upon his knees and crawled along the floor to the king's feet. It was in vain; a few days more and another head had fallen on Tower Hill.

Ringwood's beautiful manor house was the home of Lord Chief Justice Mansfield, who lived through most of the 18th century and was famous for half of it; his epitaph in Westminster Abbey tells us (using his Christian name):

> *Here Murray, long enough his country's pride,*
> *Is now no more than Tully or than Hyde.*

In the grounds of Matcham, another house on the outskirts of the town, are some noble pine trees planted by Nelson who used to stay in the old house which stood here but has now been burned down. It was the home of his sister Mrs Matcham, who was sympathetic to Nelson in all his domestic concerns and gave a home to the fatherless Horatia. She sleeps at Slaugham in Sussex.

The town has a quaint brick chapel built by the nonconformist congregation which used to meet at Moyles Court in the time of Dame Alice Lisle, the old lady butchered by Judge Jeffreys for protecting fugitives from Sedgemoor. The chapel is filled with deep box-pews and high galleries, and has a gaily painted plaster wreath of fruit and flowers on the ceiling and an 18th century lacquer clock.

The church, approached by an avenue of limes planted 200 years ago, was rebuilt last century, but it keeps its 13th century canopied piscina, the 200-year-old brass candelabra, two silver flagons, and an almsdish made in Shakespeare's time. It has also a brass portrait of one of its rectors, John Prophete, once Dean of York, who died a few years before Agincourt. He is wearing a magnificent cope engraved with figures of the Madonna and saints.

A Great Journalist

HERE lived and died Harold Begbie, one of the best-known writers of his day. For more than a generation he had been writing in papers and books. He was writing poetry for a London newspaper when poems were measured by foot-rules, and he received a cheque for 136 inches of poetry at 2s 6d an inch. He must have written as much as any man whose writing was worth reading.

He had a way that took him anywhere. He could knock at any door and be welcome. He knew everybody and everybody liked him. No man had more famous friends. He worked hard because a writer must, but he found time to travel, and he had seen all the

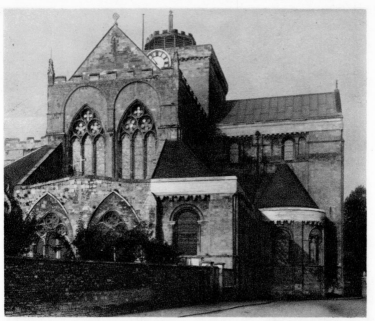

The Ancient Walls

South Aisle

The Nave

THE SPLENDOUR OF ROMSEY ABBEY

Painted Reredos

Carved Capital

Norman Doorway and Saxon Crucifix

ROMSEY ABBEY

great cities. But he loved most to be at home in the finest little country on the Earth. He loved every part of it. He bought or built or rented houses one after the other in seven counties and in London, houses with the little gardens he loved, or with the moor about him, or with a great forest seen from his windows, or with the Channel at his garden end.

Once it appeared that he had finally found himself. He had left London in a fit of gloom. Despair had possession of him, and he looked forward to a simple life away from the world of men and the excitement of affairs. Then it was that he became the Gentleman with a Duster and wrote The Mirrors of Downing Street. It was from a labourer's cottage on the Yorkshire moors that this book came into every library and club, into every section of intellectual and political society, on both sides of the Atlantic.

It is curious to look back and remember the guessing of the identity of the Gentleman with a Duster. Not a soul but the publisher knew outside that cottage; but an editor in London who handled more Begbie manuscripts than any other man was able to penetrate behind the veil by an oddity of style which nobody else would guess; and he wrote a letter to the author conveying the profound secret that he himself had written The Mirrors of Downing Street! The letter reached Harold Begbie one morning when he was at his wits' end to know how to answer persistent assertions of his authorship of the book, and he was able at last to invent the perfectly truthful formula that he had heard in confidence from an acquaintance in London that he had written the book. "Will you come," he wrote very wittily to the friend, "and write my name in your book?" So began the series of books of which the authorship was one of the best-kept secrets of our time. They have been sold on both sides of the Atlantic in hundreds of thousands.

This most versatile writer and most charming man left his mark on the world. He entertained and informed a host of readers. He gave the Salvation Army its most famous book in Broken Earthenware. He wrote a book in defence of Lord Haldane which will be read when Lord Haldane's detractors are forgotten. When Earl Grey lay dying he asked for Harold Begbie and begged him to write his last message to the world. He delighted a wide and famous company of friends in every walk of life. Perhaps he wrote too much, for the journalist's world is so full of wonder that he cannot stop; but he was a poet too, with something of the crusader in him. He could write on anything at any time with a touch of pure genius, and yet, such a fountain of life and wit was he, it seemed always that the best was yet to come.

A Masterly Mind With Clive

ROCKBOURNE. What could a village want more than this, a sheltered place in the downs wedged between Dorset and Wiltshire, dowered with fine trees, and a clear stream making its way to the Avon? It is one of those places chosen by the monks of old, and still up a chalky road leading to the downs is a farm whose mighty barns were part of a monastic house, for they have 13th century windows and doorways. The farm was once the home of Sir John Cooper, father of the first Earl of Shaftesbury.

The church (to which we come under a great arch of yew) rises above the farm on a grassy knoll, and has much beauty. A Norman archway leads us to the vestry, the nave arcade is 13th century, the barrel roof is 15th, an old table is 17th, and the spacious pews are 18th. The font is 15th century with a 17th century cover, there is a little glass 500 years old, the old dovecot remains, and the manorial chapel is now a barn. There are many monuments to the Coote family, one of the humblest bearing the proud name of Sir Eyre Coote, the masterly Irish soldier who did so much to build up English influence in India. It was to his judgment that Clive yielded when he launched the attack at Plassey, the battle which, against apparently hopeless odds, gave England command at Bengal. With an army of 3000 men Clive was faced by 55,000. He called a council of 16 officers and Clive and eight others favoured delay; Coote and six others voted for attack. Clive took an hour to think it over, and then agreed with Coote, attacked, and won. Coote came home very rich, with no criticism against him except his love of riches. He was immensely popular with his men. He had bought an estate here, and though he died in India he wished to lie at home, and here they brought him. A pillar in his grounds was set up by the East India Company.

There are three sculptures on the walls to members of the family, a bust of a young man of 33 who died in Austria, an angel comforting a woman and two children to a young man who died at Naples, and a relief to another Sir Eyre Coote, nephew of the famous soldier; he was a General and is shown here as he lay dying, beckoned to heaven by an angel and mourned by his widow and their only son.

In the chancel are some old flags, one of which was captured in the tragic Walcheren expedition at the beginning of last century, one of the most miserable failures in the history of the British Army.

The Splendour of the Abbey

ROMSEY. There is hardly a street in Romsey that has not something to delight us, something from auld lang syne. One street has delightful almshouses made new in our time with pretty porches, dark roofs, and shaped like a new moon. Above them is an enchanting white house with balconies hardly bigger than bird-cages, perfectly lovely when they are covered with wistaria, and beyond it all is the peace memorial park, with the Test flowing swiftly by, fresh from turning the wheel of a leather mill. In the square is Matthew Noble's bronze statue of Lord Palmerston standing bareheaded, and the old inn, now an inn no more but keeping the old hammered sign from which Fairfax hanged any of his followers who misbehaved themselves. We see Palmerston's home from the bridge, a fine white house called Broadlands. Here he was born and here he grew up, his favourite room overlooking the river. The house has been much enlarged since James the First stayed here; it has lofty porticos and stands in 400 acres with a lake in front of it, and we understand that his study is still kept as he knew it.

But most of all in these streets we must love Church Court. A narrow alley brings us to a row of buildings in the middle of which is one of rare romantic interest. On one side are 18th century cottages and on the other a Tudor cottage of great charm, its wattle and daub walls held together by timbers, its four doors fixed in by hand-forged nails, its oak hearth kerb held by wooden pegs, its windows opening and shutting with Tudor hasps and catches.

Set between these cottages is King John's House with walls of flint and stone, an ancient gargoyle, and some fine windows. John built it as a hunting lodge, and here he sent his daughter the little Princess Joanna, with Christiana of Romsey as a governess. He charged the mayor and bailiffs of Winchester twopence a day for her maintenance, and when she married the King of Scotland in 1221 the house was given to the abbey as a guest house. Since then it has fallen on evil days and been a workhouse and many things, but it is in good hands again and beautiful to see.

It has the original stone doorways, a battered but beautiful window with moulding inside and out, an oak roof with a Tudor kingpost, a three-handled stone mortar shaped by an axe 700 years ago, and, most marvellous of all, a set of blazoned shields, two portrait heads, and many mottoes cut in the plaster with the point of a dagger. For reasons which have satisfied the experts it is believed that these drawings were done on February 13, 1306, when Edward the Third visited Romsey with his Court. One of the things enabling them to fix the date is the crowned head of the king himself. The shields are those of well-known barons and the mottoes and messages left by these visitors have such meanings as these:

> God advise me at God's will.
> Nobody knows but God alone,
> God in whom I put my trust.

These words they wrote, this king's head they drew, one winter's night 600 years ago in the upper room of the house that John built.

Not far away from it stands the abbey founded by Alfred's son Edward. His great church was sacked by the Danes, and the impressive structure we see is Norman and English. It contains some of the finest 12th and 13th century work to be found in England, most of it due to Henry de Blois who gave us the marvellous church of St Cross at Winchester. It is bigger than Rochester Cathedral, bigger than Chester, and it has been a famous seat of learning. Its west front is one of the finest examples of 13th century work with its severe simplicity, and its low Norman tower is captivating in spite of the belfry added last century. From the top of it we see Romsey like a map at our feet, with the Isle of Wight beyond.

Very beautiful is the Norman doorway, with four twisted columns and a richly moulded arch, and by the doorway, impressing all who come into this impressive place, is a sculpture at least 800 years old, of the triumph of life over death. It is one of the most remarkable Crucifixion scenes we have seen, with Christ on the Cross erect, eyes open, with no nails in either hands or feet, the Hand of God reaching down to him from the clouds. It is remarkable that this design is almost identical with the Hand of God on coins made in Winchester nearly 1000 years ago, and one drawn in a Saxon book in the British Museum.

This wonderful stone is one of two ancient Calvarys preserved in the great treasure house of Romsey, the smaller one being indoors over the altar of the Chapel of St Anne, and under a traceried wooden canopy perhaps 600 years old. One of the very earliest Crucifixions in this country, this also expresses the note of triumph. On the arms of the Cross are angels swinging censers, below is the Madonna with St John, and at the foot of the Cross stand two Roman soldiers, one with hyssop on a rod, the other in the act of piercing Christ's side with his spear. Springing from the rood and writhing itself about these figures is the True Vine. We may owe the preservation of this crucifix to the fact that in some time of danger long ago it was built with its face in the wall to save it from destruction; it is now built into the wall of one of the five apses.

The interior of the abbey is majestic and lofty. Great columns with carved capitals carry the handsomely moulded arches, and above this march yet more arches set in pairs with slender shafts, each pair crowned by a greater arch. Above these are the clerestory windows, and all the way up to the lofty roof the columns rise in increasing beauty. The west end comes from the 13th century, but the rest (except for two 14th century windows from the vanished lady chapel) is as it came from the Norman masons.

The ancient Saxon crucifix is in the south aisle; in the north aisle are several rare treasures. One is a simple Jacobean altar table with a row of ancient tiles in front of it on which we noticed knights on horseback, dragons, lions, and lilies. In the floor are ancient gravestones with crosses, one with a hand holding a crozier. On the wall, in a glass case, is a fine piece of 14th century needlework, a green velvet cope with stars of gold thread and crimson satin, once gay with flowers and used as an altar cloth.

The transepts, too, have an interesting collection of things to see. In the north transept we may go back 900 years in the twinkling of an eye, for here is a trapdoor which gives us a peep of the foundations of the first great church, the building which grew out of the house of prayer St Morwen and her nuns would use. Stirring it is to be on ground that has been sacred so long, while Saxons and

Normans, Plantagenets and Tudors, Stuarts and Hanovers and Windsors, have ruled England; for anything we know there may be fragments here from the foundations laid by the grand-daughter of King Alfred.

The walls in this transept bring us to a chapter in history nearer our own day, for outside they have the marks of Cromwell's bullets when he fell on the carousing Royalists and drove them helter-skelter from the town. There is an archway set askew in the wall, thought to have led to an anchorite's cell, and in this transept is an old carved chair, a handsome modern reading desk, and a screen with a row of 600-year-old heads in the cresting. The screen was found among the lumber in the triforium by an old vicar who did much to restore and beautify the church. He was Edward Lyon Berthon, 54 years vicar in this lovely place, and his kindly face smiles at us from his memorial window opposite, with his microscope on one side and his boat on the other, for he it was who invented the Berthon Collapsible Boat in the days of Samuel Plimsoll, who was much interested in it.

But the rare possession of this transept is its wonderful reredos, believed to have been painted in 1520. It is over the altar of the Chapel of St Lawrence where it was first set up, though in the course of its long life it has been elsewhere. This precious possession has been restored by Professor Tristram since the days when somebody nailed the Lord's Prayer and the Ten Commandments on it, and we see it much as the artist left it four centuries ago. In the centre at the bottom Christ is rising from the tomb, to the stupefaction of four Roman soldiers watching, but to the delight of two stately angels and the great joy of a little lady kneeling in a corner, perhaps the abbess who commissioned the painting. Above are nine enchanting figures in a row, all drawn with charming simplicity. They are supposed to be these saints: Jerome in a red gown and red hat; Francis of Assisi in his monk's frock with a tiny figure of his friend Clare kneeling at his feet, in a black dress and with fair hair; Sebastian bound and pierced with arrows; Augustine of Canterbury, mitred and with a crozier and a book; Scholastica in black and white robes holding a red book; Benedict pointing to a wound in his thigh; Roche with a little red demon at his feet; Augustine of Hippo; and Anthony in a golden mitre and robes of green, red, and gold.

Sleeping in the south transept is a lady fashioned in the marble of the Purbeck hills 700 years ago. She lies sheltered under a cusped and clustered recess of great beauty, and wears a long gown and a simple headdress, with angels guarding her. On the wall is a portrait bust of John St Barbe and another of his wife; they died during the Commonwealth. He is in black and gold and his wife is plainly dressed and has long brown hair; their four enchanting little sons kneel in long frocks and big collars.

High up on a transept wall is a grotesque figure with a crook and a broad grin; it is on the wall with the bullet marks, where there is also a pretty wooden door dated 1739 in a Tudor doorway. On a bracket behind the high altar is an exquisite wooden bust of a woman at prayer.

There is no old glass, and the windows are not notable. One is to Lord Cowper Temple and another to Lord Palmerston. Another window is in memory of one of a group of faithful servants remembered here—Elizabeth Painter, who was a servant in a family for 55 years and died at 94. Here lies Honest Gaspar, who was 60 years in one service and received his Well Done in 1785, and there lies here also John Latham, who was over 80 when he finished a great book describing all kinds of known birds, and was still enjoying a hearty meal at 96.

Two monuments are in memory of a mother and a child much beloved. The mother is Maud Ashley, who died in our own century and is shown here in a medallion above a touching group of a woman clasping two children; the child is Alice Taylor, daughter of a Romsey doctor, her figure carved by the father himself. It shows the little one sleeping with a moss rose in her fingers, and the words on the tomb are: "Is it well with the child? It is well!"

On a plain stone in the south aisle we read that here lies Sir William Petty, and on a dignified monument we see this fine old man serenely sleeping in long robes. He was born here in 1623 and laid to rest in 1687, and his 64 years were as crowded with achievement as it would be possible to crowd a life. He comes into the two immortal diaries of his time, for both Pepys and Evelyn note his doings. Romsey and heredity endowed him with a touch of that universal genius which characterised the Elizabethans. From a clothier's shop in the town he took to the sea, landed on the Continent, and returned to England to teach anatomy. The money he earned at sea had paid for his education; the money he earned at Oxford enabled him to turn inventor and to provide England with its first letter-duplicating machine, which was a mechanical triumph rather than a commercial success. Appointed physician to the Army in Ireland, he carried out a brilliant survey which for the first time gave Ireland an intelligible map. Though he lost his property in the Great Fire of London he had capital enough to set up iron works, to open lead mines, and to establish fisheries.

In the meantime he excited the wildest hopes of revolutionising navigation by an invention for which he is still best remembered, the wonderful ship of which we read in Pepys. This was a double-bottomed vessel designed to do what no other ship could until the advent of steam—to sail against wind and tide. He gave his first model to the Royal Society and worked on the scheme for years, but finally relegated it to that limbo which houses perpetual motion and the defeat of gravity.

His imagination was inexhaustible. He was a great musician, one of the best doctors of the age, a born surveyor, a master industrialist, a first-rate economist with original views on taxation. He was a wit and a scholar whose company delighted that illustrious circle into whose presence Pepys so frequently brings us. So versatile a man, with so apt a tongue and so ready a pen, was bound to have enemies in the less worthy circles of a lawless London, and one of his enemies was Sir Alan Brodrick, who challenged him to a duel. In matters of this sort Petty was never at a disadvantage. Certainly he would fight, he told Sir Alan, but as he was shortsighted he proposed to balance inequalities. Being challenged, he had choice of weapons; and he decided on axes in a dark cellar!

All good men loved him. There is a magnificent tribute to his gifts and qualities in Evelyn's Diary, which accounts him the best Latin poet living, the most prudent counsellor in the State, unequalled as a manufacturer, in advance of all his contemporaries in statecraft, but never long in favour because he outwitted all the rest.

Romsey Abbey has a remarkable collection of antiquities reminding us that our churches were once thought of as museums, to which were brought all sorts of odd and curious things. In the Saxon Crucifixion we have seen a Roman soldier with his spear, but here, in a glass case at the west end of the abbey, is an actual Roman spearhead, with a pair of forceps 600 years old and two ancient stone lamps. In this case also is what is called a Test Act Certificate from the days of Charles Stuart, when it was laid down that no one might hold civil or military office unless he had taken sacrament within the year. Near the case is a magnificently carved chest 500 years old, the work of Flemish craftsmen. It is one of the best we have seen, covered with arches of scrollwork, and it has a steel lock on which is a small bearded figure holding a cross.

The documents of Romsey are worthy of this chest, for they are in an excellent state of preservation, with christenings, marriages, and burials from 1569, and we found on a page for 1643 the simple entry of the death of "a soldier whose name is unknown." He was an Unknown Warrior of those exciting days, and he is all the more interesting to us because they buried him here on August 4, the first day of that Great War of which our most famous symbol is the grave of the Unknown Warrior in the Abbey. Among the other documents of Romsey is the 500-year-old illuminated manuscript known as the Romsey Psalter, which was missed from the abbey and found again in a London bookshop. There is the deed by which the town purchased the abbey from Henry the Eighth when he broke up the monasteries; the actual deed is here and can be seen, showing that the parishioners gave the King the equivalent of £1200 of our money for this great place.

But of all the pathetic possessions of this noble shrine can any be more moving than one small thing in the glass case with the Roman spearhead and the little stone lamps? It is a woman's hair. She is believed to have been the wife of a Roman officer, and was buried here in a lead coffin under the wall of the south aisle in a position suggesting a burial older than the church, for the coffin was placed north and south. The coffin has been opened and it was found that all but the hair had fallen into dust. The hair was resting on a block of wood, dusty, reddish, and ending in a straggling plait. It is symbolical of the spirit of this fine town in which so much that is old has come down to us so little spoiled by time.

The Victorian Era Begins

ROPLEY. Tradition tells us that it supplied the honey for the Conqueror's mead. Today it is a big village reached by a winding byway climbing slowly from the Alton highway and dipping sharply down. The church, its wooden tower wearing a big tile cap, is six or seven centuries old, and has kept its old aumbry and piscina, its 15th century font, a broken stone coffin, and an Elizabethan chalice.

Here was born, the son of the vicar, one of the least impressive of all our Primates, Archbishop Howley. Millions have seen the film of the young Queen Victoria wakened in the night by two men in black. One was the Lord Chamberlain and one Archbishop Howley, who had come to Kensington Palace to tell the young princess that King William was no more. So the Victorian Era began. Archbishop Howley crowned the young queen. He was a diehard Tory who opposed most things. He stood against all the generous spirit of Liberalism in its fight for freedom for Jews and Roman Catholics, opposed Reform and Education, and was generally undistinguished. He died in Lambeth Palace and lies at Addington in Surrey.

Beautiful Ann

ROTHERWICK. It has a splendid village hall with a timbered front, and a church famous in the county for its woodwork and remarkable for the fact that the tower arch and the chancel arch are both of wood, the spaces above them timbered like a Tudor house. The nave roof is supported most elegantly on timbers probably 400 years old. The mellow red brick tower is 17th century, and one face of it is pitted with an extraordinary collection of deep holes which have left many people guessing. One suggestion is that they were made by Cromwell's men; another that volunteers in the days of Napoleon put their targets against the tower and did not shoot too straight. Two of the bells are more than 500 years old, and one seems to have come from the famous Wokingham foundry. We found here a suggestion that it was presented to his native village by John de Rutherwyk, Abbot of Chertsey in the 14th century. The church has a 13th century chancel, two old doors studded with nails, a 13th century font, some solid old pews, a handsome Tudor screen, and some old musical instruments. The reredos is copied from one in a Rheims church, and is a memorial to the 29 Rother-wick men whose names live for evermore.

On the chancel floor is the white gravestone of Ann Tylney, engraved with a rose, a tulip, and a skull and crossbones within a wreath. She died in 1681 and we read that she was young and beautiful, and hopeful of great reward in heaven, for

> *She who on earth an angel did appear*
> *Must have a great degree of glory there.*

There is also a big wall-monument to Frederick Tylney, whose epitaph tells us he was an eminent example of English hospitality in the 17th and 18th centuries, and founded three scholarships at Oxford. Anthony More, who yielded up his spirit in 1683, has a little tablet gay with coloured arms and a quaintly painted mermaid.

A Hero and a Rascal

ROWNER. It has a moated fort, an aerodrome loud with the noise of warlike craft, an iron church, and far away from it in a green field another church, small, humble, and old, with a Norman doorway leading into the vestry. It has a font older than the Reformation, and a chancel arch, a piscina, and a priest's seat of the same age. The church was long the chapel of the Brunes, and a fine monument of the 16th century to Sir John Brune has the peculiarity of being made of chalk, one of a small group of chalk monuments we have come upon which have resisted time for centuries. The chalk of which they are made comes from a great depth and is very hard.

In the graveyard lies Sir Frederick Thesiger, a gallant naval captain who served in the Russian Baltic fleet in the reign of the Empress Catherine, and, returning to his country's service, was aide-de-camp to Nelson at Copenhagen, and remained his intimate friend. He died at Elson near Rowner two months before Nelson fell at Trafalgar. At Copenhagen as a volunteer he carried to the Danish Crown Prince the flag of truce which ended the battle by appealing to the Danes as "the brothers of the English," and to do this he went straight forward through the Danish fire. Another stone is that of Rachael Burdon, widow of Captain Burdon of the Royal Navy, whose epitaph tells us that he met his death in an encounter with the ferocious pirate Paul Jones.

John Paul (Jones was his fanciful addition) was the son of a Scottish gardener of the 18th century. Apprenticed as a sailor, he became a captain busy in the slave trade, which he varied with smuggling. Then, deserting his own country during the war with the

American States, he took command of American vessels preying on English commerce. Later he took service under the French and finally joined the Russian navy and became an admiral of the fleet. Being ill requited for his services, he returned to France and died in Paris at 45, a clever seaman, fearless, but an unmitigated rascal.

The Old Medallions

ROWNHAMS. There was once a marshy patch of ground in Rownhams which was of no use in winter and put to bad use in summer, when it became dry and hard enough to use for rowdy games and brawlings. Now it is encircled by trees, and has a small stone church in its centre with a splendid cedar at its four corners. The change was brought about by Major Oliver Colt, who fell seriously ill and vowed that should he recover he would drain the bad land and build a church on it. He lived to begin the good work, but was struck down again and died in 1853 before the church was finished. His widow completed and furnished it in his memory and he lies in a stone tomb outside the chancel, near a lofty widespreading cedar.

The church has a gallery of delightful old Flemish medallions in its windows with pictures from the Bible and other subjects, 59 in all. We see David returning triumphant from his encounter with Goliath, accompanied by musicians and carrying the giant's head impaled on a sword; Tobias hauls a huge fish out of a swirling stream; Stephen kneels praying steadfastly in spite of the cruel stones; St John holds a chased goblet in his hand and watches the poison leave it in the shape of a serpent as he blesses it; Bel looks down at a fierce little dragon coiled near his feet; Charity walks surrounded by little children and carrying others in her arms; and a noble couple in rich 16th century dress kneel at the foot of a crucifix with the ladies of their household grouped behind them. This last picture possibly represents a royal betrothal or marriage. Some of the medallions are set in vivid fragments of old glass and near Charity is a demon head and the handsome head of a war horse in bright blue. The medallions are of uncommon beauty.

The painted reredos came from Italy and is thought to be part of a triptych of the Nativity, angels and richly dressed personages looking down in wonder.

One of Rownham's rectors (R. F. Wilson) wrote some of the first of the famous Oxford Tracts with Newman, Keble, and Pusey; and a sheaf of their letters is preserved at the rectory. Pusey was a familiar guest here and loved the rectory garden, massed with rhododendrons and overlooking a far stretch of the Test Valley.

The Other Neville Chamberlain

IN the churchyard is a stone with the words once on the lips of Our Lord, the prayer of the Publican; but they appear a little strangely here, in this way: *God be merciful to me, a sinner* (*by request*).

The man of great simplicity who made this request and lies in this grave was Field-Marshal Sir Neville Chamberlain. He was born at Rio de Janeiro in 1820, and lived through all the rest of the 19th century, being laid here after a life of good courage which won for him the tribute of Coeur de Lion from Sir Charles Napier.

Though he spent his life as a soldier there were times when the thought of war filled him with disgust, and it was only for his love of England that he endured it. His father was our Consul-General in Brazil, and was made a baronet for his services in negotiating a commercial treaty with that country. Neville entered the Royal Military Academy at 13, and at 17 was an engineer in the East India Company's army. He joined the expedition to Afghanistan, and took part in much fighting with the Afghans. He made a name for himself as a bold leader and a clever swordsman and had many dangerous escapades, once being wounded by a Ghazi who jumped on his horse and stabbed him.

In 1842 he marched from Kandahar to Kabul under General Nott, and was at the capture and burning of Istaliffe, which so upset him that he declared that he was "disgusted with myself, the world, and above all with my cruel profession." He was twice wounded on this march; in four years with the Afghans he had been wounded six times. General Nott appointed him to the Governor-General's body-guard. He applied for active service on the outbreak of another Sikh war in 1848, and here he did a thing that must always be remembered in war history.

It was necessary for somebody to swim the Chenab River and explore the right bank. If the Sikhs were there it was certain death to the swimmer, but Chamberlain took with him a few men of the 9th

Lancers and swam across. He found that the Sikhs had left, and he swam back to be greeted by Lord Gough as the bravest of the brave. His health breaking down, he went to South Africa and was hunting lions for a year, and on returning to India in 1854 he was given command of a force of 11,000 irregulars to guard 700 miles of frontier. He was thanked by the Governor-General, and a little later was chosen to lead troops into a territory no European had visited.

Now came the Mutiny, and Chamberlain was put in command of a movable column to crush any rebellion in the Punjab, his staff officer being the future Lord Roberts. But he was soon at Delhi, where, seeing his men hesitate before a wall lined by mutineers, he leapt over it on his horse, and was disabled by receiving a shot in his shoulder.

After a few years at home he returned to India to take command of the Madras army, and on having a mission stopped by the Ameer of Afghanistan he took up a strong attitude and declared that the British Government should lose no time in resenting insults. In five years he said farewell to India and came home to enjoy 21 years of quiet life in Hampshire.

W. H. Hudson's Fairyland

ROYDEN. It is Fairyland. To get to it we follow a road which trips along over many ups and downs between tiny fields bedecked with flowers and sunny with gorse, through a gloomy avenue of pines, and then, with a rush down a steep hill under oaks and willows, come into a green space with a noble 17th century manor house, farm buildings, and cottages. In this house W. H. Hudson spent some of his happiest Hampshire days. In the woods about it he saw a hornet and a field vole dispute the ownership of a stream of elm sap. Yews and flowers still make the small garden lovely and the little river Boldre sweeps swiftly by under the arch of a wooden bridge. It is hard work to tear ourselves away, lured on by the road through the woods, carpeted with primrose, celandine, and violet, past the last of Royden's cottages out into the road to Boldre. In Hampshire Days Mr. Hudson has this on the place he loved so well:

A small old picturesque red-brick house with high-pitched roof and tall chimneys, a great part of it overrun with ivy and creepers, the walls and tiled roof stained by time and many-coloured lichen to a richly variegated greyish red.

It was an ideal spot for small birds. I have never in England seen so many breeding close together. The commoner species were extraordinarily abundant. Chaffinch and greenfinch; blackbird, throstle, and missel thrush; swallow and martin, and common and lesser whitethroat; garden warbler and blackcap; robin, dunnock, wren, flycatcher, pied wagtail, starling, and sparrow—one could put one's hand into half a dozen nests of almost any of these species.

And very many of them had become partial to the old buildings: even in closed rooms where it was nearly dark not only wrens, robins, tits, and wagtails, but blackbirds and throstles and chaffinches were breeding, building on beams and in or on the old nests of swallows and martins. The hawfinch and bullfinch were also there, the last rearing its brood within eight yards of the front door.

One of his two nearest neighbours was a gold-crested wren. When the minute bird was sitting on her eggs, in her little cradle-nest suspended to a spray of the yew, every day I would pull the branch down so that we might all enjoy the sight. The other next-door neighbour of the bullfinch was the long-tailed tit, which built its beautiful little nest on a terminal spray of another yew, ten or twelve yards from the door; and this small creature would also let us pull the branch down and peep into her well-feathered interior.

The Old Barn and the Old Chapel

ST LEONARDS. We wonder if the quiet roads to this hamlet can have been much different when the white monks of Beaulieu came this way to build a grange; yet the cottages and farms, as we approach, seem little older than the modern church and give no hint of the surprise awaiting us. This is a mighty barn built about 700 years ago, once so huge that it measured 210 feet from end to end. It is now partly in ruin, but enough remains to show how magnificent it was with its great gables, its arched doorways and windows, and its massive buttresses. Nor is this all. In the charming garden of the manor house, itself once part of the monastery buildings and showing moulded stones from the 13th, 14th, and 15th centuries, are the ruins of a lovely chapel. There is much exquisite work left for us to enjoy, the tracery of the broken windows and the two canopied niches being beautiful. The battered walls are crowned with the colour and scent that wallflowers and aubretia bring with them to pay for their lodging in crack and cranny.

The Mighty Font

ST MARY BOURNE. The shallow Bourne winds through it, white with water-crowfoot when we called, decked with wild

musk and overhung with willows. Its hills on either side are crowned
with trees or ridged with terraces of prehistoric men. It is possible
when the crops are down to trace part of the famous Port Way on
one side of the valley, crossing the Bourne and climbing the opposite
hill on its way to Salisbury.

One of the ancient yews of Hampshire, a big decrepit fellow,
gnarled and hollow, stands by the church. He must be older than
the Tudor tower, certainly older than the porch covered with
wistaria, perhaps as old as the early village clock crumbling on a
buttress by the porch, the mass dial.

The church has grown from a Norman building and has one of
Hampshire's great treasures, a mighty font of black Tournai marble,
quarried and carved 800 years ago. Its four sides are about 14 feet
round and are magnificently decorated, the finest carving being of
vines with bunches of grapes. Several times, too, the carver has
introduced lovely doves drinking from little vases. The base, also of
Tournai marble, is copied from the original base. There are seven of
these fonts in England, the most famous being at Winchester, but
this is the biggest of all, worth going miles to see. Near it on the
floor are a few medieval tiles.

The lectern has a little history which will please all those who
think lost or stolen goods should be returned. It was sold and presented by its owner to Reading Museum, and it is good to know
that the museum gave it back to the church. The four-sided lectern
is shaped rather like a square paper boat and has two chains hanging
from it, the links made of twisted metal about three inches long. A
quaint old table, with letters cut all over it and holes charred in it,
speaks to us of ancient days in the belfry, where generations of singers
carved their initials and allowed their candles to burn too low. There
are some chained books, medieval wall-painting, and (treasured in a
glass case) a strip of red cloth, fringed with gold and embroidered
with initials, part of the altar frontal 250 years ago. Far older is the
battered stone figure of an armoured knight with his legs crossed,
believed to be the crusader Roger de Andelys. Older still is the wide
arch of the chancel with a band of beaded moulding, for it is Norman
built by the men who set up the big square piers of the nave arcades,
with their slender corner columns. The chancel was built about
1300, and the south aisle has windows with beautiful 14th century

Silchester   Church and Roman Wall

Odiham   The Ancient Castle

Selborne   **Gilbert White's Church**

Selborne   **Gilbert White's Home**

tracery. Very clear on one of the walls is a text written in black letters 300 years ago.

The beetle robber of antiquity has robbed the church of nearly all its Tudor timbers, but the village is proud that its own craftsmen have set in their places the most faithful reproductions of the medieval roofs. It is a very creditable achievement.

Gilbert White and His Village

SELBORNE. It is, of course, Gilbert White's village; he must have brought more people to it than all its natural beauty ever would have drawn without him. He was born here and here he lies, and here he studied every natural thing that happened, sun and wind and rain, and leaves on trees, and flowers in fields, and singing birds and creeping tortoises. Here he wrote his famous book.

He would know it today if he could come back. The Zigzag he made still wriggles up his beloved Hanger, a steep hill behind the village to the wishing stone at the top. The old yew, 26 feet round its trunk, still towers by the church. The inn he knew still offers food and rest to the traveller. His own home facing the church is changed but his own sitting-room remains, and on the lawn his graceful little sundial still marks the sunny hours. The small green outside the church is still called the Plestor as in his day and long before it, and his limes are growing in the street before the old butcher's shop.

Very modestly he lies in this small place he made so famous, and many travellers must have missed his grave. It is outside near the vestry door, with so small a headstone that it is easily passed over, for it bears only his initials and the date of his death. The big gravestone in the chancel floor covers the grave of his grandfather.

The beautiful site for the church was given by the wife of Edward the Confessor. The old door swung open for Gilbert White as it has swung open for all comers for about seven centuries; it still has its original ironwork. It opens into a nave with the arcades as the Normans left them, on round pillars and with fluted capitals. In it stands the font at which every baby born in Selborne has been christened for about 800 years. There are 15th century bench-ends in the nave and in the porch, and medieval tiles with flowers, foliage, birds, and dragons.

The restorers have much spoiled the church indoors, but one of its fine possessions is a beautiful window of Francis of Assisi, a memorial set up to Gilbert White by readers of his famous book. It shows St Francis with his little brothers the birds and beasts, and the window has in it the 64 kinds of birds mentioned by White in his writings. Here also is a triptych over the altar given by Gilbert's brother Benjamin when Gilbert died in 1793. It is a 17th century altarpiece by Joost van Kleef and has in its central panel the Wise Men with St George of England on one side and St Andrew of Scotland on the other. There is a lovely 14th century window in a chapel approached by a wide flight of steps 700 years old, which once had pews on them for children and have now resting on them carved coffin stones from the ancient priory here.

At the head of a mound under the old yew is an oak post carved with a trumpet marking the grave of the village trumpeter whose story W. H. Hudson told. He was notorious in the 19th century for calling out the men of the village when a fight with the Alton men was threatening, and for encouraging them with his trumpet in the fray. On the top of the Hanger is a seat set up in memory of Gilbert White, where we may sit and see the view that so rejoiced his heart, and recognise among the rolling hills around us "that noble chalk promontory, remarkable for sending forth two streams into two different seas." The two streams are the branches of the Arun and the Wey, the two seas are the North Sea and the Channel.

Much of the beauty about Selborne has been handed over to the National Trust and is in safe keeping as long as Gilbert White is read.

Gilbert White's grandfather was vicar here; his father, a barrister in London, retired and died here; and Gilbert felt it impossible to live anywhere else, so much was he in love with it. From Basingstoke Grammar School he passed to Oxford, where he became a Fellow and Dean of Oriel. His fellowship made him financially independent, and his life allowed considerable freedom of movement. To satisfy his sense of duty to the Church he took a succession of curacies himself in and near Selborne, and happy memories of him long remained in that countryside.

The one fault he had to find with it was that the whole region did not contain anyone whose special interests were like his own, watching Nature in all its forms, birds and animals and plants, and the weather in its many manifestations, and recording these things. So Gilbert White sought companionship through correspondence, in stimulation of his own ardour as an observer. He also planned tours that would enable him to compare his observations in his native Hampshire with those in other localities.

A most companionable man, with strong family feelings and relatives and friends scattered widely over southern England, he felt it a duty and pleasure to visit them with something like regularity, and he also extended his rides, for he travelled on horseback through a large part of England. His visits reached as far as the Derbyshire Peak, and he spent a week at Spalding to sample the Gentlemen's Society there. He began to write to Daines Barrington when he was about 49, and continued the correspondence for 18 years. He had been writing for several years to Thomas Pennant, priming him with knowledge for his books, before he started his interchange of letters with Barrington. It was Barrington who suggested that the correspondence might be published, and eventually in 1789, The Natural History and Antiquities of Selborne was published by the author's brother Benjamin White, who had a publishing business in Fleet Street. The book was made up of 44 letters White had written to Pennant and 66 to Barrington. Its success was instant, and it is still a continuous seller, fully established as a genuine classic.

Dealing with a medley of subjects the book could only have been written successfully in the form of letters. Through the ease of that form it develops some rare qualities—a frequent strain of delightful humour, complete openness of character, an utter absence of self-consciousness or trying to be clever. A wholly honest and unaffected man is telling us what he has seen through patiently clever eyes, telling it with a touch of quaintness that is peculiarly fitting.

The book is not the one he desired to write. He wished to make it a complete natural history of the village he loved, but it is only a gathering together of fragments of unassorted material for a work undone. Yet who would have it otherwise? It is enough to immortalise the village and the man. He died four years after the book was published, and happily was well assured of its success.

The Tale of a Gold Ring

SHERBORNE ST JOHN. Its greatest sight is the Tudor manor house a little way off, built by that Lord Sandys who was, said

Shakespeare, "mad, exceeding mad." If mad he was, then madness is a good architect, for this stately house is still, as old Leland found it, "one of the principal houses in goodly building in all Hampton-shire." Although The Vyne was altered and extended by Inigo Jones or his pupil, it is still mainly the house where Henry the Eighth brought his queen to stay and where Elizabeth was entertained. During the Commonwealth it was bought by Speaker Challoner Chute, whose descendants hold it to this day, and whose marble monument is in a room next to the exquisite little private chapel, the chief wonder of the house. We come away from it feeling that we have seen something more than ordinarily beautiful. The pews and their canopies are lovely with intricate carving, the floor has handsome tiles made by men of Michael Angelo's Italy, and the east window is filled with glowing Flemish glass showing us portraits of a youthful Henry the Eighth, Catherine of Aragon, and Margaret of Scotland, all the work of some master artist. The sacred subjects in the window are the Crucifixion, the Way of the Cross, and the Resurrection.

There is in this great house at the time this book appears one of the most remarkable Roman treasures in England, a ring stolen from a Roman temple at Lydney in Gloucestershire. The temple was dedicated to a British god named Nodens, as we know from inscriptions found in it. On a lead tablet found in the ruins was a prayer to the god Nodens begging that he would refuse to grant health to all those named Sinicianus until the thief of that name returned the ring of Silvianus to the temple. Apparently the ring was never returned. It disappeared from the Roman temple at Lydney Park when the Romans were in Britain, and found its way to the Roman city at Silchester, where it lay for over 1000 years. In 1795 the buried city at Silchester was excavated, and one of the things recovered was a gold ring engraved with the name of Sinicianus. It would seem that the ring stolen from the temple at Lydney was recovered in the temple at Silchester, being now in the possession of Mr Chute, whose family have owned The Vyne since the days of Charles the First.

In the grounds of the great house, and leaning over the road, is a colossal oak tree, high and mighty and surely one of the oldest living things in Hampshire. It is about 25 feet round the trunk.

The village church with its ancient walls of flint and plaster is full of lovely and thrilling things. The bells are a noble fellowship, the oldest having been here 500 years, and there is a mass dial which marked the time before clocks. Within its rosy brick porch is a worn stone begging us of our charity to pray for the souls of Jamys Spyre and Jane his wife, who set up the porch in 1533; and above the stone are the kneeling figures of Jamys and Jane, their poor heads gone. The church has a massive kingpost roof, a solid Norman font with a cover probably Jacobean, a desk with three chained volumes of Foxe's Book of Martyrs printed in 1641, and a charmingly carved pulpit and canopy "Mad by Henri Sly, 1634." By the altar is a 17th century portrait bust of a bearded man clasping his cloak about him, Richard Attkins looking much as we imagine Shakespeare would have looked.

By the chancel is a chapel founded by Bernard Brocas, a friend of William of Wykeham and the Black Prince, and a terrific fellow in his time. He died in 1395 and was buried with great pomp in Westminster Abbey. The chapel is full of the brasses of his family, gracious ladies and richly armoured knights, all wonderfully engraved. The earliest are those of Raulin Brocas (shown with enormous ears) and his sister Margaret, both severely dressed as in the 14th century. John Brocas, who died about 1420, has two portraits of his armoured self and portraits of his two wives and their children. Near him is a later Bernard in fine armour and a tabard, his coat of arms and a grisly skeleton, crowned and shrouded, keeping him company. Still another portrait is that of William Brocas, also in armour, kneeling at prayer with his gauntlets and helmet beside him. He was the father of Edith Pexsall, who is lying in stone by her husband's side on a 16th century tomb between the chapel and the chancel. Under their finely carved arch they are an engaging couple, he in armour and she in a long gown with a girdle from which hangs a little bag; both are holding in their fingers what seem to be hearts.

Two iron helmets hang in the chapel, and over its altar is a window filled with rather quaint old glass. One piece is a 17th century medallion of a very jovial St Lawrence in a golden cloak, dragging a harrow and waving a book in the air, his halo floating above him. In the floor of the chapel we noticed the gravestones of two beautiful Brocas sisters of Queen Anne's time, who died in the fullness of their youth. One epitaph tells how their eyes were scarcely dried for lovely

Mary when cruel death a second stroke decreed and snatched Ann from them too.

The ancient moated manor house of the Brocas family stands about two miles from the village and still bears the beautiful name of Beaurepaire. A proud family, the founder of the Beaurepaire branch was one of three brothers whose father is said to have fallen at Bannockburn, and who were brought up at the Court of Edward the Second. One member of the family is spoken of by Shakespeare as a traitor against Bolingbroke.

The Young Astronomer

SHERFIELD-ON-LODDON. Two ponds and a grey watermill by the river which Pope called "Loddon slow, with verdant alders crowned" are pleasant village belongings, with many fragments from the past in the little church along the road. It is nearly all made new, with a handsome tower and a shingled spire. Several pieces of old helmets we found sharing a windowsill with a pewter almsdish, and an old tile decorated with a horseman: and in the window above them is what appears to be a rather queer St George attacking a red dragon.

There is a heraldic brass to Edmund Molyneux, who was born in 1532, brass portraits of an Elizabethan lady called Mary Palmes and her ten children, and another of her father Stephen Hadnall, kneeling, his sword hilt peeping out under his cloak. He had the doubtful privilege of being a gentleman of the privy chamber to Mary Tudor. The sides of the doorway are scored with crosses and queer symbols believed to be marks of 14th century pilgrims.

There is a wooden cross from the battlefield grave of Arthur Tilney, hanging below the roll of honour on which we noticed the name A. J. Liddell, VC. He distinguished himself at Oxford and was to be an astronomer; there seemed to be a great future for him. But in August 1914 he went to the Front in command of a machine gun section. Quickly promoted and awarded the Military Medal, he was invalided home and joined the Flying Corps, having qualified as a pilot. A week after his return to the Front he was wounded while in the air, his right thigh broken. He almost lost consciousness, and the machine, with its control wheel smashed, dropped nearly 3000 feet. In the fall Liddell recovered sufficiently to achieve the apparently impossible feat of finishing his course and coming down safely. He had saved his observer's life and his machine, but Liddell himself, the cheerful and devoted soldier, died from his wound. The sky which was to have been his proud career had been his doom.

The City Under the Cornfield

SILCHESTER. We found ourselves here on a summer's day with a cornfield swaying in the breeze, and we thought it the most thrilling field of corn we have seen in all our journeyings, for under it lies Calleva, the lost city of Rome.

A long stone wall, plainly seen in places and traceable over a roughly octagonal space of about 100 acres, enclosed the great city now sleeping under these green fields. Outside the rambling wall with its four gateways can still be seen the great amphitheatre where 10,000 spectators made a Roman holiday; inside was a colonnaded forum, a hall of justice, a temple to the gods, and, what is most precious to us in all the city, a tiny Christian church; its foundations are intact.

Here was the life of a crowded city for hundreds of years, with streets and temples and squares and courtyards, a miniature of all the glory that was Rome, houses filled with lovely things from the hands of the potter, or the worker in bronze, or the sculptor in stone. We have only to take a long walk or a short ride and thousands of these things will lie before our eyes, as they make up one of the most astonishing collections of our long past, in the wonderful museum at Reading.

Here at Silchester we roam about and feel the wonder of it all, and here, in the church of this small village, just within the Roman wall by a neat farmhouse, is something rare and strange which has come from the city underneath—a chair made from a piece of wood which must have been a growing tree when Christ walked in Galilee, for it was used by the Roman builders of Calleva to line a water culvert. Out of it has been made a plain chair which was standing by the screen in the church when we called, rich-hued with age yet looking otherwise as if it might have been cut yesterday. Beside this piece of timber with a past the carved panels of the pulpit from Shakespeare's day seem young indeed, and the domed canopy of the pulpit, with an olive branch bearing a dove, comes only from the Commonwealth.

There is a Norman pillar in one arcade of this 700-year-old church and the rest of the arcade is 14th century. So is the fine font. The splays of two windows have painting on them 700 years old. There is a wooden chest about 200 years old. The parson's dovecot remains.

In a handsome recess in the wall is a stone lady who has been sleeping here 600 years, with small figures supporting her head. She was here when they brought the lovely chancel screen, an extraordinary piece of work by 15th century craftsmen, its tracery with the delicacy of lace, and in the cresting a row of kneeling angels with wings outspread and feathery robes. The low wooden tower is 15th century too.

Still surrounded by remnants of the Roman wall, 12 feet high in parts, lies the great field below which is the Roman city of Calleva. The city was originally the chief city of the powerful Atrebates, whose kings owned a large part of Berkshire, Hampshire, Sussex, and Surrey, and had dominions across the Channel in Gaul, where Julius Caesar met Commius, a leader of the Atrebates on both sides of the Channel. It is the one city in the country which, passing from British to Roman keeping, has yielded a British inscription set up after the legions sailed away to confront the barbarians at the gates of Rome. It is a fifth century inscription, commemorating one Ebicatus, written in the crude Celtic characters that were just beginning to find their way from Ireland into Britain after the Romans with their Latin had departed. It tells us that already Britain was losing its culture and reverting to the language of its barbaric past. Ebicatus the unknown is the silent but eloquent witness.

Forty years of excavating turned time backwards here; and the treasures found are in Reading Museum. The soil is replaced, but exact models are preserved, and from them we could rebuild Roman Silchester tomorrow. The city communicated by splendid roads with London, Winchester, Wales, and the North. The four gateways by which they entered the city have been discovered, with the continuation of the highways themselves beyond Calleva.

The wall, a mile and a half round, enclosed broad streets laid out at right angles, with great buildings and luxurious villas. The most important structure for us was the church, of which the style was unique. The only entrance was at the east end; the apse, with seats for clergy, was at the west end, and there also stood the altar, based on a platform of rich mosaics. The choir was in the west end of the nave. There are two narrow aisles and a miniature transept, and the walls were two feet thick.

Scholars agree that this, England's oldest known church, was built soon after Constantine's adoption of Christianity, and must have stood for a century before the legions left. Its design resembles that of the basilica, or hall of justice, a noble building with Corinthian columns at each side, an apse at each end, a dais for the magistrates, and a number of chambers for officials. Close to the basilica was the forum, 150 yards wide, with a red-roofed colonnade and a number of shops. The cattle market lay not far away; after that the public baths. Of a hundred buildings explored many were once fine houses, one containing 30 rooms. Remains of friezes and beautiful mosaics spoke of the wealth and luxury of the city, but a find of rare interest spoke also of industry. There were a number of hand-mills that had been used for grinding colours for dyes, and near them 12 buildings with 21 stone furnaces.

All the buildings, public and domestic, were roofed with red Roman tiles, and in such a setting the city must have been a picture of comfort and beauty. Immediately outside the east gate lay the arena, where gladiators fought. Of the treasures found there were statuary, inscriptions, marbles, columns, tools, bronze figures, bells, an imperial eagle some proud centurion once carried, objects in metal and bone, and coins dating from Mark Antony.

In this fine city Commius was king of the Atrebates. Nearly all we know of him comes from Julius Caesar, who, admiring and trusting him, had made him king. Hearing that Caesar was about to invade Britain, Commius went to him with an offer of submission, hoping to spare Britain the horrors of war. Caesar's reply was to send Commius back, accompanied by 30 horsemen, with instructions to induce the people to "embrace the protection of the Romans"; but the moment Commius arrived and declared his mission he was seized, chained, and thrown into prison, not being released till the victorious march of Caesar set him free.

After Caesar's second visit to Britain Commius accompanied him back to Gaul, while his three sons reigned here, issuing gold coins which state that they are his sons. He later revolted against Caesar in Gaul, and proved a most formidable adversary, ambushing his columns, cutting up his convoys, and inflicting a deadly wound on one of the leading Roman generals in a hand-to-hand fight.

At last the forces of Caesar were too much for him, and he had to rush to Britain, hotly pursued by Roman cavalry, and escaping by one of the most famous stratagems in history. Reaching the coast, he found the tide out and his ships aground. He ordered the sails of his stranded ships to be hoisted, and the Romans, approaching, saw the fluttering sails as they looked down from a height, and, as Commius had expected, thought he was afloat at sea and gave up the chase. He afterwards made peace with Mark Antony, and, remaining in Britain, allowed his sons to rule in his stead.

So not only are our first church and one of our first towns buried beneath this hundred acres of storied land at Silchester; there is the stuff of history here too, of the Silchester king about whom Caesar wrote as intimately and generously as about Mark Antony himself.

The Singer of the Psalms

SLACKSTEAD. Here lived Thomas Sternhold. Groom of the Robes to Henry the Eighth he must have found this hamlet's peace and shadowed loveliness a very lovely thing after the glare and racket of the Court. Here in 1549, the year when they laid him to rest at Hursley, he began that metrical version of the Psalms which was finished by Hopkins after his death and was for a long time printed with the book of Common Prayer. This version was for nearly two centuries the only hymn-book of the Church of England. The phrases are described by old Thomas Fuller as more pious than poetical, "the authors having drunk more of Jordan than of Helicon," yet their rough rigour has a great popular appeal. We may be sure these enchanting lanes and rolling hills gave Sternhold inspiration for his great achievement.

A Bishop and His Adventures

SOBERTON. Rich with treasure, its hilltop church is guarded by a noble yew, the pride of the village. For 400 years its embattled tower, one of the finest in Hampshire, has been swarming with grinning demons and savage gargoyles, and high on its west front are the heads of a man and a woman divided by a skull. Near one is a key and near the other a pail, and it is these curious things which have suggested the story that the tower was built from the savings of a butler and a dairymaid. We do not know. Its bells have been ringing since the tower was new; they were given by the lord of the manor in 1527. The tower was restored by the generous subscriptions of servants in 1880, at a cost of £113.

There are old wall-paintings in the Curle chapel, named after the famous Bishop of Winchester who sleeps here. On one splay is a little figure of St Anne, upon whose head rests the hand of the Madonna, a towering figure. The other splay has St Catherine, with a man crowned at her feet. The chancel roof of oak is about 600 years old. In the sanctuary are two fine old chairs with richly carved backs.

The chancel arch is 700 years old. The altar rails were shaped during the Commonwealth, and the box-pews are 18th century. In the vestry is a Jacobean communion table. On the walls of the Curle chapel are lovely fragments of stone carving, and here is sheltered a huge stone coffin which is believed to have lain in a field about 1600 years, and had a skeleton in it when found.

The treasure of the chancel, which has a lovely piece of 16th century glass showing the arms of Cardinal Beaufort, is the altar cloth. In the days of the Civil War some Flemish lady's clever fingers wove into this linen cloth for Soberton's altar the story of the Good Samaritan. The date is on it (1645) and it is a rare piece of work. It was used for 200 years and is now much worn, but we can distinguish a man on a horse and an inn with a sign.

Walter Curle, the most famous man sleeping here, was born at Hatfield in 1575. His father was probably the William Curle who was an auditor of Queen Elizabeth and has a monument in Hatfield church. However this may be, the Cecils helped the lad's education and he became a Fellow of Peterhouse, whose chapel he helped to build. By 1621 he was Dean of Lichfield, and eight years later Bishop of Rochester. Then Archbishop Laud, realising his worth, persuaded Charles Stuart to raise him to the see of Winchester. Here he at once proceeded to improve the cathedral, spending his own money freely. But he carried out too faithfully Laud's efforts for a uniform standard of worship, and there was much resentment among the Puritan clergy of the diocese. When the Civil War broke out the bishop held Farnham Castle; but this fell and Winchester was captured ten days later. The cathedral was plundered, but next year the Royalists recaptured the city, only to lose it again before long, the bishop escaping to his palace at Waltham. This in turn was captured and burned, the bishop escaping in a dung cart. Once more he was present at a siege of Winchester, this time by Cromwell himself. The bishop was now 70, and was set free but deprived of everything. With his family he came to live at Soberton, where he died in 1647, being laid here as he wished, rather than in one of his cathedrals.

The Squire and His Lady

SOPLEY. It is on the Avon, and its blessings and beauties are many. The road twists in and out among its cottages as if anxious lest we should miss one. It is gracious with tall trees and the green beauty of water-meadows, divided by the curving river, with the majestic ridge of St Catherine's hill beyond. But lovelier than all is the small 13th century church perched on a knoll overlooking the tranquil valley, its tower hunched about the tiny spire, somehow like a drowsy bird.

Even the porch hints at the delight in store within, for over the door is an old stone figure of St Michael. Leaning against the wall on either side of the door inside are two delightful people carved in stone, believed to be the founders (in 1270) of the church. No mailed knight he, but a quiet country squire in tunic and hood; no flaunting worldly lady she, but a gracious country wife in cloak and wimple. Though time has dealt roughly with their heads and the carved canopies over them, they are wonderfully well-preserved remembering that they were found in a lane. In the north aisle is an arch with two corbel heads thought to be Edward the Third and Queen Philippa, obviously attempts at portraiture. There are two excellent heads at an east window and two charming angels in the roof playing the double pipe and viol. In the tracery of the east window are two more angels, holding heraldic shields and sharing their eyrie with a lion's head and a flaming brazier, the badge of the Comptons, in 16th century glass.

The font was made when the nave arcade was built, in the 14th century; the piscina is 13th. There is a Jacobean pulpit, and in the chancel a handsome chair with 1604 on it. It has an extraordinarily massive back. Near some lovely linenfold panelling is a 13th century gravestone carved with a cross. The timber roof has carved and coloured bosses.

Hanging on the wall is a flag with a history, for it has been in the wars, having been taken from the tent of Arabi Pasha at the Battle of Tel-el-Kebir by General George Willis, whose grandfather was vicar here 46 years. In the churchyard is a great tomb with railings round, where sleeps John Lord Keane, a soldier who, we are here told, fought for his country in the four corners of the world. In 1839, five years before his death, he was in command of the forces which conquered Kabul, and drove the usurper Dost Mahomet from his stolen throne. After life's fitful fever he sleeps well.

Old England's Sea-Gate

SOUTHAMPTON. Whether we think of its past or its present or its future, it is one of the wonders of the world. Its building up into a great port has been the work of centuries. Its daily life keeps it in touch with 160 of the chief ports of the world. Its future is to be greater and greater yet.

When Winchester was the capital of England Southampton was the chief port, and these two towns were the nucleus of Alfred's Wessex. A thousand years ago the Danes were making war on them. Athelstan, first King of all England had a mint here, and there are those who claim that it was here that Canute sat by the waves and rebuked his flattering courtiers. From here Crusaders went out under Richard Lionheart, and troops embarked for the wars of Edward the Third and Richard the Second. Here was the moving scene which Shakespeare makes immortal for us as Henry sets out for Agincourt. Here Philip of Spain arrived and said mass on his way to Winchester to marry Mary Tudor.

It was probably in the days when the Danes were ravaging the town that the Southampton Walls appeared. They are marvellous today, but must have been a wondrous sight up to the 16th century, with seven or eight gates, great towers at the corners, and a castle within. The south and west walls fronted the River Test and were washed by the tide; the east and north walls were on the land side and were moated. These walls were the contribution of the Middle Ages to the strength of Southampton, and a mighty achievement they were, but they were child's play compared with the work that has been done here in our own time in this marvellous town at the head of the inlet from the Solent.

This ancient town is making itself the greatest seaport in the world. It was just before Trafalgar that it began its harbour works, and it was just before the Great War that they began these works which have no parallel in England as a piece of engineering. They have reclaimed 400 acres of new land and made it good with two million tons of material dredged from the bed of Southampton Water, and on these 400 acres they have made a new dock two miles farther inland than the old one, defended by a mile and a half of massive quay walls. If our statesmen could build up peace as Southampton builds up docks, humanity would have security for ever.

The building of the wall itself was something like a miracle. First a broad embankment of gravel was laid, and into this gravel were sunk 146 massive concrete monoliths, some of them sunk 100 feet. Each monolith was a complete and complicated structure with nine vertical shafts running through it, each shaft ten yards round. If we think of one of these things as something like a building in itself we shall be near the mark, and there were 146 of them. Down the nine deep wells inside each monolith mechanical grabs descended to excavate the material beneath. The monolith itself sank through the gravel, and as the material below was removed by the nine great grabs the huge structure sank by its own weight. The monolith would sink ten feet and men would add another ten feet on the top of it; another ten feet would sink, and another ten feet would be added. On and on the sinking and the building went (iron blocks weighing 4000 tons being sometimes needed to keep them upright) until the monoliths were fixed in the earth fifty, sixty, eighty, a hundred feet deep. To most of us it is an incredible feat, but it is all in a day's work at Southampton, and at last all these monoliths were part of the solid earth. When all these concrete pylons were buried, the gaps between them were bridged and filled in with concrete blocks to form the great quay wall.

So the great wall was made. At one end was the area to be enclosed and made into a dock. It was first enclosed by embankments of gravel and chalk into which were driven colossal sheets of steel-plate, then 50,000,000 gallons of water were pumped out from the enclosure, and a million cubic yards of mud removed. A train of 50 trucks arrived each day bringing cement for the concrete which was to replace the mud, and it does not astonish us that the millions of money spent here equalled the cost of a modern battleship, and more than equalled the cost of two or three cathedrals. It must have seemed like a dream to those who had planned this thing, but the dream has all come true, even the avenue of silver birches running through the reclaimed area so that passengers from the great liners are greeted by a scene more characteristic of Nature's Own Island than the slums through which we usually reach our great sea-gates.

The George the Fifth Graving Dock, opened by the king whose name it bears, can take a ship of 100,000 tons, its first ship being the Queen Mary. The dock is 1200 feet long, 135 wide, and 59 deep. Two million tons of earth were dug away to make it, its floor is over 20 feet thick, and its walls are nearly 60 feet high. It has 750,000 tons of concrete in it, and its enormous steel gate weighs 1800 tons. The dock holds 58,000,000 gallons of water weighing 250,000 tons. Three lines of blocks run along the floor of this dock, two to keep the ship upright and one for the keel to rest on. When the dock is dry these blocks are set ready for a ship, the dock is filled with water, the great gate glides back into its recess, and the ship enters and is secured by ropes. The gate comes back into its place, the electric pumps pour out the water in four hours, and the ship is dry, resting on the blocks.

The older Port of Southampton is on the tip of the land between the Test and the Itchen. Here are ten docks (six of them dry), 4219 feet of quays facing the Test and 3758 feet facing the Itchen. The outer dock, opened in 1842, is the oldest; its waters cover 16 acres and the dock is used by cross-channel steamers and cargo boats. The inner dock (10 acres) is only accessible at high tide. The Empress Dock (18 acres) has an average depth of 26 feet, but the Ocean Dock (15 acres) is 40 feet deep. The six dry docks in this area range from 51 feet wide and 281 feet long up to the gigantic proportions of the Trafalgar Dock, 100 feet wide and 912 feet long. The whole of Southampton Docks, including the new extensions, have a three-mile frontage to the two rivers, and five miles of quays.

It would be bewildering to attempt to give any impression of the coming and going, the loading and unloading, the arrivals and departures of cargoes and people, at Southampton. We will merely say that 20,000,000 tons of ships use the docks in a year, and that £1,000,000 worth of goods come or go every week.

Such is the New Southampton, and those who know it well know that this great town itself has with much public spirit tried to keep pace with the wonderful development of its harbour. It stands on 11,000 acres and has almost 1000 acres of open spaces and parks, a proud record. The time is not far off when it will have 200,000 people, and it has 9 railway stations, 16 kinemas, and more than 80 churches. About 40 consuls of other lands are stationed here. It has a Civic Centre second to none in the kingdom, one of the best examples anywhere of an architectural group for the public life of a town. It keeps its parks gay with flowers and shrubs, with statues dotted about, and one of them (Andrews Park) has an aviary and a pretty rock garden with a lily pond, a waterfall, and three small bridges. Southampton Common is bigger than Hyde Park, a mile long and nearly a mile wide in parts, and through it runs a beautiful avenue which is one of the loveliest approaches to any big town. The land on either side of it is the remnant of a forest which once covered all this space, wide stretches of heath, glades set with every kind of English forest tree, thickets of holly and hawthorn, four lakes, wide spaces for sport and recreation, and stately avenues. Immediately above the Common is the Civic Sports Centre, probably unequalled by any other English town. It lies in a natural parkland of about 270 acres, beautified with trees and shrubs, and provides all the amenities for promoting health and recreation.

It is the dramatic interest of Southampton that it bridges the centuries with such a spacious grandeur. Here stand its ancient walls, here are the ancient quays washed by the tide for ages, and here is the spirit of the 20th century, the old town renewing its strength like the eagle. We may feel the thrill of the new or the spell of the old in a very short walk in Southampton.

From its old West Quay Crusaders sailed under Richard Lionheart. Through its West Gate defiled the English troops who fought at Crecy. Here Henry the Fifth marshalled his yeomen for Agincourt, and here, five centuries having passed by, secretly and silently the never-ceasing tide of England's youth and manhood poured forth for four long years. Eight million men, fifteen thousand guns, and eight hundred thousand horses were shipped from this port to an unknown place in France.

Can we stand without emotion on the quay from which the May-

Ships and a Flying Boat

The Docks Seen From the Air

FAMOUS SIGHTS OF SOUTHAMPTON

The Famous Bar Gate

The City Walls and West Gate

DEFENCES OF OLD SOUTHAMPTON

flower and the Speedwell sailed on their perilous voyage to seek liberty for their faith beyond the seas? Near the spot where they embarked is their memorial, unveiled by Mr Walter Page, the American ambassador whose letters to President Wilson have become part of our literature. At the top of a column of Portland Stone 50 feet high is a beacon surrounded by Greek pillars and crowned by a copper model of the Mayflower as a weathervane. This is the simple inscription:

> On the 15th August 1620 From the West Quay near this spot the famous Mayflower began her voyage carrying the small company of Pilgrim Fathers who were destined to be the founders of the New England States of America.

From the century after that the story of Southampton and its port has been the story of increase and prosperity. Its place at the head of Southampton Water (up which the greatest sea-going vessels can pass), the remarkable phenomenon of its four hours of high tide, the safe harbourage protected by the natural breakwater of the Isle of Wight, and the far-sighted enterprise of its town and harbour authorities, have combined to make it one of the greatest seaports in the world.

It has three gateways, but the pride of the town is the Northern Bar Gate. One of the finest medieval gateways in the country, it forms the boundary between the narrow limits of the Old Town and the broad well-planned spaces of Greater Southampton. It was built by the Normans and the original Norman arch is seen in the middle of the passage, which is 60 feet deep from back to front: the pointed arches of the north and south faces are 14th century.

The pointed arches on either side were added to strengthen the central arch and to give space for the Guildhall over it, where the trade guilds met for their transactions. Wide buttresses and rounded flanking towers rise to the battlements, and two lions have been on guard 800 years. They are the lions we read of in the Romance of Sir Bevis of Hampton, written by a Norman scholar in the century after the Conquest. It was the only book John Bunyan had as a boy, and we cannot doubt that the adventures of Sir Bevis stirred the imagination of the Bedford Tinker as he was building up his matchless story of Pilgrim's Progress. It is thrilling to look on these lions and remember that they, too, are immortal.

What scenes this port has witnessed! While Henry the Fifth was waiting here with his army for a favouring wind to take him out to France and Agincourt, and his ships were riding at anchor outside the walls (with his tennis balls on board, a present from the Dauphin for his wilder days), the plot against his life was revealed, and on this Bar Gate the heads of three traitors were suspended as he sailed away to his triumphs. They were Richard Plantagenet, Earl of Cambridge, Henry Lord Scroop of Masham, and Sir Thomas Grey. They were tried in the Red Lion Inn still standing in the High Street; we may see its ancient hall, the scene of the trial, with an open roof and a staircase gallery on which they would look in their last hour.

Who can look at it without a thrill, not seeming to hear those words of the king to his lost friend Lord Scroop:

> What shall I say to thee, Lord Scroop?
> Thou that didst bear the key of all my counsels,
> That almost might'st have coined me into gold?
> I will weep for thee,
> For this revolt of thine, methinks, is like
> Another fall of man.

The three traitors were buried under the floor of St Julian's Church, and a tablet tells us their story.

On the southern face of Bar Gate stands George the Third in the guise of a Roman Emperor, as was fashionable in his day. The watch bell on the parapet has rung out the alarm of fire since Shakespeare was writing Henry the Fifth, and a hundred years later a sundial was set above the head of the king. The Guildhall has been used as a court of justice since Elizabeth, and it has a statue of Queen Anne, the last of the Stuarts, which was brought inside to make room for the House of Hanover.

The 13th century West Gate (looking now as it did 700 years ago and still with its portcullis grooves and the openings for dropping unpleasant things on unwanted visitors) is about halfway along the fine west wall, opposite the old landing-place. It is thrilling to realise that under these very stones for 600 years our ancestors have passed in peace and war to cross the narrow Channel.

The best piece of this great medieval wall runs from the West Gate along the shore, having with it the 12th century Castle Water Gate, the 14th century Catch Cold Tower, and the rounded Arundel Tower, 55 feet high and possibly on Saxon foundations. Only a few fragments of the castle itself are left. The sally port overlooking the water can be traced, and there is a vaulted chamber where stores were kept. On the wall at this point we found a luxuriant growth of the yellow rocket which we were told was growing nowhere else in the county.

Next to the West Gate is the 15th century Guard Room, level with the top of the walls; it was used by the watchmen. It has a Spanish chestnut roof and wattle and daub walls, and joining it is the Western Esplanade, with its striking arcades, built in the 14th century to strengthen the wall against invasion; they are an unusual series of 19 shallow arches 90 yards long and 30 feet high. From the top of each arch a parapet was built to reach the older wall, leaving space for openings through which showers of stones or molten lead could be poured down on unwelcome intruders. From this point the wall runs to the Bugle Tower.

We can trace the line of the old East Wall by passing along the street so quaintly named Back-of-the-Walls. A 15th century tower marks the south-east corner of the Old Town, and here is God's House Gateway, where the portcullis grooves can still be seen. The rooms above God's House Gate, and a gallery leading to the wall, were used as prisons in the 18th century. The East Gate has gone with most of the wall, which reappears at the north-east corner with Polymond Tower and continues towards Bar Gate.

Within the walls Southampton is rich in old houses, two of the oldest (King John's Palace and Canute's Palace) being among the most ancient domestic buildings still standing in England. For more than 800 years King John's Palace walls have stood intact, the west wall coinciding with the town wall by West Gate. They are now roofless, two feet thick, and in them the Norman doorways and the tiny Norman windows look north and west. There is a Norman fireplace and a Norman chimney. Canute's Palace, also Norman, is near the vanished South Gate; only bits of the arches are left, and the dark interior has fallen from its high estate. It should be said that neither Canute nor John were ever in these houses which bear their names.

God's House was a 12th century hospital founded by Gervase le Riche, Portreeve of Southampton, for receiving pilgrims from the

Continent on their way to Becket's tomb at Canterbury or St Swithun's at Winchester. Here they were received by holy men and women, and the hostels and the church close by were dedicated to St Julian, the patron saint of pilgrims. The two houses remaining stand on two sides of a square garden, and are occupied by four Brethren and four Sisters. St Julian's Church is on the third side and is interesting for its carved Norman capitals and because the services are in French, as they have been since 1567. Here, as we have seen, lie the three traitors to Henry the Fifth, and here is a strange memorial to a priest who died in 1569; it has a curious head of alabaster yellow with age, attached to a headless brass figure. There are 18th century hat-pegs, and an old bell of the 14th century.

The Wool House of the 14th century was used to store English wool on its way to Flanders. It has massive rounded buttresses and strong walls within which prisoners of war were kept in the 18th century; on some of the beams are names they carved.

The Undercroft, an underground chamber near St Michael's Church, contains a vaulted roof with carved stone bosses, supported by corbels representing a medieval style of headdress. With its hooded fireplace, bearing remains of ballflower ornament, it resembles part of a monastic building. The chamber was probably used by the monks of Beaulieu Abbey as a rest-house for pilgrims landing at Southampton on their way to Canterbury.

But the choicest treasure of all these old places is the glorious Tudor House at the corner of Blue Anchor Lane, built by the rich merchant Henry Huttoft. It has four storeys and is now restored to its original plan of 400 years ago. It was bought with King John's Palace, by a public-spirited townsman who restored it, and the 16th century timbered building is now appropriately a museum, carefully guarded as a priceless example of a Tudor home secured for future generations.

Built on foundations older than the fabric itself, Tudor House has Norman work in the vaulting of the cellars, and a panelled banqueting room with a minstrel gallery. The fine oak ceiling was found only after three covering ceilings had been removed from it. There is a hidden passage with a priest's hole. In the various rooms of this fine house is set out vividly the life-history of the people round about, beginning with thousands of specimens from a Stone Age flint factory on Twyford Down and remains of prehistoric beasts, and going on through Roman days into the Middle Ages. We found in one case medallions resplendent in blue and gold with early glass from Netley Abbey, and here we found also a spinet belonging to Charles Dibdin, on which that quarrelsome songster may have first played Tom Bowling. Dibdin was born in Southampton, appropriately enough for a man who gave England her most famous sea songs. He was the parish clerk's son and became a chorister at Winchester but preferred to go to London to live with Uncle Tom, a sea captain. He hung about the theatres, became a singer at Covent Garden, but he developed a quarrelsome nature, so that, although everybody sang his songs (he wrote about 1400), he was not very popular, and fell on hard times, eventually being given a pension by one Government to have it withdrawn by another; and he died dependent on charity. In this town Hubert Herkomer was a boy studying in the School of Art, and his palette hangs on the walls. Very pathetic are two other relics, a portrait and a sword of Commander Smith, captain of the Titanic, which sailed out from here and did not come back. She was the pride of England as well as of Southampton, and the words on the wall bring tears to the eye:

After doing all that man could do for the safety of the many lives in his care, his last acts were to jump from the sinking Titanic, to carry a drowning child to a boat, and then, despite entreaties, to swim back at once to his post on the bridge of the rapidly disappearing ship. His last words, many times repeated, were, Be British.

The courtyard between Tudor House and King John's Palace is planted as an old-world garden, clipped yews, stone paths, and flower beds making it delightful on a summer's day, looking out to where the River Test widens on its way to the sea.

In another house in this famous town was born a son of Southampton whose fame is as wide as the world. At 41 French Street Isaac Watts first saw the light. It is all warehouses and markets now, but we found two houses of quiet distinction sheltered by railings and a group of shrubs and trees. Little Isaac Watts played in the Queen Anne panelled rooms of one of these, and in its walled garden, which has a fine old fig tree. Here sunrise and sunset, insects and flowers and birds, came with their simple influence into his mind, and bore fruit in his songs for children. It was sad to see that his house was decaying, and apparently in jeopardy.

But something will remain if Isaac Watts's house should go. His father, in prison for his faith when the son was born, was deacon of the Nonconformist meeting-house Above Bar, and Isaac's was the first name on its baptismal register. Here was first sung that hymn which has since sung its way all round the earth, O God, our Help in Ages Past. It was sung for the first time from manuscript copies made by young Watts himself. A Congregational Chapel now stands on the old site, and the Watts Memorial Hall has a tablet reminding us that Isaac was one of the first Sunday scholars here. He will never be forgotten, for his statue stands in Watts Park, there is a memorial hall in the town, and from the tower of the magnificent Civic Buildings rings out four times a day the tune of his great hymn.

The town does well so to honour Isaac Watts, who sleeps in London near John Bunyan and John Wesley. The first book of hymns he issued preceded John Wesley's first hymn-book by 30 years; the hymns of Watts "gave an utterance, till then unheard in England, to the spiritual emotions, and made hymn-singing a fervent devotional force." He wrote about 600 hymns, and they alone do not adequately represent the output of the years when his health compelled him to live as an invalid.

The past lingers in this memory-haunted place. On the smooth sward of the green at the foot of Lower Canal Walk, Southampton men have met on summer evenings for more than 600 years to play their game of bowls. On every hand are memorials of the great and brave. In Queen's Park is a monument of slender marble columns to General Gordon, and in the Park is a statue of Lord Palmerston and another to Richard Andrews, five times mayor. In Watts Park also is the memorial (by Sir Edwin Lutyens) to the men who fell in the war, and the Titanic memorial, the town's most poignant memories in our time. The memorial to the heroes of the Great War is a massive pylon with 2003 names, crowned with a cenotaph supported by two lions in relief. On the cenotaph is a fighting man lying at rest. At the foot of the pylon are piers with emblems of eternity crowned by fir cones, and an altar stone modelled on those in the war cemeteries on the battlefields. Facing this group is the Titanic memorial, a semicircular seat of Aberdeen granite, divided by a block on which rests the bronze prow of an ancient galley, surrounded by a floral wreath and crowned with the figure of an angel. The inscription is a tribute to the engineers of the Titanic, who "showed their high conception of duty by remaining at their posts." This memorial was raised by subscriptions all over the world. A tablet to the memory of Titanic musicians is in the entrance of the public library and on it, a pathetic thing to see, is the musical score of Nearer, my God, to Thee, the hymn they played as the ship went down.

Near the Pilgrims Memorial on the southern shore a fountain pays tribute to the heroic Mary Ann Rogers of the steamship Stella, telling the story of her faithfulness unto death. She was stewardess of the steamship Stella, busy with a little crowd of Easter holiday-makers on their way to Guernsey in 1899. Backwards and forwards, down below attending to those who were none too happy in their sea-trip, Mary Rogers did not know that the sun that had smiled on them as they steamed out of Southampton was now clouded over, but a little later the moan of the ship's siren told her they had run into fog. The ship steamed on, picking her way warily, and then came a rending shock which brought her to a standstill. She had struck one of the Casquets, the dreaded rocks of Guernsey fishermen. Mary Rogers saw all her charges on deck with their lifebelts fixed, and then put on her own and climbed up after them. So steeply sloped was the deck that it seemed as if the sea was already leaping up to seize them. One lifeboat collapsed as it struck the dark swirling water, and pitiful cries were added to the turmoil. But the moment came when only Mary Rogers and one other were left of all the women. The other woman had no lifebelt and as Mary pushed her towards the last boat she slipped off her own belt and put it over the woman's shoulders. "Now, Mrs Rogers, jump in!" they cried, but she saw that one more might sink the crowded boat. The boat was lowered, and the women looked back with tearful eyes to the only woman left on the sinking ship. "Goodbye, goodbye!" she called, and with her hands upraised she prayed as the waves were rising about her feet. Seven minutes after the Stella struck the rock she sank, taking with her nearly a hundred men and one woman, the stewardess who had given away her two chances of life.

The oldest of Southampton's churches is St Michael's in the heart of the Old Town. The tower is Norman, with its four massive arches rising between the nave and the chancel; outer walls, chapels, bays, have been added since the 14th century. Very odd is the effect of this isolated Norman tower in the midst of a church of many periods. Its tall 18th century spire was raised in the 19th century to serve as a landmark to ships at sea. There are four chained books, a 16th century stone figure of Lord Chief Justice Lyster, and a wall-tablet in memory of Bennet Langton with the Latin words spoken of him by his friend Dr Johnson, "May my soul be with Langton." Johnson died first and left his black servant to the care of Langton, who is remembered by Johnson enthusiasts as the young scholar who reproved the doctor for his roughness of speech. He was buried here in 1801, beloved by all.

The chief treasure of the church is the great black font, one of seven brought to this country from Tournai in the 12th century; it is in the style of Winchester's famous font, but with weird animals round it. The fine brass eagle of the lectern is 500 years old, one of 50 remaining in England; it was buried under the floor to save it from destruction in the Commonwealth. The chalice of St Michael's is one of the most beautiful pieces of Elizabethan silver still surviving, chased and embossed inside the bowl with a picture of the meeting of Isaac and Rebecca; the border outside has in it a rabbit, a snake, a grasshopper, and a lizard, with several foxes; the stem has a knob with embossed ornament; and the foot is engraved with sea monsters. It is the work of a silversmith of 1567. There are 15th century screens, 14th and 15th century piscinas, a 17th century chest, and mason's marks on the walls.

Among all this treasure sleep the wife and daughter of Isaac Watts, and we may be sure the verse on their stone was written by the doctor:

She dyd, and, dying, did entrust
With Christ her spirit and her dust,
In faith to rise and see His face
And sing the triumph of His grace.

The 18th century All Saints Church (with 18th century benches and gallery), built in classic style on the site of an older building, has one of the biggest open ceilings of any church in the country unsupported by pillars of any kind. One of our poets laureate, Henry James Pye, wrote an ode at the laying of its foundation stone in 1795.

There is a graceful figure by Flaxman in memory of Henrietta Dillon, and a font at which Sir John Millais was baptised. He, too, was Southampton born. At nine years old he came to London and on the way was lucky enough to have the chance of sketching Sir Joseph Paxton asleep in the coach. Arrived at London he had the good fortune to meet the President of the Royal Academy, with the result that he became a student there and carried off every prize. The most popular painter of his day, it may be that he will live longest by certain portraits done in his prime: John Bright, Beaconsfield, Newman, Carlyle, Tennyson, Gladstone, and other notable men of his age. He was rich, happy, beloved. His wife was the beautiful and accomplished woman who had formerly been married to John Ruskin. He lived to see a family of delightful children about him, sharing his joys in the fullest of lives, the richest of friendships. A baronetcy and the presidency of the Royal Academy came to him just before his death, and as he lay stricken he said, "I have no enemies; there's not a man with whom I would not shake hands—except one, and I should like to shake him by the hand now." His honours were a year old when they carried him to his rest in the Painters Corner of St Paul's, where he lies by his old friend Lord Leighton (who has a painting in a church not far away at Lyndhurst).

Here also lies Sir George Carteret, who is remembered because New Jersey in America was granted to him at a rent of £6 a year. He served in Charles Stuart's navy and won back our Island of Jersey from the Parliament for the King. Charles made him its governor and an admiral, and he harried the English ships engaged in trade so that Parliament regarded him as a pirate and passed an Act against him. Charles the Second twice visited him in Jersey, and it was Charles who gave him an American island as a reward. He named his prize island New Jersey in honour of his native island in the Channel, and he died a very rich man with his new possessions. His grandson was made a peer.

In the catacombs below All Saints, where 300 people were buried, lies Admiral Philip Carteret, who died at Southampton in 1796, having won fame by important geographical discoveries during a voyage round the world. He discovered Pitcairn Island long before the mutineers of the Bounty found it.

The Church of Holy Rood is interesting because Philip of Spain called here on his way to Winchester to marry Mary Tudor; in Winchester Cathedral is the chair she sat in. The fine tower has stood 600 years, but the rest of the church was rebuilt last century. The choir has medieval misereres black with age from which the carvings have disappeared; they came from the vanished priory of St Denys, one of the archways of which is in the courtyard of Tudor House. The font is 15th century and the almsdish 17th. The magnificent brass eagle lectern is 15th century and has had the misfortune to lose its jewelled eyes. There is a very graceful organ front. A carved panel by Rysbrack has a little weeping Cupid mourning with an inverted torch in memory of Elizabeth Stanley, a friend of James Thomson, who mentions her in his poem of the Seasons:

> *O born to bloom, thou ship beneath the storm,*
> *To show us virtue in her fairest form,*
> *Yes, we must follow . . . close the willing eye,*
> *'Tis the great birthright of mankind to die.*
> *Blest be the barque that wafts us to the shore*
> *Where death-divided friends shall be no more!*
> *To join them there, here will thy dust repose*
> *Is all the hope thy hapless mother knows.*

Where now stands the modern church of St Mary's the ancient parish church once stood, the earliest in the town; its successor is a memorial to Bishop Wilberforce, whose son was rector here, and it has a lovely alabaster reredos, two marble fonts, a 17th century almsdish, a Jacobean chair, a 16th century painting by a parish artist, two old chests, and an ancient lead cross used for a burial.

The 100-year-old St Joseph's Church was built after the passing of the Roman Catholic Emancipation Bill; its chancel and its chapels were designed by Pugin.

In the pleasant garden-settlement of Pear Tree Green across the Itchen the little building of Jesus Chapel was set up 300 years ago. It was the first church consecrated in the town after the Reformation and the service arranged for its dedication is still in use. Black with age, a carved angel with a trumpet, once towering over a pulpit, now serves as a reading desk accompanying a fine Jacobean altar table in a chapel panelled with the wood of the pulpit. A marble chancel screen is in memory of a rector who died during the war after preaching here for 57 years.

Gathered within easy reach of its famous common, Southampton has a little world of wide interest with much architectural splendour. It has, for instance, our National Map Office, where the work of the Ordnance Survey has been going on for 150 years. Here are produced those delightful maps which show us the face of England with woods and rivers and bridges and churches and windmills all neatly marked. Begun in Southampton as a military service, it has become the indispensable aid of every man who would see England.

Hereabouts also, at Highfield, is University College, housed at last after its long years of waiting, the mass of Army huts which covered the site in the war years replaced by halls of residence, theatres, museums, laboratories, and whatever equipment a modern university needs. As for the Civic Centre, it is a splendour of great spaces dominated by the Guildhall, the interior of which has been equipped with a hall to hold over 2000 people, and with provisions for public service which make it the centre of the public life of the town. With the Guildhall are grouped the council offices, the law courts, the library, art gallery, and the school of arts and crafts. High above them all rises the lovely tower of the law courts, 182 feet high with a peal of nine bells which play the Westminster Chimes at each quarter and strike the hours like Big Ben. Three times a day they play the hymn written by a Southampton man, O God, our Help in Ages Past. There are magnificent lawns, a fountain, and a rose garden, with coloured lights playing on the fountain at night.

Southampton, we see, is a city of boundless energy and spacious beauty, and is, moreover, within easy reach of that other great seaport, Portsmouth, of Romsey with its lovely abbey, of Winchester and Salisbury with their great cathedrals, of the fascinating Isle of Wight, and of all the natural wonder of the New Forest. She has all these things at her doors and is in almost hourly communion with every quarter of the globe where men go down to the sea in ships and do business on the great waters.

Southampton has swallowed up the village of Bitterne across the Itchen, where is a 19th century church and a very ancient manor. Here in our own time there have been taking place excavations yielding Roman remains. Begun by an enthusiastic band of schoolboys, the discoveries developed and at last revealed relics from the Roman riverside fortress known as Clausentum—skeletons, glass, jewelry, and fragments of pavement. It appears that this was the port for the

British Navy built by the rebel emperor, Carausius, and part of a sea-wall of those days has been found. It has been claimed that Bitterne Manor is one of the oldest inhabited houses in England, and there are in its structure traces of Saxon and Norman work. The church in the park has a 17th century pulpit from King's College Chapel, Cambridge, and interesting remains from the old church of St Lawrence pulled down in Southampton last century. The little suburb of Woolston, along the coast, has the distinction of being the birth-place of the first flying boat, which was launched here in 1912. At Shirley is Hollybrook, one of the most beautiful of all our war cemeteries, two miles from the heart of the town. It is interesting for the great monument to all those sailors, soldiers, and others who lost their lives on the high seas and round our coasts, for on the monument is the name of Lord Kitchener, who was drowned on the Hampshire.

So this old town shares in the march of the new age of wonder in which we live. Southampton is ever old and ever new, a gateway with an historic past and a future of infinite promise.

The Greatest Ship Southampton Had Seen

WHEN the years have passed away, and we who read this are old and grey, and when Southampton has seen many more generations of ships leave her shores, still men will whisper of the dark night on which the Titanic sank two miles deep in the cold waters of the Atlantic Ocean.

The Titanic was a palace of light and life and wonder. She was the greatest ship that ever sailed the seas. She was the greatest thing that was ever made by the hands of men. Sixty thousand tons of water moved away when the Titanic floated upon the sea, and it is true to say that she raised the height of the Atlantic Ocean.

Her engines had the power of 46,000 horses. Every two minutes her fires consumed a ton of coal. The labour of thousands of men had made her, and she cost more to build than St Paul's. Roses grew on her decks as in a garden, ivy climbed up her sides as up a wall; she was as long as a street and as wide as many a marketplace.

A wonder that Shakespeare could never have dreamed of was this noble ship; science and art and labour and wealth had never joined hands to make so great a thing before. Men said she was unsink-able; that the moving of a lever would close so many doors that she would be like many ships in one, and float, whatever happened. She was the last-made wonder of the world. She could almost speak; the very last thing that she did, indeed, was to send out a cry which was heard for nearly a thousand miles.

On that sunny day when the Titanic left Southampton, the proudest thing that ever left this realm, this England, her flags were flying high, and her captain must have fancied that in his ears were ringing the cheers of all the captains in the world. For he was captain of the greatest ship that ever sailed; he belonged to the greatest race of sailors that has ever been; he was bidding farewell to the sea he loved, and to crown his career his last voyage was to be the first voyage of the new Titanic. The old captain was taking the new ship from the Old World to the New.

And all was well. On the Thursday and Friday and Saturday the Titanic was the pride of her captain and the glory of the seas. A little boy was spinning his top as if he were at home; a dozen millionaires were attending to their business by wireless telegraphy as if they had been in their offices; men and women were playing and writing and talking and reading; the chairman of the White Star Line, which owned the ship, was there; famous artists and authors and business men were there; and all the men and women and children on the ship would have made up a little town. There were 2206 people, and the ship could have taken 1000 more.

The sun shone brightly all the way, the sea was calm, and the first Sunday at sea dawned for the great ship. We can imagine that the first hymns sung on the Titanic would make a great impression, and the strains of thanksgiving would die slowly away as the sun went down on the ship's first Sunday at sea. There was no moon, but the stars looked down from a clear sky on the ship that carried two thousand human souls. The Titanic was ablaze with light, and a majestic sight it must have been as it moved along a quiet sea. The day drew near its end, and the ship was 300 miles off Newfoundland. A few men were playing cards, a few were walking about the deck, but nearly all the people were asleep or going to bed.

Suddenly the ship shook; the Titanic trembled like a leaf. The men playing cards looked up; women got out of bed. "There is no need for alarm," said somebody. "We have cut a whale in two," said another. So the card-players went on with their game; the women went back to bed.

But the captain ran down from the bridge to a little room where the wireless telegraphist sat. "We have struck an iceberg," he said. "Send out a call for help." So the operator sent out the call. It was twenty minutes to twelve (about three in the morning in England), and for hundreds of miles the cry of the Titanic was heard on other ships. Some were 500 miles away, but changed their course and went toward the wounded vessel. She had entered an enormous field of ice, miles of bergs and floes, floating like pieces of broken mountains from the icy shores of Greenland. She had struck her side a glancing blow on a mass of ice below the water. The greatest iceberg had come out to meet the greatest ship.

The Titanic was mortally wounded, and for hundreds of miles around her the air was filled with her cries for help. The might of man was laid low; Nature had touched the Titanic with her finger. Thus far and no farther was this great ship to go. There was no sound in the sky, no words were printed there, yet under the stars that were shining down on England there was the burden of the most fearful news that has ever reached the ears of men.

The Titanic was sinking fast. The ship that was thought to be unsinkable was plunging into the deep. The people were out of their beds with their lifebelts on, the lifeboats were lowered, 2200 people stood trembling between two worlds. Fifty-eight miles away—fifty miles away—forty miles away, the Carpathia was racing toward them, the other ships behind.

And there, in the darkness of that Sunday night, a page was written in the history of the world that will never be blotted out. It was written by 1500 men and women in the last hour of their lives. It was written by old and young, by rich and poor. There were not enough lifeboats on this great ship for all on board, and as the boats were lowered there echoed from deck to deck that cry which has been the glory of our British name throughout the ages of the sea, "Women and children first." A few boys and girls took their places in the boats, a few babies were made safe, and then every woman found was offered a place. Some women refused to go; they would not leave their husbands. "Remember our little one at home," a man was heard to say as he pushed his wife into the boat, and stayed behind himself. "We have been together many years; we won't part now," said a brave wife, as she placed her maid safely in the boat and went back to die with her husband, a member of the American Parliament. A man and his wife and their little girl were in a boat when a woman appeared, and the man rose, kissed his child and his wife, and gave the stranger his place. The boats went off in the dark, and the last chance of escape from the Titanic was gone.

Still the water was pouring in, the engines stopped, the lights were dimmed, and when all was done that human help could do the captain's shout rang from the bridge: "Every man for himself; men, I release you." Even after that the wireless operator sat tapping, and the Carpathia heard his bitter cry, and put on every ounce of steam. Then, at twenty minutes past two, the silent stars looked down upon the saddest thing that ever broke a human heart. With its brave band playing "Nearer, my God, to Thee," the Titanic turned on its end, like a duck when it dives in the water, and plunged into the sea with fifteen hundred lives. Its first journey was ended.

When the Carpathia came upon the scene all that remained of the lifeboats were there, but nothing more was left of the palace of life that had sailed out of Southampton. The survivors were taken to New York, and when they were counted there were 703, all that were left of 2206. Never in the history of ships had so many lives been lost except in battle; and the death-roll of the Titanic was greater than the British death-roll of any battle in the South African War. The Titanic was no more; never again would the eye of man look upon that marvellous thing. But the name of it, and the end of it, will be remembered as long as men remember England.

The National Map Office

THE Ordnance Survey at Southampton has been carrying on a task requiring the highest degree of accuracy since the middle of last century. It began with the needs of our armed forces for maps, and the headquarters were fixed at Southampton merely because there was available in the city a building erected for the orphans of soldiers and no longer required for that purpose.

At first the maps were on the scale of an inch to the mile, but in 1824 the six-inch scale was begun. Thirty years later, when all England and Wales except Yorkshire and Lancashire had been mapped on the inch basis, it was decided to map the whole cultivated area of England at about 25 inches to the mile, one inch representing 2500 inches exactly.

Such big maps are called cadastral maps, from an old word meaning a register of property such as Domesday Book, and they show boundaries clearly enough for legal and taxation purposes. Property in towns needs maps showing houses, and so, aided by grants from such towns, the Ordnance Survey supplies maps of five and ten feet to the mile.

The enterprise originally aroused great interest in many remote villages, especially when the engineers set up their instruments, as often they did, on the tower of a hilltop church. If we spread out these 25-inch maps they would cover an area of nearly 22 square miles, for there are 51,456 of them. The 15,000 six-inch maps, embracing every acre of our island, would cover an area 300 feet long by about 170 feet broad. Every feature on the 25-inch map is to scale, appearing the size it would to the eye of an observer 2500 feet above the ground.

It has been found that 25-inch maps are best for estate work, in which the exact shape and area of enclosures are required; but for engineering purposes the six-inch are best, as they give contours. Town-planning schemes must by law be exhibited on the six-inch scale. The first 25-inch survey was completed in 1895, a test on Salisbury Plain showing an error of only one inch in seven miles, and the first revision was completed within ten years, a new revision being now in progress.

The walker and the motorist are more familiar with the maps on the one-inch scale or less. It may be that a man spends his life driving on business; he would be able to carry all of it in a packet of eleven quarter-inch maps, on which the main roads are coloured red, woodlands green, and the outstanding physical features made clear at a glance. But the motorist and the walker who wish to study the countryside find the 146 sheets of the one-inch map invaluable.

On these maps footpaths, byways, antiquities, and many other details which give charm to the countryside are shown. A strong red indicates the first-class roads and a brown the second-class, while a lighter red gives contour lines at 50-foot intervals. All water is blue, woodland green, sandhills light buff, and railway stations red.

If we follow with our eye the route of a railway the map indicates viaducts, cuttings, embankments, level-crossings, and every bridge (and whether it runs above or below it). On canals we see the position

The Civic Centre

The Tudor House

SOUTHAMPTON, NEW AND OLD

East Meon
Norman Font of Tournai Marble

Southampton
Norman Font of St Michael's Church

Winchfield   Norman Chancel Arch

Easton   Norman Doorway

Titchfield   Medieval Floor Tile

Odiham   17th Century Pulpit

HAMPSHIRE'S ANCIENT TREASURES

of each lock, and on a river or its estuary we see where to find the ferryman, and if he will take our car or only ourselves. Dotted lines show where a road is unfenced, and warning arrows show all slopes steeper than one in seven. Every church or chapel is marked, their symbols indicating whether they have spires, towers, or neither. Every windmill is marked, with a tiny mill, and even the humble windpump; also the lightship in the sea, and the lighthouse on the land. Every post office is marked P, and a letter t is added to those which have telephones. Ancient camps, tumuli, barrows, old castles, abbeys, and crosses are shown.

It is the proud boast of this band of workers in Southampton that no other country has anything approaching their volume of publications, and, as to their accuracy, it needs an expert of no mean standing to find anything wrong in these beautifully printed maps.

The Old Roodloft

SOUTH WARNBOROUGH. All that trees and timbered cottages can do to make a village charming has been done for it. Chestnuts march down the street and form twos up to the Norman doorway of the church, a simple place with a bell turret and two small windows filled with Tudor glass. The 13th century chancel is like a private chapel of the Whites, with 27 members of this family as they were in Tudor days. Robert, who died at the manor in 1512, has his brass portrait on the wall, a young man in handsome armour kneeling on his sword, with empty scabbard hanging at his side, his helmet with its eagle's headcrest on a bracket above him. On a big canopied tomb close by kneels Thomas White, of the generation after Robert, with a procession of tiny sons behind him, none more than seven inches high. There are 14 of them, and there were 6 daughters, though only 5 are left. Many of the children carry skulls to show that not all the 20 grew up. One of the daughters is shown again above the tomb, and we see one of the sons grown up and kneeling with his wife and daughter. On the wall opposite are two more small figures, probably younger sons of Thomas.

But the great treasure of the church is matched, we believe, only once in Hampshire, and only rarely in England. It is the old roodloft, which was preserved at the Reformation when all but one other in the county were destroyed with the Calvarys on them. The other is at Greywell.

z   337

There is no chancel arch at South Warnborough, as the 600-year-old roodloft takes its place. The screen is unusually tall, and no great beauty, but the rarity of the roodloft above it gives it importance. The loft itself is seven feet wide, but so near the roof that no one could walk along it, and the steps are gone. Many churches have the roodsteps without the loft; here is the loft without the steps.

News for King Charles

SOUTHWICK. It seemed to us a village charming, with wistaria and roses climbing over its houses, all its gardens sweet with flowers, and a medieval bell ringing; but we remember it because here sleep John and Sybil Long in two forgotten graves. She was of gentle birth and he a freeman, but they were so poor that they could not afford to educate their boy, and friends sent him to Winchester. For ever now he will be linked with that great city, for he grew up to be William of Wykeham and he founded that great school to which he gave the famous motto "Manners makyth man." Also he founded a priory near his old village, and when his father and mother fell asleep he chose its peace and beauty for their resting-place.

When the priory fell on evil hands at the Dissolution of the Monasteries it was given to John Whyte, the fawning servant of Wriothesley, a creature of Thomas Cromwell. He wrecked the place and all that is left of it is a battered piece of stone wall and a few carved capitals of fallen pillars, which we found near a group of walnut trees. But in the church are two things greatly prized by the village folk, brass candlesticks from the priory, much valued both for their historic interest and their solid beauty. Close by them is the table tomb of John Whyte himself, his brass portrait on the top with his wife's, and their ten sons and daughters with them. Behind the altar is a florid 17th century painting of cherubs and a dove. The altar rails are Jacobean, probably made by the men who raised the gallery on twisted columns. The oldest possessions of Southwick are the nave arcades of the 13th century and the Norman font. In the nave is an exquisite candelabra, probably the work of an 18th century craftsman, and we noticed here an epitaph with these beautiful lines:

> *The God of Nature and of grace*
> *Has caught me to His dwelling-place.*

A dramatic story is told of a day when Charles Stuart was staying at the manor house here (now gone) with Sir Daniel Norton. On that day the Duke of Buckingham was assassinated at Portsmouth, and the story is that the king was kneeling at prayer in the chapel when Sir John Hippesley, dusty and dishevelled from hard riding, came hurriedly in, went up to the praying king and whispered in his ear the dread tidings that must have frightened their bearer. Charles gave no sign till the service was over and then, rising from his knees, broke into passionate lamentations for his lost favourite.

Out of the Grave

SPARSHOLT. It is near enough to share something of the glory of Winchester, and many pilgrims it draws to itself, for it has much Norman work to show. The ancient church has a doorway with two singularly fine oak doors carved in the days of Charles Stuart, the names of two churchwardens over the top, and lovely fragments of a stone canopy let into the wall above it outside. There are Norman arcades, a blocked-up doorway used by the priest in the 14th century, a 16th century chancel arch possibly resting on Norman stones, and 18th century beams spanning the roof. A line of oak pillars which supported a gallery 200 years ago now forms a screen for the organ, and in a glass case on the wall is an old friend of the church which led the choir before the organ came. It is the old bassoon. Near it is another small case, shaped like a house and topped by a cross. It is a precious little house, for in it are two things so rare that they are perhaps the dearest possessions of Sparsholt, among the earliest pieces of church plate in England.

From this tiny glass house a simple chalice and paten, both made of lead, look out at us after being buried in darkness for six or seven hundred years. All that time they have lain with the dead. The paten has a cross roughly cut in the centre, done by some crude craftsman in very early days. These tokens were placed in the grave of a priest, perhaps as a tribute to his long and faithful service at the altar here, and they came to light (as part of a second cup has since been brought to light), during alterations to the church. There was also found a 13th century coffin still in the churchyard, with a stone pillar for the sleeper's head. Five hundred years after this was made there was cut on a tombstone here this epitaph to Anne Fielder:

When Life has passed and Death is come,
Then well are they who well have done.

Here also we found a beautiful epitaph by one of our national benefactors, Sir George Buckston Browne. He it is who has saved for the nation, and richly endowed for science, the old Kent home of Darwin, which he bought and presented to the British Association. He has also endowed a research station in the grounds there, where we found our famous student of mankind Sir Arthur Keith carrying on his work. It was at Sparsholt that Sir Buckston Browne laid his wife to rest, among the folk of her native village, after they had kept their golden wedding, and on her tablet is a little bronze galleon and these lovely words:

She never at any time brought grief upon me save when she died.

Sparsholt has an inn belonging to the nation, it being in charge of the National Trust, with two cottages here. A story we heard in the inn was that every tramp or tradesman's boy (or every friendly caller) who opens a certain village gate helps to fill the water tank in the roof.

This is the village for Lainston House, which in 1769 was the subject of much excited tattle at the Court of George the Third. It was all about something that happened in the little ruined chapel in the garden there, and this is the story.

The Remarkable Story of Elizabeth Chudleigh

PERHAPS we may begin with the story as it was not quite properly told in the famous letters of Horace Walpole writing to Sir Thomas Mann. "Well, (he says), but to come to goddesses. After a marriage of twenty years Augustus Hervey, having fallen in love with a physician's daughter at Bath, has attacked his spouse, the Maid of Honour, the fair Chudleigh, and sought a divorce. Unfortunately, he has waited till all the witnesses of their marriage are dead, as well as the two children. The provident virgin had not been so negligent. Last year she forced herself into the house of the parson who married them, and who was at the point of death. By bullying, and to get rid of her, she forced the poor man to give up the certificate. Since then she has appeared in Doctors Commons, and sworn by the Virgins Mary and Diana that she never was married to Mr Hervey. The Ecclesiastical Court has admitted her corporal oath and enjoined silence to Mr Hervey. Next week this fair injured innocence, who is but fifty, is to be married to the Duke of Kingston.

As proof of her purity and poverty, her wedding-gown is white satin trimmed with Brussels lace and pearls. Every word of this history is exactly true."

But every word was not exactly true—it was not true at all, for what had happened was this. Elizabeth Chudleigh had come to stay at Lainston House in the summer of 1744. She was a maid-of-honour at Court and the reigning toast, proud, ambitious, and reckless. She met at Winchester races Augustus Hervey, the Earl of Bristol's grandson, and married him secretly and suddenly at midnight in the private chapel of the house, he being a naval lieutenant on leave and neither of them having much money, but both looking forward with great expectations.

He rejoined his ship and she returned to Court. They had one child and then quarrelled and parted, and for twelve years they lived separately. During that time it seemed likely that the husband would become Earl of Bristol, and the scheming wife took steps to procure proofs of her secret marriage, which had never been publicly acknowledged. It is said that she found the old rector dying, forced him to enter the marriage in the register, and took possession of it. Little did she dream of the result of this act of folly.

Her life at home and abroad had been notoriously wild, and her husband determined to seek a divorce. She, thinking she had the proofs of her marriage safe (for the old parson had died) denied that she had ever been married to Hervey, and sued him to make him refrain from calling her his wife. As she swore they had not been married and he did not produce proofs that they had, the court declared her a spinster and warned Hervey against denying it. Then she clinched this victory by marrying the Duke of Kingston, and for four years lived as the Duchess of Kingston, her real husband meantime taking steps to secure a new trial. On the death of the duke she went abroad but returned boldly to fight the case against her husband, who now had become Earl of Bristol. The case was heard in Westminster Hall by the peers, and was unanimously decided against the duchess who was not a duchess, but was a countess through her marriage with the husband she had disowned.

After this Elizabeth, Countess of Bristol, went abroad and lived there for twelve years in wealthy style on the fortune left to her by the Duke of Kingston. She died in Paris in 1788, eight years after the death of her husband, the Earl, who had a record of most gallant service in the navy and reached the rank of admiral. His life was marred by his early marriage with this dissolute and worthless woman.

The School and the Poet

STEEP. It is a steep hill that brings us to it, and at the top a group of splendid yews stands sentinel by the captivating little church, which has the pride of the village in its keeping—a silver chalice with its cover complete, made in the time of Shakespeare by a craftsman with the charming name of Affabel Partridge.

One of the yews must be almost as old as the Norman arcades in the nave, for it is 23 feet round. For at least 600 years it must have seen the children brought for christening to this Norman font; it must have seen about 20 generations of village folk stooping to pass under this low 13th century doorway. The door is not as its medieval craftsman made it, but some of its timber is 500 years old.

In this village is the famous Bedales, the school established by Mr J. H. Badley as a protest against the formalism and narrowness of the public school of his day. It was the first boarding school for both sexes, the pioneer of co-education, and Mr Badley gave to it more than 40 years of service as a man of vision, selflessness, and inspiring singleness of purpose.

It was this school which gave Captain Scott his famous pony Christopher, one of the most impish ponies he had. Poor Captain Oates was for ever chasing him, for he would break away and gallop for miles, and in the end would walk calmly back to his stable. Captain Scott said he was glad there were no more such ponies as Christopher.

One of the poets who wrote himself into literature and fell in the Great War is remembered on this Hampshire hillside, a memorial stone having been set in the midst of a clearing. It is a great sarsen stone, and on it is the name Edward Thomas, poet, with the words "And I rose up, and knew I was tired, and continued my journey."

The traveller resting by this stone sees the Sussex Downs near Midhurst, the great height of Hindhead, and Petersfield in the distance. The hillside belongs to Lord Horder, by whose generosity it is preserved for ever against invasion by the speculative builder. In unveiling the stone Lord Horder declared that the hillside, formerly the poet's, was now given to all those people who love the English country. The Poet Laureate was at the unveiling, and in paying his tribute to Edward Thomas he said that Thomas had the most beautiful voice he had ever heard from human lips, and if he had preached he would have swayed the world. A tablet was also unveiled at Berryfield Cottage, where the poet used to live.

A cot in the children's ward at Petersfield Hospital was also dedicated to the poet's memory, the poet's widow unveiling a tablet above the cot.

Edward Thomas fell in France in the middle of the war. A friend has told of him that on one of his last walks in England with the poet, while he was home from France on leave, he asked Thomas if he knew what he was fighting for, and after a moment the poet stooped, picked up a pinch of earth between his fingers, and said, "I think, literally, this." He was fighting for the earth he loved and for his Motherland. This is one of the small poems the soldier-poet wrote when he was out at the war:

> *No one cares less than I,*
> *Nobody knows but God,*
> *Whether I am destined to lie*
> *Under a foreign clod,*
> *Were the words I made to the bugle call in the morning.*
>
> *But laughing, storming, scorning,*
> *Only the bugles know*
> *What the bugles say in the morning,*
> *And they do not care, when they blow*
> *The call that I heard and made words to early this morning.*

Jane Austen's Village

STEVENTON. Who knows it? How many, when the Southampton express for London leaves Winchester and continues to climb up the Hampshire Downs past Micheldever, and plunges through the tunnels of Popham Beacon, know when and where to look out and say with a thrill, "Steventon, Jane Austen's birthplace!" Very few, we fear, for it is still an out-of-the-way place, as when Jane lived here for most of the first 25 years of her life, and it is of little importance except for her. We all come here for the sake of the woman of whom Sir Walter Scott said that she had the most wonderful talent he knew for describing the feelings and character of ordinary life. The little parsonage in which she learnt to walk and talk has disappeared, but here is the severe little church in which her father was for 44 years rector, though his pulpit and her font have gone. It is about 700 years old, with a sundial scratched on the doorway, and we found its key hanging on an old yew which must have stirred the wonder of the little Jane, for it is big enough to have been here perhaps as long as the church.

One of the bells in the tower was made in the great medieval foundry at Wokingham, and was ringing here before Joan of Arc was born; its date is said to be 1380. There is a tablet to Jane and to her brother James, who followed his father as rector and has slept in the churchyard since 1819. In the chancel is a relief of three little daughters of William Knight, who was rector last century: Mary Agnes aged 5, Cecilia aged 4, and Augusta aged 3, all cut off by scarlet fever. Never, we feel, can there have been a more touching use of the words, "Lovely and pleasant in their lives, and in their death they were not divided."

The church has still the old manor pew, but the Elizabethan manor house has fallen from its high estate to become a garage, though a garage beautiful and much cared for. The new house to which it belongs has part of a Saxon cross in one of its walls.

But it is as Jane Austen's village that the traveller seeks it out. She is one of Hampshire's immortals, the seventh and youngest child of the rector of Steventon and the neighbouring village of Deane. The other children were five brothers and a sister, and all of them outlived Jane. Two of the boys became admirals. No notable woman has lived a quieter life. The first 25 years of it were spent in her native village, living as a cultured and thoroughly domesticated daughter of a well-to-do country clergyman might be expected to live. Her relaxations were visits to Bath, where she had relatives, or to London. During her last 17 years, she spent four years in Bath, four in Southampton, and nearly nine near Alton, only moving into Winchester for medical attention shortly before her death in 1817. She had no adventures, though in her youth she was handsome and sprightly enough to make other clever women of her day rather jealous and afraid of her. She lived the kind of life, among the kind of people, depicted in her books, and she wrote. That is all there is to say of Jane except of her books, how they were produced, their quality, and their place in the history of English middle-class life.

She began to write in her teens for her own amusement. By the time she was 23 she had written three of the half dozen books that have given her a place in the front rank of our fiction, Pride and Prejudice, Sense and Sensibility, and Northanger Abbey; but they were not published till she was 36. Then Sense and Sensibility found a publisher and had a success that ensured a market for Pride and Prejudice, and set their author busy writing Mansfield Park and her masterpiece Emma. Only five years were left for her mature activity. Northanger Abbey and Persuasion were published after her death.

From the first Jane Austen's stories captured readers capable of understanding literary workmanship that does with perfection what it seeks to do. Scott bowed down to her. Disraeli confessed to having read Pride and Prejudice 17 times. Jane had too much humour to attempt anything beyond her scope or experience. What she attempted to portray was the comedy of the ordinary life she knew, and that she did so well that her writings mirror a stratum of the life of her period. Steventon gave birth to one who, in her own sphere as a novelist, is supreme among Englishwomen.

Farewell, John

STOCKBRIDGE. Familiar to all who go west by Salisbury, its long Tudor and Georgian street crosses two streams and has some fine old houses and a town hall clock older than Waterloo. It has near it the prehistoric camp called Danebury and burial mounds going back to Neolithic times, and at one entrance to it runs a road the Romans made, now a rough track between high banks which are a riot of wild flowers in summer.

We found here a great rarity among the stately homes of England, for Marsh Court, built by Sir Edwin Lutyens, is a chalk house, with mantelpieces and other interior work of chalk. We have come across chalk churches, and chalk carving on tombs, but we do not remember a chalk house before.

At one end of the town stands its oldest monument, a small building in an old graveyard sheltered by trees. It is the chancel of the ancient church, put up 800 years ago and pulled down in

1863. It has the old door ring, some wall-painting, a piscina, a 17th century altar, and the old south doorway which is built into the blocked-up medieval chancel arch. One historic memory the poor chancel has, of the day when the Empress Matilda's brother, Earl of Gloucester, was taken prisoner in it after ensuring her safe retreat from King Stephen's pursuing armies. The new church which has taken the place of the old one in the middle of the street has some of its simple 15th century windows in the nave, some old stone heads in the vestry, two 18th century chests, a table of the days of Queen Anne, and a rugged 13th century font held together by an iron band. One window has a fragment of old glass. Several of the old windows have modern glass showing the Good Shepherd, Peter, Dorcas, and an attractive Annunciation; but it is outside one of the west windows that we must look for some of the oldest things here: two queer coiled beasts carved in the 13th century, and a dial which was telling the time in this countryside long before the Conqueror came.

By the lonely walls of the old church sleeps John Bucket, under a tall stone decorated with a cherub. This is the stone's lament:

> *And is, alas, poor Bucket gone?*
> *Farewell, convivial honest John.*
> *Oft at the well by fatal stroke*
> *Buckets like Pitchers must be broke.*
> *In this same motley shifting scene*
> *How various have thy fortunes been*
> *Now lifted high, now sinking low,*
> *Today thy brim would overflow,*
> *Thy bounty then would all supply*
> *To fill and drink and leave thee dry.*
> *Tomorrow sunk as in a well*
> *Content unseen with Truth to dwell:*
> *But high, or low, or wet or dry,*
> *No rotten stave could malice spy.*
> *Then rise, immortal Bucket, rise,*
> *And claim thy station in the skies.*

John was the landlord of the King's Head Inn, clearly a popular and kindly fellow who made the best of everything. In the hotel in the middle of the street today we may see a ten-pound trout caught here in the River Test.

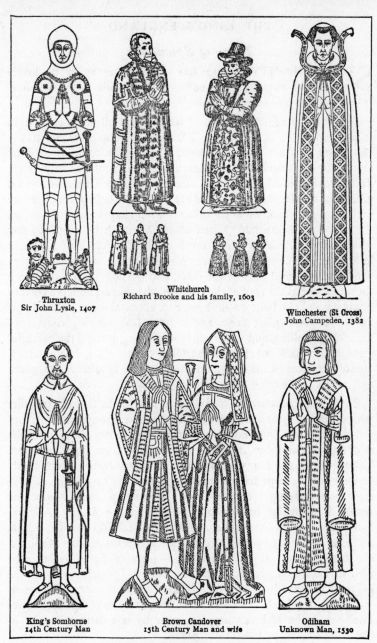

Thruxton
Sir John Lysle, 1407

Whitchurch
Richard Brooke and his family, 1603

Winchester (St Cross)
John Campeden, 1382

King's Somborne
14th Century Man

Brown Candover
15th Century Man and wife

Odiham
Unknown Man, 1530

OLD HAMPSHIRE BRASSES

347

Tomb of Splendour

STOKE CHARITY. Nature has made it worthy of its lovely name and man has packed its church with many wonders. It has six mass clocks on its walls.

The shingles of the tower and steeple were all made from oaks felled in the woods of Hursley 200 years ago; so were the sturdy pews. But far back to the Conqueror's time we come as we look about, for the splendid chancel arch, the plain font, the little north doorway seen outside, and the arcade resting on a massive central pillar, are all Norman; and there are those who believe that the tiny arch through which we enter the Hampton chapel was built before the Saxon influence had passed away. The arch is only four feet wide, and is all that is left of the first church which stood here; it led to the old chancel. The present chancel has two 13th century windows, medieval tiles in the floor, and a Tudor roof built about the same time as the roof of the nave. By the chancel arch is a curious double peephole built to look at two altars at once. The chapel has a Jacobean altar table and a little 16th century chest with linenfold panelling, and in the windows are fragments of the beautiful glass with which the Hamptons filled them in the 15th century. One of the pieces shows the Madonna and Child, another St Margaret, and others the flaming suns of the Yorkists.

But it is the astonishing collection of rich tombs that the traveller will remember most in this little place, the chief group in this Hampton chapel. On a panelled altar tomb are 15th century brass portraits of Thomas Hampton, his wife Isabel, and their eight children. Thomas is in armour with sword and spurs, Isabel is unhappily broken away except for her skirt, and two of the daughters have their hair hanging loose to show they are spinsters. Above the figures is a quaint brass representation of the Trinity. Another lovely altar tomb across the chapel has a beautiful canopy, a little niche, and painted panels in which Thomas Becket and the Madonna are fading away. It is the last resting-place of John Waller, who died in 1526, and near it, with fragments of brass heraldry, is the grave of his grandson who became lord of the manor at the age of ten. Still a third big tomb with heraldic decoration is that of Charity Phelypes in the 17th century, and near by is a little collection of ancient carved fragments including a Norman stoup and a 15th century niche.

Yet the greatest possession in this chapel remains to be told. It is a wonderful carving in stone of the legend of St Gregory. Chalice in hand at the altar, the saint gazes enraptured at the figure of Our Lord, above whose head are two angels drawing curtains, as if to reveal His presence to the saint. Another priest stands by the altar, but his face is hard and he looks away as if unaware of the miracle. It is believed to be 15th century work, and there is one like it in Exeter.

By the font is the unfinished 17th century painted tomb of Sir James Phelypes, and a tablet near it to his mother Lady Ogle, who was imprisoned in Winchester Castle during the siege and died on her way back to Stoke Charity. In the nave is yet another fine tomb to an unknown 15th century man, and a smaller one with a 15th century brass portrait of Thomas Wayte, a good-looking young man in splendid armour. Over his head is a small brass of Christ rising from the grave.

The voice of one of the bells must have been familiar to nearly all the sleepers in this church, for it was first rung about 1420 by one of the foundries attached to the abbey of Chertsey.

We shall not soon forget our last discovery at Stoke Charity. As we leave the church we pass on the left of the path two big chest tombs, and between them a flat gravestone with its inscription nearly buried by lichen. It was just possible to make out the name when we called and a thrilling name it was, for here lies the uncle of our immortal Sir Joshua Reynolds.

Wellington's Horse

STRATFIELDSAYE. When Francis Drake came home from his journey round the world the people felt they could not do enough for him and would have set his Golden Hind on the top of St Paul's. When Wellington came home from Waterloo they felt they could not do enough for him, and the nation bought him a Queen Anne house in Hampshire, in one of the oldest patches of inhabited country that England has. It is the splendid estate of Stratfieldsaye, the fine park watered by the River Loddon. At one of the gateways is Marochetti's monument of the Iron Duke, a towering column with his statue in bronze. Another gateway leads into an avenue of a mile of elms.

The house was of very little use to the conquering duke; though it cost over a quarter of a million he declared it a bad investment, which would have ruined almost any man. There is a pathetic corner in the park where lies the horse that carried Wellington at Waterloo; he was on it, we believe, for 16 hours. He called it Copenhagen, and gave it a home here for the last ten years of its life. When Copenhagen died in 1825 the brave horse was given full military honours, and the Duchess of Wellington had a bracelet made of its hair. A gravestone tells of its service at the Battle of Waterloo, and goes on to declare that

> God's humbler instrument, though meaner clay,
> Shall share the glory of that glorious day.

In the very drab 18th century church which replaced the old one there are wall-monuments with portrait busts of the second and third dukes, and to a member of the family who was Dean of Windsor and rector here. A tablet with painted heraldry is in memory of Lord Richard Wellesley who fell in the Great War. Among many other monuments is one of Sir William Pitt, Controller of the House-hold to Charles Stuart, who lies in marble with his wife. A wall-monument by Flaxman shows a man and woman weeping over an urn in memory of a Lord Rivers, and another wall-sculpture is to a rector here for 41 years, who would announce from his pulpit the death of Queen Elizabeth and the accession of Charles Stuart; it shows a little kneeling statue of him and says:

> If who this was we needs would know aright
> He was a burning and a shining light.

Another tablet tells of Walter Chapman who was rector 46 years in the 18th century, but the oldest memorials are perhaps the two 16th century inscriptions to members of the Dabrigecort family.

Under the chestnuts by the chancel door is a very quaint epitaph to John Baylie, a faithful servant who died in 1777. In 26 lines it tells us that his only sin was that he loved a drop of gin, and goes on:

> Though weak his head, to make amends
> Heaven gave him health, content, and friends.
> This little village nursed and bred him,
> And good Lord Rivers clothed and fed him.

Here follow other lines, which go on to this curious ending:

Who knows but John may find a place
Where wit must never show its face.

We found here on the roll of honour the name of J. Welch, VC. Here he was born and here he went to school. He joined the army as a private at 18, served for 11 years, and left it a sergeant. It was in 1917 that he chased and captured four soldiers single-handed, armed only with an empty revolver. While in charge of a machine gun he went out several times under heavy fire to collect spare parts and ammunition that he needed. He was wounded, but came home.

Wellington's Groom

STRATFIELD TURGIS. It is close to Wellington's home at Stratfieldsaye, and the interest it has for us all is a little link with him. In deep seclusion at the end of a lane, with a farm for its neighbour, stands a tiny church with dormer windows, a Norman font, and a brick chancel built by local men after a fire in the 18th century. Close to the porch lies John Mears, Wellington's groom. He led his master's horse in the funeral procession to St Paul's, and proud and sad he must have been on that day. He had been the Iron Duke's groom for 33 years. He was to live 20 years after his master and to remember till he was very old that day in London's streets when they buried the great Duke to the noise of the mourning of a mighty nation, when

Warriors carried the warrior's pall,
And sorrow darkened hamlet and hall.

One of the Early Christians

SWAY. It is Peterson's Folly which gives it its fame, the gaunt and stern tower seen for miles from sea and land. It is said that when it was built (probably as a tomb) a light was placed on the top of it which had an undesired effect on the vessels in the Solent, for they mistook it for a lighthouse. The next day the Admiralty sent Mr Peterson stern orders to put out his light, and it has been out ever since.

On the wild plain above Sway, half-hidden by gorse and burrowed into by rabbits, are the graves of men who may have known all about the building of the great earthworks at Buckland Rings. The moors themselves, while the sun is shining and the gorse is glad with flowers, are full of joy and beauty, but are things of threat and terror when the sun goes angrily down, or on a sullen day when there is no blossom to be seen.

Here we came upon the memory of one of the early Christians in Egypt. On a windowsill in the sanctuary of the church stands a narrow-mouthed pottery urn with three handles and a scroll pattern in red and black, and an inscription tells us that this urn, containing the ashes of a Christian convert of about the 2nd century, was found in the Christian burial ground at Ramleh in Egypt.

The Miniature Monument

SWAYTHLING. We found here, in this village almost swallowed up by Southampton, a small monument like a tiny stage, a thing a child would like to play with. It is in the chancel of the charming 13th century church (called South Stoneham, though Stoneham has the steeple and no people and Swaythling has the people and no steeple). In a little room of the church a man and woman kneel opposite one another like dolls, a prayer desk draped with green cloth between them. Below, also on their knees, is a long row of children, most of whom have lost their heads. This elegant sculpture is 300 years old, the memorial of Edmond Clerke, Charles Stuart's Clerk of the Privy Seal, who died before his master had lost his throne; he died under 50, leaving "12 children and a fair name."

But there are many other monuments, one with a bust of Edmund Dummer who died two centuries ago, his long curling hair falling over his shoulders, and another to that 18th century Thomas Lee Dummer who thought the City Cross at Winchester would look well in his park, and, having bought it, was about to take it away when the townsfolk rose against him and kept it in the awkward corner of their High Street, where it stands to this day.

There is a stone put up in the 19th century in memory of a 45-year friendship, and in the chancel is a 16th century tomb recess with lovely foliage and a helmet hanging above. Near it is a white marble monument to Mary Godden Jones, carved in Florence just over a century ago, showing an angel and poor people mourning her, above the lines she herself wrote:

> *Yet there perchance the village poor may go*
> *With tears and sable garbs of real woe*
> *To grieve for one who loved their simple train*
> *And never eyed God's image with disdain.*

The chancel and its beautifully moulded arch are Norman, and the creeper-covered tower 15th century. There is a font with a 13th century bowl recovered from the river near the church, a richly carved oak chest probably 400 years old, and a Jacobean altar table.

In the days of the Restoration there was a wise old vicar here named Roger Turner. Having to preach an appropriate sermon on the coming of the king, he took pains to warn his people against the dissipation they were too likely to indulge in, and his long oration has come down to us. One bit of it we heard when we called, this piece of excellent advice:

Do not drown your reason for your loyalty. Pray for the king's health, but drink only for your own.

Another vicar, William Harrison, served for 57 years last century, but we came upon an even more remarkable record of faithful service here—four farm servants at West End close by with well over two centuries of service between them; Robert Smith with 60 years, Sabina Smith 55, Thomas Butt 50, and Joseph Smith 46.

We do not know on what authority they base their claim, but there are those who believe that King Canute here sat by the waves and rebuked his flatterers. We believe it was at Bosham in Sussex, but the advocates for South Stoneham say it was where the Itchen runs down from the Wessex capital and opens out into the tide-water. Certainly this place (the Place of the Stone) was famous long before the days of King Canute.

Swaythling has a famous old house known as the Grange, with a Tudor mantelpiece, enormous beams, a secret room, and a Tudor wardrobe weighing about a ton. In this house lived and died Admiral Lord Hawke, and here long before him lived Richard Cromwell, Oliver coming to visit him. Perhaps it will seem to some more interesting that in South Stoneham cemetery lies a man who heard the first wireless signals sent over the sea. He was George Kemp and this is the story.

The First Wireless Taps Across the Sea

THE ordinary world had scarcely heard of George Kemp when he died at Southampton aged 75, but Marchese Marconi and many famous people knew of the part he played in the development of wireless. He was a man of Kent, and the first Englishman to help

Marconi in demonstrating his system before our Post Office in 1896. After he left the Navy he became laboratory assistant to Sir William Preece, the Post Office engineer who did so much for telegraphy and wireless, and it was Sir William who chose Mr Kemp to help Marconi. He remained with Marconi and helped him with hundreds of experiments in the pioneering days.

This grand old man of wireless would speak with obvious pride of Marconi's triumphs and of the part he had been privileged to play. He told of the experimental station established at The Needles in 1896, and of another fitted up in a tiny basement room near Bournemouth Pier. Experimental transmissions took place between these stations, but it soon became apparent that the position at Bournemouth was unsuitable, so Marconi and his first assistant decided to move their apparatus to the Haven Hotel at Parkstone, a district of Poole. That was in 1898, and from then until 1913 the Parkstone station was in regular use for experimental purposes, and many wireless problems were solved there. It was not until 1926 that the station was dismantled.

The experiments at the Haven led to the establishment of the Poldhu station, from which the first wireless signals were sent across the Atlantic. Marconi received these signals in Newfoundland in 1901, and Mr Kemp was with him and heard them too, the most thrilling sounds, perhaps, that ever fell upon human ears.

The Elizabethan Preacher

SYDMONTON. It has two magnificent examples of Norman art in its rebuilt church set among the lawns in the garden of the great house. The arch that welcomes us in and the eastern arch of the tower have exquisite carving, and the tower arch has a bold encircling band of moulding, giving it an air of strength and dignity. The church has a fine silver chalice of the days of the Restoration.

In the days of the Reformation there was born here a child who was to grow up to be a Puritan writer, Andrew Kingsmill. He was one of three great Puritan preachers left in Oxford after the persecutions of Queen Mary. It is said that he learned by heart most of the Greek version of the Bible, and that he wrote most of the sermons preached at St Mary's, Oxford, in the early days of Queen Elizabeth. He went out to Geneva and died at Lausanne on the way home.

His manuscripts were published by a college friend who described him in a vivid phrase as "a Phoenix among lawyers and a rare example of godliness among gentlemen."

For the Poor for Ever

TADLEY. Its granite peace memorial cross stands in a charming flower garden in the village, but its church, with a 17th century red brick tower, is some distance off. Tadley must be proud of its timbers. The carved and moulded doorway of the church porch is 15th century. The beautiful canopied pulpit, the plain benches, the baluster-fronted gallery, and the solid staircase with its heavy railing, are all 17th century. On the wall is the brass inscription we meet in several churches in this part of Hampshire, recording that Thomas Sympson, who died in 1676, left £15 a year to be divided among the poor of six parishes "so long as the world shall endure." A little way from the church is Tadley Place, an attractive old house with a splendid walnut tree growing near.

The Lead Font

TANGLEY. It has one precious thing, like no other in the county. No other village, nor any of the great and busy towns of Hampshire, has a font like Tangley's. Saxon, Norman, Medieval, and Tudor fonts are scattered through the county, but Tangley's is unique among them, for they are made of stone and this is lead. It is of medium size, and decorated in relief with fleurs-de-lys, Tudor roses, crowned thistles, and sceptres. It has been here about 300 years, and is one of only 38 lead fonts in England. Sad indeed were we to see scrawled over it the initials of many stupid people.

The ancient yew was the oldest friend of the old church that has disappeared, for it was all built afresh in the 19th century, not long after the 56 years rectorship of William Lance. The sanctuary is a tiny apse, and above it are two small windows which may be Saxon.

The oldest things the village has are the small sarsen stones lying in the churchyard, those great hard boulders strewn in countless numbers on the prehistoric plain of Wiltshire and raised so high in the solitude of Stonehenge.

Three Knights and a Lady

THRUXTON. It was the home of one of the treasures of the British Museum, a fine Roman tessellated pavement with Bacchus and his tiger in the centre. It is remarkable because it has an almost perfect inscription. At the corner are heads symbolising the seasons, and in the border are small crosses which would be Christian symbols. A terracotta candelabra was found at the same time.

The church has many good faces at the windows, and parts of it are 13th and 15th century. The tower arch is Norman, and within the tower a stone knight stands against a wall, battered but striking in Egyptian-like simplicity. He is believed to be Sir John Cormailles who died about 1200, and he wears a square helmet and carries a shield which hides his body. Another knight lies before the sanctuary steps, his magnificent brass portrait showing him in plate armour under a rich brass canopy, with his feet, curiously spurred, on a ferocious lion. He is Sir John Lysle, who died just after Agincourt. Still another knight lies with his lady, both exquisitely sculptured, on a double tomb under one of two lovely arches in the chancel; they, too, were Lysles who had the manor in the 15th century. He has long hair and armour embossed with lions and birds, and his smiling lady has a severe gown gracefully draping her feet.

But most intriguing of all is an Elizabethan lady carved in English oak, one of only about a hundred of such figures in all England. She was found in our time in the rectory barn, and is thought to be Elizabeth Philpotts, lady of the manor. Beautifully carved but terribly battered, she wears the ruff, puffed sleeves, and wide skirts so fashionable in her day, and a tight-fitting French cap with a veil. Close by is a rich table tomb to a 19th century lady, with a stone Bible open on the top. In the chancel is a fine tomb of someone unknown of the 14th century when the chancel arch was new; the tomb has carved panels and a canopy that serves also as the arch of a window. The pews have decorated ends, and throughout the church the woodwork is remarkable for the beauty of its carving. One of the choir seats is a tribute to Edward Nixon for his 45 years as a chorister and his 35 years as headmaster. Among the five names on the peace memorial we noticed Walter Wisewell, who perished at Jutland when his ship the Black Prince steered by accident in the darkness into the enemy line and was blown to nothing in less time than it takes to tell.

Untouched by the Reformation

TICHBORNE. An exquisite Itchen village named after its great family, lords of the manor now and apparently for ever, it is the guardian of a host of lovely things in a little church set like a stronghold up the hill. Marvellous it is to think that this chancel, with its narrow pilasters, has been here about a thousand years, and that the remains of the arcade high up in the nave wall have been here all the time (for they are Saxon). The aisles were thrown out in the 14th century, the tower and the porch are 18th, and we enter by an old door with its original ironwork centuries old. Here we found still being given away after 800 years 50 bushels of flour bequeathed to the villagers once a year in Norman times.

The chancel arch is probably 14th century, and in the 14th century east window two quatrefoils have still some of the original glass, with St Andrew in a dark robe. The altar rails are 17th century, and the pulpit and the richly carved pews go back to Shakespeare. It is thrilling to realise that the little 15th century door opening into the wall is the door the old priests would open when they mounted the stairs to declare the good news each morning from the roodloft. The font is Norman and has an old wooden cover.

Behind a stout iron railing is the Tichborne aisle, filled with the monuments of this great house. By a friendly arrangement between the Tichbornes and the Crown it ranks as a Roman Catholic sanctuary though it is part of an Anglican church; we may think of it as a tiny corner of Hampshire untouched by the Reformation.

The finest of the monuments is a great tomb of Sir Benjamin Tichborne, High Sheriff of Hampshire when Queen Elizabeth died, earning for himself rich rewards from James for having proclaimed him king on his own initiative. Sir Benjamin's tomb is one of the handsomest in the county, and handsome he looks on it, a bearded man in armour with smiling eyes.

His charming wife Amphillis lies with him, and below them kneel their sons and daughters, all delightful. Benjamin lived with his Amphillis, their epitaph tells us, with inviolate affection for 46 years. Near them is the pathetic figure of little Richard Tichborne lying on his side, wearing a gilded bonnet, a ruff, and a scarlet frock pricked out with gold. He was drowned one winter's day in 1619 in the pond near his father's house, a child of one year, six months, and two days.

In this ancient Tichborne chapel is an old helmet, and standing here are an Elizabethan altar table carved with crosses, and two ancient footstools made of rushes cut from the river.

In the Tudor days, when the Tichbornes were at the height of their fame, Chidiock Tichborne brought the family name into disrepute. He was one of the six young men to whom was allotted the task of murdering Elizabeth in Thomas Babington's conspiracy for putting Mary Queen of Scots on the throne of England. Born at Southampton in 1558, tracing descent from an ancient Norman family, he was an ardent Roman Catholic, and came under suspicion at a time when Philip of Spain was seeking every means in his power to secure the overthrow of Elizabeth and Protestantism. In 1586 John Ballard, a priest disguised as a captain and well furnished with money, who had for months been visiting all the Roman Catholic families in England, persuaded Chidiock to throw in his lot with Babington. He did so, and the group of young men met and hatched the details of their plot in London taverns. But Walsingham had a spy among them, and they were all arrested, tried, and condemned to a horrible death. Chidiock pleaded guilty and faced his fate bravely, spending the last night of his life in writing these striking verses.

> My prime of youth is but a frost of cares;
>   My feast of joy is but a dish of pain;
> My crop of corn is but a field of tares;
>   And all my good is but vain hope of gain;
> The day is fled, and yet I saw no sun;
> And now I live, and now my life is done!
>
> The spring is past, and yet it hath not sprung;
>   The fruit is dead, and yet the leaves are green;
> My youth is gone, and yet I am but young;
>   I saw the world, and yet I was not seen;
> My thread is cut, and yet it is not spun;
> And now I live, and now my life is done!
>
> I sought my death, and found it in my womb;
>   I looked for life, and saw it was a shade;
> I trod the earth, and knew it was my tomb;
>   And now I die, and now I am but made;
> The glass is full, and now my glass is run;
> And now I live, and now my life is done!

The Great Tichborne Mystery

THE most dramatic story of the Tichborne family was the claim to the title made under remarkable circumstances. At a cost of £90,000, in a trial lasting over a hundred days, the Tichbornes in 1871 successfuly resisted the claim of a Wapping butcher to be the missing Sir Roger Tichborne; and by the expenditure of an even greater sum and a trial lasting 188 days the Crown convicted the claimant of fraud.

Nothing in fiction is more wildly improbable than the story Arthur Orton and a hundred deluded witnesses sought to establish before the Court—that he was the missing heir to the Tichborne estates.

Sir Roger was the son of a French mother, and was brought up in Paris, so that he spoke French perfectly and wrote English imperfectly. Eventually he came to England, completed his education at Stonyhurst, obtained a military commission but sold out, and in 1852 went to South America. Two years later he embarked for England on a ship which was lost with all on board. Leave to presume his death having been granted, a new heir succeeded, and all the family, with one exception, were content that justice had been done. The one exception was Lady Tichborne, mother of Sir Roger. She nourished a secret enmity against the members of her husband's family, and nothing convinced her that Roger was dead. Year after year she advertised for him in English and Colonial papers. She kept a candle burning every night in the room which had been his. At last the inevitable happened.

Eleven years after the loss of Roger's ship she learned that a man trading as a butcher at Wagga Wagga in New South Wales was the long-lost heir. She entered into correspondence with him and, determined to believe, accepted him as her missing son.

Arthur Orton, the Claimant, was an ignorant man, of audacious courage and astonishing readiness of resource. He raised great sums in Australia on what he called his expectations. He got in touch with an old Negro servant of Sir Roger and learned what he could from him; he met men who had known the heir and learned what he could of him; and with amazing facility he built up a structure of falsehood and fraud with which he reached England in 1866. He visited Paris to confront Lady Tichborne. The real

Sir Roger was a little man, short, slight, with sloping shoulders, narrow head, and a beaked nose, and the Claimant was a colossal figure, of 24 stones, yet Lady Tichborne took him to her heart as her long-lost son. Her affidavits sworn, she died. Whether she was really deceived, or whether her animus against the Tichbornes had influenced her, nobody knows.

Sergeant Ballantine, who led for the Claimant, said afterwards that the case might have been settled by a single question. The Tichbornes had behind them a man who had tattooed young Roger's arms. It was only necessary to ask the Claimant to bare his arm and Orton's case must then and there have collapsed, for he was not tattooed. Yet nobody thought of it, apparently.

The case dragged on and on, the Court crowded by leaders of society, and not until it had run 102 days was a verdict returned against the Claimant. Then he was ordered into custody and indicted for perjury, and at the end of 188 days more was sentenced to penal servitude for 14 years.

The Chained Bible

TIMSBURY. Everything to do with its church is charming—its simple shape, the beauty of its surroundings, and its many links with old England. It is reached by a garden path belonging to the school. A beautiful timber porch still offers the shelter it has afforded for 500 years; the solid old pews still keep their place in the nave, with the medieval beams of the roof looking down. Little is here that has not shared with England a long period of history. The walls come from the 13th century, and the great wooden lock on the south door is 15th. The slender strips of golden glass in the chancel windows were made about the time of Joan of Arc. The chancel screen, lovely, low, and simple, is 500 years old, and the beautiful pulpit with its golden-lettered canopy was made in Shakespeare's time. A chair in the chancel is 17th century and the wide oak armchair facing it is Elizabethan, and is carved on the back with flowers and foliage. The smooth font and its workmanlike oak cover have been here together since 1681. A rare and beautiful chained Bible of the 17th century lies in a recess, wonderfully clean and in perfect condition, with the chain by which it was fastened when books were chained in churches.

There is a group of ancient tiles in the sill of a window, all that is left of the paving of the chancel and nave. One is 15th century and bears William of Wykeham's motto, others are 13th century and were probably made at Beaulieu Abbey. There is a piscina 500 years old. Under the tower is a 13th century chest, and near the door a cupboard hangs on the wall with a library of books given by Timothy Goodacker in 1713. The fine Elizabethan chalice is believed to have been made by a village craftsman.

In the churchyard is a big mossy stone basin thought to be a 15th century domestic mortar from Manor Farm. It is by the porch, and opposite is a delightful flower-bordered path running through walled gardens to the manor house. On the sunny wall of the church is an ancient mass dial.

Old Walls and Their Memories

TITCHFIELD. It has had a famous past and is famous still for its possessions. Its wide streets of timbered and plastered houses have a front line of much charm. We found the old walls nearly hidden by wide-flung draperies of crimson creeper. Here and there, under overhanging storeys, tiny windows blink and peer darkly at the passer-by, and above bows set with panes of ancient glass rise roofs green and bronze with moss and lichen and stonecrop.

One of England's noble places is its dignified and ordered church, guarding many treasures. The base of its tower was firmly laid a thousand years ago, and has at its corners unusually fine long-and-short work, so dear to Saxon builders. The Norman doorway is one of the best in the county, built of huge blocks, three rows of chevrons on its face, and the consecration crosses of five abbots who placed their hands on it ages since. Within this noble doorway, leading into the porch, are two finely-wrought iron gates of diamond design, with 1651 on their lock; they were probably made at the old iron mills on the river. The outer stairway leads to the upper tower, where we noticed at the head of its first stage a thrilling course of Roman bricks, three deep and carried round the four sides. Three times they may have been used in building here, by Romans, Saxons, and Normans; they were probably here before Christianity came. The gracefully curved shingled spire above them was added in the 15th century.

It was the 13th century which gave the church the sedilia, the tre-foiled piscina, and the priest's doorway, and the 14th century gave it a beautiful little arcade on the south of the chancel, with four winged beasts on the capitals. From the 16th century come the timbered roofs and the five-light window with elegant niches on each side. Characteristic also of the 15th century is the harmonious group of slender clustered pillars in the north arcade.

Perhaps it is the Abbot's Chapel which brings the pilgrim here, the last resting-place of those Earls of Southampton whose name will be remembered for all time because one of them was Shakespeare's friend and patron. Their tomb rises magnificent in the middle of the floor with many-hued marbles, gleaming alabaster, and rich colouring of blue and crimson and gold contributing to its beauty. On the raised central part lies Jane the first Countess, and below are her husband the first earl and their son the second earl, who put up the monument. On it with himself and his father and mother he put his two sisters, his daughter and his son, a group of sculptured people in striking contrast with the rare simplicity of a tiny exquisite figure in white lying close by. She is the little Lady Mary, daughter of Shakespeare's friend, and she died at the tender age of four. A skull rests incongruously by her little pillowed head but three cherubs smile below.

Here also is a charming white panel by Chantrey in memory of a girl of the Hornby family who died on the eve of the Victorian Era. Her graceful girlish form is lying on a couch, her face towards us, and in the lines of the drapery and the delicate carving of her hands and feet we see some of the finest work of the famous sculptor. High up on the sanctuary wall is another white marble monument, with an interesting family of Shakespeare's day kneeling at prayer, William Chamberlaine with his wife and their four children.

There are many beautiful windows of our own time, all but one by Clayton and Bell. One of the east windows has the Madonna surrounded by the ministering women of the Gospels, Martha and Salome and the other two Marys. There is a fine Good Shepherd, a Christ in Majesty, and the Presentation in the Temple.

We came here upon much rare interest of a kind a little unfamiliar in churches, for we found ourselves thinking of old and young Gobbo in the Merchant of Venice. Nobody knows, but it is more than likely that Shakespeare heard this curious name when staying with his friend the third earl in the great house now in ruin on the site of Titchfield Abbey. The vicar showed us the name in the registers, which record that in 1593 (three years before the play was written), Augustine Gobbo was buried here, and in 1637 William Gobbo was married here. Who, looking at these pages in Titchfield's register, can forget the inimitable scene between Old and Young Gobbo in Shakespeare's play?

At the west end of the nave is a big wall-painting of the miraculous draught of fishes, in memory of a vicar of last century, and another possession of the church is a valuable collection of 17th century silver plate. The roll of vicars is one of the most interesting we have seen, beautifully illuminated, and giving the vicars from 1302 with the primates and bishops of Winchester at the time. One of the names on the list is Uriah Oakes, who was deprived of his living in 1662 under the Act of Uniformity, with 2000 other ministers.

Hanging on the wall of the Abbot's Chapel, above the great Southampton tomb, is a flag which has a stirring memory for all who are old enough to understand events when this century opened. It is the first Union Jack that flew over Government House in Pretoria when Lord Roberts marched in victorious at the end of the Boer War. It was brought home by a vicar who was a chaplain through the war, and rescued this historic banner for his village.

It is the ruin, no doubt, that will stir the deepest memories here. There is a timber gateway in the street which must have been a great place in the 15th century but of which we know nothing except that it is called Old Lodge. The ruins we come to see are those of the home of the Southampton earls, standing on the site of Titchfield Abbey a mile away. It is one of the places the Office of Works is so nobly keeping up, and it is thrilling to walk about in this place remembering what it was 700 years ago, and that 600 years ago it had one of the finest monastic libraries in England, with 224 volumes.

The abbey was given by Henry the Eighth to Thomas Wriothesley, first Earl of Southampton, for the help he had given with the King's Great Business, which was the earl's polite name for Henry's abandonment of his faithful Catherine. He pulled the abbey down and built Place House with its stones. His house is now a magnificent ruin overlooking the great fishpond guarded by an ancient and mighty oak. The square gatehouse stands across the vanished nave, lofty embattled turrets rise at the corners, and there are slender chimneys of delicate and intricate design. Still intact in the massive walls are deeply mullioned windows and the huge fireplaces lined with herringbone brickwork. We can clearly see the foundations of the great abbey church, the stone coffins in their places, and all reverent and in order.

Here, we must believe, came Shakespeare to see his patron, the earl to whom he dedicated the first work he published and his immortal sonnets. Here certainly came Charles Stuart, bringing his queen in the first year of his reign, and his friend the fourth earl was faithful to the end. Henrietta Maria so loved the place that she stayed five weeks, and it may have been the memory of that happy visit which brought Charles here again a distracted fugitive one autumn day in 1647. In one of the rooms above the gatehouse he passed his last night of freedom.

The king was here with his two companions Ashburnham and Berkley when Colonel Hammond came over from the Isle of Wight, where he was governor. It was hoped he would help the king to escape to the Continent but they were not sure of him. When Ashburnham went upstairs and told the king Hammond had come, Charles cried in despair, "O, Jack, you have undone me," and Ashburnham, in a great passion of weeping, hinted that Hammond might be killed. But the king would have no murder, and kept himself alone for two hours hoping for news of the ship he had been trying to get at Southampton. No ship came; Hammond was impatient and true to the Parliament, and Charles crossed with him to the Isle of Wight, never a free man again.

Such are the memories of these walls; such scenes they witnessed in our most famous Hundred Years. As we softly tread the velvety grass, dreaming in this remote and silent solitude, we think of that long procession we are following, bishops, abbots, priests, kings, queens and nobles, soldiers and poets, yeomen and peasants and serving-men of Old England, all playing their part and passing on. It is one of our precious places, a hallowed spot.

Shakespeare's Hero

THE man whom Shakespeare loved as scholar and benefactor, the third Earl of Southampton, was a great man of his time. All the poets of his age celebrated him in verse, as the artists painted his portrait, but it was the poor poet-actor who was to make his name immortal. We identify him repeatedly in the Sonnets, though he is not named, but there is no ambiguity in the dedications of Venus and Adonis and Lucrece.

There, over the signature William Shakespeare, the two most famous dedications in the language are addressed "To the Right Honourable Henry Wriothesley, Earl of Southampton, and Baron of Titchfield." Southampton was about 20 at the time, but he was passing rich, a gifted scholar and then, as throughout his life, devoted to literature and the theatre. He was Shakespeare's sole patron, and gave him £1000 to enable him to complete a purchase. A favourite of Elizabeth, the young man came to disgrace and imprisonment through an intrigue (followed by marriage) with one of her ladies. When he sought with Essex to depose the queen he appealed to the power of Shakespeare's genius (by causing his Richard the Second to be performed at the Globe Theatre) to show England how a monarch could be dethroned, and followed the play by an appeal to arms the very next day. For that act of violence he was sentenced to death, but reprieved; and, rising to honour under James, he engaged Shakespeare and Burbage to play Love's Labour's Lost before the Court.

He never attained commanding office in the State, for he opposed the despicable Buckingham, then all-powerful. But he was a force in colonising America, and it was he who sent Henry Hudson on his tragic voyage. Converted from Roman Catholicism, Southampton ardently supported Protestantism abroad, and died for it. With his eldest son he led an expedition to the Netherlands. Then his son died, and he, returning home, died soon after, at the age of 51.

Cromwell and the Dead King

THE fourth earl, son of Shakespeare's Southampton, was a man of small stature but of great courage, both physical and moral, who, challenged to a duel by Prince Rupert, chose pistols and short range. Happily the quarrel was composed and Southampton was left to continue the efforts in which from first to last he was unwearying, to bring peace between Charles and Parliament. He was an enlightened, moderate, just man, averse to autocratic royal powers, but constant to the king when the sword was ultimately drawn. In spite of ill health he was at the King's side throughout the long strife, and it was from his home here that Charles fled to the Isle of Wight. Southampton was in London throughout the trial and after the condemnation visited him to take a last farewell before his death.

On the night following the execution the earl secured permission to watch by the body of the dead king as it lay in the banqueting hall at Whitehall. With him was a friend, and through the night they kept a sad and silent vigil. Suddenly, about two in the morning, they heard footsteps on the stairs, and someone came slowly, heavily, up. The door opened, and a man entered, muffled in a large cloak. He approached the body, ignoring the watchers, stood contemplating it attentively for some time, then shook his head slowly, and sighed out the words, "Cruel Necessity!" By the voice and gait Southampton knew that the visitor was Cromwell.

John Birte's Coffer

TUFTON. An exquisite village on the clear and lovely River Test, it lies off the main road near Whitchurch. The small church is worthy of it, with nave walls and windows built by the Normans, and the arch of a Norman doorway above the present door in the 18th century porch. On the north wall a big painting of St Christopher, said to be not less than 500 years old, is fading away; and above the chancel arch is a shadowy text painted in Stuart times, exhorting us to fear God and honour the King. The chancel arch is possibly Saxon and is dignified in its severity. The side windows of the chancel, deeply splayed and set in arches, are 700 years old and remarkably beautiful. The font is 12th century and has a single twist of cable moulding at its base. On the west wall hangs a mellowed painting of the royal arms with the Hanoverian white horse cantering across the tiny shield in the centre. Below stands a solid chest, which may be that mentioned in John Birte's will in 1536, "I give and bequeath to the church of Tofton my great coffar." That was 400 years ago, and here is the coffer still.

The Four Horses

TUNWORTH. We must drop our sixpences here into the mouths of one of two quaint faces carved on Tunworth's old Charity

Box; and glad we are to leave them, for it is an endearing little shrine which has outlived the centuries in this hidden corner of Hampshire. A narrow way between tall beeches and the jutting eave of a thatched wall leads us to its hiding-place behind an old farm. Sweet and simple it is, like the fields and woods around, with only the shingled point of its bellcot for a spire, but with a fine timber porch added last century in memory of one who loved this village. The little arch (barely five feet wide) in the solid wall between nave and chancel was made when the Conqueror was settling himself on the throne of England, though the 13th century altered its round head to a point, and the 19th gave the whole church a new look. The heads of four spirited horses make the ends of the choir-stalls look like knights in chess. So tiny is the church that one row of these stalls is all the rector has for a vestry, while the harmonium stands among the seats in the nave.

The Marriage of Mrs Fitzherbert

TWYFORD. It has three houses with a story. Twyford House is a fine old place where Benjamin Franklin wrote most of his autobiography while visiting his friend Dr Shipley, Bishop of St Asaph. Seager's Buildings, a beautiful house in a quiet corner, with dormer windows in its mossgrown roof, is the place where a little deformed boy named Alexander Pope was at school; it is the school he had to leave for writing a lampoon on the master. Brambridge House is framed in a fine double avenue of lofty limes (which were pollarded for gun-stocks in Napoleon's day) and has the River Itchen flowing by. In the older house which stood here Mrs Fitzherbert spent her girlhood after school in Paris, and it is believed that it was here that in 1785 she married the Prince of Wales who became George the Fourth.

The marriage was the sensation and the mystery of the day. The Prince of Wales was under the age when royal weddings become valid, so that it was easy to admit the marriage or deny it, and both courses were apparently taken as convenience demanded. They appeared in public together and lived together. Ten years later the prince married the Princess Caroline, and Mrs Fitzherbert continued to live with him after an interval for respectability. The time came, however, when Mrs Fitzherbert was publicly insulted at a dinner by being deprived of her rank, and it was the end of this amazing marriage. Yet it is believed that Mrs Fitzherbert was the only woman George the Fourth ever really loved, and her portrait was hanging round his neck when he died.

We can sit in the churchyard under a green sunshade hundreds of years old, for here is a magnificent yew 15 feet round. The handsome church built by Sir Alfred Waterhouse overlooks the beautiful wooded valley of the Itchen, and has a tower and spire 140 feet high. The round pillars of the nave have capitals carved over seven centuries ago, probably by the men who made the font. On the wall is a striking 18th century bust by the fashionable sculptor Nollekens. It shows Bishop Shipley, a kindly-looking man in a curly wig, wearing his mitre and with his books and pens about him.

One of the dignified pews tells us of three generations who were churchwardens from 1829 to 1929, the grandson being Henry William Hewlitt, who had been carrying on business in a little Georgian shop for nearly 60 years when we called. We looked through the square panes of the rounded window and saw the grey-haired old saddler working where his uncle and grandfather had worked before him since 1822, working with a feeling of sadness, we may be sure, that handmade saddles belong to the past, and that his little shop was likely to come down to make room for the successor of the horse, a driving power which needs no saddles.

The Disappointed Poet

UPHAM. We come up to it, as we should expect to do, but it has little except the charm that nature gives it. Nothing old remains of its 13th century church except the foundations, the registers, and the bells. An odd entry in the registers notes the cost of cleaning out the chancel after Cromwell's troopers had stabled their horses in it. But there still stands the rectory in which there was born about 250 years ago a boy who played in its garden and must have loved its grassy walks and fruit trees. Here Edward Young grew up until he followed his father the rector to Winchester School. He would have been fairly well satisfied, we feel, if he could have followed his father all the way, for the father became Dean of Salisbury and a royal chaplain while the son was much disappointed, dying old but still a vicar. He became a fashionable poet, and every reader of poetry then read his Night Thoughts. Their solemn pomp

College and Chapel from the Playing Fields

The East End of the Chapel

WINCHESTER'S FAMOUS SCHOOL

Winchester
Hall of St Cross

Alton
South Aisle of Church

Winchester
Norman Windows of St Cross

Breamore
Saxon Chancel Arch

suited the age. Now it repels us. He had more immediate fame as a poet than he deserved, but he remained unhappy because he could not be a bishop. But Upham remembers him, for he gave it a place on the literary map. He wrote many good things and bad; one of his good ones was the epigram after visiting Voltaire:

> *Thou art so witty, profligate, and thin,*
> *At once we think thee Milton, Death, and Sin.*

UPNATELY. It is reached by quiet lanes, and has a little church of the 13th century with a battlemented brick tower of the 19th. The bells are 18th century, and there is an almsdish of about the same age; but far older is the mass dial by which the village folk would tell the time in the days before clocks.

UPPER CLATFORD. It is charming with its river scenery, and above it stands Bury Hill, fortified by prehistoric man and still wearing the natural diadem he placed about its brows. The little church, in a meadow watered by the River Anton, is approached by a delightful tunnel of limes leading to its 18th century brick porch. It has walls with a mass clock carved on them and a blocked doorway built in the 12th century, and a 16th century tower, and it was strangely used by the restorers of the 17th century, who took down a Norman arcade and set part of it in front of the chancel, giving the queer effect of a double chancel arch. They also planted in the middle of the church two huge timber pillars to support the new roof. The font and the attractive canopied pulpit are both 17th century and there are 17th century chairs and benches. One of the oldest things the village has is a pillar piscina with a carved front, a relic of Norman England found in the tower. By it is a built-up Norman window.

The Lady in the Dark

UPTON GREY. It has a little shimmering lake instead of a village green. Some of the timbered cottages gather round to admire themselves in it, while others as charming climb the hill to the church. Someone has said that these cottages seem to gossip of the days of Queen Anne, perhaps because there is a lady by the altar who was maid-of-honour to the queen. She is Lady Dorothy Eyre, and her bust shows her wearing a veil over her long hair with a scarf about her shoulders, but we must strain our eyes to see her, for rarely have we come across a chancel as dark as this. Windows like arrow slits leave it almost black. We could just make out marks on the wall round the piscina and the aumbry which show that they were once surrounded by a wood frame with a door to shut over them. The church is Norman at the core, with a central tower on one pointed arch and one Norman arch unusually tall and narrow with simple moulding round the top. Its 600-year-old font has faces of a man and three monkeys, one with its tongue out, and a cover made in the time of Wren, in whose day the 13th century tower was given a plain brick top. There are faint traces of 13th century painting inside the tower, and three crosses are cut in the west wall where the bishop put his hand on Consecration Day. There is a little gallery with a balustrade, and, raised two steps from the nave, are rows of 18th century pews. The striking white figures of Simeon and Anna are in a Nunc Dimittis window above them.

VERNHAM DEAN. A fine early Tudor manor house stands at the cross roads and is full of 16th century woodcarving. The church has a Norman doorway splendid with decoration, and the pillars supporting the arch have capitals carved with leaves.

The Last of the Proud Plantagenets

WARBLINGTON. It is an old, old place, and Saxons, Normans, and 13th and 14th century men all shared in the building of the little tower of Warblington with its tiny timbered spire. The tower has two small Saxon doorways built with tiles made by the Romans, and on the sunny wall is a mass dial. Close by grows a yew with a trunk 18 feet round which must have thrown its shade across an old lady who passed this way into as sad a page of history as all the centuries have seen. She was the brave Countess of Salisbury, who lived at Warblington Castle, of which the ruined turret by the churchyard is all that remains.

She would know the church as we see it, with a massive timbered porch of the 14th century, its traceried arch probably made from the timbers of old ships, for there are marks of bolts visible on the wood. One nave arcade is Norman and the other 13th century, one with its Norman strength and one with slender marble shafts. There are two 13th century arches leading from the tower into the chancel, which has 15th century tiles in the floor decorated with animals, birds, and fleur-de-lys. There is a peephole for the altar with a groove showing that it once had a sliding panel, a curious feature we do not remember to have come upon elsewhere. The church also keeps the pitch pipe used by the choir in olden days.

In the narrow chancel (longer than the nave) is a brass of a 16th century vicar kneeling at prayer, Raffe Smalpage, and 200 years older are two ladies sleeping in the aisles, one with a long gown and a wimple, lying in a recess with the fragment of a sculpture of angels carrying her soul.

In the churchyard are many 18th century gravestones, some of them remarkable. On one is a fish swallowing a man drowned at sea, another has a sailor drowning in a ship turned upside down, and another shows a ship on fire in Portsmouth harbour. Among all these lies the first Bishop of Adelaide, Augustus Short. He was a Westminster schoolboy who was offered the bishopric of Adelaide when four colonial bishoprics were founded in the middle of last century, and he did much in those early days to build up churches and schools among the scattered people of the Bush.

Two stone huts in a corner of the churchyard are a witness of grim days of long ago, for they once sheltered men guarding graves from body-snatchers, a practice which went on till the Anatomy Act of 1832 put a stop to it. One who remembered the days when the watchers used these huts lies in the churchyard. He was old William Norris, who was rector for more than half of last century and died in 1893 at the rectory in which he had lived for 97 years.

It is the ruined turret of the old castle that brings history to mind in Warblington. In this 14th century castle was born the Henry Cotton who was Queen Elizabeth's godson, and of whom she said when she made him a bishop that she had blessed many of her godsons but never before had had a godson to bless her. But it is the undying memory of this place that it was the scene of the foulest stain on the name of King Henry the Eighth. From here he dragged the last of the Plantagenets and butchered her.

She was Margaret Pole, Countess of Salisbury, a daughter of George Plantagenet, Duke of Clarence, her mother being a daughter of Warwick the Kingmaker. Born in 1473, she married Richard Pole, a Buckinghamshire squire who had a family relationship to Margaret Beaufort, mother of Henry the Seventh. When Margaret was 32 her husband died, leaving her with four sons and one daughter. She was well aware of the danger from her family's royal descent, for as soon as Henry the Seventh had secured the throne he, as a precaution against a possible rival, had locked up her brother Edward, Earl of Warwick, in the Tower, and beheaded him. So she brought up her children to beware of the family liability to find its way to the scaffold.

The Poles were a sincere and earnest Roman Catholic family. They were thoroughly staunch, and everybody knew it. Margaret had the great advantage of being trusted by young Henry the Eighth. She had lost her husband and brother and he sympathised with her. One of the first of his acts as a king was to give her a State pension, and afterwards, on making her Countess of Salisbury, he restored to her the family estates, and she became governess of his daughter (and her god-daughter) Princess Mary. But the countess would not acknowledge Anne Boleyn as Henry's queen, and kept away from the Court while Anne held sway there.

Some of the children of the countess gave King Henry half-hearted service during the period of the dissolution of the monasteries and the risings following that upheaval, but they kept out of the work as much as they could, and Reginald Pole, Margaret's cleverest son, who had gone abroad to study with a grant from Henry, kept abroad and began to make himself a name in religious circles in Italy. Henry kept up communication with Reginald, trying through him to ascertain what was the pope's view of Henry's own attitude on religion and marriage. At last Reginald dropped a bomb on King Henry in the form of a book which told him he was quite wrong in his views, and hoping he would repent and return to the Roman fold.

The Pole family in England were staggered by this challenge to Henry. The countess, now living at Warblington, wrote to her son abroad, and to those at home, in angry protest. The truth was they agreed entirely with Reginald, but thought he ought not to have put them in danger in England from his safe place in Italy, and their letters were meant to be seen by the King's Council, so as to stave off trouble. In that they did not succeed, Henry's instant determination was to clear off all the Pole family with its aspirations to royalty. So he clapped in the Tower Margaret herself and her sons Henry and Geoffrey, with their friends Henry Courtenay, Marquis of Exeter, and Sir Edward Neville, Constable of Leeds Castle in Kent, who had long been a soldierly courtier. Courtenay had royal blood in his veins, which condemned him to extinction.

The king's method of procedure was by protracted questioning, again and again renewed, to collect evidence of guilty talk about the blood relation between the Pole family and the royal line, and then to infer conspiracy. Geoffrey Pole, who was the long-tongued member of the family, gave the case away. He admitted carrying messages from abroad, grew confused, pleaded guilty, and caused the beheading of all the rest—the countess, Geoffrey and his brother Henry, and their two friends.

The execution of Margaret, as we have said, is the blackest blot on the character of Henry the Eighth. He had been her friend. He had described her as the most saintly woman in England. She had been a second mother to his eldest child. Yet, without calling on her to answer the accusations made against her, she was ordered out for execution in her 69th year. She behaved with dignity and resignation, but the executioner was a clumsy fellow and the last scene was horrible, the headsman taking six strokes to sever her head from her body as she stood on her feet. She had erected in Christchurch Priory a beautiful chantry to be her last resting-place. Its beauty it wonderfully preserved, but she does not lie there. She, described by Macaulay as "the last of the proud race of Plantagenets," is one of five women victims of this man's heartless cruelty who are lying headless in the grim chapel of St Peter's-in-the-Tower.

The Norman Baron's Church

WARNFORD. In the lovely Meon valley, it has for near neighbour the prehistoric earthworks crowning Old Winchester Hill. The church, reached by a private path for which we ask permision at the lodge, stands in a shady corner near the great house of Warnford Park. Founded by Wilfrid of York when he came to convert the Jutish settlers 1300 years ago, it is rich in wonderful things. Two stone tablets in the outside walls of the nave tell us in Latin of the church's rebuilding by a powerful Norman baron, and beg us to pray for him:

> *Good folks in your devotion every day*
> *For Adam Port, who thus repaired me, pray.*

Sharing the shelter of the porch with this prayer is a rare treasure indeed, a tiny Saxon sundial evidently saved from Wilfrid's church. It is surrounded by carved leaves.

The massive Norman tower, has pairs of round windows and shallow buttresses and under its tower is a big roughly made chest carved with roundels by a carpenter who closed his eyes 700 years ago. The great font is also Norman, its sides with battered sculptures of strange beasts and birds. The tower is shut off from the nave by a beautiful screen, rich in carving and three centuries old. The chancel screen is the same age, panelled, and with foliage, and has a delightful little arch, Many of the benches in the nave, simple and sturdy, contain wood of the century when Caxton gave England its first printing press. In the 14th century chancel is a long bench divided into three by arms decorated with leaves. Men were sitting on it when Chaucer was riding to Canterbury with the pilgrims. The charming silver chalice was given to the village in 1687, and the paten cover used with it is an important piece of silver, being the only one of its kind in Hampshire. There are two iron helmets in the chancel.

Sir Thomas Neale, who died in 1621, has a magnificently sculptured tomb in the sanctuary. He lies by his two wives, clad in fine armour, with his beard flowing over his ruff. His wives are richly dressed and their nine children kneel below. The knight's coat-of-arms is flanked by Faith and Charity, though Charity seems to have had little part in his life if the bitter ending of his epitaph is like him, for it is a prayer that any one of us who looks on him without a tear may be turned to stone!

Close to the church, but hidden from us by trees, are the remains of a stately 13th century house. It must once have been a noble building with its lofty arcaded hall, but all that is left of it are the crumbling walls of the kitchen and the buttery, and one of the hall's slender pillars, 25 feet high, which still vies gracefully with nature's living pillars growing up about it.

The Oldest Silver Paten

WEEKE. Weeke begins where Winchester leaves off and, being so near the city of wonder and beauty, it is not surprising to find that it also has its share of thrilling and lovely things. The rarest and most precious of its treasures is a little silver paten, the oldest in use anywhere in England. Experts believe that the man who fashioned it, who so lovingly decorated its rim and engraved the little lamb in the centre, lived in the time of Roger Bacon, so that it must have been handled by over 20 generations of village folk.

The tiny manor church is a haven of quiet by the busy highroad. One of the bells was paid for nearly 450 years ago by William Compton, a great benefactor of the church, and it is his brass which is the first thing we see as we enter the building through its simple Norman doorway. This brass has a long inscription and no portrait, but over the inscription is a queer St Christopher with his head on one side, leaning on a knotty staff as he carries the Child on his shoulder through the stream. We remember only one other brass of the Saint with the Child (at Morley in Derbyshire).

In the 13th century chancel, which has a few beautiful old tiles, is a small crude stone with deeply incised letters telling us it is to the memory of Dr Harpesfield, rector of the parish at the Reformation. The east window has the Lamb of God among its subjects, as well as a patchwork of old glass including an odd face and part of a figure with a hand by a book. In the nave there is a tablet asking the reader to blush if he does not venerate the memory of Thomas Gordon, who died in 1776.

The Father and Mother of Cobden

WEST MEON. Charming with pretty cottages in a green valley, West Meon sees its river running swiftly by, as behoves one born 400 feet up on the hills. The flint church was rebuilt last century and keeps only the Jacobean altar table from the old church; but the churchyard hides in the grass three headstones bearing well-known names. On two of the stones, standing side by side and made beautiful with decoration, are the names of William and Millicent Cobden.

These two peaceful sleepers had a son whom they christened Richard, born to them when they were living in Sussex in 1804 in the old home at Heyshott which the nation enabled their son to buy back, and which is now a home of research for economic students, the Citadel of Free Trade in a world which has lost that priceless heritage. The son grew up to be a printer of calicoes famed for their good taste and quality and known as Cobden Prints, and then suddenly Richard Cobden flamed into an apostle of Free Trade and his name was on all men's lips.

The third grave is that of a man whose lasting memorial is in London, a memorial wide and green, carefully mown and rolled, and surrounded in the summer by vast crowds cheering as the ground resounds with the meeting of a well-bowled ball and a swift straight bat. It is Thomas Lord who sleeps under the grass at our feet, the founder and proprietor of the original Lord's Cricket Ground in London, which, after various changes caused by the building of houses, the cutting of canals, and the making of railways, retains its founder's name, and is the home and property of the Marylebone Cricket Club, the authoritative ruler of the national game. He came here in 1830 to spend his declining days as a farmer.

Outside the village, on the way to East Meon, is a school for boys called Westbury House, and half-hidden in its trees are the ruins of a tiny stone chapel of the 14th century, built by Robert le Ewer, lord of the manor. Though there is nothing left to show it, his grave is said to be by the font to which the little chapel still clings. This fine house is 20th century but in the Conqueror's Domesday Book there was a house with the same name on its site valued at "three hides." The ruined chapel has a medieval window looking towards the house and a stone with a relief of a knight or a priest carved on it.

We came upon three records of faithful service here, two 18th and 19th century rectors for 50 and 51 years, Stephen Unwin and John Dampier; and a cross on the green in the middle of the village to George Vining Rogers 1777–1846, more than 40 years a doctor in West Meon. He was the father of one of the most indefatigable searchers for the facts of everyday life ever known in England, James Edwin Thorold Rogers. He began his life as a Church of England curate of the High Church variety, but changed his views and desired to resign his clerical orders. Then he found it could not be done, and for about ten years he persisted in advocating the necessary Parliamentary changes. In the end the Clerical Disabilities Act was passed, and he was, in 1870, the first man to withdraw legally from the vows he had taken in his youth.

As Professor of Political Economy at Oxford he began the collection of statistics for over 500 years of the History of Agriculture and Prices in England, and in 1866 published two volumes giving the figures for 140 years. While doing this work he was very active on the public platform as an outspoken Radical, and when his re-election as professor at Oxford became due he was rejected. But he went on with his research work, and entered Parliament and after he had published six volumes of his great History of Agriculture and Prices, and two volumes of his book Six Centuries of Work and Wages he was re-elected to the Oxford professorship from which he had been ejected.

Throughout all these years Thorold Rogers was busy writing books and was always ready to enter into any electioneering hurly-burly that might occur; but his solid claim on the admiration of his country-men is the industry and care with which he dug up facts from the far-off past. The lessons to be drawn from these facts will be differ-ently read by different people, but the facts are there for anybody.

Thomas Lord and His Cricket Pitch

THOMAS LORD, who sleeps at West Meon, was Yorkshire born, but only because his parents had to leave their native Scotland after the '45 rebellion. He was born in 1757, when cricket was a favourite sport, but cluttered round with the betting crowd. Six years before England had been shocked by the news that the Prince of Wales had been killed by a hit from a cricket ball.

At 23 we find Lord acting as groundsman to the White Conduit Club, where the MCC played its matches. Another seven years and he had opened his own cricket ground on what is now Dorset Square; and such faith had the MCC members in their ex-groundsman's know-ledge of turf that they transferred their patronage to him. When building encroachments, as London's land became more and more valuable, drove him to remove his cricket pitch, turf and all, to a site near where the Regent's Canal now is, the MCC again went with him.

The making of the Canal caused Thomas Lord to look round for yet another site for his ground. But he was not dismayed. He enjoyed making cricket pitches more than anything else in the world, and this time he chose its present site. Again he took up and relaid the old turf; again the MCC followed him. Not till he was 73 could he bear to tear himself away from the green turf and the sound of leather against wood; but the old man sold out at last, bought a farm in West Meon, and tried his hand at rough fields for a change. Not for long, though, for in two years his life was over.

There is a special appropriateness in his coming to this village, which has as neighbours Hambledon and Broadhalfpenny Down, where cricket first forecast its modern importance and county matches first arranged. It is good, too, that the MCC eventually bought his ground and kept for it the name of Lords.

He Died with Kitchener

WESTON PATRICK. The church has a simple 12th century doorway scored with some of the little crosses of the faithful, and hanging on one of its walls is a case in which is kept the centre of a dark green altar cloth embroidered with the initials of the two churchwardens of 1682. The communion cup was made a few years after Queen Elizabeth came to the throne. A pillar in the nave is inscribed with the names of three men who died that we might live; one was a rector's son, and another one of 600 who sank when Lord Kitchener went on his last voyage in the ship named after this county.

Old Sir Benjamin

WEST TISTED. It is one of our little English groups at the end of a grass-grown track, just a manor house and a little grey church, yet how like a touch of history it is, especially with the hollow oak in the field and the old yew in the churchyard.

The house was one of the Tichborne dower houses and here in 1644 lived Sir Benjamin Tichborne, Royalist as the king. When General Waller had routed the king's men at Cheriton Sir Benjamin was there; he saw 2000 Englishmen fall slain and only hard riding and his knowledge of the country saved him. Just in time he reached the hollow oak in the field, scrambled up the tree, and dropped exhausted into its dark security. A few weeks went by and the house was startled by the arrival of Cromwell's troopers. Sir Benjamin fled into the priest's hole under the roof and the Puritans announced that they were under orders to occupy the house for some time—an anxious time for Lady Tichborne, with her husband hiding under the roof and his enemies in the kitchen. One night a shot rang out and the Puritan captain fell dead, accidentally shot by one of his troopers while cleaning a pistol. The scene of the tragedy is now the dining-room.

The house has much beauty still from its Tudor days, magnificent mantelpieces, archways and fireplaces, with a priest's room and the old steps leading to it from a narrow passage; but the house is in its youth compared with its neighbour, for in the church walls is a blocked-up arch with the stones laid as none but Saxons laid them, one upright and one lengthways. Children are still christened at a Norman font, and the oak roof is 700 years old. So, we doubt not, are the stout timbers on which the belfry rests. A massive Jacobean altar table is used as a side altar. We like the plain stone tablets near the pulpit reminding us that Sir Benjamin and his wife sleep below in peaceful forgetfulness of the storm and stress of 1644.

A lonely and secluded corner of our Motherland is this, and is there not something of pathos in the picture of Old Yew standing sentinel in the graveyard, looking across to its old crony the hollow oak which saved Sir Benjamin's life so long ago?

600-Year-Old Bells

WEST TYTHERLEY. It lies lonely and lovely among the trees near the Wiltshire border, with a plain 19th century church watching over it from the hill. It has a few relics of the ancient church, among them a brass of a 15th century lady, Anne Whitehead, and two 14th century bells. The altar plate is 16th and 17th century and includes an Elizabethan chalice and an Italian crucifix of gold and silver. Up in a handsome gallery is a modern organ, but down in the nave is the barrel organ which it replaced, still capable of playing thirty tunes.

The Ancient Bell

WEST WORLDHAM. A quiet little place of many lanes and rich in trees, its church made new in 1888 on its ancient foundations. We come into it by a doorway 750 years old, and it has kept its 14th century bell, its simple 15th century timbered porch, and two small medieval piscinas. In one window is a quaint collection of little diamond panes of glass, among them a green parrot, a dove carrying an olive branch, a robin, a lamb, and a tiny figure of a golden-haired woman carried on the back of a sea beast. She is holding a comb in one hand and a mirror in the other, the ruling passion strong in high adventure.

A Thrilling Discovery

WEYHILL. High up on the hills near Andover, it is famed for its centuries-old fair, a scene of much liveliness in mid-October. It has a small church, refashioned in the 19th century but still keeping its simple early Norman chancel arch, a bell perhaps 500 years old, and a silver chalice with Elizabethan engraving. From the lancets in the chancel four attractive angels look out in modern glass.

Two peace memorials there are on these walls, one to the three men from Weyhill who fell in South Africa, the other to the eight who fell in the far greater war.

The churchyard cross is unusually interesting, for its ancient base was found buried by a rector, and the cross itself, brought from Jerusalem, is fashioned of the same stone as the Stone of Unction in the Church of the Holy Sepulchre.

It was near Weyhill that a thrilling discovery was made some years ago by men excavating a Roman house. They came across a cement floor which rang hollow and on breaking it open found a wonderful set of pewter plates, cups, and dishes hidden in a recess below. Some were decorated with simple patterns and one vessel bore the Christian monogram. This fine service, once apparently in the home of a Roman Christian, is now where all may see it, in the British Museum.

Queen Elfrida's Priory

WHERWELL. Off the Roman road from Winchester to Cirencester, it has traces of a Saxon priory, many charming old cottages, and a church that was rebuilt in the 19th century but still keeps much of the interest of its ancient predecessor. The oldest possessions of the church include part of a Saxon cross, a sleeping figure under a handsome canopy, and some remarkable pieces of 13th century sculpture. The sleeping figure is believed to be a nun who was a prioress here in the 14th century, and the sculptures are among those medieval representations called the Harrowing of Hell, the story of Christ's descent into hell, where He overpowers the evil one. There is more stonework from the ancient church of Wherwell on the side of the Iremonger Mausoleum, a remarkable building with hideous faces and a line of shields.

The church also has the silver chalice from the old one, rich in tulips, daffodils, and anemones carved in Milton's England, and in the nave floor there are two old gravestones with heraldic carving, one to a five-year-old child grandly described as the Honourable John West Esquire and with an epitaph ending in this exquisite line;

Reader, shed a tear for the loss of so much innocence.

But there is more than this. Those who step through one of the churchyard gates leading to a beautiful garden will come upon two ancient stone coffins and a quaint 17th century stone in the wall telling of the "overacted zeal or avarice of King Henry" which destroyed the ancient priory in this place. In the walls of a farm we noticed stone faces peeping out, which must once have been on the walls of the priory, whose story is rather a grim one. It was founded in Saxon times by Queen Elfrida in remorse for the murder of her stepson Edward at Corfe Castle to put her own child on the throne. In remorse she founded a priory here, and little stone faces from its walls are still looking out at Wherwell.

The Saxon Lady

WHITCHURCH. A little country town where five roads meet, it has a rare and wonderful possession set near the chancel arch of its church. It is the memorial stone of a woman whose name means Pledge of Peace. She lived and died in Saxon England, a nun of Wherwell's Priory, it is believed, about a thousand years ago. There are those who think her older still, but all we have to tell us is a beautiful Latin inscription, that *Here lies the body of Frithburga, buried in peace*. Sculptured on her stone is a bust supposed to represent Our Lord with a book in His hands; the stone was long lost, and was found in use as something for a bell-ringer to stand on.

Another precious thing the church has, a flight of belfry stairs said to be unique, it is made of solid blocks of wood and cased in plain wooden walls about 500 years old, pierced by tiny traceried windows.

The church, though mainly modern, has still three Norman pillars and arches, and three of the 15th century. The font is 15th century too, and there are brass portraits of two Elizabethans, Richard and Elizabeth Brooke, he in a long furred gown and she in a lovely brocaded dress and a queer high hat. Below are their six children, also in brass, and a long quaint epitaph in rhyme, beginning:

This grave (Oh grief) hath swallowed up with wide and open mouth
The body of good Richard Brooke, of Whitchurch, Hampton South.

One of the sons, Thomas Brooke, lies in stone close by, a kindly looking bearded man with his charming wife Susan. She is richly dressed, her hair brushed up in a sort of half-moon in front of a pretty bonnet. They used to live at the vicarage when it was the manor house.

Whitchurch has eight bells collected down the centuries. Two are older than the Reformation, two are from Shakespeare's time, two are 18th century, and two part of the town's peace memorial.

Older Than History

WHITSBURY. It has one or two treasures in its 13th century church, but it is on the map for an earthwork older than history, Whitsbury Camp and Castle Ditches. The camp has a well 400 feet deep, probably sunk by the Romans. It covers 15 acres and has deep ditches with steep slopes, from a height of 402 feet it surveys a wide tract of downland across to Cranborne Chase. The camp is one of a group guarding these lonely uplands when the Saxons came, and in the land it overlooks are signs of Human activities before the time of written history—Bokerly Ditch, Grim's Ditch, and various burial mounds. The church has a silver chalice given to it in 1673, and an interesting small mazer bowl of arbor vitae mounted in silver. The bowl is probably from the 16th century. An old bell not now used is inscribed with the date 1623, the figure 3 being curiously made by turning an E the wrong way round.

The Flower of the Uvedales

WICKHAM. This endearing village, the praty townlet, as old Leland called it, has its name in the annals of fame, for all the world has heard of its son William of Wykeham; and it was beloved of Isaak Walton too. It is a charming place, memorable alike for beauty and history.

In its wide square, bounded by every description of old and charming architecture, tourneys were once held. Down the hill by the bridge over the clear River Meon is a big mill whose great beams, pitted by shot, were part of the timbers of the American frigate Chesapeake, captured off Boston in 1813 by the British frigate Shannon in one of the most spirited of naval encounters. The beams were broken up at Portsmouth.

Beyond the bridge lies the church, still preserving its Norman doorway, the capitals sculptured with King Stephen's badge, a centaur with bow and arrow, which is the zodiac sign of Sagittarius. Squeezed into a chapel is the splendid monument in Derbyshire alabaster of a descendant of the great house which gave William of Wykeham his chance in the world. William's benefactor was Nicholas Uvedale; the monument here is that of William Uvedale and his comfortable wife, who lived in Shakespeare's day. The little lines at the corners of his eyes suggest that often his kindly face was lit with smiles; she is round-faced, restful, and motherly; they are a pair in a thousand. Below kneel their nine children, the youngest boy John an enchanting rogue with impish winning smile, and thick, short curling hair, holding in his hand, as if he considered it a great joke, a skull which tells us that he died before his parents. Over the door of the chapel hangs Sir William's funeral helmet, removed from the tomb after the spurs had been stolen. An inscription asks and tells us: "Reader, would you know who lies in this tomb? It is the flower of the Uvedales and honour of his race"; and goes on:

Thy virtues, worthy knight, need not this tomb,
Men's hearts and Heaven afford them fairer room.

We noticed a memorial to William Cummins, an old man who died before the Victorian Era began, and of whom we are told that he came as a poor servant to this parish about 1763, fulfilled his humble duty with uprightness and fidelity for 60 years, and bequeathed at his death £800 in gifts of gratitude and charity. In the sanctuary is an old armchair with a richly carved back.

But the chief renown of Wickham comes from the fact that it is the birthplace of its great William, Chancellor of England and Bishop of Winchester, builder of Winchester College and New College, of whom the historian Froissart said "Everything was done through him, and without him nothing was done."

William of Wykeham

FOR a time William of Wykeham was the most powerful man in England. As he was born poor and became enormously rich, he had plenty of flattering friends and spiteful enemies whose accounts of him clashed when he had been laid to rest in the chantry he built for himself in the cathedral he had remodelled. But in spite of overstatements made by friends and enemies alike, Wykeham comes to us clearly through the centuries as a very great man.

His mother "had some gentle blood" and his father was freeborn, but they were poor, and William owed his good start in life evidently to the fact that he was the outstanding sharp boy of his native village. He caught the eye of Nicholas Uvedale, lord of the manor, who sent him to school at Winchester. All through his life he must have been grateful for this help for his great ambition was to provide similar education for later generations of boys, seventy of them at a time, and that noble work remains to this day.

The education which William obtained at the Prior's school at Winchester was not clerical in the religious sense, but practical and designed for business purposes. It included languages, mathematics, and some law. He was 38 when he entered holy orders. No doubt he was a tonsured clerk from the first, but he was not a priest, and his work till he was almost middle-aged was that of business management. Probably he owed to his Wickham patron's influence his start as secretary to the constable of Winchester Castle. Then he accompanied the Sheriff of Hampshire as his clerk when he travelled the county. Next he joined the king's service as clerk of the works where the king was building castles, and became warden of forests, and finally Keeper of the Privy Seal and the king's private secretary.

This was the time when, in constant contact with the king, he exercised great influence over him. It was said by his envious detractors that he was "Chief of the Privy Council and Governor of the Great Council," which was another way of saying that the king trusted his practical abilities and relied on his judgment. In his turn Edward heaped recompense on his unfailing servant, which took the form of appointing him prebend in various collegiate churches and cathedrals, so that he began to accumulate wealth from many sources. Four years after he took priestly orders he was elected Bishop of Winchester, but the pope delayed his sanction for a year. At this time he was the richest ecclesiastic in England, and Froissart made the note that "Sir William de Wican reigned in England." It is calculated that he had an income of £60,000 a year at present values.

All this, of course, is wrong according to our ideas, but how did this wealthy prelate spend his money? That he spent it wisely appears plainly in the linked colleges he built and endowed at Winchester and Oxford, and in remodelling his cathedral. He had had great experience in building and he used it in repairing many manor houses that were included in the endowments of the cathedral. In earlier days the bishops of Winchester had ensured their power by

Winchester   St Catherine's Hill

Winchester   Wolvesey Castle

The Window of George the Sixth and Queen Elizabeth

The Famous Norman Font

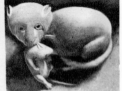

Carvings on the Choir Stalls

TREASURES OF WINCHESTER CATHEDRAL

building various castles. One of them was at the town of Bishop's Waltham, midway between his own birthplace, Wickham, and Winchester, and he transformed it into a peaceful dwelling-place and used it as his residence. As an administrator of the religious foundations he was a reformer of abuses and incurred unpopularity in certain priories. When Edward the Third fell into his dotage, and John of Gaunt led a movement for setting aside government by such ecclesiastics as Wykeham, his management of affairs was challenged, and he was suspended from his civic offices, but the charges against him were not sustained, and when Richard the Second succeeded Edward the Commons called the bishop back to be one of the advisers of the young king. His plans for the fine educational institutions which he left to posterity were wise and far-seeing, and his benefactions have proved sound and lasting. He was not an architect as some have inferred, but a great business man, who built much and knew whom to employ. His life was spent in a narrow district in Hampshire which he dearly loved. There he was born and there he died. His life was consistent and his heart true. It was typical of him that he left in his will provision for lasting prayers for the souls of the men who helped him when he was a poor boy, as he planned to help many who should follow him.

Uncle Wallop

WIELD. It is small, pretty, and far away, with a church the Normans built, a good chancel arch, an arcaded font on five pillars, and a chalice made when Shakespeare was a boy. The handsome Norman doorway has a mass dial, and on the walls are many traces of old paintings. Here on a splendid alabaster monument lie Sir William Wallop and his third wife, he in Tudor armour, she very handsome in a simple headdress and with lovely lace cuffs to her sleeves. The long epitaph dismisses Sir William Wallop briefly as High Sheriff of the county and three times Mayor of Southampton, but draws a picture full of colour of his uncle who was on good terms with Henry the Eighth and went abroad as one of our ambassadors. We are told that he was admiral of a navy and captain of a thousand adventurers against the French. He was Sir John Wallop who died in 1617, and exquisitely carved he is here. On the opposite wall is a prettily carved memorial to a mother who died bringing her child into the world in the same year.

The City Unique in the Land

WINCHESTER. The finest country in the world has nothing finer. This is how an Englishman must feel on coming from King Alfred's grave. Our noblest king could have no nobler tomb than this, our ancient capital and still our proudest southern town.

We may not see King Alfred's grave, but it is here. His dust is mingling with the soil we tread. He stands majestic in its streets, and the city is his tomb. We cannot look unmoved at this cloaked figure in bronze, fashioned by Hamo Thornycroft and set up here to celebrate his thousandth year of fame. Set on a huge block of granite, Alfred stands in his cloak, raising his sword, looking into Winchester, to that great shrine where lie our Saxon kings; to that great hall with what they call King Arthur's Table; to William of Wykeham's famous school; up this street of narrow ways thronged by pilgrims for a thousand years. Towards all this he looks, to all this wonder of our past and all this beauty of today, and we feel that he is looking at Old England carrying on. The thread of life has not broken here since Alfred walked these streets, and we may wonder if there is any name on England's map that means so much to us as Winchester.

We may come into this historic city, capital of England before London, from the historic New Forest, from the heart of nature to the heart of history, from the place where the Conqueror's son fell dead to where they brought him on a cart, a hated thing, to lay him in this noble shrine; and we feel that it is all one, the rugged strength of the Forest and these massive stones of Winchester. They are the stuff of which England is made.

Here is every kind of thing belonging to our past: the old houses and hospitals, the castle and the gateway, the ancient cross, the quaint passages and crooked ways, the cloister and the green, the great walls and the winding streets, the serenity that comes from trees and meadows and river, our oldest great school and our greatest medieval church, cloistered ways of long ago and the matchless cloister to those hundreds of Winchester scholars who went out to France and did not come back—does it not seem that this Winchester is the epitome of England from Alfred until now?

This great street of our ancient capital begins low down near where the statue of Alfred stands, and widens on its way until the ancient houses narrow it and it begins to rise. Now it narrows and climbs to the great West Gate by which the Castle stands. The gate has stood where it is for 600 years, and has the openings through which molten lead could be poured on unwelcome guests, the slits through which arrows could be shot at an enemy, and the grooves in which the portcullis was let down. The grotesque heads with big holes for mouths are said to be the openings through which the drawbridge chains were worked. At the top of the street stands this old gate; at the bottom stands Alfred on an acre as holy as any in this land.

On one side of him is a green lawn leading to blocks of small houses still known as St John's Hospital, one of the oldest charities in the country (founded in 1289). It has a lovely old tower with a charming niche over the archway, and the houses are set round a lawn. On the other side of the statue is a garden where a thousand years ago Alfred's queen founded an abbey. Some years ago remains were found which it was believed might be Alfred's and they were placed under a flat stone to the east of the parish church of St Bartholomew's, Hyde.

Looking out on Alfred's statue is the 19th century Guildhall. It has a portrait of Charles the Second by Peter Lely in the banqueting room, and set in niches or at the windows are sculptures of historic figures and historic scenes. In the niches are lifesize figures of Egbert and Alfred, both armed, of the first mayor holding the charter of the city; and of Henry the Second who granted it. Over the windows are groups of King Arthur with his knights, the coronation of Egbert, Alfred in council, Canute laying his crown on the altar, the Conqueror compiling his Domesday Book, and the marriage of Mary Tudor to Philip of Spain. Six heads at the windows are those of William Rufus, Edward the Confessor, Richard Lionheart, Queen Elizabeth, and Queen Victoria, and the man with the curious name of Dunwallo Mulmutius, who fortified the city in 500 BC.

Halfway up the street, at the place where it begins to narrow by the ancient House of God Begot (named after its Saxon owner), stands the slender cross which was one of the architectural jewels with which Cardinal Beaufort adorned Winchester in the 15th century. It stands 43 feet high and is tucked away in a corner like a bit of medieval England, caring nothing for the roaring traffic of the 20th century passing by. On it are William of Wykeham with his staff and books, King Alfred and St John, the figure of an old mayor, and eight saints in niches round the top. Time has battered it, and once it came within an ace of being carried off to a private park. That was in 1770 when a rich man thought the cross would suit his garden and was only prevented from carrying it off by a great rally of the city apprentices. The 19th century restored it and renewed its figures, all except John the Evangelist, the only old figure looking down.

Just inside the passage by the cross is a queer little building which stands on the site of the Conqueror's palace. It is the tiny church of St Lawrence which every Bishop of Winchester must visit before he is enthroned. On his way to the cathedral the bishop turns into this small church and remains alone for a few minutes as if communing with the spirit of the Conqueror. In the days of the Norman Duke new bishops came to his palace as an act of loyalty before going to the cathedral, and so strong was the hold he had on men's minds that the custom was continued after his death. It is continued to this day, and every Bishop of Winchester for more than two centuries has visited this spot where the Conqueror lived when Winchester was his capital, and where, as we see, his rule still holds sway.

It may be thought that Winchester has not the impressive exterior of some of our cathedrals, but it is delightful to approach it through the little passage from the High Street, across the square where Alice Lisle was done to death, down the little avenue leading to the great west front. If the low central tower does not impress us (it is 140 feet high and 50 feet wide, and rises only 35 feet above the ridge of the transept roofs), the west end is striking with its colossal window, its great gable, and the slender turrets rising to great heights; and the east end has a charming exterior with captivating windows. And it is something to remember that the tower has dominated this scene for 800 years. Everywhere in these precincts we feel that we are in a world far removed from our own, the Dean's Stable has over it the 14th century timber roof of the old Pilgrim's Hall, the deanery itself is the very house in which Philip of Spain stayed on the eve of his marriage to Mary Tudor, and the very doors through which we walk out by the porter's lodge have been opening and shutting for 700 years.

One of the very first churches in England must have stood in this place, for descriptions have come down to us of a church built by the Roman Lucius in 164. It was destroyed during the persecution of the Emperor Diocletian, who threatened to annihilate Christianity, which has now built a temple in the ruins of his palace. The church was built again by the Saxons, and the son of a Saxon king lies here. A Latin poem by Wulstan describes the new cathedral consecrated in the presence of King Ethelred, and we know that after the Saxons had gone a kinsman of the Conqueror, Walkelyn, pulled down the Saxon church to its foundations. The story goes that he asked the king for as much oak as he could cut in four days and nights from Hampage Wood and that he set to work an army of men who removed the forest. The wonderful transepts are his work, but his tower fell in 1107, soon after William Rufus had been buried here, being built again in the original style. In 1189 Bishop de Lucy added the choir behind and the processional aisles, removing the Norman apse; and it was the 14th century building bishop, William of Edington, who refashioned the Norman nave and built the fine west front. It is still the longest cathedral in the land, but he shortened it by 40 feet, after which William of Wykeham, the greatest Winchester man who ever lived, transformed the cathedral and gave it the magnificence that we see, raising it half as high again, cutting back the Norman work, and facing it with new stone.

It is the longest medieval church still left in England, and was long the biggest cathedral in northern Europe, 185 yards from east to west, and covering about an acre and a half of space within its walls. It is the work of five centuries of human labour. We are surprised perhaps to see the vast nave looking so young in this old place, but though it was refashioned in the 15th century its proportions are Norman, and so is the core of the pillars, monsters 12 yards round. These huge piers are the work of the men who built the marvellous transepts 850 years ago; they were little hurt by the fall of the tower in 1107, and we look on them as their builders looked on them. They are an amazing spectacle, the arches rising to a wondrous height, massive and rugged yet so neatly built that they look almost like a solid block, so clean that we may think their builders had just gone home. We can sit and look on them from the old oak settle on which the Norman monks would sit, for it is here in the south transept. We have seen Norman doors still swinging on their hinges, Norman roofs sheltering Norman naves, even a Norman screen, but to sit on this oak settle is a rather intimate touch with far-off days; we half expect to hear an old monk say, "Tomorrow will be Friday," until, we remember we are in the 20th century, and that was long ago.

In the south transept is a superb piece of Norman carving on the wall, a double arch which at one time formed a noble entrance to what is now known as the Blois Treasury. It has been built up and a plain doorway remains; but these two arches of elegant lace-like carving in stone are where the Normans put them and are unsurpassed as an example of the delicacy of the Norman craftsman at his best. In the north transept are wall-paintings of a head of Our Lord, the Descent from the Cross, the Entombment, the Nativity, the Annunciation, the Entry into Jerusalem, and the Raising of Lazarus. There is in this transept, kept under glass, a model of the Mauretania given by the Cunard Company; it has been thought that it would be interesting to future generations to have this small copy of one of the first great ships of the 20th century in a cathedral which has made one of its bays into a Mariner's Chapel.

It is a moving thing to sit here looking on these mighty walls and thinking of the ancient builders, and yet it is the 20th century that has done for Winchester the most miraculous thing of all. This great place was sinking in a bog. In the first years of our century the famous engineer, Sir Francis Fox, was summoned to Winchester to meet a very anxious dean and chapter. He was told that the cathedral had sunk in some parts more than two feet, that walls and buttresses were leaning, arches distorted, great cracks showing everywhere, stones falling from the roof. Very old men could remember when the great west door was piled up with rubbish, and the whole cathedral neglected like some old barn, but Winchester was now the precious jewel in England's crown again and it was breaking to pieces. It was one of two catastrophies that threatened two of our noblest buildings of that time. St George's Chapel at Windsor was threatened with the loss of its wonderful roof, which had rested for centuries on inadequate foundations; Winchester was threatened with the loss of its cathedral which had rested for 800 years on timbers rotting in a bog. The 20th century has saved them both.

At Winchester Sir Francis Fox had a pit sunk by the south wall and he found that eight feet below the turf the masonry stopped. Where the masonry stopped were great trunks of beech trees, and the old story leapt to mind of Bishop Walkelyn begging leave of the Conqueror to take all the timber he could from Hampage Wood within four days. He collected a crowd of men and kept their axes swinging night and day, so that not a tree was standing after the fourth day. Here they laid them in a peat bog forming a raft on which to build this great cathedral. The little wood the Bishop's men cut down had borne its burden well for 800 years, but now it was sinking into the marsh. These great walls would not stand the vibration of hammers, the marshy foundations would not stand the wholesale pumping dry: it seemed that nothing but catastrophe awaited one of the noblest buildings standing in these islands. Then it was that one man's brain and one man's hands were equal to the need of the hour; Sir Francis Fox decided to underpin this great cathedral and William Walker undertook to do it for him. You will find their names on the west wall and there they should remain for all time, especially William Walker's. He saved this wonder for posterity. The Conqueror's cousin set the cathedral on a bog, William Walker set it on a rock.

He was a diver, and for over five years he worked under Winchester Cathedral. First the fabric was strengthened with scaffolding and by grouting, a mechanical operation reversing the action of a vacuum cleaner, exerting any pressure up to a hundred pounds an inch. By grouting the dust of ages was removed from these walls and owls, martins, rats, mice, and bees lurking in the cracks were blown out. Then water was forced in to cleanse the walls, coming back at first like ink; and finally a stream of cement was poured into the cracks. Now began the work of underpinning, and Walker went down into the bog grovelling in the dark just under the graves of kings. The water was so black with peat that artificial light was useless; he toiled in the darkness guided by touch alone. He removed the peat handful by handful and laid bags of concrete in its place on the gravel bottom. Four layers of concrete bags he laid to cut off the gravel from the water, which was then pumped from the particular pit in which he was working. Then concrete blocks were built above the bags and pinned securely to the underside of the Norman masonry. From pit to pit in the cathedral bed this heroic diver made his way like a water-rat, till at last, with his unaided hands, he had remade the bed of Winchester Cathedral, and set it on solid ground.

Since the year 639 a Christian Church has stood on this spot, though for a while Saxon invaders turned it into a temple of Wotan. On St Swithun's day in 1093 the Norman Cathedral was consecrated. On St Swithun's day in 1912 a vast concourse of people headed by King George the Fifth came to give thanks that this shrine of English history was saved. We do not wonder that there was great exultation; we could almost believe that the mighty dead rejoiced, Canute and Walkelyn, William of Wykeham, Izaak Walton, Jane Austen, and Alfred himself not far away. The Archbishop of Canterbury preached from the text "Prosper Thou the work of our hands upon us, O prosper Thou our handiwork," and as he listened, William Walker sitting there with the king and queen, prelates and peers, must have felt that he would not have changed his diving helmet for a crown.

It is the spaciousness of Winchester that must impress us all. If we are spellbound by the height and vastness of the nave with its two chantries to William of Wykeham and William of Edington, our astonishment grows as we come to the transepts with Norman arches piled upon each other.

Here is the oldest iron grille in England, unique for being Norman work, and believed to have been put here to keep back the crowd of pilgrims from St Swithun's Shrine (now vanished). These beautiful gates are made up of four pieces of ironwork, scrolls branching out of the central stem so as to form an impressive mass of quatrefoils. There are about 264 rings, with leaves in them, and the general effect is that of ostrich feathers. And we go through these 13th century Pilgrim Gates into the choir; out of the choir into the aisles with two great chantries, out of the aisles into the presbytery with two fine chapels, out of the presbytery to the east end with three more chapels, the lady chapel in their midst. As we walk about in this great place the wonder grows with every step we take.

By the great west door are two bronze figures of kings by Hubert Le Sueur; they are Charles the First and James the First, and the sculptor was paid £380 for them; it is said that they were buried in the Isle of Wight during the Civil War. Above the three tiers of arches resting on the stupendous Norman piers the stone vaulting hides the original timbers cut down in four days by Bishop Walkelyn. They must have been growing in Alfred's England and were shaped

Winchester   **King Alfred**

In Winchester Cathedral Close

Two of Winchester's Old Gateways

Winchester Cathedral   **The 15th Century Altar Screen**

and fixed in the roof by Norman builders, part of the same stock of timber with which the foundations were laid in a bog.

In this great nave are two medieval features not to be missed, the minstrel gallery with flowered cusps and bosses, resting in arches springing from the piers, and the lovely chantry of William of Wykeham, one of the best survivals of 14th century England. It is lofty, elegant, and of great beauty. Round this noble tomb runs a little arcade with a famous motto William gave to Winchester, "Manners makyth man." The chantry is divided by three arches with canopies carved to the shape of the arches, and the stonework everywhere is like fine lace. Graceful shafts support the canopies, with pinnacles rising to the level of the triforium. The vaulted ceiling is richly tinted with bosses of blue and gold. William of Wykeham lies in his bishop's robes, with his hands folded on his breast, his crozier on his shoulder, a serene figure with two angels at his head and three little men praying at his feet. It was decreed that three monks were to say mass here three times a day for a penny. The chantry has been restored in our time, and has ten fine statues by Sir George Frampton; they are the Madonna and Child with angels, the Good Shepherd, the Warden of New College with a student of that college, William of Wykeham with a Winchester boy, and four apostles (James, John, Peter, Paul).

Beyond this chantry lies the simpler chantry of William of Edington, who lies in the tomb in which he was laid in 1366; it is very plain. On the other side of the nave, between the two chantries, is the remarkable font, one of seven in England which came from Tournai in Belgium. Its great square bowl of blue-black marble stands on five pillars, and its four sides are filled with primitive medallions of symbolical doves and foliage, spandrels of flowers, doves drinking out of vases, and two groups of scenes in the life of Santa Claus, the beloved St Nicholas. It is a captivating little gallery of sculpture. Here is the man who promised Nicholas a gold cup on the birth of a son and heir, and we see the saint with this boy who has fallen overboard with the cup, Nicholas having been sent for to bring him back to life. Three men are shown watching him. One of the central panels shows the cruel butcher who cut off the heads of three boys, and another shows the benefactor who, when a nobleman became too poor to give his three daughters a dowry, presented each daughter with a bag of gold. Nicholas is shown again in front of a church

393

with the nobleman kneeling at his feet, and the three daughters with plaited hair congratulating each other on their good fortune, while a servant stands by with a hawk on his wrist. At this great font Izaak Walton saw his grandson christened; it was at a special silver font that they baptised here that Prince Arthur whose death opened the way to the throne for Henry the Eighth, and so transformed the face of Europe and changed the course of history.

The east end of this long cathedral rises 19 steps above the nave, and it is worthy to be exalted. It has unfortunately an oak screen, a noble piece of work by Sir Gilbert Scott, to break the incomparable line of this interior which runs for 175 yards from east to west, but beyond the screen it is all magnificent. It is lined at the west end with some of the finest medieval stalls in England, and at the east end with medieval stone screens on the top of which rest six painted chests holding all that remains of Saxon bishops and kings. The altar screen is one of the most exquisite pieces of stonework in the land. The 62 carved stalls, facing each other in the choir, are from the first years of the 14th century. Behind each stall is a wide arch with two trefoiled arches below a circle, the spandrels enriched with many birds, animals, and a mass of foliage; there are thousands of tiny heads. The canopies are decorated with folded leaves, and everywhere the carver's work is a pure delight. The misereres are older than the canopies, among the oldest in the land, and on them are all the quaint little figures we expect to find under these seats, and some surprises. There is a bishop in a fool's cap, the fox with the goose, a monk grinning at an owl, peasants kneeling and laughing, a man attacked by a wolf, an old woman with a cat and a distaff, and a delightful group of a sow piping away while her little pigs are munching, apparently enchanted by the music. The stalls end on one side by the magnificent pulpit given by Prior Silkstede, whose name it bears. It is 16th century; the nave pulpit is Jacobean. It is thought that they laid William Rufus near the choir pulpit on that day when Walter Tyrrell's arrow killed him in the New Forest, but his ashes are now mingled with the remains in the painted chests.

These are six of the most significant chests in all England. They have been cleaned and painted in our own time, restored as they were in medieval days, but in them is all that is left of twelve Saxon saints and kings. Here are the bones and ashes of the kings who founded the first cathedral, of one who gave a manor to it, of its first Saxon bishop, of the Conqueror's son William Rufus, of King Canute.

We do not now know the chests which contain particular kings, for the chests were opened in the Civil War and the remains have been mixed up. But these are the twelve who lie in these six chests:

Kinegils, King of the West Saxons and first founder of the cathedral.
Ethelwulf, King of Wessex and father of King Alfred.
King Egbert and Kenulph, builders of the first cathedral.
William Rufus, Bishop Stigand, Bishop Wina, and Bishop Alywn.
Eldred, the king buried here by his friend Dunstan, with this inscription: "The pious Eldred rests in this tomb, who admirably well governed this country of the Britons."
Edmund, eldest son of Alfred, crowned in his father's lifetime; his chest was inscribed: "Him whom this chest contains, and who swayed the royal sceptre while his father was still living, do Thou, O Christ, receive."
Canute and his Queen Emma, the fair maid of Normandy, on whose original chest were these words: "Here rests in this chest Queen Emma, She was first married to King Ethelred, and afterwards to King Canute: To the former she bare Edward, to the latter Hardicanute. She saw all these four kings wielding the sceptre, and thus was the wife and mother of English kings."

It was the Conqueror's grandson Henry of Blois, brother of King Stephen, who first gathered together these remains and placed them in coffers, but it was Bishop Fox in the 16th century who had made the chests we now see. Two chests contained inner coffers older than the chests themselves, the chests being actually covers dropped over the ancient coffers. These coffers are plain oak boxes with gabled lids and are probably 15th century. They are painted in red, green, yellow, and black, and between the bands are roses and crowns with scrolls bearing the names. Two of these coffers have been removed from their chests and replaced with lead coffers in which the bones rest; it has been done so that we may see these examples of medieval work and they are now in the north transept. They have actually held the dust of Saxon kings, having received them from the original coffers in which the Conqueror's grandson placed them. The outer chests as we see them are of painted oak, decorated in thin gilt lead, the lids having decorated shields and helmets, and of primitive construction. It is known that they were made in the 16th century, though two are known to have been replaced in 1661. Altogether there are in the chests the remains of 12 people from the year 643 to 1100. The ashes of William Rufus would be taken from his grave to be placed in the coffer; the stone in the choir pointed out as the Rufus Stone is not his grave. It was opened in the Civil War when the chests were disturbed, and in it were found a ring and a silver chalice, from which it is inferred that Henry de Blois was buried there.

Between the stone screens on which these chests rest rises the great glory of this choir, the original altar screen with the figures replaced on the eve of our own time. In front of us as we stand looking at the chests is one of the wonders of medieval England, the great screen which is hardly to be matched elsewhere. It is 15th century, and it fills the whole space of 1700 square feet between the pillars. It is of white stone arranged in three tiers of canopied niches filled with big and little statues of angels, saints, and kings. There are 64 statues in all, 19th century work set in 15th century niches. In the centre is an exquisite figure of Our Lord on the Cross, and below is a lovely carving of the Holy Family. Each tier has big figures and small ones. The big figures being saints, apostles, and martyrs, and the smaller group more intimately human folk, among them Izaak Walton, Bishop Ken, Archbishop Alphege, King Egbert, William of Wykeham, Cardinal Beaufort, Cardinal Wolsey, Canute, Alfred, Queen Matilda, Earl Godwin, and Edward the Confessor. The marvellous screen is one of the rarest possessions of Winchester with its great array of figures, its spires and crowns and buttresses, its friezes of flowers and leaves and quatrefoils, and its two doorways with four charming groups of 15th century carving on their spandrels showing scenes in the life of the Madonna with medieval painting fading away. The altar rails in front of the screen are by Grinling Gibbons, and the altar books, bound in red velvet, were given by Charles the Second.

As we stand in the presbytery amid all this wonder it is interesting to raise our eyes to the roof and consider a remarkable thing. The roof of the cathedral is the longest in the world. In the nave the ancient timbers have been covered by the later vaulting and new timbers have been added to them for strength; but they are all unseen. The casual observer will imagine that the whole length of the roof is stone, but in fact the roof of the presbytery is of wood. It is what the artist may consider to be in the nature of a sham, but it has been held by experts that this imitation roof is not less magnificent than the vaulted roofs it imitates. It has been made to look like stone, and it has a unique collection of bosses which have been bolted over the older bosses. Those running east from the altar representing the Last Days in Jerusalem: Gethsemane, Pilate and his wife, Peter's Denial, the Betrayal, Judas with the money bag, and the Crown of Thorns. There is more wooden roofing in the vaulting of the tower lantern; it is dated 1635, and has various heraldic devices of Charles Stuart, Archbishop Laud, and others, with a central emblem of the Trinity in which is an inscription containing a hidden date in Roman numerals, certain letters being picked out in red which, regarded as figures, make up the date 1635. On four of the corbels from which the choir roof springs are heads of our first Stuart kings, each repeated.

We come from the choir into aisles with two chantries that appeal to us for their beauty and their historic interest. The beautiful chantry is that of Bishop Fox, which has no tomb, but is rich with 55 vaulted niches of which no two are alike. They are mostly empty but one or two have modern sculptures in them, one a modern figure of St Birinus, and two memorials of men who fell in the war. Under an arched recess is one of the grim skeletons put on tombs in those days to teach humility. There is a stone skeleton in the companion chantry of Bishop Gardiner; it is the only thing in the chantry except for a chair upholstered in blue velvet. It is the chair in which Mary Tudor was married to Philip of Spain one summer's day in 1554, a year before Bishop Gardiner died. He would see her sitting in it ablaze with jewels, her black velvet dress a mass of precious stones, her mantle of gold falling from her shoulders, her ladies about her looking more like celestial beings, a writer said, than mortal creatures. Here sat this woman who married the man who was to send out the Armada for our destruction, this woman at whose word were burned alive 350 of the noblest men and women in the land. By her chair is her portrait, a copy of one made for Philip by Anthony More. She is wearing her famous pearl.

The aisles lead us into the presbytery where, immediately behind the choir screen, are three tombs in a row, those of Prior de Basynge and Bishop Sumner with Prior Silkstede between them. His coffin has been opened and in it was found a body wrapped in black serge, with the boots still on the feet. Beyond these are two more chantries, Bishop Waynflete's and Cardinal Beaufort's. The 15th century chantry of William Waynflete is elaborate with cornices and battlemented screens, and in it lies the bishop in his robes with mitre, gloves, and ring, his hands clasping a heart. Of Cardinal Beaufort's chantry an old writer said that a horseload of pinnacles had fallen from its canopy, and certainly it is a marvellous mass of carving. Its roof has rich fan tracery, and the cardinal lies in his scarlet cloak with his cardinal's tasselled hat, his calm face suggesting very little of the remorse he must have felt since he stood in Rouen marketplace and saw Joan in the fire. Joan now looks across the floor at him from her place between two piers, a golden figure set up in our time. Beyond the presbytery is the lady chapel with its painted walls, set in between the chapels in which lie the earl of Portland and Bishop Langton. The Earl of Portland was Charles Stuart's Lord High Treasurer, and he lies on his tomb in bronze sculptured by Hubert le Sueur with marble busts of his people round him. Bishop Langton was waiting to be enthroned at Canterbury when he died of plague in 1501.

It is the painted walls that we come to see in the lady chapel, for 450 years they were fading away. The chapel was transformed late in the 15th century when it received its beautiful vaulting, its exquisite wood carvings, and 22 painted scenes on the north and south walls. They are an interesting group of scenes in the life of the Madonna showing her portrait carried by the bishop to ward off plague, a thief delivered from the gallows, the Madonna begging an artist to make Satan ugly, and the very quaint story of a painter falling from the scaffold, saved in the nick of time by the Madonna on his canvas thrusting out her arm to grasp him. Not only has Professor Tristram brought to light these faded pictures for us, but he has reconstructed the paintings and hung them in panels.

As no cathedral can have everything, Winchester has only a little ancient glass. There are eight canopied figures in the clerestory windows, all from the 15th and 16th centuries; and both the east and the west windows have ancient fragments. In the east window the top central light has glass of William of Wykeham's time, and the great west window has two 14th century medallions made up of fragments set in the mosaic of the old glass which fills the window.

But two 20th century windows Winchester is proud of, one the stately coronation window of George the Sixth presented by the Glaziers Company; the other a tribute to George the Fifth presented by Americans. Both are the work of Mr Hugh Easton and are companion windows. George the Sixth and Queen Elizabeth are kneeling and holding their crowns, and above figures of Henry the Fourth and Joan of Navarre who were married in the cathedral; George the Fifth kneels in his robes as a Knight of the Garter, and the inspiration of the window has come from the vision of the Rider on the White Horse in the Apocalypse. The symbolism represents the growth of England through Saxon, Norman, and Tudor days, and there are splendid figures of Edward the Confessor and William the Conqueror.

It is for its architectural beauty rather than for its monuments that Winchester is renowned, but there have been a thousand burials here since the Reformation, and the cathedral has some impressive tombs. In this noble nave lie Jane Austen and Izaak Walton with no glorious monuments because they need none, though there is a window in memory of Izaak Walton, showing him with his friend Cotton on the bank of the River Itchen, St Catherine's Hill in the background; and there is a brass on the wall in memory of Jane Austen. On a stone on Walton's grave are these lines by Bishop Ken:

Alas! He's gone before
Gone to return no more;
Our panting hearts aspire
After their aged Sire,
Whose well-spent life did last
Full ninety years, and past.
But now he hath begun
That which will ne'er be done:
Crowned with eternal bliss,
We wish our souls with his.

In the north nave aisle lies the famous Mrs Montagu, of whom we read that she had beauty, wit, judgment, reputation, and riches, and, using them for the benefit of mankind, might be justly deemed an ornament to her sex and country.

A fine bronze panel on the south wall of the nave shows General Forrest on a horse; Sir George Prevost is remembered in a sculpture of a weeping woman; Richard Willis is reclining with a book; there is a lovely marble figure of Edward Browne lying at prayer and a relief of John Wickham, a surgeon; and a charming sculptured group in memory of Joseph Warton, Master of Winchester, shows an old man teaching four boys with eager faces. A mourning angel on the wall of the nave is very beautiful, and very appealing is the simple tribute to John Vaughan who

Loved the poor and the rich and won their hearts, loved this house of God and wrote its story, loved the birds of the air and the flowers of the fields, and taught others to do likewise.

Bishop Peter Mews, who fought in the Civil War and followed Charles the Second into exile, is shown on the wall of the nave with his crozier and mitre. Another fine relief is in memory of Dean Garnier, of whom we are told that he attended a levée held by Napoleon and heard Napoleon flatter Charles James Fox by telling him that he was the greatest man of the greatest country in the world. Among the monuments in the great space at the east end is one by Chantrey, showing Bishop Brownlow North kneeling at prayer; he was the bishop in whose time a vast sum was spent on restoring the cathedral, and he also restored Farnham Castle early last century. Standing under an arch surrounded by weapons of war is the Royalist Sir John Clobery who figured in the Civil War.

The oldest figure on a tomb is the black marble effigy of an unknown Norman priest in King John's day. The only ancient military figure (between the Beaufort and Waynflete chantries) is a knight lying in complete ringed armour of the 13th century his legs crossed, his feet on a lion, his head held up by angels, his right hand grasping his sword. Between two pillars of the nave lies Bishop Morley, founder of the cathedral library, friend of Charles Stuart and Izaak Walton; he has an epitaph he wrote himself at 80. Next to him is Bishop Hoadly, whose eloquence annoyed the ineloquent poet Alexander Pope; he has a medallion portrait. A brass tablet on one of the pillars (on the left of the steps leading to the choir) brings to mind one of the sad hours of Charles Stuart, for it concerns the death of Colonel Richard Boles, who fought with him at Edgehill and died in a pulpit in Hampshire. "Bring me a mourning scarf," said Charles when he heard the news, "I have lost one of the best commanders in the kingdom."

One monument only in this great place seems not to be wanted; it is that of Bishop Wilberforce in the south transept, one of the

The Lovely Chantries Round the Choir

Norman Transept

Choir Aisle

MATCHLESS WINCHESTER CATHEDRAL

Canopied Niches Behind the Altar

The Pulpit and Choir Stalls of Winchester

worst works of Sir Gilbert Scott. It is a pity that this stately transept, one of the wonders of England in itself, should be spoiled by the pompous absurdity of this canopied structure, and that the good name of Bishop Wilberforce should be linked with a monument so entirely out of place; we feel that he must be thankful to be sleeping not here but in the little green where his wife lies with the wife of Cardinal Manning by the east wall of a village church in Sussex.

It is said that in the space behind the altar known as the Feretory, and now used as a vestry, the Conqueror's son Richard lies in a marble coffin, and hereabouts also Alfred's eldest son was buried. Our last Danish king, Hardicanute, lies near him, and among all these ancient figures lies St Swithun who, as he lay dying, asked to be buried in the churchyard here so that his grave might receive the raindrops from the roof and be trodden by the feet of devout passers-by.

Nearly 1000 years ago he was brought indoors, and as the rain fell heavily at his reburial there has been foisted on to this good man the superstition that if it rains on St Swithun's day it will rain for 40 days more. It never has been so within recorded time. Under the altar in the 13th century there was laid the heart of Bishop Ethelmar, who is shown with his mitre and crozier in a massive sculpture set in a wall behind the choir. He was Aymer de Valence, Bishop of Winchester at the age of 23, but was not consecrated for some years.

He went to Rome on Ascension day in 1260, and on his way home was taken ill in Paris, where he died and was buried, his heart being sent here. His monument has several times been moved, and a strange discovery was made in 1912, when a workman digging at one of the buttresses outside found a long-lost piece of the monument with two finely carved shields on it. In replacing this there was found a small cavity with a tiny lead casket in it. The casket was 700 years old, but contained no heart, and on a search being made it was found that 250 years ago a workman accidentally broke this monument, and under it the heart was then found in a golden cup. The heart has now been reburied in the north aisle.

The pavement has diamond-shaped stones here and there, marking children's graves, and one epitaph says: "Dear to her friends, dearer to her parents, most dear to God."

Winchester has two great libraries, belonging to the Cathedral and the College. The Cathedral library, which was built while London lay in ashes after the Great Fire, is reached by an old wooden stairway from the south transept. It has gathered to itself rare treasures covering a thousand years. It has a charter signed by King Ethelwulf and his young son King Alfred, an 11th century copy of Bede, a 12th century copy of the life of Edward the Confessor and (rarest of all its treasures) a Bible of the 12th century written in three volumes on vellum. This superbly illuminated manuscript of the Bible is the finest work known of the Winchester school of craftsmen. It is thought that it would be read aloud in the refectory of St Swithun's monastery, and we know that it was considered to be a masterpiece in its own day, for it was borrowed for a monastery in Somerset so that the monks might copy it. It is the work of three artists. Another masterpiece of Anglo-Saxon art is the Benedictional produced for Bishop Ethelwold in the 10th century; it has 28 miniatures of which almost every one is the earliest treatment of the subject in English art. Among the treasures of the library is the original Cathedral Charter of Henry the Fifth, some early books with their chains, the staff of Bishop Fox and his ring, the ring of Bishop Gardiner, and the significant ring, set with a sapphire, which was found in the tomb supposed to be that of William Rufus; the significance of the ring is that it confirms the belief that the tomb is that of Henry of Blois.

In the College library is the craftsmanship of ages past, and on the flint walls of the old building in which the books are housed now hangs a wonder of our time which the ancient scholars could hardly have conceived. It is a marvellous Empire Clock, the works designed by Mr Henry Baker and Mr Robert Stewart, and the style of the clock by Sir Herbert Baker. Above the great circle with its dial of 24 hours is Phoebus Apollo with the horses of the sun; he rides in splendour above the hour of noon. Below the dial Selene is sleeping in her crescent moon at midnight. The clock has two dials, the inner one being a 12-hour clock, the outer one marking 24 hours, showing the time at Greenwich and throughout the Empire.

For the clockmaker this timepiece is a remarkable mechanical achievement, and for all of us it must seem a wonderful achievement of 20th century ingenuity. The various time zones are marked by symbols. The lion represents Greenwich time, South Africa has a winged springbok and the protea flower, India has the Great Star of India, and Burma a peacock's feather, Singapore an anchor. New Zealand and Australia are shown by the stars of the Southern Cross. For the Pacific Ocean is a three-masted ship and for Canada a maple leaf. The United Kingdom has the leek, the shamrock, the thistle, and the rose, Newfoundland has a fish, and for the Atlantic Ocean there is a two-masted ship. The movement of the clock is driven by an electric motor running at a constant speed of 120 revolutions a minute. The works have 13 ball bearings with about 100 tiny balls. The framework of the big dial is made of stainless steel, and there is a stainless steel second hand, marking every second of time as it passes, as well as the gilded hands which mark the minutes and the hours.

All over the world the traveller meets the scholar from the school, where *Manners makyth man*. Winchester has become one of the most renowned of all our public schools. It was accepted as a model for Eton to which it gave the first headmaster, William of Waynflete. Its great block of buildings have something in them of most of the centuries from the 14th till now, with two groups of cloisters separated by 500 years, and both famous, both stirring the mind in different ways. In one we think of the medieval monks walking round a gracious square with a beautiful chantry of 1420 in the midst of it; in the other we have all those 500 Wykehamists who gave their lives for England in the Great War. The chantry chapel in the old cloisters set in the centre of a square 132 feet long on each side, is in memory of a steward of the college in the 15th century. The college stands a little way out of the boundary of the Cathedral Close, and over its massive gateway is the date 1394 with an ancient statue of the Madonna and Child. We pass into the quadrangle, and over the middle gate is another Madonna with the Archangel Gabriel, and a statue of William of Wykeham. In the inner quadrangle (115 feet each way) is the great oak panelled hall and the kitchen with bagpipes carved over their windows. Over another window is a statue of Frugality with his ironbound chest, over the master's window is the schoolmaster and a scholar, and on the wall of a passage leading to the kitchen is the famous medieval painting of The Trusty Servant repainted in the time of George the Third to give this very pleasant ass a Brunswick uniform. Here is the refectory 63 feet long and with a fine vaulted roof made new in 1817. The chapel is delightful and still has the fan tracery vaulting of Wykeham's day, carved in wood; we come into the chapel through a vestibule decorated in memory of 13 boys who fell in the Crimean War. There are medieval windows with imposing buttresses, and the chapel has some of the most varied carvings we have seen, one of them a man haunted by goblins. The east window is a Jesse Tree, copied last century from the original, and at the bottom of it are the clerk of the works, the carpenter, and the glazier. The figure of King Ahaz was missing from this tree for 121 years and has been found among some old glass fragments in our time and replaced in its original position. The sacristy has a tabernacle of gold with a gold chalice given by Henry the Sixth, and the room above has still the original window shutters cased in iron, and the ancient chest containing the college deeds. There are three new figures in the centre of the reredos all by Mr E. G. Gillick; they are in memory of the war and represent a soldier, a mother, and Christ Triumphant. The actual school is a detached building said to have been designed by Christopher Wren, and on its west wall is a piece of advice which every Wykehamist loves, translated to mean "Learn, Leave, or be Licked."

Once a year Winchester College boys visit St Catherine's Hill a mile away in keeping with an ancient custom. On the hill are the foundations of St Catherine's Chapel, and close by the ruins is an ancient earthwork maze, the story being that it was dug by the Dulce Domum schoolboy who had been kept back at school during the holidays. It is just a legend, but it is an old tradition in Winchester which tells us of the writing of this famous poem sung by schoolboys for centuries. For some misdeed the Master of Winchester had ordered a scholar to be chained to a pillar while all the other Wykehamists went home for Whitsuntide, and it is said the boy in his grief wrote the words of Dulce Domum, to which the organist wrote a tune. The song was in Latin, but it was the first English Home Sweet Home. This is how the boy at the pillar begins:

> Sing a sweet melodious measure;
> Waft enchanting lays around:
> Home! a theme replete with pleasure;
> Home, a grateful theme resound.

In the chorus he appears to find solace by indulging in memories of his happy earlier years:

> *Home, sweet home! an ample treasure;*
> *Home! with every blessing crowned;*
> *Home! perpetual source of pleasure;*
> *Home! a noble strain resound.*

Wistfully he recalls the smiling meadows where he loved to stroll. He envies the swallow who

> *seeks her dwelling,*
> *And no longer loves to roam;*
> *Her example thus impelling,*
> *Let us seek our native home.*

His thoughts turn to his mother, and he thinks of the welcome that would have awaited him:

> *O what raptures, O what blisses,*
> *When we gain the heavenly gate!*
> *Mother's arms and mother's kisses*
> *There our blest arrival wait.*

Alas and alack, so great was his grief, so keen his remorse at the disgrace befalling him, that when the scholars returned to Winchester they found him dead at his pillar.

Every year in olden days Whitsuntide would be ushered in by a procession of masters, scholars, and choristers round the pillar to which the poor boy was chained, the pillar at which he wrote the first Home Sweet Home. They would chant his verses as they walked, keeping alive the mournful tale of Dulce Domum.

The most stirring corner of the college grounds is the cloister in memory of those 500 Wykehamists who gave up their lives to preserve their country's freedom. It is one of the noblest memorials of the Great War, the work of Sir Herbert Baker with a gallant band of sculptors, carvers, and building men. Sir Herbert has put on record the energy and pride of the men (practically all from Winchester) in their work, "their hammers and hods and chisels were never idle; we have been back in the good old days." We can well believe it, for this is more than brick and stone and brass; it is the human spirit made manifest.

This memorial is between the street and the Meads, and we come into it through the Boer War Gate which brings us into a small forecourt where a stone tablet is set in the old wall with John Bunyan's immortal words on it:

Then said he, My sword I give to him that shall succeed me in my pilgrimage, and my courage and skill to him that can get it; my marks and scars I carry with me, to be a witness for me that I have fought His battles; who will now be my rewarder. So he passed over, and all the trumpets sounded for him on the other side.

In this open court are four lion heads found in the old wall. In the cloister the four paved ways meet between the grass squares at a stone column crowned with a cross, and with two sentinel crusaders facing east and west guarding the symbol of sacrifice. Round the outer walls runs a prose poem in Bible language set in a background of flints. This is what it says:

Thanks be to God for the service of these five hundred Wykehamists, who were found faithful unto death amid the manifold chances of the Great War. In the day of battle they forgat not God, who created them to do His will, nor their country, the stronghold of freedom, nor their school, the mother of godliness and discipline. Strong in this threefold faith they went forth from home and kindred to the battlefields of the world, and treading the path of duty and sacrifice laid down their lives for mankind. Thou, therefore, for whom they died, seek not thine own, but serve as they served, and in peace or in war bear thyself ever as Christ's soldier, gentle in all things, valiant in action, steadfast in adversity.

In the spaces between the arches of the four walls are arms and badges of the navy and the national forces, and symbols of various aspects of life and government. On the inside walls are great tablets with the names of 500 Wykehamists who fell. The four corners are covered with domes dedicated to India and the Dominions, and in the pavement below them are round stones quarried in these dominions, and inlaid with brass symbols. Badges of the 120 regiments in which the 500 served are blazoned on the corbels and beams of the roof, and the remaining four badges, belonging to regiments most nearly associated with Winchester, are carried by angels on the oak struts of the roof.

Looking across the cloister from the north and south walls are two sculptured reliefs, one of an angel holding the symbol of Victory, the other of Peace with Plenty. In the floor at the gateway into the Meads are four small stones from the ruins of Ypres. In another pavement is an anchor of granite brought from the base of Table Mountain. Other pavements have crosses in stone from Australia and New Zealand, the Great Bear surrounded by maple leaves carved in marble from British Columbia, and the Star of India carved in marble such as is in the buildings of New Delhi. There are carved on the walls pack camels for Arabia, the Zimbabwe Bird, (Cecil Rhodes's favourite symbol), a Pacific canoe, a fully rigged East Indiaman, St George and the dragon, a rhinoceros and a snake, the peacock in his pride, fruited palm trees, the sacred rivers of the East, and other reliefs of scenes and symbols significant of those parts of the world in which some Wykehamist fell for Winchester and England.

Winchester has two castles, the castle on the hill, on its historic site by the West Gate, and the castle of the bishops down below. Both have Norman work in the walls, but one is a ruin and the other has been transformed in modern days.

The Norman Wolvesey Castle stands in ruin by the bishop's modern house; the ruin is picturesque and has a nearly perfect keep. The modern house was built from the design of Christopher Wren. Though his front has gone, part of his work remains, with the Tudor chapel, to which a new east window of great beauty has been added, the work of Christopher Webb. It has Our Lord in Majesty in its central light, with the Nativity below and angels above, and in the other lights are Alphege and Alfred, St Swithun, William of Wykeham, Henry de Blois, Lancelot Andrewes, Cardinal Beaufort holding a model of his tower at St Cross, and Christopher Wren holding a model of his palace. The colouring of the window is charming. Some of the materials of which this bishop's palace was built were brought from the Conqueror's palace burned down in 1102. Philip of Spain and Mary Tudor stayed here at the time of their marriage in the cathedral, but the site is more interesting because of the tradition (not warranted by excavation) that here Alfred's scribes compiled most of the Anglo-Saxon Chronicle. He ordered the book to be kept on a chain, and the original copy chained here on this very spot is now at Corpus Christi College, Cambridge.

The castle on the hill is chiefly interesting for the stirring events that have happened where it stands, but its great hall is impressive with columns of Purbeck marble, stone window seats, staples which held the old shutters, remains of the dais for the king, and remains of Norman work visible in the walls. On the wall at one end hangs what is called King Arthur's Round Table, made hundreds of years too late for him; it is certainly 400 years old and may be 600. It is 18 yards round and made of stout oak planks with spaces for King Arthur and 24 knights, and there are bullet marks which probably come from the days when the castle fell to Cromwell, who himself conducted a six-day siege. In front of the table is Sir Alfred Gilbert's bronze statue of Queen Victoria, done for her Jubilee. It is said that Queen Matilda escaped in a coffin from the castle during her bitter war with King Stephen. Certainly the castle was the home of the Conqueror and of William Rufus, and it was from here that Rufus set out for the hunt from which he did not return. He set out from the castle in the state of a king and returned to the cathedral with the indignity of a man unbeloved.

Here Henry the First was married and here Henry the Third was born. Here Henry the Fifth received ambassadors, and Henry the Sixth planned Eton College. Here all the Edwards held their Court. Here came Richard Lionheart with his nobles and here Prince Arthur was born. But more stirring than the memory of those things is the thought that here Sir Walter Raleigh was sentenced to death at the bidding of a King of England to please the King of Spain. He lived under the sentence for 15 years before he was finally tried again and hounded to his doom. One other tragic memory of injustice lives with it, for it was here that the foul Judge Jeffreys sentenced Alice Lisle to death; she was beheaded in the little square which opens on to the path leading to the west door of the cathedral. Just outside the castle walls is an obelisk set up in the streets to mark the place where peasants used to bring food for poor people stricken with plague; they would leave it on a stone for the victims to take away.

Of Winchester's group of churches a few have still something from Norman days. The Church of St John the Baptist has nave arcades from the days when the Norman style was passing into English; it has two aisles and a very narrow nave. The main walls are 13th century, the tower 15th. The roodloft stairs remain from the days before the Reformation and the rood screen remains with them. From the 14th century come two side screens in the

One of Winchester's Old Houses

A Glimpse of the Cathedral

WINCHESTER, ENGLAND'S OLD CAPITAL

Winchester   **St John's Hospital**

Winchester   **The Castle Hall**

Winchester   **The College Memorial Cloisters**

Winchester   **Norman Cloisters of the Cathedral**

The Home of the Brothers

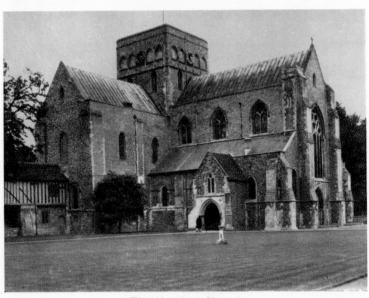

The Hospital Church

ST CROSS, WINCHESTER

chancel and stone seats for priests. The font is 15th century, the pulpit 16th, the bells 15th and 17th, and the candelabra 18th. There is a fragment of medieval glass, and still present in the church are the works of the 17th century clock. St Peter's has a tower built on a Norman base, and arches from the end of Norman days, with a little 15th century glass, a 15th century bell, and a 12th century font. St Swithun's Church has a 15th century font; St Bartholomew's with a Norman doorway has a 12th century font, an ancient pillar piscina, a 17th century altar and rails, a mass clock, and stone fragments from Hyde Abbey. The Church of St Maurice is 19th century, but has a 15th century tower and a Norman doorway, a screen in the chapel 600 years old, 15th century altar rails, and a mass dial. The 19th century Holy Trinity, in a charming churchyard, has wall-paintings of the Stations of the Cross. The Roman Catholic Church in St Peter's Street has a fine early Norman gateway which was the west doorway of a vanished church. St Michael's Church in Kingsgate Street has a mass dial on its wall which told the time of mass in Saxon days, and a 17th century font; the church has been rebuilt but the medieval tower remains. St Thomas's has been made new, and has a silver almsdish of the 17th century.

For those who think a cathedral city could have no more, a walk to St Cross brings an impressive surprise. We may come to it through the streets or over the meadows, and we shall be greeted as pilgrims have been greeted here for 800 years, with the offer of the Wayfarer's Dole, a piece of bread and a drink. Through all these centuries it has been refused to none who ask.

A gabled archway brings us to a small courtyard across which rises the noble tower of Cardinal Beaufort's gateway into one of the oldest houses of charity in England, founded by Henry of Blois for the daily feeding of 100 poor men as well as housing and clothing and feeding 13 more too old and sick to help themselves. He appointed a master to look after them, and gave them warm black gowns to wear and a silver cross as their badge. When 300 years had gone by Cardinal Beaufort, who took the king's crown as security for a loan, gave a new lease of life to this house of poverty and richly endowed it with beauty and new buildings. He built houses for 2 priests, 3 sisters, and 35 brethren, and still the good work goes on about his gateway, on which he kneels in stone under one of three lovely niches, matched by a fine modern figure of the Madonna.

Beyond the gateway lies a delightful green quadrangle, with a charming architectural group round it. In front of us is one of the finest Norman churches in these islands; on our right is the great hall and the kitchen, across the lawn are the ancient cottages of the brethren, with tall chimneys, mullioned windows, and pointed doorways; and facing them is the long 16th century timbered ambulatory, carrying above it the infirmary, whose east window opens into the church so that in olden days an ailing brother might sit there and be comforted. The oriel window resting on two brick arches and a central column belongs to the room of the nuns. A doorway in the wall here opens on to a lawn in which Dendy Sadler found the inspiration for his famous pictures of Thursday and Friday.

The church is Norman and English, a massive block with a low central tower like Winchester's, which we may climb to look out across the trees, rivers, and meadows to St Catherine's Hill or to wander along the heights of the clerestory which is a great adventure here. Outside the chancel are two lovely stone brackets on a pillar and by them an exquisite little piscina on a tiny column; and at a corner of the south transept wall is an extraordinary triple arch with beautiful carving, it may have been a doorway. At the east end is a beautiful little square turret. The walls have thirty kinds of mason's marks put here by the medieval builders.

He would be dull indeed who could move about this ancient haunt of charity and not be stirred with the thought of all the generations of old folk who have come this way before us, have lived here in the evening of their days, sat in these chairs at these tables. A raised dais faces us as we come into the old quarters of the Brethren of St Cross and still on the long table are the pewter dishes, the tall leathern jugs, the bell which rang to summon the brothers to meals, the pair of wooden candlesticks they used, and the two wooden saltcellars, all from Cardinal Beaufort's time. There are wonderful chairs with seats cut out of the round of a solid oak trunk, and a great oval table with a marble top at which sat Cardinal Beaufort, William of Wykeham, and even Henry of Blois, for it is believed that the table came from Winchester Castle, where it was used for feasting in the Conqueror's day. Far more thrilling it is than the King

Arthur's Table hanging there which King Arthur never saw. On this table of St Cross Bishop Blois would pay his hundred masons a penny a day to build his palace.

The roof of this great hall was built in the 14th century from timbers believed to have been the first Spanish chestnuts brought into England. Behind the dais is splendid panelling, the minstrel gallery with the line of leather fire buckets hanging from it, a lovely heraldic window in which we noticed the cardinal's red hat, and a wooden frame with a calendar put here 200 years ago. The kitchen, small and stone-flagged, brings us into the very heart of a homely and human past, for at this great fireplace, where the meals of the brethren, their guests, and their masters were prepared for centuries, is a stupendous tray for meats and a remarkable windlass still working, with the old brick oven, the spits and jacks for roasting, and the baking dishes, all now pensioned off after their long service for the poor.

Nothing was too good for this fine place, and we found in its windows fragments of some of the rarest glass in England, coming from the 12th century. In the passage to the kitchen is a small window with the arms of Robert Sherborne, a master in 1495, with his motto, "I have loved wisdom." But it is over the doorway that we find the 12th century glass, a speck of gold and blue above some 14th century medallions. Robert Sherborne's glass is interesting because in it is a curiously written date from the days before the figures 4 and 5 were generally used, and 4 was shown as half of 8, and 5 as half of the Roman X.

The noble church of St Cross, built for these poor brethren, is a majestic place. It was set up when our English builders were forming their own ideas, when the pure round arch was becoming pointed, the windows were becoming more important, and the walls less massive. The great piers on which the arches rest in the nave are farther round than they are high, and rest on bases with four sculptures at the corners, each group of four making a series, such as the Cycle of Man. Everywhere the work is magnificent; we see the Norman merging into the English style with all its changes, to the eve of the greatest change of all in the 15th century. Every style of Norman ornament is found in this most lovely place and the rich carving of the arches, doorways, windows and the rib of the vaulting is an unusual and captivating picture. The church is 125 feet long and 115 wide at the transepts. The windows are Norman and Transitional in the nave and choir aisles, and later in the clerestory. In the nave of three bays the work is Norman and English too; in the string course we can see where the Norman craftsmen ended and the English craftsmen took it up, a bunch of grapes marking the change. We see also the mark of the change at the Reformation, for the old roodloft was cut away with a saw and the ends of the timbers are left. The rich and intricate moulding round the windows and the vaultings is Norman; so is the massive font of Purbeck marble which came from the old Church of St Faith.

The windows in the north transept are very interesting, and one of them is set askew to allow the sunlight to fall on a Madonna niched in a pillar; the glass through which the light falls is 14th century. The best glass at St Cross is in the oldest part of the church, the four windows of the triforium in the chancel. There is an ancient portrait of St Gregory in a window of the clerestory showing him with his bishop's staff. The glass is 15th century, and has fine figures of St Catherine, St Swithun, St John, and a lovely Madonna. There is some fine modern glass from the Powell workshops, showing the Wise Men, Christ in Majesty, and the Crucifixion.

The lady chapel is rich in beauty, with carved ribs on the vaulted ceiling and running round a lovely window. The roof is remarkable and has zigzag moulding by the Normans. The chapel has two handsome Tudor screens, Elizabethan altar rails, and a piscina with a little central column and two canopies. On the altar are fragments of a painting of the martyrdom of Thomas Becket, and above the altar is a triptych by Jan de Mabuse painted about 1500 and bought for £20. It shows the Nativity, with a monk offering the Child a pear, and has two panels of St Barbara with a book and St Catherine with a wheel. Standing by the altar is Cardinal Beaufort's chair, and there are two 14th century stalls on which have been carved dolphins putting out very long tongues.

In the peace memorial chapel at St Cross is what is probably the first memorial set up in England to the men who never came back; it was erected a month before the Armistice, and is a lovely bronze of St George by Sir George Frampton. The oak reredos of the chapel is by Sir Thomas Jackson, the window is by Powell and has a very fine figure of Fortitude. There is much stone canopy work, and in the roof is a remarkable oak and acorn boss of the 12th century. In the chancel, dividing it from the choir aisle, is a medieval stone screen entirely filling a great arch, and on the chancel and chapel walls are three or four pieces from a screen of 1529 carved with quaint fancies and little figures. There is an extraordinary bird unknown to zoology on the lectern, having an eagle's body with a parrot's head, webbed feet and terrible talons. It is very old, and the story is that it was to have been destroyed long ago, but was cut up by a man so cleverly that he was able to put it together again. The choir-stalls have finely carved canopies, and the stalls themselves are scarred all over with the initials and patterns cut by the choristers.

Among other notable possessions of the church is a solid gold chalice with a diamond cross, a massive altar stone which has been rescued from a ditch, a lovely fragment of the old reredos, a brass of John Campeden who did the wonderful series of corbels in the tower, two other brasses showing Richard Harward, a 15th century warden, and Thomas Lawne, a rector of Mottisfont who died in 1518, patches of frescoes fading away, chevron carving round a window with 64 little birds in the spacings, a serpent forming an arch above a door, and two wooden crosses from France.

Such is the church with its great tradition and its true nobility, set up for the Hospital of St Cross. There is something pathetic in the sight of these old brethren ending the evening of their days in this old place, in the atmosphere sanctified by the serenity of so many generations in this ancient capital of England.

The Norman at His Best

WINCHFIELD. It has a rare good fortune in the possession of a marvellous little Norman church. It might be thought a pocket edition of the wonderful St Cross at Winchester, so rich and generous is the decoration beneath its red roof and its little red-capped tower.

Until we came to Winchfield it had seemed to us that our capacity for wonder at anything Norman had been exhausted, but, having stopped under the old porch to admire a splendid Norman doorway with richly carved arches and sides, and great fern leaves round its capitals, we entered to come upon a surprise indeed. We may wonder if there is a chancel arch like Winchfield's anywhere else. Rich and ornate beyond the habit of the Norman mason, it is remarkable also for being only six feet wide, one of the narrowest of its period in England. So rich and deep are the mouldings that they remind us of work in a Moorish shrine. Fern leaves uncurl round the capitals, a characteristic of the 13th century. The most unusual feature is a series of 11 rolls attached like miniature stone rollers to the soffit of the arch. The round piers are the only portions of this striking archway which are not elaborately carved.

The arch leads into a chancel lit by narrow windows zigzagged round with more carving. On a pillar a tiny Norman piscina blossoms among stone leaves. It is all very dark, but a switch is here to light up all this beauty, and memorable is the glow of it behind the Norman arch. So small is this chancel that it can hold only two little benches, ancient and modern, for two little choirboys to squeeze into each. The rector has his seat, another old one, just behind the splendid 17th century pulpit, a beauty covered with carving. Four upper panels have vases of flowers, and from among the curious interlaced design of the four lower panels quaint cherubs look out at us. An ancient oak pew in front of the pulpit has served as pattern for others here. Some think it 700 years old, and now it is crumbling before our eyes.

The font is Norman, with odd pillars of Purbeck marble at its base; yet it looks new, and this modern appearance is added to by the text stamped in lead which someone who should have known better has bound round it. Behind is a plain Norman tower arch. Much of the Norman work has been restored and some has been copied; but we shall never forget the glory of the real Norman work here.

On the walls the initials of this church of St Mary are repeated over and over again in wrought iron wherever a stay has been put in to strengthen the old structure outside, the initials forming a curious kind of ornamentation.

The church has few old neighbours, though one or two fields distant is the old Court House, a pleasant gabled building.

The Table's Story

WOLVERTON. It lies in lovely country made still lovelier by the fine park of Wolverton House, and has a charming red brick church in classic style, built when new churches were rare, in the 18th century. It is thought the architect may have been a pupil of Christopher Wren. The church has been attacked by fire, and has lost its minstrel gallery and some of its character at the hand of the 19th century restorer; but it has kept its fine panelled door, its delightful pews, its beautiful reredos, and the sturdy reading desk and pulpit (both exactly alike) into each of which the preacher enters by an arch. The vase-like font has been rescued from the churchyard after years of banishment, and the nave roof contains the elegant 15th century timbers from this church's predecessor. By the door is a table with a quaint little account of itself on a brass plate. It says:

> My legs were once window frames.
> My sides were part of the parish chest.
> My top belonged to the pews of the church
> Before it was restored.

Poor Rhymer

WONSTON. Its church has suffered most unhappily from fire, but it has a 400-year-old grey tower, battlemented and with a handsome traceried window in it. There is an old nail-studded door with an ancient locking-bar fitted in the wall, and under the tower is a quaint tablet put up in 1714 with these words by a struggling rhymer:

> The best Benefactor to this church (burnt by fire)
> Was (ten guineas, a gift by) John Wallop Esquire.

On the sunny wall are three dials which told the time of mass in the days before clocks. The south doorway and the pointed chancel arch with its sculptured capitals were both made about 1200. So were the deeply splayed side windows of the chancel, each filled with an attractive Bible figure in modern glass. There is an old chair richly carved in the sanctuary. The lychgate is modern and made of splendid timbers; the old rectory, in a beautiful garden, is said to have had its beginning in the 14th century.

Old Yew

WOODCOTT. A tiny place with lovely views and far horizons, we feel it is in the keeping of its mighty yew, a giant very much alive if a little decrepit. Protected by a line of noble beeches from the winds which sweep over this churchyard, the veteran is one of the biggest yews in Hampshire, with a girth of more than 27 feet. The little church has been made new more than once, and its chief delight is its old carving from Belgium. Rich and dark, the altar rails are cut with ornamental quatrefoils, the pulpit has a figure with a sword, and the reading desk has St Peter with his keys. The carving also includes quaint little angel figures, one touching his lips as if to ask our silence.

The Pictures at the Village Hall

WOODGREEN. Through quiet meadows watered by the River Avon and a hundred little streams, by an old water mill where the turning of the busy wheel drowns the ripple of the river we come to this small place where history has taken shape in beautiful form and colour on the walls of the village hall. There seems at first but a small number of houses in gardens overflowing with Spring flowers, grouped about the hall and the church room; for there is no church; but wandering in the lanes we find many pleasant homes in woodlands once part of the New Forest.

It was the happy idea of two artists staying in this fair countryside to record the daily life and pleasures of the little community on the walls of their village room, the centre of their interests and recreations. The fund for the building of the hall was started by the women of the village, and in 1930, when the hall was opened, the two friendly artists (Mr R. W. Baker and Mr E. R. Payne) began their work of love. For 18 months they painted away, having as models the men, women, and children of the village; even the local cows and pigs were pressed into the service. It was a great conception to reproduce them all on the walls of the room, looking for all the world just as they work and play and walk about the village street, so that they can see and recognise themselves and each other as they meet in daily life.

Appropriately in this land of flowering orchards the biggest scene is the apple-gathering, where strong and nimble youths among the laden boughs are plucking the ripe fruit which is collected by the less active workers below. Another group is busy with the cider-press. The local folk-dancing team is seen footing it merrily to the strains of a fiddle, and charming is a demure group of little maidens, all in their Sunday best, as they are seen in the children's choir on anniversary days at the Methodist chapel. There are well-known

William of Wykeham's Tomb

Statues in the Wykeham Chantry

SCULPTURES IN WINCHESTER CATHEDRAL

The Rich Decoration of the Triforium

Roof and Reredos of William Wayneflete's Chantry

The Bench of the Norman Monks

WINCHESTER CATHEDRAL'S ANCIENT TREASURES

faces in the cricket field and at the local flower show, and the unwearying caretaker, so proud of it all, keeping it as lovingly as her own parlour when we called, is pictured cutting bread and butter for a feast. Perhaps the loveliest bit of all is the framing of the little stage in three scenes (Morning, Noon, and Night) where the crowing cock rouses the world for the day's activities, the haymakers rest and take their noontide meal under a spreading tree, and as darkness falls while bats flit to and fro "the moping owl doth to the moon complain."

Well might Sir William Rothenstein suggest, when he came down to unveil these paintings, that this was the beginning of a new development in the history of English painting. The hall is in use nearly every day and sometimes twice a day for the many-sided interests of this delightful village. As we reluctantly leave it we realise that the happiness it holds is for the future as much as for the present, and those who now dwell here, when old and feeble, will live their youth again at the sight of the gay and gallant lads and lasses pictured on the walls.

WOOLTON HILL. It has little or nothing that is old, but it has things that are beautiful, for among several attractive windows in this church we remember a fine figure of Christ in a silver robe with a red cloak. It is here in memory of a ten-year friendship, and there is another window with St John in a green robe bearing a golden chalice in memory of a vicar. One of the porches is a mother's memory of two sons who did not come back from the war. There is a window of Faith, Hope, and Charity given by neighbours and friends in memory of a lady much beloved. The reredos is a tribute to a soldier and a sailor; it is a sculpture of the Last Supper in stone, a group of fine figures under canopies. Outside the windows is a variety of sculptured heads.

The Young Man in Armour

WOOTTON ST LAWRENCE. Although made new in the 19th century, the church has still its 14th century tower, a Norman doorway with a richly decorated arch, a sturdy Norman arcade, and four bells which have called the people to worship for over 350 years. There is an almsdish made in Dr Johnson's time and a small pewter basin engraved in 1743.

But the most striking possession of the church is a marble figure of Sir Thomas Hooke, a noble piece of work. He is a handsome young man in 17th century armour, reclining under a canopy on a rush mattress, his long curled hair falling to his shoulders, his face turned to the altar. Above him, on an iron bracket, hang his gauntlets, helmet, and spurs, and a short dagger-like sword in a velvet scabbard. There is a good modern window with expressive figures of Abraham and Moses representing Faith and Justice. The whole sanctuary is paved with old heraldic tombstones, one carved with much ornament, among which is a very quaint rabbit carrying three ears of corn. Behind the reredos we come upon a far more ancient coffin lid decorated with a cross. In the nave is a bust of William Wither, who died in 1733, his fine head reminding us of the Roman emperors.

A lovely yew in the churchyard has great branches bowing in an almost perfect ring. We imagine it has been here 200 years.

The Precious Crystal Bowl

YATELEY. Its chief treasure is a rare cup presented to the church by Mistress Sarah Cocks in 1675, and thought to be the work of Dutch artists in the Elizabethan Era. It is a delicate and very lovely thing of great worth, its bowl of rock crystal with a little medallion of Susannah and the Elders at the bottom, its metal parts of silver-gilt embossed and engraved with fruit, flowers, and cherubs. By it lie fragments of the lost cover, of which there is a reconstruction in the vestry. The cup has not been without adventures, for it was once dropped and broken by the parish clerk, and once stolen. Fortunately it was found the next day in the churchyard ditch, and now it is kept for all to see in a little safe in the wall.

The chancel is a place of great interest. The screen has graceful tracery and is partly 15th century. The glass in the 13th century east window is the beautiful work of William Morris and Burne-Jones, showing Peter and John and the King Omnipotent, each against a background of twining leaves. On the doorway is a little mass dial, and on the floor are many ancient red and yellow tiles with horsemen, dragons, kings and queer figures on them. In the north wall are a blocked archway and a little peephole to match, both from the 14th century, and together they have a story to tell, for they belonged to an anchorite's cell. The cell was paved with the tiles now in the chancel, and its foundations show that it was a little room 8 feet by 11, the usual size for such a dwelling. Within its walls, with these two openings into the chancel, there lived 600 years ago a man or a woman cut off from the world.

A brass shield by the chancel screen tells how there hung here for five years the colours of the 4th King's Own, before Yateley gave them back to the regiment. It had been carried into action in the Peninsular War, the war with America, and at Waterloo. More thrilling is the memorial on the wall with Yateley's 40 immortal names of our own time. It has the unforgettable words from the last despatch of Sir Douglas Haig, written in the hour of grief and triumph:

By the long road they trod with so much faith and with such devoted and self-sacrificing bravery we have arrived at Victory, and today they have their reward.

The chancel and nave walls are 700 years old, and the nave arches were made of chalk from Odiham 600 years ago. The north doorway is also chalk, and has still the line of moulding the Normans gave it. The south doorway has a deep hole in the wall for the reception of a locking bar. The big font is 14th century. The candlesticks are possibly medieval.

The tower is supported by huge 15th century beams criss-crossing all about us and making us think of a barn. The clock was made in Cromwell's time, and is constructed like the one in the famous Curfew Tower at Windsor. Two bells are very old, one about 1420; and in the vestry are some other old music-makers of Yateley, its little collection of instruments once used in the vanished western gallery.

On a raised platform under the tower's timbers is the 16th century brass portrait of William Lawerd, in a long furred gown, with his wife in a kennel headdress, and their nine sons and only daughter. Near by in brass is the head of pretty Elizabeth Morflett, and an unknown bearded man in a ruff and gown. On the other side of the tower is a portrait of William Rugg as he was 400 years ago, with his tall wife, four sons, and seven daughters.

The simple lychgate has been here 300 years, and its ingenious swinging gate has been on its hinges since 1800. Through it a curate passed many thousands of times last century, for he remained curate 53 years.

ISLE OF WIGHT

The Garden Island

IT has been said by one who goes sailing in the waters of the Solent that the little Isle of Wight, set in its silver sea, looks like a tapestry. Certainly it looks like what it is, an island paradise.

It is one of the most delightful regions of England, a spectacle never to be forgotten if we come to it in rhododendron time or hydrangea and fuchsia time, for everywhere these grow luxuriantly, and with a host of other flowers and ferns they make the Isle of Wight a heavenly hunting ground for botanists. Its birds and animals are exceptional, and it is closely linked with the annual migrations of Autumn and Spring.

It is not without good reason that it is called the Garden Island. It has all the interest of a piece of England where men have lived for centuries and built castles and churches and harbours and great houses, and the lover of antiquity finds here something Roman, something Saxon, something Norman, and many medieval churches; but it is nature rather than man that has made this island one of the most tranquil and entrancing spots we could wish to see, for up on the downs or down by the sea it is a rare and lovely place, and for those who come to it when Spring is breaking into Summer there is no spectacle in England more enchanting.

If we would forget the world and all its troubles we need but take a ferry-boat from Lymington, cross to the lovely little harbour of Yarmouth, looking like a rainbow with its yachts and sailing-boats, pack up our kitbag in some such lovely corner as Totland Bay, and walk slowly up the downs until we reach a height with the island stretching along in front of us, with the Solent on one side and the Channel on the other.

It may be at Tennyson's Cross, the wonderful down on which the poet loved to walk; there is no scene more delightful, more invigorating, within a few hours of London. Or it may be Brighstone Down, or Arreton, or St Catherine's Hill, or Brading, or Bonchurch, or Shanklin—it matters not where we are on these great heights; we shall find tranquillity. If we would have as thrilling a motor ride as England can afford us we can run round the south of the island from end to end with the sea hardly out of our sight, beginning at Freshwater Bay, near Tennyson's home, on to St Catherine's Point, and in the shade of the Undercliff to Ventnor and Bonchurch, Shanklin and Sandown. For those who walk, or for those who use a car to discover how nature hides her loveliness in little places, there are lanes that bring us to landscapes of surpassing beauty, fields enchanted by nature's own hand, with acres of golden buttercups and purple clover and campion; we have seen no green fields in England more beautiful than these when Sumer is a-cumen in. The banks and hedgerows are aglow, the gardens creep over the walls, the wayside is ablaze with colour. Lost in the heart of this little island, or up on the downs, or riding between the green hills and the sea, we are one with nature, and in her Island Garden there is peace.

The Isle of Wight is a little smaller than our smallest county, being only 147 square miles, 22 miles from the Foreland in the east to the Needles in the west, and 13 miles from Cowes facing Southampton Water to St Catherine's Point jutting out into the English Channel. It is interesting to look at it from the sea.

Approaching from the east we come to Bembridge Point in a bower of trees, and making our way up Spithead we pass Ryde climbing up its hill, and next come the wooded shores of Binstead, Wootton, Osborne (white and plain) and Old Castle Point. Beyond this East and West Cowes face each other across Medina River, with an estuary extending inland five miles to Newport. Newport is the island capital with Carisbrooke Castle behind it. Low-lying meadows line the shores of the Solent as far as Yarmouth in the west, a delightful little town with an inlet extending to Freshwater. We next round Cliff End barely a mile from Hurst Castle on the mainland and we are in sight of the Needles, famous all the world over, with a frowning down above them. Here is Totland Bay, and Alum Bay with the remarkable coloured strata, from where children love to bring home bottlefuls of the sands. Here we notice the beautiful lines made by flints in the long regiment of steep white cliffs crowned by Tennyson's Cross. If we climb up to this cross, as Tennyson loved to do in the quiet of the evening, we are rewarded with a glorious view of land and sea.

We round the Needles and sail east with the downs on our horizon and many chines cut in the coast, each chine with its tiny stream and many of them with landslips. Sailing on we come to St Catherine's Point with its bird-haunted lighthouse, and St Catherine's Hill behind it rising 781 feet, the beginning of another range of chalk downs running to St Boniface a few feet higher, the very top of the island. We see the edge of this range forming the inland cliffs which give Ventnor half its glory and are ever basking in the sun; and now we turn north again and pass Old Shanklin with its astonishing chine, its lovely old village, and the delightful Keats Green, Sandown with the great bay pointed by Culver's snow-white cliff, and so back to the Foreland and Bembridge.

Bembridge, always famous as a great point of the Isle of Wight, has built up a fine reputation by its school, and it has an excellent Ruskin Gallery which we may see. At the opposite point of the island we come upon the memory of Tennyson, who lived here and roamed about these downs, and here met Garibaldi. If we follow the River Yar inland from Bembridge we come to Brading, with the church that has stood 800 years and something of the villa that has been here eighteen centuries. It is a remarkable survival of the Roman Empire, with fascinating pavement mosaics. At the head of the Yar valley we come to Godshill, charming with its thatched cottages in the shadow of the medieval church tower; and on the downs at Arreton remains of the Bronze Age have been found, some of which we see in Carisbrooke's museum.

It is Carisbrooke that stirs historic memories in the island. Who can look up at this great skyline, with its towers and battlemented walls, without being moved by the thought of the captive king and his delicate little daughter? Through this Tudor gateway, through these very doors, Charles Stuart passed, still dreaming that he could escape the net stern fate was weaving round him; and when it was all over it was to this island fortress that Cromwell in a merciless moment sent the king's little daughter to languish and to die. There is no more pathetic monument in the island than her white figure sheltered in Newport church. It is sad to think of youth dying with all this beauty round it, but the thought is with us again as we think of Keats, seeking here the health and strength that never came, writing here that first line of Endymion which nowhere else could have been written more fittingly, A thing of beauty is a joy for ever. Here have come poets and writers and artists too many to remember; here George Morland painted his rustic masterpieces, and so little has the interior of the island changed since then that we seem to imagine that some of these little barns are in his pictures.

All the world knows of the enchanting spectacles seen every year at Cowes, which gives to the island ship-building, the only important industry it has with one exception—the tourist industry, which flourishes because in all our islands is no more restful little place to come to than these few square miles set like a diamond in the sea.

Eight Saxon Windows

ARRETON. It takes us back a thousand years in its wonderful church, which has a Saxon doorway and eight Saxon windows, a Saxon piscina, and a piece of Saxon sculpture. Yet not even these exhaust the interest of Arreton, for it has a perfect Jacobean farmhouse with a wing at each end, a pond sheltered by willows, charming cottages tucked away behind the inn, and groups of lovely trees with a glorious copper beech by the church gate.

A splendid Tudor porch, with a vaulted roof, leads us into one of the most charming interiors in the Isle of Wight. Nearly every building century has given it something. It is long, lofty, and wide, with a fine nave arcade, graceful chancel arches, beautiful windows, a 700-year-old font and a new one, a handsome pulpit made by a local carpenter from Jacobean panelling found in an inn, the old rood stairs, a chest made soon after Shakespeare died, and a copy of the first edition of Foxe's Book of Martyrs. In the south chapel is a beautifully carved table made by an Elizabethan craftsman, and two brasses. One brass has a poem on William Serle telling us of the charities he left and that he died a bachelor in 1595. The other brass is a headless figure in 14th century armour, all that is left of the portrait of Harry Hawles, who has a rhyme ending:

> Long tyme steward of the Ysle of Wyght
> Have m'cy on hym, God ful of myght.

The Saxon builder and the medieval craftsman bequeathed to Arreton a rich and varied legacy. Few churches can have more Saxon windows, six of them circular (three on each side of the nave with quatrefoil tracery of a later date) and two of them round-headed. One of the round-headed windows is above the tiny Saxon doorway leading into the 14th century tower. But the best of this group of Saxon windows is in the chancel, the narrow and deeply splayed window making a lovely setting for a crucifixion scene. Set in the wall of the north aisle are two fragments of sculpture, one a

Saxon carving of the Ascension fading out of recognition, the other a lifelike dragon's head from a 12th century statue of St George. The new font, which has a cover carved by a local lady, stands on an ancient pillar and has one ancient panel in the sides of the bowl. It has two fishes on it which were rescued, fittingly enough, from a stream in the vicar's garden, where the panel was found.

There are some delightful corbels in the chancel, and there is a relationship which would hardly be guessed at between two stone heads in an arch near the pulpit; they look across at one another as they often did in life, representing a curate and his clerk. There are two Westmacott monuments to an ancient family of the island, one in memory of a boy drowned in a storm-tossed boat, which is shown in relief, and a third monument is to the last baronet of the family, Sir Leonard Worsley Holmes, whose wife and daughters are seen mourning for him. His youngest daughter died a few days after him and was buried in his grave. Two more famous names we found in Arreton—Queen Mary's in the visitor's book, and Henry Cromwell, the most capable of Oliver's sons. Henry's son William lies with his wife Martha under a red brick tomb by the south door, and their initials are still readable on a stone at the gate of their old home here.

So this old church thrills with its touch of history down a thousand years, and we were interested to find its sanctus bell still hanging in the belfry. The vicar rang it for us, that we might hear its mellow tone. In the churchyard, where the weathervane has been showing the way of the wind for 200 years, are two stones standing together, marking the graves of two sisters, one famous in the island as the heroine of one of the tales of Legh Richmond. She is Elizabeth Wallbridge, and at the death of her sister she was a servant at a great house. Legh Richmond, who was a curate on the island at the time, took the funeral service, and from the letter of gratitude written to him by Elizabeth sprang up a great friendship. Richmond made her the heroine of his story of The Dairyman's Daughter, a story which was printed in six languages and had a sale of two million copies. Her father's cottage is a plain slate-roofed house at Hale Common.

There are three fine old manor houses within easy reach of Arreton, and above the village is Arreton Down, with traces of Saxon and earlier civilisation and a magnificent view 444 feet up.

Ruskin and Nansen

BEMBRIDGE. It lies in the south-east corner of the island, a quiet, restful place amid much natural beauty, the sea, a harbour, and the downs. It has a school founded in our own time by Mr Howard Whitehouse and most deservedly famous already, built on the cliffs a mile or two from the village. Its handsome, buildings are spread over extensive grounds, and the chapel is remarkably beautiful, with an impressive tower which is an island landmark. We may climb it if we will ask permission.

Mr Whitehouse, founder and first warden of Bembridge, has infused into the atmosphere of the school the spirit of two of the noblest men of his time. He knew John Ruskin and has preserved for the nation his home on Lake Coniston. He knew Dr Nansen and sent out his boys to Oslo to pay homage to him. They made a model six feet square illustrating Nansen's journey Farthest North. Round the margins were models of the Fram and of many of the accessories Nansen took with him. On the day it arrived at the explorer's house a happy party of boys were sitting on the top of its packing case, and so they arrived with their motor lorry in a sort of triumphal procession. This is from the little speech in which the model was presented to Nansen:

Some of us are too young to remember from contemporary accounts the days of your epic adventures in the Arctic seas, but we have all read the imperishable story. At the end of the war we remember that you led the civilised world in the attempt to fight the forces of disease, famine, and pestilence, which followed in its wake. In those years, too, you took under your care the oppressed remnant of the Armenian nation, whose story is one of the tragedies of the world. Today you are the foremost champion of those who seek to make the brotherhood of nations a reality and to banish war from the earth. We beg your acceptance of this gift, the work of our hands, as a symbol of our affection and homage.

Dr Nansen was much moved. They would all be explorers in one field or another, he told them, and he begged them to stick to whatever they began "till the task is finished and finished well, whatever it may be." It is one of the mottoes of Bembridge school.

As for John Ruskin, the founder has built up an association from which the school cannot escape, for in the grounds are the Ruskin Galleries, housed in a building of great beauty, and containing a unique collection of pictures, 300 of them original drawings by Ruskin in water colour, pen, and pencil. It is the most important collection of his drawings in existence, and includes many of the original plates for his books. The collection also includes works by artists associated with Ruskin, among them Sir Edward Burne-Jones, Walter Crane, T. M. Rooke, and Arthur Severn. There is also an art library, with many original Ruskin manuscripts.

Near Bembridge School is the great Culver cliff, a natural sanctuary for wild sea birds, and notable in literary history, for our poet Swinburne knew it and loved it, and as a boy climbed its precipitous slopes.

The small Brading Harbour comes into the Anglo-Saxon Chronicle with the description of one of Alfred's naval battles. Danish pirate ships were constantly appearing off the coast, and it was to deal with these that Alfred turned shipbuilder. His ships were twice as long as the Danish; some had 60 oars, some more. What may have been the first British naval battle is described with much detail in the Chronicle under the year 896 AD. The pirate fleet had been plundering along the South Coast, and had taken refuge in some land-locked harbour of the Isle of Wight. Alfred's new ships besieged the Danes. At low water the opposing crews fought on the sands; but before the battle could be decided the tide turned, and the sands which had witnessed the fight were covered with the incoming waters. One by one the boats righted themselves and were once more afloat; but the Danish boats, being smaller, were able to get out of the harbour first. Two of them were wrecked before they passed the cliffs of Beachy Head, and the crews were captured and brought before the King at Winchester. It is sad to read that Alfred ordered them to be hanged, an unusual decision, for he was truly merciful.

The Poet's Farewell

BINSTEAD. A delightful corner of the island, it has views of Spithead through its trees, and quarries to which Winchester and Chichester cathedrals sent for stone. The Norman church was built by a most exclusive Abbot of Quarr, who "would not have all his tenants and the inhabitants of Binstead come to trouble the Abbey Church." The 19th century church has kept its Norman chancel and a medieval bell, and some of the carvings of the old nave are built into the west wall of the new one. The old south doorway (1150) is made into a gateway of the churchyard; the stout little man with a beard sitting above it on the head of a queer beast must have looked down on many generations of Binstead folk. From this Norman gateway we have the best view of the fine little chancel. There is a grinning face curiously set in curling feathers below the bell turret, and a tiny heraldic beast at the head of the two lancets. Some of the early herringbone work has been preserved. The chancel is lined with beautiful quatrefoil panelling, and stalls once in the chapel of St Mary's College, Winchester. Between the two uprights of a reading desk is a striking piece of old Flemish craftsmanship carved in wood, representing Aaron and Hur supporting the hands of Moses while the Israelites fought the Amalekites. A vigorous scene carved on a smuggler's gravestone in the churchyard by the east end shows the smuggler trying to outsail the officers of the law, who won the race by shooting him on board his ship. It was in the porch of this church that Horace Smith, writer of the famous Ode to an Egyptian Mummy, wrote these lines on leaving the island:

> Farewell, sweet Binstead! take a fond farewell
> From one unused to sight of woods and trees,
> Amid the strife of cities doomed to dwell,
> Yet roused to ecstasy by scenes like these;
> Who could for ever sit beneath thy trees,
> Inhaling fragrance from the flowery dell.

By a farmhouse at the end of a lane, with lancet windows, a parapet, and a bellcot, is a stretch of grey ruined wall which is all that remains of old Quarr Abbey, consecrated by Henry de Blois 800 years ago. The whole island came feasting here to crown so good a work, in which every inhabitant had lent a helping hand. The feast was on a summer's day in 1150; we called on a summer's day in 1932 and found cattle grazing where the proud founder lies—Baldwin de Redvers, who sleeps hereabout with his wife Adeliza and two sons Richard Lionheart loved. There are no marks for their graves, but in this little place they lie, proud folk of Norman England, their glory passed away.

But they are not forgotten, for a new abbey has arisen, built by French monks in our own time, its walls of pure red brick inside and out, its pinnacled turrets designed by one of the brothers. It is the only church we have seen of its size built with entirely new ideas, and its short nave and long choir, with the continuous line of arches from west to east, is one of the striking spectacles of the island.

A Remarkable Group of Men

BONCHURCH. It looks out to sea from the slope of St Boniface Down, the noblest height in the island, rising 787 feet; the down and the village are both named after the Saxon saint to whom the tiny church is dedicated, a Devon man who was educated in Hampshire, evangelised Germany, and was murdered at Dokkum.

The old church, standing on a Saxon site, has been fashioned through the centuries and has a doorway believed to be made up with the curved stones of a Norman arch. The door itself is of very great age, studded with nails and built up of two layers of planks. The altar rail is made from the old roof beams. It is thought that the first church on the site was founded by Boniface before he left the monastery of Nursling for his lifework on the continent.

In a new church on a site given by the wife of James White of Punch worshipped Elizabeth Sewell, whose tales for children were much read last century. In this church are six windows filled with old glass, painted with saints in rich robes by 15th century Flemish artists. There is also a charming little window with a figure of St Edith in memory of another worshipper, Edith Swinburne, the companion window with a figure of St Benet being to the memory of Admiral Swinburne. They were both friends of the church, and the most famous member of their family, the poet, lies in the churchyard, which is like a garden with little vales and hills among trees and flowers and shrubs. The Swinburne graves lie close by the path, all alike with grey stone; the poet had a home here called East Dene, the charming old white house backed by trees with the wide sweep of the lovely bay in front of it.

Every visitor to Bonchurch knows the beautiful water bordering the village street, and every bird knows it, too. It was part of the garden of Mr H. de Vere Stacpoole, the novelist, but its charm belongs to all who pass. It has an inscription to Margaret de Vere Stacpoole, and is a memorial to the novelist's wife which has now been presented to the village, and is to be kept, we hope, always as beautiful as we found it.

The history of Bonchurch is linked with a remarkable group of names. Here Macaulay lived for a time (at Madeira Hall on the Ventnor road). He would walk up this winding drive flanked by the rocks to which the coast here owes its rare beauty. Here Tennyson loved to come, though once he had the unpleasant experience of being set upon by unmannerly ladies who seized his hat and cut it into pieces—like rosemary, for remembrance. Here also is a hilltop which Mr Howard Whitehouse, the founder of Bembridge School, has given to the National Trust, naming it Nansen Hill. Here Scouts and Guides may camp, catching, let us hope, something of the indomitable spirit of the man whose name it bears. We must hope that the Isle of Wight is proud to have his name on its map.

Bonchurch was the birthplace of Sir Thomas Hopsonn, who became a tailor's apprentice but for ever heard the call of the sea and ran away to join the Fleet. His resourcefulness and his love of high enterprise earned him swift promotion, and his courage and skill won him a knighthood from Queen Anne.

Not yet is the list of famous men of Bonchurch exhausted, for in the graveyard of the old church sleep not only Swinburne but two other Victorians, William Adams and John Sterling. William Adams was a preacher and writer beloved by all throughout the island. He lived at the house called Winterbourne, and is still remembered by old folk as the Good Gentleman. As we look at his grave we are reminded of the best known of his beautiful allegories, The Shadow of the Cross, for an iron cross casts its shadow across the grave when the sun is shining. John Sterling was one of the early Liberals. Everyone who knew him felt that he was remarkable, but the sum total of his achievements did not suffice to make him famous. Yet the world has been told how he impressed one of his friends so vividly and attractively that it is willing to accept the testimony.

His father, Edward Sterling, was a famous writer on the staff of The Times, who between 1830 and 1840 wrote its chief articles with such reverberating energy that the paper was given the nickname of The Thunderer. The family was Scottish in origin, but had lived in Ireland for over a century, and was on its way to England when John was born in the Island of Bute on July 20, 1806. He was educated at

Glasgow and Cambridge, and made useful friendships. He knew Coleridge, Wordsworth, and Carlyle. In the first few years after leaving Cambridge he became secretary of an organisation which aimed at abolishing the East India Company's monopoly of trading in the East, plunged into journalism, wrote a novel and some poetry, joined in a revolutionary conspiracy in Spain, and married. He was 24, and ill-health began an attack which never ceased.

Those years were spent in fighting for his existence against tuberculosis. He tried the West Indies, where he had property; served for eight months as a curate in Sussex; travelled abroad; and at last tried the Isle of Wight. All this time he was writing stories, poems, and essays, and corresponding brightly with his friends. But what could be expected from one so pursued by death? He died at Ventnor in his 37th year, and this is what his biographer, Thomas Carlyle, said of him:

A more perfectly transparent soul I have never known. He was good and generous and true; joyful where there was joy, patient and silent where endurance was required of him; shook innumerable sorrows and thick-crowding forms of pain gallantly away from him, and faced frankly forward. There was no guile or baseness anywhere found in him.

While the memory of Carlyle lasts the memory of John Sterling will last, for it is the simplest and most understanding and understandable book the sage of the Victorian Era ever wrote.

The Poet Apart from the World

ALGERNON CHARLES SWINBURNE was endowed with the gift of song, but his use of it will always be questioned. Much of his writing, whether in verse or prose, was an expression of intense prejudice. He had no stability of character and judgment, and was not fit to go about the world alone.

He was born in London in 1837, the son of a bluff admiral and an earl's daughter. As a child he was frail and had no school experience of the ordinary kind. At Eton he was a curiosity, apart from the customary life of the school. As a desultory reader he was from infancy a prodigy. He had learnt French and Italian with English as a child, was familiar with Shakespeare at the age of six, and when he left Eton probably knew more about English literature than any

The Castle Gateway

Steps to the Norman Keep   15th Century Gates

CARISBROOKE CASTLE

Cowes   Osborne House

Freshwater   Tennyson's Home

FAMOUS HOUSES IN THE ISLE OF WIGHT

Eton master knew. A diminutive figure, with a huge head and a shock of red hair, small hands and feet that could not be kept still when he became excited, he read and read—apart. His pastimes were all individual, and never led him into teams.

Swinburne entered Balliol when he was 18 and attracted the notice of the great Jowett, who was then Professor of Greek. Jowett proved himself a most patient friend for many years, but Swinburne never accommodated himself to the routine work of the university. In boyhood he had passionately accepted High Churchism, but in the freedom of Oxford he wholly discarded Christianity and in politics became an ardent republican. If he had any religion left it was the paganism of Greece and Rome, and so it remained. He left Oxford without taking a degree, and his withdrawal was a great relief to Jowett, who feared that his opinions and his conduct would end in his being expelled as Shelley had been.

When he had reached the age of 42 the poet, who had become a physical wreck, was placed in charge of his friend Theodore Watts-Dunton, a lawyer with literary tastes; and he remained under his control for the last 30 years of his life. Clearly it was a necessary constraint. His health was restored, and deafness was the chief drawback of this long quiet period. He died of pneumonia in 1909, and was buried at Bonchurch, the resting-place of his family.

Swinburne was born to be a poet, and his uprearing was entirely favourable to that career except that he never had any touch with average human life. He revelled in books and met all the chief poets of his day, and his poetry is all derived from bookish sources. Those sources were romances picked up from history, the most persistent being the hackneyed theme of Mary Queen of Scots; the study of Greek drama; a view of love on the level of the demi-monde, revolutionary ideas centring on Mazzini's work for the liberation of Italy; and, in prose, rhapsodic criticisms based on his boyish reading of Elizabethan writers. The body of thought in these writings is never substantial, but the lyrical quality and poetical charm are often delightful, and Swinburne's real contribution to literature is his invention of rhythms and rhymings that distinctly add a smoothness and fluency to the language.

The prevailing spirit of Swinburne is one of profound pessimism. His world is a place without God and without hope. He had a clear view of poetry, and an active mind, but it was easily susceptible to outside influences, and he had no ballast of common sense. He allowed his stereotyped beliefs, his unrestrained impulses, and his profusion of words to run away with him, and carry him into the ranks of poetic curiosities.

The Three Wooden Statues

BRADING. It is said that when Wilfrid sailed from Selsey to convert the Jutes in the Isle of Wight he chose this place for his first sermon, so that it has been a place for pilgrims since the 7th century began. The church goes back 800 years, and has two of its consecration crosses still seen; but Brading goes back farther yet. It has three wooden statues of a family 800 years old, and remains of a house 800 years older, and it is believed that the narrow road near the church, leading past the vicarage to the old quay, was used by the Phoenicians who came to Britain for tin 4000 years ago.

The statues represent three Oglanders, members of a family holding land in the Island since they landed with the Conqueror at Pevensey. It was Sir John of the days of Cromwell who wrote the history of the island, and he is one of the three statues which make this church a place of pilgrimage. They are in the 15th century chapel, panelled with a low wooden screen and decorated with small coloured shields. There are two imposing wooden figures and a small replica. The big ones are to Sir William Oglander, who died in 1607, and Sir John who died in 1655; the small one, in a niche behind his father's tomb, is of Sir John's only son George, a mite two feet long. The best of the three is the earliest, the work of a master craftsman of Shakespeare's day; it shows Sir William with a noble head, wearing an Elizabethan beard and ruff; he has black and gold armour and his sword-hilt is beautifully carved and gilded. Sir John's statue shows him as a grey-bearded man in black and gold, his feet on a lion and his shield emblazoned with a gold bird on a blue ground. He was in this church one Sunday in 1647 when the news of Charles Stuart's arrival in the Island came to him. He rode over the next day to Newport to offer the king his homage, and the king came to see him at Nunwell, where Sir John went on his knees and offered him a purse of gold.

Near by is the table tomb of Oliver Oglander, older than all these, for he died in 1530. He kneels with his wife and seven children on one side of the tomb, facing a group of crippled beggars who have evidently thrived upon their charity.

The oldest monument in the church is a stone in the chancel floor, engraved with the delicate outline portrait of John Curwen, Constable of Porchester Castle, who died in 1441. His armoured figure stands under a beautiful canopy with the symbols of the Evangelists and six saints in niches. The stone was precious to antiquarians because the head, hands, and the sword-hilt were filled-in with enamelled metals, which have now been stolen. The handsome altar in the Oglander chapel is Jacobean; it has lovely silver and crystal candlesticks. The altarpiece is a modern reproduction of the Pieta by Francia in the National Gallery. The chapel has also a beautiful Stuart chair inlaid with flowers in variously toned woods.

The arcades belong to the first period of English building, the arches resting on round pillars with carved capitals shaped by the Normans. There is a chest with iron handles and a slot for coins made in 1637, a charming marble font bowl of about the same time on a 13th century stem, and a brass candelabra of 1798, made in Holland.

A sundial on the post of an old cross has been marking the hours since the year of Waterloo, and some sad little processions it has seen. In that terrible year for Europe 1848 this church had its great sorrow too, for within ten days they laid here four girls from one house, the youngest one year old and the oldest six. They were lovely and pleasant in their lives, wrote the stricken parents on the stone, and in their death they were not divided. They brought here some years afterwards the tiny Elizabeth Theresa Agnes Rollo, Lord Rollo's child, and a little angel she looks in white marble on her black tomb, sleeping in a nightgown with her head on a pillow and her hands clasped in prayer.

The fine tower is about 700 years old and like no other in the Island, for it is pierced with arches so that medieval Sunday processions round the church might pass through unhindered. The beacon irons once fixed to the top of the tower are in the porch.

When the 18th century met the 19th Brading had a popular curate named Legh Richmond, whose moral tales were printed as The Annals of the Poor. They were very popular, and three of his stories of rural life are often remembered. One was called Jane the Young

Cottager. Jane was real, a delicate girl who attended Legh Richmond's Bible class and won his heart. She died when she was but 15; her grave is just beyond the chancel, and on it is written:

A child reposes underneath this sod,
A child to memory dear, and dear to God;
Rejoice; yet shed a sympathetic tear;
Jane the Young Cottager is buried here.

Her cottage was prettily covered with creeper when we called.

In this churchyard also sleeps an old man, Benjamin Maund, a chemist and bookseller of Worcestershire who made himself a name by his love of flowers, and has a collection in the British Museum. By the church are some half-timbered houses and the little town hall, which keeps the village stocks and whipping-post. Let into the ground at the top of the hill above the station is an iron block with a hole in it; it is the old bull ring.

A mile or two away is a splendid hill 400 feet high called Ashey Down, with one of the noblest views of the Island, and on it are 12 burial mounds in which lie Britons of the Bronze Age.

We have a glimpse of Nunwell, Sir John Oglander's house, from the road; parts of it are modern, the oldest parts Tudor. But young indeed is Nunwell compared with the oldest house in Brading. It was found by shepherds who were pitching fold and were puzzled by striking something hard in the turf. A search was made and there was brought to light (in 1880) one of the finest Roman villas in the land. It has been carefully excavated and preserved, and can be seen by all.

The House With the Wonderful Pavements

THE size of the Roman Villa and its elaborate mosaic floors show that it must have been the home of an official of some consequence. There were two blocks of buildings to the right and left of the villa, one with a hypocaust having 54 little tile pillars to support the floor. These were not so interesting as the villa proper, however, and one of them has been covered up, part of the other being left to show the hypocaust. The villa has 12 rooms, some with plain tessellated floors, others with patterned pavements mostly in a good state of preservation and looking like carpets.

The hall of the house is 50 feet long and has for the subject of its pavement one that was popular with the early Christians, Orpheus charming the wild things with his lyre. A peacock, a coot, a fox, and a queer little monkey in a red cap are listening to the young god's music. The monkey is an unusual addition. There are the remains of a pavement in another room, with a gladiator, a fox under a tree, a little house with a flight of steps, the watchman, with the head and legs of a cock, and two fabulous winged animals, as part of its decoration. In the middle is a head.

The best pavements are in a room about 40 feet long which appears to have been divided by a curtain, as one end is wider than the other. Between the two ends is a strip of pavement divided into three panels. Its central subject is a black-bearded astronomer seated by a pillar with a sundial on it, pointing with a stick to a globe below it, and a vase with what seems to be a pen sticking out of it is on his other side. It has been suggested that he is Hipparchus, the first great astronomer. Each part of this long room has picture pavements. One has been rather badly damaged; the subject of its remaining panel is the rescue of Andromeda by Perseus, who carries the Gorgon's head. At each corner is a bust of one of the seasons. Spring has almost entirely gone, but Summer has poppies in her hair; Autumn is garlanded with corn; Winter has a clock fastened on her shoulder by a brooch, and is holding a bare branch with a dead birch hanging from it. A peacock inquisitively examining a vase of flowers, his long tail trailing, has fortunately escaped damage.

The best of these rich pavements has in the centre Medusa, with dark eyes and snaky locks furiously writhing. Four square panels hedge her about, and in each are two graceful figures, a man and a woman, some wearing quaint costumes. Four horn-blowing satyrs fill the triangles between the base of these squares and the edge of the pavement, and the whole is bound together by borders of intricately interlaced designs. Another narrow strip joins this fine pavement. It is decorated with queer creatures, half-man, half sea-beast, two of them carrying off plump damsels who do not seem to be in much distress, and one of them with a shepherd's crook over his shoulder.

There are cases filled with all manner of things found during the uncovering of the villa. Pottery, bronze ornaments, lovely fragments of glass, a red tile bearing the imprint of a man's foot and the paw mark of his dog; the hook and catch of a gate, horses' bits, locks and keys, huge nails, and shear of a hand plough, gimlets, and a piece of plaster with a beautiful bird painted on it. A quantity of charred wood suggests that this fine house was lost through fire, an interesting bit of news from the days of Roman Britain.

Thomas Ken

BRIGHSTONE. It shelters under the great height of Brighstone Down, a delightful place. The top of the down (it is 700 feet up) is the highest point of the middle range, and from it we see almost from end to end of the island, from Culver Cliff above Sandown to Freshwater Bay, 20 miles as the crow flies. The little church (which has an old mass clock on its sunny wall) has a beautiful interior, with a Norman arcade for the north aisle and medieval arches on the south, a 13th century doorway, a 14th century tower, and a 15th century font. There is a pretty trefoiled niche in one of the piers, and in the splay of a window are the remains of the roodloft stairs. Two chairs in the sanctuary were given by Charlotte Yonge, who spent the profits of her books on Hampshire churches.

In this pulpit there preached that valiant and saintly man Thomas Ken; the sanctuary pavement is a memorial to him by Winchester College. He was rector here before he was Bishop of Winchester, and in the rectory garden (where gentian from Switzerland flourishes as though still on its native heights) is a row of trees he planted. Beneath their shade he wrote those two hymns which morning and evening rise from Christian hearts wherever the English tongue is spoken the whole world round, *Awake, my soul, and with the sun*, and *Glory to Thee, my God, this night*. He was with Charles the Second on his deathbed, stood by that king's son Monmouth on the scaffold, and was one of the Seven Bishops whose courage ended the Stuart tyranny. Here also came another famous man, William Wilberforce, who freed the slaves. His son Samuel, famous as the Remodeller of the Episcopate owing to his diocesan reforms, was ten years rector, and the father spent many of his later days climbing these downs or strolling along the shore. A third bishop who was rector here was Dr Moberley, Bishop of Salisbury.

The Pine Raft

BROOK. Its coast is beautiful with chines cut by busy little streams, but is dangerous to shipping, and not once or twice but many times have seafarers owed their lives to the courageous men of Brook, hazarding their own lives in their lifeboat. When the tide is low here it leaves behind on the beach what looks like a mass of rock, jumbled up and covered with seaweed. But they are not rocks; they are pine trees from a forest of the days before history, and are known as the Pine Raft. After the Pine Raft even the green mound on Brook Down 500 feet up does not seem very old, and the battered 13th century archway of the tower of the little church, rebuilt last century on the hill above the village seems like a thing of yesterday.

The church (in which the only old possessions are a blocked arch in the tower and a stone carving of a lion) stands at the top of a steep God's Acre with the graves in front of it and in due season a glorious mass of rhododendrons behind, with Brook House as if in the sky beyond. The house is the old home of the Seelys, whose graves lie in a simple group on the slope of the hill, shaded by a great pine. In the shade of the tree is the grave of Henry George Gore Brown, VC, "a soldier who tried to do his duty," and more than tried, for he did it. He was a great grandson of Arthur Browne in whose arms Wolfe is said to have died at Quebec. He won his VC at the siege of Lucknow by rushing into a battery and spiking two heavy guns. With him here sleeps his grandson who, we read, at fifteen gave his young life for England.

Brook House set high above the island was owned in Tudor days by Dame Joan Bowerman who here entertained Henry the Sixth. He left her his drinking-horn and the promise of a buck every year from Carisbrooke forest which the good Joan apparently deserved, for she founded a chantry in which a priest was to sing for her, her husband, her father and her mother and all Christian people. In the days when Sir Charles Seely was living here last century Garibaldi slept under this roof and planted some trees which we understand are still flourishing. The gardens and the rhododendrons, a wonderful sight, run down to the churchyard.

Tennyson's Prince of Courtesy

CALBOURNE. The island has few more comely villages. It has a green and a group of great elms, delightful cottages, an old stone house in a wooded park, an ancient church, and Winklestreet, entrancing Winklestreet—a row of small houses watching the busy stream tumbling over its tiny falls on its way to the meadows.

Most of the church is as the builders left it 700 years ago when they refashioned the work of the Normans, but the tower was heightened in the 18th century, when the builders left on the wall an old tablet saying "I am risen from ye ruins of near 70 year." On an outer wall is an ancient mass dial and on one of the inner walls of the tower is a doorway nine feet from the ground, and near it is a deeply splayed window which once enabled the schoolmaster to keep an eye on the children sitting in what was the choir gallery. The font is 13th century. The east windows are lovely and unusual, two slender lancets wide apart with a trefoil in a ring between them. On the chancel walls is a brass to Daniel Evance, who was rector here in Cromwell's day. It has a verse, the figure of Time with a scythe and hourglass, a skeleton armed with an arrow, and an anagram on his name, *I can deal even.*

There is a brass portrait of a knight in armour, his feet resting on a dog, his hands folded in prayer, who may be William Montacute, Earl of Salisbury, a 14th century Governor of the island. A pathetic story has come down to us about his death. He was killed while jousting with his father, who, broken-hearted, set up an altar tomb with a brass portrait of his son in the church of every village where he held lands or houses. A tablet on one of the houses in Calbourne marks it as the birthplace of William Long, author of a work on the Isle of Wight dialect and editor of the Memoirs of the Oglanders, an ancient family of the island.

Through the trees on the road to Carisbrooke we catch sight of a beautiful house called Swainstone, mainly 18th century as we see it, but the successor of a palace founded for the Bishops of Winchester 800 years ago and still with a 13th century hall intact. It is suggested that Warwick the Kingmaker feasted in the hall, and his brave grand-daughter Margaret Pole, last of the Plantagenets, whose execution is the foulest blot on the memory of Henry the Eighth. Swainstone is the home of the Simeons; the last generation of the family has a memorial chapel in the church, with elaborately carved and canopied recesses. Tennyson loved to come here and they loved to go to Farringford. The death of Sir John Simeon was one of the most sorrowful events during Tennyson's life in the Isle of Wight,

and in the shadow of the cedar on these lawns the poet sat down one
day and wrote with a heavy heart these lines:

Nightingales warbled without
Within was weeping for thee;
Shadows of three dead men
Walked in the walks with me.
Shadows of three dead men, and thou wast one of the three.

Nightingales sang in his woods:
The Master was far away:
Nightingales warbled and sang
Of a passion that lasts but a day;
Still in the house in his coffin the Prince of Courtesy lay.

Two dead men have I known
In courtesy like to thee:
Two dead men have I loved
With a love that will ever be:
Three dead men have I loved and thou art last of the three.

Two of these shadows of three dead men were Arthur Hallam,
his youthful friend, and Henry Lushington, his brother-in-law,
and the third was Sir John Simeon. He it was to whom we owe one of
Tennyson's greatest poems, for it was he who suggested that the
poet should write Maud. Sir John was one day in Tennyson's study
when he came upon a verse beginning:

O! that 'twere possible
After long grief and pain
To find the arms of my true love
Round me once again.

Those were the days before Tennyson had found fame, and when he
was a struggling poet on a few hundred pounds a year. Sir John
would give his friend no rest until he had made him promise to write
a poem round this verse, and so it was that the long drama of Maud
came to be. Much of it was written at Swainstone, and it is said to
have been out of the profits of Maud that Tennyson bought Farringford, his own home at Freshwater. Another Simeon is remembered
by the drinking trough at the village cross-roads, given by "his
friends at home" to the memory of Sir Barrington Simeon.

Charles Stuart and his Little Daughter

CARISBROOKE. We come to it for the castle in which a king
was a captive and in which his daughter died, but Carisbrooke

has something older than our English dynasties. The ruins of the castle are young compared with the ruin under the vicarage garden, where is a Roman bath, the central heating arrangement of a Roman village, and the remains of a tessellated pavement with a pattern of flowers. We can see the outline of the villa in the grass.

Halfway up one of the lofty hills stands the church with its 15th century tower, and a spire rising 100 feet. The tower has a beautiful stone turret, battlements, and crocketed pinnacles, and is decorated with rows of gargoyles and queer animals. Halfway up are two figures holding a book on which is carved the date 1471. Its eastern buttresses grow up in the nave, and between them rises a majestic arch. The beautiful south doorway and its stone porch are 600 years old, and most of the 12th century arcade was refashioned by the builders of that time.

The elegant pulpit, with a monk's doorway over it, was made in the time of Cromwell; the font cover is about the same age. The big chest with a slot for coins is Elizabethan. The oldest of three ancient gravestones has on it a quaint portrait of a prior, like a drawing of a child on a slate; it was done about 800 years ago. The other two stones are 13th century. On the wall is a canopied recess with an angel carrying a shield; it shelters Lady Margaret Wadham, aunt of Jane Seymour, Queen of England. Lady Margaret, a solitary figure on her fine tomb, was a great friend of cripples, and is kneeling before a group of beggars and cripples, each one in a lovely little panel. A picture painted on wood hangs on a wall in the nave in memory of William Keeling, an East India Adventurer who discovered the Cocos Islands and attended James the First. The picture shows a ship with Death at the prow, a beautiful woman at the stern, and William Keeling in armour in a gay attitude by the mast. The frame of the picture is painted with gruesome devices, and we read:

> *Forty-two years with vessel frail,*
> *On the rough seas of life did Keeling sail.*

One of the treasures of the church is the finely wrought silver processional cross, 500 years old, made in Venice and carried by pilgrims of the Middle Ages to the Holy Land. It was brought back to Italy and given by Princess Beatrice to the church. It is in a glass case where all can admire the exquisite delicacy of the 13 Bible scenes on it, each in a separate compartment with many perfect figures. Another lovely cross on the altar was given in memory of his brother, a young soldier of the Great War, by Sir Victor Corkran, the buttons of the hero's uniform being set in the cross as jewels.

A little way from the church there stood in ancient days a priory of which nothing now is seen save what is in this church, and a few scribblings by some of its impish scholars. They are precious scribblings now, preserved in one of two recesses on the outer wall of the nave, one 12th century and one 13th. There are drawings of a woman's head, a few unreadable sentences, and something like a ship and Prince of Wales Feathers. The monks of the old abbey had the teaching of boys fortunate enough to get schooling in those days, and it is believed that the scribblings are the work of these young scholars in their idle moments. They are all that is left of the abbey built by William Fitzosbern, a kinsman of the Conqueror.

He laid the foundations of the castle, too, and this famous ruin stands on his earthworks. The flagstaff from which its flag flies is interesting because it was the boom of the Spinnaker sail on King George the Fifth's yacht Britannia. It is a 52-foot Norway pine. Keats wrote part of Endymion while staying here, and of this noble mass of masonry he said that he did not think he would ever see a ruin to surpass it. It is believed to have been on this spot that the Conqueror with his own hands arrested his brother Odo as he was leaving for Rome in the hope of obtaining the Papacy. The castle's outer gateway is Elizabethan and has the queen's initials; but it opens on to a stone bridge crossing the dry moat and leading to the splendid twin towers of a 14th century gatehouse. The towers were raised higher by Anthony Woodville, whose sister married Edward the Fourth but whose chief distinction is that he translated the first book printed in English. The gatehouse he used is now a museum, and has three portcullis grooves, 500-year-old gates with ancient hinges, and a knocker which has worn a hole through the wood. Facing the gatehouse across the neat lawns of the courtyard are the Constable's lodgings, refashioned in the 14th century, with a hall and staircase built by Anthony Woodville and a bigger hall older still, having a 12th century window. Keeping it company in the ground, just through the entrance doors through which the king would walk, is a mountain ash from his birthplace, Dunfermline Abbey.

In an upper room of the Constable's lodgings Charles Stuart had his Presence Chamber, and leading off from it is a wing with a little room in which his daughter Elizabeth died. Here also her brother, the little Duke of Gloucester, described by Clarendon as a prince of extraordinary hopes, was captive till Cromwell set him free.

Beyond the stately Governor's house is a 16th century well-house, sheltering the shaft sunk probably 800 years ago when the old well failed. A mighty wheel about 50 feet round was hauling the bucket up when we called, worked by a gamely stepping donkey. The wheel was made in 1587; its frame is oak and its shaft is chestnut. The donkey walks about 300 yards to bring the bucket to the top, and the life seems to do the donkey little harm, for one of them is said to have seen his fiftieth birthday.

A long flight of steps leads us to the top of the outer wall, where we can look across the valley stream with its nesting swans, and see the village with its noble tower, the grey castle buildings, cedars, and many blossoming trees. The path brings us to the ruined keep in which is still the ancient well which failed Baldwin de Redvers when he held the castle against King Stephen, so that he built the new well out of which our game little donkey is still bringing his bucketfuls of fresh spring water. We can still see the water glistening faintly through the ferns lining this old well.

We may walk across the grassy square where Charles Stuart used to walk, and through the ruins of the rooms he lived in. We may sit and meditate in the chapel of St Nicholas which stands where there has been a chapel since the Conquest, though the place we see is a beautiful reconstruction in celebration of the 250th anniversary of the execution of the King. The tracery of the windows is beautiful, and the carving of the reredos clear and fine. In a vestibule is Bernini's bronze bust of Charles with the starry crown of martyrdom below it, and his last word on the scaffold, Remember.

The church has been furnished as a memorial to the 2000 men of the island who never came back. The statuettes in the sanctuary are the patron saints of all the island churches, and in the window recesses are stone figures of the warrior saints of Christendom. The seats are made of battleship timbers.

The little museum in the gatehouse has much to attract us with its memory of the past. It has some extraordinarily delicate jewelry work of the Bronze Age, one fragment truly enchanting, showing a running hare inlaid with enamels. It is from the burial mounds on the hills, where there was also found a necklace made from animal claws. But it is the Stuart relics that thrill us most. There is a small red and gold Bible given by the king to his valet; the ivory top of the walking stick he used here; a crystal locket with a lock of his hair, the lace cap he wore on his last night; and a fragment of the lace cravat he wore on the scaffold. There is also James the Second's baby shirt and a ring with a fragment of the white silk dress Princess Elizabeth was wearing when she died. In a small box are some pathetic ringlets of the princess, who was sent here after the execution.

Sad it must have been for her to share the last scenes in which the king had been a captive, the place where he used to read Spenser's Faerie Queen, and the Bible; he used to say that his best living companion here was an old little crumpling man who made his fires. Cromwell sent Elizabeth here for safety, though she begged not to have to go to her father's prison. One day, as she was playing bowls on the green laid down for her father, she was caught in a sudden storm. She was not strong, being "deformed and bowed down by an unconquerable malady," and she fell in a fever. A maid came to her room one morning and found her sitting in a chair by the window, her cheek resting on a Bible the king had given her. She was in the sleep that knows no waking in this world.

The Broken-Hearted Princess

BORN in 1635, when her father was ruling England without a Parliament, her troubles began when she was only seven, her father having gone to set up his standard at Nottingham and her mother having crossed the sea to Holland.

For five years she never saw her father, and spent her time in studying languages, including Greek and Hebrew, with a view to a better understanding of the Bible, which was her constant companion. When she was ten she and her brother Henry were placed under the care of the Earl of Northumberland at Syon House, Isleworth, where her elder brother James was sent to join her on the surrender of Charles Stuart in 1646. The proud Elizabeth did not like it, and told James that if she were a boy she would not long remain a captive, however light or glittering might be her fetters.

445

One summer day in 1647 her long-hoped-for meeting with her father took place at Caversham, where they spent two long days together. Fairfax and other army officers who were present fell in love with her gentle bearing and gave her the Puritan name of Temperance. During the next few months the children were often taken to Hampton Court, where their father was playing the Army off against the Parliament. Elizabeth and her brothers were at length brought to London and began to plan the escape of James, at last succeeding. James was dressed up in woman's clothes, there was an exciting game of hide and seek, and he was spirited away.

When Elizabeth was told of her father's sentence the shock nearly killed her. On January 29 she was brought to St James's Palace to say farewell. She wept bitterly and Charles took her on his knee. Thomas Herbert, who was with them, has left an account of the sad scene:

The King then gave them all his jewels, save the George he wore, and, again kissing his children, had such pretty and pertinent answers from them both as drew tears of joy and love from his eyes; and then, praying God Almighty to bless 'em, he turned about, expressing a tender and fatherly affection. Most sorrowful was this parting, the young princess shedding tears and crying lamentably, so as moved others to pity that formerly were hard-hearted; and, at opening the bedchamber door, the king returned hastily from the window and kissed 'em and blessed 'em; so parted.

The little princess never recovered from the blow. Next summer came tidings of the landing in Scotland of her brother Charles. The Council of State sent her to Carisbrooke, though she pleaded desperately against being sent to a castle which had been her father's prison, and she had not been there a week when she was stricken by fever and passed away, a broken-hearted child of fourteen. They laid her by the altar in the church at Newport, and for 200 years only the letters ES marked her grave.

The Lonely Tower on St Catherine's Point

CHALE. There is much to see and remember here—the lofty downs 780 feet high, the bay three miles from Atherfield Point with its treacherous ledge to St Catherine's Point with its famous light, the fine old manor house with a 15th century barn 100 feet long, the beautiful church, the chine, the old beacon, and the column on the downs.

The all-devouring sea has left its mark on this beautiful coast. At the beginning of the Undercliff, along which we could once go from here to Ventnor, is Blackgang Chine, a deep chasm cut in the cliffs by a stream trickling to the sea, and beyond are the tumultuous tumbled slopes with the ragged cliffs above, and the green woods in which there was built a graceful little temple in honour of Shakespeare's 300 years. The temple was built about 1864, and a spring below is dedicated to the memory of Shakespeare with an inscription from Two Gentlemen of Verona.

Chale's 15th century church has a fine turreted and pinnacled tower, and we come into it through a pointed door with rows of moulding. The oldest parts are two low bays of the south arcade which have come from the end of the 12th century. The church is lighted by candles, and the candlesticks on the canopy posts of the altar are four golden angels with outstretched wings. The fine candelabra in the sanctuary are to the memory of a rector who was once Bishop of North-West Australia. There are some lovely painted windows by Kempe, five of them given by an American in memory of ancestors who were rectors. In the west window are six warrior saints resplendent in golden armour.

A century older than the church is the shrine on the summit of St Catherine's Hill, nearly 800 feet above the moving waters. Here a small stone tower has stood 600 years, 36 feet high, with a pointed cap and pierced with openings all the way round. On one side are two doorways, one above the other, and over them are the marks of an old gable roof. The little tower in its impressive solitude is a remarkable survival, actually a medieval lighthouse. It is mentioned in the Winchester registers of 1328 as having been endowed by Walter de Godston. It was a shrine in the old days, when an oratory which has now vanished joined on to it, the keeper being a priest whose duty it was to see that a light was burning all night, and to offer mass for those who were lost at sea.

The oratory had two storeys, the lower one where the priest lived and kept his stores, the upper one for a chapel. The tower had four storeys, the two upper ones reached by ladders. Night after night the lonely priest would climb the ladders to tend his beacon, and night after night his prayers would go up to heaven for the souls of the drowned or for some desperate ship of whose lights he would catch fleeting glimpses from his eyrie above this treacherous coast.

One night in 1536 the solitary priest of St Catherine's Down came down from his lonely tower for the last time. Henry the Eighth and Thomas Cromwell had dissolved the monasteries, and the light on the summit went out. Somewhere about two centuries later Trinity House began the building of its modern lighthouse near the forsaken tower, but, realising that at such a height the weather would spoil its light, they gave up building and restored the tower as a daytime landmark. The unfinished 18th century lighthouse still stands hard by.

But this dangerous coast is not, of course, without its light. At St Catherine's Point, the most southerly point of the island, is the lighthouse built in the 19th century, with a light equal to more than 15 million candles, and one of the most powerful sirens in the world. The lighthouse tower rises 80 feet from the ground but the lamp is 136 feet above high water. At this height the horizon is 17 miles off and ships at that distance can easily see its powerful beam, which moves through 220 degrees, nearly two-thirds of a circle. In the vast area thus covered by the light its flashing can be seen for a fifth of a second every five seconds. There is another lamp in the lighthouse tower 22 feet below the first, showing a fixed red light visible 16 miles away.

Beyond Walter de Godston's tower on the inland run of the downs is a column 72 feet high with a ball on top. It was erected by Michael Hoy, a merchant in Russia, in memory of Tsar Alexander's visit the year before Waterloo, and (Mr Hoy adds) in remembrance of many happy years he lived in the emperor's domains. In 1857 a lieutenant had a second inscription cut, allowing the emperor to share his column with those brave men who fell in the Crimea.

The downs hereabouts look across the lovely woods and valleys, and in the distance is the great white wall of Freshwater Bay, majestic in the sunlight and crowned by Tennyson's Cross.

Queen Victoria's Island Home

COWES. Here come all the best and most beautiful yachts afloat to strive against each other. It is the home of the most famous yacht club in the world, the Royal Yacht Squadron. It is a delightful picture as we approach it from the sea, with the houses coming

St Boniface Down

Luccombe Common

THE BEAUTY OF THE ISLE OF WIGHT

Cowes   St Mary's Church

Godshill   Church Tower and Thatched Roofs

TWO ISLE OF WIGHT CHURCHES

almost to the water's edge. The sound of 22 little cannon starts the races and welcomes the victors; they are the only ornament on the curved platform in West Cowes where the Royal Yacht Squadron building stands. There is little or nothing left of the Tudor forts or of the old castle. Near the Squadron is Holy Trinity Church, a last century building with many tablets to members of the Squadron; one of them has on it a yacht sailing swiftly towards the rising sun.

In an 18th century house called Westbourne lived a collector of customs whose son, born here in 1795, lived to become immortal as Dr Arnold, headmaster of Rugby School. Northwood House, in a beautiful park where all may walk, was the home of the Wards, one of whom (William George) was Tennyson's great friend, in whose memory the poet wrote six lines, including these:

Farewell, whose living like I shall not find,
My friend, the most unworldly of mankind.

Close by Northwood House is the church founded during the Commonwealth and made new last century. George Ward built the tower, and inside is a wall-monument to himself and his wife. In the south aisle is a brass to the famous Dr Arnold. A little way down the road is the Roman Catholic Church, which has a small picture of the death of the Madonna by Antonello da Messina, who is said to have taught the Venetian artists the use of oils. The church has also a great altar-painting of the Descent from the Cross. Beyond Princes Green, a lovely stretch of turf by the Solent, past the small column carrying a powerful light for ships, the road runs along the water's edge to Gurnard, where the remains of a Roman villa have been found and where it is thought the old tin route ran. Gurnard Head is rich in fossils. On the parade is a plaque set up by the people of Maryland in memory of the sailing of the Ark and the Dove, which carried the first settlers to Maryland 300 years ago.

Over the ferry is East Cowes, with its busy shipyards and two big houses in lovely parks: Norris Castle, whose grounds join those of Osborne House, and East Cowes Castle, the towered mansion built for himself by John Nash, who died here in 1835 after having given London its old Regent Street and Brighton its Pavilion. There is an odd story of John Nash and his castle which is good enough to remember. He was travelling in Ireland when he came upon Lough

Cutra Castle and he made it the model of the castle he built for himself at Cowes. The owner of Lough Cutra in course of time became hard up, sold his estates, and as a poverty-stricken old man of 70 went to Paris and met a rich old lady named Mrs Tudor. It was not long before rich and poor were happily united, and during their honeymoon she said to him "You must come down now and see our country home." They came to the Isle of Wight, and as they reached the avenue he remarked that this was very odd, remarkably like Lough Cutra. When they pulled up at the front door the old gentleman fell into a state of agitation, rushing into the hall and exclaiming, "Don't tell me that is the drawing-room on the right." But it was, and, standing in the middle of the room, the bewildered old man cried "If there is a picture gallery through there, I shall faint." There was.

But it is, of course, for Osborne House that the public comes to East Cowes. It was the seaside home of Queen Victoria. Here she died. Here ended the life which ended the Victorian Era, the most famous and prosperous 60 years in the history of the English people. Today the house is a memorial to the queen. Part of it is a convalescent home for officers, something perhaps of a white elephant. It was built in the classical style in 1846. There are lofty apartments filled to overflowing with furniture, ornaments, curios, china, pictures, and sculpture. The Durbar Room is a mass of teak carving and ornamental plaster work, with a handsome ceiling. A plaster peacock in his pride stands over the mantelpiece, and in glass cases are examples of Eastern craftsmanship, a fish with gold and silver scales and shining eyes among them. In the dining-room hangs a picture of the queen as a happy young mother with her children about her and Prince Albert at her side, and let into the floor is a brass plate showing where her coffin lay in state.

The grounds are a sanctuary for birds, and are very beautiful, especially the wilder parts with the trees growing in copses and the Solent glittering through. A long path leads us to the Swiss cottage where the children played at housekeeping; it is now a small museum. Here is Queen Victoria's writing desk and the royal cradle, a lovely little boat suspended between two posts with a satin pillow embroidered with the queen's initials. There is a model of Jerusalem given to the queen by Dean Stanley, a case of porcelain ornaments collected by her as a child, and an enchanting model shop with the name Spratt over the door and the words "Grocer to Her Majesty." There is King Cetewayo's hide shield, the skull of an Australian crocodile, and fossils and curios from all over the world.

In the Swiss cottage is a white kitchen with pots and pans we could make mirrors of, and floors and walls as clean as the china. The only people who have cooked in this kitchen are princes and princesses, the children of Queen Victoria. They would stand in rows with their sleeves rolled up and their pinafores on, mixing their cakes, and here is the kitchen as they knew it, unused since their day. It was their domestic school to which their mother sent them.

The queen died on the evening of January 22, 1901, having lived from the end of the second decade of the 19th century into the first month of the 20th. The queen of peace died in the midst of war, and almost her last act was to greet Lord Roberts on his return from the Boer War, where he had laid down the command for Lord Kitchener; the earldom she conferred on Lord Roberts was the last title she gave. On the 10th of January she saw Mr Joseph Chamberlain, her last interview with the minister being to receive news of war; on the 15th she took her last drive; on the 19th she had grown very weak, and her children were summoned. The German Emperor arrived and was present when the queen passed away, 81 years old, having reigned 63 years, seven months, and two days, the longest reign in British history. On the first of February her coffin was placed on the yacht Alberta, passing between long lines of warships, from which a last salute was fired as the queen left for ever her island home.

The Home of Tennyson

FRESHWATER. The granite column on the summit of High Down marks the height to which Tennyson would come on all days in all weathers, climbing the down he loved and rejoicing in its sweeping views over land and sea, woodland and meadow. He found this place before he was famous and when he was a struggling poet. He had a little money invested in a railway and thought he could get on with that and the £500 he was earning from his poems, so he came to Farringford. He thought the view from its windows a miracle of beauty, and he loved to roam about, doing a little farming, sweeping up the leaves on the lawn, mowing the grass, gravelling the walks. He became so interested in his garden that he began making a flower dictionary. He went exploring with the local geologist.

He kept himself aloof from the village folk, but would go about in his green coat and his big-brimmed hat, concerning which the local people used to say that "once round Tennyson's hat twice round Freshwater."

The gardens and the meadows of Farringford sloped down to the sea, cloaked behind by a crescent of trees. Tennyson was soon describing it all in some verses he sent to Frederick Denison Maurice asking him to Farringford. Maurice was then beginning the movement for Christian Socialism which so deeply interested him and Charles Kingsley; he had founded one college for working men and another for women, and had been expelled from his professorship in London on account of his theological essays, and Tennyson begins by saying that, even if every clergyman foam in spite at him he would find welcome here,

> *Where, far from noise and smoke of town,*
> *I watch the twilight falling brown*
> *All round a careless-ordered garden*
> *Close to the ridge of a noble down.*

He should have no scandal while he dined, said Tennyson; they would hear the magpie gossip, and might discuss the wars, and

> *How best to help the slender store,*
> *How mend the dwellings, of the poor.*

Maurice came. He read family prayers in the morning, and the poet said that it was the most earnest and holiest reading he had ever heard.

Here years afterwards came another famous man, Garibaldi. He was staying with the Seelys at Brook, and Tennyson went to see him, "a most striking figure in his picturesque white poncho lined with red, his embroidered red shirt and coloured tie over it." It was arranged that Garibaldi should plant a tree at Farringford, and they chose a Wellingtonia which had been raised from a cone from a tree 300 feet high in California; it is flourishing by the drive. Garibaldi told Tennyson that he could never doubt England—he loved her. "She never alters; next to God I never cease to have faith in her," he said. They talked poetry together and repeated some of each other's lines, for Garibaldi had written songs and hymns.

We may see over the house at times during the summer. In the drawing-room hangs G. F. Watt's lovely portrait of Lady Tennyson, and in Tennyson's study (still practically as he knew it) is his high-backed chair, the desk in the window, his candle stand, and his tobacco jar. A turret stair leads from it to the playroom, now filled with touching and intimate things. Here is a cast of the poet's hand, manly and strong, a little manuscript book containing a poem called Armageddon written when he was 15; his pipes, his paper-knife, his pruning knives, pens, quills, some of his tobacco, his paint-box, and some seals. There are some of his favourite books: Don Quixote in Spanish, the Bible in Hebrew, Goethe, and Virgil. A little collection of things associated with his last days includes the very last book he asked for, Shakespeare opened at Cymbeline, and with it is his New Testament, his nightcap, and the glass he took his medicine in. There is a white pall embroidered with flowers, and Queen Victoria's laurel wreath with the card on which she wrote the tribute to a poet whose fame will outlast her own: "A tribute of true regard and affectionate admiration from his sovereign."

The garden path, running among the trees and over the little bridge where he would stand watching the moonlight over the sea, takes us to the small ivied summerhouse in which he wrote Enoch Arden. Its walls were painted with peacock's feathers by Tennyson himself. The church and the village are not far away. The poet died on Blackdown in Sussex and lies in the Abbey, but Lady Tennyson's grave is by the east wall of the churchyard with the River Yar winding peacefully past. They died at the same age with four years between them, and the happiness of their long married life is expressed in the words on Lady Tennyson's grave: "Dear, near, and true, no truer Time himself can prove you, though he make you evermore dearer and nearer." There is a stone in memory of the poet telling us that his happiest days were passed at Farringford, and on it are two lines:

> *Speak, living voice, with thee death is not death;*
> *Thy life outlives the life of dust and breath.*

The church was restored while Tennyson lived at Farringford, and looks almost new outside, but the impressive arcades are about 800 years old, and in the north aisle, hidden between two doors, is a small Norman doorway. The font is also on a Norman base. The chancel arch is 15th century, and by it are two tablets in marble frames in memory of Tennyson and his son Lionel, who died on his way back from India in 1886 and was buried at sea. The poet was profoundly grieved by the loss of his affectionate boy, who had grown up at Farringford and gone into the India Office, and was on a visit to Lord Dufferin in India when he caught jungle fever and hung for three months between life and death. He died in the Red Sea and they stopped the ship under a silver moon and lowered the coffin.

> *Not there to bid my boy farewell,*
> *When That within the coffin fell,*
> *Fell and flashed into the Red Sea,*
> *Beneath a hard Arabian moon*
> *And alien stars.*

The tablet to Lionel in the church has these four lines by the poet:

> *Truth, for truth is truth, he worshipt, being true as he was brave,*
> *Good, for good is good, he followed, yet he looked beyond the grave:*
> *Truth for truth and good for good! the Good, the True, the Pure, the Just!*
> *Take the charm for ever from them, and they crumble into dust.*

There is another memorial to Lionel by the altar, one of two statues at each side. Lionel's is a statue of St John, and the other is a statue of St Peter to Canon Isaacson, rector here for 50 years. There is also a tablet to the poet's grandson Harold, who gave his life for England in HMS Viking during the Great War. He was the son of Hallam, the second Lord Tennyson, who was killed in action in the Channel, his last message being, "I have only done my duty as a man is bound to do, and I die with a joyful spirit." He lies with his mother in the churchyard. There is a tablet to his mother, Audrey Tennyson, which tells us that "she went about doing good." Another tablet records the death of Hallam's second wife, and another is to his second son Alfred Aubrey, who was killed in action. The names of both these brothers are on the peace memorial in the churchyard, and on the wall of the church is a tribute to Hallam Tennyson himself (in all there are seven Tennyson memorials). In a lovely window of the baptistry are figures of the Madonna, St Elizabeth, St Paul, and John the Baptist in memory of a father and son of the Worsleys, one of the oldest and best-known families on the island. Philip Worsley's death deeply moved the Tennysons. He was a poet, and his poems had just arrived at Farringford when Garibaldi called; the thought of him dying of consumption in his lodgings near the bay mingled strangely, said Lady Tennyson, with the sounds of welcome to Garibaldi as he passed through the village, where people on foot and horseback and in carriages had waited for two hours. Dr Richard Garnett wrote of Worsley that as a poet he achieved what no one else had achieved, making Homer speak like Spenser in his translation.

In one of two small chapels here, both 13th century, is a small brass portrait of a man in armour with his feet on a lion; he is thought to be Adam de Compton, who would be living when the chapel was built. It is a lovely brass. At the eastern end of the south aisle are the matrices of two brasses very effectively painted black on the white walls.

The voyager to the Isle of Wight, if he is crossing in the evening, must always remember that it was while crossing here that Tennyson wrote the most familiar and most moving of all his poems, the 16 lines of Crossing the Bar. They came in a moment, he said to one who described the poem as crowning his life's work, but Dr Jowett was right when he predicted that they would be immortal:

> *Twilight and evening bell,*
> *And after that the dark!*
> *And may there be no sadness of farewell,*
> *When I embark;*
>
> *For though from out our bourne of Time and Place*
> *The flood may bear me far,*
> *I hope to see my Pilot face to face*
> *When I have crossed the bar.*

It is thrilling, as we read these lines, to remember that exactly fifty years after the poet crossed the bar the sound of his voice spoken here at Farringford was heard again in his old home on Blackdown in Surrey. In 1939 a number of those who knew him met there and heard Tennyson's voice on a gramophone record made from the wax cylinders on to which the poet spoke in 1889, little imagining, perhaps, how pathetic it would seem in half a century to friends who, longing in vain for the touch of a vanished hand, could at least listen to "the sound of a voice that is still."

In the end Tennyson left the Isle of Wight for Blackdown on the border of Surrey and Sussex, where he died. In his last years at Farringford he was much annoyed by tourists, and once, when some Americans pressed to see him and he was refusing, he was only moved to give way by a friend who pleaded for them, saying that these people had come three thousand miles to see a lion and had found a bear. The poet relented, but he was not too ready to see his hero-worshippers, and at last changed his address, moving from one lovely down to another.

The Little Crooked Boy

THERE was born at Freshwater, a parson's son, one of the most extraordinary men of the 17th century, Robert Hooke. He started life in the summer of 1635 as the most miserable slip of humanity that can be imagined, but this poor little crooked boy became the cleverest man of his age, though because he was a little quarrelsome history has never given him his due. As a child he made amazing mechanical toys, and book-learning came to him easily: he mastered the six books of Euclid in a week. He brought out most of his inventions without help, and claimed that a hundred discoveries were entirely due to him. Yet he never boasted of his work. The experiments he performed before the Royal Society must have numbered hundreds. Being very poor, he had to make most of his own instruments.

He realised before Sir Isaac Newton the idea of gravitation. He had a distinct conception of a mechanical flying-machine. He found out all about the function of air in regard to breathing and combustion, and made pneumatic tyres possible. He worked out the law relating to falling bodies. By the use of a pendulum he proved the movement of the earth, and he invented a circular pendulum for watches. He made a workable model on which to fashion electric clocks. He ascertained how sound is caused, and explained to Samuel Pepys how many times a second the wings of a humming insect beat. He described how light is composed, and what heat is. He displayed the wonders of the microscope, improved the telescope, and laid the foundations of astronomy. He had not the wealth or health to carry through a fraction of the schemes he worked out on paper, but he set science on its feet and made learning rational.

The Young Captain of Gaza

GATCOMBE. Nature made it lovely and man has not spoiled it. At the foot of the New Barn Down (539 feet high) and in the green serenity of the park, is Gatcombe church, with precious memories of the centuries and a treasure of our time. It has the last monument fashioned by one of our great sculptors in memory of one of our young heroes. The sculptor was Sir Thomas Brock and the monument to Charles Grant Seely, who gave up his life in 1917; he was wounded three times and fell leading his men on the Turkish stronghold of Gaza. We read that he is greatly beloved (for he was a very gallant gentleman) and that he lies at Gaza surrounded by the men of his regiment who fell with him that day. The sculptor, whose last piece of work this was, has shown the young captain with the calm of the Great Peace on his face, lying with his sword across his breast, his hands folded restfully above it, his head a little to one side. In the panels of the tomb are low reliefs of his battlefield grave and of an eastern city, with shields bearing coloured badges set in laurel wreaths. It is a monument of poignant dignity, moving us deeply, as if the sculptor had felt that it was to be, as indeed it is, his own memorial too.

One other figure of a warrior has this 13th century church; one of the rare wooden figures of knights (there are only about a hundred in the country). He is here with sword ready, an angel at his head and a lion at his feet. His name is unknown, but he lies in a recess which, with the chancel arch and a lancet window in the nave, is all that remains of a 700-year-old church built by the Estur family of Gatcombe Manor. He was perhaps an Estur and this may be a Jacobean copy of an older figure which has vanished. The arcaded font has been here 700 years. The tower itself is 500 years old, built in three stages, and the top stage is garlanded with a stringcourse of angels and gargoyles, one of them a winged and grinning demon. The stone porch has a cross on its gable supported by another of these fearful heads with clenched teeth. There is a Jacobean altar table, and the finely carved altar rails of the same period now form part of a screen. Some fragments of glass showing four angels in pale yellow are all that is left of the angelic glory which once made the windows beautiful.

The Odd Little Weepers

GODSHILL. Its delightful cottages are scattered along the road and grouped about all that is left of its lost priory, the biggest old church in the island, mainly from the 15th century. The porch has for a companion the pillar of a cross 700 years old, with a sundial on it and on the top of the porch gable is a square head with bared teeth and glaring eyes. We come into the church by a studded door which has kept its wooden lock and an original iron hinge reaching across the top, and we find ourselves in a noble interior with a black oak roof in which are over half a mile of timbers.

The church is remarkable for the tombs in the chancel, which go back to Tudor days. Here sleeps Sir James Worsley, whose family came over with the Conqueror. One of them went crusading and lies buried on the Island of Rhodes, but Sir James stayed at home, brought up at Court as a page to Henry the Seventh, and having as his playfellow the boy who grew up to be our Bluebeard King. So it was that many honours came his way when his young friend was crowned; he was made Master of the Robes at a time when it fell to him to organise the glittering pageant of the Field of the Cloth of Gold. Sir James is seen here kneeling with his lady under a canopy on which three boys are supporting shields, and above them hangs a medieval tilting helm, no mere funeral helmet, but worn in the tournaments, flaunting in the lists on some victorious head with some proud lady's favour blowing from its crest. It was probably the helmet of the knight himself, and he may have worn it on that glittering field. The pageant he organised was the most brilliant array of nobles the world has ever seen. Nearly 6000 people and over 3000 horses took part in the great cavalcade across the Channel. A palace was built for them 320 feet square, and there were 820 tents set up on the field. Such was the English pageantry alone; and two kings left their palaces to meet in a tent of gold.

By the high altar is what the historian once called the fairest tomb in our island, on which lie Sir John and Dame Agnes Leigh, nobly carved in alabaster by the famous Chellaston craftsmen. Dame Agnes is daintily dressed in a tight-fitting gown and a long cloak with heraldic embroidery, her head resting on a cushion supported by angels. Sir John's head rests on a tilting helmet, and he wears armour, his feet resting on a boar, as do his wife's. They are the most interesting pair of feet in the Isle of Wight, for at their soles are seated two tiny mournful monks with long beards, each resting his head sorrowfully on one hand while from the other hand dangles a rosary. Odd little weepers, these, and very rare in sculpture; we have come upon them in Cornwall, in Kent, and in Westminster Abbey and in St George's at Windsor, but there are only a few examples in all England. It is thought that the idea is to suggest the humility of the servant or the pride of the master. Sir John lies in his pride by the altar, still teaching these monks to be not too proud.

On a wall-monument in the north transept are the busts of two other Worsleys of the 18th century, with figures of Faith and Hope, and there is a big cenotaph which has been locally christened the Bath, set up a hundred years ago to Sir Richard Worsley.

The ancient font has a cover 200 years old. There is a beautiful Elizabethan chair with strap work and a delicately carved scroll, an 18th century almsdish, a 17th century chest, and the altar rails and altar table are Jacobean. In the chancel are two 17th century stools. A fresco which has been here about 500 years has been rescued from many coats of whitewash on the wall of the south transept; it shows Our Lord nailed to a tree with three branches from which spring willow-like leaves, the form of the tree being known as the Budding Cross. The fine cradle roof of the south transept has faces on its wooden bosses, two of the heads wearing gold crowns. The stone corbels of the transept have queer devices, one a dog's head with a padlock in its teeth. On the north wall hangs an oil painting of Daniel with the lions, and in the sanctuary is a small painting of the Madonna by Tiorelli. One of the east windows is lovely with figures of the Madonna and Child, St Michael, and St Gabriel in robes of green, blue, and purple, a nave window has a blue Madonna and a woman looking up appealingly to her in a garden, and another east window has a beautiful Crucifixion scene. There is a processional cross 600 years old, made by an Italian craftsman.

Beneath a broken stone near the porch sleeps a man of the 17th century, Richard Gard, who was apparently not beloved, for he is described as being "as crafty a knave as any, a penurious base fellow of little religion," and we are told that he lies only just below the stone, apparently lest he should fail to hear the Resurrection trumpet. Another stone covers the grave of Bartholomew Jacobs, and on it runs this 18th century rhyme:

> Man is the seed, God is the sower;
> Man is the grass, Death is the mower.

A sundial has been set on the churchyard's 13th century cross, and looking down on it are many green creatures creeping round the battlements.

The Great House and the Little Church

KINGSTON. A quiet way brings us to the church perched on a knoll and sheltered by the downs, with a beautiful manor house at its feet. Smooth green banks and flower beds slope down to the grey garden walls and the Elizabethan front, where from a wide buttress rise five tall red chimneys, towering above the mossy tiled roof. From the drive we climb 20 worn and narrow steps to the tiny manorial church, refashioned last century but keeping 13th century sedilia and the delightful brass portraits of Richard Mewys and his four sons in long gowns and square-toed shoes. Richard died 400 years ago, and he looks like a lawyer; his family lived in the island 300 years and held the manor from the 15th to the 18th century. It is all very simple and neatly kept, and the 20 narrow pews are lighted by candles.

The list of vicars, which goes back 600 years, has on it the name of John Atkinson, who was here for nearly half of last century.

Lord Mottistone's House and the Wonderful Horse

MOTTISTONE. It is a place of enchantment, with all the blessings country near the sea can lavish on a village it loves. Mottistone Down is 667 feet up, and there are trees in profusion, green fields and wild flowers, and in the summer the air about it is scented with sea, gorse, and hay all magically blended.

The winding road slips between the church and a 16th century manor house, with smooth green lawns and exuberant flower beds. It was once the home of the Chekes, kinsmen of that Sir John Cheke who was Cambridge's first Professor of Greek, tutored Edward the Sixth, and comes into Milton's sonnets:

Thy age, like ours, O soul of Sir John Cheke,
Hated not learning worse than toad or asp,
When thou taughtest Cambridge and King Edward Greek.

A great landslide from the hill behind this charming Elizabethan house buried much of it under 1500 tons of sand, and for a long time it was abandoned and no one had the courage to reclaim it. But a few years ago Lord Mottistone (known to our time as Jack Seely), Lord Lieutenant of Hampshire, excavated the house from its great mass of sand and gave to the 20th century a notable example of a lovely Tudor house. The date 1559 is on a stone over the doorway, and tradition says that our boy king Edward the Sixth once stayed here with his tutor.

A narrow path climbing past the manor house takes us through oak woods carpeted with bluebells up to the lower heights of the downs, where we come suddenly on two huge stones which are probably the oldest man-made monuments on the island, and may possibly be the remains of a dolmen raised by Stone Age men. One stands upright about 15 feet high, the other lies like a fallen warrior guarded by a friend. There are several ancient barrows on the downs, the biggest a huge mound called Black Barrow, and the view of sea, woods, and downs from here is one of the things the traveller in the Isle of Wight does not forget.

The church is small and charming; in it meet several centuries. The nave arcades and the chancel are probably 15th, and there is in the chapel a delightful Tudor arcade on clustered columns. By the altar is the table tomb of Sir Robert Dillington's wife Jane, who died in 1674. The base of the 13th century font is Norman and of unusual design, being solid and almost square, with a pillar at each corner. A Jacobean carpenter made the pulpit and filled its panels with charming designs; and some village carpenter long ago must have furnished the chancel with its reddish roof, for it is made of cedar from the cargo of a timber ship wrecked off this coast. On the wall of the nave we read of two brothers who gave themselves for England, John Edward Guy Brown, who fell in action in France, and Alexander Claud Brown, who, wounded in aerial combat, landed his plane and saved his observer.

Over Mottistone Down about the time we called a noble horse was seen carrying his master. This is his story. He was the luckiest horse on the Western Front, says Lord Mottistone, who was then General Seely. He took Warrior with him to the war, and the two became so devoted that when the General for some reason rode another horse Warrior jumped out of his box and followed him, bridleless, like a dog. He became used to shell fire, but never lost his fear of the sharp rattle of the machine gun and the rifle, though he was always self-controlled. He did not move when a horse standing next to him fell dead. When he was resting in the stables near Messines Ridge General Seely barely escaped with his life from some heavy shells; but, covered with plaster and tiles from a falling roof, he ran out in his pyjamas to the stables, where Warrior gave him a loud whinny of welcome. He took him away and in an instant the stall was blown to pieces.

Once he was stabled in a drawing-room with a precious table as a manger for his oats; and though the house was wrecked General Seely ran to the ruins to hear the well-known whinny and rescued Warrior just in time. He survived the first and second battles of Cambrai, when hundreds of horses were killed, and escaped with his life at the capture of the ridge of the forest of Morueil, where 800 horses were lost.

He cannot know that Sir John French would often ride him up and down among the troops, making speeches to keep up the men's spirits; nor can he know how proud a horse he is; but Lord Mottistone knows; never were a horse and his master greater friends.

His Last Amen

NEWCHURCH. It is on a hill near Sandown, with a view from its churchyard across a lovely valley to a range of downs. It is delightful to see the great spread of wistaria at one end of the street, and the little red steeple on the wooden tower at the other. Here a sundial has marked the hours since the 17th century. The church goes far back to the Conquest, though the oldest work we see is in three small Norman windows and in the nave arcades by our earliest English builders (notably a crude arch at the east end of the south arcade). We wonder at the size and spaciousness of the building, but it was once the only church of a parish which stretched across the island and included Ryde and Ventnor.

The church tower is weatherboarded, and built over the south porch, in which the ancient door is still swinging on its hinges. The panelled 17th century pulpit has a big canopy held by chains, with an angel holding a Bible. The beautiful gilded lectern came here last century after having been a century and a half at Frome in Somerset. It is carved with an eagle and its eaglets. There are 15th century rood stairs, an 18th century barrel organ, and altar vases of Roman pottery; perhaps the first time we have come upon Roman remains on a Christian altar.

In this small place good Richard Forward spent his long and useful life from 1750 to 1826; he sleeps by the path at the west of the churchyard. He was parish clerk 54 years and schoolmaster 53, and for about half that time was church clerk too. The stone on his grave was paid for by a penny subscription among his old pupils, and we were able to read this verse upon it:

> *In yonder sacred pile his voice was wont to sound,*
> *And now his body rests beneath the hallowed ground.*
> *He taught the peasant boy to read and use the pen;*
> *His earthly toils are o'er; he's cry'd his last Amen.*

A mile away at Knighton are the ruins of a 13th century chapel.

A Town of Famous Folk

NEWPORT. It is not now the lovely place it must have been when Keats sat down in Newport and wrote the first line of Endymion, A thing of beauty is a joy for ever. It has become the business capital of the Isle of Wight, but it has many attractive things to see and pathetic links with history. It takes us back to old Rome and gives us intimate touches with Charles Stuart, for here he was a captive and here his little daughter lies.

Yet Newport is an engaging place to see, with its delightful old grammar school, its 17th century houses, the little harbour on the River Medina, and 1000 acres of forest a pleasant mile's walk away. The town stands on a pleasant slope of the hills watered on one side by the river and on another by a stream.

In Tudor days the town gave Queen Elizabeth three of her most trusted servants: Dr Edes her chaplain, Dr James her physician, and Thomas Fleming her Lord Chief Justice. She used to say of these three that one was for her soul, one for her body, and the other for her goods. Judge Fleming has a statue in the 19th century Guildhall, showing him sitting in a chair on which is a carving of the trial of Guy Fawkes, at which he presided. The Guildhall was built by John Nash, and has balconies on two sides with a clock tower at one corner. It has some fine portraits, two magnificent silver maces, and some sea pictures, and one of its odd possessions is a pair of long poles with a glove at the end of each. The gloves were new in 1821, and in the olden days they were hung out from a balcony to let revellers know at fair time that they might dance in the streets.

We may no longer see the panelled room in which Charles Stuart received the Parliamentary Commissioners, for it disappeared with the old town hall which the Guildhall replaced. In that room Charles held his Court, with Bishop Juxon in his retinue and Brian Duppa, the bishop at whose deathbed Charles the Second was to kneel imploring blessing. But we may see the old grammar school where the king lodged, with the windows through which he looked out on the street and the schoolroom which was used as a presence chamber during the negotiations between the king and 15 commissioners which resulted in the vain Treaty of Newport. It was from here that the king was taken to Hurst Castle. He demanded to see their orders, but was refused, and it is recorded that his servants were filled with alarm as to what might happen to him. Never at one time, wrote the king's faithful servant Thomas Herbert, was beheld more grief in men's faces or greater fears in their hearts than when the king was in such a manner hurried away they knew not whither.

From this pathetic place we come to the grave of the king's little daughter in the church, where she lies in front of the altar, a brass marking the spot. The old church has gone, and the coffin was removed from its chancel, some workmen having come upon it while digging another grave. Prince Albert laid the foundation stone of the new church, and Queen Victoria set up the monument in memory of the princess fashioned from Carrara marble by Baron Marochetti. She lies a simple and beautiful white figure under a canopy of broken prison bars, symbolising that she is free from her captivity at last, and the inscription says that the monument is a token of respect for her virtues and sympathy for her misfortunes.

The tower of the church (from which curfew still rings out on nearly every winter's night) is 132 feet high. Under its central canopy is Our Lord giving His blessing to a child, and set in two other canopies are figures of Thomas Becket and St Thomas the disciple. Inside is a medallion of Prince Albert by Baron Marochetti, and a fine monument to Sir Edward Horsey who died of plague a few years before the Spanish Armada. A grand fellow he looks in marble, his bearded face dignified with repose, his body cased in armour, and his actual sword sheathed at his side. His helmet hangs above him, and his glowing epitaph attributes to him all human virtues. He was in truth a bold sea captain and something of a conspirator.

One of the most beautiful pieces of craftsmanship in the island is the delightful oak pulpit, an octagon crammed with cravings. It

The Old Village of Shanklin

Shanklin's Cliff Walk to Sandown

THE CHARM OF THE GARDEN ISLE

St Catherine's Old Lighthouse   **Newport Guildhall**

The White Walls by the Needles, Seen Across the Solent

comes from the old church and is the work of a 17th century craftsman, with a canopy magnificently carved, Justice with Mercy in its cresting, and angels blowing trumpets. Below hangs a dove, and the book-rest, supported on charming brackets, has two rows of seven panels with figures of Faith, Hope, Charity, Justice, Prudence, Temperance, and Fortitude in the top, and figures of the sciences below. Also from the old church are two almsboxes of the 17th century, the reading desk is made of wood from the old chancel screen, the bells are from the old tower, and the old font is here as a companion for the new one. One of the memories of the church is that Bishop Wilberforce here conducted his last ordination before he was thrown from his horse and killed.

Newport has many memories of interesting people who have walked its streets. Prince Albert laid the foundation-stone of its church, and Wellington, Canning, and Palmerston sat for it in Parliament. One of the Simeons, who were friends of Tennyson, has a monument on the Carisbrooke Road. The fine library centred here was founded by Sir Charles Seely, the first baronet of the family. Keats lived here while trying to get rid of the disease which finally carried him from the world of the living. John Hamilton Reynolds, a man who knew Keats and a small poet on his own account, lies in the churchyard. John Milne, the earthquake man lived and died here, doing his work at Shide and being buried at Barton. Albert Midlane, who wrote the hymn "There's a friend for little children," lived here beneath the bright blue sky of the island, and in the old burial ground is a pathetic little monument which must have interested that great friend of children. It is to the memory of Valentine Grey, a little sweep of ten who died in 1822. The brutal master whose cruelty and neglect caused his death was sent to prison for 12 months, and on a memorial raised by a penny fund is this:

To the memory of Valentine Grey, the little sweep. In testimony to the general feeling for suffering innocence this monument is erected by public subscription.

The most interesting of the old houses in the town are Chantry House, built in 1612; Hazard's House, built in 1684; and God's Providence House, with a fine doorway and stairway, and an inscription saying "God's Providence is my Inheritance." The peace memorial is in St Thomas's Square, a handsome stone cross with 341 names on bronze panels. In the marketplace is a memorial to Queen Victoria, showing three figures, Sympathy, Charity, and Fortitude supporting a crown.

A Friend of Keats

JOHN HAMILTON REYNOLDS, who lies in the old churchyard of Newport, missed being famous as a poet and died as a county court clerk. He is remembered today chiefly as the friend to whom Keats wrote many of his letters. His father was a master of the Bluecoat School and the boy became an insurance clerk, writing poetry meanwhile under the influence of Byron and Wordsworth. Byron thought so much of one of his poems that he asked a friend to review it gently. Leigh Hunt introduced Reynolds to Keats, who regarded him as a young man of high intellectual achievements. It was Reynolds who inspired Keats's poem on Robin Hood and it was Reynolds's sister who played over to Keats again and again a Spanish air which led Keats to write a song to fit it: Hush, hush, Tread Softly.

Reynolds wrote a sonnet to Keats and Keats wrote back:

> *Dear Reynolds! as last night I lay in bed,*
> *There came before my eyes that wonted thread*
> *Of shapes, and shadows, and remembrances,*
> *That every other minute vex and please:*
> *Things all disjointed come from north and south—*
> *Two Witch's eyes above a Cherub's mouth,*
> *Voltaire with casque and shield and habergeon,*
> *And Alexander with his nightcap on;*
> *Old Socrates a-tying his cravat,*
> *And Hazlitt playing with Miss Edgeworth's cat;*
> *And Junius Brutus, pretty well, so so,*
> *Making the best of's way towards Soho.*

In the end Reynolds became a lawyer and after his marriage dropped poetry and wrote for the Reviews. For a short time he was a friend of Tom Hood, who married his sister Jane; then he became clerk to the county court at Newport, where he was noted for his sarcastic wit and a not very happy disposition. His health was failing and fortune had not smiled on him, perhaps because he seems to have had a lack of purpose in his life.

The Mysterious Benefactors

NEWTOWN. The oldest town of the island, it is called New because it was made new after the French burned it down 600 years ago. It is on one of the five creeks of the Newtown river which, like the fingers of a hand, run far into the low-lying land between Cowes and Yarmouth. In the days of its prosperity it had anchorage for 50 ships of 500 tons and had a busy market where the green is now. It was the island's best haven for shipping in the 18th century, when it was twice the size of Newport. Today the tides have deserted it and its trade and its people have moved to other centres. It was one of the most notorious of the "rotten boroughs" of the days of corruption, and used to send two members to Parliament; among them the first Duke of Marlborough and Canning the Prime Minister.

The old town hall, built soon after the Restoration of the Stuarts, was for many years neglected and almost a ruin, but by the generosity of a mysterious band of benefactors it has been restored and put under the protection of the National Trust. This beneficent achievement was the work of one of the oddest companies of good people working in our time, a group of men and women who went about doing good in the name of Ferguson's Gang. One member of the Gang, wearing a mask and giving the name of Kate O'Brien, slipped into the office of the National Trust one day in 1934, all unnoticed, and dropped on the secretary's desk £500 for saving this town hall, the document she handed in being sealed with blood and full of misspellings.

It is a pretty little building the Gang has saved, with its old oak door and a dainty portico of fluted pillars. The silver seal and the mace (one of the most beautiful of its kind) are in the hands of the lord of the manor.

The church is 19th century, built in imitation of the 13th, and the sign of the ship on the house which used to be the Old Inn is a copy of the town's seal in its great days six centuries ago.

There has been found here in our time a bronze urn of the Iron Age, in which were ashes 2500 years old, and on the beach was found a complete skull of the earliest known type of wild ox, which has been extinct in this country thousands of years.

The Lovely Street

NITON. It lies in the midst of some of the finest down scenery on the Island, and when we called its sloping street was a lovely sight, with great bushes of fuchsia hanging their tassels like crimson bells over grey garden walls, a brook babbling below along its stony bed. It is sheltered by St Catherine's Hill.

We come into the church, which has Norman and medieval walls, under a yew reaching over the path. The tower is 400 years old with a little stone spire, perhaps added in Cromwell's time. The church has a 14th century porch, a big Norman font with a band of moulding, slightly pointed arches on round pillars about 700 years old, and a chancel of the 15th century. On the wall is a memorial to a friend of the village whose portrait is here by Flaxman; with it is a relief showing a woman holding young pelicans in her hand, while the mother bird is on her nest feeding them. The battlemented modern reredos is glorious in painted and gilded oak, with Christ in majesty attended by angels. In canopied recesses inlaid with gilt mosaic are oak figures of saints. There are three old chairs, a French one of the 16th century and two Jacobean. A brass tablet tells of Henry Charles Haynes, who was wrecked in a sloop off Bermuda in 1926 while on an errand of mercy.

The churchyard has a modern cross mounted on the steps of the old one; and in this peaceful place sleeps Edward Edwards, who lived through most of the 19th century and is remembered as one of the founders of public libraries. High on the downs is seen the medieval lighthouse, where for generations a solitary priest kept a light burning for ships in trouble on this treacherous coast.

A Poem to Two Children

NORTHWOOD. Away from the red village overlooking the River Medina, its church stands among the trees on a hill with a fine view of the distant downs. We come into it by a doorway with a Norman arch on two little pillars to find ourselves in a nave with arcades by the earliest English builders, the arches on the south having a graceful line of moulding round them. The chancel is 15th century; the panelled pulpit is 17th century and has a graceful carved canopy. The dignified reredos is carved with trefoils, and the plain altar was made of old oak from Carisbrooke. An oil painting of the Baptism is thought to be the work of the 16th century artist Bassano. On the windowsill we found a wooden frame, painted with cherubs, skulls, and crossbones, in which is a beautifully written manuscript poem to two children of the 17th century, and in a glass case is kept the old clarionet which helped the village choir to keep in time in the far-off days. One of the wall-monuments is unusually rich in the gruesome things so fashionable in the 17th and 18th centuries; it has a grinning skull at each side, a skull and a heap of bones below, and a winged hourglass to remind us that time flies.

The Escape of an Empress

RYDE. It is the delight of thousands every summer, a popular seaside town of the Isle of Wight, with seven miles of beach, an esplanade with trees and lawns and lovely gardens, a lake where young and old love to sail their model boats, and Puckpool Park reached by a little walk along the front past the Appley watchtower. Puckpool Park was once a military fort, but today, instead of the tramp of soldiers, we hear the laughter of the holiday maker, and round about the ramparts, bastions, and gun-emplacements are tennis lawns and bowling greens and delightful woodlands. And, of course, it overlooks Spithead, river and sea together, so that here has been witnessed the pageantry of naval history, the great ships coming to and going from Portsmouth and Southampton.

Ryde was one of the first places in England to have a pier, and now it has one of the most remarkable of all piers, three in one, running out for half a mile for trains, for trams, and for those who walk. All its churches are new. All Saints has a pulpit with saints and martyrs carved in alabaster, and a tall pinnacled tower tempting climbers with its magnificent view from the top; it is one of Sir Gilbert Scott's best works. The Roman Catholic St Mary's was designed by the designer of the hansom cab, and has survived the cab as a much more beautiful monument of its creator, who was buried at Fulham when there were still 7000 hansoms on the streets of London. It is one of the most pleasing churches on the island. Its pillars are painted; its blue chancel roof is picked out with golden stars; it has a tablet to Lady Hamilton, for 55 years a worshipper here; and a brass portrait of a lady kneeling near the pew in which she died kneeling in 1861. Over the altar is an excellent copy of the Crucifixion that hangs in the Sistine Chapel at Rome.

The theatre at Ryde is interesting because it stands on the site of an old theatre in which the famous Mrs Jordan appeared for the last time in England and Ellen Terry for the first time on the stage. Fielding the novelist stayed here to gain strength for that famous voyage to Lisbon in 1754 which he described in the last work he wrote.

In one of the climbing streets is a charming white house (now a hotel) which entertained an empress unawares. In the small hours of a September morning in 1870 a yacht stole up and anchored off the pier, and Mr Sadler of the York Hotel was awakened by urgent knocking at his door. He found two ladies and two gentlemen there, asking for the best suite of rooms he had. They left that night, and not till then did Mr Sadler know that he had sheltered the Empress Eugenie, who had escaped from France in Sir John Burgoyne's yacht.

That exciting journey had begun on the night the news of the catastrophe of Sedan reached Paris. The mob was crying for a Republic outside the Tuileries, and the empress was alone in the Louvre except for two foreign ambassadors, her attendant Madame le Breton, and the famous M. de Lesseps. There was only one hope of escape, by way of the Louvre, with which there was continuous communication. Even so there was half a mile of corridors and picture galleries to pass; and on reaching the door to the Louvre the empress found it locked, and the key gone. The mob was hurling itself against the Tuileries and all seemed lost till, with a stroke of genius, de Lesseps flung open the main doors and let the crowd stream in and through the building, and so out into the Place du Carrousel beyond.

In the meantime the missing key had been found and Eugenie and Madame le Breton reached the street and called a cab. As they did so an urchin cried, "Look, the Empress!" but his cry passed unnoticed and the cab drove off. Before they had gone far the ladies found that they had only half-a-crown between them, so, not daring to risk an altercation with their driver, they got out, gave him all their money, and continued on foot through the raging city.

Not one of the many doors at which they knocked was opened to them until they reached the house of Dr Evans, an American dentist. He sheltered them for the night and afterwards drove them, disguised, to Deauville, Eugenie pretending to be insane and on her way to an asylum. At Deauville they went aboard the yacht of Sir John Burgoyne and crossed in a terrible storm to the Isle of Wight. Arriving at Ryde in the middle of the night, the poor storm-tossed women looked so sadly disreputable that the proprietor of the York Hotel, called from his bed, hesitated about receiving them. Their stay was not long, for after a brief rest they passed on to Hastings to meet the Prince Imperial, just arrived after his own sensational escape.

This was a nine-day memory for Ryde, but one tragic memory it has that will not soon pass away, for in a field where the esplanade now runs were buried many of the victims of the wreck of the Royal George in 1782. Every schoolboy knows Cowper's poem. The ship was at anchor for repairs with officers, men, and visitors on board. The admiral was writing in his cabin when suddenly the Royal George rolled over on her side, dipping her masthead in the water. She righted herself again and then heeled over till her yards touched the sea on the other side; then she righted herself again and sank with twice 400 men. She sank because she was rotten.

The White Tower

ST HELEN'S. In a little patch of woodland overlooking the harbour, where at low tide the horses and lorries go out to cart away the mud shingle, stands the tower of its old church. It is shored up by buttresses, and has little round-headed windows and a doorway through which no bellringer passes in now. But, though no services are held within, it renders service to others still, for it is a landmark which sailors have known about 700 years, and its seaward side is kept white for their sakes.

Some way from the village is the church rebuilt in the 19th century on the site of one consecrated in 1719 by Bishop Trelawny, one of the Seven Bishops who challenged the King, hero of the ballad And Shall Trelawny Die? In the chancel is a tablet flanked by the emblem of Roman law to the memory of a judge who died in the year before Waterloo, and another decked with flags and arms of his son, who, after coming safely through many battles, was killed at Waterloo. The glowing colours from two painted windows in the east and west transepts meet on the pavement before the chancel steps. One is of Christ as the Light of the World, with St Helen and St Wilfrid. He was the saint who landed in the island in 704 and settled at Brading, where he preached the Kingdom of Christ and taught the natives to fish with hooks and nets instead of spears. In the other window is the scene of the Sermon on the Mount.

A Great Ship Goes Down

SANDOWN. It has glorious cliffs where many famous men have loved to walk. Lewis Carroll would spend long holidays here. Darwin loved it as much as any place he knew by the sea. John Wilkes built a house here which he called his "Villakin"; there is a memorial plaque on the site of it at the corner of the High Street. On Sunday mornings John Wilkes would go to Shanklin church, and after the service would walk across the fields to Knighton with David Garrick and his wife. Sir Isaac Pitman is said to have worked on his shorthand dictionary here, and to bring our history up to date Sir Hall Caine wrote his first novel here.

There are delightful gardens on the cliffs between Sandown and Shanklin, beautiful with rockeries and flowerbeds, and a wide view over the bay which runs from the gleaming white walls of Culver Cliff, rising 250 feet out of the sea, to the sunburnt cliffs on the way to Dunnose.

Sandown has no ancient church, but its nineteenth century church has a west doorway built in Norman style; it was put here in memory of Sir Henry Oglander, the last of the family which came over with the Conqueror and was part of the life of the Isle of Wight until Sir Henry died in 1874. They would be great people in the island when Sandown Castle was built by Henry the Eighth. It was second in importance only to Carisbrooke, but the sea destroyed it and Charles Stuart rebuilt it. It was demolished in 1864 and the stones were used for the present fort. Not many minutes walk away are the remains of a building a thousand years older, for we are within easy reach of the famous Roman villa at Brading. A low square mound with an anchor marks the graves of men who perished in the wreck of the Eurydice and were buried in the churchyard. The ship foundered in a squall in 1878 and only two lives were saved out of 300.

She was a training ship on her way home from the West Indies, and was almost in safe waters. A falling barometer gave the only suggestion that the morning's fair breeze would not last, and off Dunnose she was under all plain sail, with port-holes open, when the squall hit her. A heavy snowstorm travelled the length of England that March afternoon, accompanied by a strong north wind. Over the downs it came, bursting furiously upon the unprepared Eurydice before sails could be shortened. She heeled over; water rushed in between decks through the port-holes. It was impossible to lower lifeboats for those on deck. Some grabbed lifebuoys as the ship went down, but the sea was so rough and cold that most of them were overcome. Owing to the snow their plight could not be seen by coastguards, and it was not until the weather cleared that a passing ship picked up all who were still afloat, five men only, of whom three died before they could be landed at Ventnor.

The Island's Oldest Tower

SHALFLEET. It lies in the hollow and climbs the sharp slopes on a switchback hill on the Yarmouth road. We found its thatched roofs showing through masses of fruit blossom, the grey tower of the church rising grandly above. It is the oldest tower in the island, and has been saved by the engineering genius of the 20th century, for it was found that it was standing in 10 feet of clay and water, and the foundations have been relaid in concrete. Here on a small scale the miracle of the saving of Winchester Cathedral has been accomplished. The walls of the tower are five feet thick and it stands 20 feet square. The sturdy Norman doorway has a sculptured tympanum in which is a man looking very much like the Mr Noah of our nurseries, standing between two lions with tails curved above their backs. He is probably Daniel.

The spacious church has the splendid simplicity of the 13th century builder, with a lofty tower arch, a noble arcade on slender pillars of porphyry, and tracery windows with rare oval lights. The chancel screen made from ancient timbers is in memory of Thomas Hollis, who was sexton here for 55 years until just before the Great War. The reredos is made of old linenfold panelling, and the remains of the 17th century altar table. The Jacobean pulpit has carved brackets and two rows of carved panels. The wooden crucifix by the pulpit was found among old rubbish. The roof timbers of the nave and the south porch of stone are both 500 years old. Two faint sculptures are fading away after 700 years; they are on the gravestone by the south door, and are carved with shields and spears and a helmet. It is thought the helmet may mark the grave of Pagan Trenchard, a knight who lived here when men were still talking of William Rufus.

The memorial to those who did not come back from the war is a window in lovely colouring of the Light of the World, with St Nicholas and our patron St George.

Enchanting Place

SHANKLIN. Two poets have loved it, and we do not wonder, for it is the best little town in the island, old village and new town together, sheltered by Shanklin Down and with the extraordinary fissure in the cliffs called Shanklin Chine, a ravine about 60 yards wide and 100 yards deep, made by a stream cascading into pools in the green depths below, falling musically down. Ferns and flowers cling to its steep sides. There are wonderful walks through the trees and shrubs of Luccombe Chine with its hidden talkative spring, and at the Landslip where great boulders thrust themselves up ruggedly among low twisted trees. The hydrangea hedge on the sunny strip of turf, known as Keats Green, was in its glory when we called, running for three-quarters of a mile along the cliff walk, and Luccombe Common was covered with gorse and daisies and little trees. Even without the ceaseless murmuring of the sea through the trees it would be a captivating place and we can well believe that, walking or living here, Keats would think out the immortal opening line of his Endymion, A thing of beauty is a joy for ever.

At the top of the Chine stands the village with its old cottages, its ancient yews, vigorous elms and cedars, and a gabled and thatched inn with little bow windows. The town is rich in public gardens where we may sit and watch the ships pass up and down the Channel or listen to the community singing when the gardens are aglow with fairy-lights. It is good to know that Shanklin's community concerts have attracted attention far and wide and that singing is heard here not only in English but in French, German, Danish, and Welsh.

The old church stands a little aloof, drawing its cloak of ash trees about it in the shelter of the Down. It has lost much of its ancient aspect, but keeps one of its 14th century windows, a 14th century piscina, two 17th century chairs, and a splendid 16th century chest carved with the name of a 15th century prior. The timbered lychgate, handsome with its clock and bell, was set up in memory of a lord of the manor.

The two poets who loved this place were Longfellow and Keats. Keats began his long poem Lamia in a cottage under the cliff in the days when he came to the island in his pathetic search for health; and Longfellow came to the inn on the slope of Shanklin Chine in the old part of the town. This verse he wrote is let into a brick pillar from which water trickles for the thirsty traveller:

> *O, traveller, stay thy weary feet;*
> *Drink of this fountain pure and sweet;*
> *It flows for rich and poor the same.*
> *Then go thy way, remembering still*
> *The wayside well beneath the hill,*
> *The cup of water in His name.*

The little spring discovered by the court physician to Charles the Second is still running bravely. We do not wonder that the population of Shanklin has gone up 50 times in 100 years, for it is an enchanting place, with an average of five hours of sunshine every day, with heights about 800 feet above the sea, and with down and copse in the safe keeping of the National Trust. Darwin thought there was no place like it by the sea and did some writing here.

The Earthquake Man

SHIDE. It is a hamlet by Newport, and actually part of it, and is known to scientists for two considerable reasons, having to do with Roman Britain and world earthquakes. Here in 1926 were unearthed the foundations of a Roman villa. They were part of the Roman settlement known as Meda. Three of the eight rooms have mosaic pavements fairly complete and well preserved. An interesting find was an open fireplace, very unusual in a Roman house. The arrangements for the heating of the baths were astonishingly elaborate for so small a house. Part of the villa has now been completed with walls and roof, so that it can be pictured as a dwelling-place and not a mere foundation, and in it we may see many coins and pieces of pottery.

As for earthquakes, time was when, if an earthquake happened anywhere, Shide was almost always the first to record it. Professor John Milne built an earthquake observatory here and made this quiet green village famous through the scientific world. Now the observatory is no more. The good work is carried on at Oxford, and Shide is left peaceful and forgotten. But it seems a good place to remember good John Milne, who died here in the year before the war and lies at Barton, a little way off.

This remarkable man, after interesting experiences in Central Europe, Newfoundland, and Palestine, found himself at 24 a servant of the Japanese Government, and it was on his first night in Tokyo that he was so impressed by an earthquake that he resolved to study earthquakes for the rest of his life. He lived another 40 years and kept his word. The Japanese Government made him the first Professor of Seismology in the Imperial University. The practical and scientific results of the novel study Professor Milne thus initiated have been of capital importance. It has saved an incalculable number of lives, and prevented an inestimable amount of damage. He discovered methods of building houses and bridges which make these structures comparatively immune from the effects of earth tremors. Having spent twenty years in Japan, and visited the principal earthquake regions of the Pacific coast, he returned to England in 1895 and settled at Shide, where he established a highly equipped observatory.

From this quiet situation his researches extended over the whole earth. He was able to promote the establishment of sixty seismological observatories in various parts of the world, from which he received regular reports, so that by the comparison of their records the source, direction, and extent of each earthquake was known.

Sir John and Little Barnabas

SHORWELL. Perhaps more than a fair share of the island's treasures are to be found in this small place, for it has some noble houses. Yet its chief treasure is probably that confronting us as we pass through the ancient doorway of its church.

It is a big 15th century fresco of St Christopher carrying the Child, painted by a master hand and in splendid preservation. It has scenes from the saint's life round it, an unusual addition in such pictures. The river is full of fish, and a hermit stands on the right bank before his hut holding a lighted lantern. Three ships sail the waters, and from the mast of one is a light, seemingly an answering signal to the lantern on the bank. The smaller pictures show the saint riding beside the devil, and then comes his joyous renunciation of his fearful companion, this scene showing him beside a crucifix, with a staff blossoming in his hand. Next we see his martyrdom, when he is bound and wounded by arrows, the executioner in long pointed shoes holding the sword which finally ended his suffering. Among his enemies is a crowned figure with an ill-aimed arrow entering one of his eyes. The colours are red, yellow, black, and green, the draughtsmanship is remarkably good, and the whole fresco is full of conviction and vigour.

Another great rarity of this small church is its enchanting stone pulpit, about 500 years old. There are only about sixty of these medieval pulpits left in England. This one grows out of a pillar in the north arcade and is entered by an archway cut in the pier. It has a delightful wooden canopy made in 1620, and near it is an hourglass stand with an old hourglass in it.

A fine copy of Cranmer's Bible, printed in 1541 and in excellent condition, is in a glass case, and there is a copy of Richard Hooker's Ecclesiastical Polity opened at its elaborately printed title page, with a seal bearing Cranmer's arms and another seal blank, the empty space having been for Thomas Cromwell's arms, which were removed on his falling into disfavour. This Bible was restored to the church in 1891 after it had been away more than 100 years. On the wall of the south aisle hangs a small oak panel of the Crucifixion.

The font was new when the church was refashioned in the 15th century; its Jacobean cover has a dove on the top. The old Tudor gunchamber, built on to the church at the time when every village on the island was ordered to keep a cannon, has been panelled with wood from Shorwell elms and turned into a vestry.

In the south chapel is an Elizabethan altar with carved legs, and over it a quaint painting on wood of the Last Supper, brought from Iceland and given to Shorwell in 1898. On the east wall is Elizabeth Leigh's heraldic brass.

There are two portrait brasses, one of Sir Richard Bethell, a 16th century rector, in a long full-sleeved gown and a tippet fastened by a rosette on one shoulder. By an economical arrangement the upper part of the stone in which this brass is inlaid was used later for another inscription to John Godsall, a vicar here for 54 years, who died in 1732. The other portrait brass is of two pretty women with 15 children, the "deare and loyal wives" of Barnabas Leigh. The 10 sons and 5 daughters belong to Mistress Elizabeth Bampfield, resplendent in handsome Elizabethan gown and headdress. The second wife has lovely clothes too, but no headdress hides her beautiful hair.

In the north aisle is the canopied alabaster monument of Sir John Leigh, who died in 1629. He kneels at a prayer desk and has the beard, ruff, and hose of the day. Behind him in a long gown on a high hassock kneels his great-grandson Barnabas. When Sir John had died and was lying in the house awaiting burial, Barnabas, a lovely little fellow here, only nine months old, fell sick and died, and they sleep together, their epitaph ending:

> *Inmate in grave, he took his grandchild heir,*
> *Whose soul did haste to make to him repair,*
> *And so to heaven along as little page*
> *With him did post, to wait upon his age.*

Sir John, who built the splendid many-gabled house across the way (North Court), gave the church its stone spire with the weathercock dated 1617. The old knight would be thrilled to know that two Leigh brothers fell for their country on Gallipoli; we read on a mosaic memorial to them that "Nature might stand up and say to all the world that these were men."

Old Thomas Urry

THORLEY. A quiet place off the road not far from Yarmouth, Thorley has two churches. In the new one is the ancient font of the old one, 700 years old, resting on a squat pillar and having a curious base with carved corners and a little arch below. In the painted glass of four small lancets are pictured the Good Shepherd, the Light of the World, St Catherine, and St Cecilia.

Close to an old farm is all that remains of the old church, a porch and a buttressed belfry. From the road we see, over the farm buildings, a cross above an ivy-clad gable. It is roofed with tiles and looks like a small barn, but still has its charming 13th century doorway, with a beautiful image niche inside. On the floor is the grave of Thomas

Urry, who died on Christmas Day in 1631. He has a heraldic brass and these lines:

His aged years (almost) were twelve times seven,
He's called to keep his Christmas now in Heaven.

Near the door is an ancient stone coffin with a place for the sleeper's head, showing how long this church had been a place of prayer before it was put on one side and left.

Peacocks are to be met with, it seemed to us, in any of Thorley's lanes. When we called two were resting in the dead branches of a fallen tree, their brilliant feathers aglow against the silver bark.

The Beautiful Bay

TOTLAND BAY. The Farthest West inhabitable bay, one of the most impressive points of the island, and one of the most comfortable places in the world for the traveller, it is easily reached from Lymington, with the ferry landing us at the delightful little harbour of Yarmouth, in which we found the king's yacht. From the windows on the bay we look across to the mainland with Hurst Castle in good view by day, the lights of Bournemouth by night, and with clear visibility the white cliffs of Swanage in sight. Many great liners pass this way.

A little way off is Alum Bay with the coloured sands which every child loves and the near view of the Needles, and within an easy walk is Tennyson's Down, the house where he lived, and the church with seven memorials of his family and the grave of his wife. The 19th century church has little for the traveller to see, but the all-red church of St Saviour's, built by the Roman Catholics, is delightful, with its walls of neatly patterned brick, its elegant tower, its projecting baptistry, the five arches along its west front, and an interior with three big and three small bays, half-moon windows in the sanctuary, and other windows shining with the Madonna, the Good Shepherd, and saints. Hereabouts is Weston Manor, with a private chapel built by the theologian William George Ward, near neighbour and great friend of Tennyson, who thought him among the "most worthy of mankind," whose living like he would not find again.

Not far from Totland Bay in the last years of last century the first British wireless transmitting station was set up by Marconi. The first readable signals were exchanged with a steamer at sea on

479

November 6, 1897, and in June of the following year the first paid Marconigram was sent from this station by Lord Kelvin. The station has entirely disappeared, but a granite memorial has been set up to mark the spot on which it stood.

The Terrace Seven Miles Long

VENTNOR. We may think ourselves on the Riviera, with the precipitous slopes of St Boniface Down above us, the summit of the island, and facing the sea all the beauty and wonder of the famous Undercliff. The houses rise in terraces on rocky ledges, one above the other on the edge of zigzag roads. What was within living memory a grassy field is now a lovely park. There are miles of fine walks, and for those seeking physical fitness there is a tempting run up (or down) a hundred and one steps.

The great coastal terrace of the Undercliff is seven miles long and in some parts half a mile wide, running from Dunnose Point to Blackgang Chine. The terrace is believed to be the result of a pre-historic disaster when the whole face of the downs fell suddenly into the sea. There have been many landslips since that first fall, but the Undercliff as a whole, the geologist tells us, came to rest before the dawn of history. The road (surely one of the loveliest in the land) winds along it, climbing and falling at the caprice of this natural ledge, and leading us through peaceful avenues to surprise us suddenly with wild open slopes covered with gorse and rocks and mighty tumbled boulders. These slopes are the scars that refuse to heal, and will never let us forget the terror and magnitude of the disaster which turned this land into a playground of rare beauty. Under the gracious trees, covering some parts of it so thickly that we see neither cliffs nor sea, and in among its happy army of wild flowers, we can easily forget, but out on these slopes it is hard to think of anything else. The Undercliff is never really at rest; its enemies are too many. Rain, frost, the hungry sea, and that traitor within the gates called Blue Slipper (the grey, slippery clay that causes so many of the falls) are constantly at work. So here and there the movements go on, mostly making no great difference, sometimes more serious. Enchanting paths fight their way resolutely to the top of the cliffs where glorious views are the rich reward of those who follow them. At Chale it ends in the vast chine called Blackgang.

On the Undercliff are two big estates with something to make them interesting—Wolverton because in its gardens is the ruin of a little 14th century house with slits only six inches wide for windows; and the Orchard because its garden comes in the dedication of Swinburne's poem The Sisters:

Between the sea-cliffs and the sea there sleeps
A garden walled about with woodland, fair
As dreams that die or days that memory keeps
Alive ...

St Lawrence is now part of Ventnor though greatly its senior, for Ventnor is modern and St Lawrence had its church in the 13th century. Ventnor itself has a group of modern churches, including St Catherine's in 13th century style with an embattled tower, and Holy Trinity, built by three daughters of Bishop Percy. St Lawrence also has a 19th century church with a 17th century altarpiece and a chest of 1612. Its old church, before the addition of its chancel in 1830, was only 25 feet long by 11 feet wide, among the smallest in England. It has a big 15th century font, a 13th century piscina niche, a sturdy movable stoup about 500 years old, and over the doorway a row of 18th century hat pegs. There is a lovely view from the churchyard.

Steephill Castle, in its beautiful grounds at the west end of the town, was built by John Hamborough in 1833. Before it was finished he became blind and never saw the lovely home he planned. Two ill-fated queens have stayed there, the Empress of Austria in 1874 and Empress Eugenie of France in 1877. It was bought later by John Morgan Richards, the father of the novelist who wrote under the name of John Oliver Hobbes, and much of her work was produced in the study overlooking St Lawrence's Point. Craigie Lodge between Ventnor and Blackgang was for six years her other home; with its Italian gardens of three acres; it is said to be the most perfect dwelling in the island.

One of the most remarkable stories we have heard in our journeyings we heard at Ventnor. It was of the Great War, when wounded men from France were brought to Ventnor for their convalescence. The story of what happened to one of them was told long afterwards by the chairman of the Public Health Committee of the island. One of the soldiers developed tetanus in spite of having been previously injected with serum. It was an unusually delayed case, and the

Ventnor convalescent home was not prepared for having to give anti-toxin treatment, nor was there any serum to be had at the island hospital. Some was ordered from a mainland hospital, but it was feared it would arrive too late. *At that critical time a box was washed up on the shore with the very thing they wanted.*

Worrying over the man's case Dr Robertson happened to mention it to a chemist. "Why," said the chemist, "only last night the coast-guards brought me a small box picked up on the beach. It obviously contained some anti-toxin, but I did not examine it." When the box was opened this bit of driftwood from the sea was found to contain the serum which would save the man's life. The doctor rushed back to the home with it, injected the patient, who recovered. Other medical requisites were washed ashore in time, and it was dis-covered that they came from a hospital ship torpedoed in the Channel; but the little box came first, and it performed its miracle.

Queen Victoria's Church

WHIPPINGHAM. It is the tiny village on the banks of the Medina, with a medley of a church built close by the seaside palace of Queen Victoria, Osborne House. The church stands on a hill overlooking the river and is reached through a lychgate of Indian teak and an avenue of cypresses. Built into the porch is a much-worn sculpture of two men on horseback with a tree between them, a fragment from a church built here by Fitzosbern, kinsman and councillor of the Conqueror. His church has been twice replaced, the present building being erected on the site by the Prince Consort.

Queen Victoria came here when staying at Osborne House and the place is full of memories of her. The marble reredos of the Last Supper, sculptured by the Queen's architect at Windsor, was given in her memory by King Edward. In the north chapel is the marble tomb of Prince Henry of Battenberg. On the chapel altar is a bronze group designed by Princess Louise of an angel freeing a man from a cross. A richly decorated gunmetal screen by Sir Alfred Gilbert separates the chapel from the chancel, and has an inscription etched on a plate by Queen Victoria herself, saying that the screen is in Prince Henry's memory. The prince was married in this church to Princess Beatrice. Opposite this chapel is the pew furnished in memory of his mother by King Edward the Seventh. It has wall-tablets with portrait medallions of the Prince Consort, the Duke of Albany, and Princess Alice, and another tablet with a charming cherub on it, in memory of two children of the Empress Frederick. There is a memorial window to Princess Elizabeth, Charles Stuart's daughter, who died a prisoner at Carisbrooke; it shows St Elizabeth of Hungary with a crippled child at her side in a setting of trees with a distant landscape showing through.

It was at Osborne House that the famous Victorian Era came to its end with the passing of the Queen, and there is here a curious remembrance of those days, the spoon with which the last sacrament was administered to the dying Queen. It is in a glass case. The carved pulpit was given by the people of Osborne estate in memory of the Queen; the font, with the Four Evangelist symbols carved on it by Princess Louise, is a memorial to Prince Albert. There is a portrait medallion of Sir Henry Ponsonby, a handsome man who was Queen Victoria's secretary; and a tablet to an interesting 18th century man, William Arnold, who used to come to this church, close to the birthplace of his famous son Thomas Arnold of Rugby.

Many graves in the churchyard have headstones raised by the Queen in memory of her faithful servants. We read that Jane Forester attended her for 34 years, and among others remembered are head keeper William Laud, and the farm bailiff William Scott. Opposite the church is the peaceful group of red-brick houses built to Queen Victoria as homes for retired royal servants.

The Curious Pillar

WHITWELL. Seven centuries old, and in a garden blooming with flowers in due season, the church has a Tudor porch and a Tudor tower. It has lost its ancient fresco but keeps its ancient bell. A water colour of the fresco hangs in the aisle; the original fell away after being recovered from many coats of whitewash. The old bell stands under the west window, ringing no more.

The oldest part of the walls is on the north side of the chancel arch, where there is 12th century carving. Long ago the chapel and the chancel were two places, used by two parishes and divided by a wall; in the 16th century the wall was transformed into a fine arch and became part of the Tudor church. There is a curious pillar which forms part of the chancel arch and nave arcades; it is of Purbeck marble and unlike any of the other pillars, evidently a misfit and much too short, for a long upper capital has been added to it. There is a tub-shaped font and a Jacobean pulpit and table. For altar rails the church has some delightful old carved benches, black and polished with age. A glass case on the wall holds a strange relic found when the roof was repaired in the last century, a finely carved wooden model in minature of the Hands of Our Lord, bearing the prints of the nails.

It is delightful to meet Joan of Arc in this small place; there is a small statue of her by the handsome chancel screen, which is Whitwell's monument to the men who never came back.

Alice Lisle's Family

WOOTTON. The tide comes up to it and works an ancient mill; and it has a heronry, and a tiny church founded in the time of William Rufus. Its south doorway is the work of 11th century builders and is charming, with a pillar on each side and a double roll of moulding. The chancel is 13th and 14th century and the lovely pulpit is Jacobean, with carved panels and a canopy.

It is the simplest of little buildings, with nave and chancel in one and a tiny chapel for the organ. The nave is plain to severity, but the chancel is bright with colour. The arms of King Edmund the Martyr, the patron saint, are in a chancel window, and in four glowing lancets are the Four Evangelists. The roof is painted between its old beams, and the stone reredos has pillars and background of coloured marbles. Modern paintings of St Michael and St Gabriel are on the chancel walls, and the lovely east window by Kempe represents the Crucifixion. A pathetic page of history comes to mind as we catch the name on a grey heraldic tombstone in the chancel floor, for it is to one of the Lisles who lived at the manor house here; one of them built the church. It was into this family that Dame Alice came, the first victim of the brutal Judge Jeffreys in his terrible Assize, when he ordered her to be beheaded for sheltering two fugitives from Sedgemoor.

In the sunny churchyard sleeps Admiral Sir John Baird, who died in 1908, "a man greatly beloved." Above his tomb is an anchor roped to a cross, and the comforting words, "And so He bringeth them unto the haven where they would be."

The Stolen Statue

YARMOUTH. If we set out from the pleasant ferry of Lymington this is the first place to welcome us to the Garden Isle; it is like a piece of tapestry as we approach, and on arriving is a veritable picture with its little harbour full of sail. There is no more delightful scene in the island than Yarmouth Harbour on a sunny day when the ferry arrives and the yachts of many colours (red, green, yellow, and white) are lying here. It is among the oldest towns in the island, and was once the seat of the Governor. It has still a castle which was one of four blockhouses built by Henry the Eighth for defence against the French, who twice set Yarmouth on fire; but the castle, garrisoned until last century, is now dismantled in the grounds of a hotel. It has a fine Queen Anne staircase.

There is a tiny 18th century town hall standing over what was once the market, and in it is a lovely mace of solid silver, with Charles the Second's arms on the top and his initials at the foot. There are beautiful old charters written on vellum, with seals attached by coloured plaits of silk, of which the earliest goes back to 1334. But the old books of Yarmouth are at the bottom of the sea, and this is how they went. At a Court Leet dinner in 1784 one of the guests was a captain from a ship in the harbour, and, having dined not wisely but too well, he saw as he left a case of what he thought to be wine, and secretly carried it off to his ship. There he discovered that the case was full of books, and in his disgust he threw them overboard.

Many pilgrims are drawn to the 17th century church by a monument which has had a strange adventure. It is on the tomb of Sir Robert Holmes, the bluff admiral who twice entertained Charles the Second and is renowned for deeds that made their mark upon the world. He stands under a canopy supported on porphyry columns, an impressive but singular figure in rich armour, his face rather out of keeping with the rest of him for a reason that is no fault of the sculptor. The statue was not made for him but for Louis the Fourteenth of France. It was finished except for the head, which the sculptor wished to fashion from life, and the marble was on its way to Versailles for this purpose when it was captured by the admiral, who thought it would do splendidly for his tomb and had his own head put where the French king's should have been.

485

Sir Robert was an Irishman who became a captain at the Restoration, and he is frequently mentioned by Pepys, who objected to his appearing in church in a gold lace suit, so diverting attention from prayers. He went out to protect our traders against the Dutch when they were claiming the monopoly of West African trade, and later crossed the Atlantic to help to capture New Amsterdam when the name was changed to New York in honour of the Duke of York, to whom Charles the Second gave the whole of the Atlantic coast. Holmes was now made an admiral, and in 1666, the year of the Great Fire, he lit a fire of his own which made him famous (as such things did in those days), attacking Dutch ships with fire ships and destroying 150 East Indiamen, richly laden. For the remainder of his life he served in Parliament, unaffected by the Revolution and the flight of his patron James.

On the wall near his stolen statue in the church are two tablets in memory of his grandson Lord Holmes and his small son. Lord Holmes was Governor of the island in the 18th century and left money to be distributed on every anniversary of his little boy's death, it having been given away without a break from 1752 till now.

The church has the stand of the hourglass which marked the time for the sermons 300 years ago and an old clock which was telling the time as long ago as 1679.

The Island's Finest Norman Work

YAVERLAND. Where Bembridge slopes southward to the sea the small church and the stately 17th century manor house of Yaverland stand side by side, both with something from the past. Yaverland was an island until the 13th century, when the lord of the manor made a causeway to Yarbridge. The church was built about 1150 as the private chapel of the manor. The house, with tall wide gables and an imposing front, is one of the finest on the island. Part of the 12th century walls are left; the side wings were added in 1620. Its chief beauty is in the carving of the fine door and the oak staircase with grotesque corbels on the wall.

The best part of the church is in the doorway and the chancel arch, which are counted the best Norman craftsmanship in the island. The doorway (near which is a mass dial) has a lovely tympanum of diapered pattern, and wide mouldings of short pilasters and zigzags.

A friendly face smiles from above it, and the two pillars are rich in a shell-like pattern. The chancel arch is not surpassed for its impressiveness in any Hampshire church. Its slender pillars are completely covered with similar designs, and the deeply cut mouldings are exquisitely carved. There is a small movable holy water stoup with a broken bowl which was found when the church was restored in the 19th century; it is 15th century, and preserved with it is another vessel discovered at that time, a big Celtic urn that must have seen twenty centuries. It rests on a carved bracket which was once part of the ancient roof. The font is 14th century. There is a 15th century holy water stoup, and the rood stairs have survived the Reformation.

In this small country church is a wealth of modern painted glass which might well grace the lady chapel of a cathedral. The east window of the Crucifixion (by Clayton and Bell) has in the lower lights small scenes from Our Lord's life. In the west window is a glorious pair of figures of the Archangels Raphael and Gabriel, and an angelic group with musical instruments illustrating the words of Te Deum, "To Thee all Angels cry aloud." Four small figures of Faith, Hope, Charity, and Humility are in the chancel, and there is a magnificent Archangel Michael by Frank Frampton.

The church owes many of its lovely possessions to a rector of the end of last century, who gave the reredos, a masterpiece of dazzling colour and beauty. It is in alabaster, and on a background of golden mosaic Our Lord is seen with adoring angels, with Evangelists in richly coloured recesses and angels in canopied niches.

HAMPSHIRE TOWNS AND VILLAGES

In this key to our map of Hampshire are all the towns and villages treated in this book. If a place is not on the map by name, its square is given here, so that the way to it is easily found, each square being five miles. One or two hamlets are in the book with their neighbouring villages; for these see Index.

INDEX

This index includes all notable subjects and people likely to be sought for, and a special index of pictures appears at the beginning of the volume.

INDEX

494